Dictionary of cultivated plants and their regions of diversity

Second edition revised of: A.C. Zeven and P.M. Zhukovsky, 1975, Dictionary of cultivated plants and their centres of diversity

Dictionary of cultivated plants and their regions of diversity

Excluding most ornamentals, forest trees and lower plants

A.C. Zeven and J.M.J. de Wet

Centre for Agricultural Publishing and Documentation

Wageningen — 1982

CIP-GEGEVENS

Zeven, A.C.

Dictionary of cultivated plants and their regions of
diversity: excluding most ornamentals, forest trees and
lower plants / A.C. Zeven and J.M.J. de Wet. - Wageningen
: Pudoc. - Ill
Herz. uitg. van: Dictionary of cultivated plants and their
centres of diversity / A.C. Zeven and P.M. Zhukovsky,
1975. - Met index, lit. opg.
ISBN 90-220-0785-5
SISO 632 UDC 633
Trefw.: plantenteelt.

ISBN 90-220-0785-5

Contents

Preface

The aim of this work is to give the reader quick reference to the regions of diversity of cultivated plants. For important crops, regions of diversity of related wild species are also presented. Wild species are often useful sources of genes to improve the value of crops.

Species cultivated primarily as ornamentals and timber crops, and useful lower plant species are not included.

Taxa are arranged alphabetically first by family, secondly by genus and thirdly by species within genera. The more common taxonomic synonyms, as well as the better known (English) names are listed. Taxonomy is based primarily on Willis's dictionary (1966) and the Baily Hortorium, Hortus Third (1976).

Somatic chromosome numbers and genome formulae are presented where known. Most of the chromosome numbers are derived from Bolkhovskikh et al. (1969). Where the chromosome number could not be traced, a space has been left open. Chromosome number and genome constitutions may indicate the relationships of a species.

The work included many more species than we could know. Corrections, criticisms and additions including data on chromosome number would be highly appreciated. They should be sent to the senior author, Institute of Plant Breeding (I.v.P.), Agricultural University, P.O.B. 386, 6700 AJ Wageningen, the Netherlands.

We hope that this work may help the plant breeder to ease shortages of food and other agricultural products. We hope that it will also encourage the establishment of natural wild plant reserves in anticipation of needs for wild genes.

Anton C. Zeven
Jan M.J. de Wet

History of the work

FIRST EDITION

In 1968 Prof. P.M. Zhukovskij published a paper 'New centres of origin and
new gene centres of cultivated plants including specifically endemic microcentres of species closely allied to cultivated species'. This paper was
issued in Botanical Journal, Moskov 53:430-460 and was abstracted in Plant
Breeding Abstracts (1968). I wrote to Prof. Zhukovskij asking whether he
would prepare an English version. He wrote back that he was preparing a
booklet in Russian on the 'World genofund of plants for breeding: world gene
centres of cultivated plants and their wild progenitors', which was published in 1970. The text was translated by Dr E.E. Leppik, Research Botanist of
the New Crops Research Branch of the US Department of Agriculture, Beltsville,
Maryland, who invited me to edit the manuscript and to seek a publisher.

The publishers suggested that the work be extended to include more cultivated plants. Prof. Zhukovskij agreed to this proposal and the work has now
been enlarged from 700 species to about 2300 species.

A.C. Zeven

SECOND EDITION

In October 1975 my co-author, Professor Dr P.M. Zhukovskij died at
Leningrad after a long and fruitful life which he dedicated to cultivated
plants: their botany, their taxonomy and their agriculture and use. He
worked almost to the last day of his life to spread knowledge of cultivated
plants. A few months before his death, he received copies of the first edition of this Dictionary and he expressed his happiness with the work.

In 1979, Pudoc informed me that the stock of the book was almost exhausted
and that they considered reprinting the work. However as many scientists are
working on cultivated crops, many new data were available for a new edition.
Furthermore, colleagues and myself had discovered mistakes and omissions and
so it was a good opportunity to prepare a revision. I am very grateful to
those who have suggested additions and improvements.

To help in preparing a revised edition, I asked help from Professor J.M.J.
de Wet, Crop Evolution Laboratory, Department of Agronomy, University of
Illinois, Urbana-Champaign, Illinois, United States. He is an excellent taxo-
nomist of cultivated plants and I was extremely happy that he took up the
invitation despite a busy life as scientist. The present edition has greatly
benefited from his encyclopaedic knowledge of cultivated plants.

A.C. Zeven

Origins of agriculture and domestication of plants

INTRODUCTION

Man was not always a farmer. Only during the last fifteen thousand years or so has he learned to some degree to control his food supply. Before the advent of agriculture, man was a hunter and food gatherer. Gradually, however, some of the animal species he used to hunt were protected, and selected species of food plants were brought into cultivation. Plant and animal husbandry were initiated, and these plants and animals eventually became so dependent on man that they could no longer compete successfully with their wild relatives for natural habitats. They became domesticated.

The antiquity of this shift in man's activities from food gathering to food producing is not known with certainty. Plant and animal husbandry were probably well established long before noticeable phenotypic changes occurred in species under domestication, and became preserved in archaeological records of man's history. Be that as it may, man had abandoned his nomadic food-gathering way of life some 10 000 years ago for one of sedentary food-production in several parts of both the Old and New Worlds.

In many regions, even with a high level of agriculture, man still gathers wild and semiwild plants or fruits, such as brambles, blueberries, raspberries, mushrooms, herbs for food, heath for brooms, wood for buildings, fuel or paper-making, and grass for domestic animals. However man does not depend on these plants; he only collects them for economic or recreative reasons. If he depended on them, he would grow them or find a substitute. Some people may grow plants while others collect the same species in the wild.

We may ask why man started to cultivate plants, why he started to do so only 'recently' and why only certain plant species or varieties were domesticated.

ORIGINS OF AGRICULTURE

Much has been written about man's shift from plant collecting to plant growing. Some authors have put forward 'deterministic' hypotheses, such as a higher mental or social level leading to the cultivation of plants, or climatic changes causing a progressive desiccation of the country and enforcing the application of artificial methods of food production (Spinden, 1971; MacNeish, 1964a). Sauer (1952), however, thought that agriculture could not have originated solely from chronic food shortage, as four conditions had to be fulfilled before plant or animal husbandry could be initiated:
- Previously acquired skills in other fields to start experiments.
- Sedentary way of living.
- Presence of wooded lands easier to clear than savannas or forests. Large river-valleys subject to periodical flooding are unsuitable, because man was not able to control floods.
- A marked diversity of plant populations must be present, so that a large reservoir of genes is available for selection.

Sauer concluded that the ancestors of the earliest agriculturists were relatively prosperous progressive fishermen living in a mild climate along fresh waters.

Little is known about the skills of the first farmers, and information on the correlation between earlier fixed dwelling and incipient food production is limited. The earliest sites with year-round occupation were discovered in the Nile Valley of Upper Egypt (15 000 to 10 500 B.C.) but they show no evidence of plant of animal domestication (Churcher & Smith, 1972). Early occupation sites found in southern Africa dating from 47 000 B.C. (Border Cave in Zululand), 43 000 B.C. (Howieson's Poort near Montagu, southwest Cape Province), 42 000 B.C. (Rose Cottage Cave near Ladybrand in eastern Orange Free State) belong to this category. But, it is not clear whether these sites were occupied all the year round. The botanical material associated with them has not yet been analysed (Dart & Beaumont, 1971; Beaumont & Boshier, 1972).

Sites where agriculture developed first must have been in areas where plant collectors/hunters/fishermen roamed. It is most likely that they lived in wooded lands for hunting game, or near water for fishing. Fishing communities led a sedentary life. Nomads roam, but return to sites known for their richness in animal and plant food. This may have led to annual occupation of sites for a few weeks until the food supply was depleted. On such sites, the soil may have become bare because of disturbance by man; paths, loam pits, graves dilapidated mudhouses and abandoned compounds. Near water, there would be natural bare lands such as riverbanks, gravel, rocks, landslides and esturian plains. Plants pre-adapted to such environments would colonize them. Around dwellings, many plants would derive from plant parts collected by man and brought home. Plants adapted to disturbed habitats are weedy in habit and prefer 'open' rich soils. They grow quickly and have large food reserves that enables them to survive adverse conditions. These characteristics make them suitable for cultivation. They may grow wild in mountains or hills with a wide topographical diversity. In such areas with many microclimates, variants have most chance to survive. After they had migrated into the artificial habitat, man may have found some useful types among them. Some of the plants may have been genotrophes adapting quicker to man-made conditions than expected (Zeven, 1975).

Other sites where agriculture may have arisen would be middens on the compounds. Many parts of plants (fruits, seeds, tubers, roots) must have been accidently or purposefully thrown away. They must have developed into plants with a luxurious growth on these fertile places (Anderson, 1952; Burkill, 1952; Chang, 1970; Engelbrecht, 1916; Flannery, 1965; Harlan & de Wet, 1965; Hawkes, 1969).

The sequence by which crops arose may be summarized as follows:
- Wild plants collected by man.
- Wild plants migrated into temporary or permanent dwelling sites of man either by accident as gathered plant parts or spontaneously. This must have continued for an extremely long time.
- Plant preadapted to disturbed habitats colonized areas around dwellings. Man gathered wanted plant parts from some of these weedy plants.
- Natural selection was reduced and selection pressures introduced for adaptation to man-made habitats. Decrease in variation was counteracted by hybridization and mutation, followed by isolation, protection and conscious selection by man. Selected deviants from the wild phenotypes would survive. This state can be called proto-agriculture.
- The dependence of man on selected plants increased in such a way that when demand exceeded availability, man eradicated undesirable plants and started to improve useful plants. When man moved outside the natural range of a

species on which he depended, he was forced to plant. Thus man learned to retain seeds and other propagules when the plant was to grow outside its natural range, to purposefully prepare a habitat in order to reap a better harvest of the colonizer, now turned into crop. This stage represents incipient agriculture. Near-eradication has led to incipient cultivation of Tabernanthe iboga and Camassia leightlinii.
- Crops were further improved intentionally by cropping methods. This stage represents effective agriculture.

The change-over from food collector/hunter/fisher to full-time agriculturist must have been very gradual. Once the process started, it became practically automatic (Hawkes, 1969) or self-generating. This gradual change - including the change to animal husbandry - resulted in
- less energy to obtain more food,
- people becoming tied to the(ir) land
- spare time for other pursuits (MacNeish, 1964).

By inventing agriculture, mankind gained more from solar energy. Raising crops (and husbanding animals) are man's major means of exploiting that form of energy (Rappaport, 1971).

PLANT DOMESTICATION

Two kinds of organisms, weeds and domesticates, prosper in man-made habitats. Organisms adapted to habitats not notably disturbed by man are wild. Among wild organisms are kinds adapted to various degrees of natural disturbance. They occupy different positions in seral succession. Plants at the pioneer end of succession can also invade man's disturbed habitats. When the habitat is continously being disturbed by man, however, a different set of species becomes established.

Plants that are spontaneous and persistant in habitats that are continually being disturbed by man are weeds. There are degrees of weediness. Wild colonizers will invade man-disturbed habitats, but cannot survive continual disturbances by man or by natural means. If not continually disturbed, waves of species will become established until dynamic but essentially stable populations are achieved. When habitats are continually being disturbed, only weeds can survive spontaneously. One need only drive along highways to observe the strict adaptation of weeds to man-disturbed habitats. Roadside species rarely form part of the adjacent natural vegetation, even of cultivated fields.

Plants tended by man are cultivated but not necessarily domesticated. They may be wild, weed or domestic in adaptation. Man maintains cultivated plants in the man-made habitat because they are of sufficient value. Cultivation includes all kinds of agricultural practices, from merely protecting individual plants to actual planting or sowing, and tending of planted populations. Villages in West Africa are often built around one or more giant baobab trees (Adansonia digitata). These trees provide shade as well as fruits from which a refreshing drink is produced. Baobab is cultivated but wild, and survives continuous disturbance by man of its habitat because it is perennial and not because it is a weed. On the other hand, weeds can be cultivated. Animal fonio (Brachiaria deflexa) is a cultivated cereal in West Africa (Portères, 1976). It is widely distributed across the African savanna and often harvested as a wild cereal (de Wet, 1979). In Angola, however, a weed race of Brachiaria deflexa is often encouraged by local growers of sorghum (Sorghum bicolor) to invade their cultivated fields, and forms a considerable part of the annual cereal harvest (de Wet, 1975).

Domesticates are strictly adapted to habitats specially created for them by man. They have evolved under domestication to the point where they depend

on man both for habitat and propagation. Domesticated seed-plants have lost
the natural ability to disperse seed efficiently natural seed dispersal and
domesticated root and tuber crops are often poor seed producers or are completely sterile sexually. Crops in an early stage of domestication often become
weedy, and many weeds represent species in various stages of domestication.
Indeed, weeds differ from domesticated primarily in degree of dependence on
man for success in the continually disturbed man-made habitat.

Ecological boundaries, as well as boundaries of usefulness to man between
wild, weed and domestic taxa are not always sharp. Higgs & Jarman (1969,
1972) correctly point out that the wild class of organisms merge into the
domestic class by a continuous series of degrees of intimacy with man. The
question thus arises whether domestication occurs from wild across bridging
weedy races. This certainly has been one route. The majority of weeds, however, do not represent a stage in the evolution of crops.

Origins and evolution of weeds

Weeds evolved and are still evolving in man-made habitats in one or more of
four principal ways (de Wet & Harlan, 1975). First, they evolve from colonizer species by selection for adaptation to habitats that are continually
being disturbed. Second, weeds originate as derivatives of hybrids between
wild and cultivated races of domestic species. Third, they evolve from domesticates that are abandoned by man or escape cultivation, by selection for
a less intimate association with cultivation. Fourth, weedy races of crops
originate as a result of introgression with related wild species of the
domesticate.

A majority of weeds have evolved from wild colonizers that invaded the
man-made habitat. Their wild ancestors are aggressive colonizers of all
disturbed habitats, and many of them have been distributed by man well beyond
their natural ranges. The common weeds of North America are Eurasian in
origin (Reed & Hughes, 1970). In their new habitats these species are obligate weeds, while in their native habitats races are known that form part of
the natural habitat. Dandelion (Taraxacum officinale), henbit (Lamium
apoplexicaule), crabgrass (Digitaria sanguinalis) and many other urban weeds
are natives of Europe, and have been introduced to the New World since the
Fifteenth Century.

Weed races of domestic species originate by natural selection as a by-
product of domestication, by selection from partially domesticated or abandoned domesticates, or from hybrid between wild progenitors and their domestic relatives. Weedy hybrid derivatives are known for most, if not all,
crops (Harlan, 1965, 1969). There are, for instance, weed sunflowers
(Helianthus annuus), weed carrots (Daucus carota), weed maize (Zea mays) and
weed watermelons (Citrillus vulgaris). Indeed, even domestic species that
are regularly propagated by vegetative means, such as cassava (Manihot
esculenta), sweet potatoe (Ipomoea batatas) or potato (Solanum tuberosum)
have weed races. Weed races that originate as a result of introgression
(Anderson, 1949) between wild and domestic taxa are often strictly agricultural weeds. They rarely invade natural habitats of their wild relatives
with any success. Adaptive traits acquired under domestication have little
selective value in primary habitats, and gene exchange in the direction of
wild taxa is not extensive. Gene flow in the direction of the crop, however,
may not only produce successful weeds, but may actually benefit the crop
(Harlan, 1969). In the Nobogame Valley of Chihuahua in Mexico, ears of maize
showing traces of introgression from teosinte (Zea mays ssp. mexicana) are con-
sciously selected by farmers as seed stock (Lumholz, 1902; Wilkes, 1970).

Weed races of domestic species often mimic the cultivated race they accompany in vegetative and inflorescence traits, except for retaining natural seed dispersal. Such weeds are particularly obvious in pearl millet (Pennisetum americanum) and are widely distributed with this crop across the West African savanna. Scholz (1979) suggests that these mimetic weeds are actually degenerate domesticates. Brunken et al. (1977) indicate, however, that although shibras closely resemble pearl millet in gross morphology, in more detailed inflorescence traits they are widely variable, and generally intermediate between pearl millet and its wild progenitor. Weed-crop mimicry may also become established between unrelated species. It was already known in Biblical times that darnel (Lolium temulentum) grains were difficult to separate from those of the wheat or barley it accompanies as a weed. Similarly, false flax (Camelina sativa ssp. linicola) is an obligate weed of flax fields in southern Russia, where it mimics races of cultivated flax in growth habit, time of flowering and seed size (Sinskaja & Beztuzhera, 1931). These weeds originated from ssp. sativa by selection in fields of cultivated flax.

Cultivated races of domestic species can revert back to weed habit. Many fence and hedgerow weeds of Europe are derived from species once grown in herb or vegetable gardens. The common Queen Anne's lace, the weedy spring annual of temperate Eurasia and North America is a weed race of the vegetable carrot. In cereals, where natural seed dispersal mechanisms have become lost under domestication, new dispersal mechanisms need to become established after the crop is abandoned as a cultigen. Seed dispersal in grasses commonly occurs as a result of an abscission layer that forms below the glumes or between the glumes and the florets. In the genus Sorghum disarticulation is commonly below the glumes. This is true of both wild and weed races of Sorghum bicolor in Africa. Mississippi chicken corn (ssp. drummondii) in the United States, however, disperses its grain by breaking of the rachis below the spikelet. This dispersal mechanism evolved in an escaped domesticate and is also encountered in parts of Ethiopia where wild relatives of S. bicolor are absent (de Wet, 1978). There are weed sorghums in the United States with the usual means of seed dispersal. These represent derivatives of introgression between diploid cultivated sorghum and tetraploid Johnson grass (Sorghum halepense), an introduced Mediterranean weed. This weed was introduced into the eastern United States some 100 years ago and has been extending its range by absorbing genes from cultivated sorghum. The initial hybrid is triploid and partially sterile. When backcrossed with the cultivated parent, some fully fertile tetraploid offspring are produced. Diploid offspring are also produced from such introgression. They resemble cultivated grain sorghum in habit and habitat preference, and have in recent years become obnoxious weeds in the cornbelt of the United States.

Weeds are not restricted to the plant kingdom. Numerous animal species are weedy. The housefly is a cosmopolitan 'weed', European rabbits are 'weedy' in Australia, and the Holy Brahmin cow is an obnoxious though revered weed in Hindu India. Indeed, by definition civilized man is the ultimate weed, being obligately confined to totally disturbed man-created habitats.

Evolutionary dynamics of plant domestication

Domesticates are adapted to permanently disturbed man-made habitats. Plant husbandry must have been initiated to protect and increase population and density of selected food-plants. Phenotypic changes that accompanied adaptation under domestication probably resulted from a combination of natural and conscious and unconscious selection. Sauer (1952) and Anderson (1960), among others, suggested that wild food-plants invaded the man-disturbed

habitat, became weedy around waste places, and eventually adapted to cultivation. This is probably true of aggressive colonizers such as the several
cultivated species of Chenopodium (Sauer, 1950) and probably some vegetatively propagated tuber-crops. Parts of edible tubers must have made their
way to rubbish heaps where they sprouted to produce vigorous plants, and
such dump heaps are notorious habitats for colonizers. Man certainly could
not have failed to notice these plants nor failed to realize the convenience
in having them readily available for harvesting. Plant husbandry is an obvious next step, and domestication of selected food-plants would be initiated.

Sowing or planting, however, is only part of plant domestication, and
these practices were probably known to man long before the advent of agriculture. Domestication is initiated with planting or sowing, but the domestication process continues only as long as the crop is grown one generation
after another in habitats specially created by man. Food collecting, sowing,
planting or any other husbandry by food gatherers does not necessarily lead
to domestication. Digging for edible underground parts, and stripping plants
of edible leaves, stems or fruits are as extensively practiced by other
animals than man. Plants that are uprooted during food-gathering are frequently allowed to set seed before harvesting (Burkill, 1952) and, even if
not allowed to fully mature, seeds produced in previous generations will
insure continuation of the gene pool of the species. Similarly, when populations are harvested for their mature fruits or seeds, sufficient seeds
usually escape the harvester to insure establishment of a new generation.
Individuals in a wild population do not all mature at the same time and inflorescences on the same individual usually mature at different times. Among
the many thousands of plants regularly harvested in the wild as food, few
have become domesticated. Even harvesting followed by sowing or planting will
not necessarily lead to domestication. Wild cereals, as an example, are often
sown by nomadic food gatherers to increase natural populations (Steward,
1941). This practice, however, will only maintain natural evolutionary development. These food gatherers rarely try to improve the habitat, except
perhaps for burning the area to be sown, and very rarely repeat the experi-
ment with the same population more than twice.

Adaptation to man-made habitats is complex. The ability to colonize disturbed habitats is characteristic of wild progenitors of all seed-crops as
well as other food plants propagated by sowing. Sowing in prepared habitats
selects for an increase in colonizing ability. It increases competition
among individuals. Seedlings that germinate first when conditions become
favourable, and those that grow most vigorously when crowded will provide
most seeds from which the next sown generation will become established. With
each successive man-sown generation, selection pressure for survival in the
man-made habitat increases. Domesticated seed-crops therefore lack dormancy
and tolerate crowding by their own kind, but are poorly adapted to compete
with natural colonizers.

Harvesting alone selects to enforce wild-type survival mechanisms. The
deepest rooted individuals of tuber-bearing species or individuals with the
most efficient means of seed dispersal escape the food gatherer, and transfer their genes for survival to the following generations. Wild seed-crops
are harvested by beating, swinging of a basket, hand stripping, by uprooting
whole plants, or by cutting inflorescences with a knife or sickle for later
threshing. Wilke et al. (1972) point out that harvesting in any way other
than for later threshing will not encourage loss of seed-dispersal ability,
even if followed in successive generations by sowing. Cereals such as sauwi
(Panicum sonorum) in northwestern Mexico, or raishan (Digitaria cruciata) in
northeastern India (Singh & Arora, 1972) are commonly harvested by uprooting

plants before the individuals are fully mature. They retain efficient seed-dispersal mechanisms although the species are fully domesticated in the sense that cultivated races can no longer compete successfully with their wild progenitors for natural habitats. Harvesting and later threshing, however, select for individuals with the most persistent florets or fruits at maturity. Major seed-crops therefore lack the ability of natural seed-dispersal, and domesticated races depend on man both for a suitable habitat and seed dispersal (sowing). They are never successfully spontaneous (weedy) in the man-made habitat for more than a few generations.

Food gatherers harvest an array of annual and perennial edible plants, seeds and fruits. Relatively few of these were domesticated. The sites of early agriculture must have limited the number of species available for cultivation. Numerous desirable food plants, however, do not lend themselves to domestication. Some have exact habitat requirements and are not already pre-adapted to man-made habitats. The progenitors of all seed-crops are aggressive colonizers, and the progenitors of vegetatively propagated crops readily adapt to transplanting by man. Many desirable food plants give a poor return for the effort and for time invested in sowing or planting, and were probably soon abandoned by man as cultigens. Still others were probably never brought into cultivation.

Plant domestication is sympatric evolution. The wild progenitors of crops are commonly sympatric with their domestic conspecific races. They usually differ strikingly in phenotype and adaptation, but remain sufficiently related genetically to cross and produce fertile hybrids. Hybridization is common and genes are exchanged, particularly in the direction of cultivated races. Divergence and introgression are opposing evolutionary processes. Evolutionary divergence depends on isolation. Burkill (1952) suggests that the initial isolation that led to domestication was provided by man when he transported his favourite food plants beyond their natural ranges. This would also have forced man to plant, replant seed harvested from populations planted in specially prepared habitats. However, selection pressures associated with domestication themselves act as isolating mechanisms. In domestication, isolation between wild and cultivated races becomes disruptive. Thoday (1972) demonstrates that under conditions of disruptive selection associated with differences in adaptation, population divergence continues, even with hybridization. When divergence has progressed to the stage where parent and daughter populations have distinctly different adaptive norms, interpopulation gene flow is effectively eliminated, since hybrids between them are poorly adapted to either parental habitat. Only with a change in selection pressures does divergent evolution come to an end. Racial isolation in domestic species is achieved by gametophytic and sporophytic barriers, and differences in flowering time. The principal isolating force between domestic races and their progenitors, however, is ecological adaptation. Wild races of domestic species do not successfully invade cultivated fields, and cultivated races are totally adapted to habitats specially created for them by man. Hybrids between wild and cultivated races, and derivatives of such introgression survive in 'intermediate' habitats as weeds and provide a bridge between them for occasional gene exchange.

Evolutionary dynamics of plant domestication

Crane (1950) and Masefield et al. (1969) present classes of selection schemes from wild plant to the present cultivated crop. The possible changes of a species caused by domestication were listed by Polunin (1960) and Purseglove (1968).

Domesticated plants
- spread to a more diverse environment and have a wider geographic range
- may have a different ecological preference
- may flower and fruit simultaneously
- may lack shattering or scattering of seeds and may have lost dispersal
mechanism completely
- may have larger fruits and seeds, and so lower efficiency of dispersal
- may have been converted from a perennial to an annual
- may have lost seed dormancy
- may have lost photoperiodic controls
- may lack normal pollinating organs
- may have a different breeding system (Usually the change is from complete
or partial cross-fertilization to partial or complete self-fertilization.
This change may result from a change in flower morphology, or a change from
self-incompatibility to self-compatibility.)
- may lack defensive adaptation such as hairs, spines and thorns
- may lack protective coverings and sturdiness
- may have better palatability and chemical composition, rendering them more
likely to be eaten by animals
- may be more susceptible to diseases and pests
- may develop seedless parthenocarpic fruits
- may have undergone selection for double flowers, which may involve con-
version of stamens into petals
- may have become sexually sterile and vegetatively reproduced.
    Speed of domestication depends on the duration of a generation and inten-
sity of selection pressures. For cereals, a generation usually takes one
year, whereas for vegetatively propagated plants, fast changes are not
usual. Braidwood & Howe (1962) estimated that all major changes in wheat
and barley under domestication had taken place within 2 000 years. Helbaek
(1966) suggested even 1 500 years.
    Some crops were domesticated for several uses. Examples are:
- Sorghum bicolor: annual forage grass, syrup sorghum, grain sorghum, broom
corn, popping sorghum used for confectionary, inflorescenses in floral
arrangements,
- Cannabis sativus: fibre, drugs, oil seeds,
- Brassica napus: rape, swedes, hungary gap kales, oil-seed colzas,
- Brassica campestris: rapeseed, turnip, leafy vegetables,
- Brassica oleracea: vegetable, forage, ornamental, walking stick, construc-
tion material,
- Helianthus annuus: oil, cattle feed, ornamental, bird food, ceremonies,
- Elaeis guineensis: mesocarp oil, kernel oil, wine
- Vicia faba: dry seed, fresh seed, forage, green manure.
    This list can easily be extended. Some plants may have been domesticated
for one use that eventually became obsolete. If no alternative use were
found, its cultivation would be abandoned and it would be lost as a cultigen, but may survive as a weed. Crops may have been abandoned until use was
found for them. For instance, several medicinal crops and herbs are also
grown as ornamentals, as are Viola tricolor and Digitalis purpurea. Some
former medicinal species are nowadays grown only as ornamentals. Similarly
reverse plants used in ritual became ornamentals. Many fencing or hedging
plants, grown to stop domestic animals from running away and wild animals
from entering protected areas, are used nowadays as ornamentals or for
hedges. Anderson (1960) and Chang (1970) supposed that the first crops were
not food plants. Anderson suggested that plants were first domesticated for
body paints, hedges, poisons, chewing, fatigue drugs and ritual purposes.

Chang believes the early domesticated plants were used for making containers (bamboo trunks, fruits of bottle gourd), cordage or as herbs. These plants were useful and, when man became dependent on them, he started to cultivate them. Most experts on crop history, however, believe that food crops are among the first domesticants. Burkill (1952) listed the sequence in which he believed crops were domesticated:
- cereals
- pulses
- greens
- oil seeds
- 'roots'
- herbaceous fruits
- fibre
- woody plants, chiefly fruit trees
- various industrial plants.

Numerous species of wild grasses are adaptable to domestication; they yield well, grow gregariously, so that their caryopses could be collectively harvested, they have edible caryopses, their foliage is excellent for fodder, and the caryopses are good to store. Man did not overlook these advantages of grasses (Burkill, 1952). Pulses must have followed grasses in domestication. Subsequently, several plants collected for the leaves came into domestication as oil crops. Many woody plants received particular attention. Purseglove (1968) stated that cereals were first domesticated in arid and semi-arid regions, whereas in the wet tropics cultivation started with root and tuber crops. Archaeological research will eventually elucidate the correct sequence of domestication. It may differ from region to region and different kinds of crops may have been domesticated simultaneously.

The plant families have not contributed equally to the present supply of domesticated species. Among the 173 families (see table) 48 families are represented by only one item, 24 by 2 items, 10 by 3 items, and 4 by more than 100 items. The family with most items is the Gramineae (379, 15.2% of the total number of items); most of them coming from Region 8: Africa. This continent is well known for its forage grasses. The Leguminosae follow with 337 items (13.5%); Regions 2, 7, 8 and 10 are the main sources. Gramineae and Leguminosae contribute about one third of the number of items. Rosaceae rank third with 158 items (6.3%), most of them come from Regions 1 and 9. Solanaceae rank fourth with 115 items (4.6%), most of them come from Regions 10 and 11.

Region 2 has contributed the highest number: 331 items (12.5%), closely followed by Region 1 (295 items, 11.8%), and Regions 8 and 10 (each 292, 11.7%). These four regions contribute almost half of all items.

Table.   Number of items per family per region, per family and per centre

Family	Region												uni-den-ti-fied	Total
	1	2	3	4	5	6	7	8	9	10	11	12		
Acanthaceae				1				2		1				4
Aceraceae											1			1
Actinidaceae	4													4
Agaraceae		1	1	1				6		2	17		1	29
Aizoaceae								3		1				4
Alismataceae	1													1
Alliaceae	9			1	3	4	2		2					21
Alstromeriaceae											1			1
Amaranthaceae	1	3		2			1	1		6	3	3	1	21
Amaryllidaceae							2							2
Anacardiaceae	2	7		1	1		1			5	4	1	1	23
Annonaceae		2						1		4	8			15
Apocynaceae		1		2			1	4		2			1	11
Aquifoliaceae	1									1				2
Araceae	1	7		4					1	8	2	1		24
Araliaceae	5	4										1		10
Aristolochiaceae									1					1
Asclepiadaceae		1		1			1	1				1		5
Averrhoeaceae		2												2
Azollaceae	1	1												2
Balanitaceae							1							1
Balsaminaceae	1													1
Basellaceae		1								2	1			4
Berberidaceae									1			1		2
Bignoniaceae								1			3			4
Bixaceae										1				1
Bombacaceae		4						1		1	1			7
Boraginaceae	1	1			1		2		1					6
Bromeliaceae										3	1			4
Burseraceae	1	4						2						7
Cabombaceae	1													1
Cactaceae										18	36			54
Campanulaceae	2								1			1		4
Cannabidaceae	4			1					2			1		8
Cannaceae								1		1				2
Capparidaceae							1							1
Caricaceae										3	1			4
Caryocaraceae										1				1
Caryophyllaceae							2		2					4
Casuarinaceae			1											1
Celastraceae	4													4
Chenopodiaceae	4		1	2	4	6	6		5	2	1	2	1	34
Chloranthaceae	1													1
Chrysobalanaceae										1				1
Cleomaceae								1						1
Combretaceae		4												4
Compositae	10	7		3	5	3	18	9	16	6	4	5		86
Convulvulaceae	2	1		1			1			2	3			10
Cornaceae						1								1
Corylaceae	4					3	1							8
Corynocarpaceae													1	1
Crassulaceae								1	2					3
Cruciferae	8			3		5	11	4	12	1			1	45
Cucurbitaceae	5	2		9	1	2	3	17	2	2	7	1	2	53
Cupressaceae								1				1		2
Cyperaceae	5	3					3		2	1			2	16
Datiscaceae					1									1
Dioscoreaceae	2	8		1			15			2	1			29

Family	Region												uni-den-ti-fied	Total
	1	2	3	4	5	6	7	8	9	10	11	12		
Dioscoreaceae	2	8		1			15			2	1			29
Dipsacaceae						2								2
Dipterocarpaceae		1												1
Ebenaceae	3	2			1						1	1		8
Ehretiaceae							1				1	3		5
Elaeagnaceae					1									1
Elaeocarpaceae	3	1									1			5
Ericaceae							1							1
Erythroxylaceae										2				2
Eucommiaceae	1													1
Euphorbiaceae	4	13		3			2	7		10	2	1	1	43
Euryalaceae	1													1
Fagaceae	5			1			1					2		9
Flacourtiaceae		6		2				1						9
Geraniaceae							2	7						9
Ginkgoceae	1													1
Gnetaceae		1												1
Gramineae	35	47	2	32	12	34	37	72	39	22	20	25	2	379
Grossulariaceae	3						1	6				2		12
Guttiferae		9		4				1		2				16
Hippocastanaceae				1			1							2
Hydrastidaceae											1			1
Hydrophyllaceae		1									1			2
Illiciaceae	2													2
Iridaceae	2					1	2				1			6
Juglandaceae	4				1	1			1	1	2	4		14
Labiatae	5	6			1		17	9	10		3	1		52
Laminariaceae	1													1
Lauraceae	2	3		1			1			2	3			12
Lecythidaceae										2				2
Leguminosae	14	45	9	23	6	20	49	54	33	44	14	10	6	337
Lemnaceae		1												1
Liliaceae	8	1		1	1	1	3	1	2			2		20
Limnanthaceae											1			1
Limnocharitaceae		1												1
Linaceae				1	1	1	1	1	1					6
Lythraceae								1						1
Magnoliaceae	1	1												2
Malpighiaceae										3	2			5
Malvaceae	6	4	5	8	2	6	2	14	1	9	9	1	3	70
Marantaceae								1		2				3
Martyniaceae											1			1
Melastomataceae								1						1
Meliaceae		3		1										4
Menispermaceae	1							2						3
Moraceae	3	6		4	2	2	1	4			2	1		25
Moringaceae				1				1						2
Musaceae	1	4	1	3				2						11
Myricaceae	1													1
Myristicaceae		2												2
Myrtaceae		10	40	2				3		13	5			73
Nelumbonaceae						1								1
Nyctaginaceae		1								1				2
Oleaceae	5			2	1		3							11
Onagraceae										1	1			2
Orchidaceae											2			2
Oxalidaceae										1				1
Paeoniaceae									1					1
Palmae	1	10		3			1	9		4	2			30
Pandaceae		4						1						5

Family	Region													uni-den-ti-fied	Total
	1	2	3	4	5	6	7	8	9	10	11	12		
Papaveraceae						1	1				1			3
Passifloraceae										17	1	1		19
Pedaliaceae	1			2				4						7
Pentaphragmaceae		1												1
Peperomiaceae										1				1
Perioplocaceae				1				1						2
Phytolaccaceae	1									3		1		5
Phytolaccaceae	1									3		1		5
Pinaceae		1					1							2
Piperaceae		5		2				2		1				10
Pistaciaceae							2							2
Plantaginaceae	1			1			2		1					5
Polygalaceae								1						1
Polygonaceae	8	1		1	1	1		1	5		2			20
Portulacaceae								4	1		1	2		8
Protaceae			3											3
Punicaceae						1								1
Ranunculaceae	2						2		3					7
Resedaceae				1		1	3		1					6
Rhamnaceae	3						3		2	1				9
Rosaceae	41	2		1	26	22	2	1	37	4	1	21		158
Rubiaceae	1	4		4		1	6	1	2					19
Rutaceae	12	15	1	4		1	5	3			2		1	44
Salicaceae					1				7			1		9
Sambucaceae									2					2
Santalaceae		1												1
Sapindaceae	3	5		1				1		3				13
Sapotaceae		3		3				3		5	6			20
Saurucaceae		1												1
Saxiphragaceae										1				1
Scrophylariaceae	1						1		3					5
Simaroubaceae		1								1	1			3
Simmondsiaceae											1			1
Solanaceae	1	2	6	4			2	12	4	47	31	5	1	115
Sterculiaceae								4		4	2			10
Stilagninaceae		1												1
Strychnaceae				1										1
Styraceae		1												1
Taccaceae		1												1
Tamaricaceae					1			1						2
Taxaceae	1													1
Tetragoniaceae	5													1
Theaceae				1										1
Thymelaeaceae	2									1				3
Tiliaceae	1			2				1						4
Trapaceae	3													3
Tropaeolaceae										3				3
Typhaceae	1													1
Ulmaceae					2		2							4
Umbelliferae	5	3		2	2	4	13		11	1				41
Urticaceae	1	1		2			1						2	7
Valerianaceae						1	2		4			1		8
Verbenaceae				1			1	2		1				5
Violaceae	1						1		1					3
Vitadaceae	2				1	2	1		1			7		14
Zingiberaceae	4	16		9				2						31
Total	295	311	70	166	82	129	246	292	231	292	225	113	27	2489
% of total	11.8	12.5	2.8	6.7	3.3	5.2	9.9	11.7	9.3	11.7	9.0	4.5	1.1	

Cradles of agriculture and regions of diversity

Geographic centres of plant domestication cannot be found without studying the origins, hearths or 'cradles', and spread of agriculture and of domestic plants.

Wild plants are still entering cultivation, whereas an important crop like the oil palm in West Africa is still largely semi-domesticated (Zeven, 1967; 1973). Other examples of semi-domesticates are secondary crops, i.e. crops that were first weeds in primary crops but were later themselves domesticated.

Sites of prehistoric farms have been discovered in Thailand, the Near East and Mexico. They showed that incipient agriculture existed in Thailand at about 11 000 B.C. (Gorman, 1969), in the Near East at about 9 000 B.C. (Cambel & Braidwood, 1970) and Mexico at about 6 000 B.C. (MacNeish, 1964a; 1964b). In other parts of the world no such early sites have yet been found, and it is generally accepted that from these cradles agriculture spread to other parts of the world. There are good arguments for independent origin of agriculture in China (Ho, 1969). But agriculture may have reached China and Japan, and S.E. Asia from Thailand, while agriculture probably reached Europe, Africa, W. and S. Asia from the Near East.

Alexander Von Humboldt was probably the first author to refer to the origin of crops. In his work Essai sur la Géographie des Plantes (1807) he said: "The origin, the first home of the plants most useful to man and which have accompanied him from remotest epochs, is a secret as impenetrable as the dwellings of all our domestic animals. We do not know what region produced spontaneously wheat, barley, oats and rye. The plants which constitute the natural riches of all inhabitants of the tropics, the banana, the pawpaw, the cassava, and maize have never been found in wild state" (cited by Hawkes, 1970). If he were alive now, Von Humboldt would be delighted to learn how much we know of the origin of cultivated plants.

The next study was by Alphonse De Candolle in "Géographie Botanique Raisonée" (1855). Then came Charles Darwin (1868) with his book "Variation of animals and plants under domestication". However Darwin was not interested in the origin of cultivated plants, but in evolution of animals and plants, whether in nature or under domestication.

De Candolle's thoughts on tracing the origins of cultivated plants were published in 1882 in his book Origine des Plantes Cultivées. His work is still largely up to date (Harlan, 1961). He based his investigations on:
- classical botany (plant geography, knowledge of adventive and ruderal species, understanding of history of development of whole floras),
- bio-archaeology (plant remains, pictorial records, especially from Egypt),
- palaeontology,
- philology.
He concluded that the region where a species was abundant was not necessarily its centre of origin. Perhaps De Candolle (1882) was the first to indicate regions where plant domestication might have taken place (Smith, 1968):
- China
- S.W. Asia and Egypt

- tropical Asia.

In De Candolle's time, it was quite natural to include Egypt as much of the knowledge of plant history came from that country.

After De Candolle, Nicolai Ivanovič Vavilov suggested cradles of agriculture. At the height of his career he had more facilities than anyone before (Harlan, 1951). With his abundant energy, he exploited them to the full. During the Fifth International Genetics Congress at Berlin in 1926, Vavilov (1928) developed his theory of centres of origin or gene centres indicating that several regions of the world possess concentrations of variation of certain cultivated plants and that these regions overlap for several cultivated plants. These regions can be identified by the Differential Method, described by Burkill (1952):

- Take a map
- select major cultivated plants
- mark the sites where recognizable botanical varieties and races of these cultivated plants are found. The identification of the botanical varieties was done by investigating the morphology, cytology, genetics and resistance to diseases, pests and unfavourable climatic conditions of the plants
- Where those marks often coincide is a centre of origin. In such centres the greatest diversity of the cultivated crop is observed.

Vavilov concluded that a centre of origin was characterized by dominant alleles and that the frequency of recessive alleles increased and diversity decreased towards the periphery. The cause was inbreeding, geographical isolation and drift.

At the periphery, secondary gene centres may develop; new areas with a great diversity conditioned by recessive alleles. In 1926, Vavilov reported that Asia Minor lies in the Asiatic, Mediterranean, Balkan and Transcaucasian gene centres of wheat and other crops. In 1931, he extended this idea by distinguishing seven gene centres. In 1935, he raised this number to eight by splitting SW Asia into Central Asia and the Near East. Later Zohary (1970) proposed to reunite them. The centres recognized by Vavilov were:

I.   China
II.   India
IIa.   Indo-Malaya
III.   C. Asia, including Pakistan, Punjab, Kashmir, Afghanistan and
        Turkestan (USSR)
IV.   Near East
V.   Mediterranean coastal and adjacent regions
VI.   Ethiopia
VII.   S. Mexico and C. America
VIII.   S. America (Peru, Ecuador, Bolivia)
VIIIa. Isle of Chiloe (Chile).

These centres lie between 20 and 45° latitude north and south in mountainous regions and often in areas with a temperate climate. They are separated by great deserts or lie on different continents. According to Vavilov, agriculture in these eight regions developed independently, because of the differences in agricultural methods, implements and domestic animals.

Vavilov may have been influenced by Willis' Age and Area hypothesis (Willis, 1922): in comparing wild species with similar modes of dispersal, those with the wider distribution are the older, and that the longer a species has been present in an area, the more diverse the derived species and subspecies found there. Vavilov may also have been influenced by the agro-

geographical work of Engelbrecht (Zeven, 1973). However time is not the
only factor that influences the dispersal of a species and its increase of
variation.

In the 1930s, Vavilov established an 'ecological passport' for the accessions of his large collections by sowing them at various sites ('geographical
sowing') after which he estimated:
- differences in growth during the vegetative period
- differences in length of the various development stages, including growth
rhythm
- economic characters, such as size of fruits and seeds
- vegetative characters
- resistance to different kinds of drought
- resistance to cold
- differences in flowering
- resistance to bacteria and viruses
- resistance to insects
- ecological growth form: xerophyte, hydrophyte, mesophyte.
The diversity was enormous but within limits and with certain regularities.
Vavilov discovered parallelisms that are especially clear for plants of the
same general group (annuals, herbaceous), characterized by the same area of
distribution and following the same geographical route in their evolution.
Since it seemed as though each species differentiated into different agro-
ecological and geographical groups, he was able to establish the 'ecological
passport' for annual cereals, grain legumes, oil and fibre flax. In 1940,
Vavilov divided the Old World (excluding Africa south of the Sahara and
tropical Asia) into 19 areas, each characterized by the plants with essentially the same 'ecological passport':

1. Syrian Group Agricultural Territory: chiefly foothills of Syria, Palestine
and Jordania. Characteristics of cultivated and wild plants: relatively
small; with small leaves, flowers and seeds; thin, stiff stems; non-
shattering spikes or indehiscent pods; high maturing temperature; short
vernalization stage. Examples: types of wild and domesticated Triticum
species; barley; oats; peas; lentils; grass-peas; chick-peas; domesticated
flax and vetch.

2. Anatolian Group Agricultural Territory: mountainous parts of Turkey.
Characteristics: medium-size; thin, stiff stems; medium-sized spikes, fruits
and seeds; resistant to drought; short development stages; requiring considerable warmth during last stage of development. Examples: as Group 1.

3. Armenian Xerophytic Mountain Group Agricultural Territory: arid, mountainous steppes of Soviet and Turkish Armenia. Characteristics: markedly xerophytic (small narrow leaves); small seeds. Examples: Triticum vavilovii
(also resistant to shattering, and winterhardy); early dwarf, small seeded,
xerophytic chick-peas; a large number of relatives of domesticated wheat;
Secale vavilovii.

4. Caucasian Mesophytic High-Mountain Group Agricultural Territory: high
mountain plateaux of Daghestan and Georgia, Northern America. Characteristics: thin stems; comparatively smooth awns; small or medium-sized seeds;
short or medium vegetation period. Examples: original ecotypes of soft
wheat; prototypes of European steppe winter and spring bread-wheats; Triticum carthlicum; a specific group of barley with narrow leaves; many xerophytic and mesophytic types of Secale montanum and S. cereale ssp. segetale
(many with a great diversity of red and brown forms).

5. Daghestan-Azerbaijan Foothill Group Agricultural Territory: coastal regions of Daghestan and Azerbaijan. Characteristics: mesophytic; long vege-

tation period; tall; leafy; large seeds; rather resistant to leaf rust.
Examples: giant forms of soft and durum wheats; barley, rye; peas, vetch,
winter types of durum.

6. Transcaucasian Humid Subtropical Group Agricultural Territory: West
Georgia and Black Sea coast, humid regions of Turkey and S. Azerbaijan
(Lenkoran), N.Iran. Characteristics: hydrophytic, tall. leavy; late;
rather resistant to various European fungus diseases, Examples: endemic
Triticum ssp. such as T. macha and T. timopheevi, and some other diploid and
tetraploid Triticum types; late types of prostrate fibre-flax sown in autumn
and winter; transitory and very late spring varieties of cereals.

7. Iran-Turkestan Group Agricultural Territory: irrigated and unirrigated
regions of Iran, Afghanistan, Soviet Central Asia (Uzbekistan, Tadjikistan,
Turkmenia). Characteristics: low to medium-high; rather non-shattering rough
spikes; weak stems subject to lodging; slow growth during early stages of
development; drought-resistant during late stages; high temperature requirement at maturity; extremely susceptible to all European fungus diseases when
sown in steppe or wooded steppe regions of Europe. Two subgroups:
a. Khiva Subgroup: near mouth of Amu-Darya river, late varieties of wheat,
barley, flax and peas
b. Kashgar Subgroup: high plateaux near the Pamir, extremely cold-resistant
varieties of soft wheat and relatively late varieties of flax (frequently
with white flowers and seeds).

8. Pamir-Badakhstan Group Agricultural Territory: Soviet and Afghan Badakh-
stan (Pamir Agricultural District), C. and N. Kafirstan, at very high altitudes (even 3000 m or more). Includes types from Upper Himalayas and Tibet.
Characteristics: mesophytic types; of medium height; broad leaves; short
vegetative period; extremely susceptible to all European fungal diseases.
Furthermore a giant type of rye with large anthers and pollen grains, big
kernels and large spikes; liguleless, soft and compactum wheat; large broad-
leaved, naked, six-rowed barley; small seeded, early peas, beans and grass-
peas.

9. Indian Group Agricultural Territory: N. India. Characteristics: as those
for the Pamir-Badakhstan Group; despite the diversity in ecological circum-
stances quite uniform; not bushy; thin, stiff stems; small narrow leaves;
early; short; development stages and rapid development rhythm; resistant to
drought; need high temperatures, especially during last stages of development; rapid filling-out of seeds; small seeds (in cereals, flax and grain
legumes); spikes of wheat and barley smooth with non-shattering grain.
In Kashmir, a subgroup has been established based on a special wheat type
characterized by medium height, thin stems, long narrow leaves, small kernels, rather smooth awns, winter habit, and less susceptibility to brown
rust than the plants of Group 7. (The reason why Group 8 and 9 have been
separated, despite identity of characteristics, was not stated.)

10. Arabian Mountain Group Agricultural Territory: Yemen, where high-mountain agriculture is subject to the influence of the surrounding deserts.
Characteristics: short spring annuals with extremely rapid growth; thin stiff
stems; narrow leaves; relatively large seeds. No examples are given.

11. Ethiopian (Abyssian) Group Agricultural Territory: Ethiopia and Eritrea.
Divided into two subgroups;
a. varieties sown at beginning of main rainy season; cosmopolitan, hydrophytic types of tall large-seeded varieties of barley and peas. (Ethiopian
wheats, though not notably cosmopolitan, may be included here.)
b. varieties sown at the end of the rainy season: flax, chick-peas, lentils,
beans, grass-peas, and an Arabian type of pea (xerophytic, early, low, small-
leaved, small-seeded). Origin: very probably linked with India and mountain-

ous Arabia.

12. Chinese-Japanese Group Agricultural Territory: China and Japan. Very likely, the original material was imported from Asia Minor by way of India several millenia ago, but very important new characters have developed in this group. Characteristics: short development stages; low or medium height; extremely small seeds; rapid filling of grains. Examples: rapidly filling wheats with small kernels, awnless or awnletted.

13. Mediterranean Group Agricultural Territory: Mediterranean Area. Characteristics: rather tall, bush; large spikes; long awns; large light-coloured seeds; high yields; usually solid straw, short first development stage; resistant to low air humidity, requiring much warmth at maturity; resistant to fungal diseases. (No examples were given.)

14. Egyptian Group Agricultural Territory: Egypt. Characteristics: barley and durum with short stiff stems, medium-sized spikes and short first development stages. Similar types have been found on Cyprus.

15. South European Group Agricultural Territory: S. France, N. Italy, part of Yugoslavia, Bulgarian coast. Characteristics: tall plants; large leaves; big fruits; high yields. Examples: Triticum turgidum sensu stricto, soft wheats; in Lombardy, giant forms of oats, chick-peas, horse beans, and a polonicoid wheat have been found.

16. European Steppe Group Agricultural Territory: European Steppe from Tirol to the Urals; transferred to N. America, especially to the prairies. Examples: xerophytic spring and winter types of cereals and grain legumes, the winter types winter-hardy, the spring types drought-resistant; rather small seeds, weak straw, narrow leaves. (Vavilov divided this Group into two subgroups, but gave no ground for them.)

17. West European Group Agricultural Territory: W. Europe including S. Finland and S. Sweden. Characteristics: tall hydrophytic plants; thick; stiff stems; large broad leaves; large dense, highly productive spikes; medium-sized or large grain; ripening late. Local varieties have lax spikes, and are tall and early.

18. Central European Group Agricultural Territory: forest and wooded steppe of C. Europe. Characteristics: high-yielding mesophytes. Examples: long-fibre flax, high-yielding peas, awnless soft wheats.

19. Northern (Boreal) Group Agricultural Territory: N. European Soviet Union, Siberia, N. Scandinavia. Characteristics: mesohydrophytic; precocity; medium-sized; low warmth requirement; cold-resistant. Examples: self-compatible rye and very early types of forage barley.

Vavilov worked on his concept of gene centres, modifying it, until his death. These agro-ecological groups need not coincide exactly with gene centres. The purpose of all his effort is obvious. There are groups of plants possessing certain characteristics not present in other groups. So when looking for a certain property in a species, it is not necessary to study its entire area of distributuion, but it is sufficient to look for it in the group(s) where this property has already been found.

The gene microcentres of Harlan (1951) are a further breakdown in geobotanical patterns of variation. They are small areas in which evolution is still proceeding at a rapid rate. For wheat, Harlan identified three microcentres in Turkey. Undoubtedly many more exist elsewhere. With the introduction of high-yielding foreign wheat varieties, these microcentres are disappearing. Harlan also identified gene microcentres in Turkey for a number of other crops. He found that such centres frequently coincide. They may be in the plains or in mountainous regions, near civilization or remote from it, in areas with very primitive or more advanced husbandry.

With increasing knowledge of cultivated, weedy and wild plants, it is becoming evident that some parts of Vavilov's theory had to be changed (review-
ed by Kuckuck, 1962). Nevertheless it still forms a good basis to search for
wild or semi-wild relatives of particular crops. The large collections made
by Vavilov and his introduction of a genetic element in investigation still
render these discussions pertinent. One point in Vavilov's theory was that a
primary centre was marked by a high frequency of dominant alleles. Gökgöl
(1941) showed that it was impossible to indicate such a centre for wheat.
Brieger (1963) did not find one for maize, Zeven (1967; 1972) not for oil
palm and Hanelt (1972) not for Vicia faba. Besides it has been pointed out
that a great diversity may also arise from the variation of the environment.
Hence the relation between mountain regions and centres of origin. Such a
great diversity may also develop when two populations of a (partial) cross-
fertilizing species meet, as has been shown for Carthamus tinctorus. Vavilov's theory that where the greatest diversity is found is also the centre
of origin, is no longer tenable, as was shown for crops such as Triticum
dicoccum and Hordeum vulgare in Ethiopia. These crops show a great diversity
there, but no wild relatives are present.

Kuckuck (1963) concluded that Vavilov would certainly have altered his
theories with present knowledge. Indeed, he introduced changes as his research progressed.

The number of cradles of agriculture has been extensively discussed. Va-
vilov believed in several, others suggested two (Sauer, 1952); one for the
Old World (Burma and adjacent area) and one for the New World (C. America).
Darlington (1952, 1969) also suggested two: the Fertile Crescent of the Near
East and Mexico. From these nuclear areas agriculture was supposed to have
spread across the Old World and the New World, respectively. After the intro-
duction of agriculture, new centres of plant domestication developed. Thus,
Darlington & Janaki Ammal (1945) distinguished twelve 'centres of origin':

1. Ethiopia
2. Mediterranean coast
3. Iran, incl. the Caucasus and E. Turkey
4. Afghanistan
5. Indo-Burma
6. Siam-Malaya-Java
7. China
8. Mexico
9. Peru
10. Chile
11. Brazil-Paraguay
12. United States

As compared with the list of Vavilov (1926), they proposed continental Chile
instead of the Isle of Chiloe, and added the Brazil-Paraguay and the United
States centres.

They considered the Mediterranean centres as diffuse, for cultural rather
than botanical reasons. "The Mediterranean, a barrier to wild plants, has
been a means of dispersal and a bond of union for plants of established
cultivation".

In 1956, Darlington added Europe (for no indicated reason), Central Africa
(perhaps based on Portères' views - see below) and C. America (already mentioned by Vavilov). He also switched inexplicable to 'region', though the
captions of his table and figure still mention 'centres'. This resulted in
the following centres:

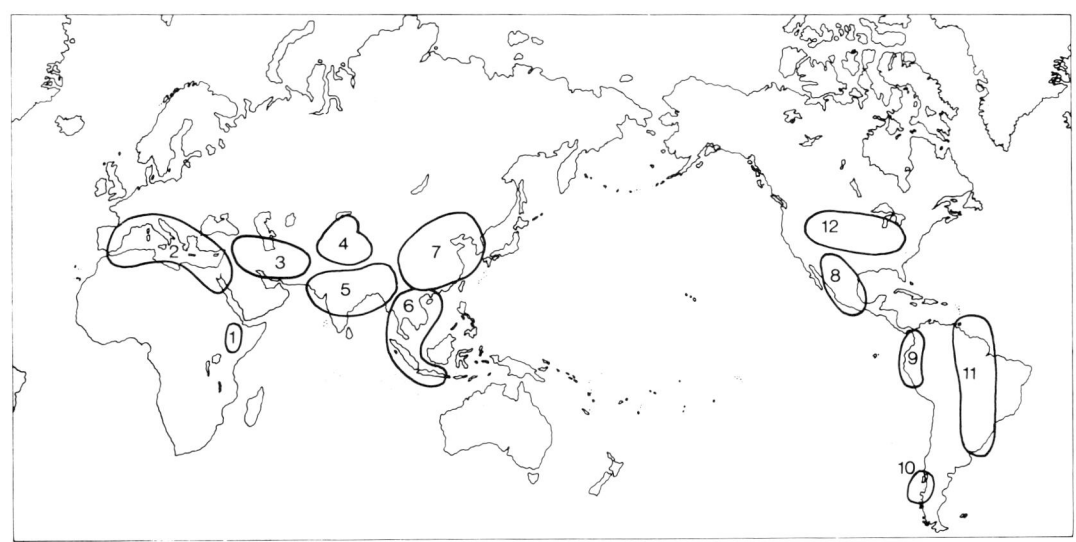

Gene centres of cultivated plants of Darlington & Janaki Ammal (1945) derived from Vavilov

1. S.W. Asia
2. Mediterranean
2a. Europe
3. Ethiopia
3a. C. Africa
4. C. Asia
5. Indo-Burma
6. S.E. Asia

7. China
8. Mexico
8a. United States
8b. C. America
9. Peru
9a. Chile
9b. Brazil-Paraguay

In 1950, Portères suggested independent cradles of agriculture in Africa south of the Sahara, one in E. Africa, the other in Tropical W. Africa. He divided the latter into:
- the Senegambian 'Subcradle',
- the Central Niger 'Subcradle',
- the Benin 'Subcradle' and
- the Adamawa 'Subcradle'.
Other African cradles of agriculture are in N. Africa and Ethiopia. In 1962, he changed his concept by dividing and subdividing Africa into:

A. West African Cradle
   I. Tropical Sector
      a. Senegambian Subsector
      b. C. Niger Subsector
      c. Chad-Nilotic Subsector
   II. Subequatorial Sector

B. Nilo-Abyssinian Cradle
   I. Nilotic Sector
   II. Abyssinian Sector
C. E. African Cradle
D. C. African Cradle

The Nilo-Abyssinian Cradle coincides with Vavilov's Ethiopian and part of the Mediterranean Centre of origin. The last two cradles have not been further elaborated. Portères (1950; 1962) decided on a W. African Cradle because of the presence of several crops typical to that area. In this he was supported by Murdock (1959), who established four regional agricultural complexes:

1. S.W. Asian Agricultural Complex, developed by Caucasoids
2. SE. Asian Complex, developed by Mongoloids
3. C. American Complex, developed by American Indians
4. W. African Complex, developed by the W. African Negroes.

His decision on an independent West African Agricultural Complex is based on grounds similar to those of Portères.
  Anderson (1960) started from quite another characteristic, in dividing agriculture into floral and non-floral seed-crop agriculture in C. Africa and a 'pole' of floral agriculture in Indonesia. He supposed that the floral type of agriculture spread into Oceania, China and Japan, India and Afghanistan, and the non-floral type remained in Africa. The almost complete lack of interest in flowers and ornamental plants among the African peoples is really astonishing, whereas in the region of the floral type even the poorest man grows some ornamentals (Anderson, 1960). This is not due to an absence of ornamental species in Africa. Many species are commonly grown elsewhere now. The claim of an African cradle of agriculture has been refuted by Wrighley (1960), Clark (1962), Baker (1962), Harris (1967) and Harlan (1967). Baker (1962) summarized his objections as follows:
- few of the domesticates are definitly known to originate from W. Africa
- several of the domesticates have so little differentiated from their wild progenitors that they cannot be of great antiquity as cultivated plants
- if cultivation had been practised locally for seven millenia, an associated weed flora rich in indigenous species would have evolved.
  Harris (1967) concluded that typically W. African crops are local additions to an intrusive agricultural complex, rather than compounds of an ancient indigenous one. After the introduction of agriculture into N. Africa it spread into the Sahara. With the desiccation of this area in the third millenium BC, agriculture became established in the savanna zone stretching from the Atlantic to Lake Chad and further to Cape Horn in E. Africa. In this centre, the many typically African plants, listed by Harlan (1971) were domesticated.
  Kupzov (1955, cited by Darlington 1956) showed regions of the world that belong to certain hearths of agriculture. He identified ten, grouped into 5 'main agricultural regions':

Hearth of agriculture	Main agricultural region
1. Indian 2. Indonesian	I. Australoid
3. Chinese	II. Mongoloid
4. C. Asiatic 5. Near East 6. Ethiopian 7. Mediterranean	III. Europoid
8. Nigerian	IV. Negroid
9. Mexican 10. Peruvian	V. Americanoid

  Except for Nigeria they derive from a neolithic stage.
  Zhukovskij (1965) was the first to refer to Siberia as a gene centre for crops. Many Malus, Prunus, Pyrus and other species were domesticated there. Further, it is a rich source of wild relatives of these species.

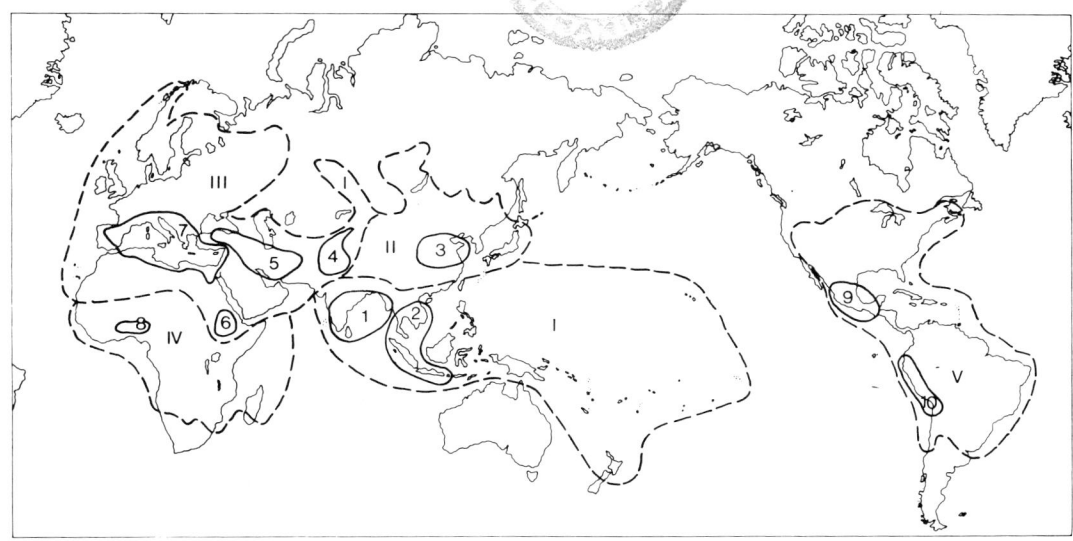

Primary regions of agriculture (——) and regions of expansion (---) of
Darlington (1956) derived from Kupzov (1955)

Megacentres of cultivated plants of Zhukovskij (1968)

In 1968, he heralded his idea about 'megagene centres'. As so many crops
originate outside one of Vavilov's centres of origin, it was necessary to
enlarge the areas in which species were domesticated. These megacentres en-
gulf much of the world's land surface and extend over vast areas. They are:

1. China	7. Mediterranean coastal and adjacent regions
2. Indochina-Indonesia	8. Africa (8a Ethiopia)
3. Australia-New Zealand	9. Europe-Siberia
4. Indian Subcontinent	10. C. America
5. C. Asia	11. Bolivia-Peru-Chile
6. W. Asia	12. N. America

Megacentres 1, 2, 4, 5, 6, 7, 8a, 10 and 11 as recognized by him, are based on Vavilov's concepts though much enlarged. Zhukovskij proposed as new ones 3 (Australia-New Zealand), 8 (whole Africa) and 9 (Siberia). Megacentre 12 (N. America) had already been presented by Darlington & Janaki Ammal (1945) and 9 (Europe) by Darlington (1956). Zhukovskij (1968) did not draw boundaries between 2 and 4, 5 and 6.

In 1970, Zhukovskij made some amendments; some megacentres were enlarged and boundaries were drawn between 2 and 4, and 5 and 6. Obviously the greater the number of investigated crops, the larger the areas. Therefore Harlan (1971) developed the idea of centres and non-centres. He suggested that agriculture began independently in three areas and that there was a system composed of a centre and a non-centre, many indigenous plant species were domesticated, after agriculture was introduced. Harlan (1971) preferred the term 'non-centre' because of the large area involved. His classification was:

Centre	Non-centre
A1. Near-Eastern	A2. African
B1. Chinese	B2. SE. Asian and S. Pacific
C1. C. American	C2. S. American

Major crops domesticated in the 'non-centres' may sometimes have spread to their centres in early times.

Zhukovskij's (1970) classification has been used as basis for the following list, though possibly some megacentres still have to be enlarged. This

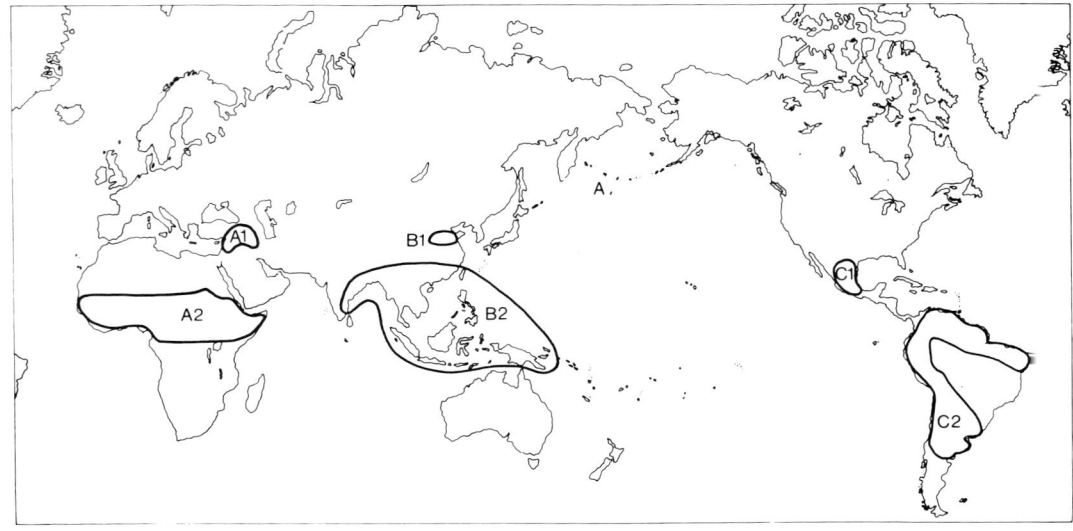

Centres and noncentres of agricultural beginnings of Harlan (1971)

holds especially for S. America, where a shift of the eastern boundary may include Brazil and Paraguay and the land west of these countries, as proposed by Darlington & Janaki Ammal (1945).

We preferred the term Region to Megacentre.

Future research will show whether there have actually been three cradles of agriculture:
1. E. Asia (China and Burma)
2. the Near East (Fertile Crescent)
3. C. America,
and how agriculture spread from these cradles over the world.

1 Chinese-Japanese Region

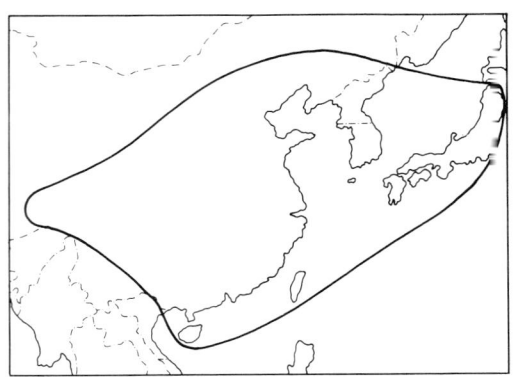

Vavilov called the Chinese-Japanese Region the 'East Asian Centre of Origin'. For several crops, Japan is a secondary centre of diversity. The Chinese-Japanese Region is the primary region of diversity for several fruit-crops from the Amur-Ussuri Region. Li (1966, quoted by Chang 1970) divides China into two regions: (1) N. China with a seed and vegetable agriculture; (2) S. China, which forms a buffer zone between N. China and Region 2, with its vegetatively produced crops. Chang (1970) and Harlan (1971) suggest an independent origin of agriculture in the N. China Region, which resulted in a wholly original assemblage of cultivated plants. Harlan calls the B1 North Chinese Centre of Origins for Agriculture.

The earliest known site of agriculture in China is at Yang-Shao. It is strictly Chinese, with no appreciable foreign influence before 1300 BC. It is at present assessed to date back as far as the 4th millenium BC. Older agricultural sites will probably be found in China (Ho, 1977).

China contributed several major crops. These include several species of fruit trees, Camelia sinensis, Corchorus sinensis, Glycine max, Panicum miliaceum and Setaria italica. It is a secondary centre of diversity for Oryza sativa and other crops.

Actinidiaceae

ACTINIDIA ARGUTA Sieb.& Zucc. Tara vine. 2n= c. 116. China, Japan, Korea and the Primorye Territory, USSR. Very frost resistant. Used in crosses with A. chinensis* (Schroeder & Fletcher, 1967).

ACTINIDIA CHINENSIS Planch. Chinese gooseberry, Strawberry peach, Yang tao. 2n=c. 116, c. 160. W. and C. China. Extensively cultivated in the Yangtse valley and elsewhere for its large, fragrant, juicy fruits. Luther Burbank used it as a pollen donor with the frost resistant A. arguta*.

ACTINIDIA KOLOMICTA Maxim. Kolomikta. 2n=c. 112. NE. China and the Primorye Territory, USSR. Very winterhardy. With delicious berries containing much Vitamin C. It is cultivated.

ACTINIDIA POLYGAMA Miq. Silver vine. 2n=c. 58, c. 116. N. and W. China, Korea and Japan.

A polygamous, trioecious ornamental. In Japan the leaves are boiled and eaten.

Alismataceae

SAGITTARIA SAGITTIFOLIA L. Arrowhead. 2n=22. Europe and Asia. A herb cultivated in China and Japan for its edible corms.

Alliaceae

ALLIUM CHINENSE G. Don (syn. A. bakeri Regel). Rakkyo, Ch'iao T'ou. 2n=(x=8) 16, 24, 32. China (Li, 1970). Cultivated in China, Japan, California and elsewhere by the Japanese and Chinese.

ALLIUM FISTULOSUM L. Welsh onion, Cibol, Stone leek, Spring onion. 2n=16. Siberia and China (Li, 1970). Cultivation started probably in N. China. Cultivated in China and Japan. Related to A. altaicum Pall. (2n=16) from N. Mongolia. A. wakegii Araki. (2n=16) and A. microbulbum Prokh. The latter is considered a hybrid of A. fistulosum* and A. altaicum. Cultivars with blue-green leaves and white bulb are sometimes separated as A. bouddbae O. Deb. (2n=16) (Purseglove, 1972).

ALLIUM LEDEBOURIANUM Roem. & Schult. Asatsuki. 2n=16. From USSR to Japan. Cultivated in Japan (Kihara, 1969).

ALLIUM MACROSTEMON Bunge. Chinese garlic. Chromosome number varying with parts of the plant from diploid (2n=2x=18) to hexaploid (2n=2x=72). Including aneuploids. Ancient Chinese garden plant with very big bulbs. Introduced in W. Georgia (USSR) during the Middle Ages.

ALLIUM NIPPONICUM Franch. & Savat. 2n=16, 32. Formerly cultivated in China but now it only grows wild there (Li, 1969).

ALLIUM RAMOSUM L. Chinese leek. 2n=32. N. China and Siberia. Cultivated in N. China. An autotetraploid. It differs from A. porrum*.

ALLIUM SATIVUM L. Garlic. 2n=16, genome formula SS. C. Asia (p. 81). Var. pekinense Makino sometimes considered a native of N. China. Cultivated in N. China and Japan (Li, 1969).

ALLIUM SCHOENOPRASUM L. Chive. 2n=16, 16 + 1B, (24, 32). Europe, Asia and N. America. Very polymorphous. Domesticated in USSR (region not given) (Kazakova, 1971). Cultivated over the whole world.

ALLIUM TUBEROSUM Rottl. ex Spreng. (syn. A. odoratum L.). Kui ts'ai, Nira, Chinese chive. 2n=16, 32. Primary centre of origin unknown, as it easily runs wild (Jones & Mann, 1963). At present from E. Mongolia to Japan, the Philippines and through Thailand to N. India. Its tetraploid type may derive from an autotetraploidization of a diploid species or from an amphiploidization of a hybrid of two diploid species. Cultivated in China for its edible leaves and young inflorescenses, and as an ornamental.

Amaranthaceae

AMARANTHUS GANGETICUS*

Anacardiaceae

RHUS SUCCEDANEA L. Waxtree. 2n=30. China and Japan.

RHUS VERNICIFERA DC. (syn. R. verniciflua Stokes). Varnish tree. 2n=30. China and Japan. It is the source of a varnish, Japanese lacquer.

Aquifoliaceae

ILEX INTEGRA Thunb. 2n=   . Japan. A tree cultivated for its bark which is pounded and used as bird lime.

Araceae

COLOCASIA ESCULENTA (L.) Schott var. antiquorum (Schott) Hubbard & Rehder (syn. C. antiquorum Schott, C. esculenta var. globulifera Engl. & Krause). Eddoe, Taro, Dasheen. 2n=2x= 28, 3x=42. SE. Asia (p. 49). Many socalled wild specimens are probably derivatives of run wild plants. From SE. Asia it spread to China and Japan where var. antiquorum developed. In 500 AD. some cultivars are mentioned in China (Li, 1969). At present many cultivars are described. Some of them are triploid (Bai et al., 1971). Their vernacular names are also used for Xanthosoma spp. Dasheen is a corruption of 'eddo de la China'. In Japan a secondary centre of diversity developed.

Araliaceae

ARALIA CORDATA Thunb. Udo. 2n=28. Japan. Cultivated in Japan as a vegetable (Kihara, 1969).

PANAX GINSENG C.A. Meyer. Ginseng, Chinese ginseng, Korean ginseng. Ussuri region, China, Manchuria and Korea. Exterminated in the Chinese provinces Shansi and Shensi. There it was cultivated for a long time in SE. Manchuria, N. Korea, Japan and also USA and USSR (Baranov, 1966). Radix Ginseng comes from the cultivated ginseng, and Radix Ginseng Sylvestris from the wild (Hu, 1976).

PANAX PSEUDO-GINSENG Wall. San-ch'i. 2n=   . China. Wild and cultivated for its roots used in medicine (Hu, 1976).

PANAX REPENS Max. (syn. Aralia repens Max.). China and Indochina. A herb cultivated in Yunaran, China and elsewhere for its medicinal roots.

TETRAPANAX PAPYRIFERUM (Hook.) Koch. Rice-paper plant. 2n=24. N. Formosa and S. China (Hunan, Szechwan, Yunnan, Kweichow, Kwangsi and Kwangtung provinces). Cultivated in the (sub)tropics as an ornamental (Perdue & Kraebel, 1961).

Azollaceae

AZOLLA PINNATA R. Brown. Water velvet, Water fern, Mosquito fern. 2n=   . Domesticated in China and Vietnam (p. 50) and grown for its symbiosis with the N-fixing alga Anabaena axollae Strassburger. In China, several cultivars have been developed: Red azolla, Green azolla, Wild azolla-Whole river red and Vietnam azolla. See further p. 50.

Balsaminaceae

IMPATIENS BALSAMINA L. Balsam, Garden balsamine. 2n=14. Indo-Malaya and China. Cultivated in China as a cosmetic plant and elsewhere as an ornamental.

Boraginaceae

LITHOSPERMUM OFFICINALE L. Var. erythrorhizon (Sieb. & Zucc.) Hand.-Mazz. (syn. L. murasaki Sieb., L. erythrorhizon Sieb. & Zucc.). 2n= 28. Cultivated in N. China and Japan for a red dye. Ssp. officinale is cultivated in Bohemia (p.   ).

Burseraceae

CANARIUM ALBUM (Lour.) Raeusch. White Chinese olive. 2n=   . China. Cultivated in S. China and Cochinchina.

Cabombaceae

BRASENIA SCHREBERI J.F. Gmel. Watershield, Junsai. 2n=28. Asia, Africa, Australia and N. America. Cultivated in Japan as a vegetable (Kihara, 1969).

Campanulaceae

CODONOPSIS TANGHEN Olivier. Szechuan tang-sêng. 2n=   . China. Cultivated for seng.

PLATYCODON GRANDIFLORUM DC. Chinese bellflower. 2n=(16), 18, (28). Cultivated in China and Japan as a medicinal crop.

Cannabidaceae

CANNABIS SATIVA L. Hemp. 2n=20. Its origin is described on p. 149. In NE. Asia including Japan, Korea and the Peking area exceptionally tall plants are grown (Small et al., 1975).

HUMULUS JAPONICUS Sieb. & Zucc. 2n=16 in male plants and 17 in female plants with an X-Y_1-Y_2 sex chromosome system. E. Asia (Japan, Taiwan, China, Korea and Manchuria). Naturalized in E. N. America, Europe and sporadically elsewhere. An annual aggressive weed (Small, 1978).

HUMULUS LUPULUS L. Hop. 2n=2x=20 with X-Y sex chromosome system. Var. cordifolius (Miquel) Maximowicz (syn. H. cordifolius Miquel) is wild and cultivated in Japan and China. A perennial mainly propagated by rhizomes (Small, 1978a).

HUMULUS YUNNANENSIS Hu. 2n=   . Dioecious. Yunnan, China. It looks similar to the female plant of H. lupulus and is often confused with it.

Celastraceae

EUONYMUS JAPONICUS Thunb. (syn. E. pulchellus Carr.). 2n=32. S. Japan. A shrub. Cultivated in Spain and elsewhere for rubber.

TRIPTERYGIUM WILFORDII Hook.f. 2n=   . China, Japan and Taiwan. Cultivated in Chekiang, China as a source of insecticide.

Chenopodiaceae

KOCHIA SCOPARIA (L.) Schrader. Summer cypres. 2n=18. S. Europe and Asia. Cultivated in Japan and China as a potherb, and as an ornamental.

SALSOLA KOMAROVII (Iljin.) Oka-hijiki. 2n=36. Japan. Cultivated there (Kihara, 1969).

SALSOLA SODA L. 2n=18, 36. Mediterranean area and Asia. A herb cultivated in Japan.

SUAEDA GLAUCA Bunge. Matsuna. 2n=   . Japan. Cultivated there (Kihara, 1969).

Chloranthaceae

CHLORANTHUS SPICATUS (Thunb.) Mak. (syn. Ch. inconspicuus Swartz.). 2n=30. China. Cultivated in China, Indochina and Japan as a tea aroma.

Compositae

ARCTIUM LAPPA L. 2n=32, 36. Europe and Asia. Cultivated in China and Japan as a root vegetable and in China and Europe (p.   ) as a medicinal plant.

ARTEMISIA CAPILLARIS Thunb. 2n=18, (36). E. Asia. Cultivated there and elsewhere as a medicinal plant.

CHRYSANTHEMUM CORONARIUM L. Garland chrysanthemum, Crown daisy. 2n=   . China. Cultivated in S. China (Li, 1970), later in whole China and Japan and elsewhere. Used as a vegetable.

CHRYSANTHEMUM SEGETUM L. 2n=18. Europe and Asia. Cultivated especially in China. Leaves are used as a vegetable in the Near-East. Malaya and Indochina.

CHRYSANTHEMUM SINENSE Sab. (syn. Pyrethrum sinense DC.). 2n=   . China and Japan. Cultivated there as a vegetable.

GYNURA PINNATIFIDA DC. (syn. G. japonica Mak.). San ch'i, Tien ch'i. 2n=20. China. A perennial herb cultivated for its medicinal properties.

LACTUCA DENTICULATA Maxim. 2n=10, (20). It was cultivated in China.

LACTUCA INDICA L. Indian lettuce. 2n=18. India, Japan, Philippines and Indonesia. Cultivated in China, Japan and other countries. Many varieties exist in China.

PETASITES JAPONICUS F. Schmidt. Fuhi. 2n=87. Sachalin and Japan. Cultivated for its flower buds and leaf stalks (Uphof, 1968; Kihara, 1969).

XANTHIUM STRUMARIUM L. Cocklebur. 2n=36. In China it was used as vegetable. Now it is a weed in fields and along roadsides (Li, 1969).

Convolvulaceae

CALYSTEGIA SEPIUM (L.). R.Br. 2n=22, (24). Subtropics and tropics. A perennial herb cultivated in China for its roots which are used as a vegetable.

IPOMOEA AQUATICA Forsk. (syn. I. reptans Poir.). 2n=30. Throughout the tropics. Var. aquatica is an aquatic plant and a paddy vegetable in S. India and SE. Asia. Propagated by cuttings. Cultivated in fishponds to provide spinach, pig and fishfood (Purseglove, 1968). Var. reptans is an upland vegetable in SE. Asia propagated by cuttings or seed.

Corylaceae

CORYLUS CHINENSIS Franchot. 2n=   . China. Cultivated especially in the Szechuan and Yunnan provinces.

CORYLUS HETEROPHYLLA Fischer. Siberian hazel nut. 2n=28. N. China, Japan, Korea and the Primorye Territory, USSR. Cultivated in China. The seed has a medium-good taste. The shell is very hard.

CORYLUS MANSHURICA Maxim. Manchurian hazel. 2n=   . China, Japan and the Primorye Territory, USSR. Cultivated in China.

CORYLUS SIEBOLDIANA Blum. Siebold's hazel. 2n=28. Japan. Cultivated there.

Cruciferae

BRASSICA CAMPESTRIS L. 2n=20, genome formula AA. See p. 150 for the origin of this species. In Region 1 four (sub)species developed. Ssp. chinense (L.) Makino (syn. B. chinensis*) is an annual, fast-growing, precocious, leafy vegetable. The juicy leaves only contain 3.5-4% dry matter. Ssp. nipposinica (Bailey) Olsson (syn. B. japonica Sieb., B. rapa var. laciniifolia (Bailey) Kitam). It has finely dissected deep-green leaves (7% of fresh leaves is dry matter). It grows slowly and has little winterhardiness. Ssp. pekinensis (Lour.) Olsson (syn. B. pekinensis Rupr.) is one of the oldest vegetables in China. It forms large, compact heads. Ssp. narinosa (Bailey) Olsson, Broad-beaked mustard forms a tight rosette of small, curley leaves (see B. narinosa*).

BRASSICA CHINENSIS L. (syn. B. campestris L. ssp. chinensis (L.) Makino). Chinese cabbage, Celery cabbage, Pak-choi. 2n=20, genome formula AA. Primary centre China where it was domesticated. Cultivated in SE. Asia and elsewhere. It is a vegetable, a salad and an oil crop (var. oleifera). Var. pekinensis (Rupr.) (syn B. pekinense Rupr.), pe-tsai. (2n=20) has

blanched heart (see B. campestris*). Var. parachinensis Bailey (Sinsk.) is B. parachinensis Bailey, mok pak-choi. B. japonica* has also the same genome formula. This genome is related to the Ad genome (n=7) of B. adpressa Boiss. (2n=14), the F genome (n=8) of B. fruticulosa Cyr. (2n=16) and the T genome (n=10) of B. tournefortii Gouan (2n=20) (Mizushima, 1969). Prakash & Narain (1971) concluded that the genomes of B. tournefortii are younger than the A genome, and that this species has evolved from the oleiferous plants of the species carrying the A genome.

BRASSICA NARINOSA L. (syn. B. campestris L. ssp. narinosa L.). Kou T'sai, Broad-beaked mustard, Chinese Savoy. 2n=20. Only known as a cultigen. Cultivated in E. China esp. around Shanghai. Introduced to Japan and later to the USA (Helm, 1963b). Related to B. chinensis* and other A genome carrying diploid Brassica-species. It has entire, deep dark-green leaves.

BRASSICA OLERACEA L. Chinese kale. 2n=18, genome formula CC. Formerly described as B. alboglabra Bailey, but Phelan & Vaughan (1976) showed that Chinese kale belongs to B. oleracea, however Snogerup (1979) suggested that this vegetable may derive from introductions of B. cretica* ssp. nivea.

NASTURTIUM INDICUM DC. 2n=   . In China it was cultivated as a vegetable. Near Saigon var. apetala Gagnep. is grown as a medicinal crop.

PUGIONUM CORNUTUM Gaertn. 2n=   . A herb cultivated as a vegetable in Mongolia.

RAPHANUS SATIVUS L. Radish, Small radish. 2n=18, genome formula RR. This is a very polymorphic species including biennials with large, fleshy roots and annual forms. Japan and the opposite coastal areas of the mainland are suggested as primary centre. If so the radish would have derived from the wild R. raphanistrum L. (2n=18) and spread over the Old World probably introgressing with other ecotypes and other wild species as R. maritimus Smith (2n=18) and R. rostratus DC. Wein (1964) suggested that R. maritimus is the parent of radish, while R. landra Moretti (2n=18) is the parent of the small radish. He indicated the E. Mediterranean region as its gene centre (p. 107).
In Japan and China large rooted forms: daikon (R. acanthiformis de la Blanch., R. sativus var. acanthiformis Mak., var. macropus Mak., var. longipinnatus Bailey) have been developed. A giant form, the Sakurajuma Daikon (f. gigantissimus), is cultivated in Japan. The roots weigh up to 20 kg. Vavilov (1949/50) called these giant cultivars, the champions of plant breeding.
Var. oleiformis* Pers., the oil-seed radish is cultivated in China and Japan and also

elsewhere.

WASABIA JAPONICA (Miquel) Matsumura (syn. Eutrema wasabi (Sieb.) Maxim.). Wasabi, Japanese horseradish. 2n=28. Cultivated for its pungent rhizomes.

Cucurbitaceae

CUCUMIS MELO L. Melon, Muskmelon, Canteloupe. 2n=24. Centre of origin in Africa (p. 124). Secondary centre in China. Chinese and Japanese melons have small fruit and an unpleasant strong taste. The genotypes are convar. chinensis (Pang.) Greb., convar. monoclinus (Pang) Greb., ssp. conomon (Thunb.) Greb. (syn. C. conomon Roxb.), oriental pickling melon.

CUCUMIS SATIVUS L. Cucumber, Gherkin, 2n=14. Centre of origin in India (p. 72). Secondary gene centre a mesophytic type with elongated fruits arose in the Far East. Sources of resistance to powdery mildew are found there.

HODGSONIA MACROCARPA Cogn. (syn. H. heteroclita Hook.f. & Thomson, Trichosanthes kadam Miq.). Lard fruit. 2n= . Cultivated in Yunnan and elsewhere in China for its oily seeds.

TRICHOSANTHES CUCUMEROIDES Max. Japanese snake gourd. 2n=44. The chromosomal number suggests and autoploidization or alloploidization, which may have happened in Japan or China where their roots are used to prepare starch.

TRICHOSANTHES JAPONICA Regel. 2n=22. Japan. There starch is prepared from the roots.

Cyperaceae

CAREX DISPALATA Boott. 2n=78, 84. Japan. Cultivated there in rice fields for its leaves which are made into hats.

CYPERUS CEPHALOTUS Vahl. (syn. C. natans Buch-Ham.). 2n= . Trop. Asia and Australia. A perennial herb cultivated in the rice fields in Japan for mat making (Uphof, 1968).

CYPERUS GLOMERATATUS L. Wangul. 2n= . Korea. Old fibre crop. Rarer than C. iwasakii*.

CYPERUS IWASAKII M. Wangul. 2n= . Korea. Old fibre crop. Much more common than C. glomeratatus*.

ELEOCHARIS DULCIS (Burm.f.) Trinius (syn. E. plantaginea R.Br.). Water chestnut. 2n= . W. Africa, upto India, China, Japan, Philippines, Fiji and New-Caledonia. A herb. Cultivated in S. China for its tubers. Probably derived from E. tuberosa Schultes which grows wild in trop. Asia.

Dioscoreaceae

DIOSCOREA JAPONICA Thunb. 2n=40. Japan. Cul-

tivated in Japan, China and neighbouring islands. Some taxonomists include this species in D. opposita*.

DIOSCOREA OPPOSITA Thunb. (syn. D. batatas Decne.). Chinese yam, Cinnamon vine. 2n=c. 140, c. 144. China. Cultivated in China, S. Japan, Taiwan and the Ryukyu islands.

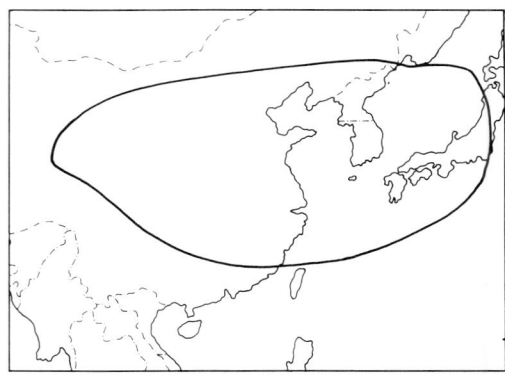

Dioscorea opposita (Harris, 1972)

Ebenaceae

DIOSPYROS KAKI L.f. (syn. D. chinensis Blume). Kaki, Japanese persimmon. 2n=c. 54-56, 90. Mountains of C. China. Centre of origin and primary centre of diversity in China. Secondary centre is Japan. Cultivated in Mediterranean countries and USA for its edible fruits.

DIOSPYROS LOTUS L. Caucasian persimmon. 2n=30. Subtropical China, in Talysk and W. Georgia, USSR and adjacent Iran (p. 82). All three are countries of primary diversity. Naturalized in the Balkan peninsula and elsewhere. The fruit is excellent when dried.

DIOSPYROS MAJOR (Forst.f.). Bakh. (syn. D. andersonii P.S. Green). 2n= . Pacific islands. Cultivated for its fruits which produce oil that can be used to scent other oils. The seeds are edible (Smith, 1971).

Elaeagnaceae

ELAEAGNUS MULTIFLORA Thunb. Cherry eleagnus 2n= . China, Japan and Korea. Cultivated for its edible nuts (Mansfeld, 1959).

ELAEAGNUS PUNGENS Thunb. 2n=28. N. China and Japan. Cultivated for its edible fruits.

ELAEAGNUS UMBELLATA Thunb. 2n=28. China, Korea and Japan. Cultivated for its edible nuts (Mansfeld, 1959).

Eucommiaceae

EUCOMMIA ULMOIDES Oliver. Gutta percha tree, Tuchung. 2n=34. The upland regions of W. and C. China. Cultivated as a medicinal plant. A polygamous plant, dioecious forms have been found.

Euphorbiaceae

ALEURITES CORDATA (Thunb.). R.Br. Tung oil tree. 2n=22. Primary gene centre: Japan. Cultivated there and in Taiwan. Its cross-ability with A. fordii* and A. montana* points to an affinity.

ALEURITES FORDII Hemsl. Tung oil tree. 2n=22. C. China, between 26° and 33°N. Hybrids may occur between wild and cultivated forms. Secondary gene centre of cultivated tung trees probably in USA (p. 202). Cultivated in other American countries, in USSR and Madagascar. With A. montana* natural hybrids may occur. It also crosses with A. cordata.

ALEURITES MONTANA (Lour.) Wils. Tung oil tree. 2n=22. China south of 25°N. Cultivated in Malawi, Brazil and elsewhere. With A. fordii* natural hybrids may occur. It also crosses with A. cordata*.

SAPIUM SEBIFERUM Roxb. Chinese tallow tree. 2n=36. Cultivated in the tropics.

Euryalaceae

EURYALE FEROX Salisb. 2n=58. Tropical Asia. Cultivated in S. China.

Fagaceae

CASTANEA CRENATA Sieb. & Zucc. Japanese chest-nut. 2n=22, 24. Japan. Cultivated in Japan and in USA for its nuts.

CASTANEA MOLLISSIMA Blume. Chinese chestnut. 2n=24. N. and W. China. Cultivated in China and elsewhere for its nuts. It is source of resistance to Endothia parasitica, a fungus causing damage to chestnut (C. sativa) in USA.

QUERCUS ALIENA Blume. 2n= . Japan, Korea and C. China. Cultivated as food for the Japanese oak spinner (Mansfeld, 1959).

QUERCUS DENTATA Thunb. Daimyo oak. 2n=24, 48. Japan, Taiwan, Korea and Manchuria and W. and N. China. Cultivated as food for the Japanese oak spinner and also used for timber (Mansfeld, 1959).

QUERCUS MONGOLICA Fisch. Mongolian oak. 2n=24. N. China, Korea and N. Japan. Cultivated as food for the Japanese oak spinner and also for timber.

Ginkgoaceae

GINKGO BILOBA L. Gingko, Maidenhair tree. 2n= . E. China. Cultivated in China and Japan as an ornamental. The seeds are eaten.

Gramineae

ARUNDINARIA AMABILIS McClure. Tonkin bamboo, Tonkin cane. 2n= . Only known as cultigen and may have originated in Vietnam. Secondary gene centre: China - Province Guandun and adjacent regions of Guancy. Cultivated for its stems which have many technical properties. Used for hand work, including fishing rods.

AVENA SATIVA L. convar. nuda Nord. (syn. A. nuda L.). Naked oats. 2n=42, genome formula AACCDD. The origin of oats has been described on p. 109. Cultigen of NE. China and Mongolia, the Tibetan-Himalaya highlands, in Turkestan and W. China. It is characterized by 5 to 7 florets per flower and by big seeds.

BAMBUSA GLAUCESCENS (Willd.) Sieb. ex Munro. (syn. B. nana Roxb.). Hedge bamboo. 2n=72. China and Japan where it is cultivated. In Indochina it is grown as a border plant.

BAMBUSA MULTIPLEX Raeusch. 2n=72. Cochin China and Japan. A shrubby, woody grass. Cultivated in trop. Asia for various purposes.

BAMBUSA STRICTUS Nees. 2n=70, 72. India (p. 73) and provinces Guancy, Guandun, China and in Hongkong, in tropical evergreen forests. Stems are about equal to those of the best Indian species B. arundinaceae*. Secondary centres: Indochina (p. 53) and S. China.

BAMBUSA TEXTILIS McClure. 2n= . Province Guancy, China.

BAMBUSA TULDOIDES Munro. 2n= . S. China. Cultivated for various purposes.

CHIMONOBAMBUSA QUANDRANGULARIS (Fenzi.) Mak. 2n=48. Continental China and Taiwan. Culti-vated in Japan, China and Taiwan and occa-sionally on the shores of the Black Sea in Caucasus, USSR.

ECHINOCHLOA CRUS-GALLI L. Barnyard grass. 2n= 36, (42, 48), 54, (72). Japan and China. Close affinities with the cultivated E. fru-mentacea*. The hexaploid type, 2n=6x=54 is an allopolyploid with E. oryzicola Vasing., 2n=36 as one parent. According to Yabuno (1968) this species has the same genomic con-stitution as E. utilis (see E. frumentacea*).

ECHINOCHLOA CRUS-PAVONIS Schult. 2n=36, 54. Subtropics and tropics. A grass cultivated in Yunnan, China.

ECHINOCHLOA FRUMENTACEA (Roxb.) Link. (syn. Panicum frumentacea Roxb.). Japanese millet.

Billion dollar grass, Sanwa millet. 2n=36, 54, (56). China. Primary centre in China. Cultivated in Korea, China, USSR and N. America for human consumption, and as a fodder crop. Closely related to E. crus-galli*. Ohwi and Yabuno separated E. utilis Ohwi & Yabuno (2n=54) from E. frumentacea because they found differences in the genomic constitution, geographical distribution and panicle morphology of these two species (Yabuno, 1968). Yabuno considers that the genome formulas of E. utilis and E. crus-galli* are the same and that the genome formulas of E. frumentacea and E. colona are also the same.

ELYMUS ARENARIUS L. Sea lyme grass, Sand elymus. 2n=56. Europe and Asia. A perennial grass. Cultivated in Japan for its culms and elsewhere as a dune stabilizer.

HORDEUM VULGARE L. ssp. humile Vav. & Bacht. 2n=14. Barley. The origin of barley is described on p. 91. Japan and C. China. Ssp. humile is short, has small leaves, hexastichious ears which are apically awned or awnless.

LINGNANIA CHUNGII McClure. 2n=   . S. China (Provinces Junjan and Guancy) in tropical evergreen forests.

MISCANTHUS SACCHARIFLORUS (Maxim.) Hack. 2n= 4x=76. E. Siberia, N., C. and NW. China, Mongolia, Manchuria, Korea, Japan. Erect types near Hongkong were cultivated as 'arrow plants'. This species probably played a role in the development of Chinese sugar-canes (Saccharum officinarum* Sinense group). It is also used as an ornamental (Grassl, 1977).

ORYZA SATIVA L. ecospecies japonica (syn. ssp. japonica Kato). Japonica rice. 2n=24, genome formula AA. Indochina. The origin of rice is discussed on p. 74. Ecospecies japonica consists of ecotypes japonica and nuda. Spread to Japan, Korea, N. China, Himalaya region, Egypt, Italy and Spain.

PANICUM MILIACEUM L. Preso millet, Shu. 2n=36, (40, 54, 72). Primary centre: N. China. From here it has spread upto Italy. In China it was an important cereal till the introduction of wheat and barley (Li, 1970). P. spontaneum Lyssev. (2n=   ) might be a weedy type of this species. It grows in Afghanistan, Kazakstan and may be wild in Mongolia (Mansfeld, 1959).

PASPALUM DISTICHUM L. 2n=40., genome formula X_5X_5WW, (48), 60. Lowlands of the world. In Japan, it is valued as a forage crop in ricefields. See also p. 202.

PHYLLOSTACHYS BAMBUSOIDES Sieb. & Zucc. Madake, Giant timber bamboo, Japanese timber bamboo. 2n=48. China where its primary gene centre is located. Secondary gene centre is Japan. Many forms occur there under the name 'Madake'.

PHYLLOSTACHYS DULCIS McClure. Sweetshoot bamboo. 2n=   . C. China. It is cultivated there. The young shoots are edible.

PHYLLOSTACHYS HENONIS Mitf. 2n=48, 54. C. China (Szechwan). It is cultivated there. Secondary centre is in Japan. One of the forms developed under cultivation, is black bamboo, kenon bamboo ('Nigra', syn. Ph. nigra (Lodd.) Munro, which is cultivated for its young shoots.

PHYLLOSTACHYS MAKINOI Hayata. 2n=48. Taiwan. It is cultivated in Japan.

PHYLLOSTACHYS MEYERI McClure. 2n=48. China (Chzesian). Apparently cultivated in Japan where a strain with deformed internodes arose.

PHYLLOSTACHYS PUBESCENS Mazel ex de Lehaie. 2n=48. Mountains of SE. China. Secondary gene centre in Japan. This species has the largest plants in the genus. Used in the timber industry and for its shoots.

PHYLLOSTACHYS VIRIDIS (Young) McClure. 2n= China. It is cultivated there for pulping.

SACCHARUM OFFICINARUM L. Sugar-cane. 2n various. On New Guinea, the New Guinea Noble canes developed (p. 54) and via Indonesia and Philippines they reached S. China where they hybridized with a 4x Miscanthus species (probably M. sacchariflorus*) to produce the Tekcha clones of the new Sinense group. This must have taken place 705-220 BC. during the Yueh culture. The Tekcha clones have 2n=138. From these basic Sinense clones, younger clones originated with 2n=106-120. They crossed with Chinese S. spontaneum*, 2n=96 to produce still younger Sinense clones, including the 'S. sinense Roxb. clone'. During its migration to India it must have hybridized again with S. spontaneum and probably other grasses. Its migration to India (p. 75) may have been promoted by the red rot disease which affected the S. officinarum clones, which had reached N. India via S. India from Indonesia. This must have taken place ca 150 BC. In N. India, the Sinense group was described as the Pansahi group (Grassl, 1977).

SETARIA ITALICA L. (syn. Panicum italicum L.). Foxtail millet, Liang. 2n=18, genome formula AA. N. China. From here it spread throughout Asia and Europe in prehistoric times. In China it was an important cereal till the introduction of wheat and barley (Li, 1970). It derives from S. virides (L.) Beauv. (2n=18), genome formula AA. It is possible that S. pallidifusca Stapf & C.E. Hubbard (2n=36) is an allotetraploid with S. italica as one of the diploid parents.

SINOBAMBUSA TOOTSIK (Sieb.) Makino. 2n=48. Japan (Ryu-Kyu Islands).

SINOCALAMUS BEECHEYANUS (Munro) McClure. 2n=

. S. China. It is cultivated there.

SINOCALAMUS EDULIS (Odashima) Kenf. 2n= .
China. Its shoots are edible.

SINOCALAMUS OLDHAMII (Munro) McClure. 2n= .
Taiwan.

SORGHUM BICOLOR (L.) Moench. Chinese Amber
Canes and Kaoliang. 2n=20. Sorghum was domesticated in Africa (p. 133). Chinese amber
canes are found on the coast of China and
Korea, and also in India and Burma. They very
likely arrived in China and the Far East by
sea traffic. They are related with the E.
African sorgo. After introduction of sorghum
from India into S. China it came into contact
with S. propinquum (Kunth.) Hitchc., 2n= ,
and by hybridization kaoliang arose (Doggett,
1970).

TRITICUM AESTIVUM L. Thell. ssp. vulgare
(Vill.) MK. (syn. T. vulgare Vill.). Bread
wheat, Common wheat. 2n=42, genome formula
AABBDD. Centre of origin: Transcaucasia and
adjacent regions (p. 93). It arrived through
Korea and Japan in about 300 BC. (Kihara,
1969). Secondary centre of diversity in both
countries. The Chinese wheats are characterized by very broad leaves, with 5 to 7 florets
per spikelet, with squarehead ears, with daylength neutrality, with fast ripening grain,
and by precocious forms. In the mountains of
the Sinkiang Province of China very frost resistant wheats developed. Chinese and Japanese
wheats cross easily with rye, probably because
there was no selection pressure against this
characteristic due to absence of Secale ce-
reale-types. Some Japanese and Korean wheats
are short and this character was introduced in
wheat varieties of Italy, Japan, USA, Mexico
and elsewhere.

ZEA MAYS L. Maize. 2n=20. Maize was domesticated in C. America (p. 190). Secondary centre: China (Brandolini, 1970). The mutant
ceratina Collins originated in E. Asia. Cultivated in China, Japan, Manchuria, Burma and
the Philippines.

ZIZANIA LATIFOLIA Turc. Manchuria water-rice,
Gau Sun, Chiaopai. 2n=30, 34. China and adjacent regions. Cultivated as a cereal in N.
China in ancient times. Later its cultivation
moved to the south and its use as a cereal
gradually decreased. It is cultivated as the
vegetable Chiaopai or Gau Sun. The fungus
Ustilago esculenta P. Henn. infects the leaf
bases, which swell and are eaten.

Grossulariaceae

RIBES ALPESTRIS Decne. 2n= . Himalaya up to
3000 m. In China used as a hedge plant.

RIBES LONGERACEMOSUM French. 2n= . W. China.
Cultivated there for its fruits. It could be

used to improve the strig length of cultivar
R. nigrum*.

RIBES USSURIENSE Jancz. 2n= . E. Asia. It is
a source of resistance to black-current gall
mite, Phytoptus ribes Nal., a pest of R.
nigrum*. It easily hybridizes with R. nigrum.

Illiciaceae

ILLICIUM ANISATUM L. Japanese star anise. 2n=
28. China, Korea and Japan. Cultivated for its
medicinal seeds.

ILLICIUM VERUM Hook.f. (syn. L. religiosum
Sieb. & Zucc.). Star anise. 2n=28. SE. Asia.
Cultivated for its medicinal fruits. It is not
known wild.

Iridaceae

BELAMCANDA CHINENSIS (L.) DC. Blackberry lily,
Leopard flower. 2n=32. China and Japan. Cultivated there as a medicinal crop.

IRIS ENSATA Thunb. 2n=40. Temp. Asia upto
Himalaya. Cultivated in China for its leaves
(binding material).

Juglandaceae

CARYA CATHAYENSIS Sarg. Chinese hickory.
2n= . E. China. Cultivated in Yunnan, China
(Mansfeld, 1959). It closely resembles C.
tonkinensis Lecomte.

JUGLANS AILANTIFOLIA Carr. 2n= . Japan.
Var. ailantifolia (syn. J. sieboldiana Maxim.),
Siebolds walnut. Var. cordiformis (Maxim.)
Rehd. (syn. J. cordiformis Maxim.). Cultiva-
ted in N. America.

JUGLANS DUCLOUXIANA Dode. 2n= . Mountain
regions of Asia. Cultivated in China.

JUGLANS MANDSHURICA Maxim. Manchurian walnut.
2n=32. NE. China and the Primorye Territory,
USSR. It is winterhardy and is used as rootstock.

Labiatae

ELSHOLTZIA CRISTATA Willd. 2n= . China and
Japan. A perennial plant introduced in other
parts of Asia, Europe and America as an oil-
seed crop.

MENTHA ARVENSIS L. var. piperascens Mal. Japanese mint. 2n=96, genome formula R^{a}R^{a}SSJJAA.
Japan. Cultivated in Japan, China and Brazil.
It is the main source of menthol. Var. agrestis (2n=72, genome formula R^{a}R^{a}SSJJ) is very
likely a hybrid of var. piperascens and M.
japonica Makino (2n=48). It is a source of
early maturity and rust resistance (Ikeda et
al., 1970). M. arvensis is one of the parents
of M. x gentilis (see M. cardiaca*).

PERILLA ARGUTA Benth. 2n=   . China and Japan. Cultivated for various purposes. It is sometimes included in P. frutescens*.

PERILLA FRUTESCENS Britt. (syn. P. ocymoides L.). Suttsu, Perilla. 2n=38, 40. Himalayas, China and Japan. Primary centre: China. The red-leaved strains (syn. P. crispa (Thunb.) Nakai) are sometimes used as ornamentals and the green-leaved plants (P. crispa var. ocymoides) for the seed oil. Cultivated in China, Japan and Korea as a drug plant (Li, 1969) and formerly as a leafy vegetable.

STACHYS SIEBOLDII Miq. Chinese artichoke. Japanese artichoke. 2n=   . It is one of the few tuber crops domesticated in China. Cultivated there, Japan, Belgium and France.

Laminariaceae

LAMINARIA JAPONICA Aresch. Haidai. 2n=   . China. Cultivated as a food plant and as a source of iodine.

Lauraceae

CINNAMOMUM CAMPHORA (L.) Nees & Eberm. Camphor tree. 2n=24. China, Japan and Taiwan. Cultivated in these countries and other tropical countries.

CINNAMOMUM ZEYLANICUM Breyn. 2n=24. Sri Lanka and SW. India. Cultivation started in Sri Lanka in 1770. Cultivated now in several countries.

Leguminosae

ASTRAGULUS SINICUS L. (syn. A. lotoides Lam.). Genge, 2n=16. China. Cultivated there on rice soils as a soil improver.

CANAVALIA GLADIATA (Jacq.) DC. var. alba (Makino) Hisauchi (syn. C. ensiformis (L.) DC. var. alba Makino). Siro-nata-name. 2n=22. Cultivated in Japan (Sauer, 1964). Characterized by white seeds.

GLEDITSIA JAPONICA Miq. 2n=   . Japan. Cultivated for fruit juice, which is used for washing.

GLYCINE MAX (L.) Merr. Soya, soybean. 2n=40. China. Available evidence suggests that soya was domesticated around the 11th Century BC. in E.N. China. Since the 1st Century AD., it became widely introduced and land races evolved in China, Korea, India and other parts of Asia. The species is today widely cultivated in most agricultural regions of the world (Hermann, 1962; Hymowitz, 1970).

GLYCINE SOJA Sieb. & Zucc. Wild soya. 2n=40. Widely distributed in N., NE. and C. China, adjacent USSR, Korea, Japan and Taiwan. The weedy G. gracilis Skvortz. occurs where G.

soja and G. max are sympatric and represent derivatives of hybrids between wild and cultivated soybean (Hymowitz & Newell, 1980).

LESPEDEZA CUNEATA (Dum. Cours.) G. Don. (syn. L. sericea Benth.). Perennial lespedeza. 2n= (18), 20. E. Asia. Cultivated in the USA for erosion control.

LESPEDEZA STIPULACEA Maxim. Korean lespedeza. 2n=20. E. Asia. Cultivated in the USA for hay making.

LESPEDEZA STRIATA Hook. Common lespedeza, King grass. 2n=22. E. Asia. Cultivated in the USA in pastures and for hay making.

MUCUNA HASSJOO (Piper & Tracy) Mansf. (syn. Stizolobium hassjoo Piper & Tracy). Yokohama bean. 2n=   . Japan and China. Cultivated there and in the USA for the seeds.

PHASEOLUS ANGULARIS Wight. Adzuki bean. 2n=22. Primary gene centre C. China. It is unknown wild. Cultivated in China, Manchuria, Korea and Japan. Secondary gene centre Japan.

PHASEOLUS VULGARIS L. var. chinensis (syn. Ph. chinensis Hort. ex Schur.). Asparagus bean. 2n=22. Its origin is discussed on p. 194. It reached China from the Americas after Columbus' voyage. In China a secondary gene centre arose. The main character, a parchment-like layer in the pod wall was lost and the pod became edible.

PUERARIA THUNBERGIANA (Sieb. & Zucc.) Benth. Kudzu. 2n=24. China and Japan. Cultivated as a cover crop, green manure and hay crop, in New Guinea and New-Caledonia as a tuber crop (p. 58).

VICIA UNIJUGA A.Br. (syn. Orobus lathyroides L.). Two-leaved vetch. 2n=12, (24, 36). E. Siberia, Manchuria and Japan. Occasionally cultivated.

WISTERIA BRACHYBOTRYS Sieb. & Zucc. 2n=16. A vine. Cultivated for its fibrous bark.

Liliaceae

ANEMARRHENA ASPHODELOIDES Bunge. 2n=22. N. China. A medicinal plant occasionally cultivated.

FRITILLARIA VERTICILLATA Willd. 2n=24. Var. thunbergii Baker. Cultivated in China as a medicinal plant.

LILIUM AURATUM Lindl. Gold band lily, Yama-yuri. 2n=24. Japan. Cultivated there for its large bulbs (Kihara, 1969).

LILIUM CORDIFOLIUM Thunb. 2n=24. Japan. Cultivated there for its starchy bulbs.

LILIUM LANCIFOLIUM Thunb. Oni-yuri. 2n=24. Japan Cultivated there for its bulbs (Kihara, 1969).

LILIUM MAXIMOWICZII Regel. Ko-oni-yuri. 2n= 24. Japan. Cultivated there as a food crop (Kihara, 1969).

LILIUM TIGRINUM Ker-Gawl. Tiger lily. 2n=(24), 36. China. Cultivated there and in Japan for its edible bulbs.

OPHIOPOGON SPICATUS Kunth. 2n=   . China. A herb cultivated in Chekiang as a medicinal plant.

Magnoliaceae

MICHELIA FIGO (Lour.) Spr. (syn. M. fuscata Andr.). Banana shrub. 2n=38. China. Cultivated there for its banana-scented flowers used for scenting hair oil.

Malvaceae

ABELMOSCHUS MANIHOT*

ABUTILON AVICENNAE Gaertn. (syn. A. theophrasti Medic.). Button weed, Chinese jute, Velvet weed, Butter print chingma. 2n=42. Cultivated in China (many local varieties), USSR and elsewhere for its fibre called jute or Indian mallow.

GOSSYPIUM ARBOREUM L. Tree cotton. 2n=26, genome formula A_1A_1. Arose in India (p. 77). Race sinense, Chinese cotton, Nanking cotton, developed in E. China. It is the earliest fruiting form of this species. It has short lint and requires a long daylength. First cultivated as an ornamental. At present it has a low breeding value.

HIBISCUS SYRIACUS L. Rose of Sharon. 2n=80, 80-84, 90, 92. China and Taiwan. Cultivated first in China as a hedge plant and later elsewhere as an ornamental.

MALVA SYLVESTRIS L. High mallow. 2n=42. Probably the early vegetable K'uei mentioned in Chinese literature. At present a weed in China (Li, 1970). Cultivated in Europe as a medicinal crop and ornamental.

MALVA VERTICILLATA L. (syn. M. crispa L., M. mohileviensis Graebn., M. pamiroalaica Ilj.). Mallow. 2n=c. 84, c. 112. E. Asia. It was an early Chinese domesticate there. About 500 AD. it was there an important vegetable with several varieties like purple and white stemmed, large and small leaves. During the 7-10th Century the cultivation in China declined. In 1848 it was only observed in remote areas. Introduced to Japan, where it is a weed now (Li, 1969). Also in W. Asia and Europe. Cultivated in Europe as a medicinal crop. This plant has often been described as M. crispa

being a cultigen of M. verticillata.

Menispermaceae

COCCULUS THUNBERGII DC. 2n=   . A woody vine cultivated in Japan for basket making.

Moraceae

BROUSSONETIA KAZINOKI Sieb. 2n=26, 39. A tree cultivated in Japan and Korea for its bark which is a source for paper production.

BROUSSONETIA PAPYRIFERA (L) Vent. Paper mulberry. 2n=26. China and Japan. In the Far East this tree is used for making paper and barkcloth (Purseglove, 1968).

MORUS ALBA L. White mulberry. 2n=28. China. Cultivated there and elsewhere for its leaves eaten by silk worms, for its fruits and for paper making. It is often planted as a roadside tree. cv Makado has 2n=3x=42.

Musaceae

MUSA BASJOO Sieb. & Zucc. 2n=22. Japan. Species of the Eumusa section. Used for making fibre.

Myricaceae

MYRICA RUBRA Sieb. & Zucc. (syn. M. nagi Thunb.). Chinese strawberry tree, Ioobai, Yama momo. 2n=16. Cultivated in China for its fruits.

Oleaceae

FRAXINUS CHINENSIS Roxb. 2n=92, 138. W. and C. China. Especially var. acuminata Lingelsh. (syn. F. koehneana Lingelsh.) is cultivated as a host plant of the insect Coccus pela for wax production.

LIGUSTRUM JAPONICUM Thunb. Japanese privet. 2n=44. A shrub. Cultivated in Japan for its seeds.

LIGUSTRUM LUCIDUM Ait. 2n=46. A tree cultivated in China as a host plant of the insect Coccus pela for wax production.

LIGUSTRUM OVALIFOLIUM Hassk. 2n=46. Japan. A shrub widely planted for hedges in Europe and elsewhere. It may have run wild there.

OSMANTHUS FRAGRANS Lour. 2n=46. Himalaya, China and Japan. A tree cultivated in E. Asia for its very scented flowers used to aromatize tea.

Palmae

TRACHYCARPUS FORTUNEI (Hook.) H. Wendl. Windmill palm, Chusan palm. 2n=36. China. Often planted in E. Asia for its fibres.

Pedaliaceae

SESAMUM INDICUM L. Sesame, Beni seed. 2n=26.
Primary centre is discussed on p. 144. Secondary centre in China/Japan. There ssp.
quadricarpellatum developed.

Phytolaccaceae

PHYTOLACCA ACINOSA Roxb. 2n=36. Trop. Asia,
China and Japan. A perennial herb cultivated
in India as a vegetable. In the Chinese phar-
macy the berries are used.

Plantaginaceae

PLANTAGO MAJOR L. 2n=12, (18, 24). Europe and
temp. Asia. Var. asiaticum Dcne. is cultivated
in China as a vegetable and as a medicinal
herb.

Polygonaceae

FAGOPYRUM TATARICUM (L.) Gaertn. Tatary buckwheat. 2n=16. Primary centre is probably in
East Asia. There, it is often found as a weed
of barley and wheat fields. It is a source
of rutine.

POLYGONUM HYDROPIPER L. Tade, Knotweed. 2n=
20, (22). Cultivated in Japan (Kihara, 1969)
and formerly, also in China. Var. maximowiczii
is the edible type. In China and elsewhere
it is a weed now (Li, 1969).

POLYGONUM MAXIMOWICZII Regel. 2n=   . Japan.
Cultivated there as a vegetable.

POLYGONUM TINCTORIUM Ait. 2n=40. China. Formerly it was cultivated as a blue dye-plant.
It is naturalized for instance in the Ukraine.

RHEUM HYBRIDUM Murray. Rhubarb. 2n=   . Ori-
ginating probably in Mongolia. Probably a hybrid of R. rhaponticum, 2n=44 and R. palmatum*.

RHEUM OFFICINALE Baill. Medicinal rhubarb. 2n=
22, (44). Cultivated in China as a medicinal
crop.

RHEUM PALMATUM L. East Indian rhubarb, China
rhubarb, Turkey rhubarb. 2n=22, (44). Mongolia, or W. China. Cultivated formerly as a
purgative (root) and at present as an ornamental. It is probably one of the parents of
R. hybridum* (syn. R. rhabarbarum L.). It is
related to R. rhaponticum*.

RHEUM UNDULATUM L. 2n=22, 44. China. Cultivated as a vegetable.

Ranunculaceae

ACONITUM CARMICHAELI Debeaux (syn. A. wil-
sonii Stapf ex Mottet). 2n=64. China. Cultivated there as a medicinal crop.

COPTIS CHINENSIS Franch. 2n=   . W. China. A
herb cultivated as a medicinal plant.

Rhamnaceae

HOVENIA DULCIS Thunb. Japanese raisin tree.
2n=24. China, Korea and Japan. Cultivated in
E. Asia upto India for its edible inflorescence
and as an ornamental.

ZIZIPHUS JUJUBA Mill. non Lam. (syn. Z. vulgaris Lam.). Jujub, Chinese jujube. 2n=24,
(40), 48, (60, 72), 96. Primary gene centre
of the wild and cultivated types is probably
in C. and S. China. Wild type grows in many
Asian countries.

ZIZIPHUS MAURITIANA Lam. (syn. Z. jujuba (L.)
Lam. non Mill., Z. sosoria Roem. & Schult.).
Indian jujube. 2n=48. Tropical Africa and
Asia. Cultivated in India, Cochinchina and
China since ancient times.

Rosaceae

AMYGDALUS BESSERIANA Schott. (syn. A. nana
L.). Dwarf almond, Russian almond, Steppe almond. 2n=16. Primary gene centre is in E.
Europe and Siberia (p. 158). Ssp. rosiflora
types from China are sources of winterhardiness, precocious fruiting and prostrate-grow-
ing. Disadvantages are its small and white-
fleshed fruits.

AMYGDALUS KANSUENSIS Skeels. (syn. Persica
kansuensis (Rehd.) Kov. & Kost., Prunus kansuensis Rehd.). Chinese bush peach. 2n=   .
NW. China. It tolerates -35°C. It could be
useful as a rootstock (Zylka, 1970).

AMYGDALUS MIRA (K.) Koch (syn. Prunus mira
Koehne). Smoothpit peach. 2n=   . W. China
It might be used as a source of late flower-
ing (Zylka, 1970) and winterhardiness.

AMYGDALUS PERSICA L. (syn. A. pumila Lour.
Persica vulgaris Mill., Prunus persica (L.
Batsch.). Peach. 2n=16. Primary centre: moun-
tane areas of Tibet and SW. China (Holub,
1969). Secondary centres: Iran, C. Asia (p
84), Caucasus, Crimea (p. 100). Moldavia (US-
SR) (p. 158), Italy, Spain (p. 118) and California, USA (p. 204). Cultivated for its
fruits and as an ornamental. Holub (1969) divided the cultivated varieties according to
their morphology and geography into four
groups viz. 1. Chinese, 2. Central Chinese,
3. Western Chinese and 4. Yellow-fleshed from
Europe.

ARMENIACA MANDSHURICA (Koehne) Kost. (syn.
Prunus mandshurica (Maxim.), P. armeniaca
var. mandshurica Maxim.). Manchurian apricot.
2n=16. S. Ussuria, E. Manchuria upto N. Korea.
It resists intense cold.

ARMENIACA MUME (Sieb. & Zucc.) Sieb. ex Carr.

(syn. Prunus mume Sieb. & Zucc.). Japanese apricot. 2n=16, 24. Mountains in C. and N. China. Cultivated as an ornamental in China, Korea and Japan. Its kernel is eaten. It is not frost resistant.

ARMENIACA VULGARIS Lam. (syn. Prunus armeniaca L., P. tiliaefolia Salisb.). Apricot. 2n= 16. Primary gene centre: NE. China. Secondary gene centre in E. Tien-Shan and in Trans-Ilii and Dzhungar-Alatau. A small area of wild apricots is found in Daghestan (p. 100) and in the Kotur Bulak canyon in the Alma-Ata region. Evreinoff (1954) believed that it occurred in a much larger region up to Armenia and Iran. The related A. ansu (Max.) Kost. (syn. Prunus ansu Komar) (2n=   ) could be used as a source of resistance to fungal diseases.

CHAENOMELES SINENSIS (Thouin) Koehne. Chinese quince, Japanese quince. 2n=32. Its fruits have the aroma of quince. Therefore it is mistakenly described as a species of Cydonia.

CRATAEGUS HUPEHENSIS Wils. 2n=   . Hupeh, China. Cultivated there for its fruits.

CRATAEGUS PENTAGYNA Waldst. & Kit. (syn. C.

Prunus bessyi

pinnatifida Bunge). Chinese hawthorn. 2n=34. N. China, Korea and Siberia. Cultivated in China for its fruits (Li, 1970).

DUCHESNEA FILIPENDULA (Hemsl.) Focke. (Syn. Fragaria filipendula Hemsl.). 2n=   . A herb of China cultivated for its fruits.

ERIOBOTRYA JAPONICA (Thunb.) Lindl. Loquat, Japanese plum, Japanese medlar. 2n=32, 34. Cultivated in China, Japan, California and S. Europe.

FRAGARIA ITURUPENSIS Staudt. 2n=56. Island of Iturup, S. Kuriles.

MALUS ASIATICA Nakai (syn. M. prunifolia var. rinki). 2n=   . NW. China. Used for cultivation.

MALUS BACCATA (L.) Borkh. var. mandchurica (Max.). Schneid. (syn. Pyrus baccata L.). Manchurian crab apple. 2n=34. Primary gene centre: the Shansi, Shensi, Kiangsi and other provinces in China. Centre of origin probably Siberia, SE. of Lake Baikal (p. 159). Used for rootstock material.

MALUS HALLIANA Koehne. 2n=34. Gene centre in China and Manchuria. A wild ornamental.

MALUS HUPEHENSIS (Pamp.) Redh. (syn. Pyrus hupehensis Rehd.). Chinese crab-apple, Tea crab-apple. 2n=3x=51, 4x=68. C. and W. China and southwards into Assam. It is mainly used as a rootstock. Also a source of resistance to Podosphaera leucotricha. The 3x is male-sterile and 80% of the seeds are apomictic.

MALUS MICROMALUS Makino. 2n=34. China and Japan. Cultivated there. Its fruits are edible (Rehder, 1947). It is thought to be a hybrid of M. spectabilis* and probably M. baccata.

MALUS PUMILA var. niedzwetskyana Dieck. 2n=34. Tian-Shan mountains. China.

MALUS SIEBOLDII Rehd. (syn. Pyrus toringo Sieb.). Toringa crab. 2n=34. Primary centre Japan. It is a profusely branching salt-tolerant shrub used as rootstock for dwarf plantings.

MALUS SPECTABILIS (Ait.) Borkh. Zamechatelnaya. 2n=34, 51. Primary centre: C. China. It is not known wild. It is probably a parent of M. micromalus*.

PRUNUS subgen. cerasus Pers. There are probably 150 species belonging to ssp. cerasus. The greatest number is located in the mountain regions of W. China. Some big fruited species are valuable for breeding.

PRUNUS CANTABRIGIENSIS Stapf. (syn. P. pseudocerasus Koids.). Chinese sour cherry, Yingtao cherry. 2n=   . Yangtze Valley in China. Cultivated in China (Uphof, 1968).

PRUNUS DAVIDIANA (Carr.) Franch. (syn. P. persica var. davidiana Maxim., Persica davidiana Carr.). Chinese wild peach. 2n=16. Vladivostok, SW. through Charbin upto Dacin-San and Ala-San (China). Cultivated as an ornamental. It is frost, drought and heat resistant. Probably it is valuable as a rootstock for Amygdalus persica* and Prunus domestica* (Zylka, 1970).

PRUNUS PSEUDOCERASUS Lindl. (syn. P. paniculata Edwards). 2n=32. W. Hupei, China. A tree cultivated there for its fruits.

PRUNUS SALICINA Lindl. Chinese plum, Japanese plum. 2n=16. Primary gene centre: the forests of N. China. Second gene centre: Japan. Cultivated in Japan, China and also in California. It crosses easily with the North American plum species. A new stone fruit 'cherry plum' was derived from crossing the wild P. cerasifera* with P. salicina var. Burbank. Because of its winterhardiness this fruit tree can be grown where apricot will not fruit.

PRUNUS SARGENTII Rehd. Sargent cherry, Mountain cherry. 2n=16. Japan, Manchuria, Korea and rarely in the Far East of USSR. Used as

Prunus davidiana

an ornamental. It is frost resistant and fast growing. The fruits are not very palatible.

PRUNUS SIMONII Carr. Apricot plum, Simon plum. 2n=16. Primary centre: probably N. China and Japan. No wild plants are found. Also cultivated there. Crossing with P. triflora Roxb.* (2n=16) from the same area has led to the development of cultivars which are especially grown in N. America.

PRUNUS TOMENTOSA Thunb. (syn. P. trichocarpa Bunge). Nanking cherry, Manchur cherry, Chinese bush cherry. 2n=16. N. and W. China, Japan, Himalaya, Turkestan and in the Far East of USSR. Cultivated as a fruit tree and ornamental in the Far East of USSR, N. China and Japan.

PRUNUS USSURIENSIS Kov. & Kost. (syn. P. triflora Roxb. var. mandshurica Skvoro.). Ussurian plum. 2n=16. Cultivated or run wild in Manchuria, E. of USSR and for some years also in Siberia and N. Kazakhstan (Zylka, 1970). It is a source of good fruit flavour and cold resistance. This species is sometimes considered as a subspecies of P. cerasifera*.

PYRUS BETULAEFOLIA Bgb. 2n=34. N. and C. China. Used as rootstock. Resistance against scab (Venturia) is found in this species.

PYRUS BRETSCHNEIDERI Rehd. 2n=34. Hupei and Shansi, China. Primary gene centre: N. China. There it was domesticated. It is the commonest cultivated pear in this region. The fruits are characterized by hard, crisp, white sweet flesh.

PYRUS CALLERYANA Dcne. 2n=34. China, Japan and Korea. Primary gene centre: the Tsinling mountain range, China. It is used as rootstock.

PYRUS PHAEOCARPA Rehd. 2n=34. N. China.

PYRUS PYRIFOLIA (Burm.) Nakai (syn. P. serotina Rehd.). Sand pear. 2n=34. Primary gene centre: the highlands of N. and C. China. Var. culta (Mak.) Nakai is drought resistant, but not very winterhardy. The leaves reach 15 cm in length. The fruits are outstanding for their preserving quality. It crosses easily with the wild European pear, P. communis*.

PYRUS USSURIENSIS Maxim. Ussuri pear. 2n=34. SE. Siberia upto the Manchurian-Chinese area. Primary gene centre: NE. China and the Primorye Territory, USSR, along the Ussuri river. The ancient var. culta is widely distributed over N. and C. China. It is adapted to cold, dry regions. It is the most winterhardy wild pear. As this species originated outside the Chinese centre proper it has no resistance to scab and other diseases. It probably played a part in the origin of P. communis*.

ROSA MULTIFLORA Thunb. 2n=14. E. Asia. Used as rootstock.

ROSA RUGOSA Thunb. 2n= . China and Japan. The rose hips are used by the Ainu. Used as an ornamental and in hedges as one parent to breed for rootstocks.

RUBUS ILLECEBROSUS Focke. Strawberry raspberry, Balloon berry. 2n=14. Japan. Cultivated in N. America.

RUBUS PHOENICOLASIUS Maxim. Wine raspberry. 2n=14. Japan and N. China. Cultivated for its fruits and as an ornamental.

RUBUS PUNGENS Oldhami. 2n= . Korea. Used in breeding with R. idaeus*.

Rubiaceae

GARDENIA JASMINOIDES Ellis (syn. G. florida L.). Cape jasmin. 2n=22. Probably S. China. Cultivated in E. Asia for perfumery oil.

Rutaceae

CITRUS ICHANGENSIS Swing. 2n=18. S. of Tsin 'lin range in W., C. and SW. China. It is very frost resistant. Therefore it has been crossed with cultivated Citrus species. Used as a rootstock.

CITRUS JUNOS Tan. Juzu. 2n=18. Han'su province, China at 1372 m altitude. It is frost resistant and therefore used as a rootstock. Its fruits are big but sour. It was already known in the time of Confucius (about 2500 years ago). Because of introgression, characters of 12 Japanese and 2 Chinese wild Citrus species are recognized in juzu.

CITRUS RETICULATA Blanco. (C. nobilis Andr. non Lour.). Mandarin, Tangerine. 2n=18. See for its possible origin p. 63. Secondary centre: Japan. New types such as the Satsuma (var. unshiu, syn. 'C. unshiu') and the Natsudaudau ('C. natsudaidai') arose through bud mutation and spontaneous hybridization. Satsuma tangerine (unshiu mikan) is probably a derivative of So-kitsu or Man-kitsu.

CLAUSENA LANSIUM (Lour.) Skeels. Wampi. 2n= 18. It is a small-fruit tree of S. China. Cultivated in several tropical countries.

FORTUNELLA CRASSIFOLIA Swing. Meiwa kumquat. 2n=18. China and Japan. It is occasionnaly cultivated.

FORTUNELLA HINDSII (Champ.) Swing. Wild kumquat. Hongkong kumquat. 2n=18, (36). The Tziulun mountains of Hongkong. It has no great value. The 4x form originated spontaneously (Cameron & Soost, 1969).

FORTUNELLA JAPONICA (Thunb.) Swing. (syn.

Citrus japonica Thunb.). Round kumquat, Marumi kumquat. 2n=18. Primary centre Japan. This fruit tree is unknown in a wild state. It is occasionally cultivated.

FORTUNELLA MARGARITA (Lour.) Swing. (syn. Citrus margarita Lour.). Oval kumquat, Nagami kumquat. 2n=18. Japan. Cultivated in Japan, China and Florida, USA. Fortunella species cross easily with each other and with Citrus species.

PONCIRUS TRIFOLIATA (L.) Raf. Trifoliate orange. 2n=18, (36), N. China, also primary centre. This area is its centre of diversity. Cultivated in China as an ornamental, and in USSR and Japan it is used as a rootstock. Hybrids with sweet orange (Citrus sinensis) are citranges used as rootstocks, with sour orange (C. aurantium*) are citradias, crosses of citrange with kumquat (Fortunella margarita*) resulted in citrangequat. Other hybrids are citrandarin (P. trifoliata x C. reticulata) and citrangedin (citrange x calamondin (see C. reticulata)).

TRIPHASIA TRIFOLIA (Burm.f.) P. Wilson (syn. T. aurantiola Lour., T. trifoliata DC.). Lime berry, Trifoliate lime berry. 2n= . Centre of origin possibly China (Mansfeld, 1959). Cultivated for its edible fruits.

ZANTHOXYLUM PIPERITUM DC. Japanese prickly ash, Japan pepper, Sanshô. 2n=70. China and Japan. Cultivated there (Uphof, 1968; Kihara, 1969).

ZANTHOXYLUM SIMULANS Hance (syn. Z. nitidum DC., Z. bungei Planch.). 2n=32. China. A shrub cultivated in C. and S. China for its seeds. This seed is a source of Chinese pepper.

Sapindaceae

LITCHI CHINENSIS Son. Litchi, Lychee, Leechee. 2n=28, 30. S. China. Leenhouts (1978) described three subspecies: ssp. chinensis, ssp. philippensis (Radlk.) Leenh. and ssp. javensis Leenh. Ssp. chinensis is the cultivated litchi. It was first mentioned ca 100 BC. when Emperor Wu Ti tried to introduce it from N. Indochina into S. China. It is grown now in N. India, S. Africa, Florida and Hawaii. There are many races. Those from China can be grouped as Water litchi and Mountain litchi. Water litchis are grown in the lowland and have smooth fruits, while the Mountain litchi is used as stock or as a fruit-tree in hilly regions. Its fruits are smaller and more prickly. Leenhouts (1978) thinks that the Mountain litchis are similar to wild types. Ssp. philippensis is found in the Philippines, where it is not cultivated; its fruits bear sharp pyramidal warts and are not eaten. It is not a wild type (Leenhouts, 1978). Ssp. javensis has fruits like the original ssp. chinensis. It is occasionally grown in Indochina and W.

Java. Van den Berg (1978) believes that ssp. chinensis and ssp. javensis developed independently from ssp. philippines. However more material should be collected and studied to support this.

NEPHELIUM LONGANA (Lam.) Camb. (syn. Euphoria longana Lam.). Longan. 2n=30. C. and S. China. Cultivated there for its fruits.

SAPINDUS MUKOROSSO Gaertn. Chinese soapberry. Soapnut tree. 2n=   . China, Burma and Himalaya. Cultivated in China, Japan, India and elsewhere for its fruits.

Scrophulariaceae

VERONICA ANAGALLIS L. 2n=36. Temperate zone. Cultivated in Japan as a lettuce.

Simaroubaceae

AILANTHUS VILMORINIANA Dode. 2n=   . W. China. Cultivated there as a source of food for silk worms.

Solanaceae

SOLANUM MELONGENA L. var. esculentum Nees. Chinese eggplant. 2n=24. Domesticated in India (p. 79). Secondary centre: China. There the small fruit-form already existed before 500 AD. (Li, 1969).

Taxaceae

TORREYA GRANDIS Fort. Chinese torreya. 2n=   . China. Cultivated in Szechuan and Anhwei, China.

TORREYA NUCIFERA Sieb. & Zucc. Japanese torreya, Kaya. 2n=   . Japan. Cultivated there.

Tetragoniaceae

TETRAGONIA EXPANSA Murr. New Zealand spinach, Tsuruna. 2n=32. Japan. Cultivated there (Kihara, 1969). However, Uphof (1968) restricted its native area to Australia and New Zealand.

Theaceae

CAMELLIA JAPONICA L. Camellia. 2n=30. From Taiwan northwards through the Ryu Kyu islands and Yakushima to S. Japan, also in S. Korea and Dagelet islands (Sealy, 1958). Cultivated for its Tsubaki Oil and as an ornamental. C. wabiske* might be a natural hybrid of C. japonica and C. sinensis*. Attempts to cross the latter species seem to have met success (Kato & Simura, 1978). If so, cold resistance of C. japonica can be introduced into C. sinensis.

CAMELLIA OLEIFERA Abel. (syn. C. sasanqua Thunb.). Sasanqua camellia. 2n=allo 6x=90.

China. Cultivated there and Indochina to yield 'tea oil' (Sealy, 1958).

CAMELLIA SINENSIS (L.). O. Kuntze (syn. C. thea Link., Thea sinensis L.). Tea. 2n=30, (45, 60). Primary centre: the mountains of China, north of NE. India (Simura et al., 1967). It spread to SE. China, Indochina, Assam and later to other countries. Secondary centres: Assam, other parts of India (p.79) and Sri Lanka. Hashimoto & Shimura (1978) consider SE. China (Szechwan - Yunnan) to Assam, India as centre of origin. The taxonomy of Camellia is confusing. Some group the cultivated escapes and putative wild plants in one species C. sinensis, and recognize subspecies, varieties and types; others have given some subspecies/varieties/types specific rank. Wu et al. (1970) suggested that the wild tea populations originated from heterogeneous populations of species hybrids. The main types are China tea (C. sinensis var. sinensis L., syn. C. sinensis L.) and Assam tea (C. sinensis var. assamica (Masters) Wight, syn. C. assamica Masters). The latter type includes the Cambodia race (C. assamica ssp. lasiocalyx Planch.-MS, syn. Thea lasiocalyx Planch.). At Tocklai, Assam Wilson's Camellia (C. irrawadiensis P.K. Barau) is found. The Forest's Camellia (C. taliensis Sealy) produces tea of low quality. It is probably a hybrid of C. sinensis and C. irrawadiensis and should be included in the latter species. Darjeeling tea also is a possible product of C. sinensis introgression in C. assamica (C. irrawadiensis) (Visser, 1969). Leaves are widely used to make tea; in Burma leaves are used to prepare pickled tea as food (Simura et al., 1967).

C. wabiske* might be a natural hybrid of C. sinensis and C. japonica* (see however C. wabiske*) and so are the 'China hybrids' and Cambodian varieties of tea (Bezbaruah & Gogoi, 1972).

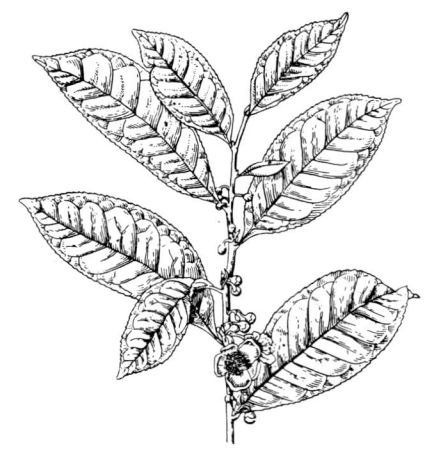

Camellia sinensis

CAMELLIA WABISKE Kitamura. Wabisuke. 2n=30. Cultivated in Japan. This species is considered as a natural hybrid of C. sinensis* and C. japonica* L. If so,. it could probably be used as a bridge species between these two species, because hybridization has failed so far. However Nagato (1979) stated that this species is a hybrid of C. japonica with a species other than C. sinensis.

Thymelaeaceae

DAPHNE ODORA Thunb. 2n=(18, 27), 28, 30. Japan. A shrub cultivated there for its fragrant flowers.

EDGEWORTHIA PAPYRIFERA Sieb. & Zucc. (syn. Daphne papyrifera Sieb.). 2n=36, (72). Japan. Occasionally cultivated there.

Tiliaceae

CORCHORUS OLITORIUS L. Jute, Tossa jute, Jew's mallow. 2n=14. S. China and probably taken to India/Pakistan. Cultivated as a spinach in the Ganges-Brahmaputra delta, where it may have run wild and in the Middle East, Egypt, Sudan and trop. Africa.

Trapaceae

TRAPA BICORNIS L. 2n=   . China. A waterplant cultivated there, Korea and Japan.

TRAPA BISPINOSA Roxb. Singhara nut. 2n=   . India, China and Japan. A waterplant cultivated for the seeds in India.

TRAPA NATANS L. Water chestnut, Water caltrop. 2n=c. 36, 40, 48, c. 48. Europe, Mediterranean region and Asia. It was cultivated in S. China (Li, 1970). Elsewhere the seeds have been consumed since neolithic times.

Typhaceae

TYPHA LATIFOLIA L. Cat-tail, Reeds mace, Bull rush, Marsh beetle. 2n=30. A cosmopolitic plant cultivated in China.

Umbelliferae

ANGELICA KIUSIANA Maxim. 2n=22. China. An old Chinese vegetable. It is a weed now (Li, 1969).

ANGELICA POLYMORPHA Maxim. 2n=22. China. Cultivated there as a medicinal crop.

CRYPTOTAENIA JAPONICA Hassk. Mitsube. 2n=(18), 20, 22. Cultivated in Japan.

GLEHNIA LITTORALIS F. Schmid. Northern Sand Sêng. 2n=22. N. and E. Asia. Cultivated in Shantung, China.

PHELLOPTERUS LITTORALIS Benth. Hama-bôhû. 2n=22. Sachalin, Japan and China. Cultivated

in Japan (Uphof, 1968; Kihara, 1969).

Urticaceae

BOEHMERIA NIVEA (L.). Gaud. Ramie, Rhea, China grass. 2n=28, (42). S. and C. China, on Taiwan and S. Japan. Cultivated in China since ancient times, where there are many varieties, Japan, Philippines and other trop. countries. Var. chinensis, Chinese ramie, White ramie, (2n=28) may have originated in SW. China, while var. indicum (syn. B. utilis Blume, B. tenacissima Gaud. (2n=   ), Indian ramie, Green ramie might be a derivative of a cross between var. chinensis and an unknown species.

Violaceae

VIOLA VERUCUNDA A. Gray. Chin. 2n=24. China. An old chinese vegetable. Now it is a weed (Li, 1969).

Vitadaceae

VITIS AMURENSIS Rupr. (syn. V. thunbergii Regel, V. shiragai Makino). Amut grape. 2n=38. Primorye and Khabarovak and NE. China. This species belongs to the Chinese centre of origin of Vitis-species. It withstands -40°C. It is a possible source of winter-hardiness for V. vinifera . Occasionally cultivated.

VITIS DAVIDII (Rom.) Foex. Spring vitis. 2n=   . The Tziansu and Yunna Provinces, China. Occasionally cultivated there.

Zingiberaceae

ALPINIA CHINENSIS Rosc. 2n=48. China and Indochina. The rhizomes are used in Chinese medicine and the leaves for fibre. Sometimes cultivated.

ALPINIA OFFICINARUM Hance. Lesser galangal, Small galangal. 2n=   . E. and SE. Asia. Cultivated in China.

AMOMUM GLOBOSUM Lour. Round Chinese cardamon. 2n=   . China. Cultivated there.

ZINGIBER MIOGA (Thunb.) Rosc. Mioga ginger, Myôga. 2n=55. Japan. Cultivated there (Kihara, 1969).

2 Indochinese-Indonesian Region

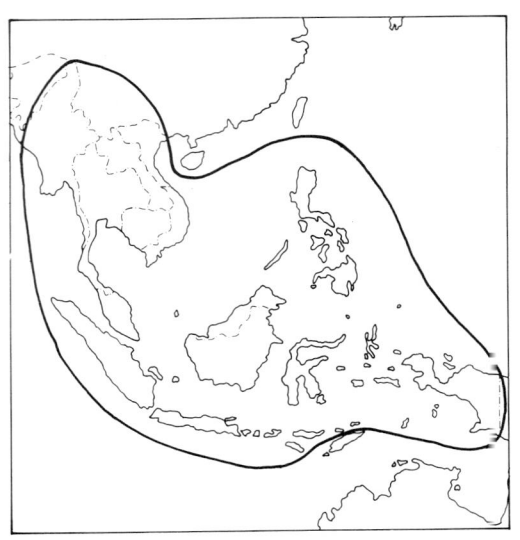

Vavilov called the Indochinese-Indonesian Region the Tropical Asian Centre of Origin. Darlington (1956) and Li (1966 cited by Chang, 1970) divided this region into S. Asia: Burma, Thailand and Indochina, and SE. Asia: Malayan Peninsula and the Malaysian Archipelago. Li described an agriculture based mainly on vegetatively propagated crops. Harlan (1971) considered this region as B2 Southeast Asian and South Pacific noncentre, as agriculture may have been introduced there.

The oldest known agricultural remains from Region 2 come from Spirit Cave 60 km N. of Mae Hongson, NW. Thailand (Gorman, 1969). This agrees with Sauer's (1952) conclusion that the Old World centre of development of agriculture was situated in the NW. part of Region 2 (about present day Burma). Spirit Cave was inhabitated from ca. 10 000 to 5 600 BC. Solheim (1972) proposed that horticulture may have developed in 20 000 - 15 000 BC. and there was a further domestication of plants and also of animals in 15 000 - 8 000 BC. resulting in large-scale agriculture and animal husbandry.

Another early archaeological site is at Non Nok Tha, NE. Thailand. It dates from around 5 000 BC.

In Spirit Cave remains of Prunus, Terminalia, Areca, Vicia or Raphia, Lagenaria and Trapa, and in another layer Piper, Madhuce, Canarium, Aleurites and Areca were found, and in a third layer Canarium, Lagenaria and Cucumis (Gorman, 1969). Further research is needed to support the taxonomic identifications. For instance Schultze-Motel (1972) does not accept that Vicia faba could have been present. Chang (1970) used the presence of Vicia faba, Lagenaria, Trapa and Cucumis as proof that these plants were actually cultivated.

The region is important for crops such as bamboos, tropical fruit trees, ginger, Cocos nucifera, Colocasia esculenta, Dioscorea spp., Musa spp., wild and weedy Oryza spp., Piper spp., and Saccharum officinarum.

Agavaceae

CORDYLINE TERMINALIS Kunth. Palm lily. 2n=ca
152. SE. Asia, Australia and most of Oceania.
Cooked roots will keep for several weeks.
During the 17th and early 18th Century, roots
were fermented and distilled to produce spir-
its (Barrau, 1961).
One clone is extensively cultivated for the
fleshy roots that contain laevulose (Ezumah,
1970).

Amaranthaceae

AMARANTHUS GANGETICUS L. 2n=34. Asia. Cultivated in India, Malaya, China and Japan as a
spinach. See also A. mangostanus*.

AMARANTHUS MANGOSTANUS Juslen (syn. A. tricolor L. var. mangostanus Thell.) 2n=32.
Trop. Asia. Cultivated as a pot-herb. In A.
tricolor are sometimes included var. gangeticus and var. tricolor (syn. A. melancholicus
L.). See A. gangeticus*.

AMARANTHUS PANICULATUS L. 2n=32. Used as a
pot-herb and grain crop in SE. Asia. It might
be conspecies with A. cruentus* (Sauer, 1950)
or a synonym.

Anacardiaceae

BOUEA MACROPHYLLA Griff. 2n=   . A fruit tree
of the wet tropics of SE. Asia.

MANGIFERA CAESIA Jack. 2n=40. Primary centre
Indonesia. This fruit tree is cultivated
there and elsewhere.

MANGIFERA FOETIDA Lour. Bachang mango. 2n=40
Indochina and Malaysia. Cultivated in Java.

MANGIFERA ODORATA Griff. Kurwini mango. 2n=
. Malaysia. Cultivated in Java. It is
closely related to M. indica* (Rhodes et al.
1970).

SEMECARPUS ANACARDIUM L.f. (syn. Anacardium
orientale L.). Cashew marking nut tree,
Oriental cashew nut. 2n=60. Trop. Asia and
Australia. Cultivated in the tropics.

SPONDIAS LAOSENSIS Pierre. 2n=   . Trop.
Asia. A tree cultivated for its fruits.

SPONDIAS PINNATA (Koen. & L.f.) Kurz (syn.
S. mangifera Willd.). Hog plum. 2n=   . Trop.
Asia. A fruit tree whose flower clusters are
also eaten.

Annonaceae

CANANGA ODORATUM Lamb. Ylang-ylang. 2n=16.
Malaysia. Cultivated there and in other
countries for the flowers which are a source
of essential oils.

STELECHOCARPUS BURAHOL (Bl.) Hook.f. & Thoms.
(syn. Uvaria burahol Bl.). Burahol. 2n=   .
Malaya and Java. Cultivated in Java for its
fruits.

Apocynaceae

ERVATAMIA CORONARIA Stapf. (syn. Tabernae-
montana coronaria Willd., T. divaricata
R.Br.). Grape jasmine. 2n=22. Malaya. Cultivated there for various purposes.

Araceae

ALOCASIA INDICA (Roxb.) Schott. 2n=28. Centre
of diversity SE. Asia. Cultivated there for
its stem which is eaten and as an ornamental.
Introduced to other countries such as India.
This species is sometimes included in A. macrorrhiza*.

AMORPHOPHALLUS CAMPANULATUS (Roxb.) Blume.
Elephant yam. 2n=28. SE. Asia. Cultivated in
C. and E. Java and India (p. 71).

AMORPHOPHALLUS HARMANDII Engl. & Gehr. 2n=
. Occasionally cultivated in Tonkin.

AMORPHOPHALLUS RIVIERI Dur. 2n=24, 26, 32,
39. Indochina. Var. konjac (Schott) Engl.
Philippines. Cultivated in China and Japan
(Mansfeld, 1959).

COLOCASIA ESCULENTA (L.) Schott. Dasheen,
Taro, Cocoyam. 2n=2x=28, 3x=42. SE. Asia or
NE. India (p. 71). It was introduced into
China and Japan, where var. antiquorum de-
veloped. It is also grown in the Mediterra-
nean region, W. Africa, the Pacific islands,
New Guinea, Samoa and New Zealand. In SE.
Asia, var. esculenta (syn. C. esculenta sensu

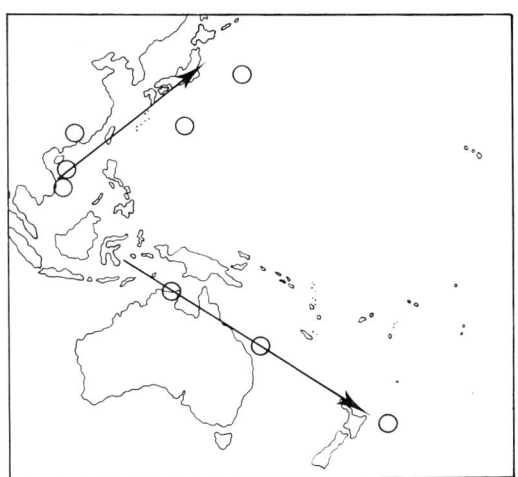

Distribution of somatic chromosome numbers for
taro (Colocasia esculenta)(Yen & Weeler, 1968)
0=3x.

Colocasia esculenta

stricto, C. esculenta var. typica A.E. Hill) developed.

Many wild populations are probably derivates of escapes from cultivation (Purseglove, 1972). Yen & Wheeler (1968) showed that the first introduction of taro into the Pacific, including the Philippines, composed of 2n=28 cultigens and 2n=42 cultigens were introduced later into Indochina-China-Ryu Kyu-Japan area and into Timor-New Caledonia-New Zealand area. Chromosome counts are needed of Indonesian taro cultigens.

CYRTOSPERMA CHAMISSONIS (Schott) Merr. (syn. C. edule Schott, C. merkusii (Hassk.) Schott.). 2n=   . Indo-Malaysian area. Introduced into many Pacific islands. Cultivated for its tubers (Purseglove, 1972).

PISTIA STRATIOTES L. Water lettuce. Tropical duckweed. 2n=28. Subtropics and tropics of the Old and New Worlds. A floating plant. Cultivated in Java in fishponds for edible shrimps that live below the plants (Uphof, 1968).

Araliaceae

NOTHOPANAX FRUTICOSUM Miq. (syn. Panax fruticosum L., Polyscias fruticosa (L.) Harms). 2n=22, 24. SE. Asia and Polynesia. Cultivated in Java for its roots and leaves.

NOTHOPANAX GUILFOYLEI Merr. (syn. Panax guilfoylei Cogn., Aralia guilfoylei Bull.). 2n=

. Probably the Pacific islands. Perhaps it is a cultigen of N. pinnatum* or a closely related species (Mansfeld, 1959).

NOTHOPANAX OBTUSUM Miq. (syn. Panax obtusum Blume, Polyscias obtusa (Bl.) Harms). 2n=   . Probably SE. Asia. Cultivated in Java.

NOTHOPANAX PINNATUM Miq. (syn. Panax pinnatum Lam., Polyscias rumphiana Harms). 2n=   . SE. Asia and New Guinea. Cultivated for its leaves.

Asclepiadaceae

GYMNEMA SYRINGIFOLIUM Boerl. Sajor pepe. 2n= . Cultivated in Malaya as a vegetable.

Averrhoaceae

AVERRHOA BILIMBI L. Bilimbi. 2n=22, 24. Malaya. Its fruits are very acid.

AVERRHOA CARAMBOLA L. Carambola. 2n=22, 24. Indonesia. Cultivated for its fruits. Some varieties have been developed.

Azollaceae

AZOLLA PINNATA R.Brown. Water velvet, Water fern. Mosquito fern. 2n=   . Domesticated in Vietnam and China (p. 33) for its symbiosis with the N-fixing alga Anabaena azollae Strassburger and therfore used to enrich soils with N, especially of rice fields. For this purpose, it has already been grown for several centuries. In Vietnam, the cv. Beo Giong was developed. It dies at the time of the maximum tillering of the rice plants and its nutrients become available at this crucial stage. Other cultivars have been developed in China (p. 33). Water fern may also be used to suppress pest weeds and as fodder. In some areas like New Zealand, it is itself a pest weed, blocking water channels and pipes (Lumpkin & Plucknett, 1980).

Basellaceae

BASELLA RUBRA L. Indian spinach. Ceylon spinach. Malabar nightshade. 2n=44, 48. Probably S. Asia (Winter, 1963). Cultivated as a vegetable, now throughout the tropics. Formerly it may have been used for dyeing. The commonest synonyms are B. alba L. (2n=48), with white flowers, and B. cordifolia Lam. (2n=   ) with heart-shaped leaves.

Bombacaceae

CEIBA PENTADRA Gaertn., var. indica (DC.) Bakh. Kapok tree, Silk cotton tree. 2n=72, 80, 88. Secondary gene centre: SE. Asia. Introduced from Africa (p. 123) probably via India. Cultivated in SE. Asia (Zeven, 1969). The Indonesian cultivar Reuzenrandoe (giant kapok) bears some characteristics of the var. caribaea*.

DURIO KUTEJENSIS (Hassk.) Beccari. Lai. 2n= . Along the foothills of the central ranges of Borneo. It has now spread to E. and N. of Borneo.

DURIO OXLEYANUS Griffith. Kerantongan. 2n= . Malaya, Sumatra and Borneo. The fruits are eaten and seeds are dispersed around the (temporary) settlements. Occasionally cultivated. Other wild species of which the fruits are eaten are D. graveolens Beccari, tabelak (2n=), D. dulcis, lahong (2n=), and D. grandiflorus (Mast.) Kostermans & Soegeng, durian munjit (2n=). D. graveolens grows wild in Borneo, Malaya and Sumatra, D. dulcis in Borneo.

DURIO ZIBETHINUS Murray. Durian. 2n=56. W. Malaysia. Unknown wild. Cultivated throughout SE. Asia, W. Irian, Moluccas, Celebes, S. Philippines. Introduced to Indochina, Thailand, Burma, Sri Lanka and elsewhere. It is often semi-cultivated, i.e. semi-wild trees result from dispersal of seeds. In this way, durian groves have arisen.

Boraginaceae

TOURNEFORTIA ARGENTEA L.f. (syn. Messerschmidia argentea (L.f.) Johnston). Velvet leaf. 2n= . Trop. Asia. A shrub cultivated for its leaves which are used as smoking tobacco.

Burseraceae

CANARIUM COMMUNE L. Java almond. 2n= . Moluccas. Cultivated in many other tropical countries. The kernels are eaten and oil is extracted from them. Sometimes they are planted as shade trees and as ornamentals.

CANARIUM MOLUCCANUM Blume. 2n= . Moluccas, New Guinea and W. Polynesia. Cultivated in Malaysia.

CANARIUM OVATUM Engl. Pili, Pili nut. 2n= . S. Luzon (Philippines). The kernels contain 70-80% pili-nut oil.

CANARIUM PIMELA Koenig. Black Chinese olive. 2n= . E. Asia. Cultivated in S. China and Cochin China.

Combretaceae

QUISQUALIS INDICA L. Rangoon creeper. 2n= . SE. Asia. A woody vine. Cultivated as an ornamental, vegetable and as an anthelmintic.

TERMINALIA BELLIRICA (Gaertn.) Roxb. (syn. Myribalan bellirica Gaertn.). Bellirica, Terminalia. 2n=26, 48. India and Malaysia. Cultivated as a source of myrobalan which is used for tanning leather, for black dye and for making ink.

TERMINALIA CATAPPA L. Indian almond, Myrobalan, Almendro. 2n=24. Trop. Asia, N. Australia and E. Polynesia. Widely cultivated in the tropics. The kernels contain about 55% oil. Used for manufacturing edible fats, cosmetics and pharmaceutic preparations. Used for timber; leaves and bark are used for preparation of medicines. The fruits are edible.

TERMINALIA CHEBULA Retz. 2n=14, 24, 26, 48. India to Malaysia.

Compositae

BLUMEA BALSAMIFERA (L.). DC. 2n=20. Himalaya, India, Malaysia, S. China and Taiwan. Cultivated in Java as a medicinal crop.

BLUMEA MYRIOCEPHALA DC. 2n= . India, Vietnam, Malaya and Indonesia. Occasionally cultivated in Vietnam.

ENHYDRA FLUCTUANS Lour. (syn. E. helonchu DC., Hingtsha repens Roxb.). 2n=22. India, Indochina, Thailand, China and Indonesia. A water plant occasionally cultivated in Cambodia and Malaya for its leaves.

EUPATORIUM STOECHADOSUM Hance. 2n=40. Vietnam. Cultivated there.

PLUCHEA INDICA Less. 2n=20. Cuttings of this shrub are planted as hedges in Indonesia. Young leaves are eaten as a vegetable or used to prepare a medicinal tea.

SPILANTHES PANICULATA Wall. ex DC. 2n= . SE. Asia and New Guinea. Cultivated as a vegetable or salad.

VERNONIA ANTHELMINTICA Willd. Kinka oil iron weed. 2n=20, 54. Trop. Asia. It might be a source of epoxy fatty acids.

Convolvulaceae

IPOMOEA MAMMOSA Chois. 2n= . Abouana. Philippines. Cultivated in Indochina. Formerly it was erroneously believed that this species was the ancestor of I. batatas*.

Cucurbitaceae

BENINCASA HISPIDA (Thunb.) Cogn. (syn. B. cerifera Savi). Wax gourd, White gourd. 2n=24. Java. Cultivated throughout Trop. Asia (Purseglove, 1968). It was already mentioned as a vegetable in China in 500 AD. (Li, 1969).

TRICHOSANTHES ANGUINA L. Edible snake gourd. 2n=22. Trop. Asia from India (p. 73) to Australia.

Cyperaceae

FIMBRISTYLIS GLOBULOSA (Retz.) Kunth. 2n= . Trop. Asia, Sri Lanka, India, Malaysia and

Mariannes. Cultivated on Malaysia for mat-
making etc.

LEPIRONIA ARTICULATA (Retz.) Domin. (syn. L.
mucronata Rich.). 2n=   . SE. Asia, Malaysia,
Australia and Fiji. Cultivated in Indonesia.

SCIRPODENDRON GHAERI (Gaertn.) Merr. (syn. S.
costatum Kurz.). 2n=   . Trop. Asia, Samoa
and Australia. Cultivated in Sumatra for mat
making.

Dioscoreaceae

DIOSCOREA ALATA L. Greater yam, Water yam,
Winged yam, Ten months yam. 2n=(20), 30, 40,
50, 60, 70, 80. SE. Asia, in the Assam-Burma
region it is the cultigen of D. hamiltonii
Hook., 2n=   , or D. persimilis Prain & Burk,
2n=   , or a similar species (Burkill, 1935).
Some types have been described as D. atropurpurea Roxb., 2n=   , and D. purpurea Roxb.,
2n=   . It is virtually sterile (Ayensu &
Coursey, 1972).

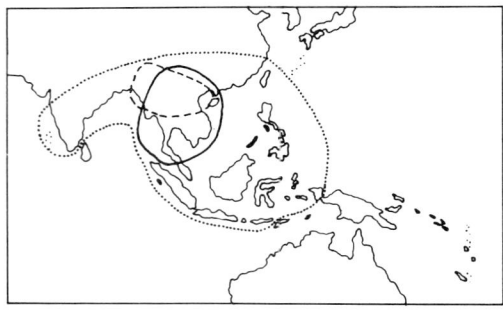

Dioscorea alata (———), D. esculenta (---) and
D. hispida (···) (Harris, 1973)

DIOSCOREA BULBIFERA L. Potato yam, Aerial
yam, Bulbil-bearing yam. 2n=36, 40, 54, 60,
80, 100. Trop. Asia and Africa. Possibly it
was domesticated in Asia as well as Africa
(p. 125). Cultivated in Trop. Asia, Africa,
Oceania and the W. Indies. The tubers and
bulbils are edible. The African form (p. 125)
has been described as D. latifolia Benth.,
2n=   . There are many types which often have
been described as species e.g. D. heterophylla
Roxb., 2n=

DIOSCOREA ESCULENTA (Lour.) Burk. Lesser yam,
Asiatic yam, Potato yam, Fancy yam, Chinese
yam. 2n=40, 60, 80, 90, 100. Indochina. Cultivated in S. China, and later throughout the
tropics. Most flowers are male (Ayensu &
Coursey, 1972).

DIOSCOREA FLABELLIFOLIA Prain. & Burk. 2n=
. Malaya. Occasionally cultivated there.

DIOSCOREA HISPIDA Roxb. (syn. D. hirsuta

Dennst, D. triphylla L.). 2n=40, (80). India
(p. 73) and SE. Asia. Closely related to the
African D. dumentorum (Coursey, 1967).

DIOSCOREA NUMMULARIA Lam. 2n=   . SE. Asia.
Cultivated there and in Indonesia and Oceania.
It closely resembles D. cayenensis*.

DIOSCOREA QUARTINIANA A. Rich. 2n=   . Throughout Trop. Asia. Cultivated in E. Nigeria
(Coursey, 1967).

DIOSCOREA PENTAPHYLLA L. 2n=40, 80, 144, c.
144. SE. Asia. Cultivated throughout Indonesia
and the Pacific islands.

Dipterocarpaceae

SHOREA STENOCARPA Burck. 2n=   . Malaya. Cultivated for its seeds, a source of a Borneo
tallow.

Ebenaceae

DIOSPYROS DISCOLOR Willd. (syn. D. blancoi
How.). Malobo, Velvet apple. 2n=   . Malaysia
and Philippines. Occasionally cultivated for
its edible fruits.

MABA MAJOR Forst.f. 2n=   . Cultivated for its
fruits on the Friendship Islands.

Elaeocarpaceae

ELAEOCARPUS FLORIBUNDUS Blume. 2n=   . From
Bangladesh to Java. Cultivated in Bengal and
Assam for its fruits.

Euphorbiaceae

ALEURITES MOLUCCANA Willd. Tung oil tree. 2n=
44. Autotetraploid. Indonesia. Its wild parent is not known. Crosses between this species
and A. montana did not succeed (Wit, 1969b).

ALEURITES TRISPERMA Blanco. Tung oil tree,
Banucalang. 2n=22. Philippines. Cultivated
there, in Malaya and Indonesia. Crosses with
A. montana did not succeed (Wit, 1969b).

BACCAUREA DULCIS Muell.-Arg. Tjoopa. 2n=   .
Malaya and Indonesia. Cultivated there for
its fruits (Uphof, 1968).

BACCAUREA MOTLEYANA Muell.-Arg. Rambai. 2n=
. SE. Asia. Cultivated there for its fruits
(Uphof, 1968).

BACCAUREA RACEMOSA Muell.-Arg. 2n=   . Malaysian Archipelago. Cultivated there for its
fruits.

GLOCHIDION BLANCOI Lowe. 2n=   . A tree cultivated in Far East and Philippines for the young
leaves and shoots (Terra, 1967).

HEVEA BRASILIENSIS (Willd.) Muell.-Arg. Brazilian hevea, Para rubber tree. 2n=36. Amazon basin (p. 169). A secondary gene centre: Malaya. Domesticated in SE. Asia at the end of the 19th Century (Purseglove, 1968).

MANIHOT ESCULENTA Crantz. Cassava. 2n=36. America (p. 170 and 190). Secondary centre of diversity in Indonesia.

PLUKENETIA CORNICULATA Smith. (syn. Pterococcus corniculatus Pax & Hoffm.). Painapaina. 2n= . SE. Asia. Cultivated as vegetable.

PHYLLANTHUS DISTICHUS (L.) Muell.-Arg. (syn. Ph. acides (L.) Skeels. Otaheite gooseberry. 2n=26, 28. India and Madagascar. Cultivated in the tropics for its fruits (Purseglove, 1968).

PHYLLANTHUS EMBLICA L. Emblic, Myrobolan. 2n=28, 98. Trop. Asia. Cultivated in the Old and New Worlds for its fruits (Uphof, 1968).

SAUROPUS ALBICANS Blume (syn. S. androgynus Merr.). 2n= . Cultivated as a vegetable in SE. Asia.

TRIGONOPLEURA MALAYANA Hook.f. Gamber ooran. 2n= . Malaysian Archipelago. Cultivated there for its leaves which substitute for Uncaria gambir*.

Flacourtiaceae

FLACOURTIA RAMONTCHI L'Hér. Botoko plum, Madagascar plum, Governor's plum, Ramontchi. 2n=22. Malaya and Madagascar. Cultivated in the tropics for its fruits.

FLACOURTIA RUKAM Zoll. & Mor. Rukam. 2n= . Malaysia and Philippines. A tree cultivated for its fruits.

HYDNOCARPUS ALCALAE C. DC. 2n= . Philippines. Cultivated for its seeds which are a source of oil used to cure leprosy.

HYDNOCARPUS ANTHELMINTHICUS Pierre ex Lanessan. 2n=24. Indochina and Thailand. Cultivated in many tropical countries for the seeds which are a source of oil used to cure leprosy.

HYDNOCARPUS KURZII (King) Warb. 2n= . Ssp. kurzii in Burma Highlands and Assam. Ssp. australis in Burma Lowlands and N. Siam. Ssp. kurzii is cultivated in many trop. countries for the seeds which are a source of oil used to cure leprosy.

PANGIUM EDULE Reinw. Pangi. 2n= . Malaysia. Cultivated in Java.

Gnetaceae

GNETUM GNEMON L. Bulso. 2n= . From Assam to Malaysia and Fiji. Var. ovalifolium (Poir.) Bl. is considered the wild type while var.

gnemon is the cultivated type planted in Java. Introduced to Java, Sumatra and elsewhere. Cultivated in SE. Asia for its seeds and leaves. A large dioecious shrub.

Gramineae

ANDROPOGON ACICULATUS Retz. (syn. Chrysopogon aciculatus Trin.). 2n= . The tropics. Cultivated in Vietnam for its roots which contain Chiendent grenille à brosse (Uphof, 1968).

BAMBUSA ARUNDINACEA (Retz.) Willd. Spiny bamboo. 2n=70. Primary centre: India and Burma (p. 73). Secondary centre: Malaysia and E.Java.

BAMBUSA CORNUTA Munro. 2n= . Java. A woody grass cultivated for its tender shoots, which are used as a vegetable.

BAMBUSA SPINOSA Roxb. 2n= . Philippines and Indonesia. A woody tall grass cultivated as a timber bamboo and also for its young shoots used as a vegetable.

BAMBUSA STRICTUS Nees. 2n=70, 72. India and Burma (p. 73). Secondary centres: Indochina and S. China (p. 37).

BAMBUSA TULDA Roxb. 2n= . India, Burma (p. 73) and Tahiti. Secondary centre: Java.

BAMBUSA VULGARIS Schrad. ex Wendl. 2n=72. Probably Malaysia or India. It is unknown in the wild. Cultivated in the tropics for its young shoots and for its stems.

COIX AQUATICA Roxb. 2n=10. S. Asia. Grown as fodder in India, also collected as a wild cereal in Orissa, India.

COIX GIGANTEA Koenig ex Roxb. 2n=20, 40. S. Asia. Involucres are used as beads and poultry are fed on the grains in NE. India.

COIX LACRYMA-JOBI L. Job's tears, Adley. 2n= 20, genome formula BB. S. Asia. Wild races have indurated involucres of various colours used as beads. Domesticated races have soft involucres and are widely grown as cereals in NE. India and SE. Asia. Cultivated kinds are often referred to as C. Ma-yuen Romanet (Arora, 1977; Jain & Banerjee, 1974; Kaul, 1973).

CYMBOPOGON CITRATUS (DC.) Stapf (syn. Andropogon citratus DC.). Lemon grass. 2n=40, 60. Probably Malaysia or Sri Lanka. Unknown wild. Cultivated in S. Asia, Indochina and elsewhere for its lemon grass oil.

CYMBOPOGON NARDUS (L.) Rendle (syn. Andropogon nardus L.). Citronella grass. 2n=20, (40, 60). Cultivated in Indonesia, Sri Lanka and elsewhere for its citronella oil. There are two types of oil: (1) Sri Lanka type obtained from var. lenabatu which is cultivated in S. Sri Lanka; (2) Java type obtained from var.

mahapengiri (syn. C. winterianus Jowett, 2n= 20). The latter was introduced into Java from Sri Lanka early in 20th Century. It is now widely distributed throughout the tropics. The wild type in Sri Lanka has a different oil composition (Wijesekera et al., 1973).

DENDROCALAMUS ASPER (Schult.) Becker ex Heyne (syn. Bambusa asper Schult.). 2n=   . Probably from the Malay Peninsula and adjacent areas. Unknown wild. Secondary centre: Malaysian Archipelago. It has strong stems and edible shoots.

DENDROCALAMUS BRANDISII Kurz. 2n=72. Burma, Thailand, Cambodia and Vietnam. Its stems are used as building material.

DENDROCALAMUS MERRILLIANUS Elm. 2n=   . Primary centre: Philippines. Its stems are used as building material.

DINOCHLOA GIGANTEA Munro. 2n=   . Lower Burma. Primary centre: Lower Burma. Its stems are used as building material. The plant of this species is the largest among the bamboos.

DINOCHLOA MACLELLANDII Kurz. 2n=   . Cambodia, Laos and Vietnam. Its stems are used in the basket industry.

DINOCHLOA PENDULUS Ridb. 2n=   . Malay Peninsula. Its stems are used for baskets.

GIGANTOCHLOA APUS (Schult.) Kurz. 2n=   . Burma and Indochina. Several species are cultivated in Java, Borneo and Philippines and on the Malay Peninsula (Tenasserim). Secondary centre: Java.

GIGANTOCHLOA LIGULATA Gamble. 2n=   . N. part of Malay Peninsula and Thailand. The timber is used and the shoots are eaten.

GIGANTOCHLOA MAXIMA Kurz. 2n=   . Unknown wild. Secondary centre: Java. Its stems are an excellent material for building.

GIGANTOCHLOA SCORTECHINII Gamble. 2n=   . Malay Peninsula. Its stems are used as building material.

GIGANTOCHLOA SCRIBNERIANA Merr. 2n=   . Laos and Cambodia. Its stems are used as building material.

GIGANTOCHLOA VERTICILLATA (Willd.) Munro. 2n=   . SE. Asia. Cultivated in W. Africa, W. Indies, Fiji and elsewhere (Purseglove, 1972).

ISCHAEMUM INDICUM (Houtt.) Merr. Batiki blue grass. 2n=   . SE. Asia. Cultivated in W. Africa, W. Indies, Fiji and elsewhere (Purseglove, 1972).

MISCANTHUS FLORIDULUS (Lab.) Warb. 2n=38.

New Guinea. This species together with M. sinensis* from Fiji played a role in the origin of the Edule group of Saccharum officinarum* (Grassl, 1977).

ORYZA GRANULATA Nees & Arn. (incl. O. meyeriana Baill.). 2n=24, 48. Malaya. It belongs to the 'officinalis' group of Oryza.

ORYZA LONGIGLUMIS Jansen. 2n=48. New Guinea.

ORYZA MINUTA Presl. 2n=48, genome formula BBCC. This wild species has the same genomes as the African O. eichingeri*. It belongs to the 'officinalis' group.

ORYZA NIVARA Sharma & Shastry. 2n=24. S. and SE. Asia and N. Australia. This is the wild annual close relative of O. sativa*.

ORYZA OFFICINALIS Wall. 2n=24, genome formula CC. This wild species is the parent of the species belonging to the 'officinalis' group.

ORYZA PERENNIS Moench. 2n=24, genome formula AA. The distribution of this wild species is discussed on p. 74. In Oceania, the Oceanian race (2n=24) of this species developed. See also O. rufipogon* and index.

ORYZA RIDLEYI Hook.f. 2n=48. SE. Asia.

ORYZA RUFIPOGON Griff. (syn. O. montana Lour.). 2n=24. Several SE. Asian countries. It is a pernicious weed of rice land. It easily crosses with rice. It might be a hybrid product of natural crosses of rice and O. perennis* and would then be of the same nature as O. sativa var. fatua*. According to recent views of taxonomists, O. rufipogon includes O. perennis*, O. fatua*, O. sativa f. spontanea*, O. perennis ssp. balunga*, O. perennis ssp. cubensis*. See also O. nivara*.

ORYZA SATIVA L. Rice. 2n=24, genome formula AA. Primary centre: SE. Himalaya area (p. 74). Ecotype Tjereh and Bulu developed in Indonesia. Tjereh belongs to the ecospecies 'aman' (ssp. indica Kato) (Morinaga, 1968).

ORYZA SCHLECHTERI Pilger. 2n=   . New Guinea.

PASPALUM SCROBICULATUM*

SACCHARUM OFFICINARUM L. Sugar-cane, Noblecane. 2n=40II=80. New Guinea. Modern clones resulting (2n=100-125) from hybridization. Sugar-cane derives form S. robustum Brandes & Jeswiet ex Grassl, which grows wild in New Guinea, Celebes, Borneo up to New Hebrides Basic types of N. coast of New Guinea, Celebes and Borneo have 2n=60, while those from southern coast of New Guinea have 2n=80. The first basic type may have originated in Borneo The second basic type may have been the wild parent from which primitive sugar-cane developed.

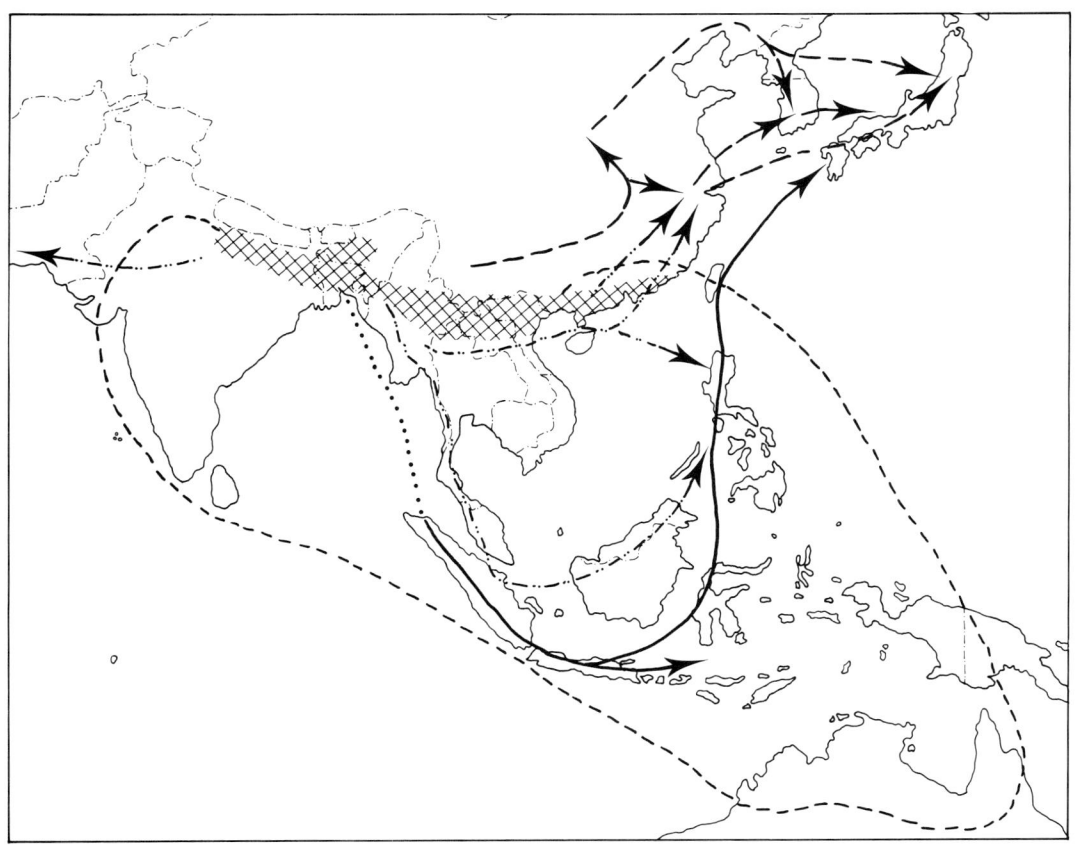

Dispersal of races Oryza sativa across Asia. Area of origin (grey), "Indica" ($\cdots-\cdots$), "Japonica" (---), "Javanica" (—), extend of wild relatives ($\cdots\cdots$) (Chang, 1976).

S. robustum is cultivated for its large stalks used for fences and for construction. During the domestication of sugar-cane, geographic types may have hybridized. Through selection, sugar-cane has a much lower fibre content, increased juiciness and sugar content throughout the stalk. These are the New Guinea Noble canes which must have originated ca 700 BC. On New Guinea, these Noble canes hybridized with Miscanthus sinensis . With hybridization, and backcrossing and perhaps other intergeneric hybridization (Roach, 1972), the Edule group of canes developed (Grassl, 1964, 1967, 1968, 1977). This group has also been described as S. edule Hassk. The Edule canes have been subdivided into Vitho canes (syn. Erianthus maximus Brongn. and E. pedicelare Trin.), 2n=87-100 and Nduruka canes (syn. S. edule Hassk.), 2n=70.

From Fiji, sugar-cane was taken to Hawaii, which lies outside the Miscanthus area. There the Hawaiian (Original) Noble canes developed, which are thicker and are used as chewing canes and as ornamentals.

The New Guinea Noble canes were also transported northwards and northwestwards to other parts of Indonesia, Philippines, S. Japan, S. China (p. 38) and India (p. 75).

SACCHARUM SPONTANEUM L. Wild sugar-cane. 2n= (x=10)40-128. SE. Asia. In Philippines three groups are found: 2n=56, 2n=72 and 2n=80. Plants with 2n=80 occur in many habitats for instance on mountains and river banks, and in grassland (Rithidech & Ramirez, 1974). In the Indo-Gangetic Plain, plants with 2n=40-72 are found (Mehra & Sood, 1974). In Indonesia and especially in Java and Sumatra, plants with 2n=112 occur. They may be of hybrid origin, deriving from S. officinarum (2n=80) x S. spontaneum (2n=64). Used as fencing for pigs by the Austronesians from SE. Asia.

SCHIZOSTACHYUS BRACHYCLADUS Kurz. 2n=   . Java and E. Malaysia. Secondary centre: the Malay Peninsula.

SCHIZOSTACHYUS GRANDE Ridl. 2n=   . Malay

Peninsula.

SCHIZOSTACHYUS LULAMPAO Merr. 2n= . Centre
of origin Philippines. Used in the paper
industry.

SCHIZOSTACHYUS ZOLLINGERI Steud. 2n= . Malay Peninsula, Java and Sumatra.

SINOCALAMUS LATIFLORUS (Munro) McClure (syn.
Dendrocalamus latiflorus Munro.) 2n= . Burma, Thailand, Taiwan and Philippines. Its
stems are used as building material. The
young shoots are eaten. They are also canned
and exported.

TRITICUM TURGIDUM (L.) Thell. Durum wheat
(syn. T. durum Desf.). 2n=28, genome formula
AABB. For origin see p. 94. In India a secondary centre of diversity (Jain et al.,
1976).

VETIVERIA ZIZANIOIDES Stapf (syn. V. odorata
Virey, Andropogon muricatus Retz.). Vetiver.
2n=20. A grass of Trop. Asia. Cultivated for
volatile oils in its rhizomes and as a hedge
plant.

ZEA MAYS L. Maize. 2n=20. Domesticated in C.
America (p. 190). Secondary centre arose in
S. and SE. Asia (Brandolini, 1970).

Guttiferae

CALOPHYLLUM INOPHYLLUM L. Alexandrian laulal,
Undi. 2n=32. Coastal regions from E. Africa
upto Australia and Polynesia. Often planted.
In India it has a rather restricted economic
importance. The kernel yields Domba oil.

GARCINIA ATROVIRIDES Griffith. Gelugur. 2n=
. Assam and Malaya. Occasionally cultivated.

GARCINIA COCHINCHINENSIS (Lour.) Choisy. 2n=
. Cochin China. Cultivated for its fruits.

GARCINIA DULCIS (Roxb.) Kurz. Baniti. 2n= .
Philippines to Java. The bark yields a green
dye and the fruits are edible. Occasionally
cultivated in Java.

GARCINIA INDICA Choisy. Kokum, Kokan, Ktambi.
2n=48, c. 54. Trop. Asia. Cultivated for its
fruits. In India, it is a minor oil-seed
plant (p. 75).

GARCINIA MANGOSTANA L. Mangosteen. 2n=c. 76,
96. Malaysia. It is considered to be the most
delicious of all tropical fruits. It is derived from wild G. silvestris, which is also
found in India (p. 75).

GARCINIA MULTIFLORA Champ. (syn. G. tonkinensis Vesque). Cây giôc, Bira tai. 2n= .
N. Vietnam, Laos, Hainan and Hongkong. Cultivated in N. Vietnam for its fruits.

GARCINIA PEDUNCULATA Roxb. Tikul. 2n= .
Bengal and Silhat (Bangladesh). Cultivated for
its fruits.

GARCINIA TINCTORIA (DC.) W.F. Wight. Matau,
Gamboge tree. 2n=c.80. India (p. 75) and Malaya. Cultivated in the tropics for its fruits.

Hydrophyllaceae

HYDROLEA ZEYLANICA Vahl. 2n= . Trop. Asia.
Cultivated in Java for its young leaves.

Labiatae

COLEUS AMBOINICUS Lour. (syn. C. aromaticus
Benth.). Indian borage, Dacon ajenton 2n=68.
Indonesia. Cultivated in SE. Asia and W. Indies for its aromatic leaves. These leaves
are used in stuffings and for flavouring
meats. They may substitute for sage (Salvia
officinalis*) and borage (Borago officinalis*)
(Purseglove, 1968).

COLEUS PARVIFLORUS Benth. (syn. C. tuberosus
Benth.). 2n=56, 64. This tuber crop is cultivated in SE. Asia.

OCIMUM GRATISSIMUM L. 2n=40, 48, 64. Trop.
Asia, esp. India. Cultivated in India as medicinal crop.

OCIMUM SANCTUM L. Holy basil. 2n=64. Shrub of
trop. Old World. Cultivated as a sacred plant
in India and elsewhere.

ORTHOSIPHON STAMINEUS Benth. (syn. Ocimum
grandiflorum Blume). 2n= . SE. Africa to
Australia. A shrub cultivated in Java as medicinal plant.

POGOSTEMON CABLIN (Blanco) Benth. Patchouli.
2n= . Philippines. Cultivated for its essential oil.

Lauraceae

CINNAMOMUM BURMANI Blume. Batavia cinnamon.
2n= . Malaysia. Cultivated there.

CINNAMOMUM CASSIA Blume (syn. C. aromaticum
Nees). Cassia cinnamon, Chinese cinnamon.
2n= . Cultivated in S. China for its bark
and flower buds. Cassia oil is obtained from
the leaves (Purseglove, 1968).

LITSEA CALOPHYLLA (Miq.) Mansf. (syn. L. te-
tranthera Mirb., L. sebifera Blume). 2n= .
Malaya and Indonesia. Cultivated esp. in
Bangka, Indonesia for its fruits.

Leguminosae

ALBIZIA LEBBECK Benth. Lebbek, Indian walnut.
2n=26. Trop. Asia to N. Australia. Cultivated in tropics and subtropics as fodder crop
and as shade tree.

ALBIZIA MOLUCCANA Miq. (syn. A. falcata (Stickm.) Backer). 2n=   . Malaya. Cultivated there and elsewhere as shade tree and as green manure.

ALBIZIA MONTANA (Jungh.) Benth. 2n=   . Malaysia. Cultivated as green manure and shade tree.

ALBIZIA SUMATRANA. 2n=   . Indonesia. Cultivated in Zaïre as soil cover, green manure and shade tree.

CANAVALIA GLADIATA (Jacq.) DC. Sward bean. 2n=22, 44. Old World. Probably derived from C. gladiolata Sauer (2n=22), which occurs in the Burma-Yunnan area (Sauer, 1964). Wild in Trop. Asia and Africa. Cultivated in Asia, especially in India as food, forage and cover crop or as green manure. In some areas, it has naturalized (Purseglove, 1968). In Japan, the white-seeded cultigen (var. alba) is cultivated (p. 40).
    C. polystacha (Forsk.) Schweinf. (2n=   ). Cultivated from SW. China upto Ethiopia/Somalia as pulse and seed. It is also considered the parental type of C. gladiata.

CASSIA DIDYMOBOTRYA Fresen. Candelabra tree. 2n=28. A shrub used as green manure in Malaya and Sri Lanka.

CASSIA HIRSUTA L. 2n=28, 56. Vigorous bush used in Malaya, Indochina and Uganda for soil cover. C. intermedia Sharma, Vivek. & Rathak (2n=   ) is a natural hybrid of C. occidentalis L., (2n=26, 28) and C. hirsuta (Sharma et al., 1974).

CASSIA LESCHENAULTIANA DC. 2n=48. Shrub used in India and Indonesia as green manure.

CASSIA MIMOSOIDES L. 2n=16, (32). Trop. Asia and Africa. Tree used in Indochina and Indonesia as green manure.

CASSIA OCCIDENTALIS L. Coffee senna, Negro coffee, Stink weed. 2n=26, 28. Tropics. Used in Indochina as green manure.

CASSIA PUMILA Lam. 2n=   . Cover crop in Indochina.

CASSIA SIAMEA Lam. (syn. C. florida Vahl.). 2n=28. India, Malaya and Indonesia. Cultivated in Malaya and India as fodder crop. Introduced on Cuba as green manure.

CASSIA TORA L. Sickle senna, Wild senna. 2n=26, (28, 56). Tropics. Occasionally cultivated as a green manure in China and Indonesia.

CLITORIA LAURIFOLIA Poir. (syn. C. cajanifolia Barth). 2n=24. Tropics. Occasionally cultivated in Sri Lanka and Indonesia and formerly in Tanzania as green manure.

CROTALARIA ALATA Ham. 2n=16. Malaysian Archipelago. Excellent green manure.

DERRIS DALBERGIOIDES Baker. 2n=   . Used as shade tree in SE. Asia.

DERRIS ELLIPTICA Benth. Derris. 2n=22, 24, 36. From E. India to New Guinea except S. Malaya. Clones are distributed locally except one which is found in many places in SE. Asia. This clone has a high content of rotenone (Toxopeus, 1952).

DERRIS MALACCENSIS Prain. Derris. 2n=22, 24. Malaysian Archipelago, where also cultivated types are found. Like D. elliptica*, it is a source of rotenone (Toxopeus, 1952).

DERRIS MICROPHYLLA (Miq.) Jackson. 2n=   . Used as shade tree in SE. Asia. Introduced into Indochina.

DERRIS ROBUSTA Benth. 2n=   . Used as a shade tree in SE. Asia.

DESMODIUM GYROIDES DC. 2n=20, 22. Trop. Asia. A shrub used as a green manure.

INDIGOFERA TEYSMANNII Miq. 2n=32. SE. Asia. It is a green manure.

INOCARPUS EDULIS Forst. Tahiti chestnut. 2n=20. From Malaysia to Polynesia, where it is cultivated for seeds and as shade tree.

MELILOTUS SAUVEOLENS Ledeb. (syn. M. graveolens Bunge). Daghestan sweet clover. 2n=16. E. Asia and Indochina. Cultivated in USA. Some annuals are found in this biennial plant.

MIMOSA SEPIARIA Benth. 2n=   . Trop. Asia. Used for hedges (Mansfeld, 1959).

MUCUNA ATERRIMA (Piper & Tracy) Holland (syn. Stizolobium aterrima Piper & Tracy). Mauritius bean, Bengal bean. 2n=22. Trop. Asia. Cultivated there and elsewhere as a green manure and soil cover.

MUCUNA CAPITATA (Roxb.) Wight & Arn. 2n=   . India and Java. Cultivated as a vegetable and for its seeds.

MUCUNA COCHINCHINENSIS (Lour.) A. Cheval. (syn. M. nivea DC., Stizolobium niveum O. Kuntze). 2n=22. Cochin China. Cultivated in tropics as vegetable, for seeds, as green manure and soil cover.

MUCUNA DEERINGIANUM (Bort.) Small. (syn. Stizolobium deeringianum Bort.). Florida velvet bean. 2n=22. Probably trop. Asia or Malaysia. Cultivated as cover crop, green manure and forage crop.

MUCUNA PRURIENS DC. var. utilis Wahl. (syn. Stizolobium aterrimum Piper & Tracy). Bengal

bean. 2n=22. Probably Trop. Asia. Widely
cultivated as cover crop and green manure in
tropics.

NEPTUNIA OLERACEA Lour. 2n=c.52, 54. Tropics.
Aquatic, cultivated as a vegetable in Indochina.

PARKIA SPECIOSA Hassk. 2n=   . Malaysia. It
is cultivated.

PELTOPHORUM PTEROCARPUM Backer (syn. Caesal-
pinia arborea Zoll., Inga pterocarpa DC.).
Soga. 2n=   . SE. Asia to Australia. Cultivated on Java for its bark, which is a source
of brown dye.

PITHECELLOBIUM BIGEMINUM Mart. 2n=   . E. and
SE. Asia. Cultivated on Java for edible seeds.

PITHECELLOBIUM JIRINGA Prain. 2n=   . Malaysia and Philippines. Cultivated on Java for
edible seeds.

PITHECELLOBIUM LOBATUM Benth. 2n=   . SE.
Asia. Cultivated for leaves, fruits and flowers, which are eaten as vegetable

PSOPHOCARPUS TETRAGONOLOBUS (L.) DC. Goa bean,
Asparagus bean, Winged bean, Manilla bean.
2n=18, (20). It very likely originates from
E. African Ps. grandiflora (p. 138). It has
been domesticated as a trans-domesticate in
Asia, where it now occurs widely.

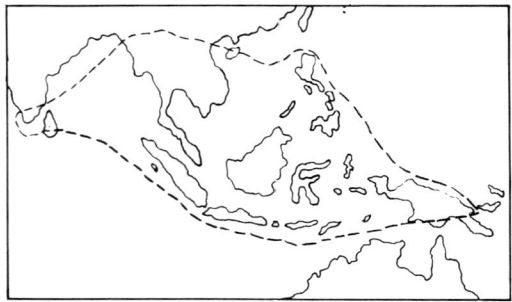

Winged bean (Psophocarpus tetragonolobus)

PUERARIA PHASEOLOIDES (Roxb.) Benth. Tropical
kudzu. 2n=22. Malaysia. Used as cover crop
and green manure throughout the tropics.

PUERARIA THUNBERGIANA (Sieb. & Zucc.) Benth.
(syn. P. lobata (Willd.) Ohwi). 2n=24. Asia
and W. Pacific islands. Cultivated in C. Highlands of New Guinea and in New Caledonia for
edible tubers. Formerly it may have been a
staple crop, replaced by Ipomoea batatas*
(Watson, 1968). See also p. 40.

SESBANIA AEGYPTIACA Poir. (syn. S. sesban
(L.) Merr.). 2n=12. E. Africa, S. Asia and
Australia. In India and Java, it is used as
hedge and shade plant.

SESBANIA GRANDIFLORA (L.) Poir. Agati sesbania. 2n=14, 24. E. India to Australia. Cultivated in tropics for flowers and green pods,
used in S. Asia as vegetable.

TEPHROSIA CANDIDA DC. White tephrosia. 2n=22.
Asia. Used as a green manure and cover crop.

VIGNA HOSEI (Craib) Backer. Sarawak bean. 2n=
20. The origin of this cover crop is not clear.
It is only known that material cultivated
in Malaya was obtained from Sarawak. It rarely
fruits in those areas. Morphologically it is
very similar to V. parkeri Bak. ssp. acutifolia Verdc., which is found in E. Africa.
The number of chromosomes of that subspecies
is not given, but ssp. maraguensis (Taub.)
Verdc., (syn. V. maraguensis (Taub.) Verdc.,
(syn. V. maraguensis (Taub.) Harms.) has 2n=
22. Ssp. maraguensis also grows in E. Africa
(Verdcourt, 1970).
   With no evidence for the origins of V. hosei,
this species is included in Region 2. Further
research into its origin is needed. For instance, its karyotype could be compared with
those of other species. The cause of its near
lack of fruits (propagation by cuttings)
could be studied. And interspecific crosses
should be made to study its affinities.

VIGNA RADIATA (L.) Wilczek (syn. V. glabres-
cens Maréchal, Mascherpa & Stainier, Phaseolus
aureus Roxb., Phaseolus radiatus L.). Green
gram, Golden gram, Mung bean, Moong, Oregon
pea. 2n=22. India and Burma. This crop derives from the wild var. sublobata (Roxb.)
Verdc. (syn. Phaseolus sublobatus Roxb.), 2n=
22, which grows wild in India and Burma.
Spread to S. China, Indochina and Java, and
later to other countries. It is closely related to V. mungo*.

VIGNA UMBELLATA (Prain) Maréchal, Mascherpa
& Stainier (syn. Phaseolus calcaratus Roxb.).
Rice bean. 2n=22. Himalaya and India. Primary
centre: India. Cultivated in many Asian countries and elsewhere. Characterized by late
maturing and dehiscent pod.

Lemnaceae

WOLFFIA ARRHIZA Wimm. Khai-nam. 2n=   . Burma,
Laos, Thailand, Bangladesh and India. An a-
quatic plant cultivated as vegetable by Bur-
mese and Laotians. Cultivated in N. Thailand
in rain-fed open ponds. It is very rich in
protein, much richer than the traditional
crops including soya bean.

Liliaceae

TAETSIA FRUTICOSA (L.) Merr. 2n=   . Pacific
islands and Malaya. The leaves were used for
cloths. Cultivated in Samoa for this purpose.

Limnocharitaceae

LIMNOCHARIS FLAVA (L.) Buch. Vegetable water-lettuce. 2n=20. A weed of canals and lakes. On Java, cultivated in rice fields and ponds. The young shoots are used as cuttings.

Magnoliaceae

MICHELIA CHAMPACA L. 2n=38. Cultivated for perfumery.

Malvaceae

ABUTILON INDICUM (Torner) Sweet. Country mallow, Indian abutilon. 2n=(36), 42. Malaysia, India and Philippines. Cultivated in India and elsewhere for its fibres and its oily seed. It is now a weed in the tropics.

GOSSYPIUM ARBOREUM L. Tree cotton. 2n=26, genome formula A_2A_2. Probably originated in India (p. 77) or Africa (p. 175). Race burmanicum was selected in Indochine. It is an annual form requiring a very short day and characterized by short hairs resembling wool.

GOSSYPIUM HIRSUTUM L. Cambodia. 2n=52, genome formula AADD. The origin of this species is given on p. 176 and 194. Cambodia type developed in Cambodia. Introduced into India where it is cultivated on a large scale. There it was named Cambodia.

THESPESIA POPULNEA (L.). Sol. ex Correa. Portia tree, Tulip tree. 2n=26, 28. The New Guinean species T. patellifera Borss., T. robusta Borss., T. fissicalyx Borss., T. multibracteata Borss. belong together with T. populnea to the section Thespedia of this genus. This may point to an E. New Guinean origin of T. populnea. It is widely distributed in trop. countries as shade tree. This wide distribution is due to the capacity of the seeds to float in sea-water for months and remain alive.

Meliaceae

LANSIUM DOMESTICUM Jack. Langsat. 2n=72. Malaysian Archipelago and Indochina. Cultivated there and elsewhere for its fruits.

MELIA AZADIRACHTA L. (Melia indica Brand., M. japonica Hassk., M. parviflora Moon, Azadirachta indica A. Juss.). Margosa, Nim, Neem. 2n=28. Dry region of Irrawaddy Valley. Cultivated and naturalized throughout India and in Pakistan, Sri Lanka, Burma and Malaya. It is a minor oil crop in India; the seeds are the source of margosa oil.

SANDORICUM KOETJAPE (Burm.f.) Merrill. Santol. 2n=22, 44. Malaysia and Indochina. Cultivated in this area and elsewhere for its fruits.

Moraceae

ALLAEANTHUS LUZONICUS F. Vill. 2n= . This tree is cultivated in Philippines.

ARTOCARPUS ALTILIS (Park.) Fosberg (syn. A. communis Forst.). Breadfruit. 2n=54, 56, c.81. Wild in forests of Malay Peninsula and of Moluccas. Secondary gene centre: islands of Oceania.
Diverse forms are found in Philippines. They are products of hybridization between the breadfruit and A. blancoi (Elm.) Merr., which grows in that country. Similarly variants are observed in Micronesia being products of introgression between breadfruit and the wild A. mariannensis Trécul. The introgressed characters of this wild species are seeded fruits, entire leaves and reddish hairs on veins (Fosberg, 1960a; Coenen & Barrau, 1961).

ARTOCARPUS CAMANSI Blanco. Kamansi. 2n= . Philippines. Cultivated near Manila for its fruits.

ARTOCARPUS CHAMPEDEN (Lour.) Spreng. Champedak. 2n= . Malaya. Selected forms are cultivated in SE. Asia.

ARTOCARPUS LAKOOCHA Roxb. 2n= . India and Malaysia. Cultivated in tropics for fruits.

ARTOCARPUS RIGIDUS Blume (syn. A. dimorphophylla Miq.). Monkey jack. 2n= . Malaysian Archipelago. Cultivated for fruits.

Musaceae

MUSA (Eumusa) edible cultivars. Banana. 2n=22, 33, 44. The genus Musa is divided into four main sections of which Eumusa includes the important cultivars. The edible cultivars are improved types of M. acuminata Colla (2n=22, genome formula AA), triploids of that species and diploid, triploid and tetraploid hybrids of this species and M. balbisiana Colla (2n=22, genome formula BB) (p. 78). The latter types have often been named M. x sapientum L. and M. x paradisiaca L. M. acuminata is a polymorphous species. The primary centre of origin is Malay Peninsula, but the greatest diversity is known in New Guinea (Simmonds, 1964).
The cultivars of the AA group are found throughout the tropics. In Malay Peninsula, the primary centre of diversity is observed. A secondary one is found in E. Africa (p. 141). The main cultivars like Gros Michel, Cavendish subgroup and Red/Green Red belong to the AAA group. The Dwarf Cavendish cultivars of the Cavendish group grown, for instance, on Samoa and in the Canary Islands originated from Indochina. These cultivars have often been referred to as M. cavendishii Lambert or M. sinensis Sweet ex Saget (Simmonds, 1964).
The first M. x acuminata x balbisiana hybrid group is the diploid AB group, which is of S. Indian origin (Simmonds, 1964) (p. 78).
The second hybrid group is the triploid

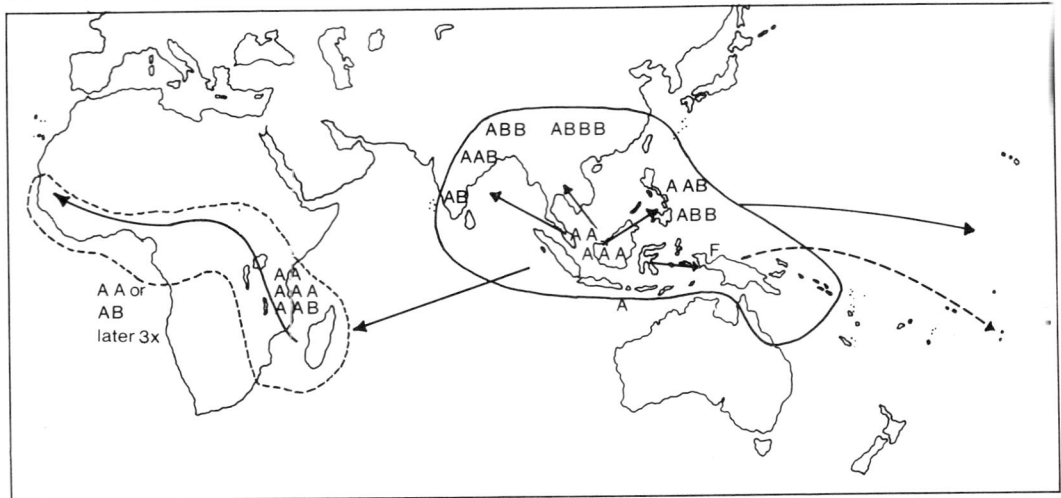

Distribution of wild bananas (——) and cultivation in Africa (---). Origin and movements of Eumusa groups (AA-ABBB) and of Australimusa series (open arrow) (Simmonds, 1962).

AAB group. Its major centre of origin lies in India (p. 68), while a clone (Maio maoli) may have arisen in Philippines (Simmonds, 1964).

The third hybrid group is the triploid AAB group. S. India is a major centre of origin. It is quite likely that a second centre is found in Philippines.

The fourth hybrid group, consisting of one clone, is the tetraploid ABBB group. Its centre of origin very probably lies in Indochina (Simmonds, 1964).

MUSA* cultivars of the ABB group. 2n=33. Most ABB cultivars originated in S. India (p. 68). However it is possible that after the cultivated M. acuminata (AA) reached Philippines, hybrids arose with M. balbisiana*.

MUSA* BALBISIANA

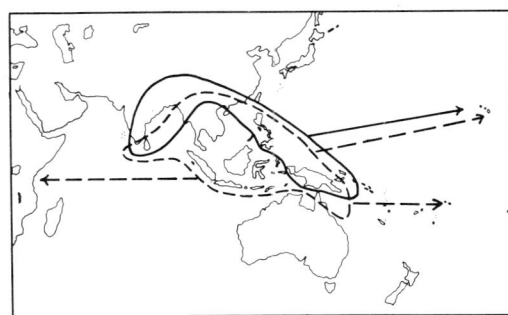

The wild Musa balbisiana (——) and M. acuminata (---) types (Simmonds, 1962).

MUSA* TEXTILIS Nee. Abaca, Manilla hemp. 2n= 20. Philippines. A tall perennial. Cultivated there and elsewhere in the tropics for its fibre. Canton fibre is obtained from a natural completely sterile hybrid (2n=21) of M. textilis x M. balbisiana*.

Myristicaceae

MYRISTICA ARGENTEA Warb. Papuan nutmeg. 2n= . New Guinea, where it is also occasionally cultivated (Flach & Cruickshank, 1969).

MYRISTICA FRAGRANS Houtt. Banda nutmeg. 2n= 42, 44. Centre of origin: Moluccas. It is not found there wild. From there, it spread throughout the tropics (Flach & Cruickshank, 1969).

Myrtaceae

EUGENIA AQUEA Burm.f. (syn. Syzygium aqueum (Burm.f.) Alston). Watery roseapple. 2n= . Bangladesh, Burma, Sri Lanka, Sumatra and Moluccas. It is also cultivated.

EUGENIA CARYOPHYLLUS (Sprengel) Bullock & Harrison (Syzygium aromaticum (L.). Merr. & Perry). Clove tree. 2n= . The wild clove tree, sometimes named E. obtusifolia Reinwardt (Caryophyllus sylvestris T. & B.), grows on many islands of Moluccas and in New Guinea. It has bigger leaves and flower buds, and is less aromatic than the cultivated tree. Cultivated for a long time.

Some variation exists in and outside its centre of origin.

EUGENIA FORMOSA Wall. (syn. Syzygium mappaceum (Korth.) Mansf.). 2n= . Trop. Asia.

Tree cultivated in Cochin China for fruits.

EUGENIA JAMBOLANA Lam. (syn. Syzygium cumini (L.). Skeels, Eugenia obtusifolia Roxb., E. cumini (L.) Druce). Java plum, Jambolan plum. 2n=33, 44, 46, 55. India to Malaysia, China and N. Australia. It is cultivated there and elsewhere. In India, a large-fruited type is cultivated (Mansfeld, 1959).

EUGENIA JAMBOS L. (syn. Syzygium jambos (L.) Alston). Roseapple. 2n=28, 33, c.42, 44, 46, c.54. Tree cultivated for a long time in Indo-Malaysia. Its centre of origin is not known.

EUGENIA JAVANICA Lam. (syn. Syzygium semarangense (Bl.) Merr. & Perry). 2n=33, 42, 44, 45, 66, 88, 110. Malaysia to India. Much cultivated in Java.

EUGENIA MALACCENSIS L. (syn. Syzygium malaccensis (L.) Merr. & Perry). Pomerac, Malay apple. 2n=22. Malaya. Some varieties are known.

MELALEUCA QUINQUENERVIA L.f. (syn. M. leucadendra L.). Cajéput tree. 2n= . Australia to Burma. Planted in forestry projects in Philippines, Hawaii and elsewhere. Also planted to drying out swamps, and as ornamental.

PIMENTA ACRIS Kostel. 2n=22. Indonesia. Cultivated there for oil distilled from the leaves (Purseglove, 1968).

RHODOMYRTUS TORMENTOSA Wight. Downy rose-myrtle. 2n= . India and Malaysia. A shrub cultivated in the (sub)tropics for its fruits.

Nyctaginaceae

PISONIA ALBA Span. Maluko, Lettuce tree. 2n= . Malaya. Wild tree is called P. sylvestris Teijsm. & Binn. (syn. P. grandis R. Br.) (2n=). Cultivated for leaves, which are used as vegetable.

Palmae

ARECA CATECHU Merr. Betelnut palm. 2n=32. Trop. Asia. Cultivated for nuts.

ARENGA PINNATA (Wurmb.) Merr. Sugar palm. 2n=26, 32. Primary centre: the Indonesian-Hindustani gene centre (p. 78). Possible secondary gene centre: India.

BORASSUS FLABELLIFER*

CALAMUS CAESIUS Blume. 2n= . Malaya, Borneo and Sumatra. Cultivated for stems.

COELOCOCCUS ARMICARUM Warb. Polynesian ivory-nut palm. 2n= . Carolina Islands. Cultivated in Philippines for its ivory-like nuts.

METROXYLON SAGU Rottb. Sago palm. 2n= . Malaya, Moluccas and New Guinea. Sago is obtained from the marrow of the stem. This species is occasionally split in M. sagu - the wild type and M. rumphii (Willd.) Mart. (2n=) - the cultigen.

NYPA FRUTICANS Wurmb. (syn. Nipa fruticans Thunb.). Nipa palm. 2n=16. SE. Asia upto Australia. Cultivated on Sumatra for its leaves and for wine production. Introduced to the mangrove area of S. Nigeria, where it has run wild (Zeven, 1973).

PRITCHARDIA GAUDICHAUDII H. Wendl. 2n= . Sandwich Islands. Cultivated there for its leaves which are used for thatching.

PRITCHARDIA PACIFICA Seem & Wendl. 2n=36. Fiji and Samoa. Cultivated for its leaves, which are used for thatching.

SALACCA EDULIS Reinw. 2n= . Malaysian Archipelago. Cultivated on Java for its edible fruits.

Pandaceae

PANDANUS AMARYLLIFOLIUS Roxb. (syn. P. odorus Ridl.). 2n= . Cultivated in Malaya for its fragrant leaves.

PANDANUS BROSIMAS Merr. & Perry. 2n= . Cultivated in the highlands of New Guinea for its seeds, which have a pleasant flavour and are rich in oil (Purseglove, 1972).

PANDANUS SPURIUS Miq. (syn. P. moschatus seu laevis Rumph., R. moschatus Rumph. ex. Miq., P. tectorius Soland. var. moschatus (Rumph. ex Miq.) Merr., P. laevis Lour., P. odoratissimus L.f., P. inermis Roxb.). Thatch screw pine, Putat, Pudak. 2n=c.51, 54, 60. Cultivated in SE. Asia to the extremes of Polynesia for its leaves for thatch and for its fruits. The cultivar is one clone, probably originated as a bud sport on a staminate plant of some wild species of section Pandanus. Perhaps the mutation occurred on a specimen of P. spurius some millenia ago (St. John, 1965).

PANDANUS WHITMEEANUS Martelli. Paogo. 2n= . Cultivated in New Caledonia, New Hebrides and elsewhere. On Futuna, it is used only for personal adornment. The fruit oil is used to perfume coconut oil (St. John & Smith, 1971).

Pentaphragmaceae

PENTAPHRAGMA BEGONIAEFOLIUM Wall. 2n= . A fleshy herb cultivated as vegetable in Malaya (Terra, 1967).

Pinaceae

PINUS MERKUSII Jungh & de Vriese (incl. P. merkusiana Corling & Gaussen). Merkus pine.

2n=   . Burma to Philippines and south to
Sumatra. Planted in tropics as a source of
turpentine and paper, and to control erosion.

Piperaceae

PIPER BETLE L. Betel pepper, Betle vine, Be-
tal, Sirih. 2n=32, 64, (78). C. and E. Malaysia. Cultivated in the tropics. The leaves
are chewed together with betelnut (Areca
catechu*).

PIPER CUBEBA L.f. Cubeb, Cubebe, Tailed pepper. 2n=24. Cultivated there and in neighbouring countries.

PIPER METHYSTICUM Forst. Kava pepper. 2n=
. Polynesia. Cultivated there. The roots
and rhizomes are used to prepare a non-al-
coholic beverage. In small amounts it is a
stimulant; in large amounts a narcotic.

PIPER RETROFRACTUM Vahl (syn. P. officinarum DC.). Javanese long pepper. 2n=   . Malaysia. It resembles P. longum*. Cultivated
for its spike, which is used as a spice.

PIPER SAIGONENSE C. DC. Lolo. 2n=   . Indochina. Cultivated there occasionally. Closely
related to P. lohot C. DC., which comes from
Tonkin district.

Polygonaceae

POLYGONUM ODORATUM Lour. 2n=   . Indochina.
Cultivated as a pot-herb in Vietnam.

Rosaceae

RUBUS ALBESCENS*

RUBUS ROSAEFOLIUS Smith. Cape bramble, Mau-
ritius raspberry. 2n=   . Tropical Asia.
Introduced in other continents. Cultivated.
It is considered a parent of R. probus Bailey,
Queensland raspberry, a shrub from Australia.
The other parent is R. ellipticus Smith,
the Yellow Himalayan raspberry from E. India.

Rubiaceae

MITRAGYNA SPECIOSA Korth. 2n=   . Malaya and
S. Thailand. Cultivated as a substitute for
opium.

MORINDA TRIFOLIA L. Indian mulberry. 2n=   .
Indonesia and Malaya. Cultivated on Java
as a dye crop.

OLDENLANDIA UMBELLATA L. Indian madder. 2n=
36. Trop. Asia. Cultivated as a dye plant.

UNCARIA GAMBIR (Hunt.) Roxb. Gambier. 2n=
. Malaya. Formerly cultivated in SE. Asia.
Its leaves and young branches contain a tannin.

Rutaceae

AEGLE MARMELOS (L.) Corr. Indian bael, Bengal
fruit. 2n=18, (36). Cultivated in SE. Asia
and some other trop. countries for its fruits,
which are used medicinally.

CITRUS AURANTIFOLIA (Christm.) Swing. Lime.
2n=18, (27). Probably Malaysian Archipelago
or N. India. It may derive from a cross of
C. medica* with a biotype of the primitive
subgenus Papeda (Scora, 1975). Wild trees are
reported to grow in N. India. Spread throughout tropics. The cultivar Tahiti is triploic.
Interspecific hybrids have been obtained.
Mandarin lime is probably a hybrid with C.
reticulata*, sweet lime with C. medica* and
limequat with Fortunella margarita*. The
nakoor lime (named C. nakoor) is a complex
natural hybrid with some Papeda group parentage. The Rangpur lime belongs to C. reticulata*.

CITRUS AURANTIUM L. Sour orange, Seville
orange, Bigarade. 2n=18. Probably SE. Asia or
Cochin China. Unknown wild. It may derive
from C. reticulata* x C. grandis* (Scora,
1975). Spread throughout (sub)tropics. In
some areas, it has run wild. Ssp. bergamia
(Risso & Poit.) Wight & Arn., Bergamot (2n=
18) is cultivated especially in Calabria, S
Italy for the production of bergamot oil
(p. 105). Crosses with C. sinensis* (Sweet
orange) gave Bitter sweet orange. The var.
myrtifolia Kergawl., Myrtle-leaved orange is
a bud mutant. Its fruits, Chinottos, are can-
died in Italy and S. France.

CITRUS GRANDIS (L.) Osbeck (syn. C. decuma-
nus L. 2n=18, 21; C. maxima (Burm.) Merr.
2n=18, 36). Pummelo, Shaddock. 2n=18, 36.
Probably SE. Asia. Primary centre of diversity: SE. Asia. Spread to China, India and
Iran, and later to other tropical countries
(by Captain Shaddock to Barbados in 17th Century). Unknown wild. The best fruits come
from Thailand where the plants are cultivated on ridges surrounded by brackish water.
Self-incompatible and monoembryonic perennial.
Introgression with C. reticulata* occurs
(Scora, 1975).

CITRUS HYSTRIX DC. Mauritius papeda. 2n=
Philippines and Burma to Malaya. A small
type cultivated for its fruits.

CITRUS JAMBHIRI Lush. Rough lemon. 2n=   .
It derives from C. medica* x C. reticulata*
(Scora, 1978).

CITRUS LIMETTA Risso. Sweet lemon. 2n=18.
Trop. Asia. Small tree cultivated in some
countries.

CITRUS LIMON (L.) Burm.f. Lemon. 2n=18, 36.
Centre of origin somewhere in SE. Asia. The
area east of Himalayas in N. Burma and S.
China has been suggested. Unknown wild. Has
a complex origin (Torres et al., 1978). A

secondary centre: the Mediterranean Region
(p. 118). Scora & Malik (1970) suggested that
this species might be a stabilized hybrid of
C. medica* - C. aurantifolia* assemblage.
Cultivated in several (sub)tropical regions.

CITRUS MEDICA L. Citron. 2n=18. Subtrop. Asia.
A basic Citrus species (Torres et al., 1978).
It may be one of the parents of C. limon* and
C. jambhiri*. Monoembryonic.

CITRUS MITIS Blanco. Calamondin. 2n=18. Philippines. It derives from C. reticulata var.
austera x Fortunella sp. A tree occasionally
cultivated in (sub)tropics. Hybrids of this
species have been produced, for instance
Calarin and Calashu are hybrids with C. reticulata* (Satsuma). Calamondin is a hybrid of
C. reticulata x Fortunella sp.

CITRUS PARADISI Macf. Grapefruit. 2n=18. SE.
Asia. Unknown wild. Probably derived from C.
grandis* x C. sinensis* (Torres et al., 1978).
Chiranja is a hybrid with C. sinensis and
citrumelo with Poncirus trifoliata*.

CITRUS RETICULATA Blanco (C. nobilis Andr.
non Lour.). Mandarin, Tangerine. 2n=18. Probably Philippines, or Cochin China. Unknown
wild. Secondary centre arose in Japan (p. 45).
Minessy et al. (1970) found close relationship with C. sinensis* 'Balady Blood'. Its
relationship with C. paradisi* 'Duncan' and
'March' is moderate and with C. grandis*
remote. Var. austera Swing is the sour mandarin. It probably includes the Rangpur lime
(Purseglove, 1968).
    Hybrids with other species have been made.
For instance Oranguma is an artificial hybrid
of Satsuma x C. sinensis* (Orange), and Tangor
is a natural hybrid of the same parents. Its
origin is in Thailand. Tangor has been described as C. nobilis Lour. Citrandarin derives
from Poncirus trifoliata* x C. reticulata,
calamondin (see C. mitis) from C. reticulata
x Fortunella sp., and chironja from orange x
C. reticulata.

CITRUS SINENSIS (L.) Osbeck (syn. C. aurantium
L. var. sinensis L.). Sweet orange. 2n=18, (27,
36). Probably S. China or Cochin China. Unknown
in wild. It may derive from C. reticulata* x
C. grandis* (Scora, 1975). Secondary centres:
Israel and Spain (p. 118). It was already mentioned in Chinese sources dated 2200 BC. It
has the same origin as C. aurantium* but the
wide genetic variation of C. reticulata causes
differences in the derived species. It is
widely distributed in the (sub)tropics. There
are many cultivars. Citrange is a hybrid with
Poncirus trifoliata* and chironja is a spontaneous hybrid with C. paradisi*. It originated in Puerto Rico. By apomixis, it breeds
true.

MURRAYA EXOTICA L. Limonia. 2n=18. Trop. Asia.
Used for hedges.

MURRAYA PANICULATA (L.) Jacq. Cosmetic bark-
tree, Orange jasmine. 2n=18. SE. Asia. Cultivated in the tropics as an ornamental and
for hedges. The wood (Satinwood) is used in
Java to make cutlery.

    Santalaceae

SANTALUM ALBUM L. (syn. Sirium myrtifolium
L.). Sandel wood. 2n=10. E. India to Malaysia. Cultivated there and elsewhere for
scented wood.

    Sapindaceae

ERIOGLOSSUM RUBIGINOSUM (Roxb.) Blume (syn.
E. edule Bl.). 2n= . Trop. Asia to New
Guinea and Australia. A small tree cultiva-
ted in Indonesia and elsewhere.

NEPHELIUM LAPACCEUM L. Rambutan. 2n=22. Malaysian Archipelago. Cultivated for its delicious fruits. Many varieties have been developed.

NEPHELIUM MUTABILE Blume. Pulasan. 2n= .
Malaysia. Cultivated in SE. Asia and in
other countries.

POMETIA PINNATA Forst. Matoa, Taun. 2n= .
Malaysia, Indonesia, Papua New Guinea and
Pacific islands. A forest tree used for timber and for its fruits. Cultivated for its
edible fruits. On W. Irian alongside the
banks of the Sentani Lake.
This crop will probably be replaced by higher
-yielding exotic fruit trees (Rappard, 1961).

SAPINDUS RARAK DC. 2n= . Cochin China and
Malaysia. Planted in Java, India and elsewhere for its fruits.

    Sapotaceae

MANILKARA ELENGI (L.) Chev. 2n= . Origin
uncertain (Uphof, 1968). Cultivated in the
Malaysian Archipelago.

PALAQUIUM GUTTA (Hook.) Burck. Gutta percha.
2n=24. Malaysia. It is tapped for its latex.
In general, the tree is first felled.

PAYENA LEERII (Teijsm. & Binn.) Kurz. 2n=
Burma and W. Malaysia. Cultivated on Java as
a source of gutta percha.

    Saururaceae

HOUTTUYNIA CORDATA Thunb. 2n=56, 96, c.96,
100-104. Indochina and China. Cultivated in
Vietnam for salad and as medicinal crop.

    Solanaceae

LYCINUM CHINESE Mill. Chinese wolfberry. 2n=
24. E. Asia. Cultivated in Java as vegetable.

SOLANUM UPORO Dunal. 2n=   . Polynesia. Cultivated in Fiji for its fruits.

Stilagninaceae

ANTIDESMA BUNIUS (L.) Spreng. Bignay, China laurel. 2n=117. India to Australia. Cultivated in Malaysia and elsewhere for its fruits (Purseglove, 1968).

Styraceae

STYRAX BENZOIN Dryander. 2n=   . Malaysian Archipelago. Planted in Sumatra.

Taccaceae

TACCA PINNATIFIDA Forst. (syn. T. involucrata Schum. & Thonn., T. leontopetaloides (L.) Kuntze). Tacca pin, Tahiti arrowroot. 2n=30. SE. Asia (Massal & Barrau, 1956). Possibly domesticated by Polynesians for its starchy roots and introduced into Malaysia and Madagascar. Also found from Ethiopia to W. Africa.

Umbelliferae

CARUM ROXBURGHIANUM Benth. (syn. Trachyspermum roxburghianum (DC) Wolff). Ajmud. 2n(wild)= (20, 40) 42, (44); (cultivated)=20. Trop. Asia. Cultivated in Indochina, Sri Lanka and India.

LIGUSTICUM MONNIERI Calest. (syn. Selinum monnieri L.). 2n=   . E. Europe, Siberia, China and Vietnam. Occasionally cultivated in N. Vietnam.

OENANTHE JAVANICA DC. (syn. O. stolonifera Wall.). Oriental celery, Water dropwort, Batjarongi. 2n=20. From Indochina to Malaya, Philippines, China, Korea, Japan and Australia. Cultivated in Indochina, Japan, China (Kihara, 1969) and Java. A leafy vegetable that often occurs as a weed.

Urticaceae

LAPORTEA DECUMANA Wedd. 2n=   . Moluccas. Cultivated as a medicinal plant.

Zingiberaceae

ALPINIA CONCHIGERA Griff. (syn. Languas conchigera Burk.). 2n=   . Malaya. It is a common village plant there.

ALPINIA GALANGA (L.) Willd. Langwas, Greater galangal. 2n=48. Trop. Asia. Cultivated for its rhizomes. It is a common village plant. Several varieties have been observed.

ALPINIA MALACCENSIS (Burm.f.) Rosc. 2n=48. Malaysian Archipelago and E. India. This perennial herb is cultivated.

AMOMUM CARDAMOMUM Willd. Cardamon. 2n=   . Ma-

laysia. Cultivated there.

AMOMUM KEPULAGA Sprague & Burk. Round cardamon. 2n=   . Cultivated in Malaysia and Java.

AMOMUM KRERVANH Pierre. Krervanh. 2n=   . Cambodia. Cultivated in Indochina.

AMOMUM MAXIMUM Roxb. Java cardamon. 2n=   . Malaysia. Cultivated in Java.

BOESENBERGIA PANDURATA (syn. Gastrochilus pandurata Ridl.). 2n=   . Malaya and Java. Cultivated over wide area for its rhizome.

CURCUMA HEYNEANA Valeton. 2n=   . Java. The rhizomes are a source of an arrowroot.

CURCUMA PIERREANA Gagn. 2n=   . Malaya. Cultivated in Annam (Vietnam).

CURCUMA XANTHORRHIZA Roxb. 2n=   . Amboina. Occasionally cultivated in Java and Malaya.

KAEMPFERIA GALANGA L. 2n=22, 54. Trop. Asia Widely cultivated for its rhizomes.

KAEMPFERIA ROTUNDA L. 2n=33, 54. Trop. Asia Cultivated for its rhizomes.

PHAEOMERIA MAGNIFICA Schum. (syn. Alpinia magnifica Rosc., A. speciosa D. Dietr., Amomum magnificum Nenth.). 2n=   . Malaya. Cultivated there.

ZINGIBER CASSUMUNAR Roxb. Cassumunar ginger. 2n=22. Cultivated in Cochin China and Malaya. In Malaya as a village medicinal crop.

ZINGIBER ZERUMBET (L.) Smith. Zerumbet ginger. 2n=22. Trop. Asia. Cultivated in Cochin China, Cambodia and elsewhere.

3 Australian Region

The Australian Region was not described by Vavilov, but it was marked out by Zhukovskij (1970) because of the domestication of several plant species to important crops or the use of wild species as breeding parents. The main crops derived from this Region are Eucalyptus species. Wild species useful for tobacco breeding are Nicotiana debneyi and N. goodspeedii. It is a secondary centre of diversity for Trifolium subterraneum.

Agavaceae

PHORMIUM TENAX J.R. et G. Forst. New Zealand flax, New Zealand hemp, Harakaka lily, Formio. 2n=32. New Zealand. Cultivated there. Introduced into S. America and other countries. The only other species of this genus Ph₀ colensoi Hook., mountain flax (2n=32) produces a weak fibre. It might be used as a breeding parent.

Casuarinaceae

CASUARINA EQUISETIFOLIA Forst. Swamp oak, Bull oak, Polynesian iron wood, Horsetail tree. 2n=18. It is often cultivated as soil stabilizer.

Chenopodiaceae

ATRIPLEX SEMIBACCATA R.Br. Australian salt-bush, Berry saltbush. 2n=18. Australia. Cultivated as fodder crop on the saline soils of California and Arizona, USA.

Gramineae

HOLCUS LANATUS L. Yorkshire fog, Soft meadow grass, Woolly softgrass, Velvet grass. 2n=14. See p. 153. A secondary centre of diversity has developed in New Zealand (Jacques, 1974).

ORYZA AUSTRALIENSIS Domin. 2n=24, genome formula EE. Australia. All research into the affinity of the species to other Oryza species uses plants derived from one collection (Chang, 1970).

Leguminosae

ACACIA CYANOPHYLLA Lindl. 2n=26. Australia. Cultivated as an ornamental and in Europe to stabilize coastal dunes.

ACACIA DEALBATA Link. Silver wattle. 2n=26. SE. Australia and Tasmania. Cultivated as an ornamental, for its timber and as soil stabilizer. It is the familiar florist's mimosa.

ACACIA LONGIFOLIA (Andrews) Willd. (syn. A. cibaria F.V. Muell.). 2n=26. New South Wales, Australia. Cultivated as ornamental and as stabilizer of coastal dunes in Europe.

ACACIA MEARNSII De Wild. Black wattle. 2n=26. Cultivated in several countries mainly for its tannin and as ornamental. Sometimes the names A. decurrens (Wendl.) Willd. or A. mollissima Willd. are wrongly used for black wattle.

ACACIA PYCNANTHA Benth. Golden wattle. 2n=   . South Australia and Victoria, Australia. Cultivated for tannin and as ornamental.

GLYCINE CANESCENS F.J. Herm. 2n=40. A close

relative of G. max*, being a possible source
of resistance to powdery mildew, Microsphaera
diffusa Cka. & Pk.

LUPINUS COSENTINI Guss. (syn. L. varius L.
ssp. varius Franco & P. Silva). Western Australia blue lupin, Sandplain lupin. 2n=32.
Along the coast of Morocco and scattered in
W. Mediterranean region. Introduced into
W. Australia about 1850 as a source of flour.
Cultivated for summer sheep feed and soil improvement. It is now widely naturalized (Gladstones, 1970).

PHASEOLUS LATHYROIDES L. Phasemy bean. 2n=22.
Queensland, Australia. Used in E. Africa in
pastures (Whyte et al., 1953). This species
and Vigna radiata* possess a high homology of
chromosomes, which points to a close relation
(Biswas & Dana, 1975).

TRIFOLIUM SUBTERRANEAUM L. Subterranean clover,
Sub clover. 2n=16. Primary centre in the Me-
diterranean Region (p. 115). Secondary centre:
Australia.

Malvaceae

GOSSYPIUM AUSTRALE F.V. Muell. 2n=26, genome
formula C_3C_3. N. Australia.

GOSSYPIUM BICKII Prokh. 2n=   , genome formula G_1G_1. Queensland, Georgina River.

GOSSYPIUM ROBINSONII F.V. Muell. 2n=26, genome
formula C_2C_2. W. Australia.

GOSSYPIUM STURTIANUM J.H. Willis. 2n=2x=26,
genome formula CC. C. Australia.

GOSSYPIUM STURTII F.V. Muell. 2n=26, genome
formula C_1C_1. C. and S. Australia.

Musaceae

MUSA (Australimusa). Fe'i banana. 2n=20. The
fe'i banana originated from one or more wild
Australimusa species in New Guinea-Solomon Islands area. Probably carried by man in an
easternly direction. Cultivated especially in
Tahiti, where many bunches are harvested from
semi-wild plants. Some clones have been described as M. fehi Bert. ex Vieill., M. aiori
Sagot, M. seemanii F.V. Muell. and M. troglo-
dytarum L. (Simmonds, 1964).

Myrtaceae

EUCALYPTUS ALBA Reinw. ex Blume. 2n=22.
Timor and Flores and to the south of New
Guinea. Cultivated in Brazil. The wood is
reddish-brown. The cork contains much tanning
material.

EUCALYPTUS AMYGDALINA Labill. (syn. E. salicifolia Cav.). Willowleaf eucalyptus, Peppermint tree. 2n=22. Tasmania. Cultivated in

Gossypium sturtii

Chile, Zaïre and W. Georgia (USSR). Closely
related to E. regnans*.

EUCALYPTUS ASTRINGENS Maiden. Brown mallet.
2n=22. SW. Australia. Cultivated in Morocco,
S. Africa and Cyprus. The bark used for the
tanning industry. It is very drought-resistant.

EUCALYPTUS BOTRYOIDES Smith. Blue gum, Banga-
lay eucalyptus, Bastard mahogany. 2n=22.
Coastal areas of SW. Australia. Cultivated in
Algeria and Zaïre. E. trabutii Vilm. (2n=22),
is a hybrid of E. botryoides ♀ and E. camaldulensis* ♂ arisen in Italy.

EUCALYPTUS BROCKWAYI Gardn. 2n=22. S. Australia. Its area of distribution is limited.
Cultivated in N. Africa. Extremely drought-
resistant.

EUCALYPTUS CAMALDULENSIS Dehn. Longbeak eucalyptus, Australian kino, Red gum. 2n=22.
Australia, excluding Tasmania. It is culti-
ted almost in all countries that grow Eucalyptus. Secondary centres: the Mediterranean
region (p. 117), Brazil (p. 127) and Argentina (p. 127). In cultivation, many spontaneous hybrids have arisen. E. trabutii Vilm.
(2n=22) is a hybrid of E. botryoides ♀ and E.
camaldalensis ♂. A new form developed in
Israel (p. 117).

EUCALYPTUS CINERA F.V. Muell. 2n=22. S. areas
of New South Wales, Australia. Used as ornamental. It is a valuable source for breeding
cold-resistant forms of Eucalyptus.

EUCALYPTUS CITRIODORA Hook. Spotted gum, Lemon-scented gum. 2n=(20), 22, (28). N. coast

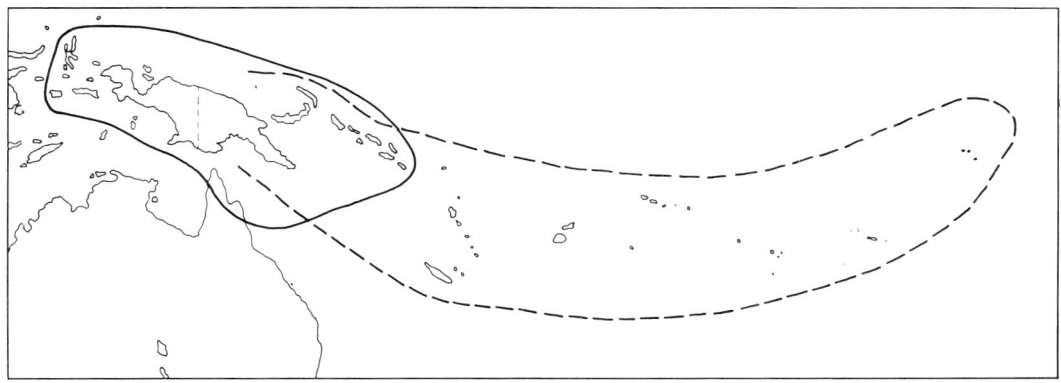

Wild Australimusa (——) and Fe'i bananas (---)(Simmonds, 1962).

of Queensland, Australia. Cultivated in many (sub)tropical countries for essential oil rich in citronellal.

EUCALYPTUS CLADOCALYX F.V. Muell. (syn. E. corynocalyx F.V. Muell.). Sugar gum. 2n=22. S. Australia. Cultivated in Australia, Mediterranean area and in some African countries. The wood is of excellent technical value.

EUCALYPTUS COCCIFERA Hook.f. 2n=   . Tasmania. Because of its hardiness, it is used for breeding types for W. Georgia (USSR).

EUCALYPTUS CREBRA F.V. Muell. 2n=   . Queensland, reaching New South Wales, Australia. Cultivated in several countries of Africa, India and Argentina. Some spontaneous hybrids are known.

EUCALYPTUS CYPELLOCARPA L. Johnst. (E. goniocalyx pl. anct.). 2n=22. SW. Australia attaining 900-1200 m altitude. Cultivated in Mediterranean area, S. America and on Hawaii.

EUCALYPTUS DALRYMPLEANA Maiden. Mountain gum. 2n=22. SE. Australia, attaining 1350 m altitude and in C. Tasmania attaining 900 m altitude. Cultivated on the coasts of the Black Sea in the Caucasus. It is a promising economic species on Hawaii and in China. It is considered to be of hybrid origin. Natural and artificial hybrids are known. It can be used in breeding better types.

EUCALYPTUS DELEGATENSIS R.T. Baker. (syn. E. gigantea Hook.f.). Alpine ash, Woollybutt, Red mountain ash, White top stringbark. 2n= . The mountains of SE. Australia up to 1350 m and in Tasmania up to 900 m. Cultivated in New Zealand, Hawaii and W. Georgia (USSR). Used for cultivation and as breeding parent in USSR.

EUCALYPTUS DIVERSICOLOR F.V. Muell. Karri. 2n=22. Coasts of SE. Australia. Cultivated

in countries of Mediterranean area, in Africa and New Zealand. It is one of the most valuable economic species.

EUCALYPTUS EUGENIOIDES Sieb. (syn. E. scabra Dum-Cours.). White stringybark, Pink blackbutt. 2n=   . Coasts areas of SE. Australia. Cultivated in S. Africa, Kenya, India and Hawaii. The wood is used in industry. Some natural hybrids are known.

EUCALYPTUS GLAUCESCENS Maiden & Blakely. 2n= . Mountains of SE. Australia. Its distribution is very limited. Used for crossing with species of poor hardiness.

EUCALYPTUS GLOBULUS Labill. Fever tree, Blue gum. 2n=20, 22, 28. SE. Tasmania. Cultivated. Secondary centre: the Mediterranean region. Used for wood and oil. Spontaneous hybrids are known under cultivation in Tasmania.

EUCALYPTUS GOMPHOCEPHALA A.DC. 2n=22. SW. coasts of West Australia. Cultivated in countries of the Mediterranean region. Africa esp. Cameroon, Hawaii and New Zealand. It has the heaviest and strongest wood among all Eucalyptus species. In Algeria, some spontaneous hybrids are known.

EUCALYPTUS GRANDIS Hill. ex Maiden. 2n=   . Coast areas of the N. part of New South Wales and SE. Queensland up to 650 m. Cultivated in Cameroon, Nigeria and Madagascar. It is thought that E. 'saligna' or E. 'saligna/grandis' are African strains developed after introduction of Queensland material (Larsen & Cromer, 1970).

EUCALYPTUS GUNNII Hook.f. 2n=22. Cultivated in USSR, Great Britain, Japan and Hawaii. Used for industry and breeding on the Caucasus coasts of the Black Sea.

EUCALYPTUS LEUCOXYLON F.V. Muell. (syn. E. conoidea Benth.). White ironbark, White gum.

2n=22. C. areas of Victoria and South Australia. In the latter area, it is rare. Cultivated in the Mediterranean area esp. Cyprus
and S. America esp. Argentina. Used for its
wood and oil. Some geographic races and
spontaneous hybrids have been described.

EUCALYPTUS MACARTHURI Dean & Maiden. 2n=22.
C. New South Wales, Australia. Cultivated in
Africa esp. Zaïre, Hawaii, New Zealand, S.
France and W. Georgia, USSR. It produces an
essential oil. Some spontaneous hybrids are
known. In the USSR many (poly)hybrids have
been produced.

EUCALYPTUS MACULATA Hook.f. (syn. E. varie-
gata F.V. Muell.). Spotted gum. 2n=22. Coastal
areas of SE. Queensland, New South Wales and
E. Victoria. Cultivated in Africa esp. Cameroon, Zaïre, Kenya and Madagascar; the
Mediterranean region esp. Spain, France; Chile
and Uruguay. The wood is very valuable.

EUCALYPTUS MAIDENII F.V. Muell. Maiden's gum,
Spotted blue gum. 2n=22. Mountains of SE.
Australia. Cultivated in Africa esp. Cameroon,
Congo and Kenya; the Mediterranean area esp.
Italy and Spain; Brazil and New Zealand. Its
wood is valuable, containing essential oil.
Some spontaneous and artificial hybrids have
been reported.

EUCALYPTUS MELLIODORA A. Cunn. Yellow box.
2n=22. Australia. Cultivated in the Mediterranean area, in Africa esp. Zaïre and Eritrea. Used for its wood and as an ornamental
tree. It is extremely melliferous. There are
geographic races and spontaneous hybrids
known.

EUCALYPTUS MICROCORYS F.V. Muell. Fallow wood.
2n=   . Coastal areas of the N. part of New
South Wales and SE. Queensland. Cultivated in
Mediterranean area and Africa esp. Zaïre and
Eritrea. Used for wood. Some spontaneous
hybrids are known.

EUCALYPTUS NIPHOPHILA Maiden & Blakely. 2n=
  . Alpine zone of SE. Australia, up to 2000
m. It tolerates -24°C and hence is of great
importance for hybridization with valuable
economic species.

EUCALYPTUS PANICULATA Sm. (syn. E. fergusoni
R.T. Baker). Grey ironbark. 2n=22. The coasts
of New South Wales. Cultivated in Africa esp.
Kenya and Tripoli; Mediterranean area, esp.
Spain and Tripolitania; S. America, esp. Paraguay and Uruguay, and India. The wood is especially strong, heavy and durable.

EUCALYPTUS PAUCIFLORA Sieb. ex Spreng. 2n=
Sub-alpine zone of E. Victoria and the mountains of New South Wales and Tasmania, up to
1650 m. Cultivated in England, France, Japan
and W. Georgia (USSR). On the fringe of its
area, it is very hardy. It is valuable in

breeding hardy strains. Some geographic races
and spontaneous hybrids are known.

EUCALYPTUS PERRENIANA F.V. Muell. ex Rodway
2n=   . Tasmania. Cultivated in the USSR. I-
is hardy (it tolerates -13°C).

EUCALYPTUS REGNANS F.V. Muell. Mountain ash
Swamp gum, Australian oak. 2n=   . Mountains
of S. Victoria up to 900 m and in Tasmania up
to 600 m. Cultivated in Kenya, New Zealand
and other countries. This is the biggest and
most valuable species in this genus. Some
trees are recorded up to 96 m high. It is
closely related to E. amygdalina*.

EUCALYPTUS RESINIFERA Smith (syn. E. spectabilis F.V. Muell., E. hemilampra F.V. Muell.).
Kino eucalyptus, Red mahogany, Forests mahogany. 2n=22. Coastal zone of S. Queensland
and C. part of New South Wales. Cultivated in
Argentina, Sri Lanka, Ethiopia, Cameroon and
other countries. The wood is very valuable.

EUCALYPTUS ROBUSTA Smith. Beakpod eucalyptus,
White mahogany, Swamp mahogany. 2n=   . Coasts
of S. Queensland as far as S. of New South
Wales, Australia. Cultivated in Mediterranean
area, Africa esp. Cameroon, Zaïre and Kenya;
Argentina, India and other countries. Often
cultivated on swampy grounds. The wood is economically valuable.

EUCALYPTUS SALIGNA Sm. Sydney blue gum, Saligna gum. 2n=22. Coasts and slopes of mountains
in New South Wales and SE. Queensland. Cultivated in Africa, esp. Cameroon, Kenya and Zimbabwe; S. America esp. Argentina and Brazil.
After E. globulus*, the most widely distributed species in cultivation. The wood is extremely valuable. This is the most rapidly
growing species in the genus.

EUCALYPTUS SIDEROXYLON A. Cunn. ex Benth. Red
ironbark. 2n=22. The W. slopes of New South
Wales upland and in the N. part of Central
Victoria, Australia. Cultivated in Africa esp.
Cameroon, Kenya, Zaïre and Rhodesia; the Mediterranean area, esp. Spain, Portugal, Algeria, Morocco, Cyprus and Israel; Japan, USA
and New Zealand. Its wood is economically very
valuable. It contains essential oil. Some
spontaneous hybrids are known.

EUCALYPTUS TERETICORNIS Smith. (syn. E. suba-
latum Cunningh.) Red gum, Flooded gum, Grey
gum, Blue gum. 2n=22. Almost the whole coast
of E. Australia. Cultivated almost in all the
countries of the world where Eucalyptus is
grown. The wood is very valuable. In USSR,
interspecific hybrids are produced. The strains
'C' of Zanzibar and 'Mysore Hybrid' of India
belong to this species (Larsen & Croner,
1970).

EUCALYPTUS VIMINALIS Labill. (syn. E. mann-
fera Cunning, E. persicifolia Lodd.). Ribbon

eucalyptus, White gum, Swamp gum. 2n=22. SE. Australia and E. Tasmania. Cultivated in Mediterranean area, in countries of C. and S. Africa, India, New Zealand and USA. In subtropical areas of USSR, it is the commonest Eucalyptus species. The wood is of moderate value. An essential oil is obtained. Many spontaneous and artificial hybrids are known.

LEPTOSPERMUM LAEVIGATUM F.V. Muell. Australian tea-tree. 2n=22. Australia. Cultivated there for the reclamation of moving sand. Dried leaves are used for tea-making.

MELALEUCA PREISSIANA Schan. 2n=   . Australia. Var. leiostachya Schan. (syn. M. parviflora Lindl.) is a soil stabilizer.

Proteaceae

HAKEA SALICIFOLIA (Vent.) B.L. Burtt. 2n= SE. Australia and Tasmania. Cultivated for reclamation of arid land in Spain and Portu gal. It has run wild in those countries.

HAKEA SERICEA Schrader. 2n=20. E. Australia. Cultivated for reclamation of arid land in Portugal and Spain. It has run wild in those countries.

MACADAMIA INTEGRIFOLIA L.S. Smith. (syn. M. ternifolia F.V. Muell., M. ternifolia var. integrifolia and M. tetraphylla L.A.S. Johnson). Queensland nut, Macadamia nut, Australian bush nut, Australian hazelnut. 2n=28, 56. E. Queensland, Australia. Cultivated in Hawaii. M. integrifolia is known as the smooth-shell type and M. tetraphylla as the rough-shell type. M. ternifolia is now considered to apply correctly only to a species with bitter cyanogenic seeds less than 25 mm in diameter, inedible and never cultivated (Kraus & Hamilton, 1970).

Rutaceae

EREMOCITRUS GLAUCA (Lindl.) Swing. 2n=18. This tree is capable of withstanding 6 months drought. It easily crosses with Citrus species giving fertile hybrids.

Solanaceae

DUBOISIA HOPWOODII F.V. Muell. Pituri, Pitchery. 2n=   . Australia. Cultivated for some decades to yield atropine.

DUBOISIA LEICHHARDTII R.Br. 2n=60. Australia. Cultivated for some decades for atropine.

DUBOISIA MYOPOROIDES R.Br. Corkwood, Mgmeo. 2n=60. Australia. Cultivated for atropine.

NICOTIANA DEBNEYI Domin. 2n=48. Australia. Used as a source of resistance to blue mold caused by Perenospora tabacina Adam.

NICOTIANA GOODSPEEDII Wheeler. 2n=40. New South Wales to SE. of West Australia. It has a short growing period. It is very resistant to Peronospora tabacina Adam. Some natural introgression with the closely related N. exigua Wheeler, 2n=32, N. nuaveolens Lehm., 2n=(24), 32, (48, 64), and N. rotundifolia Lindl., 2n=44.

SOLANUM LACIANIATUM Aiton. Cut-leaved nightshade. 2n=92. Australia and New Zealand. Cultivated in Europe and elsewhere for its foliage, which is a source of steroid precursors.

4 Hindustani Region

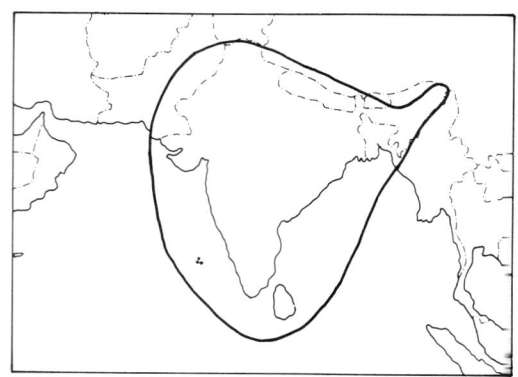

The Hindustani Region of diversity was included by Vavilov in his Tropical South Asian Centre of Origin. Zhukovskij (1968) distinguished this centre only by number (IV), but in 1970 he indicated a distinction between this and the rest of S. Asia. He based his distinction on the existence of species specific for this Region 4.

Although this region is near known old farming sites in Thailand, agriculture must have been introduced from the NW. adjacent area. Early farming sites have so far revealed few details of native cultivation. At Mūan-jo Daro (Mohenjodaro) and Harappa on the River Indus in Pakistan, almost on the boundary between Regions 4 and 5, a site of the Harappan culture was discovered dating from 2500 - 2000 BC. Some remains of Gossypium arboreum were discovered. At a site, Navdatoli-Mahesvar on the Narbada River, in C. India, dating from 2000 BC., remains of wheat, peas, broad beans, lentils, Lathyrus sativus and rice were found. Except for rice, these crops were domesticated outside India.

Important crops of the region include bamboos, fruit trees, Cucurbita sativa, Mangifera indica, Musa sp., Oryza sativa, Phaseolus mungo, Piper sp., Saccharum sinense and Vigna sinensis.

Species of this region have influenced the development of crops elsewhere, mainly by active distribution between this region and areas such as Ancient Egypt, Assyria, Sumeria and the Hittite Empire. Exchange also took place with Africa. Crops were distributed especially to the Mediterranean area by the Arabs in the 8th-10th Centuries AD. Such crops include citrus trees, cotton species, jute, rice and sugar-cane.

Acanthaceae

BARLERIA PRIONITIS L. 2n=30, 40. Trop. Africa and Asia. Cultivated in India as a medicinal crop.

Agavaceae

SANSEVERINIA HYACINTHOIDES (L.) Druce (syn. S. zeylanica Willd.). Ceylon bowstring hemp. 2n=   . Sri Lanka. A fibre plant cultivated there.

Alliaceae

ALLIUM AMPELOPRASUM L. Levant garlic, Perennial sweet leek. 2n=16, (24), 32, genome formula AAA'A", (40, 48). S. Europe, Asia Minor, Caucasus to Iran and N. Africa. Some cultivation in Germany and France (p. 148), Iran (Taree irani, 2n=32; Tahbaz, 1976) and in Kashmir (Koul & Gojil, 1970). The wild and cultivated types are both extremely variable. This species is related to A. sativum*, A. porrum*, A. kurrat* and A. scorodoprasum*.

Amaranthaceae

AMARANTHUS ANGUSTIFOLIUS Lam. 2n=32, (34). S. and C. Europe, SW. Asia up to India and Turkestan and to Africa. In India var. polygonoides Thell. is cultivated.

CELOSIA ARGENTEA L. Quail grass. 2n=(36), 72. India. Var. cristata Kuntze (syn. C. cristata L.). Cockscomb grass. 2n=36. It is a pot-herb, fodder and fibre crop and an ornamental.

Anacardiaceae

MANGIFERA INDICA L. Mango. 2n=40. Assam and
the Chittagong Hills. Spread to many tropical
countries. Rhodes et al. (1970) classified
cultivars into:
1. polyembryonic group with oblong fruits, common in SE. Asia,
2. monoembryonic group with roundish fruits
common in India and
3. a group intermediate in fruit shape, also
common in India.
4. the Sandersha-Haden complex, consisting of
hybrids developed in Florida and Hawaii. M.
odorata* and M. zeylanica Hook.f. are not
closely related. Natural cross-fertilization
ranges from 5 to 62%. A secondary centre of
diversity has developed in Florida (p. 199).

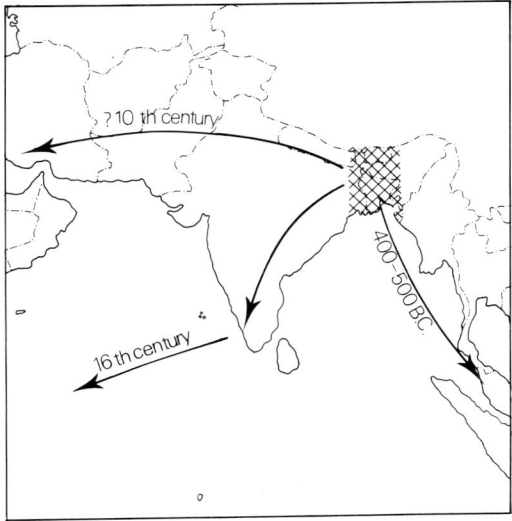

Centre of domestication and routes of migration of Mangifera indica (Singh, 1976).

Apocynaceae

NERIUM INDICUM Mill. (syn. N. odorum Soland.).
2n=22. Trop. Asia, especially India. Cultivated as a medicinal plant.

RAUVOLFIA SERPENTINA Benth. 2n=(20), 22, (24,
44). India, Sri Lanka, Burma and from Thailand
to Java. Because of the high demand for this
medicinal crop, it became (nearly) extinct in
some areas. To provide sufficient roots, some
hospitals in India set up small gardens of it.
Its cultivation could be extended to India and
elsewhere (Dutta et al., 1963).

Araceae

ALOCASIA CUCULLATA (Lour.) Schott. Giant taro.
2n=28. India and Sri Lanka. Cultivated for

its corms.

ALOCASIA MACRORRHIZA (L.) Schott. Giant alocasia. 2n=26, (28). Probably Sri Lanka. Spread
in the Malaysian Archipelago and to India and
further to Trop. America. Several varieties
are cyanogenic. A. indica is often included
in this species.

AMORPHOPHALLUS CAMPANULATUS Blume. Whitespot
giant arum, Oroy. 2n=(14), 28. Trop. Asia
(p. 49). Cultivated in India and elsewhere
as a tuber crop.

COLOCASIA ESCULENTA (L.) Schott. Taro, Dasheen.
2n=2x=28, 3x=42. The centre of domestication
is not certain. Some authors suggest Malaysia,
others like Kuruvilla & Singh (1981) NE. India, Assam or Upper Burma. These authors found
2x cultivars in the plains of India and 2x
and 3x cultivars in the hills of NE. India.

Asclepiadaceae

MARSDENIA TINCTORIA R.Br. 2n=   . Himalaya to
China, Malaysia. Cultivated in India as a dye
plant.

Cannabidaceae

CANNABIS SATIVA L. Hemp. 2n=20. Centre of
origin C. Asia (p. 149). Spread to India in
early times. The Indian type is cultivated
for its narcotic properties. Thence it must
have spread to the Middle East and elsewhere.
'C. ruderalis Janesch' is a weedy non-toxicant
type.

Chenopodiaceae

BETA VULGARIS L. Indian spinach. 2n=18, genome formula VV. For origin see p. 104. Indian
spinach is cultivated mainly for its leaves
and occasionally for its roots. There is a
red-leafed and a green-leafed type. As it
differs in chromosome pattern and for its
phenolic compounds from table beetroot, Basu
& Mukherjee (1975) described it as B. palonga.
However, more research is needed. It very
likely derives from early introductions from
the Near East via Afghanistan, whereas the
table beetroot was introduced later from Europe (Basu & Mukherjee, 1975).

KOCHIA INDICA Wight. 2n=18. Introduced into
Egypt where it is cultivated as a forage crop.

Compositae

INULA RACEMOSA Hook.f. 2n=20. Cultivated on
a small scale in the Labaul Valley in NW.
Himalaya for its aromatic roots. Cultivation
is reported from N. Africa, Asia Minor, Ethiopia, Iran, E. India and some European countries.

SAUSSUREA LAPPA Clarke. 2n=26. Grown in the

Valley of Kashmir and adjacent area for its aromatic roots.

VERNONIA AMYGDALINA Delile. Bitterleaf. 2n= . Trop. Africa. Occasionally cultivated.

Convolvulaceae

IPOMOEA ERIOCARPA R.Br. 2n=   . India. Used as a spinach and as a green fodder.

Cruciferae

BRASSICA CAMPESTRIS L. 2n=20. genome formula AA. See p. 150 for the origin of this species. In Pakistan/India the var. toria Duthrie & Fuller, Indian rape, Toria, and var. sarson Prain, Indian colza, Brown sarson are cultivated. Brown sarson can be divided into (1) self-compatible and (2) self-incompatible types. These two types can be differentiated by disruptive selection for flowering time, genetic drift in isolated populations, and chromosomal inversions suppressing recombination in connection with a recessive mutation of a major gene, independent of the S locus but inactivating that locus (Swamy Rao, 1971). A considerable diversity is observed in Bihar and E. Utter Pradesh (Anand et al., 1975).

ERUCA VESICARIA (L.). Cav. (syn. E. sativa L.). 2n=22. Mediterranean Region (p. 107) and Asia. Cultivated in India for jamba oil.

RAPHANUS SATIVUS L. Serpent radish, Snakelike radish, Rat-tailed radish, Tree radish from Java. 2n=18. Cultivated from Java to NW. India. The plant requires a short daylength to develop roots. Var. mougri Helm (syn. R. caudatus L., R. sativus var. indicus Sinsk. is characterized by small long fleshy fruits and glabrous leaves. Var. oleiformis Pers.* is also grown in India.

Cucurbitaceae

CITRULLUS COLOCYNTHIS*

CITRULLUS LANATUS (Thunb.) Mansf. Water melon. 2n=22. Var. fistulosis (Stocks) Duthie & Fuller (syn. C. fistulosis Stocks), Round melon (2n=24) is cultivated in India for its round fruits. It differs in chromosomal number and leaf phenolics from C. lanatus and should probably be raised to a species (Kaur et al., 1973).

COCCINIA CORDIFOLIA Cogn. (syn. C. indica W. & A.). Ivy gourd, Small gourd. 2n=24, (36). Trop. Asia, and Red Sea area to Sudan. In S. India, forms occur with long less bitter fruits.

CUCUMUS SATIVUS L. Cucumber, Gherkin. 2n=14. Primary gene centre probably the Himalayas. Introduced into Europe. Near East, China and elsewhere. Secondary gene centres in China and Near East (p. 36 and 89). In India, cucum-

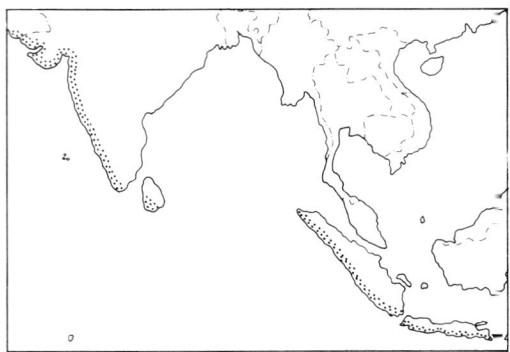

Raphanus sativus var. mougri (Sinskaya, 193).

bers have been cultivated for at least 3 000 years (Leppik, 1965). Three varieties have been described: (1) var. hardwickii (Royle) Alef. (syn. C. hardwickii Royle) (a weedy type); (2) var. sikkimansis Hook. (the 'Indian type'); (3) var. squamosus Gab. Sources of resistance to powdery mildew Sphaerotheca fuliginea (Schlecht. ex Fr.) Poll are found in cucumber material from China, Japan, Indonesia and India.

CUCURBITA MAXIMA Duch. ex Lam. Pumpkin. Winter squash. 2n=40. Its origin is described on p. 169. Secondary centre in India and adjacent areas.

LUFFA ACUTANGULA (L.) Roxb. Sponge gourd, Angled loofah, Sinkwa towel gourd. 2n=26. Probably India. Primary gene centre probably there. It was found in Karakoram/Hindu Kush in 1955 (Tozu, 1965). Cultivated in China and Japan.

Dutt & Roy (1971) suggested the following evolution of the various related Luffa species. They considered the wild monoecious L. graveolens Roxb. (2n=26) as the primary species. From it, two species derived: the wild dioecious L. echinata Roxb. (2n=26) and the cultivated monoecious L. aegyptica*. They considered dioecism as a derived factor that arose after divergence from the monoecious L. graveolens.

From L. aegyptica, the monoecious type of L. acutangula and later the hermaphrodite type of that species arose, which is also called L. hermaphrodita*.

LUFFA AEGYPTIACA Tull. (syn. L. cylindrica (L.) Roem.). Smooth loofah, Suakwa, Sponge gourd, Vegetable gourd. 2n=26. Domesticated probably in tropical Asia, possibly in India. Cultivated in almost all tropical regions where it may have run wild. Used for producing vegetables or sponges. It is also used for a medicine and for insulation.

This species includes L. racemosa Roxb. (2n =) with L. hermaphrodita* the only two 'species' with bisexual flowers.

LUFFA HERMAPHRODITA Singh & Bhandari. Satputia. 2n=   . Cultivated in Bihar and Bengal, India. It crosses easily with L. acutangula*, the F_1 being monoecious. It is similar to L. acutangula* and to L. cylindrica (see L. aegyptiaca*), but has bisexual flowers, oblong-ellipsoidal fruits and smooth shiny black seeds. It may be a hybrid of one of those two species. Types described as L. racemosa Roxb. and included in L. cylindrica are also bisexual (Singh & Bhandari, 1963).

Dutt & Roy (1971) included L. hermaphrodita in L. acutangula*. They condidered it as the hermaphrodite type of that latter species.

TRICHOSANTHES CUCUMERINA L. (syn. T. anquina L.). Snake gourd. 2n=22. India to Australia. Cultivated for a long time in India.

Dioscoreaceae

DIOSCOREA HISPIDA*.

Euphorbiaceae

BACCAUREA SAPIDA Muell.-Arg. 2n=   . Malaysia, India and China. Cultivated by Hindus for its fruits.

CROTON TIGLIUM L. Purging croton. 2n=   . SE. Asia. Cultivated now in India and Sri Lanka for its seeds (Purseglove, 1968).

Flacourtiaceae

DORYALIS (DOVYALIS) HEBECARPA (Gardn.) Walb. (syn. Aberia gardneri Clos.). Ceylon gooseberry. 2n=   . Trop. Asia especially India and Sri Lanka. Cultivated for its berries.

HYDNOCARPUS LAURIFOLIUS (Dennst.) Sleumer (syn. Hydnocarpus wightianus Blume). 2n=24. India. Cultivated in several trop. countries for its oil, used to cure leprosy.

Gramineae

BAMBUSA ARUNDINACEA (Retz.) Willd. Spiny bamboo. 2n=70. India. Cultivated there. In forests bordering rivers and on mountains up to 900 m. Much cultivated in Java, rarely in Indochina. Secondary gene centre in Java (p. 53). Used as building material and in the paper industry. This is one of the largest bamboo species. Its stems can be 30 m long.

BAMBUSA POLYMORPHA Munro. 2n=72. Bangladesh. Cultivated there and in Burma. Used as building material and in the paper industry.

BAMBUSA STRICTUS Nees. 2n=70, 72. In India (except Assam) and Burma. Secondary centres in Indochina (p. 53) and S. China (p. 37). In dry areas of forests. It is drought-resistant.

BAMBUSA TULDA Roxb. 2n=   . India. Burma (p. 53) and Tahiti. Secondary centre Java.

CEPHALOSTACHYUM CAPITATUM Munro. 2n=   . Burma and Himalaya. Its shoots are edible.

CYMBOPOGON FLEXUOSUS (Nees ex Steud.) Wats. (syn. Andropogon flexuosus Nees). Malabar grass, Cochin grass. 2n=20(+1-2B), 40(+1-2B), x=10. India. Cultivated for its essential 'East India lemon-grass oil'. Var. coimbatorensis Gupta (2n=40) is a cultigen.

CYMBOPOGON MARTINI (Roxb.) Wats. Roshagrass, Palmarosa, Ginger grass. 2n=20, 40(+1-2B), x=10. E. India. Cultivated in India and Indonesia for palmarosa oil and ginger grass oil. The cultigen var. motia (syn. C. motia Gupta, syn. var. martinii), 2n=20, produces palmarosa oil, while var. sofia Gupta, 2n=40(+1-2B) produces ginger grass oil.

CYMBOPOGON PENDULUS Wats. 2n=20, 60. India. Recently taken into cultivation (Jagadish-chandra, 1975).

CYNODON DACTYLON (L.) Pers. Bermuda grass. 2n =(x=9) 18, genome formula AA; 36, genome formula AABB; 45, 54, genome formula AAAABB. Widely distributed in the Old World tropics. Malik & Tripathi (1968) and Harlan & de Wet (1969) indicate that the two diploid genomes of the tetraploid are essentially homologous. Var. aridus Harlan & de Wet (2n=18) and var. afghanicus Harlan & de Wet are excellent fodders tolerant to drought. Several selections of var. dactylon are grown as lawn grasses. Var. elegans Rendle is a major natural grass of Africa, and var. coursii (Camus) Harlan & de Wet is a major fodder in Madagascar (Harlan et al., 1970). See p. 128.

DENDROCALAMUS HAMILTONII Nees & Arn. 2n=   . C. and E. Himalaya up to 900 m and Upper and Lower Burma up to 1 200 m altitude. Used as building material and in the paper industry. It grows in humid areas along rivers and in low places, and forms large thickets.

DENDROCALAMUS LONGISPATHUS Kurz. 2n=72. Bangladesh and Burma (Arakan). Used for paper making. It is found in humid mixed forests along rivers on fertile clay soils.

DIGITARIA CRUCIATA (Nees) A. Camus. 2n=   . Var. cruciata grows wild in a large area of E. India and China. Probably domesticated in the 19th Century in the Khasi Hills, E. India, by selecting var. esculenta Bor with longer stems, longer spikes, larger inflorescences and much bigger grains. It grows slowly and yields little. Its advantage is the production of straw in an area where little grass grows (Bor, 1955; Singh & Arora, 1972).

DIGITARIA SANGUINALIS (L.) Scap. Manna. 2n= 18, 36, 54, 72. Cultivated in Kashmir and adjacent Afghanistan, and in SE. Europe. The species is a weed of temperate regions in all continents (Portères, 1955a). Cultivated kinds differ little from their close wild relatives in floral morphology.

ECHINOCHLOA COLONA (L.) Link. Shama millet, Jungle rice. 2n=(36, 48), 54, (72). Cultivated in India as a fodder grass and as a cereal. Formerly it was grown also in Egypt. Yabuno (1968) considered the genome formula of this species to be the same as that of E. frumentacea*.

ELEUSINE CORACANA (L.) Gaertn. Finger millet, Ragi. 2n=36. Introduced from Africa (p. 129). Kempanna (1969) recognized various types in India. Hilu & de Wet (1976) described how the African lowland race must have reached India from the south or south-west. The introduction must have taken place by sea routes c. 1000 BC. In S. India, the crop developed a secondary centre of diversity. Thence it spread to the north. In NE. India, the Indian race developed and in N. India the North Indian type. It is not clear whether the last taxon evolved from the lowland race or from the Indian race or from both.

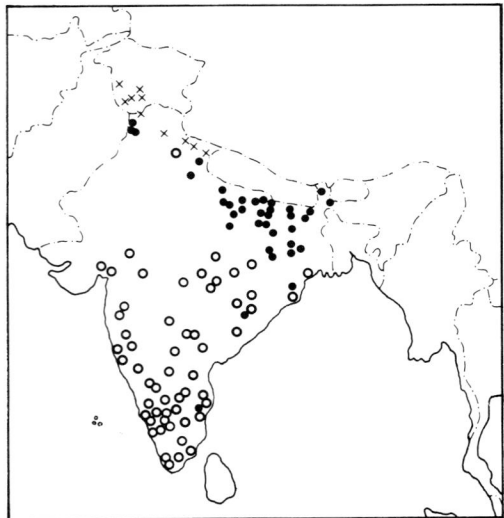

Various types of Eleusine coracana in India, (o) lowland race, (•) Indian race,(×) Indian highland type (Hilu & de Wet, 1976).

MELOCANNA BACCIFORA (Roxb.) Kurz. 2n=   . Burma from Garo to Arakan. Primary centre: Bangladesh. Its stems are used as building material.

NEOHOUZEAUA DULLOSA (Munro) A. Camus. 2n=   . S. and SE. Burma. It has a very long fibre and is used widely to produce paper.

OCHLANDRA TRAVANCORICA Bedd. 2n=c. 72. Pri-

mary centre: the Travancore Mountains and Tinneville (altitude 900 - 1 650 m). It is used in the paper industry.

ORYZA MALAMPUZHAENSIS Krish. & Chand. 2n=48 India.

ORYZA RUFIPOGON Griff. Perennial wild rice. 2n=24. The more commonly accepted epithet O perennis Moench probably does not refer to Asiatic wild race (Tateoka, 1964). Widely distributed in Asia and Australia. As recognized by Chang (1976a, b), it includes the annual O. nivara Sharma & Shastry (1965a, b). The perennials are weakly rhizomatous with extra vaginal branching and are adapted to continuously flooded habitats. Cytogenetic studies suggest that under cultivation this perennial (Nayar, 1973) gave rise to the annual cultivated O. sativa (Chang, 1964). Spontaneous annuals of Asia (O. sativa var. fatua Prain) are probably weedy derivatives of hybrids between O. sativa and O. rufipogon (Oka and Chang, 1961), whereas Oceanic annuals may represent truly wild O. nivara (Oka, 1974).

ORYZA SATIVA L. Rice. 2n=24, genome formula AA. S. Asia. The antiquity of rice cultivation is uncertain. Rice was probably collected as a wild cereal across the humid tropics of Asia. In parts of India and in Sri Lanka, perennial wild rice is still harvested as a cereal (Vishnu-Mittre, 1974). The oldest known rice remains in the archaeological record (Allchin, 1969; Solheim, 1972) are from Mohenjodaro in Pakistan (2500 BC.), India (2300 BC.) and Thailand (3500 BC.). According to esterase isozyme genotypes, the centre of diversity of rice is in Assam-N. Burma-Yunnan. In Assam types resembling the African O. glaberrima are found (Seetharam & Ghorai, 1976).

Three races of rice are commonly recognized. (1) The basic tropical race indica probably originated over a broad region spreading from the Ganges Plains of India to Vietnam and S. China (Chang, 1976a, c). It includes the floating rices of South Asia. (2) Race indica was introduced into the Yellow River (Huang Ho) Valley and the lower Chang (Yangtze) River

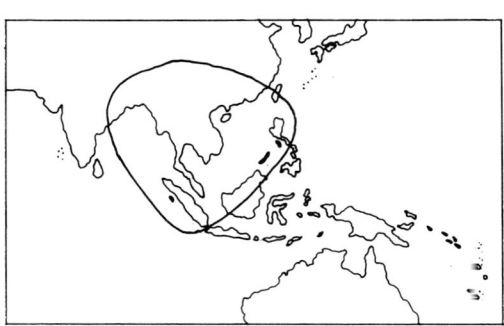

Centre of origin of rice (Chatterjee, 195_).

Basin, where the temperate race japonica e-
volved. Race japonica was introduced to Korea,
and later Japan around the 3rd Century BC.
(Morinaga, 1968). (3) Race Indica also spread
SE. into the Malaysian Archipelago, where
the large-grained race javanica evolved,
which is widely cultivated across the islands
of SE. Asia. The wet rice cultivation of
Philippines, Malaysia and Indonesia is quite
a recent introduction (Spencer, 1963).

PANICUM ANTIDOTALE Retz. Blue panic grass,
Giant panic grass. 2n=2x=18. India, W. Saudi
Arabia. Introduced into Australia as a forage
grass.

PANICUM SUMATRENSE Roth ex Roem. & Schult.
(syn. P. miliare Lamk.). Little millet. India and Sri Lanka. P. psilopodium Trin. (2n=
54) might be its ancestor (Mansfeld, 1959).
It is possible that cytotypes with 36 chromosomes occur.

PASPALUM SCROBICULATUM L. Khodo millet. 2n=
20, 40. C. India. Widely cultivated in the
Indian Plains as a cereal. Its closest wild
relative, P. orbiculare Forst., is widely distributed and collected as a wild cereal across
S. Asia.

SACCHARUM OFFICINARUM L. Sugar-cane. 2n various. Sugar-cane originated in New Guinea (p.
54) about 600-500 BC. New Guinea Noble canes
must have reached S. India via Indonesia. It
was transported northwards to reach N. India
ca 400 BC. C. 250 BC., it was severely attack-
ed by red rot disease, which must have promoted the introduction of Sinense sugar-cane
from China (p. 38). During migration, it
hybridized with S. spontaneum*, as also happened in Orissa and Bihar (Parthasarathy, 1946;
1948; Bremer, 1966). Originally the Sinense
group of sugar-canes were named Pansahi sugar-
cane.
    In N. India (Punjab to Assam), the Barberi
group (S. barberi Jesw.) of sugar-canes developed. Its origin is not yet fully understood. The group can be classed into subgroups: (1) Mungo, 2n=81, 82, 83, without S.
spontaneum introgression; (2) Dhaulo, 2n=82,
83; (3) Nargori, 2n=105-124 with Sinense
introgression; (4) Saretha, 2n=91.

SACCHARUM SPONTANEUM L. Wild sugar-cane, Kas-
soer, Thatch grass, Bagberi, Djarb, Khus. 2n
=40-128, with euploids 40, 48, 64, 80, 96,
104, 112, 128 and possibly 54. Probably India
in the foothills of the Himalaya Mountains.
Now it is distributed in innumerable groups of
various ranks and significance from Africa
over Asia to Japan and the Solomon Islands.
One group (2n=112) is found in Indonesia (p.
55), while another one (2n=104-128) occurs in
E. Africa (p. 133). Recently introduced into
New Guinea and hence its influence there is
still limited.
    S. spontaneum is used as a source of disease

resistance of S. officinarum*. In N. India, it
has hybridized with S. sinense* group Saretha.

SINOCALAMUS GIGANTEUS (Walb.) Keng. 2n=   .
India, Indochina and S. China. Cultivated
there. Used as building material. It is one
of the largest bamboos.

SORGHUM BICOLOR (L.) Moench. Juar, Jowar. 2n=
20. Primary gene centre: Africa (p. 133). Secondary centre: India. No hybridization has
occurred with wild sorghums, because they are
tetraploids (Doggett, 1970).

TRITICUM AESTIVUM (L.) Thell. ssp. sphaerococcum (Perc.) MK. (syn. T. sphaerococcum
Perc.). Indian dwarf wheat. 2n=42, genome
formula AABBDD. Transcaucasia and adjacent regions (p. 93). Ssp. sphaerococcum is indigenous to NW. India, Pakistan and adjacent parts
of Afghanistan. It is characterized by short,
non-lodging culms, erect leaves, globular
grains and susceptibility to diseases.

VETIVERIA ZIZANIOIDES (L.). Nash. Vetiver.
2n=20. Sri Lanka, India up to Burma. A grass
cultivated in the tropics for its essential
oil.

ZEA MAYS L. 2n=20. Domesticated in C. America
(p. 190). Secondary centre: S. Himalayas (Brandolini, 1970), where flint maize (indurata
Sturt.) is common.

    Guttiferae

GARCINIA INDICA*.

GARCINIA SILVESTRIS Boerl. Wild mangosteen.
2n=   . Malaysia (p. 56) and India. Parental
species of G. mangostana*.

GARCINIA TINCTORIA*.

MESUA FERREA L. Nahor, Nagas tree, Indian rose
chestnut, Ironwood. 2n=32. Trop. Asia, India
and Malaysia. Cultivated in India as a timber
tree and for its flowers and fruits. The flowers are used in the perfume industry, the
fruits are edible and the seeds contain oil
for lamps.

    Lauraceae

CINNAMOMUM TAMALA Nees & Eberm. 2n=   . India.
A tree, whose bark is used as a substitute
for the spice from C. zeylanicum*.

    Leguminosae

ALBIZIA STIPULATA Boiv. (syn. A. chinensis
(Osb.) Merr.). 2n=   . Cultivated in India
and Sri Lanka for its high-quality fodder.
Elsewhere it is cultivated as a shade tree,
green manure and cover crop.

BAUHINIA PURPUREA L. Camel's foot. 2n=28. China to India. A tree cultivated in India for various purposes and in Trop. Africa as a fodder plant.

CAJANUS CAJAN (L.) Millsp. Pigeon pea. 2n=22, 44, 66. India, where wild plants of this species and the closely related wild Atylosia cajanifolia Haines, 2n=   occur (De, 1974; van der Maesen, 1980). De (1976) suggests the forests of Upper W. Ghats as the domestication centre of pigeon pea. A secondary centre of diversity developed in Africa.

The cultivars can be grouped into two groups: (1) var. bicolor DC. primarily large long-lived late maturing with red or purple stained flowers and hairy purplish pods containing 4-5 usually purple-mottled or dark seeds; (2) var. flavus DC. mostly smaller and early maturing with all-yellow flowers and light-green pods containing 2-3 seeds.

CANAVALIA ENSIFORMIS (L.) DC. Jack bean, Horse bean. 2n=22. S. America (p. 173). Secondary centre: India.

CASSIA AURICULATA L. Tanner's cassia. 2n=14, 16, 28. Cultivated there for tanning material, obtained from the bark (Purseglove, 1968).

CASSIA FISTULA L. Indian laburnum, Purging cassia. 2n=24, 26, 28. India. Cultivated in the tropics for its pods, the pulp around the seeds being used as a purgative (Purseglove, 1968).

CASSIA SIAMEA*.

CICER ARIETINUM L. Gram, Chick-pea. 2n=14, 16, (24, 32, 33). Probably W. Asia (p. 96). Probably a secondary centre in India. Introduced into India in early times and now much cultivated there. Strains with fine dark-brown and black seed have been cultivated for a long time. 'Kabuli' types were introduced from Afghanistan about 1700 (van der Maesen, 1972).

CROTALARIA BURHIA Buch.-Ham. 2n=16. This fibre crop comes from E. India.

CROTALARIA JUNCEA L. Sunn hemp, Sann hemp. 2n =16. Probably India. Unknown wild. A bast-fibre crop. Cultivated in many tropical countries as a green manure (Purseglove, 1968).

CYAMOPSIS TETRAGONOLOBA (L.) Taub. (syn. C. psoralioides DC.). Guar, Cluster bean. 2n=14. Probably domesticated in Africa (Anderson, 1960). However Hymowitz (1973) described how seeds of C. senegalensis* arrived in Africa with Arab-Indian horse trade. Subsequently it came into domestication in India. Cultivated in India, Pakistan and elsewhere for fodder, food and as a source of gum. No wild forms in the Indo-Pakistan subcontinent.

DOLICHOS UNIFLORUS Lam. (syn. D. biflorus

auct. non Linn.). Horse gram. 2n=20, 22, (24). Tropics of Old World, especially in India and Himalayas where it is also cultivated.

INDIGOFERA PILOSA Poir. 2n=16, 32. Used in Sri Lanka as a green manure.

MELILOTUS INDICUS All. Indian clover, Yellow annual sweet clover, Sour clover. 2n=16. Punjab, India to the Mediterranean area and Turkestan. Cultivated in N. India as a fodder crop and in USA as cover crop.

MUCUNA CAPITATA*.

MUCUNA PACHYLOBIA (Piper & Tracy) Rock (syn Stizolobium pachylobium Piper & Tracy). Fleshy pod bean. 2n=   . India. Cultivated as vegetable.

MUCUNA UTILIS Wall. ex Wight. Velvet bean. 2n =   . India. Cultivated as vegetable, cattle food and green manure.

SESBANIA ACULEATA (Pers.) Poir. Dhanchia. 2n =(12), 24, 32. Cultivated in Bengal for its fibre and especially as green manure.

SESBANIA AEGYPTIACA*.

SESBANIA SPECIOSA Taub. ex Engl. 2n=12. India (?). Cultivated there as green manure in rice fields.

VIGNA ACONITIFOLIA (Jacq.) Maréchal (syn. Phaseolus aconitifolius Jacq., Vigna lobata (L.) Verdc., Phaseolus trilobus Wall.). Mat bean, Moth bean. 2n=22. India, Bangladesh and Burma. Cultivated in these countries and also on Sri Lanka and in China. In USA it is cultivated as a fodder crop.

VIGNA MUNGO (L.) Hepper (syn. Phaseolus mungo L.). Black gram, Urd, Urid. 2n=22, (24). India. Unknown wild. Closely related to V. radiata*. V. radiata var. sublobata (Roxb.) Verdc. (syn. Phaseolus sublobatus Roxb.) (2n= 22) is most likely the wild parent. In Pantnagar, strains of this variety are intersterile (Singh & Ahuja, 1977).

VIGNA UNGUICULATA (L.) Walp. (syn. V. sinensis (L.) Savi, Dolichos sinensis L.). Cowpea, Black eye, Southern pea. 2n=22, 24. Primary centre of diversity: W. Africa. Secondary centre: India. Probably originally domesticated in W. and C. Africa (p. 138).

From Africa, cowpea was taken to India and later it spread from both those regions over the world.. Ssp. mensensis Verdc. grows wild in the African forest zone and ssp. dekindtiana Verdc. wild in the African savanna zone. Most cultivars belong to ssp. unguiculata and the yard-long bean and asparagus bean cultivars to ssp. sesquipedalis (L.) Van Eseltine are rare in Africa. These last two subspecies evolved from ssp. unguiculata (Summerfield et al., 1974).

In N. Nigeria, a form developed for the fibre obtained from the peduncles. Other uses are food, green manure, forage and cover crop.

Liliaceae

IPHIGENIA STELLATA Blatter. 2n=   . W. India. A source of colchicine.

Linaceae

LINUM USITATISSIMUM L. Flax. 2n=30, (32). Its possible origin is given on p. 99. In India and adjacent areas, flax of ssp. indo-abyssinicum Vav. & Ell. is found. It is identical to flax of Ethiopia including Eritrea and it may have originated there. It hybridizes with ssp. mediterraneum* resulting in a hybrid ssp. hindustanicum Vav. & Ell.

Malvaceae

ABELMOSCHUS ESCULENTUS (L.) Moench (syn. Hibiscus esculentus L.). Okra, Lady's finger, Gombo. 2n=72-132. Probably a cultigen developed from a wild species A. tuberculatus Pal & Singh (2n=   ) in trop. Asia. It could be the ancestral or wild form of A. esculentus (van Borssum Waalkes, 1966; Bates, 1968). It is a N. Indian species differing from A. esculentus only in having strigose pubescence on the stems and shorter capsules beset with bristly tuberculate hairs. Van Borssum Waalkes suggested that A. tuberculatus be included in A. esculentus.

ABELMOSCHUS MANIHOT (L.) Medikus. (syn. Hibiscus manihot L.). 2n=60, 66. India, Pakistan, through S. China to New Guinea and N. Australia. Cultivated for its immature fruits.

Ssp. manihot is the cultigen that must have been selected by man from wild hairy and prickly types (ssp. tetraphyllus (Roxb. ex Hornem.) Borss., syn. Hibiscus tetraphyllus Roxb. ex Hornem.).

ABELMOSCHUS MOSCHATUS Medikus. (syn. Hibiscus moschatus L.). Musk mallow. 2n=72. India, S. China, Indochina to Indonesia and SW. Pacific islands to New Guinea and N. Australia. Centre of origin possibly E. India (Mansfeld, 1959). Cultivated for its seeds, which are used as perfume, for its immature edible fruits, its fibre and often as an ornamental.

ABUTILON INDICUM*.

GOSSYPIUM ARBOREUM L. Tree cotton. 2n=26, genome formula A_2A_2. Primary centre: Indian subcontinent. Unknow wild. Spread E. and SE. to Burma, Indochina and the Malaysian Archipelago. Centre of domestication probably Gujarat, which is the westernmost state of India (Hutchinson, 1971). Close to this area, a fragment of textile and a string dated 2500-1700 BC. have been found at Mohenjo-Daro, Pakistan.

Race indicum of Indian subcontinent is more closely related to cottons belonging to G. herbaceum* than are other races of G. arboreum. It includes both perennial and annual forms. It is very likely that the perennial forms are primitive and that the annuals were selected later.

In N. India and Pakistan, race bengalense was cultivated. Perennial forms are occasionally found in remote places in Rajputana and in the Ganges Valley. It spread S., SE. and W. The African race soudanense* was probably the cotton cultivated by the people of Meroë (an ancient Nubian civilization), who were the first in Africa to spin and weave cotton. Chowdhury & Buth (1970) suggested, that this race might be indigenous to Africa rather than introduced from India as a textile crop.

GOSSYPIUM STOCKSII Masters. 2n=26, genome formula E_1E_1. Sind, India and SE. Arabia. It is drought-resistant.

HIBISCUS RADIATUS Cav. 2n=72, genome formula AABB. India to Burma. Introduced into Africa and elsewhere where it is cultivated. Mainly used as ornamental; cultivated in Java as vegetable and drug plant. It is a source of resistance to root-knot nematode for H. sabdariffa . It is an allotetraploid of H. cannabinus* and another diploid species. If it is indigenous to India, the amphiploidization must have taken place there after the introduction of H. cannabinus as a fibre crop. However the only known diploid B-carrier is the African H. surattensis* (Menzel & Martin, 1971). If the origin of H. furcatus Roxb. non Willd. (2n=144), genome formula BBGGWWZZ from India and Sri Lanka is studied, the origin of H. radiatus may also be solved.

SIDA RHOMBIFOLIA L. Queensland hemp, Broomjue sida, Cuba jute. 2n=14, 28. Tropics. Cultivated in India and later in Queensland as a fibre crop (var. retusa L.). It is an extremely variable species.

Moraceae

ARTOCARPUS HETEROPHYLLUS Lam. (A. integra (Thunb.) Merr., A. integrifolia L.f.). Jack fruit, Jak. 2n=56. Unknown wild. It has a very ancient cultivation in India. There and in Sri Lanka it is popular; it is also cultivated elsewhere in the tropics (Purseglove, 1968).

FICUS ELASTICA Roxb. Indian rubber tree, Karet tree. 2n=26, (39). India and Malaya. Cultivated in India, Java and elsewhere. It is also cultivated as an ornamental house-plant (Purseglove, 1968).

FICUS RELIGIOSA L. Pipal tree, Peepal tree, Bot tree. 2n=26. This strangling fig is sacred to Hindus and Buddhists. It is propagated by cuttings and layering. A scion planted at cuttings and layering. A scion planted at Anuradhapura in Sri Lanka in 288 BC. (Purseglove, 1968) died in 1971.

FICUS ROXBURGHII Wall. 2n=   . Cultivated for its figs.

Moringaceae

MORINGA OLEIFERA Lam. Horse-radish tree, Drumstick tree. 2n=28. India. Cultivated throughout the tropics as a vegetable, in hedges and for its fruits, whose oil is used for lamps and cosmetics.

Musaceae

MUSA cultivars of the AB group. Ney poovan (and other names). 2n=22. Cultivated on a small scale now. See p. 52 for discussion.

MUSA cultivars of the AAB group. 2n=33. Mostly India. Only the clone Maia maoli has probably arisen in Philippines.

MUSA BALBISIANA Colla. Pisang bau, Klue Tani. 2n=22, genome formula BB. India, Burma, Sri Lanka and E. New Guinea. Cultivated for its leaves as a packing material or as a fibre plant (de Langhe, 1969). It is not very variable. It is one of the parents of the AAB, ABB and ABBB groups (p. 59) of cultivated bananas.

Myrtaceae

EUGENIA JAMBOLANA*.

RHODOMYRTUS TORMENTOSA*.

Oleaceae

JASMINUM GRANDIFLORUS L. Catalonian jasmine, Italian jasmine. 2n=26. Himalayas. Cultivated for its fragrant flowers and used in perfumery.

JASMINUM SAMBAC (L.). Ait. Arabian jasmine. 2n=26, 39. India and Sri Lanka. Cultivated in tropics. Flowers are used for scenting tea and as source of an essential oil.

Palmae

ARENGA PINNATA (Wurmb.) Merr. Sugar palm. 2n= . Primary centre: possibly Malaysian Archipelago (p. 61). Secondary centre: India. Cultivated in many trop. Asian countries.

BORASSUS FLABELLIFER*.

COCOS NUCIFERA L. Coconut palm. 2n=32. SE. Asia, Indonesia and W. Pacific islands. Possible secondary centre: India.

Pedaliaceae

SESAMUM INDICUM L. Sesame, Beni seed. 2n=26. Primary centre: Africa (p. 144). Secondary centre: India. Thence it is believed to have spread E. through China, Indochina into Japan, and W. through Afghanistan, Asia Minor and Iran to the Mediterranean area including N. Africa.

Perioplocaceae

CRYPTOSTEGIA GRANDIFLORA*.

Piperaceae

PIPER LONGUM L. Indian long pepper, Jaborandi pepper. 2n=24, 48, 52, 96. The foot of Himalayas. Cultivated in India and Sri Lanka for its spike, which is used as a spice. It resembles P. retrofractum Vahl*.

PIPER NIGRUM L. Black pepper. 2n=36, 48, 52, 60, 104, 128. The slopes of mountains in the Ghats, Malabar, SW. India at an altitude between 150 and 2 400 m. Spread to SE. Asia and Philippines. Now cultivated in other trop. countries (Gentry, 1955; de Waard & Zeven, 1969).

Plantaginaceae

PLANTAGO OVATA Forsk. (syn. P. decumbens Forsk.). 2n=8. Mediterranean area, C. Asia and India. Cultivated in India (esp. Gujarat) for its seeds used in medicine.

Polygonaceae

RUMEX VESICARIUS L. 2n=18, (20). Greece, N. Africa, India and Malaysia. Cultivated in India as a medicinal plant.

Resedaceae

RESEDA ODORATA L. Mignonette. 2n=12 (14). For origin see p. 118. Var. neilgherrensis (Muell. -Arg.) Abdallah & de Wit is found on Nilagiri Mt and in Bombay area and Decca Peninsula (Abdallah & de Wit, 1978).

Rosaceae

RUBUS ALBESCENS Roxb. Mysore raspberry. 2n= . Mountains of India, Sri Lanka, Malaya and Indonesia. Occasionally cultivated, especially in Puerto Rico.

Rubiaceae

COFFEA BENGALENSE Heyne ex Willd. 2n=22. Bengal, Burma and Sumatra. Occasionally cultivated in India (Purseglove, 1968).

MORINDA ANGUSTIFOLIA Roxb. 2n= . Trop. Himalayas, Assam and adjacent areas. Cultivated for bark and wood, as source of yellow dye.

MORINDA CITRIFOLIA L. (syn. M. bracteata Roxb.). Indian mulberry. 2n= . S. India and Malaysia up to Pacific isles. Cultivated in India as a dye crop.

RUBIA CORDIFOLIA L. Indian madder. 2n=22. Trop. and temp. Asia. Cultivated in India as a dye plant.

Rutaceae

CITRUS LATIPES (Swing) Tan. 2n= . Hills of NE. India. The fruits are not edible. It can be crossed with other Citrus species, including the cultigens.

CLAUSENA DENTATA (Willd.) Roem. (syn. C. willdenowii Wight & Arn.). 2n=18, 36. India. This small tree is known for its edible berries.

FERONIA LIMONIA (L.) Swing. (syn. Limonia acidissima L.). Indian wood apple. Elephant apple. 2n=18. India and Sri Lanka. Now cultivated in several trop. countries for its fruits.

MURRAYA KOENIGII (L.) Spreng. Curry-leaf tree. 2n=18. India. Cultivated for its leaves.

Sapindaceae

SAPINDUS TRIFOLIATUS L. Soap-berry tree, Soap-nut tree, Arceta. 2n= . India, Pakistan and Sri Lanka. Cultivated for its fruits, which yield soap.

Sapotaceae

MADHUCA INDICA Gmelin (syn. M. latifolia (Roxb.) Macbr. Moa tree. 2n= . N. and C. India. Cultivated for its flowers, which are rich in nectar.

MADHUCA LONGIFOLIA (Koenig) Macb. (syn. M. indica J. F. Gmel.). Mahua, Mowra butter tree. 2n= . India. Cultivated there.

MANILKARA HEXANDRA (Roxb.) Dubard. 2n= . S. Asia. Cultivated in India.

Solanaceae

ATROPA BELLADONNA L. Belladonna. 2n=(50), 72. From Spain, the Balkans, Asia Minor to India. Medicinal plant. In India, var. acuminata (syn. A. acuminata Royle, 2n=72) is found. It is cultivated there.

CAPSICUM ANNUUM L. Bell pepper, cayenne pepper. 2n=24. Mexico (p. 196). Secondary centre: Asia.

DATURA METEL L. Hindu datura. 2n=24. India. Medicinal plant introduced into many parts of (sub)tropics. Often cultivated as ornamental.

SOLANUM MELONGENA L. Egg-plant, Aubergine, Bringal, Melongene. 2n=24, (36, 48). Very probably India. A wild-looking form with many small fruits, sometimes called var. insanum, is found on the Bengal Plain of India. Perhaps it is a de-domesticated run-wild type. Martin & Rhodes (1979) found associations of some characteristics of cultivars. This could point to reproductive isolation of this self-fertilizer or to human selection pressure. Primary centres in India, secondary in China (p. 46). S. melongena is closely related to S. incanum*.

Strychnaceae

STRYCHNOS NUX-VOMICA L. Strychnine tree. 2n= 24, 44. India, Sri Lanka and Indonesia. Cultivated for its nux vomica used in medicine.

Theaceae

CAMELLIA SINENSIS (L.) O. Kuntze (syn. C. thea Link., Thea sinensis L.). The origin of tea is discussed on p. 39. Secondary centres: India, Assam and Sri Lanka.

Tiliaceae

CORCHORUS CAPSULARIS L. Jute, White jute, 2n=14. Unknown wild. Primary centre: India and Pakistan. It has been cultivated there for a long time. Spread now throughout the tropics.

GREWIA ASIATICA L. Phalsa. 2n=36. Salt Range, Puna, India (Mansfeld, 1959). Cultivated in India, Sri Lanka and elsewhere for its fruits.

Umbelliferae

ANETHUM GRAVEOLENS L. (syn. Peucedanum graveolens (L.) Hiern.). Dill. 2n=22. Eurasia. Cultivated in Greece, the district of Rome and Palestine (p. 118). Indian types have longer fruits. This species includes A. sowa*.

CARUM COPTICUM (L.) Benth. & Hook. (syn. Trachyspermum ammi (L.) Sprague). Ammi, Lorage. 2n=(16), 18. India. It yields an essential oil.

Urticaceae

GIRARDINIA HETEROPHYLLA Dcne. (syn. Urtica heterophylla Roxb.). Nilgeri nettle. 2n=20. From NW. Himalaya to Malaysia. In the Nilgeri area, India var. palmata is cultivated.

MAOUTIA PUYA Weddell (syn. Boehmeria puya Hassk., Urtica puya Wall.). 2n= . Perennial herb of trop. Himalaya, Khasia and Burma. Occasionally cultivated for its fibres.

Verbenaceae

NYCTANTHES ARBOR-TRISTIS L. Tree of sadness. 2n=44. C. India. Planted near temples. It is a source of a saffron-yellow dye. The oil is used in perfumery. Cultivated as ornamental.

Zingiberaceae

AMOMUM AROMATICUM Roxb. Bengal cardamon, Nepal cardamon. 2n= . India and Pakistan. Cultivated there.

AMOMUM XANTHIOIDES Wall. 2n=   . Burma. Cultivated in India.

CURCUMA AMADA Roxb. 2n=42. India and Pakistan. Cultivated in India for Mango ginger.

CURCUMA ANGUSTIFOLIA Roxb. East Indian arrowroot. 2n=42, (64). Himalayan area. Cultivated for its edible starchy rhizomes.

CURCUMA CAESIA Roxb. Kalihaldi. 2n= . Bengal. Occasionally cultivated for its edible rhizomes.

CURCUMA DOMESTICA Val. (syn. C. longa Koenig non L.). Turmeric, Curcuma. 2n=(32), 62, (63, 64). A completely sterile triploid, which probably arose with the wild C. aromatica Salisb. (Wild turmeric, Yellow zedoary; 2n=42) as one parent. C. aromatica grows in India. At first, turmeric may have been used as a sacred plant; later it was cultivated for its rhizomes, which are used for flavouring, and for colouring food and cloth. It spread in early times to China, SE. Asia and later to other parts of the tropics. There it may have run wild (Purseglove, 1972).

CURCUMA ZEDOARIA Rosc. Zedoary. 2n=63, 64. E. India. Cultivated in SE. Asia, Sri Lanka and Madagascar. Rhizomes are a source of a condiment. Young flowers are used for flavouring food.

ELETTARIA CARDAMONUM (L.) Maton. Cardemon. 2n=48, (52). S. India and Sri Lanka. Cultivated in India and Malaysian Archipelago. Seeds of cardamon are used to flavour coffee and in cooking; the oil is used for perfumery. The cultivated types can be divided into three varieties and two groups: group major Thwaites includes the Sri Lanka variety; group minuscula Burkill (syn. var. minor Watt) includes the Malaban variety and Mysore variety. Wild types have also been described as belonging to major. Plants of this group are marked by anthocyanin pigmentation.

ZINGIBER OFFICINALE Rosc. Ginger. 2n=22. Unknown wild. Probably domesticated in India. It was known in China and Trop. Asia at an early date. Cultivated now throughout the tropics.

5 Central Asian Region

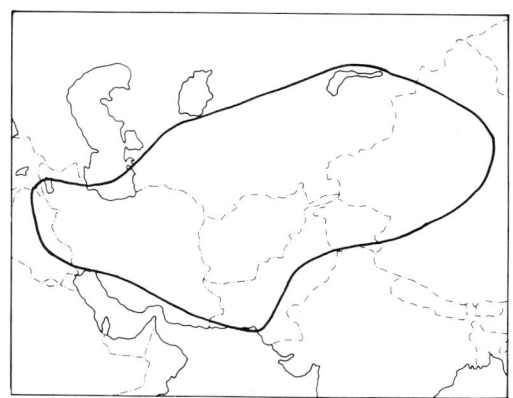

The Central Asian Region was called Southwestern Asian Centre by Vavilov. Zohary (1970) preferred to join it with Region 6, the Near Eastern Centre, as did Zhukovskij (1968), who separated both areas by number only. But in 1970, both centres were on the map, separated by a line, and Region 5 was extended northwards (Zhukovskij, 1970).

This centre served as a transfer zone between Regions 1 and 4. Furthermore, the Himalayas have provided many species as parental stock for crops. Agriculture must have reached this centre from Region 6 about 5 000 BC.

Major crops of this centre include fruit-trees, Allium cepa, A. sativum, Daucus carota, Lathyrus sativus, Spinacea oleracea and Vicia faba. Cucumis melo has there a secondary centre of diversity.

Alliaceae

ALLIUM CEPA L. Onion. 2n=16. Cultivated since 1 000 BC. Probably C. Asia and esp. NW. India, Afghanistan, Uzbekistan and W. Tien Shan, where related species A. pskemense O. Fedtsch. (2n= 16) and A. vavilovi Popov & Vved. (2n=16) grew wild (Vavilov, 1949/50). Secondary centre is Region 7. Another related wild species is A. oschaninii O. Fedtsch. (syn. A. cepa var. sylvestre Regel) from Pamirs, Alai and Tien Shan. This species is used as food. Wendelbo (1971) and McCollum (1974) suggested this species to be the wild A. cepa or the wild ancestor of A. cepa.

The top onion, tree onion or Egyptian onion (A. proliferum*, syn. A. cepa viviparum (Metzger) Alefeld) is a hybrid of A. cepa and A. fistulosum* (Fiskesjö, 1975). Such hybrids have also been described as A. aobanum Araki, 2n=16 and A. wakegii (see A. chinense*). A. cornutum G.C. Clementi ex Vis., 2n= near Budva, SW. Yugoslavia is probably a bulbilliferous form derived from extinct cultivation (Tutin et al., 1976). Var. ophioscorodon (Link) Döll has a stem coiled in one or two wide loops before anthesis.

ALLIUM PROLIFERUM. 2n=16. Tree onion, Egyptian onion. Formerly described as A. cepa* var. proliferum and as A. fistolosum*, but a true natural hybrid of both these species (Fiskesjö, 1975; Vosa, 1976). Propagated by bulbs. Viviparous.

ALLIUM SATIVUM L. Garlic. 2n=16, genome formula SS. Some consider A. longicuspis Regel (2n=16) as the wild parent of garlic. This species occurs in C. Asia. Var. pekinense (Prokh.) Makino came into cultivation in China (p. 53). Secondary centres developed in Regions 6 and 7 (Kazakova, 1971). Garlic was already known in Egypt before 3 000 BC. Sterile, propagated with bulbils.

Anacardiaceae

PISTACEA VERA L. Pistacio. 2n=30. Mountain slopes, sometimes forms sparse forests. Cultivated in this centre and elsewhere for its seeds. In Turkmenia, there are relic populations, which indicate the once wide distribution of this species (Kabulov, 1969). Dioeceous. In orchards of P. atlantica (2n=28) grown for rootstocks in USA, hybrids with P. vera form and develop female and male branches. They could perhaps be used to breed monoeceous trees.

Chenopodiaceae

BETA VULGARIS L. Beet. 2n=18, (27, 36). Primary centre is discussed on p. 104. Secondary centre developed in Region 5.

SPINACEA OLERACEA L. Spinach. 2n=12. Iran to Manchuria. Primary centre in Afghanistan and Tajikistan. Related to S. tetrandra* and S. turkestanica*. An anemophilous species of which the very young seedlings are eaten as a vegetable.

SPINACEA TETRANDRA Stev. 2n=12. A wild relative of S. oleracea* occurring in the stony steppes of Caucasia including Armenia, and Kurdistan. A weedy anemophilous species.

SPINACEA TURKESTANICA Iljin. 2n=12. A wild relative of S. oleracea* occurring in the loess foothills of the Kara Kum, the southern foothills of Uzbekistan and Turkmenia, and along the Syr Darya. A weedy anemophilous species.

Compositae

ARTEMISIA CINA Berg. Levant wormseed plant. 2n=18. The Orient and Russian Turkestan. Cultivated in Russia and W. of USA.

ARTEMISIA DRACUNCULUS L. Tarragon, Estragon. 2n=18, 36, 54, 72, 90. USSR and from W. Asia to Himalaya. Perennial widely cultivated as a condiment. 'Russian' tarragon (2n=90), a decaploid, is fertile, whereas the 'French' tarragon (2n=36), a tetraploid, is sterile and propagated vegetatively. The types with (2n=45, 54, 72) may be hybrids (Rousi, 1969).
A. dracunculoides Pursh (2n=18) from N. America has often been included in this species.

CARTHAMUS TINCTORIUS L. Safflower. 2n=24, genome formula BB. Primary centre in Region 6 (p. 88). Secondary centre near Kabul, Afghanistan. The great variation of the safflower population there, that led Vavilov to believe that area to be a centre of origin, is very likely caused by the meeting of the Middle Eastern and West Pakistan safflower types there (Knowles, 1969).

INULA HELENIUM L. (syn. Helenium grandiflorum Gilib.). Elecampane, Elfdock, Horseheal, Yellow starwort. 2n=20. Probably C. Asia. Also wild westwards to C. and S. Europe. It used to be cultivated and had various uses.

TARAXACUM KOKSAGHYZ Rodin (syn. T. bicorne Dahlst.). Kok-saghyz. 2n=16. Turkestan. Cultivated in USSR as rubber crop.

Cucurbitaceae

CUCUMIS MELO L. Melon, Musk melon, Canteloupe 2n=24. Probably Africa (p. 124). Secondary centre in Region 5, in which are found ssp. melo Pang., convar. chandalak (Pang.) Greb., convar. ameri (Pang.) Greb., convar. zard (Pang.) Greb., ssp. flexuosus (L.) Greb.

(snake melon) (2n=24), var. tarra Pang. and ssp. agrestis (Naud.) Greb. (2n=24), var. agrestis Pang. The last is a weedy field melon.

Datiscaceae

DATISCA CANNABINA L. 2n=22. C. Asia. A herb. Cultivated as a source of yellow dye.

Ebenaceae

DIOSPYROS LOTUS L. Caucasian persimmon. 2n=30. Subtrop. China (p. 36) in Talysk and W. Georgia (USSR) and adjacent Iran. Both these areas form primary centres.

Elaeagnaceae

ELAEAGNUS ANGUSTIFOLIA L. (var. E. argenta Moench). Silverberry, Russian olive. 2n=12, 28. From S. Europe to C. Asia, China and Himalayas. Primary centre in C. Asia. Cultivated there and in Iran for its edible nuts.
E. orientalis L. has been included as var. orientalis (L.) O. Kuntze. in this species.

Gramineae

AEGILOPS CAUDATA*

AEGILOPS CYLINDRICA*

AEGILOPS JUVENALIS*

AEGILOPS KOTSCHYI*

AEGILOPS LORENTII*

AEGILOPS OVATA*

AEGILOPS SQUARROSA auct. non. L. (syn. Ae. tauschii Cosson, Triticum tauschii (Coss.) Schmalh.). 2n=14, genome formula DD. E. Turkey, Iraq, Crimea and Caucasia (Zohary et al. 1969) in the west, and Pakistan and Kashmir in the east. Primary centre to the south of the Caspian Sea. This wild species is the D

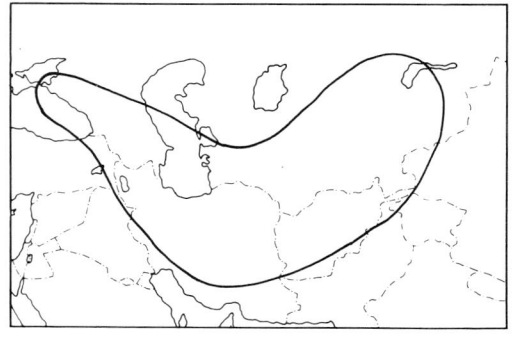

Aegilops squarrosa

genome parent of T. aestivum*. Ssp. eusquar-
rosa Eig (syn. Ae. tauschii ssp. tauschii)
usually has short anthers and is generally
strictly autogamous, whereas ecotypes with
long anthers are facultatively allogamous and
resemble ssp. strangulata (Eig) Tzvel. (Hammer & Knüpffer, 1979).

AEGILOPS TRIARISTATA*

AEGILOPS TRIUNCIALIS*

SECALE CEREALE L. Weedy and cultivated rye.
2n=14. The origin of this species is discussed on p. 91. Secondary centre in E. Iran
and Afghanistan, where S. afghanicum (Vav.)
Roshev. (syn. S. cereale ssp. afghanicum
(Vav.) Khush) originated. The main stream
of cultivated rye spreading over Europe and
Asia comes from the secondary centre (Khush,
1963). Khush based his conclusion on the pig-
mented ears of all cultivated rye varieties
and those of the weedy rye types in Afghanistan. They occur in grain fields with a habit
and growth rhythm similar to wheat (Stutz,
1972).
    Var. eligulatum Vav., liguleless rye was
found by Vavilov in the secondary centre.

SECALE TURKESTANICUM*

TRITICUM AESTIVUM (L.) Thell. ssp. compactum
(Host.) MK. (syn. T. compactum Host.). Club
wheat. 2n=42, genome formula AABBDD. Ssp. compactum developed in the mountains of the Hindu Kush.

TRITICUM TURGIDUM ssp. turgidum conv. polonicum (L.) MK. 2n=28, genome formula AABB. The
type 'T. ispahanicum Heslot' was found in
Isfahan (Iran) where it is adapted to irrigated cultivation. It is marked by its narrow
and elongated glumes.

    Hippocastanaceae

AESCULUS HIPPOCASTANUM*

    Juglandaceae

JUGLANS REGIA L. Walnut. Persian walnut, English walnut. 2n=32, 36. Secondary centre: Moldavia, SE. Europe and SW. Europe (p. 155).
Many varieties have been described.

    Labiatae

LALLEMANTIA ROYLEANA (Wall. & Benth.) Benth.
2n=14. From Iran to Himalayas. Cultivated in
E. India as an oil crop.

    Leguminosae

CICER ARIETINUM L. Chick-peas, Gram. 2n=14,
16, (24, 32, 33). Secondary centre in Afghanistan, whence the 'Kabuli' types of India
derive. They were introduced there about 1700

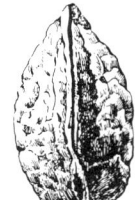

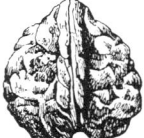

Juglans regia

(van der Maesen, 1972).

CICER MICROPHYLLUM Royle (syn. C. songaricum
Steph., C. jaquemontii Jaub. & Spach.). 2n=
14. Tibet, Afghanistan and W. Himalayas. Cultivated in W. Himalayas for its seeds.

FLEMINGIA VESTITA Benth. ex Baker (syn. Mog-
henia vestita (Benth. ex Baker) O. Kuntze.
Sohphlong. 2n=22. W. Himalayas, N. India.
Cultivated for its edible tubers, especially
in Assam.

LATHYRUS SATIVUS L. Grass pea, Chickling pea.
2n=14. Probably W. Asia. A centre of diversity
in the Mediterranean Region. Cultivated in
Europe since ancient times and in Region 7
(p. 114). Unkown wild.

MEDICAGO SATIVA L. Lucerne, Blue alfalfa. 2n=
16, genome formula SS, 32, genome formula
SSSS. Transcaucasia (p. 97). The centre of
diversity of blue lucerne is in NW. Iran and
adjacent regions to Tibet.

VICIA FABA L. (syn. Faba vulgaris Moench.).
Field bean, Broad bean, Horse bean, Tick bean,
Windsor bean, Faba bean. 2n=12, 14. Probably
SW. Asia (Ladizinsky, 1975c) or Mediterranean
region (Zohary, 1977). Wild ancestor uncertain. It may derive from the weed V. angustifolia L. (2n=14). Formerly it was believed to
derive from V. narbonensis, but Ladizinsky
(1975c) and Abdalla & Günzel (1979) showed
that this species was not related to the field
bean. Ladizinsky (1975c) also showed that V.
galilaea Plit. & Zoh. (2n=14) and V. hyaenis-
cyamus Mount. (2n=14) were not related either.
Related species are V. bithynica (L.) L. and
V. johannis Tamanschian. The field bean is
divided into three varieties according to the
size of the seed: var. minuta (Alef.) Mansf.
(syn. var. minor (Pieterm.) Harz.,), pigeon
bean or tick bean, var. equina Pers., horse

bean, and var. faba (syn. var. major Harz.),
broad bean.

From its centre of domestication, the field
bean spread to Europe, China and the Mediterranean. In the Mediterranean region, a secondary centre of diversity arose (p. 116). The
pigeon and horse beans are used as animal feed,
and the broad bean as a vegetable.

Schultze-Motel (1972) has listed all data on
archaeological remains of the field bean. Almost all these remnants belong to var. minuta.
He did not find a sharp distinction between
long-seeded and roundish types, so the development of the field bean from two original forms
is not very likely. Only once was var. faba,
the broad bean found, in Iraq. It dated from
about 1 000 AD., which may point to late development of the large seed.

Liliaceae

FRITILLARIA IMPERIALIS L. Crown imperial. 2n=
24. Iran and Turkestan. The bulbs were a
source of starch and used in medicine. It is
an ornamental.

Linaceae

LINUM USITATISSIMUM L. Flax, Linseed. 2n=30,
(32). Origin of flax is discussed on p. 99.
Primary centre of origin probably in Region 5
(Vavilov, 1957). This conclusion is based on
the great diversity of flax in India and adjacent northerly area. Spread from Region 5
into Region 4 (p. 76).

In the mountains of C. Asia, the 'curly oil
flax' developed. It is characterized by the
large number (140-150) of seed capsules per
plant.

Malvaceae

GOSSYPIUM BARBADENSE L. Sea Islands cotton.
2n=52, genome formula $(AADD)_2$. Peru. Spread
to reach Africa and Asia in historical times.
Secondary centre in Turkmenia, Tajikistan and
S. Uzbekistan, USSR.

GOSSYPIUM HERBACEUM L. Short staple American
cotton. 2n=26, genome formula A_1A_1. S. Africa
(p. 139). Introduced into Ethiopia, S. Arabia
and Baluchistan, where race acerifolium
(p. 99) developed (Hutchinson, 1962).

Meliaceae

MELIA AZEDARACH L. China berry, Bakayan, Pride
of India, Persian lilac, Bead tree. 2n=28.
SW. Asia up to W. China. Cultivated in tropics as an ornamental and shade tree. Seeds
produce oil. They are also used as beads.

Moraceae

MORUS NIGRA L. Black mulberry. 2n=(89-106),
308. C. Asia. Cultivated at higher altitude
in the tropics (Purseglove, 1968), and also

throughout S. Eurasia for its fruits. The
Black Persian mulberry is probably a variety
(Purseglove, 1968).

URTICA CANNABINA L. 2n=   . C. and N. Asia.
Cultivated for fibre.

Oleaceae

JASMINUM OFFICINALE L. Common white jasmine
2n=26. From Iran to Kashmir and China. Cultivated especially in S. France for its flowers, which contain essential oil used in
perfumery.

Polygonaceae

RHEUM RHAPONTICUM L. Rhubarb. 2n=44. SE. USSR.
Cultivated as vegetable. Probably one of the
parents of R. hybridum*. Related to R. palmatum*.

Rosaceae

AMYGDALUS BROWICZII Freitag. 2n=   . Afghan-
stan. Related to A. communis* and A. korshinskyi Hand.-Mazz, 2n=   .

AMYGDALUS BUCHARICA Korsh. (syn. Prunus bucharica (Korsh.) Fedtsch.). Bukhara almond.
2n=16. W. Tien Shan, Pamirs and Alai, and
in Afghanistan. It may form a source of sweet
pits, of high oil content and of a good kernel
to shell ratio.

AMYGDALUS COMMUNIS L. (syn. Prunus amygdalus
Batsch.). Almond. 2n=16. W. Kopet-Dagh (Tur-
menia), Afghanistan and W. Tien Shan (p. 100).
Primary centres: W. Kopet-Dagh (Turkmenia) and
W. Tien Shan. Extensively cultivated in S.
Europe and California. In this centre and in
Region 6 (p. 100) other Amygdalus species are
found. In Georgia (USSR) A. georgica Desf.
(2n=16) is found. In Kopet-Dagh and Badkhyz
A. turcomanica Lincz. occurs. In Armenia A.
nairica Fed. & Takhi. and A. urartu* with A
fenzliana are native. In this area and in
Nakhichevan A. fenzliana* (syn. Prunus fenzliana Fritsch) (2n=16) grows. This species is
very cold resistant and crosses freely with
cultivated species. Further A. scoparia Spach.
(syn. Prunus scoparia (Spach.) Schneid.) (2n=
16) is found in Kopet-Dagh and Iran.

AMYGDALUS PERSICA L. Peach. 2n=16. Primary
centre: China (p. 42). Secondary centre in
Iran and C. Asia.

AMYGDALUS PETUNNIKOWII Litvin. (syn. Prunus
petunnikowii (Litvin.) Rehd.). Turkestan almond. 2n=16. W. Tien Shan, in Kazakhstan, Tad-
shikistan and Uzbekistan and partly in Kirgizi-
stan, USSR. It is an ornamental. It has a
high oil content. It is drought resistant. It
easily crosses with A. communis*.

AMYGDALUS SPINOSISSIMA Bge. (syn. Prunus

spinosissima (Bge.) Franch.). Thorny peach
brush. 2n=16. C. Asia from Kopet-Dagh (Turkmenia) through Pamir-Alai to W. Tien Shan,
in Iran, Afghanistan and Kurdestan. It is late
flowering and has a high oil content.

AMYGDALUS TANGUTICA Korsh. (syn. Prunus de-
hiscens Koehne). Tangut plum. 2n=   . W. China. Cultivated in some parts of China for the
kernels.

AMYGDALUS ULMIFOLIA (Franch.) M. Pop. (syn.
Prunus triloba Lindl.). 2n=16. C. Asia.

AMYGDALUS VAVILOVII M. Pop. (syn. Prunus vavilovii M. Pop.). Vavilov almond. 2n=16. Kopet Dagh (Iran and Turkmenia), W. Tien Shan,
the Pamirs and Alai. At one time it was believed that this species was a hybrid between
A. spinosissima* and A. communis*.

ARMENIACA DASYCARPA (Erhr.) Borkh. (syn. A.
atropurpurea Lois., Prunus dasycarpa Ehrh.).
Purple apricot, Black apricot. 2n=   . Unknown
wild. Cultivated in C. Asia, Transcaucasia
and Iran. The fruits are very sour and may be
used in marmalades. It might be used as a
source of late flowering, and of cold resistance of the flower buds.

ARMENIACA VULGARIS L. Apricot. 2n=16. Primary
centre in NE. China (p. 42). Secondary centre
for the cultivated apricot E. Tien Shan. For
the wild apricot, this primary gene centre
was formerly continuous with the main part in
China (p. 42).

CRATAEGUS AZAROLUS L. (syn. C. aronia Bosc.).
Azarolier. 2n=   . S. Europe, Africa (p. 118)
and the Orient. In Uzbekistan, a large-fruited
type, var. turcomanica Popoff, is found. It
is poor in vigour.

FRAGARIA BUCHARICA Losinsk. Bukhara strawberry. 2n=   . Region 5.

MALUS KIRGHIZORUM Al. & Fed. 2n=   . W. Tien
Shan in the underbush of wild walnut (Juglans regia L.). Primary centres are in the
basins of the Pskem, Ugam, Kok-Su and other
rivers. It is a polymorphous species. It is
likely that it introgressed into the cultivated apple (Malus pumila*).

MALUS PUMILA*

MALUS SIEVERSII (Ledeb.) M. Roem. 2n=   .
W. Tien Shan and in Ala Tau of N. Xingiang
Uygur (Sinkiang Province) in the underbush
of the wild walnut (Juglans regia L.). Var.
hissarica (Kudr.) Ponomarenko is also described as P. hissarica Kudr.

MALUS SYLVESTRIS (L.) Miller. 2n=34. Much of
Europe, in Transcaucasia and probably into W.
Turkestan. In the Caucasus, this species is not
always distinct from M. pumila*. It is very

Malus kirghizorum

Malus sieversii

winter-hardy. Used as a root-stock. Where it
grows together with M. pumila, hybrids occur
and so M. sylvestris must have been involved
in the distant origin of the cultivated apple.
One subspecies, ssp. praecox (Malus praecox
(Pall.) Borkh.), is early-maturing. Primary
centre in C. Asia. Occasionally cultivated
in N. Africa (Uphof, 1968).

PRUNUS subgen CERASUS Pers. In Region 5, there
occur wild cherries with small fruits (sect.
Microcerasus Webb.).

PRUNUS CERASIFERA Ehrh. Cherry plum. Myrobalan. 2n=16, genome formula CC, (24, 32, 48).
Primary centre is in Caucasia (p. 101). Secondary centre: the W. Tien Shan. It is characterized by high yield, early flowering, early
ripening, wide adaptability and high acid content.

PRUNUS FERGANICA Lincz. Ferghana plum. 2n=   .
Ferghana ridge in Tien Shan and in the Pamirs
and Alai (USSR). It is a true-breeding hybrid
of a spontaneous cross Amygdalus communis

and Prunus cerasifera*.

PYRUS BUCHARICA Litv. 2n=   . W. Tien Shan
and the mountains of Tajikistan. It is thought
to be a hybrid of P. regelii* and P. korshinskyi* (Vavilov, 1930a).

PYRUS KORSHINSKYI Nak. & Kik. 2n=   . Pamirs,
Alai and W. Tien Shan. It is considered as
one parent of P. bucharica*.

PYRUS REGELII Rehd. 2n=   . W. Tien Shan,
Pamirs, Alai and Bukhara Uplands. It is very
resistant to drought.

PYRUS SOGDIANA S. Kudr. 2n=   . Shakhrisyabz
region of Uzbekistan.

PYRUS VAVILOVII M. Pop. 2n=   . E. Ferghana.
It is considered a hybrid of P. communis* x
P. korshinskyi* (Vavilov, 1930a).

ROSA MOSCHATA J. Hermann. 2n=14, (28). Himalayas and Iran. Cultivated as ornamentals. It
is a parent of R. x bifera*.

   Salicaceae

SALIX ALBA L. (syn. S. Aurea Salisb.). White
willow. 2n=76. Europe (p. 161), Asia and N.
Africa. Cultivated in the Kashmir for lopping
as fodder (Heybroek, 1963).

   Tamaricaceae

TAMARIX GALLICA L. Tamarisk. 2n=24. W. Himalayas and NW. India. Cultivated for shelter
and as an ornamental.

   Ulmaceae

ULMUS VILLOSA Brandis ex Gramble. 2n=   .
Himalayas. Cultivated in sacred places or for
ornamental purposes. It is lopped for fodder
(Heybroek, 1963).

ULMUS WALLICHIANA Planch. 2n=   . Large-leaved
elm. Himalayas. Cultivated in Kashmir and
lopped for fodder (Heybroek, 1963).

   Umbelliferae

CUMINUM CYMINUM*

DAUCUS CAROTA L. Carrot. 2n=18. Wild types
occur in Europe, SW. and C. Asia and N. Africa.
These wild types have been grouped into two
aggregates: (1) ssp. agg. gingidium including
former sspp. gummifer Hooker f., commutatus
(Paol.) Thell., hispanicus (Goüan) Thell.,
hispidus (Arcangeli) Heywood, gadecaei (Rouy
& Camus) Heywood, drepanensis (Arcangeli) Heywood, and rupestris (Guss.) Heywood.
(2) ssp. agg. carota with the former sspp.
carota, maritimus (Lam.) Batt., major (Vis.)
Arcangeli and maximus (Desf.) Ball.
   There are some intermediate types (Small,

1978b).
   Carrot was domesticated in Afghanistan (primary centre of diversity) and from there is
spread over Europe, the Mediterranean area
and Asia. During spread, it introgressed with
local wild types.
   The domesticated types are divided into two
groups:
(1) the 'Eastern (or Asian) carrots' (var.
atrorubus Alef.), with mainly purple and yellow roots.
(2) the 'Western carrots' (var. sativus Hoffm.)
with mainly orange roots (Small, 1978b). The
purple types have a short storage time.
   In Turkey and Japan, hybrids between the
two groups occur, in Turkey because the two
groups grow near together and hybridize naturally. Turkey is therefore a secondary centre of diversity (p. 101). In Japan, breeders
developed varieties from artificial crosses
of these two groups.
During its spread, the yellow and white carrots probably originated by mutation (but
see p. 162). The white mutants (albus) were
used for fodder and did not participate in
the development of the European carrot (Banga,
1957).
   After reaching Iran, it probably spread
thence to China (Banga, 1962).

   Vitadaceae

VITIS VINIFERA L. Common grape. 2n=38. Deep
valleys of Tien Shan and adjacent areas. Primary centre for the cultivated grape lies in
that Region (see further p. 102).

6 Near Eastern Region

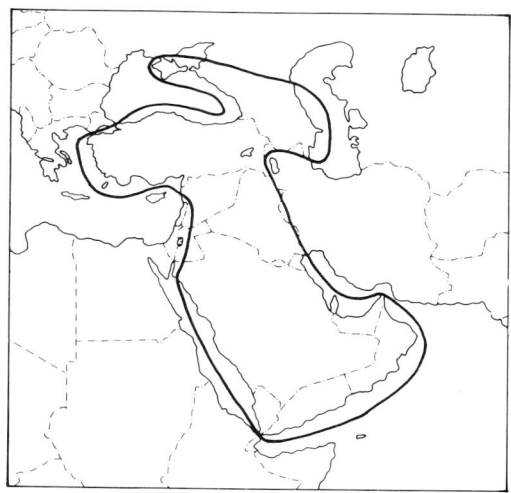

The Near Eastern Region was described by Vavilov. It included a part of Region 5.

Darlington (1956) called the area the SW. Asian region. Zhukovskij (1968) recognised two regions 5 and 6, and in 1970 he separated these on his map. Zohary (1969) preferred to combine these regions into one. Within the Region lies the Fertile Crescent. Here agriculture probably evolved around 9000 BC. (Çambal & Braidwood, 1970). Harlan (1971) called the area of the Fertile Crescent, A1 Near East centre. Agriculture spread from there to Europe, the Mediterranean Region, Afghanistan, India and possibly Africa.

Major crops include several fruit-tree species of Brassica oleracea, Hordeum vulgare, Lens esculenta, Medicago spp., Secale spp., Triticum spp., Vicia faba and Vitis vinifera.

In Georgia (USSR), a secondary centre of diversity developed for Glycine max, Lupinus albus, Phaseolus vulgaris, Setaria italica and Zea mays. Maize entered USSR by way of Georgia.

In Turkey, Harlan (1951) described microcentres for Amygdalus spp., Cucumis melo, C. sativus, Cucurbita moschata, C. pepo, Lens esculentum, Lupinus spp., Malus spp., Medicago sativa, other annual Medicago spp., Onobrychis viceaefolia, Phaseolus vulgaris, Pistacea spp., Prunus spp., Pyrus spp., Trifolium spp., Vicia faba, Vitis vinifera and Zea mays.

Alliaceae

ALLIUM AMPELOPRASUM L. Levant garlic, Perennial sweet leek. 2n=16, (24), 32, genome formula AAA'A'', (40), 48, genome formula AAA'A'-A''A'', AABBBB. Europe, Asia Minor, Caucasia to Iran and N. Africa. A type resembling ssp. iranicum P.W. is cultivated near Tehran (Tahbaz, 1971). In Israel the diploid is rare, but the triploid is a vegetatively propagated triploid weed (Kollmann, 1972). Var. babingtonii (Borrer) Syme (syn. A. babingtonii Borrer) of W. Ireland and SW. England and var. bulbiferum Syme (syn. var. bulbilliferum Lloyd) of the Channel Islands and W. France

are possible relics of former cultivation (Tutin et al., 1976).

ALLIUM ASCALONICUM L. Shallot. 2n=16. N. Africa, E. Mediterranean area. Closely related to A. deserti-syriaci Feinbrun (2n=) from Syria and Iraq (de Wilde-Duyfjes, 1976). Also described as a variant of A. cepa* (Vosa, 1976; and others).

ALLIUM KURRAT Schweinfl. Salad leek, kurrat. 2n=32. Probably Arabia and Sinai (Uphof, 1968). The geographic destribution is not known. Cultivated in the Nile area, Arabia and Palestine for its leaves (Uphof, 1968) It might be

derived from A. ampeloprasum* (Kuckuck & Kobabe, 1962). Because of its close relationship to A. ampeloprasum*, it is often included in that species as var. kurrat Schweinf.
ex Krause or in A. porrum* (de Wilde-Duyfjes,
1976).

ALLIUM PORRUM L. Leek. 2n=32. Asia Minor. Probably gene centre for cultivated forms (Kuckuck, 1962). Leek is a cultivated form derived
from A. ampeloprasum*. If so, it is included
as var. porrum (L.) Cav. in the latter species.

ALLIUM SATIVUM L. Garlic. 2n=16, genome formula SS. Wild type in C. Asia (p. 81). Secondary centre in Region 6 (Kazakova, 1971).

Boraginaceae

SYMPHYTUM ASPERUM Lepechin (syn. S. asperri-
mum Donn.). Prickly comfrey. 2n=40. Caucasia
to Armenia and N. Iran. Cultivated as forage
crop. It is probably one of the parents of
S. x uplandicum Nyman, (2n=36), a forage crop.
The other is S. officinale L., common comfrey
(2n=26, c. 36, 40, c. 40, 48), which is native
to Europe, W. Siberia and Asia Minor.

Chenopodiaceae

BETA COROLLIFLORA Zosimovich ex Buttler. 2n=
36, genome formula CCCC and aneuploids of 36.
Turkey, Georgia (USSR) and Azerbaijan (USSR
and Iran). Self-incompatible and frost-resistant.

BETA INTERMEDIA Bunge. 2n=36, genome formula
possibly LLCC. Plants which are probably hybrids of B. lomatogona* and B. trigyna* have
been described as B. intermedia. They occur
where the two species grow together. It is a
source of resistance to yellow mosaic disease.

BETA LOMATOGONA Fisch. & Mey. 2n=18, genome
formula LL, (22), 36. Asia Minor and E. Transcaucasia. It is a weed characterized by 'mono-
germ fruits'. Where the distribution of this
species and of B. trigyna overlap, tetraploid

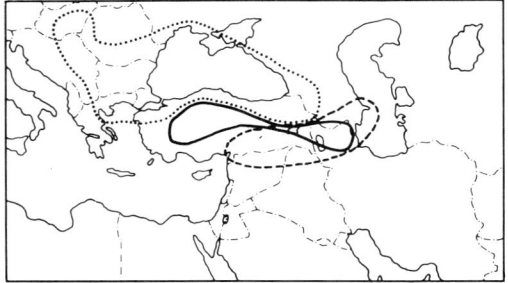

Beta lomatogona and B. intermedia (———), B.
macrorrhiza (- - -) and B. trigyna (· · ·)(Ulbrich, 1934).

B. lomatogona is found. The hybrids are probably identical to plants described as B. intermedia*.

BETA MACRORRHIZA Stev. 2n=18. (Sub)alpine zones
of mountains in Iran, Turkish Armenia (Lake
Van) and the Caucasus. A winter-hardy species
containing sugar (8-12%) and white pulp.

BETA TRIGYNA Wald. & Kit. 2n=54, genome formula LLCCCC. Around the Black Sea with outliers
to the Caspian Sea, Iran, Ukraine and Hungary.

CHENOPODIUM CAPITATUM (L.) Asch. 2n=16, 18.
The Orient. Cultivated (Mansfeld, 1959).

Compositae

CARTHAMUS TINCTORIUS L. Safflower. 2n=24,
genome formula BB. Vavilov (1951) and Kupzov
(1932) proposed three areas of origin for the
cultivated safflower: in India, based on variation and ancient culture; in Afghanistan, ,
based on variation and proximity of wild
species; and in Ethiopia, because of the presence of wild safflower species. However Hanelt (1961), and Ashri & Knowles (1960) placed
the centre of origin in the Near East because
of the similarity of cultivated safflower to
two closely related wild species: C. flavescens Spreng. (syn. C. persicus Willd. (2n=
24, genome formula BB), found in Turkey, Syria
and Lebanon; and C. palaestinus Eig. (2n=24,
genome formula BB), found in deserts of W.
Iraq and Israel (Khidir & Knowles, 1970). In
that area, introgression may still occur between wild and cultivated safflower.
    The great variation in the Afghanistan
safflower population must be caused by the
meeting of the Middle Eastern and the Pakistani
types (Knowles, 1969) (p. 82). The wild safflower of Ethiopia cannot be the progenitor
of safflower in the Near East because it has
32 pairs of chromosomes, whereas the cultivated species has 12 pairs (Knowles, 1969). Safflower is or has been cultivated in many areas
of the Old World and in North America. Many
improved USA varieties derive mainly from Su-
danese material. They are now cultivated in
Egypt, Spain and some other countries too,
where they may cross with local varieties and
so produce new genotypes or they may replace
the local varieties so that gene material is
lost. Cultivated mainly for its flowers, which
were a source of pigment, it is now cultivated
for its seeds which yield an edible oil, whose
high polyunsaturation due to its high content
of linoleic acid makes it very suitable for
consumption.
    Imrie & Knowles (1970) suggested that C.
palaestinus is a wild species. The weedy species C. flavescens and C. oxyantha M. B. (2n=
24, genome formula BB) and the cultivated
species C. tinctorius derive from that species.

CHRYSANTHEMUM COCCINEUM Willd. (syn. C. roseum
Adam). 2n=18. Wild in N. Iran, Caucasia and

Armenia. Cultivated as a garden plant. The flowers contain the insecticide pyrethrin, but their toxity is less than C. cinerariaefolium*.

TANACETUM PARTHENIUM*

Cornaceae

CORNUS MAS L. (syn. C. mascula Hort.). Cornelian cherry. 2n=18, 54. Caucasia and Asia Minor as an underbush of deciduous forests. Cultivated for its edible fruits and as an ornamental shrub. The fruits are also used to produce vin de Cornouille, an alcoholic beverage.

Corylaceae

CORYLUS AVELLANA L. European hazel. 2n=22, 28. Europe and Caucasus. Primary centre in the Caucasus. Cultivated widely for its nuts: hazel nut or cobnut.
   In this same centre there is a wealth of other Corylus species; C. maxima*, C. pontica C. Koch (2n=28), C. colchica Alb., C. iberica Wittm. & Kemular, C. imoretica Kemular, C. cervorum Petr. and C. colurna*. Trazels are hybrids of C. avellana and tree hazels (C. colurna*). They have a high kernel quality, are winter-hardy and vigorous.

CORYLUS COLURNA L. Turkish hazel. 2n=28. Occasionally cultivated in Turkey for its nuts. It is also used as a rootstock and as a source of resistance of diseases of C. avellana*. Hybrids of that species are called 'trazels'.

CORYLUS MAXIMA Miller. Filbert, White filbert, Red filbert. 2n=22, 28. Caucasia, W. Asia and SE. Europe. Cultivated for its nuts.

Cruciferae

BRASSICA OLERACEA L. Wild and cultivated cabbages. 2n=18, genome formula CC. In Asia Minor, varieties belonging to convar. oleracea*, convar. capitata* and convar. acephala* are common.

CAMELINA SATIVA (L.) Crantz. False flax. 2n=40. In SE. Europe and SW. Asia, the wild parental form occurs, probably C. microcarpa Andrz. (2n=40). It became a weed in cereal crops and flax. Later is was cultivated for its oily seeds, the cultigen being called C. sativa. An intermediate form is C. pilosa (DC) Zinger. Another weed of flax fields is C. alyssum (Miller) Thell. (2n=40). All these species have also been grouped in one species, C. sativa, being divided into subspecies microcarpa (Andrz.) Hegi, sativa, pilosa (DC.) Hegi and alyssum (Miller) Hegi. It has almost disappeared from cultivation.

CRAMBE ABYSSINICA Hochst. ex. R.E. Vries. 2n=90. Distribution in the wild is obscure. Three introductions from Turkey into USA have been

used to develop an oil-producing crop.

CRAMBE CORDIFOLIA Steven (syn. C. tatarica Jacq.). Tatar sea-kale. 2n= . Highlands of Asia Minor, India and Ethiopia. The perennial herb is cultivated for the young leaves.

IRATIS TINCTORIA L. (syn. I. canescens DC., I. littoralis Steven, I. taurica Bieb.). 2n=28. Most of Europe. Cultivated as source of dye, and therefore probably introduced.

Cucurbitaceae

CUCUMIS MELO L. Melon. Musk melon, Canteloupe. 2n=24. Africa (p. 124). Secondary centre arose in Region 4, in which convar. cassaba (Pang.) Greb. (cassaba melon, winter melon) from Asia Minor, convar. cantalupa (Pang.) Greb. (cantaloupe melons), convar. adana (Pang.) Greb., (kilik melons) convar. flexuosus (L.) Greb. (tarra melons, adjur melons, snake melons, serpent melons) are found.

CUCUMIS SATIVUS L. Cucumber, Gherkin. 2n=14. India (p. 72). Secondary centre (bethalpha type) arose in this region.

Dipsacaceae

CEPHALARIA SYRIACA (L.) Roemer & Schultes. Pelemir. 2n=10. This pestweed of wheat fields is occasionally cultivated on the C. Anatolian peneplane as an oil crop.

DIPSACUS SATIVUS (L.) Scholler. Teasel. 2n=16, 18. Cultivated in Europe and elsewhere. It has probably derived from D. ferox Loissel (2n=16, 18), which grows in Corsica, Sardinia and some sites in C. Italy or from D. fullosum L. (syn. D. sylvestris Hudson, 2n=16, 18), which grows in S., W. and C. Europe to NE. Ukraine.

Fagaceae

CASTANEA SATIVA Mill. (syn. C. vesca Gaertn.). Sweet chestnut, Spanish chestnut. 2n=22, 24. From Italy northwards to Hungary and eastwards to Asia Minor and W. Georgia (USSR). Cultivated for its nuts and timber. Outside that range, it is naturalized.

Gramineae

AEGILOPS CAUDATA L. (syn. Triticum dichasians (Zhuk.) Bowden, T. caudatum (L.) Godr. & Gren.). 2n=14, genome formula CC. Greece, Turkey, Iraq and Afghanistan. Its cytoplasm has a male-sterilizing action om the T. aestivum* nucleus.

AEGILOPS COLUMNARIS Zhuk. 2n=28, genome formula $C^u C^u C^m C^m$. Turkey, Iraq, Iran and Caucasia. It is a weed of cultivation and looks quite like Ae. triaristata* (Bor, 1970). The C^u genome will be renamed U.

AEGILOPS COMOSA*

AEGILOPS CRASSA Boiss. (syn. Triticum crassum (Boiss.) Aitch. & Hemsl. 2n=28, genome formula DDM^{cr}M^{cr}, 42, probably DDD^{2}D^{2}M^{cr}M^{cr}. Turkey, Iraq, Iran, Afghanistan and Palestine. Its cytoplasm resembles that of Ae. squarrosa (Tsuji & Tsunewaki, 1976).

AEGILOPS CYLINDRICA Host. (syn. Triticum cylindricum Ces., Pass. & Gib.). 2n=28, genome formula CCDD. It originated from the cross   Ae. squarrosa* x   Ae. caudata* (Maan, 1976). Balkan peninsula, Crete, Turkey, Caucasia, S. USSR, Iraq, Iran and Afghanistan. It is a weed in fallow fields and on hillsides.

AEGILOPS JUVENALIS (Thell.) Eig. (syn. Ae. turcomanica Roshev., Triticum turcomanicum (Rosh.) Bowden). 2n=42, genome formula DDC^{u}C^{u}M^{j}M^j. Iraq, Iran, Turkmenia and Turkistan, USSR. Its cytoplasm resembles that of 4x Ae. crassa* (Tsuji & Tsunewaki, 1976). The C^u genome will be renamed U.

AEGILOPS KOTSCHYI Boiss. (syn. Ae. triuncialis var. kotschyi (Boiss.) Boiss., Triticum kotschyi (Boiss.) Bowden). 2n=28, genome formula C^{u}C^{u}S^{v}S^v. N. Africa, Palestine, Iraq, Iran, Afghanistan and Caucasia. Probably identical with Ae. variabilis*. The C^u genome will be renamed U.

AEGILOPS LORENTII Hochst. (syn. Ae. biuncialis Vis., Ae. macrochaeta Shuttl. & Huet., syn. Triticum macrochaetum (Shuttl. & Huet. ex Duval-Jouve) Richter, Triticum lorentii (Hochst.) Zeven. (2n=28, genome formula C^{u}C^{u}M^{b}M^b. S. Europe, USSR, Turkey, Israel, Iraq and Iran. The C^u genome will be renamed U.
   The name Ae. lorentii antedates Ae. biuncialis Vis. (Bor, 1970).

AEGILOPS MUTICA Boiss. (syn. Triticum tripsacoides (Jaub. & Spach) Bowden. 2n=28 (+B), genome formula C^{u}C^{u}CC. Anatolia and Armenia. Jones & Majisu (1968) consider it related to the A, S or D genomes (p. 93 and p. 82), but not to the B genome (p. 93). The C^u genome will be renamed U. It is a cross-fertilizer.

AEGILOPS OVATA L. (syn. Triticum ovatum (L.) Raspail. 2n=28, genome formula C^{u}C^{u}M^{o}M^o. Mediterranean Region, Palestine, Syria, Turkey, Iraq, Iran, Afghanistan. A weed in cultivation. Its cytoplasm has a male-sterilizing action on the nucleus of T. aestivum* and T. turgidum*. The C^u genome will be renamed U.

AEGILOPS SPELTOIDES Tausch. (syn. Triticum speltoides (Tausch.) Gren. ex Richter. 2n=14, genome formula SS (formerly it was believed that the S genome was identical with the B genome of T. turgidum* and T. aestivum*. However new investigations showed that this was not so (Johnson, 1972; Kimber & Athwal, 1972). Primary centre: S. Turkey, N. Syria and N.

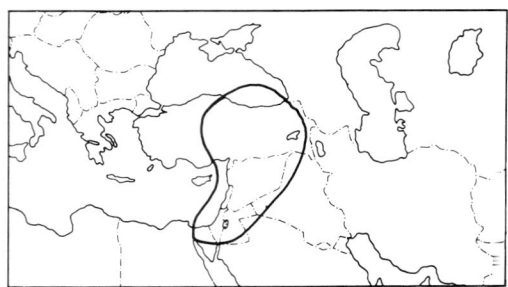

Aegilops speltoides

Iraq. It is less common in the remaining part of Turkey and Thrace, Greece and in Syria, N. and C. Israel. It is often found together with the wild T. boeoticum*.
   The species includes Ae. speltoides sensu stricto, Ae. ligustica (Savign.) Cosson and probably Ae. longissima Schweinf. ex Muschl. genome formula S^{b}S^b and is synonymous with Ae. sharonensis Eig., genome formula S^{b}S^b, and Ae. aucheri Boiss. Ssp. speltoides is a B-chromosome carrier and a cross-fertilizer.
   Waines & Johnson (1969) considered Ae. sharonensis (Triticum x sharonense (Eig.) Waines & Johnson as a hybrid of Ae. longissima and Ae. bicornis*. They based their conclusion on the similarity of grain-protein electrophoretic patterns of the hybrid and that of the summation of its putative parents, the intermediate spike characters, the intermediate ecological preference and on its distribution in Israel: the area of overlap between the two parent species. At present Ae. sharonensis is effectively reproductively isolated.
   Maan (1973) concluded from his nucleo-cytoplasmic and cytogenetic studies that the cytoplasm of Ae. speltoides is closely related to that of T. timopheevi* and differs from that of T. monococcum* and T. turgidum*. A type occurring in the Judean mountains, Samaria, Gihad, Ammon and Moav has been described as Ae. searsii Feldman & Kislev, 2n=14, genome formula S^{s}S^s(syn. Triticum searsii (Feldman & Kislev) Feldman & Kislev). It is suggested to be the B genome parent of T. aestivum*. But as it occupies the same habitats as T. dicoccoides*, it could be a derivative of that species and Ae. longissima* (A.C. Zeven in Discussion of paper by Feldman, 1978; Feldman et al., 1979).

AEGILOPS SQUARROSA*

AEGILOPS TRIARISTATA Willd. (syn. Triticum triaristatum (Willd.) Godr. & Gren.). 2n=28, genome formula C^{u}C^{u}M^{t}M^t, 42, genome formula C^{u}C^{u}M^{t}M^{t}M^{t}M^{t2}M^{t2}. The Mediterranean area, W. Asia, Iraq, Iran and S. USSR. The hexaploid is also called Ae. recta (Zhuk.) Chenn. The C^u genome will be renamed U.

AEGILOPS TRIUNCIALIS L. (syn. Triticum triuncialis (L.) Raspail. 2n=28, genome formula C^uC^uCC. The Mediterranean area, Turkey, Palestine, Syria, Lebanon, Iraq, Iran, Turkmenia, Afghanistan and Caucasus. Derived from a hybrid of ♀ Ae. caudata and ♂ Ae. umbellulata that originated in W. Turkey (Nakai, 1977; Maan, 1980). The C^u genome will be renamed U.

Ae. bushirica Rosh. might be a synonym. However Bor (1970) suggested that it could be a hybrid product of Ae. triuncialis and Ae. cylindrica*.

AEGILOPS UMBELLULATA Zhuk. (syn. Triticum umbellutatum (Zhuk.) Bowden). 2n=14, genome formula C^uC^u. Moist steppe, dry hills and as a weed in cultivation in the Greek islands, Turkey, N. Syria, Iraq, N. and W. Iran and Transcaucasia. Used in wheat breeding as a source of resistance to leaf rust, Puccinia triticina Eriks.

The C^u genome will be renamed U.

AEGILOPS VARIABILIS*

AGROPYRON INTERMEDIUM (Host.) Beauv. (syn. A. glaucum). Wheatgrass. 2n=(28), 42, genome formula $B_2B_2E_1E_1E_2E_2$. See p. 151. Ssp. podgerae (Nabel.) Dewey (syn. A. podgerae Nabel.), 2n= 42 is found in the mountains of Turkey, Iran and Iraq, where it is used as a wild forage grass.

AGROSTIS TENUIS*

CYNOSURUS CRISTATUS*

HORDEUM VULGARE L. Barley. 2n=14, genome formula VV. The wild parent of barley is H. spontaneum C. Koch (2n=14). E. Mediterranean Region - W. Asia as far as Turkmenia and Afghanistan. In the peripheral areas it only grows as a weed. In the catchment of the Upper Jordan Valley, there are robust types with very large seeds and very long awns. A slender type occurs in dry steppes of Negev, Jordan-Turkish border area - Iran - Afghanistan. In E. Galilee, small grassy types are found and everywhere are observed intermediates (Zohary, 1969).

H. spontaneum is two-rowed and has a brittle rachis. It was probably domesticated in the Fertile Crescent resulting in the two-rowed type (ssp. distichon, syn. H. distichon L.). The start of its domestication might have been about 7000 BC. Helbaek (1966) suggested that the barley found at Beidha dating from c.7000 BC was cultivated wild barley.

Braidwood et al. (1969) found 'evidently domesticated barley' at Çayönü, Turkey in layers dated c.7000 BC. However, grains of domesticated barley have been found in Egypt dating from the Egyptian Late Paleolithic (16 000-15 000) BC (Wendorf et al., 1979).

Domesticated barley has a tough rachis and the change from brittle to tough rachis may have taken place in 7000 - 6000 BC. The tough rachis is conditioned by two recessive alleles

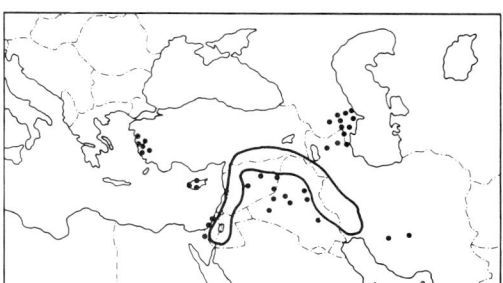

Hordeum spontaneum (Harlan & Zohary, 1969).

bt and bt_2.

Both genes are closely linked and the genotype for tough rachis is either $BtBtbt_2bt_2$ or $btbtBt_2Bt_2$. No plants with $btbtbt_2bt_2$ have yet been found or bred, probably because of the close linkage of the genes. Takahashi (1964) observed that the genotype $BtBtbt_2bt_2$ is very common (90-100%) in the 'Oriental' region: C. and S. Japan, S. Korea, China, Tibet and N.C. Nepal (naked forms), and the genotype $btbtBt_2$ Bt_2 is common (60-95%) in the 'Occidental' region: N. Japan, N. Korea, Manchuria, India, Nepal (hulled forms), Kashmir, Turkey, Europe, USSR, Egypt and Ethiopia. In Pakistan, Afghanistan, Iran, Iraq and Syria both types occur (65-75%).

C.7000 BC. 'naked barley' was first cultivated at Beidha, Aceramic Haçilar and Ali Kosh (Bus Mordesh period). In that material, the first six-rowed types (ssp. hexastichon, syn. H. hexastichon L.) appears (Braidwood et al., 1969).

Formerly H. agriocrithon Åberg was thought to be the wild parent of six-rowed barley. It has a brittle rachis. It is, however, a hybrid product of H. spontaneum and six-rowed barley. It was first observed in Tibet as weeds in barley fields. Later is was also found elsewhere where H. spontaneum came into contact with cultivated six-rowed barley. Lagunculiforme (H. lagunciliforme) and intermedium (H. intermedium Carlet) have a similar origin. Zohary (1971) suggested that these brittle types were ill-adapted to survive under stable wild conditions (at least in Israel).

In Region 6, ssp. humile* arose and in 7, ssp. mediterraneum*.

POA BULBOSA L. 2n=14, 28, (39), 42, 45, (40-58, 56). A grass of Europe, W. Asia and W.N. Africa. Cultivated in USA.

Var. vivipara of C. and Ante-Asia is a very valuable forage plant of dry steppe.

SECALE ANATOLICUM Boiss. (syn. S. montanum var. anatolicum (Boiss.) Boiss.) 2n=14. Turkey, and W. Iran and Iraq. It is a highly polymorphic weed.

SECALE CEREALE L. Weedy and cultivated rye.

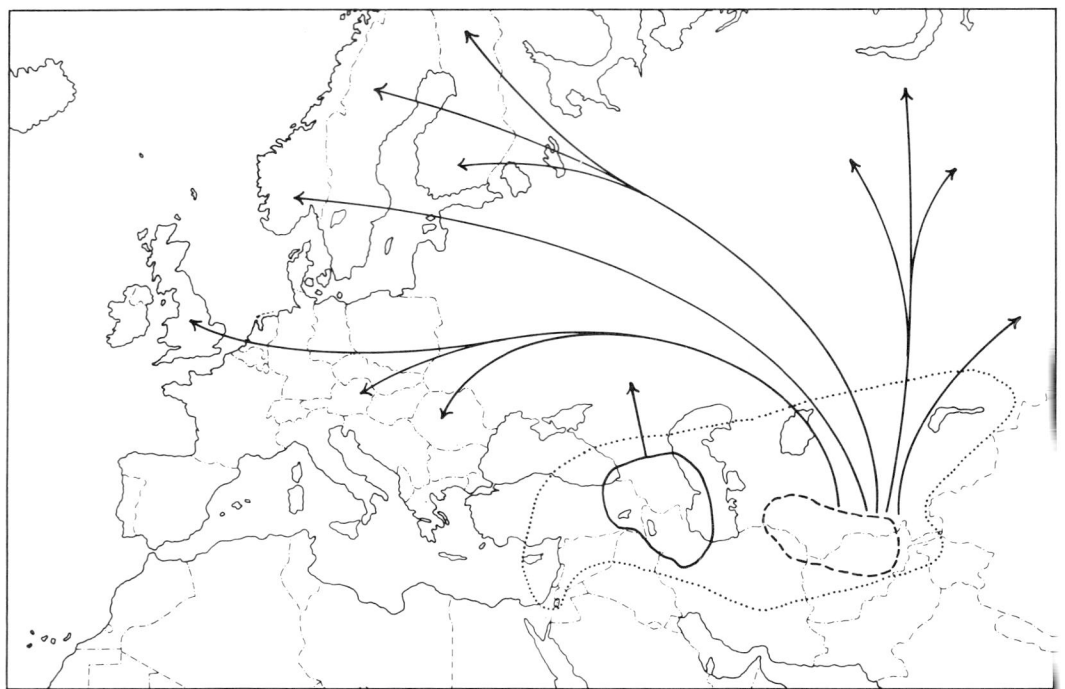

Primary centre (——), secondary centre (- - -) and distribution of wild and weedy Secale cereale types and ways of their introduction and that of rye into Europe and N. Asia (...) (Khush, 1962).

2n=14, genome formula $R^C R^C$. Primary centre of annual and perennial rye species and forms: NE. Turkey - NW. Iran. Khush (1963) suggested that a secondary centre (p. 83) is in Afghanistan and that the cultivated rye of Europe and N. and C. Asia derives from that centre. Only a few come from the primary centre. In the primary centre, S. vavilovii* and S. montaneum* hybridize with each other and introgress, resulting in a mixture of genetic variants described as 'S. segetale', 'S. afghanicum', 'S. daralgesii', 'S. cereale', 'S. turkestanicum' and 'S. dighoricum' (Stutz, 1972). Stutz (1972) suggested that from this highly variable population the annual S. cereale types invaded cultivated fields to become weeds.

S. cereale includes cultivated rye and a number of weedy rye types occurring in grain fields and along ditchbanks and roadsides throughout the Middle East (Stutz, 1972). These weedy types are:

S. afghanicum*

S. dighoricum (Vav.) Roshev. (syn. S. cereale L. ssp. dighoricum (Vav.) Khush). It is a weed in grain fields of N. Ossetia (USSR).

S. segetale (Zhuk.) Roshev. (syn. S. cereale L. ssp. segetale (Zhuk.) Khush.). This is a polymorphic weed in grain fields throughout E. Europe and the Middle East (Stutz, 1972).

S. ancestrale Zhuk. (syn. S. cereale L. ssp. ancestrale (Zhuk.) Khush). It is a robust tall (up to 2.4 m) weed with small invested seeds and fragile rachis restricted to sandy ditchbanks and fence rows near Aydin, SW. Turkey. It is reproductively isolated from domesticated rye (Stutz, 1976).

S. turkestanicum Bensin. A self-compatible cultigen of C. Asia (p. 83) and Transcaucasia.

The weedy types have derived mainly from S. vavilovii* by introgression with S. montanum* and its derivative species S. anatolicum*. In some places less favourable for wheat and barley, rye may have been developed to become fully domesticated. It is generally proposed that S. ancestrale and S. segetale are the parental types of S. cereale; however Stutz (1972) suggested that S. ancestrale derives from S. cereale. There is no introgression into S. ancestrale of other Secale genetic material, in spite of contact with other species, because a high incidence of geno-typically controlled chromosomal breaks in outcrossed hybrids leads to sterility (Stutz, 1971).

Hybridization between wheat (p. 93) and rye may have increased in the variability of wheat. Rye is a source of resistance to diseases used in wheat breeding and is a parent of octaploid and hexaploid triticales.

The closest wild relative of cultivated rye is S. ancestrale and this taxon probably gave rise to the weedy S. segetale complex. Wild rye

is characterized by spikelets that all disarticulate at maturity, while in the weed complex the lower one quarter or more of the
spikelets are not deciduous at maturity. Cultivated rye is known from the Neolithic of
Austria, but it became widespread as a cereal
in Europe only since the Bronze age.

SECALE MONTANUM Guss. Mountain rye. 2n=14, genome formula R^{m}R^m. From the C. Atlas Mountains
of Morocco and the Sierra Nevada Mountains of
Spain, eastwards in isolated pockets in the
mountains of Sicily, Italy, Yugoslavia, Greece,
Lebanon, Turkey, Iran and Iraq (Stutz, 1972).
It is a highly polymorphic cross-fertilizing
perennial. Some of the isolates have been described as distinct species or varieties:
  S. ciliatoglume (Boiss.) Grossh. (syn. S.
montanum var. ciliatoglume Boiss.). A weedy
population with pubescent culms in orchards
and vineyards near Mardin, SE. Turkey.
  S. dalmaticum Vis., population growing within the walls of the old St. Johannis Fortress
above Kotor, S. Jugoslavia.
  S. daralgesii Thum., a weedy form with non-
fragile rachis along roadsides and ditchbanks
of Armenia.
  S. kuprijanovii Grossh., a broad-leaved form
of mountain meadows of the N. Caucasus Mountains.
  S. montanum has the same chromosomal arrangement as S. anatolicum*, S. silvestre* and S.
africanum*. Its chromosomal arrangement differs
from that of S. vavilovii and S. cereale and
from its closely related forms in reciprocal
translocations involving 6 of the 14 chromosomes.
  It derives from S. silvestre* (Singh & Röbbelen, 1975) and is the parental species of S.
anatolicum (Stutz, 1972), S. africanum, S.
vavilovii and S. cereale.

SECALE SILVESTRE Host. (syn. S. fragile
Marsch.). 2n=14. C. Hungary eastward throughout the sandy steppe of S. Russia up to W. Siberia and the Pamirs and Alai (Bor, 1970;
Stutz, 1972). A low-growing annual psammophyte
with fragile rachis. It has the same chromosome arrangement as S. montanum*. This species is believed to be phylogenetically the
oldest species and is probably the ancestor
of S. montanum* (Rimpau & Flavell, 1974; Singh
& Röbbelen, 1975) from which S. cereale* derives.

SECALE VAVILOVII Grossh. 2n=14. Common to the
lower slopes of Mount Ararat and along the banks
of the Araks River. It is a wild low-growing,
annual self-compatible psammophyte with fragile rachis. It has the same chromosome arrangement as S. cereale (see S. montanum*). Bor
(1970), strongly suspected this species of
being the same as S. afghanicum*. Khush (1960)
suggested that it derived from S. montanum,
but Stutz (1972) made it clear that is is the
ancestor of S. cereale*.

TRITICUM AESTIVUM (L.) Thell. Wheat. 2n=42,
genome formula AABBDD. Primary centre: Transcaucasia and adjacent areas. There, natural
cross-fertilization is still taking place within the species and between subspecies, other
Triticum species and related species of Aegilops and Secale. This species is a natural amphiploid of emmer and Aegilops squarrosa*.
This amphiploidization must have taken place
after the development of emmer from its wild
ancestor T. turgidum ssp. dicoccoides* in the
area south of the Caspian Sea (Nakai, 1979).
  This hybridization has led to hexaploid types
with a very brittle ear. This is a 'wild' character and so one could say that there are
wild hexaploid wheats. However these segregants
cannot really be called wild.
  The main division of T. aestivum is into ssp.
spelta (L.) Thell. (syn. T. spelta L.), spelt;
ssp. vavilovi (Tum.) Sears (syn. T. vavilovii
(Tum.) Jakubz.); ssp. macha (Dek. & Men.) MK.
(syn. T. macha Dek. & Men.). Makha wheat, ssp.
vulgare (Vill.) MK. (syn. T. vulgare Vill.),
common wheat, bread wheat; ssp. compactum
Host.) MK. (syn. T. compactum Host.), club
wheat; and ssp. sphaerococcum (Perc.) MK. (syn.
T. sphaerococcum Perc.), Indian dwarf wheat.
The origin of some subspecies has not yet been
assertained. They have originated in another
centre.
  Spelt wheats have been found in Iran, in C.
Europe (p. 154) and Africa (p. 135). The spread
of bread wheat during Neolithic times has been
described (Zeven, 1979; 1980).
  Ssp. vavilovi wheat is indigenous to Armenia.
It is characterized by its branching spikelet.
  Makha wheat is indigenous to W. Georgia (US-
SR). It is often mixed with T. turgidum ssp.
paleocolchicum*.
  The spread of bread wheat during Neolithic
times has been described (Zeven, 1979; 1980).
Bread wheat is now widespread. Primary centre
in Transcaucasia and adjacent regions. Secondary centres in Hindu Kush and adjacent regions (p. 83), in China and Japan (p. 39) and
probably in African Sahara (p. 135).
  Club wheat developed in Afghanistan and adjacent regions (p. 83) and probably in Swit-
zerland/Austria (p. 154). A secondary centre
of diversity is Armenia.
  Indian dwarf wheat originated in NW. India
and adjacent regions (p. 75). Its presence
has been reported in N. Africa.
  Dorofejev (1971) suggested that ssp. macha
is the oldest hexaploid. From it, ssp. vulgare
developed. Ssp. spelta and ssp. vavilovii are
secondary spelts. They may have derived from
ssp. vulgare.
  There has been much research to identify the
donor species of the B genome. However in vain,
because it probably does not exist (see T.
turgidum*).

TRITICUM AESTIVUM (L.) Thell. ssp. compactum
(Host) MK. (syn. T. compactum Host.). Club
wheat. 2n=42, genome formula AABBDD. This subspecies developed in the Hindu Kush (p. 83).

Secondary centre Armenia.

TRITICUM MONOCOCCUM L. Wild and cultivated einkorn. 2n=14, genome formula AA. The wild ssp. boeoticum (Boiss.) Mac Key (syn. T. boeoticum Boiss.) includes the types aegilopoides (T. aegilopoides (Link) Bal. and thaoudar (T. thaoudar Reut.), as well as 'T. spontaneum Flaksb.' and 'T. urartu Tuman.'. It is spread over Greece, Turkey, Syria, N. Iraq and Transcaucasia. Aegilopoides is characterized by one grain and one awn per spikelet, whereas thaoudar has two grains and two awns. There are two distribution centres: in the Fertile Crescent and in Turkey. In peripheral areas, it is segetal. In the Fertile Crescent thaoudar is found. Aegilopoides type occurs in the colder part of Balkans and W. Anatolia. In Anatolia, intermediate types and mixtures are found. In Armenia the type urartu has been described. It has two awns and a winter habit.

In the Fertile Crescent, the wild einkorn was domesticated to become ssp. monococcum, which has a tough rachis.

Its earliest appearance is from Ali Kosh dating from c. 6500 BC., thus later than the first appearance to T. turgidum ssp. dicoccum.

Einkorn was spread over Europe, N. Africa, Asia Minor, Caucasia, Iraq and Iran. Cultivated in some areas as a fodder crop. It forms a component of the Zanduri wheat, which is a mixture of einkorn. T. timopheevi ssp. timopheevi* and T. zhukovskyi*. This population is cultivated in Georgia (USSR). This species forms a useful source of disease resistance.

There is still a natural gene flow between diploid and tetraploid species (Vardi & Zohary, 1967).

TRITICUM TIMOPHEEVI Zhuk. 2n=28, genome formula AABB (or AAB'B', AAGG). This species consists of two subspecies ssp. araraticum (Jakubz.) Mac Key (syn. T. araraticum Jakubz.) and ssp. timopheevi. Ssp. araraticum grows wild in Transcaucasia. N. Iraq, W. Iran and E. Turkey. It was first described as T. dicoccoides ssp. armeniacum Jakubz. and as T. armeniacum Mak. Some types closely resemble T. dicoccoides . However the subspecies only crosses easily with ssp. timopheevi.

Ssp. timopheevi is part of the Zanduri wheat cultivated in Georgia (USSR). It is an ancient cultivated wheat. Its rather brittle rachis causes difficulties in threshing. It is difficult to cross with other Triticum species; It is a source of disease resistance. (Timopheevi) durum and aestivum plants often are male-sterile.

Maan (1973) concluded from his nucleo-cytoplasmic and cytogenic studies that T. timopheevi ssp. timopheevi and ssp. araraticum and T. dicoccoides var. nudiglumis ex Turkey-Iran -Iraq area have the same type of cytoplasm and the genome formula AAGG. The cytoplasm of Ae. speltoides* is closer to the above cytoplasm than to T. turgidum*-cultivated wheats.

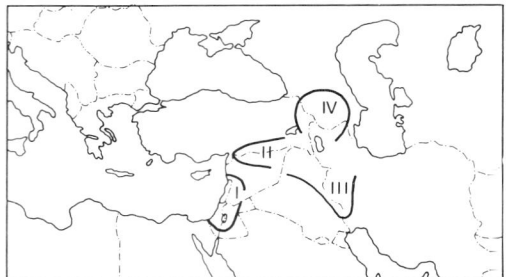

Wild tetraploid Triticum species: Triticum turgidum ssp. dicoccoides (I,II,III,), ssp. dicoccoides var. nudiglunis (III) and T. timopheevi ssp. araraticum (IV) (Johnson, 1972).

TRITICUM TURGIDUM (L.) Thell. Wild emmer wheats. 2n=28, genome formula AABB. The distribution of the wild ssp. dicoccoides can be divided into two regions. The N. region is S. Turkey - Iran - Iraq, where var. nudiglumis is found; the S. region is Israel, S. Syria and Jordan. The cytoplasm of var. nudiglumis is similar to that of T. timopheevi*, whereas that of ssp. dicoccoides of the southern region is the same as the cultivated T. turgidum* (Maan, 1973). Ssp. dicoccoides (Körn.) Thell. (syn. T. dicoccoides Körn.). derived from a natural amphidiploidization of an unknown diploid species and T. monococcum ssp. boeoticum . This amphidiploidization must probably have occurred in Syria and Palestine, probably at several places. There has been much research to identify the unknown diploid parent. However in vain.

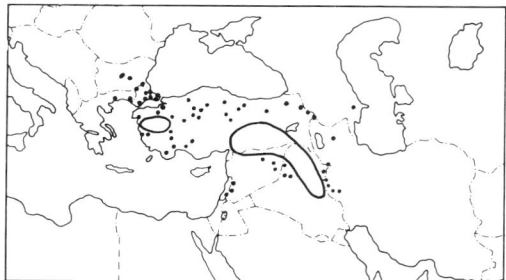

Triticum boeoticum (Harlan & Zohary, 1969).

The research has failed because the B genome of this species and of its donor have evolved of the first tetraploid Triticum species - some 100 000 years ago. Evolution followed different paths, which branched to give rise to several species with related but different B genomes.

From ssp. dicoccoides, several cultivated subspecies have been derived. These are dicoccum*, palaeocolchicum*, turgidum* and carthlicum*. The ssp. turgidum includes conv. turgidum, conv. durum, conv. turanicum and conv. polonicum. Ssp. dicoccoides is a source

of disease resistance; it also carries a re-
storer gene of (timopheevi) cytoplasmic male-
sterility.

TRITICUM TURGIDUM (L.) Thell. Cultivated emmer wheats. 2n=28, genome formula AABB. The
cultivated tetraploid wheat can be subdivided
as follows (MacKey, 1966):
ssp. dicoccum (Schrank) Thell. (syn. T. dicoccum Schubl.)., emmer,
ssp. palaeocolchicum (Men.) Mac Key (syn. T.
palaeocolchicum Men.,
T. georgicum Dek.), Georgian emmer, Kolchic
emmer,
ssp. turgidum including conv. turgidum, Pou-
lard wheat, English wheat, conv. durum (Desf.)
Mac Key (syn. T. durum Desf.), durum wheat,
hard wheat, conv. turanicum (Jakubz.) Mac Key
(T. turanicum Jakubz., T. orientale Perc.),
Khurasan wheat, conv. polonicum (L.) Mac Key
(syn. T. polonicum L.) Polish wheat,
ssp. carthlicum (Nevski) Mac Key (syn. T. carthlicum Nevski, T. persicum Vav. ex Zhuk.),
Persian wheat. They have originated by cultivation from ssp. didoccoides* and perhaps by
intergeneric and interspecific hybridization.

Primary centre in Near Eastern Region. Secondary centres in Ethiopia (p. 135) and in
the Mediterranean Region (p. 112).

Emmer is the oldest cultivated wheat. Its
cultivation is declining. Until recently, it
was cultivated in Ethiopia (p. 135), Iran, E.
Turkey, Transcaucasia, Volga Basin, Yugoslavia,
Czechoslovakia and India. It may have been domesticated c.8000 BC. in the Fertile Crescent.
The first appearance of domesticated emmer
dates from c.7000 BC. at Aceramic Neolithic
Beidha, Ali Kosh, Jericho and Ramad. Already
in 4000-3000 BC., it had reached the Atlantic
coast from Scandinavia to Spain and the Nile
Delta. Helbaek (1960) was surprised by the uni-
formity of emmer. However plants are called
dicoccum when they correspond to a certain
morphological description. It is unknown whether the idiotypes of the various dicoccum populations also correspond to each other for
characteristics other than morphological ones.

The disease-resistant khapli (khapli is the
vernacular name of emmer) of India and Yaro-
slav emmer from USSR belong to ssp. dicocum.

Durum wheat is cultivated over a large area:
Mediterranean coastal region, Ethiopia where
a secondary centre exists (p. 135) and in
areas north of the Black Sea. Another centre
of diversity is in India (Jain et al., 1976).
It is rarely observed in wheats of Iran and
Afghanistan. It is also cultivated in the
Americas and elsewhere. Distribution in the
Old World is shown by Ciferri (1939). It is
the second most important wheat in the world.

Turanicum wheat originally involved as an
oasis ecotype. Its cultivation is restricted
to irrigated fields (Mac Key, 1966). Mac Key
suggested a wide occurrence in Asia, but Kuckuck (1970) and Bor (1970) limited it to Iran
and Iraq. Kuckuck (1970) suggested that it is
a hybrid of durum x polonicum.

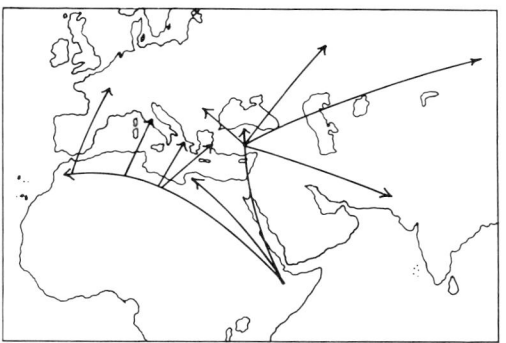

Spread of durum wheat in the Old World (Ciferri,
1939).

Polonicum wheat, distinguished by long glumes
and kernels was cultivated in S. Europe, Turkey, Iraq, Iran, Afghanistan and NW. India.
According to Kihara et al. (1956), in includes
T. ispahanicum Heslot.

Carthlicum wheat is characterized by the presence of the Q (vulgare) gene. It is not known
whether this gene arose independently in this
wheat or came from vulgare wheat. Carthlicum
wheat was cultivated in Iraq, Iran and Caucasia. It is a source of disease resistance.

Georgian emmer, Kolchic emmer (ssp. palaeocolchicum) was formerly cultivated in a mixture
with T. aestivum ssp. macha* in W. Georgia
(USSR).

English wheat (conv. turgidum) was at one
time cultivated in Europe and elsewhere. From
time to time, it was reintroduced into cultivation because its branching habit (Osiris
wheat, Wonder wheat) convinced farmers that
its yield must be high.

TRITICUM ZHUKOVSKYI Men. & Er. Zanduri. 2n=
42, genome formula AAAABB or $A^zA^zA^tA^tB^tB^t$. It
was cultivated in W. Georgia, USSR. Zanduri
was composed of einkorn, T. timopheevi ssp. timopheevi* and T. zhukovskyi. The latter is a
hexaploid but its genome formula differs from
those of the common hexaploid subspecies. It
is a natural amphiploid of ssp. timopheevi
and einkorn. Its cytoplasm has the same male-
sterilizing action on the durum and aestivum
nuclei as ssp. timopheevi. It carries genes
for resistance to stem rust and mildew.

ZEA MAYS L. Maize. 2n=20. Secondary centre in
the Near East (Brandolini, 1970). Domesticated
in C. America (p. 190). Flint maize - indurata
Sturt. is common in the Near East.

Iridaceae

CROCUS SATIVUS*

Labiatae

LALLEMANTIA IBERICA Fisch. & Mey. Lallemantia.
2n=16. Asia Minor and some regions of USSR.

Cultivated in Iran and S. USSR for its oil seeds.

Leguminosae

ALOPHOTROPIS FORMOSUM (Boiss.) Lamprecht (syn. Pisum formosum (Stev.) Boiss., Vavilovia formosa (Stev.) Fed.). Wild perennial pea. 2n= 14. Montane and submontane zones of Asia Minor, Transcaucasia, Armenia and Iran.

CICER ARIETINUM L. Chick-pea, Gram, Garbanzos. 2n=14, 16, (24, 32, 33). Unknown wild. Secondary centres of diversity probably developed in Regions 4 (p. 76), 5 (p. 83) and 7 (p. 113). Cultivated in S. Europe and N. Africa from the Atlantic eastwards, the Nile Delta and Ethiopia, and northwards and eastwards to NW. Burma, W. China, Kazakhstan (USSR). Some of the Cicer species indigenous to Anatolia may have played a role in its ancestry, particularly C. pinnatifidum Jaub. & Spach., 2n=16, (from Anatolia, Soviet Armenia, Syria, N. Iraq and Cyprus), C. echinospermum P.H. Davis, 2n=   , (from E. Anatolia) and C. bijugum K.H. Rech., 2n=16 (from SE. Anatolia, N. Syria, and N. Iraq) (van der Maesen, 1972).

Ladizinsky (1975a) found a wild annual species in Turkey: C. reticulatum Lad., 2n=   , which is cross-compatible with chick-pea, producing a fertile F_1. This species resembles chick-pea and could be the wild parent of the cultigen. So Moreno & Cubero (1978) proposed to include it as ssp. reticulatum (Lad.) Moreno & Cubero in C. arietinum.

Race orientale Pop. is characterized by very small seeds (1000-seed weight 100-120 g). It is common in Ethiopia, Sudan, Egypt, India, the Pamirs, Tajikistan and Iran. Those from Ethiopia are black-seeded.

Race asiaticum Pop. has somewhat bigger, but still small, seeds (1000-seed weight 140-200 g). It occurs in C. Asia, Afghanistan, W. China, Iran and E. Turkey.

Race eurasiaticum Pop. has moderately large seeds (1000-seed weight 200-300 g). It is cultivated in the Near East, Armenia, Azerbaijan, Ukraine up to C. USSR, and near large cities in the eastern part of the area of cultivation. The seeds are white.

Race mediterraneum Pop. has the largest seeds (1000-seed weight over 350 g). It is found in Spain, Italy, Morocco, Algeria, Tunisia and W. Turkey. The seeds are white. However Moreno & Cubero (1978) grouped the cultivars into two races: the small-seeded in race microsperma, and the large-seeded in race macrosperma. The latter is selected from the first.

GALEGA ORIENTALIS Lam. 2n=16. Caucasia. Cultivated as a fodder and as an ornamental.

LENS ESCULENTA Moench (syn. L. culinaris Medik., Ervum lens L.). Lentil. 2n=14. Zohary (1972) suggested that L. orientalis (Boiss.) Hand.-Mazz., 2n=   , is the wild ancestor of lentil; it grows wild in Region 6. L. orientalis is a dwarf lentil, as was confirmed by Williams et al. (1974). Ladizinsky (1979) too found a close affinity between the two species and L. nigricans (M.B.) Godr., 2n=   . So Williams et al. (1974) concluded that lentil and its wild ancestor belonged to one species L. esculenta, both types being ssp. culinaris (Medik.) Williams, Sanchez & Jackson for lentil, and ssp. orientalis (Boiss.) Williams, Sanchez & Jackson for wild lentil.

Lentil had been divided by seed size into varieties: var. macrosperma, a large-seeded form from the Mediterranean Region, var. syrica Barul., a medium-seeded form from the inner mountainous region of Asia Minor, and var. afghanica Barul., a small-seeded form of the highlands of Afghanistan. Another division is ssp. macrosperma (Baumg.) Barul. and ssp. microsperma (Baumg.) Barul. However Williams et al. (1974) concluded that such division is meaningless as macrosperma and microsperma form the extremes of a cline for seed size. Microsperma is found in all prehistoric exca-

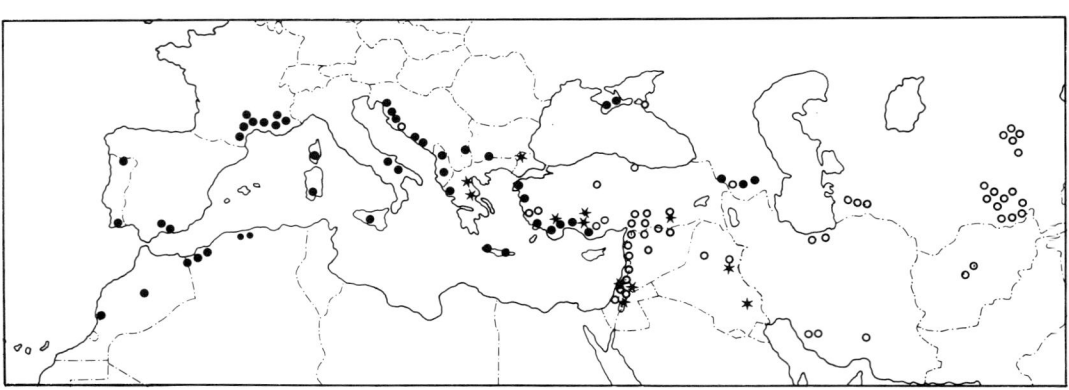

Lens nigricans (●), L. orientalis (○) and early records 6-7th millenia BC of lentil (✳)(Zohary, 1976; Ladizinsky, 1979).

vations (van Zeist & Bottema, 1971).

Agro-ecological groups meet in Turkey, where there are microcentres of diversity (Harlan, 1951).

MEDICAGO CANCELLATA Bieb. 2n=48. SE. European USSR and N. Caucasia. Useful as gene source for adaptation of M. sativa* to poor soils.

MEDICAGO DZHAWAKHETICA Bordz. 2n=16, genome formula DD, 32. The (sub)alpine zones of the Alkhalak uplands, Georgia, USSR and a part of Asia Minor. A wild perennial species. Var. timofeevi Troitz., (2n=32) is endemic to Transcaucasia. It crosses fairly easy with M. sativa (Lesins and Lesins, 1966). Some include this species as var. dzhawakhetica Bordz. in M. papillosa Boiss. (2n=16).

MEDICAGO GLUTINOSA Bieb. 2n=32. Causasus. Useful as gene source for M. sativa*.

MEDICAGO ROMANICA Prod. 2n=16. Caucasia. A wild variable perennial species.

MEDICAGO SATIVA L. Lucerne, Alfalfa. 2n=16, genome formula SS; 32, genome formula SSSS; (48). The species probably evolved around the Caspian Sea, whence it spread as a wild plant. It was the first species to be cultivated as a forage crop, probably in association with the increasing use of horses and the development of light horse-drawn chariots in the first part of the 2nd Millenium BC. It was probably intentionally sown and the more vigorous tetraploid crowded out the diploid. During the

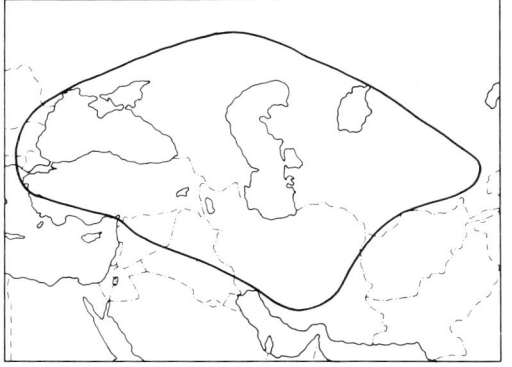

Medicago sativa (Fischer, 1938).

Persian-Greek War in the 5th Century BC., lucerne (from Provencal, meaning shining) and its older name alfalfa (from Arabic and ultimately Old Iranian aspo-asti, horse fodder) was introduced into Greece, whence it spread to S. Italy and Europe, and later to other parts of the world (Lesins & Lesins, 1979).

MEDICAGO SAXATILIS Bieb. 2n=16. Yaila Range of

Mountains in Crimea. Useful as gene source for M. sativa*.

ONOBRYCHIS ALTISSIMA Grossh. 2n=14. Transcaucasia.

ONOBRYCHIS VICIIFOLIA Scop. Esparcette. 2n=28. Cultivation of this fodder crop started in S. France (p. 157). In Transcaucasia, var. transcaucasia (syn. O. transcaucasia Grossh.) is endemic.

PISUM SATIVUM L. (syn. P. arvense L.s.l.). Pea. 2n=14. This species may be divided into six subspecies: ssp. abyssinicum (p. 137), ssp. jomardi (p. 115), ssp. syriacum Berger, ssp. elatius (Stev.) Alef., ssp. arvense Poir., and ssp. hortense Asch. et Graeb. (Gentry, 1971).

Ssp. syriacum (syn. P. humile Boiss. et Noë, P. sativum var. humile, P. syriacum Berger) is found in N. Iraq, Jordan, Syria, N., NW. and W. Iran, Israel, Turkey and Cyprus. Some forms are robust (30-70 cm tall), others slender and small (20-40 cm) (Ben-Ze'ev & Zohary, 1973). This is Zohary's (1973) 'steppe' type. It is the primary wild progenitor.

Ssp. elatius (syn. P. elatius Stev.) is found in Syria, N. Israel, Lebanon, S. coast of Turkey, Aegean belt of Turkey and Greece, Cyprus, Adriatic coast of Yugoslavia, S. Italy, Sicily, Sardinia and scattered localities in Morocco, Algeria, Tunisia, S. Spain, S. France, N. Italy and the Black Sea coast of Turkey, Crimea and Caucasia (Ben Ze'ev & Zohary, 1973). This is Zohary's (1973) tall 'maquis' type.

In the E. Mediterranean countries (esp. S. Turkey), intermediate types are found.

Ben Ze'ev & Zohary (1973) suggested that ecotypes of Turkey and Syria may have formed the parental material of the domesticated types ssp. arvense (P. arvense L.), field pea, and ssp. hortense (ssp. sativum, P. sativum L.), garden pea.

It may also derive from ssp. elatius, or from hybrids of ssp. elatius x ssp. arvense. Secondary centre in the Mediterranean Region (p. 115). It may have been domesticated in SW. Asia. The crop reached the Greeks by way of the Black Sea, who passed it on to Latin and Germanic tribes. It spread to India and China through the Himalayas and Tibet, and to Ethiopia and E. Africa (Purseglove, 1968).

TRIFOLIUM AMBIGUUM M.B. Caucasian clover. 2n= 2x=16, (32; allo-6x=48). Caucasia, Crimea and Turkey. This valuable fodder plant forms an essential part of pastures and meadows. In Australia, an allohexaploid cultivar derives from an introduction from USSR. It withstands periods of 6 weeks submerged in water.

TRIGONELLA FOENUM-GRAECUM L. Fenugreek. 2n=16, (4x=32). Probably SW. Asia. Cultivated in S. Europe, N. Africa and India as a fodder. The seeds are also eaten in India and used in medicine.

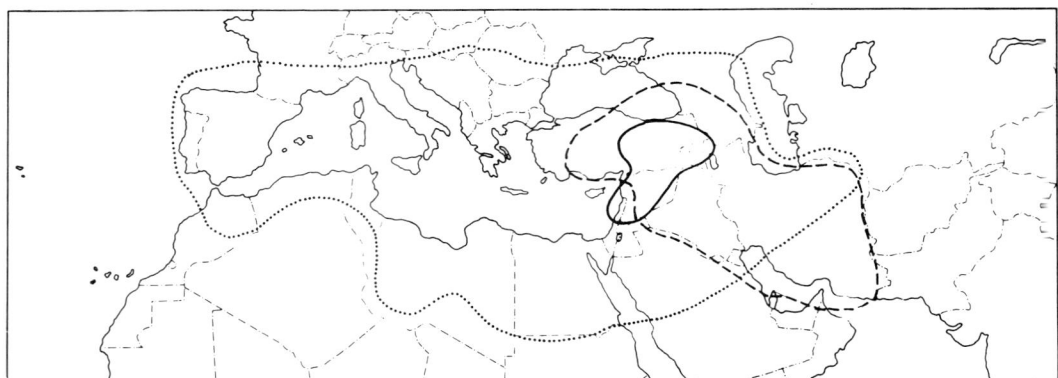

Pisum humile (——), P. elatius (···) and Alophotropis formosum (---)(Govorov, 1937).

VICIA ERVILEA (L.) Willd. Bitter vetch, Ervil.
2n=14. Primary centre in the Mediterranean Region (p. 116). In Asia Minor, a characteristic
group developed.
   It is now cultivated as a fodder but in prehistoric times it was cultivated for food. It
was already cultivated in Turkey in 5750 BC.
and probably in Greece about 5500 BC. (van
Zeist & Bottema, 1971).

VICIA NARBONENSIS L. Narbonne vetch. 2n=14.
Primary gene centre probably E. Georgia. Secondary gene centre in the Mediterranean Region. This species is a weed in wheat and barley fields of Transcaucasia and other areas in
SE. Asia. It is not cultivated there.

VICIA PANNONICA Crantz. Hungarian vetch. 2n=
12. Primary gene centre in Georgia (USSR), on
the plateau of Akhalkalak, where it grows wild
and is cultivated. Secondary gene centre in
Hungary.

VICIA SATIVA L. Common vetch. 2n=10, 12, 14.
The V. sativa aggregate is complex because of
variation in form, in chromosome number and
in karyotype, and of irregular cytogenetic
affinities between the types with different
karyotypes (Ladizinsky & Temkin, 1978). The 3
cytotypes are found among the wild, weedy and
domesticated types (Zohary & Plitmann, 1979).
In the wild types, they are partially isolated
by ecological barriers, partial hybrid sterility and predominance of self-fertilization.
Human disturbance of the land has removed
these barriers and increased variation, including that of the karyotypes.
   Zohary & Plitmann (1979) divided the aggregate up as follows:
1. ssp. sativa, 2n=12, 7 karyotypes found.
From Atlantic fringe of Europe through Mediterranean to W. India, weedy, escapes and cultivars (seed and hay), run wild in New World
2. ssp. macrocarpa (Moris) Arcang., 2n=12, 2
karyotypes. W. Mediterranean, cultivars (seed)
3a. ssp. nigra (L.) Ehrh. var. nigra (syn. V.

sativa L. var. angustifolia L.), 2n=12, more
than 25 karyotypes. Mediterranean Basin and
Europe, run wild in the New World, cultivated
for hay.
3b. ssp. nigra (L.) Ehrh. var. segetalis
(Thuill.) Ser. in DC (syn. V. segetalis Thuill.),
mostly 2n=12, more than 80 karyotypes. Mediterranean Basin deep into C. Europe, very
weedy, recently cultivated for hay.
4. ssp. cordata (Wulfen ex Hoppe) Aschers. &
Graebn. (syn. V. cordata Wulfen ex Hoppe), 2n=
10, more than 30 karyotypes. Mediterranean
Region, very weedy, some domesticated types
(hay)
5. ssp. incisa (M.B.) Arcang. (syn. V. incisa
M.B.), 2n=14, karyotypic variation unknown.
Near East
6. ssp. amphicarpa (Dorth.) Aschers. & Graebn.
(syn. V. amphicarpa Dorth.), 2n=14, karyotypic
variation unknown. Mediterranean Area and Near
East. This type is unique for its subterranean
pods and is according to Ladizinsky (1978) an
advanced form
7. ssp. pilosa (M.B.) Plitm. & D.Zoh. (syn. V.
pilosa M.B.), 2n=14, karyotypic variation unknown. Crimea and Caucasia.
By further hybridization of cytotypes and
karyotypes, and by natural and human selection,
the variation of this species may still increase considerably.

VICIA VILLOSA Roth. Sand vetch, Hairy vetch,
Winter vetch. 2n=14. W. and C. Europe, Medi-
terranean Region, N. Iraq, N. Iran and SW. of
USSR. Primary centre probably W. Asia and An-
te-Asia. Spread to the Mediterranean area and
Europe as a cereal weed.

   Liliaceae

HYACINTHUS ORIENTALIS L. Common hyacinth.
2n=16, (24, 32). Syria, Asia Minor, Greece and
Dalmatia. Cultivated in the Netherlands as an
ornamental and in S. France as a source of an
essential oil used in perfumery.

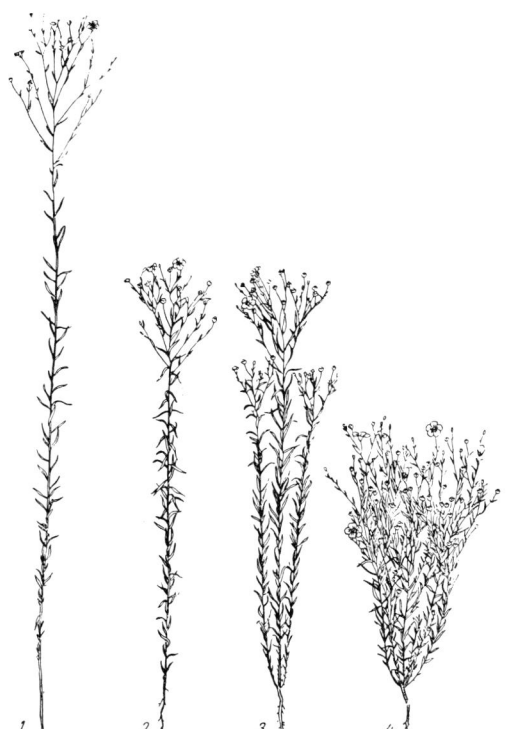

Linum usitatissimum, various length and branching types

Linaceae

LINUM USITATISSIMUM L. Flax, Linseed. 2n=30, (32). Primary centre probably in Central Asian Region (Vavilov, 1957), since flax varies widely in India and adjacent northerly areas. However as the progenitor of flax, L. bienne Mill. (Pale flax, 2n=30) is not found in this area it cannot have been domesticated there (Helbaek, 1956). Helbaek suggested that flax was domesticated about the same time as emmer and barley in the mountains of the Near East. Thence it spread to other parts of the Old World. So it must have been domesticated before c.6200 BC.(van Zeist & Bakker-Heeres, 1975).

L. bienne can be divided into two main geographic races. The first is the continental winter annual of the semi-arid foothills of Iraqi Kurdistan and Iran. It might be the parent of the prostrate multi-stemmed type cultivated since ancient times along the N.coast of Turkey, the Caspian coast of Azerbaijan and some parts of Colchis bordering the Black Sea. According to Helbaek (1956), this type is the ancestor of the small-seeded flax cultivated by the prehistoric C. European pile-dwellers. The latter is the parent of 'Winterlein', a winter annual cultivated in mountainous S. Germany.

The second is the Atlantic-Mediterranean coastland race, a perennial, also described as L. angustifolium Huds. (2n=30). It has the highest seed oil content and the highest seed weight of all wild species (Seetharam, 1972).

During domestication and furter development, types for fibre (flax) and oil (linseed) developed.

Malvaceae

ALTHAEA OFFICINALIS*

ALTHAEA ROSAE*

GOSSYPIUM AREYSIANUM Deflers. 2n=26, genome formula E_3E_3. S. Arabia. It is drought-resistant and early maturing.

GOSSYPIUM HERBACEUM L. Short-staple cotton. 2n=26, genome formula A_1A_1. S. Africa (p. 139). Introduced to Ethiopia, S. Arabia and Baluchistan, where race acerifolium* developed. In Iran, a characteristic group of annual forms has arisen, named race persicum. It spread to W. India, where it was the first annual cotton cultivated. Varieties of G. herbaceum are now often cultivated. In C. Asia, race kuljianum developed. It matures in three months from sowing, giving a small crop.

GOSSYPIUM INCANUM (Schwartz) Hillcoat. 2n=26, genome formula E4E4. S. Yemen. It is drought-resistant.

GOSSYPIUM STOCKSII*

Moraceae

FICUS CARICA L. Common fig. 2n=26. Probably S. Asia. Primary gene centre in SE. Asia. Spread to Asia Minor, Mediterranean countries and W. Europe (Storey & Condit, 1969). Long cultivated. In 4000 BC., figs were already cultivated in Egypt. In Transcaucasia, Crimea, C. Asia, Baluchistan and the Mediterranean countries, it ran wild a long time ago.

Aweke (1979) suggests that Ethiopia or at least Africa might be the area of origin of the fig and that F. palmata* is its ancestor. Var. transcaspica from the Kopet Dagh of Turkmenia is a source of frost resistance.

FICUS SYCOMORUS L. Sycomore fig. 2n=26. Its distribution is given on p. 116. Galil et al. (1976) suggested that the sycomore was domesticated in the Middle East where man was forced to propagate the tree vegetatively because of the lack of the specific pollinator.

Nelumbonaceae

NELUMBO NUCIFERA Gaertn. Indian lotus. 2n=16. Centre of diversity probably lies in N. Iran, the Kura Estuary in Transcaucasia and Volga Delta. Cultivated in China, Japan and elsewhere for its rhizomes and fruits. Formerly it was also grown in the E. Mediterranean Region

(Hjelmquist, 1972).

Papaveraceae

PAPAVER SOMNIFERUM*

Polygonaceae

FAGOPYRUM ESCULENTUM Moench. (syn. F. vulgare T. Nees, F. sagittatum Gilib., Polygonum fagopyrum L.). Buckwheat, Silverhull. 2n=16, 32. C. Asia. Introduced into several countries as a grain crop. It is often found as a ruderal. It is insect-pollinated.

Punicaceae

PUNICA GRANATUM L. Pomegranate. 2n=16, 18, 19. Wild in the Near East and C. Asia. An ancient fruit-tree, which was even cultivated in the Hanging Gardens of Babylon. Cultivated now in many countries. The only related species is P. protopunica Ralf. found wild on Socotra in the Indian Ocean.

Resedaceae

RESEDA PHYTEUMA*

Rosaceae

AMYGDALUS BESSERIANA*

AMYGDALUS COMMUNIS L. (syn. Prunus amygdalus Batsch.). Almond. 2n=16. Primary gene centres in C. Asia (p. 84) and in the Near Eastern Region.

AMYGDALUS FENZLIANA (Fritsch) Lipsky (syn. A. divaricata Fenzl., A. urartu S. Tam., Prunus fenzliana Fritsch.). Fenzel almond. 2n=16. S. Transcaucasia and Anatolia. An ornamental. It easily crosses with A. communis* and it might be a source of cold and drought resistance for that species.

AMYGDALUS PERSICA L. Peach. 2n=16. Primary centre in China (p. 42). Secondary centre in Caucasia and Crimea.

ARMENIACA VULGARIS L. Apricot. 2n=16. Primary centres in NE. China (p. 42) and in Daghestan on the slopes of the Khunzakh Plateau at an altitude of 1200-1800 m. The latter centre probably formerly linked with the main one (p. 42). The tree has a shrubby habit. Cultivated over the entire Near East.

CYDONIA OBLONGA Mill. Quince. 2n=34. Talysh Mountain Range (S. Daghestan), the Ior Valleys and Azalan (Georgia), in the Terter Valley (Soviet Azerbaijan) and in the canyons of Aidero and Yuz-Begi, Kopet Dagh (USSR). Primary centre lies there. Long cultivated.

MALUS ORIENTALIS Uglits. 2n=   . This is the only wild Malus species in the especially

sparse oak forest of Caucasia. It is polymorphous. Through introgression, characteristics such as tallness, late ripening, good transportability of fruits, high sugar content and, unfortunately, low hardiness entered the cultivated apple (Malus pumila Mill.), as can still be recognized in Caucasian, Crimean and even Italian cultivars.

MALUS PRUNIFOLIA (Willd.) Borkh. (syn. Pyrus prunifolia Willd.). Chinese apple. 2n=34, 51, 68. Primary centre in N. China. Cultivated in E. Asia for its fruits. In the USSR, this species is represented in wild forms in E. Siberia. It is highly resistant to frost and drought, much used by I.V. Michurin to breed hybrid varieties such as Kandil Kitaika   (Kitaika = Chinese), Bellefleur Kitaika, Saffran Peppin, Saffran Kitaika.

Malus prunifolia

MALUS PUMILA*

MALUS TURKMENORUM Juz. & M. Pop. 2n=   . Turkmenia, in the gorges of the Kopet Dagh. Primary gene centre also there. The cultivated form is known in Russian as 'Baba-arabka' (old arab woman). This name refers to the dying-down of the main stem at an age of about 20 years and its replacement by soboles permanently rejuvenating the tree.

MESPILUS GERMANICA L. Medlar. 2n=34. Caucasia, N. Iran and Asia Minor. Cultivated elsewhere and run wild there. It crosses with Crataegus oxyacantha* and Sorbus aucuparia*.

PRUNUS AVIUM L. (syn. Cerasus avium Moench.). Sweet cherry, Mazzard. 2n=16, (24, 32). Primary centre in Asia Minor and Transcaucasia. Wild trees also in other parts of Europe, W. Asia and N. Africa. The wild trees of Ukrainia could be grouped into four classes: 1. dark-coloured fruit: a. bitter and b. sweet and 2. light-coloured fruit: c. bitter and d. sweet. The sweetfruited types had elongate stones and longer fruit-stalks and petioles than the bitter-fruited types (M'yakushko & M'yakushko, 1970). It is likely that man selected the sweet-fruited types.

Rjadnova (1967) suggested that domestication occurred in various places. This resulted in several ecotypes differing, for instance, in resistance to unfavourable conditions and qual-ity of fruit. Constant selection resulted in large-fruited hardy types.

P. avium is one of the parents of P. cerasus*. Hybrids with P. cerasus (P. x gondounii (Poi-teau & Turpin) Rehder are known in W.Europe as 'Duke' cherries. These hybrids and P. cerasus are sources of resistance to bacterial canker caused by Pseudomonas syringae Van Hall.

PRUNUS CERASIFERA Ehrh. (syn. P. divaricata Led.). Cherry plum, Myrobalan. 2n=16, genome formula CC, (24, 32, 48). Wild in Caucasia, Iran, Asia Minor, Altai and C. Asia. Primary centre C. and S. Caucasian coast of the Black Sea, whence it spread eastwards and westwards. Secondary centre in W. Tien-Shan (p. 85). It is highly polymorphic.

This species is one of the parents of P. do-mestica*. It is also planted as a rootstock and in hedges. Var. pissardii (Carrière) L.H. Bailey has dark red leaves and flowers tinged with reddish pink. It is an ornamental.

PRUNUS CERASUS L. (syn. Cerasus vulgaris Mill.). Sour cherry, Pie cherry. 2n=32. Unknown wild, although trees that have run wild grow mainly in Caucasia and Asia Minor, but also in the European USSR, W. Balkan countries and Germany. Probably an allotetraploid of P. fruticosa* x P. avium*. Sour cherry can be divided into the true Sour cherries and 'Duke' cherries. The first can be subdivided into Morellos (austera L.) and Amarelles (caproniana L.) (Zylka, 1971a).

A special population 'Vladimir cherry' ori-ginated in Region 9 (p. 160).

PRUNUS DOMESTICA L. Garden plum, Domestic plum. 2n=48, genome formula CCSSSS or $CdCdSSS_1S_1$ or $CdCdD_1D_1D_2D_2$. Caucasia. This species is thought to be a natural hexaploid of P. cerasifera* and P. spinosa*. This alloploidization apparently took place in Caucasia, where both species oc-cur and natural hybrids with 2n=24 and 48 are still found. However it may have happened else-where. For instance Werneck (1958) considered the garden plum to have arisen in Upper Austria (p. 160).

Rybin (1936) resynthesized the garden plum. Artificial hexaploids resembled the natural ones.

PRUNUS SPINOSA L. Blackthorn, Sloe. 2n=32, ge-nome formula SSSS of SSS_1S_1 or SSC_sC_s. Wild throughout the entire territory of this centre and in Europe and N. Africa. Volga Basin types carry genes for high hardiness. It is one of the parents of P. domestica*. Some natural hybrids with P. domestica are described as P. fruticans Weihe (2n=40).

PYRUS. The Near East is the main geographic centre of origin of Pyrus species. Of about 60 Pyrus species in the world, about 25 have been described for Caucasia. Some of them also occur in Iran or in Asia Minor.

PYRUS CAUCASICA Fed. 2n= . The entire forest zone of Caucasia except the Talysh Mountain Range (Soviet Azerbaijan). A polymorphic spe-cies. In open areas, it spreads quickly and vigourously.

PYRUS SYRIACA Boiss. 2n= . Armenia. It is cold-resistant and probably played a part in the origin of the cultivated pear (Evreinov, 1944). Cultivated locally.

PYRUS TAKHTADZHIANA Fed. 2n= . Habit of a cultivated tree. Cultivated in ancient times but later ran wild.

ROSA CENTIFOLIA L. (syn. R. gallica L. var. centifolia Reg.). Provence rose. 2n=28, E. Caucasia. Cultivated for its flowers. The pe-tals are used in the perfume industry.

SORBUS DOMESTICA L. Service tree. 2n=34. Its distribution is given on p. 161. Large-fruited forms are found in forests of Crimea.

Rubiaceae

COFFEA ARABICA L. Arabica coffee. 2n=22, 44, (66). The primary centre in SW. Ethiopia. Se-condary centre in Yemen. This area is the source of Arabica coffee now cultivated in Latin America, Kenya, India, Java and else-where (Meyer, 1965).

Rutaceae

CITRUS MEDICA L. Citron. 2n=18. Probably SW. Asia. although India has often been mentioned as centre of origin. Unknown wild. It has now spread through the (sub)tropics.

The Etrog citron (var. ethrog Engl.) is used by Jews at the Feast of Tabernacles, and the fingered citron (var. sarcodactylis Noot.) Swing) by the Chinese as a medicine and an or-namental.

Umbelliferae

CUMINUM CYMINUM*

DAUCUS CAROTA L. Carrot. 2n=18. For origin see p. 86. By hybridization between the 'Eastern' and 'Western' carrots in Turkey, a secondary centre of diversity has developed there.

MALABAILA SECACUL (Mill.) Boiss. Sekakul. 2n=
. Asia Minor and Syria. Cultivated for its
roots, used as a aphrodisiac.

PIMPINELLA ANISUM L. (syn. Anisum vulgare
Gaertn., Anisum officinarum Moench). Anise
plant. 2n=18, 20. Probably the Orient. Cultivated for aromatic fruits.

Valerianaceae

VALERIANA PHU L. 2n=   . N. Anatolia. Cultivated for its rhizome, which yields the drug
valerian.

Vitidaceae

VITIS LABRUSCA L. Fox grape. 2n=38. N. America
(p. 206). Introduced into W. Georgia (USSR) as
a cultivated grape.

VITIS VINIFERA L. Common grape, European grape.
2n=38, (40, 57, 76). Primary centres: the
Central Asian (p. 86), the Near Eastern and
the Mediterranean Regions (p. 119). The wild
vine, ssp. sylvestris Gmel., is found in regions bordering the Mediterranean Sea, except
Libya and Egypt, up to Turkestan and Kashmir.
Primary centre: probably Armenia (USSR) and
N. Iran. The western wild types have been
called ssp. silvestris, and the eastern types
ssp. caucasia Vav. The wild type is dioecious
and the domesticated type (ssp. sativa DC,
ssp. vinifera) is hermaphrodite derived from
the male wild plants.
    The vine may have been domesticated in SE.
Europe where types with large bunches, and
seedless grapes have developed. Natural hybrids
are still forming in several areas, e.g. the
mountains of S. Tajikistan (USSR), where many
new forms are observed. From crosses between
the wild grape and cultivated types in Europe,
old and new cultivars developed.
    The common grape has been crossed with the
North American V. labrusca*. The fruits are
used to prepare wine, currants and raisins.
    V. amurensis* is a possible source of hardi-
ness.

7 Mediterranean Region

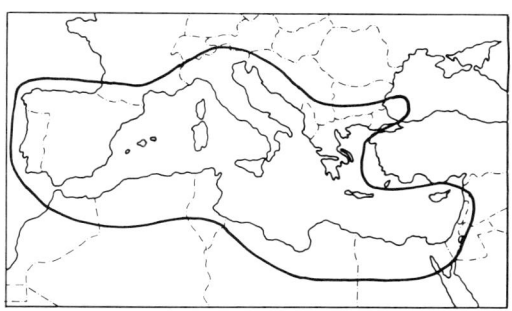

The Mediterranean Region was described by Vavilov. Darlington (1956) suggested the name Mediterranean Region of Origin.

Its situation near the Cradle of Agriculture in the Near East led to an early introduction of plant cultivation. Early farming sites have been found at Nea Nikomedeia in Greece dating c.5470 BC. (van Zeist & Bottema, 1971) and at Fayum in Egypt dating from the 5th Millenium, reaching the coast of the Atlantic perhaps c. 3rd Millenium. A very old site at Kom Ombo in the Nile Valley of Upper Egypt dated from 15 000-10 500 BC. It is a non-farming site occupied the whole year round (Churcher & Smith, 1972).

Many crops have been domesticated in the region including Avena sp., Beta vulgaris, Brassica napus, B. oleracea, Lathyrus sp., Linum usitatissimum, Lolium sp., Lupinus sp., Olea europaea, Raphanus sativus, Trifolium sp. and Vitis vinifera.

Alliaceae

ALLIUM CEPA L; Spanish onion. 2n=16. See p. 81. Secondary centre in the Mediterranean Region.

ALLIUM SATIVUM L. Garlic. 2n=16, genome formula SS. C. Asia (p. 81). Secondary centre in the Mediterranean Region (Kazakova, 1971).

Amaranthaceae

AMARANTHUS LIVIDUS L. 2n=34. Spread through Europe, Asia and to the tropics of the Old and New World. Var. ascendens Thell. (syn. A. viridis L., 2n=34) is native to S. Europe and E. Mediterranean Region. Cultivated there in the Middle Ages. Var. lividus is unknown wild. It might be a cultigen of this species. It was cultivated in the 16th and 17th Centuries as a vegetable and medicinal crop and in the 18th Century as pig food.

Var. oleraceus Thell. (syn. A. oleraceus L., 2n=) is probably a cultigen of var. ascendens. Cultivated in Europe and elsewhere as a vegetable (Mansfeld, 1959).

Amaryllidaceae

NARCISSUS JONQUILLA L. Jonquille. 2n=14. Europe, Ante-Asia to Iran and Algeria. Commonly cultivated as an ornamental and in S. France for its essential oil.

NARCISSUS POETICUS L. Poet's narcissus. 2n=14, 21. Portugal, Spain, France and Italy. Cultivated as an ornamental and in S. France for its essential oil.

Anacardiaceae

RHUS CORIARIA L. Sicilian sumach. 2n= . Mediterranean area. A shrub cultivated in Sicily and S. Italy for the leaves, which are a source of tanning material.

Apocynaceae

NERIUM OLEANDER L. Oleander. 2n=16, 22. A shrub of Mediterranean area. Cultivated as an ornamental.

Asclepiadiaceae

CYNANCHUM VINCETOXICUM*

Balanitaceae

BALANITES AEGYPTIACA Del. Betu, Desert date. 2n=16, 18. This shrub grows wild in Arabia, Palestine, N. Trop. Africa and Angola. Cultivated in Egypt for its edible leaves and flowers (Cufodontis, 1957; Terra, 1967).

Boraginaceae

ALKANNA TINCTORIA (L.) Tausch. Alkanna. 2n=
14. S. and E. Europe and Turkey. A herb cultivated as a source of a red pigment.

BORAGO OFFICINALIS L. Borage. 2n=16. Mediterranean Region. A herb cultivated as an ornamental, as a pot-herb and for bees.

Capparidaceae

CAPPARIS SPINOSA L. Caper bush. 2n=24, 38. The
cultivated forms with large flower-head, var.
spinosa, and small flower-head, var. parviflora
J. Grey probably derived from the wild var.
aegyptia (Lam.) Boiss. This variety grows wild
in S. and SE. Mediterranean area to the Sudan
and Eritro-Arabia. Var. spinosa developed in
the N. Mediterranean Region, whence it spread
to other areas, where it is cultivated as a
condiment. Var. parviflora is also cultivated
and might be a mutant of var. spinosa. Hybrids
with C. ovata Desf. are found.

Caryophyllaceae

DIANTHUS CARYOPHYLLUS L. Carnation, Clove,
Pink, Picotee. 2n=30. Mediterranean Region. A
perennial herb cultivated as an ornamental and
also as a source of an essential oil.

GYPSOPHILA PANICULATA L. Baby's breath. 2n=
34. S. and C. Europe and Caucasia. Cultivated
formerly for its roots, which contain saponin.

Now it is an ornamental.

Chenopodiaceae

BETA PATELLARIS Moq. 2n=18, (36). Mediterranean and Atlantic coasts of NW. Africa, Canary
Islands, Cape Verde Islands and Madeira. A
source of resistance to nematodes and Cercospora and tolerance to yellow mosaic for B.
vulgaris*.

BETA PROCUMBENS Chr. 2n=18. Canary Islands and
Cape Verde Islands. A source of nematode resistance for B. vulgaris*.

BETA VULGARIS L. Beet. 2n=18, genome formula
VV. The parental form is the wild sea-beet
(ssp. maritima (L.) Thell., syn. B. maritima
L.). Primary centre probably in the E. part of
the Mediterranean Region. Spread in a westerly
direction along the Mediterranean, Atlantic
coast of Europe and to Cape Verde Islands and
Canary Islands. In the Mediterranean Region,
leaves and roots of the wild plant may have
been collected, perhaps leading to development
of Swiss chard and Spinach beet (var. cicla,
var. vulgaris), whose leaves and stalks are
eaten, and to garden beet, table beet and red
beet (var. cruenta, var. esculenta). Development may have been influenced by hybridization
with wild types like ssp. macrocarpa (syn. B.
macrocarpa Guss.) in N. Africa. In California,
such hybridization still continues (McFarlane,

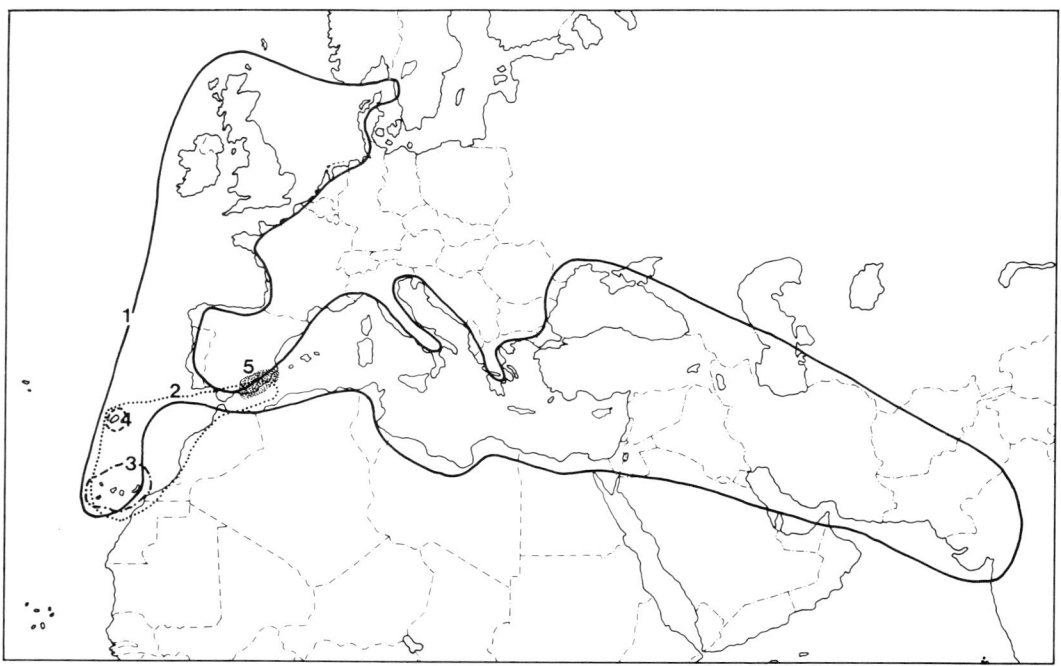

Beta vulgaris (1), B. patellaris (2), B. procumbens and B. webbiana (3), B. patula (4) and B.
atriplicifolia (5)(Ulbrich, 1934).

1975). The fodder beet (var. rapa) probably developed in the Netherlands (p. 149), after introduction of types from Spain, and the sugar -beet in Silesia (Poland) (p. 149). The wild B. macrocarpa Guss. from the coasts of the Mediterranean Region and Canary Islands, B. patula Ait. from Madeira and B. atriplicifolia Rouy from S. Spain easily hybridize with B. vulgaris, with which they may be included as subspecies.

In NW. Europe, hybrid plants of cultivated sugar-beet and ssp. maritima are occasionally observed. They derive from material propagated in France and Italy. Such hybrids bolt in the first year, producing seed. The seed drops and may result in a weed (F$_2$ plants) for several years. It is possible that, on a very small scale, wild genes derived from these hybrids introgress into the cultivated population.

The wild plants may form sources of resistance to disease such as Cercospora, yellow mosaic and increase the variation for selection of new high-yielding types.

BETA WEBBIANA Moq. 2n=18. Canary Islands. A source of nematode resistance for B. vulgaris*.

CHENOPODIUM AMBROSIOIDES L. American wormweed, Indian wormweed. 2n=16, 32, 36, 64. Probably S. Europe. Widespread in the tropics and introduced into N. America. The cultivated type, var. anthelminticus L. is a source of medicinal and essential oils.

HALOGETON SATIVUS (L.) Moq. 2n= . NW. Africa. Cultivated in the Mediterranean Region for the base-rich ash it yields when burned.

Compositae

ANACYCLUS OFFICINARUM Hayne. Bertram. 2n=18. Probably the Mediterranean Region. Formerly cultivated in C. Europe.

ANACYCLUS PYRETHRUM (L.) Link. Pellitoria of Spain. 2n=18. N. Africa, Arabia and Syria. Formerly cultivated in Europe as a medicinal plant and now in Algeria for an essential oil.

ARTEMISIA JUDAICA L. 2n= . Cultivated in the Mediterranean Region.

CALENDULA OFFICINALIS L. Marigold. 2n=(28), 32. Centre of origin probably in the Mediterranean Region. Cultivated as an ornamental, but formerly as a medicinal plant.

CICHORIUM ENDIVIA L. Endive, Escarolle. 2n=18. S. Europe to India. Cultivated as a vegetable.

CNICUS BENEDICTUS L. (syn. Centaurea benedicta L., Garberia benedicta Adans.). Blessed thistle. 2n=22. Mediterranean Region to Transcaucasia, Syria and Iran. Formerly cultivated in Germany.

CYNARA CARDUNCULUS L. (Wild) cardoon. 2n=34.

W. and C. Mediterranean area. Cultivated for its leaf stalks. Probably together with C. syriaca*, one of the parents of C. scolymus* (Zohary & Basnizky, 1975).

CYNARA SCOLYMUS L. Artichoke, Globe artichoke. 2n=34. Mediterranean area. Cultivated for soft fleshy edible receptacles of young flower heads and thick bases of the scales around the flower heads as well as for a source of a bitter compound. Several varieties are known. If it derives from C. syriaca* with introgression of C. cardunculus*, it originated in W. Mediterranean area; if it derives from C. cardunculus with introgression of C. syriaca, it originated in E. Mediterranean area (Zohary & Basnizky, 1975).

CYNARA SIBTHROPIANA Boiss. & Heldr. 2n= . Mainly on Aegean Islands, Crete and Cyprus. Related to C. cardunculus* and C. scolymus* (Zohary & Basnizky, 1975).

CYNARA SYRIACA Boiss. Wild Syrian artichoke. 2n= . Levant and S. Turkey. Probably one of the ancestors of C. scolymus*.

LACTUCA VIROSA L. Bitter lettuce, Lettuce opium. 2n=18. Primary centre round the Mediterranean (Lindqvist, 1960). Cultivated on a small scale in some parts of Europe for its latex, which has narcotic properties.

SCOLYMUS HISPANICUS L. Golden thistle, Spanish oyster plant. 2n=20. Mediterranean area. A root vegetable. Its cultivation is declining.

SCORZONERA HISPANICA L. Scorzonera, Black salsify. 2n=14. C. Europe, Mediterranean area, Caucasia and S. Siberia. A vegetable especially of S. Europe. Perhaps it was first cultivated in Spain (Mansfeld, 1959).

SILYBUM MARIANUM (L.) Gaertn. Holy thistle, Milk thistle, Lady's milk. 2n=34. S. Europe. Cultivated as a medicinal plant and as an ornamental.

TANACETUM CINERARIIFOLIUM (Trev.) Schultz Bip. (syn. Chrysanthemum cinerariifolium (Trev.) Brocc. Pyrethrum. 2n=18. Dalmatian coast including Yugoslavia and Albania. Introduced into many countries. Kenya is the main producer of the insecticide pyrethrin.

TANACETUM PARTHENIUM (L.) Schultz Bip. (syn. Chrysanthemum parthenium (L.) Bernh., Leucanthemum parthenium (L.) Gren. & Godron, Pyrethrum parthenium (L.) Sm) Feverfew, Wild camomile. 2n=18. Mediterranean area, Balkan, Asia Minor and Caucasia. Cultivated as medicinal plant and as an ornamental.

TRAGOPOGON PORRIFOLIUS L. Salsify, Oyster plant, Purple goats beard. 2n=12. Mediterranean Region. This vegetable was first cultivated for its roots long ago. It may have been domesticated by the Greeks and Romans (Mans-feld, 1959). The wild types belong to ssp. australis (Jordan) Nyman of the Mediterranean area to E. Rumania and ssp. cupani (Guss. ex DC.) I.B.K. Richardson of S. Italy and Sicily. The cultivated types belong to ssp. porrifolius (incl. ssp. sativus (Gaterau) Braun-Blanquet) (Tutin et al., 1976).

Convolvulaceae

CONVOLVULUS SCAMMONIA L. 2n=24. Mediterranean Region and Asia Minor. Cultivated for medicinal purposes.

Corylaceae

CORYLUS TUBULOSA Willd. Lambert's filbert, Kentish cob. 2n=   . Cultivated. Hybrids with C. avellana* have been cultivated.

Cruciferae

BRASSICA CAMPESTRIS*

BRASSICA NAPOBRASSICA (L.) Mill. Swede, Rutabaga, Swedish turnip. 2n=38. Secondary gene centre in Europe. The cultigen developed in the Mediterranean Region and further into Europe (p. 151).

BRASSICA NAPUS L. Rape, Colza. 2n=38, genome formula AACC. This species is an amphiploid of B. oleracea ssp. oleracea (2n=18, genome formula CC, see p. 106) and B. campestris (2n= 20, genome formula AA, see p. 151). The first amphiploid was the "primitive leaf-rape" (ssp. pabularia (DC.) Jancken). This primitive type may have developed in the W. Mediterranean Region. From it, cultivated types like ssp. oleifera DC., rape, and ssp. rapifera Metzger derive. B. napobrassica , formerly described as B. napus var. napobrassica (L.) Reichenb., is probably a derivative of B. oleracea* x B. napus. The wild var. napus may be the weedy derivative. B. napus is one of the parents of the artificially made B. napocampestris (2n= 58, genome formula $AAA_1A_1C_1C_1$).

BRASSICA OLERACEA L. s. lato. Cole. 2n=18, genome formula CC; the C genome is related to the T or D genome of B. tournefortii Gouan, 2n=20; it is the donor of the C genome of B. carinata* and B. napus*. Mediterranean area and Atlantic Fringe of Europe.
   The taxonomy is complicated and was recently dealth with by Snogerup (1979; 1980). He prefers to reserve the name B. oleracea s.str. for the wild kale of the Atlantic coast of Europe. However if so, the name cannot be used for cultivated cole crops, as they derive from wild kales from the Mediterranean area. The name B. oleracea L. is used here as a synonum of Snogerup's B. oleracea group, including:
1. B. cretica Lam., 2n=18, Aegean area, SW. Turkey and S. Greece, where it may have been introduced. Also introduced into Lebanon. The yellow-flowered type is ssp. cretica and the white-flowered type ssp. nivea (Boiss. & Sor.) Onno. This species may have played a role in the origin of B. oleracea var. botrytis. It is suggested that material was introduced into China, where it developed into 'B. alboglabra' (p. 35 under B. oleracea).
2. B. hilarionis Holmb., 2n=18, Cyprus.
3. B. insularis Moris., 2n=18, four relic populations on Corsica and 13 on Sardinia (Widler & Bocquet, 1979); also found in Tunisia (Snogerup, 1979). A species usually with white flowers; the yellow-flowered type is var. ayliesii Litard. & Simon. The species includes B. atlantica (Coss.) O.E. Schultz.
4. B. macrocarpa Guss., 2n=18, Isole Egadi (W. Sicily).
5. B. montana Pourr., 2n=18, S. France, N. Italy and probably NE. Spain. Synonymous with B. robertiana Gay.
6. B. oleracea L. s.str.
7. B. rupestris(-incana) complex, 2n=18, Sicily, W. to C. Italy, W. Yugoslavia and Crimea. To this complex belong B. botteri Vis., B. cassae Ginzb. & Teyb., B. drepaneus (Car.) Dam., B. incana Ten., B. mollis Vis., B. rupestris Rafin., B. linei Lojac. and B. villosa Biv. Some species may have played a role in the origin of the cultivated types of B. oleracea. Some primitive cultivars are cultivated in Yugoslavia.
   The types of Crimea are probably derived from old introductions.

   B. balearica Pers., 2n=18, B. scopulorum Coss., 2n=18, and B. spinescens Pomel., 2n=18, are not related to B. oleracea (Snogerup, 1979).
   There are several classifications of the cultivated B. oleracea types, e.g. Helm (1963a). The origin of these types is not yet fully understood and it is supposed that they developed gradually from several wild cabbage populations by introgression with wild species and other cultivated types, and by mutation with human selection. A simplified pedigree is presented by Helm (1963a). He suggested that from the wild cabbage (var. sylvestris, syn. var. oleracea) developed var. ramosa DC. (cottager's kale), convar. acephala (DC.) Alef., var. medullosa Thell. and convar. botrytis (L.) Alef. Cottager's kale was used as fodder. It has almost disappeared now. From it, var. gemmifera DC. (Brussels sprouts) derived, perhaps in Belgium (p. 151). From the Brussels sprouts, monstrosities such as var. dalechampii Helm derived. However, Nieuwhof (1969) suggested that the monstrosity pictured by Dalechamp (Helm, 1963a) is a cabbage with the axillary buds developed after the head had been removed.
   Convar. acephala can be subdivided into many types:
   var. acephala (kale, borecole, collard, cow cabbage). This cabbage type belongs to the oldest cultivated types. The main use is as a fodder. On Jersey and Guernsey, f. exaltata (Caesarean cabbage, Jersey cabbage) was cultivated. When closely planted, the branches and

stalks can be used as walking sticks (Jersey canes) and in house building. Other varieties belong to this group. These are var. selenisia L., var. sabellica L., var. palmifolia DC., var. medullosa Thell. and var. gongylodes L.

var. selenisia. Parsley colewort, Ornamental kale. Used as an ornamental.

var. sabellica. Curled kitchen kale, Ornamental Scotch kale, Curlies, f. sabellica mostly cultivated as a vegetable and f. rubra used as an ornamental.

var. palmifolia. Palm-leaved kale. Probably originated in Portugal. It is probably used only as an ornamental.

var. medullosa. Marrow-stem kale. Fodder crop. Pliny's Pompeian cabbage is an ancestor of this type. From that type or from marrow-stem kale, var. gongylodes (Kohlrabi, Turnip kale) derives.

From the old cultivars of convar. acephala, convar. capitata (L.) Alef. developed. The oldest type is probably var. costata DC. (Tronchuda kale, Portugese kale), which developed in Portugal and gave rise to var. sabauda and var. capitata.

Var. sabauda L. Savoy cabbage, Savoy, Milan cabbage. Probably developed in Italy.

Var. capitata L. Cabbage and Red cabbage. Developed from the same stock as var. sabauda. Their history is not known.

Convar. botrytis consists of var. italica Plenck (Sprouting broccoli, Asparagus broccoli) and var. botrytis L. (Cauliflower), which may have derived from var. italica. Both types developed in the E. Mediterranean area. B. cretica* perhaps played a role (Jensma, 1957).

Jensma suggested that from Cyprus and elsewhere in the E. Mediterranean the cauliflower was brought to Venice and to Vienna, whence it spread to NW. Europe.

CAPSELLA BURSA-PASTORIS (L.) Medik. Shepherd's purse, Capsell. 2n=32. Mediterranean area. Spread over almost the whole world. Cultivated in China as a vegetable.

CHEIRANTHUS CHEIRI L. Wallflower. 2n=14. S. and C. Europe. Herb commonly cultivated as an ornamental, formerly as a medicinal crop.

CRAMBE HISPANICA L. 2n=60. Mediterranean area. Cultivated in the Ukraine for its oil.

ERUCA VESICARIA (L.) Cav. (syn. E. sativa L.). Rocket salad, Roquette. 2n=22. Mediterranean area and Asia. Cultivated since ancient times as a salad plant and in India as a source of jamba oil (p. 72).

LEPIDIUM LATIFOLIUM L. Dittander. 2n=24. Europe, Temp. Asia and N. Africa. A perennial herb. The Ancient Greeks once cultivated it as a salad plant.

RAPHANUS SATIVUS L. Radish, Small radish. 2n= 18, genome formula RR. Primary centre probably E. Mediterranean Region, according to Wein (1964). He suggested that the radish is derived from R. maritimus Smith (2n=18). He stated that the radish could not derive from R. raphanistrum L.* (2n=18) because of the difference in structure of the fruits. Various vari-

Wild and weedy Raphanus species: R. raphanistrum (——), R. maritimus (black) and R. landra (grey) (Sinskaia, 1931).

eties have been described (Mansfeld, 1959):
var. oleiformis Pers. (R. chinensis Mill.) is
the oil-seed radish cultivated in India, Japan,
China (p. 35) and on a small scale in Rumania
and Spain; var. mougri Helm* (syn. R. caudatus
L.); var. sativus, the radish, small radish;
var. niger Kerner, radish, Spanish radish. Recently fodder radish has been bred. It is a re-
puted selection from oil-seed radish in France.
More research is needed to ascertain the origin of radish and the various botanic varieties
and cultivars. Through natural (and artificial)
hybridization with Brassica spp., genes may
introgress into R. sativus.

SINAPIS ALBA L. (syn.Brassica alba (L.)Boiss.).
White mustard. 2n=24, Mediterranean area. The
wild plant is low-growing and much-branched,
with siliquae containing browny black seeds
(melanosperma) (Hemingway, 1976). Weedy or naturalized plants may be found from Spain
through Asia Minor to E. India. Young seedlings are used as salad. Seeds are the source
of white mustard.

Cucurbitaceae

BRYONIA CRETICA*

CITRULLUS COLOCYNTHIS (L.) Schrad. Colocynth.
2n=22, (34). Arid regions of N. Africa and
Trop. Asia. Cultivated in India and the Mediterranean area for its purgative fruits.

ECBALLIUM ELATERIUM (L.) A. Rich. Squirting
cucumber. 2n=(18), 24. Mediterranean area,
Azores, Asia Minor and Crimea. Cultivated in
England as a medicinal plant.

Cyperaceae

CYPERUS ALOPECUROIDES Rottb. Mat sedge. 2n=
. Trop. Old World. Cultivated in Egypt for
mat-making (Mansfeld, 1959).

CYPERUS ESCULENTUS L. Chufa, Earth almond,
Tiger nut, Rush nut, Zulu nut, Yellow nutgrass.
2n=(18), 108. White Nile region and in the
tropics. Introduced to S. Europe by the Arabs.
Cultivated in Spain, Italy and elsewhere for
its flavoured tubers. The wild form is var.
aureus (Ten.) Richt. and the cultivated form
is var. esculentus.

CYPERUS PAPYRUS L. Papyrus plant. 2n=c.102.
Africa. Formerly cultivated in Egypt, Palestine and the Mediterranean Area. Now rarely
cultivated. It could probably remedy and pre-
vent eutrophication of tropical lakes by nu-
trient extraction. 'More active' extractor
genotypes could perhaps be obtained by breeding.

Ericaceae

ARBUTUS UNEDO L. Strawberry tree, Arbutus. 2n=
26. Mediterranean Region. Occasionally cultivated for its edible fruits.

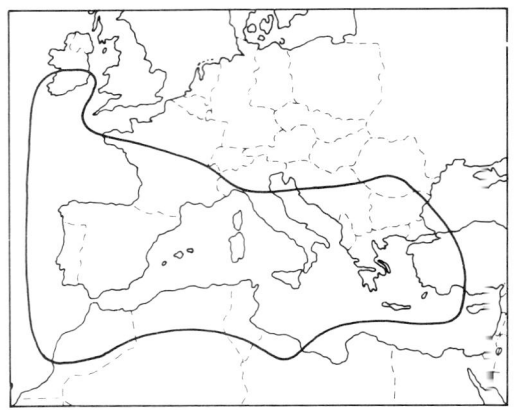

Arbutus unedo (Hutchinson, 1969).

Euphorbiaceae

CHROZOPHORA TINCTORIA (L.) Juss. Giradol. Mediterranean Region, France, Yugoslavia, Crimea to W. Asia, NW. India, Arabia. Formerly
cultivated in S. France as a source of red and
blue dye. The red dye was used for colouring
Dutch cheeses.

EUPHORBIA LATHYRUS L. 2n=20. S., W. and C.
Europe. A ruderal and weedy plant occasionally
cultivated as a medicinal. Probably only native to E. and C. Mediterranean Region.

Fagaceae

QUERCUS SUBER L. Cork oak. 2n=24. W. Mediterranean Area. A very variable species. Cultivated in S. France, Portugal, Spain, Sardinia,
Corsica, Istria, Dalmatia and Algeria.

Geraniaceae

ERODIUM CICUTARIUM (L.) L'Herit. ex Ait. Storksbill, Red-stem filaree, Alfilaree. 2n=(20, 3-
40, 36), 40, (48, 54). S., W. and C. Europe,
Mediterranean area, Temp. Asia. Cultivated as
fodder for sheep in N. and S. America.

ERODIUM MOSCHATUM (L.) L'Herit. ex Ait. Musk
storksbill, White-stem filaree. 2n=20. Mediterranean Region. Formerly cultivated as a
medicinal crop.

Gramineae

AEGILOPS BICORNIS (Forsk.) Jaub. & Sp. (syn.
Triticum bicorne Forsk.). 2n=14, genome formula S^bS^b. Xeric sandy soils of S. Israel,
Lower Egypt and Cyrenaica (Libya). It is sometimes believed to be the B donor of tetraploid
and hexaploid Triticum spp. (p. 93).

AEGILOPS COMOSA Sibth. & Sm. (syn. Triticum
comosum (Sibth. & Sm.) Richter). 2n=14, ge-

nome formula MM. Mediterranean Greece, the Aegean Islands and W. Turkey. Used as a source of resistance to yellow rust (Puccinia strii- formis West.).

AEGILOPS CYLINDRICA*

AEGILOPS KOTSCHYI*

AEGILOPS LORENTII*

AEGILOPS OVATA*

AEGILOPS TRIARISTATA*

AEGILOPS TRIUNCIALIS*

AEGILOPS UNIARISTATA Vis. (syn. Triticum uni- aristatum (Vis.) Richter). 2n=14, genome for- mula $M^u M^u_1$ The Mediterranean Greece, around the Sea of Marmara and the Adriatic coast of Yugo- slavia.

AEGILOPS VARIABILIS Eig. (syn. Ae. peregrina (Hack.) Maire & Weill., Triticum peregrinum Hack & Fraser). 2n=28, genome formula $C^u C^u S^v S^v$. N. Africa, Egypt, Palestine, Greek Islands, Turkey and Iraq. Probably identical with Ae. kotschyi*.

AEGILOPS VENTRICOSA Tausch. (syn. Triticum ventricosum Ces., Pass. & Gib.). 2n=28, ge- nome formula $M^v M^v DD$. W. Mediterranean Area. It is a source of resistance to the wheat di- sease eyespot caused by Cercosporella herpo- tricoides Fron. Natural hybrids with Triticum turgidum group durum have been found and de- scribed as Triticum rodeti Trabut. Amphiploids with tetraploid Triticum species have been named Aegilotricum.

AGROPYRON JUNCEUM (Jusl.) Beauv. Sea wheat- grass, Bent grass. 2n=28, 42, (84). Coasts of Europe, N. Africa and Asia Minor. Occasionally cultivated to stabilize dunes.

AGROSTIS TENUIS*

ARUNDO DONAX L. Giant reed. 2n=(c.60), 110. Mediterranean area to Caucasia and Syria. A grass cultivated since ancient times in S. Europe. Also cultivated elsewhere now.

AVENA CANARIENSIS Baum, Rajhathy & Sampson. 20=14, genome formula AcAc. Uplands of Fuerte- ventura, Canary Islands. It is the donor of the A genome of the evolutionary complex of maroc- cana*, A. murphyi* and A. sterilis* (Craig et al., 1974; Leggett, 1980).

AVENA CLAUDA Dur. 2n=14. The whole Mediterra- nean Basin from Morocco, eastwards. It usually grows together with A. sativa type sterilis* and A. strigosa type barbata* (Ladizinsky & Zohary, 1971). This wild species includes type eriantha (syn. A. eriantha Dur., A. pilosa MB; genome formula CpCp) and type clauda (A.

clauda Dur.).

AVENA DAMASCENA Rajhathy & Baum. 2n=14, ge- nome formula AdAd. An area 60 km north of Da- mascus, Syria. It has a high degree of genome homology with A. prostrata*. Both species are considered relics of a once common population, but are now separated by some 2500 km (Raj- hathy & Baum, 1972). Cahana & Ladizinsky (1978) consider A. damascena to derive from A. pros- trata*. It resembles A. strigosa*.

AVENA LONGIGLUMIS Dur. 2n=14, genome formula AlAl. The coastal fringe of Mediterranean coun- tries and Morocco, Portugal and Spain. Medi- terranean and Negev desert ecogeographic races have been recognized (Ladizinsky & Zohary, 1971). It derives from A. prostrata* (Cahana & Ladizinsky, 1978).

AVENA MAROCCANA Gandog (syn. A. magna Murphy & Terrell). 2n=28, genome formula AACC. Moroc- co. Probably not an ancestor of A. sativa* (Leggett, 1980). An annual belonging to the A. maroccana (magna)-A. murphyi*-A. sterilis com- plex. It is often confused with A. sterilis.

AVENA MURPHYI Ladizinsky. 2n=28, genome formu- la AACC. Between Tarifa and Vejer de la Fron- tera, S. Spain. Probably not an ancestor of A. sativa* (Leggett, 1980). It belongs to the A. maroccana* (magna)-A. murphyi-A. sterilis* complex.

AVENA PROSTRATA Ladizinsky. 2n=14, genome for- mula ApAp. SE. Spain. Parental genome donor of A. longiglumis* and A. damascena* (Cahana & Ladizinsky, 1978). It is not the ancestor of the A. maroccana*-A. murphyi* complex (Leg- gett, 1980).

AVENA SATIVA L. Oat. 2n=42, genome formula AACCDD. Two species of hexaploid oats are commonly recognized: A. sativa, characterized by florets that separate by fracturing of the rachilla, leaving a section of rachilla at- tached to each floret after threshing; and A. byzanthina C. Koch in which the basal floret leaves an abscission scar on threshing. It is widely held that these two complexes were in- dependently domesticated (Bell, 1965) but a monophyletic origin of oats is equally likely (Coffman, 1946), as becomes obvious if A. sterilis is accepted as the wild progenitor of domesticated oats. Florets of A. sterilis occur among remains of cultivated wheat and barley in agricultural settlements from Europe to China. In the northern extremes of wheat cul- tivation the better adapted weed was eventually adopted as a cultivated cereal. The cytoplasm comes from a diploid species with A genome (Steer & Thomas, 1976). The winter crop Dorm- oats is an oat with a deep dormancy deriving from A. septentrionalis* (A. fatua) x A. sa- tiva.

AVENA STERILIS L. (syn. A. athenathera Presl,

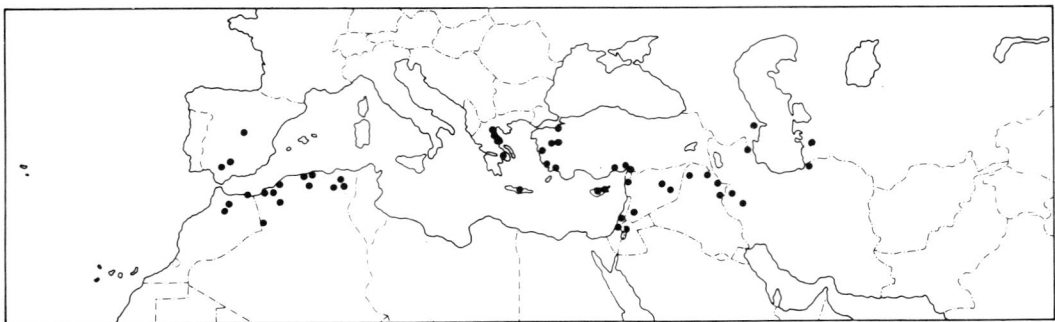

Avena clauda (Ladizinsky & Zohary, 1971).

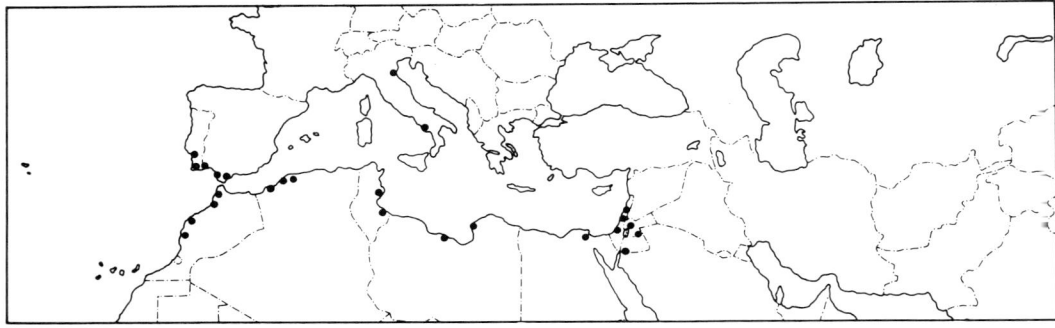

Avena longiglumis (Ladizinsky & Zohary, 1971).

A. trichophylla C. Koch), Wild oats. 2n=42.
Near East, Mediterranean Region of Europe and
North Africa. Wild oats is characterized by
dispersal units that disarticulate through
abscission callus below the basal floret of
each spikelet. Florets separate later by fracturing of rachilla segments.

It is often assumed that the mimetic weed
oats (A. fatua L., A. hybrida Petterm., A.
occidentalis Dur. as recognized by Baum, 1977)
are progenitors of domesticated oats. This is
unlikely. These weeds are characterized by
florets that disarticulate individually by
formation of abscission callus. Lack of a
mechanism for seed dispersal in domesticated
oats is genetically dominant over fatua-type
seed dispersal. A more likely explanation is
that the fatua-type dispersal evolved after
oats became domesticated.

AVENA STRIGOSA Schreb. Black oat, Bristle oat.
2n=14, genome formula AsAs, 2n=28, genome formula AsAsBB, AABB or AsAsAsAs. The As and B
genomes are partially homologous and may derive from a common parent (Ladizinsky & Zohary, 1971; Ladizinsky, 1973). The As genome
might be the prototype of the A genome of the
polyploid species (Rajhathy et al., 1971).
Ladizinsky & Zohary (1971) included in this

species the wild A. hirtula Lag. (2n=14), A
wiestii Schreb. (2n=14), A. barbata Pott. (2n=
28) and A. vaviloviana Malz.* (2n=28), and he
cultivated A. strigosa Schreb. (2n=14) and A.
abyssinica Hochst.* (2n=28). Leggett (1980)
gives the following genome formulas: A. hir-
tula-wiestii oat group AsAs and A. barbata
AABB.

All over the Mediterranean area, wild and
weedy diploid and tetraploid forms are found,
hybridizing freely. "A. hirtula" is common
in Spain, Morocco, Algeria, Italy, Greece,
Turkey and Israel. "A. wiestii" grows in the
drier steppe of the northern fringes of the
Sahara and the Arabian Desert. The cultivated
strigosa of W. and N. Europe derives from the
weedy forms common in cereal fields and edges
of cultivation in the Iberian peninsula. The
As and B genome are partially homologous and
may derive from a common parent (Ladizinsky
& Zohary, 1971). The As genome might be the
prototype of the A genome of the polyploid
species (Rajhathy et al., 1971).
Diploid and tetraploid cytotypes introgress
by means of triploids.

AVENA VENTRICOSA Balansa. 2n=14, genome formula CvCv. This wild species includes ssp.
bruhnsiana (Gruner) Malzew (syn. A. bruhnsiana

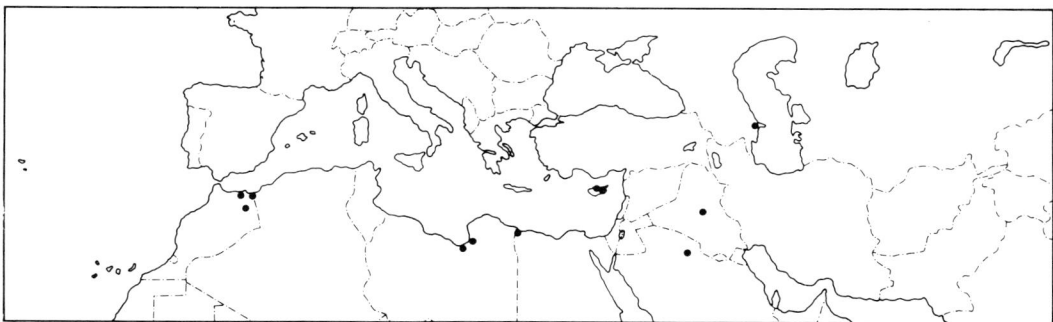

Avena ventricosa (Ladizinsky & Zohary, 1971).

Gruner) and ssp. ventricosa (Balansa) Malzew (syn. A. ventricosa Balansa s. str., genome formula AvAv).
Ssp. bruhnsiana is found in the Apsheron Peninsula of Soviet Azerbaijan and ssp. ventricosa in Algeria and Cyprus. The karyotype of ssp. ventricosa is $c_v{}^1$ and of ssp. bruhnsiana $c_v{}^3$ and $c_v{}^2$ (Rajhathy, 1971).
A. ventricosa is also found in Cyrenaica (Libya) and Iraq (Ladizinsky & Zohary, 1971).

CHRYSOPOGON GRYLLUS (Torner) Trin. (syn. Andropogon gryllus Torner). 2n=20, 40. Mediterranean area to India. Cultivated in the Po plain, Italy for its essential oil.

HORDEUM VULGARE L. 2n=14. For origin of barley see p. 91. The Mediterranean Region is the centre of origin of ssp. mediterraneum Vav. & Bacht.

LOLIUM MULTIFLORUM Lam. ssp. italicum (A.Br.) Volkart ex Schinz & Kell. Italian ryegrass. 2n=14. The irrigated lands of Lombardy in N. Italy. Probably cultivated there in the 13th or 14th Century (Beddows, 1953). Spread to N. Europe.

LOLIUM PERENNE*

PHALARIS CANARIENSIS L. Canary grass. 2n=12. W. Mediterranean area: Canary Islands, Spain, Portugal. Cultivated for birdseed.

PHALARIS TUBEROSA L. (syn. Ph. aquatica L.). Toowoomba grass, Harding grass. 2n=28. Mediterranean area. Cultivated in warm countries.

SORGHUM BICOLOR (L.) Moench. Broomcorn. 2n= 20. Sorghum originated in Africa (see p. 133). The broomcorns developed in the Mediterranean area from material that came from India/Iran or Africa through the Middle East.

SORGHUM HALEPENSE (L.) Pers. (syn. S. milia-ceum (Roxb.) Snowden, S. controversum (Steud.) Snowden). Johnson grass. 2n=40. Mediterranean area to Pakistan and S. India. This rhizoma-

Sorghum halepense.

tous perennial was introduced as a fodder to all warmer parts of the world. The leaves and stems contain HCN but make excellent hay. In the Americas, S. halepense has widely introgressed with grain sorghums (Celarier, 1958). Derivatives of such introgression are known as S. almum Parodi (Columbus grass) in Argentina (Saez, 1949) (p. 171).

Some new perennial diploid types were selected from the cross S. halepense x S. bicolor. These types combine high yield and palatibility with some frost tolerance and disease resistance. Their origin is similar to S. almum*.

STIPA TENACISSIMA L. Halfa, Alfa, Esparto. 2n=32, 40. Mediterranean area. In Spain, some cultivation is done with cv. Albardin, which has a larger fibre than wild ones. The variety

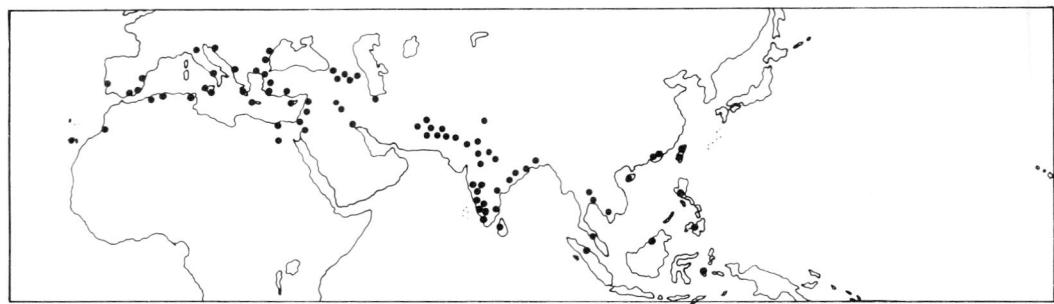

Sorghum halepense (de Wet & Huckabay, 1967).

seems to have developed there. In N. Africa
and Spain, wild halfa yields a fibre for paper-
making.

TRITICUM TURGIDUM spp. turgidum conv. durum
(Desf.) Mac Key. 2n=28, genome formula AABB.
It originated during cultivation of emmer (p.
95). Secondary centre in the Mediterranean
area.

ZEA MAYS L. 2n=20. Maize was domesticated in
C. America (p. 198). Secondary centres in
Mediterranean area and in the Nile Basin (Bran-
dolini, 1970).

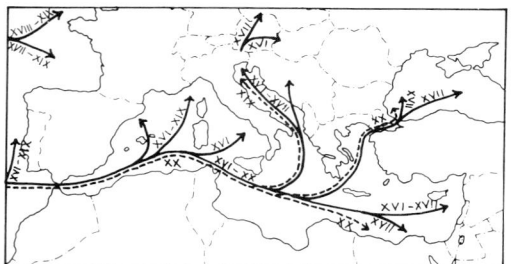

Spread of maize in the West European and the
Mediterranean region, indurata (—), indentata
(---), century of introduction (roman number)
(Brandolini, 1970).

Grossulariaceae

RIBES MULTIFLORUM Kitt. 2n=16. Mediterranean
area. It is one of the parental species of
present-day red currant cultivars (p. 155).

Hippocastanaceae

AESCULUS HIPPOCASTANUM L. Horse-chestnut. 2n=
40. C. Balkan Peninsula, E. Bulgaria, W. Iran
and the Himalayas. Cultivated as an ornamental
or shade tree, and for its timber. A. carnea
Hayne (2n=40, 80) is a hybrid with the N.
American A. pavia L., Red buckeye (2n=40).

Iridaceae

CROCUS SATIVUS L. Saffron crocus 2n=(14, 16),
24, (40). Mediterranean area and Ante-Asia.
Cultivated since ancient times for its styles,
which are a source of saffron. Formerly cultivated for this purpose in Europe and N.
America, and now in S. Europe, Asia Minor,
Iran, N. India and China.
  The origin of present-day cultivars is not
known.

IRIS GERMANICA L. German iris, Flag iris. 2n=
24, (34, 36), 44, 48, (60). Mediterranean area.
A perennial herb widely cultivated as an ornamental and for its rootstocks, which are used
in perfumery.

Labiatae

HYSSOPUS OFFICINALIS L. 2n=12. Mediterranean
area, Asia Minor and Iran. Cultivated for its
essential oil, as a medicinal plant and as an
ornamental.

LAVANDULA LATIFOLIA Medik. Broad-leaved lavender. 2n=54. Cultivated in S. France and
occasionally in C. Europe for its Oil of Spike.
The cultivated plants are often hybrids with L.
officinalis*.

LAVANDULA OFFICINALIS Chaix. (syn. L. angustifolia Mill., L. spica L.). Lavender. 2n=(36),
54. Primary centre. An old cultivated plant
for perfumery. First used as an insect repel-
lant. Many cultivated varieties are hybrids
with wild plants and L. latifolia*.

MELISSA OFFICINALIS L. Common balm. 2n=32, 64.
E. Mediterranean area to Caucasia, SW. Siberia,
S. Iran, Turkestan and Syria. Cultivated formerly in Europe and elsewhere for diverse purposes. The commonest cultivated type var.
officinalis is perhaps derived from var. hirsuta Pers. (syn. M. hirsuta (Pers.) Hornem.),
a variety from the Balkans.

MENTHA AQUATICA L. (syn. M. citrata Ehrh.).
Bergamot mint. 2n=(36, 60), 96, genome formula
$R^aR^aSSJJA^{aq}A^{aq}$, c.96. S. Europe, Asia and N.
Africa. It is a source of an essential oil.
Its A^{aq} genome is partial homologous with the

A genome of M. arvensis var. piperascens*
(Ikeda & Ono, 1969). It is one of the parents
of M. x piperita*. M. aquatica is cultivated
as M. citrata in the USA for its lavender-like
oil used in perfumery (Todd & Murray, 1968).
Patented hybrids with M. crispa L. (syn. M.
spicata* var. crispata Schrad.) are also cultivated in the USA (M.J. Murray, pers. comm.,
1971).

MENTHA LONGIFOLIA (L.) Huds. (syn. M. spicata
L. var. longifolia L., M. sylvestris L.).
Horse-mint. 2n=18, 24, (27, 36, 48). S. and
C. Europe, N. Africa, Ethiopia, Arabia, Ante-
Asia and C. Asia. Formerly it was much culti-
vated. Now only var. crispa Benth. is culti-
vated. It is related to M. rotundifolia* and
M. spicata*.

MENTHA PULEGIUM L. Penny royal, Pudding grass.
2n=(10), 20, (30), 40, (40-42). Mediterranean
area and Europe to Iran. Formerly cultivated
in Europe and elsewhere.

ORIGANUM MAJORANA L. (syn. Majorana hortensis
Moench.). Marjoram. 2n=30. Wild on Cyprus, in
SW. Turkey, Palestine and E. Egypt. Subsponta-
neous in the Mediterranean area. Cultivated
all over the world. Hybrids with O. vulgare*
have been described as O. x applii (Domin)
Bores, 2n=   and O. x majoricum Cambessedes,
2n=   . O. x applii occurs in gardens in W.
and C. Europe. O. x majoricum grows wild on
the Balearic Islands, Spain and Portugal (Ietswaart, 1980). Cultivated as medicinal plant.

ROSMARINUS OFFICINALIS L. Rosemary. 2n=24.
Mediterranean area. Cultivated as ornamental
and for its aromatic oils.

SALVIA OFFICINALIS L. Sage, Dalmatian sage.
2n=14, (16). Mediterranean area. A culinary
herb now cultivated in many gardens in temperate and tropic countries.

SALVIA SCLAREA L. Clary sage, Clary wort. 2n=
22. Mediterranean area to Iran and Transcaucasia. Formerly cultivated in the Mediterranean Region and S. Europe for various purposes, e.g. flavouring wine and beer.

SALVIA VIRIDIS L. Bluebeard. 2n=16. Mediterranean area to Iran. Cultivated locally for
its oil to flavour wine and beer.

SATUREJA HORTENSIS L. (incl. S. laxiflora C.
Koch and S. pachyphylla C. Koch). Summer savory. 2n=45-48. Mediterranean area, C. Europe
and Siberia. Cultivated for oil of savory and
as a pot-herb.

SATUREJA MONTANA L. (syn. S. obovata Lag., S.
illyrica Host). Winter savory. 2n=12, 30. Mediterranean area to Ukraine. Cultivated in S.
Europe and Germany.

TEUCRIUM CHAMAEDRYS L. (syn. T. officinale

Lam.). Common germander. 2n=32, 60, 64. Mediterranean area, France, C. Germany to S. Ural,
Iran, N. Syria and Morocco. Formerly cultivated as a medicinal crop.

TEUCRIUM MARUM L. 2n=   . W. Mediterranean
area and S. France. Cultivated in S. Europe
and formerly in Germany.

THYMUS VULGARIS L. Thyme. 2n=30. Mediterranean
Region. Now cultivated in temperate and tropical countries.

Lauraceae

LAURUS NOBILIS L. Laurel, True bay, Sweet bay.
2n=42, 48. Mediterranean Region. Primary centre also there. Cultivated there and elsewhere
for its leaves, which are used as a condiment.

Leguminosae

ASTRAGALUS BOETICUS L. Milk vetch, Loco. 2n=
16, 30. S. Europe and Mediterranean area. Cultivated as a substitute for coffee.

CERATONIA SILIQUA L. Carob, Locust tree, St.
John's bread. 2n=24. Mediterranean area, Syria
and adjacent countries. Primary centre in this
Region. Cultivated especially on Cyprus as
a fodder crop. The fruits are eaten and the
seeds are used to prepare carob coffee. More
uses are given by Uphof (1968).

CERCIS SILIQUASTRUM L. Judas tree. 2n=14. A
tree of the Mediterranean Region to Crimea
and Iran. Cultivated for its leaves (vegetable).

CICER ARIETINUM L. Garbanzos, Chick-pea. 2n=
14, 16, (24, 32, 33). Probably W. Asia (p.
96). Secondary gene centre in the Mediterranean
area. Especially large-seeded types, race mediterraneum Pop., are cultivated.

CYTISUS CANARIENSIS (L.). O. Kuntze. Genista.
2n=46. Canary Islands. Cultivated elsewhere.
Used in Mexico as hallucinogen.

CYTISUS PALLIDUS Poir. 2n=   . Canary Islands.
Cultivated as a forage crop.

CYTISUS PROLIFER Kit. (syn. C. pullilans Kit.).
Tree lucerne, Tree alfalfa, Tagasaste, Esca-
bon. 2n=48. Canary Islands or, according to
Uphof (1968), Hungary. Cultivated there as a
forage plant. Introduced into New Zealand.

GLYCYRRHIZA GLABRA*

HEDYSARUM CORONARIUM L. Spanish esparcet. 2n=
16. Mediterranean area. Cultivated as a fodder
crop.

LATHYRUS ANNUUS L. 2n=14. Mediterranean area
and Portugal. Sometimes cultivated as a fodder.

LATHYRUS CICERA L. Vetchling, Flat-pod pea-vine, Jurosse, Garousse. 2n=14. Mediterranean area, Canary Islands, Iraq, Iran and Trans-caucasia. Cultivated in S. Europe as a fodder crop and as a green manure.

LATHYRUS CLYMENUM L. (syn. L. purpureus Desf., L. alatus Sibth. & Sm.). Cicerchia porporina. 2n=14. Mediterranean area and Madeira. Culti-vated in S. Europe.

LATHYRUS HIRSUTUS L. Rough pea, Caley pea, Singletary pea. 2n=14. Mediterranean area. Cul-tivated especially in USA as a pasture hay, winter cover and for soil improvement.

LATHYRUS OCHRUS DC. 2n=14. Mediterranean area. Occasionally cultivated in Greece as a fodder.

LATHYRUS ODORATUS L. Sweet pea. 2n=14. Medi-terranean area. Seeds of wild plants were sent from Sicily to NW. Europe in 1667 by a monk, Francesco Cupani. It is commonly cultivated as an ornamental. Its flowers are also used as a source of an essential oil.

LATHYRUS SATIVUS L. Grass pea, Chickling pea. 2n=14. Probably domesticated in W. Asia (p. 83). Primary centre in the Mediterranean area.

LATHYRUS TINGITANUS L. Tangier pea. 2n=14. Mediterranean Region. It has a micro-centre in Morocco. Cultivated as a winter annual, also in USA.

LOTUS EDULIS L. Asparagus pea, Winged pea. 2n= 14. Mediterranean area to Asia Minor and Syria. Occasionally cultivated for its young pods.

LUPINUS ALBUS L. (syn. L. sativum Gaertn.). White lupin, Mediterranean white lupin. 2n= 50. Wild in Balkan, Crete and W. Turkey. Pro-bably domesticated in the Balkans (Gladstone, 1977). All cultivars have white seeds, the pro-duction of pigment being suppressed by two independent pairs of inhibitor genes. These genes must already have been selected for by farmers some 4000 years ago (Kazimierski, 1960).

L. albus is closely related to L. termis. According to Kazimierski (1960) both derive from L. graecum (see L. termis*). This lat-er species would derive from L. jugoslavicus Kazim. & Now. (2n=50) which is found in Yugo-slavia. Gladstone (1970) considered L. termis, L. graecus and L. jugoslavicus as synonyms of L. albus.

LUPINUS ANGUSTIFOLIUS L. (syn. L. varius L., L. linifolius Roth, L. reticulatus Desv.). Narrow-leaved lupin, Blue lupin. 2n=40. Pri-mary centre in the Mediterranean area. The present European cultivars probably derive from wild types of Palestine. Cultivated also in S. Africa and Australia as a forage. Widely cultivated as an ornamental too.

LUPINUS COSENTINI Guss. (syn. L. varius L., spp. varius Franco & P. Silva). Western Aus-tralian blue lupin, Sand-plain lupin, Geral-ton lupin. 2n=32. Coastal Morocco and other sites in W. Mediterranean area. Introduced into W. Australia about the middle of the 19th Century and naturalized. Since 1910, it has been cultivated for summer sheep food and soil improvement. Described as L. pilosus L., L. varius L. and L. digitatus Forsk.

LUPINUS LUTEUS L. (European) yellow lupin. 2n =(46, 48, 50), 52. Mediterranean area, where its primary centre lies. The present European cultivars derive probably from wild Palestinean plants. Cultivated as a fodder crop, green manure and ornamental. Closely related to L. hispanicus Boiss. & Reut. and L. rothmaleri Klink (2n=50, 52).

LUPINUS PILOSUS L. (syn. L. varius L. ssp. orientalis Franco & P. Silva). Greater blue lupin, Hairy lupin. 2n=42, (50). NE. Mediter-ranean Region. It may occasionally be cultiva-ted. It is characterized by its big seeds, the biggest of all Lupinus-species. The cultivated type has 2n=50.

LUPINUS TERMIS Forsk. (syn. L. graecus Boiss., L. albus ssp. albus). Egyptian lupin. 2n=   . Palestine and Egypt. Cultivated in Egypt since ancient times and in Nigeria. The seeds con-tain alkaloids, which have to be removed be-fore consumption. Closely related to L. albus. L. termis and L. graecus may be varieties of L. albus*.

MEDICAGO ARBOREA L. Cytisus. 2n=32, 48. Canary Islands, Balaeric Islands, S. Europe to Asia Minor. The 4x type is common while the 6x type is found on Esparta, Balearic Islands only. A shrub formerly used for fodder and for making

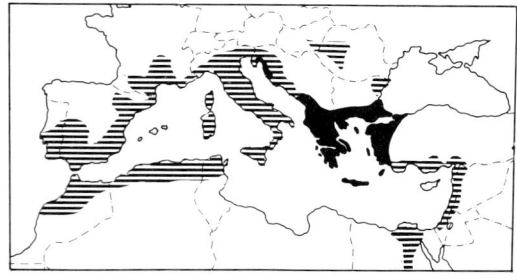

Distribution of Lupinus albus in the Mediter-ranean as a wild and cultivated plant. Hatched: cultivated (var. albus only); black: cultivated (var. albus) and native (var. graecus)(Gladstone, 1976).

baskets (Lesins & Lesins, 1979).

MEDICAGO POLYMORPHA L. (syn. M. hispida Gaertn. and M. denticulata Willd.). Bur clover. 2n= 14. Mediterranean area. Spread world wide. Cultivated as a green manure, for pasture and as a hay crop in Australia, S. America and S. USA.

MEDICAGO SATIVA L. Lucerne, (Blue) alfalfa. 2n=16, genome formula SS, 32 genome formula SSSS, 64. Transcaucasia (p. 97). Secondary centre in N. Africa, especially Algeria.

MELILOTUS INFESTUS Guss. 2n=16. A plant of W. Mediterranean area, being a source of resistance to the sweet clover weevil of M. albus* and M. officinalis*.

MELILOTUS MACROCARPA Coss. & Dur. 2n=16. N. Africa. Cultivated in Algeria for its large fruits used as spice.

MELILOTUS SULCATUS Desf. 2n=16, (32). S. Portugal and the Mediterranean area. Plants belonging to ssp. brachystachus Maire are coumarin deficient and resistant to drought, and most pests including the sweet clover weevil. Ssp. segetalis (Brot.) Maire has also been described as M. segetalis Ser. (2n=16).

ORNITHOPUS COMPRESSUS L. 2n=14. Spain, Portugal and Mediterranean area. Its northernmost point of occurrence is Brittany in France. It has a high leaf and seed production. It might be useful as a breeding source for O. sativus*.

ORNITHOPUS SATIVUS Brot. Serradella. 2n=14. Wild plants in NW. Portugal, N. Spain and SW. France. From here its cultivation spread over W. and N. Europe, since the beginning of the 19th Century. A green manure and fodder. Ssp. sativus (syn. O. roseus Dufour) is native to SW. France, N. Iberian Peninsula and the Azores. Cultivated elsewhere.
    A related species is O. isthmocarpus Coss. (syn. O. sativus ssp. isthmocarpus (Cosson) Dostal) (2n=14). A Mediterranean-Atlantic species, where it grows together with O. sativus, hybrids, described as O. macrorrhynchus (Willk.) Klinkowski & Schwz. (syn. O. sativus var. macrorrhynchus Willk.) are found.

PISUM SATIVUM L. ssp. hortense Asch. & Graeb. Garden pea. 2n=14. Ssp. hortense is domesticated in SW. Asia (p. 97). Secondary centre in the Mediterranean area.

PISUM SATIVUM ssp. jomardi (Schrank) Alef. (syn. ecotype arvense s.str., P. elatius (M. B.) Stev., P. jomardi Schrank, P. transcaucasicum Stankov). 2n=14. Cultivated in Egypt. Closely related to ssp. abyssinicum (p. 137) (Fouzdar & Tandon, 1976).

PSORALEA BITUMINOSA L. Asphalt clover. 2n=20. Mediterranean area and Canary Islands. Cul-

tivated for fodder.

SPARTIUM JUNCEUM L. Spanish broom, Weaver's broom. 2n=48, 52, 52-56. Mediterranean area and Europe. Cultivated in France near Aspiran (Hérault).

TRIFOLIUM ALEXANDRINUM L. Alexandrian clover, Egyptian clover, Berseem. 2n=16. E. Mediterranean area. Cultivated in the Near East and India. It is the oldest clover cultivated and is closely associated with agriculture in Egypt. Secondary centre in Egypt. T. alexandrinum derives from T. berytheum Boiss. (syn. T. alexandrinum var. berytheum) and T. salmoneum Mout., 2n=   . T. alexandrinum is self-compatible while its progenitors are self-incompatible. Self-compatibility may be a characteristic of domestication.

TRIFOLIUM FRAGIFERUM L. (syn. T. neglectum Fisch & Mey). Strawberry clover. 2n=16. Europe, Canary Islands, Madeira, N. Africa and W. Asia. Cultivated as fodder.

TRIFOLIUM INCARNATUM L. Crimson clover. 2n=14. C. and S. Europe, Balkans and N. Africa. The cultivated type (var. sativum Duc., ssp. incarnatum) probably derives from the wild var. molinerii (Balbis ex Hornem.) Syme. The latter is found in Spain. Long cultivated in Catalonia (Spain) and S. France. Spread to E. and N. Europe and later to N. America.

TRIFOLIUM ISRAELITICUM D. Zoh. & Katzn. (syn. T. subterraneum L. var. telavivensis Eig). 2n =14. N. Israel. It is not a parent of T. subterraneum as has been suggested. It only has 14 chromosomes while T. subterraneum has 16. Formerly it was considered as the "Israeli race" of this species.

TRIFOLIUM REPENS L. var. giganteum. Lodi clover, Ladino clover. 2n=32. Probably, Lodi, N. Italy. Cultivated first in N. Italy and the Netherlands (p. 157). An excellent fodder crop.

TRIFOLIUM SUBTERRANEUM L. Subterranean clover, Sub clover. 2n=16. Mediterranean area, SE. and W. Europe, Caucasian Region and N. Iran. It is possible that the westward migration followed the course of clearing and cropping by man (Katznelson & Morley, 1965a, 1965b). Secondary centre in Australia (p. 66). Naturalized in Australia, S. Africa, and N. and S. America.
    T. subterraneum can be divided into three subspecies: 1. ssp. subterraneum (syn. T. blesense Dodart) which is the commonest taxon sympatric with the species; 2. ssp. yanninicum Katzn. & Morley, which occurs in Istria, Dalmatia, Albania, Serbia and N. Greece; 3. ssp. brachycalycinum Katzn. & Morley (syn. var. oxaloides Eig) which occurs from W. Thrace to Caspian Sea. These subspecies are almost completely intersterile (Katznelson & Morley, 1965a). The existence of two closely related but more primitive species (T. batmanicum

Katzn. (syn. T. anatolicum Katzn.) (2n=16) in Diyarbakir Province, and T. chlorotrichum Boiss. & Balansa (2n=   ) in Phrygia) in Turkey and the absence of these and other close relatives elsewhere indicates the origin of T. subterraneum in Turkey. However, the greatest variation is found in Greece (Katznelson & Morley, 1965a).

Bailey & Francis (1971) found that the iso-flavone pattern of T. batmanicum closely resembles that of spp. brachycalycinum. They concluded that T. batmanicum might be the ancestor species of T. subterraneum and ssp. brachycalycinum is probably the earliest form of subterranean clover. They postulated that ssp. subterraneum evolved later and colonized a wider range of environments.
The isoflavone pattern of T. batmanicum is very similar to that of T. globosum L. (syn. T. radiosum Wahlenb., T. nidificum Griseb.) (2n=16). However, that species belongs to another subsection.

TRIFOLIUM VAVILOVII Eig. 2n=16. Israel.

VICIA ARTICULATA Hornem. One-flowered vetch. 2n=   . Mediterranean area, Asia Minor, Madeira and Canary Islands. Cultivated.

VICIA BENGHALENSIS L. (syn. V. atropurpurea Desf.). Purple vetch. 2n=12, 14. Mediterranean area. Naturalized in the USA. Cultivated as a clover crop and green manure, and as a winter and spring forage.

VICIA CALCARATA Desf. Demehi. 2n=12, 14. Sahara Oasis, where it is cultivated for its seeds. Also Iran & cultivated in Tripolitania (Libya).

VICIA ERVILEA (L.) Willd. Bitter vetch, Ervil. 2n=14. Primary centre in the Mediterranean area. Cultivated in Spain. A characteristic group developed in Asia Minor (p. 98). Used as forage and for grain.

VICIA FABA L. (syn. Faba vulgaris Moench). Field bean, Broad bean, Horse bean, Pigeon bean, Tick bean, Windsor bean. 2n=12 (14). SW. Asia (p. 83) or Near East or Mediterranean area (Zohary, 1977). Wild ancestor uncertain. See p. 83 for discussion of origin.

Schultz-Motel (1972) found no evidence for a supposed division of the small-seeded type into two geographical races: a long-seeded type in the W. Mediterranean area and a round-seeded type in the eastern part. So there is no reason to suppose that the broad bean originated in two separate areas. Whether V. pliniana (Trabut) Moratova found in Algeria and Morocco, is a type of V. faba or a related species is not known.

VICIA NARBONENSIS L. Narbonne vetch. 2n=14. SW. Asia (p. 98). Secondary gene centre in Mediterranean area where it is cultivated.

Liliaceae

ALOE BARBADENSIS Mill. (syn. A. vera L.). Curaçao aloe, Barbados aloe. 2n=(10), 14. Mediterranean area, S. Arabia, E. Africa, NW. India and S. China. The wild var. barbadensis of the Mediterranean area has run wild in C. America, W. Indies to Bolivia. It probably arrived there through Spain. Cultivated in W. Indies.

LILIUM CANDIDUM L. Madonna lily, Bourbon lily. 2n=14. Mediterranean area and SW. Asia. Cultivated especially in S. France for its flowers. These are a source of an essential oil. It is the oldest lily of European gardens.

URGINEA MARITIMA (L.) Baker. (syn. U. scilla Steinh.). Sea onion. 2n=20, (30), 40, 60. Mediterranean coast; most common in E. Algeria. Wild and cultivated plants are used for their pharmaceutical properties and in rat poison.

Linaceae

LINUM USITATISSIMUM L. Flax, Linseed. 2n=30, (32). For origin see p. 99. In the Mediterranean area, the oil-flax (spp. mediterraneum Vav. & Ell.) is cultivated. In Italy, hybrid forms (spp. transitorium Vav. & Ell.) of ssp. eurasiaticum and ssp. mediterraneum are found. Large-seeded types are cultivated in N. Africa. Those from Algeria are a source of Fusarium resistance.

Malvaceae

ALTHAEA OFFICINALIS L. Marsh mallow. 2n=42, (c.42, 40-44). Europe, E. Mediterranean area and W. Asia. Cultivated for its roots, which are a source of medicine.

ALTHAEA ROSEA (L.) Cav. Garden hollyhock, Hollyhock. 2n=(26), 42, (56). Asia Minor, Balkans and Crete. Ran wild in Italy, S. France and S. Tyrol. Cultivated in Europe since the 16th Century, especially var. nigra hort., which has blackish purple petals used to colour wine and as medicine. Cultivated now in many types as an ornamental.

Moraceae

FICUS SYCOMORUS L. Sycomore fig. 2n=26. Its area of distribution can be divided into two parts: 1. the main part is the E. Coast of Africa from S. Africa to Sudan, where trees produce viable seed and grow wild; 2. the northern area is the Middle East and N. Africa where trees do not produce viable seed and have to vegetatively propagate. The tree was perhaps domesticated in the Middle East (p. 99). The southern boundary of the domesticated sycomores runs through Sudan (Galil et al., 1976).

Myrtaceae

EUCALYPTUS CAMALDULENSIS Dehn. Longbeak eucalyptus. 2n=22. Primary centre in Australia
(p. 66). Secondary centres in the Mediterranean Region and S. America (p. 177). It was
believed that the trees of this species cultivated in Israel came from S. Australia, but
the leaves of the Israeli trees contain three
polyphenols which have not been found in the
species anywhere in Australia.

EUCALYPTUS GLOBULUS Labell. Fever tree, Blue
gum. 2n=20, 22, 28. SE. Tasmania. Cultivated.
Secondary centre in the Mediterranean Region.

MYRTUS COMMUNIS L. Myrtle. 2n=22. Mediterranean area and SW. Europe. Cultivated since ancient times for its fruits and for its medicinal properties.

Oleaceae

FRAXINUS ORNUS L. Flowering ash, Manna ash.
2n=46. A tree of C. and E. Mediterranean area.
Cultivated on the N. coast of Sicily.

OLEA CHRYSOPHYLLA Lam. Golden-leaved olive
tree. 2n= . Wild over a large part of the
Old World, including the Mediterranean area.
It is possibly the wild ancestor of O. europaea*. If so, it is a synonym of O. europaea
var. sylvestris Brotero.

OLEA EUROPAEA L. Olive tree. 2n=46. Mediterranean area. Primary centre in the Mediterranean Region. Its domestication started there
in ancient times. Var. sylvestris Brotero includes the wild forms and the possible naturalized cultivated types. Var. europaea is the
cultivated form. The main differences of var.
sylvestris are spiny lower branches and small
leaves and drupes. Some cultivars are developed
for table olives, others for oil. See also O.
chrysophylla*.

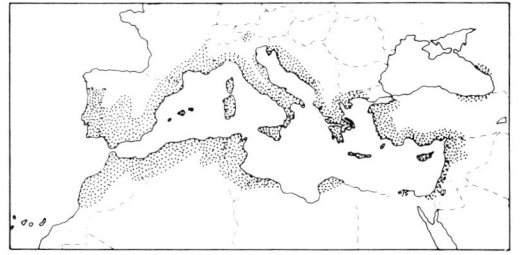

Olea europaea (Polunin & Huxley, 1972).

Palmae

CHAMAEROPS HUMULIS L. Dwarf palm. 2n=36. Wild
in the W. Mediterranean area. Cultivated in
some parts of Morocco. Often planted as an ornamental. A source of fibre (crin végétal).

Papaveraceae

PAPAVER SOMNIFERUM L. Opium poppy. 2n=2x=22,
4x=44. The cultigen ssp. somniferum derives
from the wild ssp. setigerum (DC) Corb. (syn.
P. setigerum DC), 2n=2x=22, 4x=44, which occurs
in the Mediterranean Region from the Canary
Isles eastwards. In Greece and Cyprus, tetraploid types are found, which are more ruderal
than the diploid and hence spread easier (Hammer & Fritsch, 1977). Schültze-Motel (1979)
stated that the poppy was domesticated in the
W. Mediterranean area. The cultigen is grown
for the dried latex obtained from unripe capsules, which is used in medicine and as a narcotic, for its ripe seeds, which are eaten or
pressed for poppy oil, and as an ornamental.
It often escapes from cultivation. There are
several taxonomic classifications to divide
the cultigen into various subspecies on the
basis of phenotypic variation.

Pinaceae

PINUS PINEA L. Stone pine, Pinie. 2n= . S.
Europe. A tree often cultivated for its edible
seeds.

Pistaciaceae

PISTACIA LENTISCUS L. Lentisk pistache. 2n=24.
Mediterranean area. A small tree cultivated
for its chewing gum.

PISTACIA TEREBINTHUS L. Terebinth pistache.
2n= . Mediterranean area. On the Aegean
islands, a type with big fruits and large
leaves was cultivated.

Plantaginaceae

PLANTAGO INDICA L. 2n=12. C., S. and E. Europe and W. Asia. Cultivated in S. France as
a medicinal herb (Mansfeld, 1959).

PLANTAGO PSYLLIUM L. Psyllium. 2n=12. Mediterranean area.

Ranunculaceae

AQUILEGIA VULGARIS L. Columbine. 2n=14. S.
and C. Europe (p. 158), N. Africa and temp.
Asia. Cultivated widely as an ornamental, formerly also for medicinal purposes.

NIGELLA SATIVA L. Black cumin. 2n=12. C. (p.
158) and S. Europe, N. Africa and W. Asia. Cultivated for its seed in the Mediterranean area
and in the Orient. Cultivated formerly in C.
Europe.

Resedaceae

RESEDA LUTEOLA L. Weld. 2n=24, (26, 28). C.
Europe (p. 158), Mediterranean area, Iran and
Afghanistan. Formerly cultivated as a source
of deep yellow dye.

RESEDA ODORATA L. Mignonette. 2n=12, (14). N. Africa. It may derive from R. phyteuma* with introgression of R. arabica Boiss., 2n=24 and R. orientalis (Muell.-Arg.) Boiss., 2n=   . R. arabica is found in Africa north of the Sahara, Egypt, Palestine, Syria and upto the Persian Gulf, while R. orientalis occurs in S. Turkey, Cyprus, Lebanon, Syria and Palestine. Between 1733 and 1737 material was sent to Paris and from there its cultivation as a perfumery plant started and spread (Abdallah & de Wit, 1978). Var. neilgherrensis is grown in India (p. 78).

RESEDA PHYTEUMA L. 2n=12. N. and S. of the W. and C. Mediterranean area. Said to be eaten as a vegetable in Greece. It may be the main ancestor of R. orientalis* (Abdallah & de Wit, 1978).

   Rhamnaceae

RHAMNUS CATHARTICUS*

RHAMNUS FRANGULA*

RHAMNUS PRINOIDES L'Hér. 2n=14. Ethiopia. Cultivated for leaves and branches which are used to flavour beverages, and for medicine (Jansen, 1981).

ZIZIPHUS LOTUS (L.) Lam. 2n=24. Mediterranean area. A tree cultivated in Italy, S. Spain and Egypt. It is probably the lotophagus of the ancient peoples of Libya.

   Rosaceae

AMYGDALUS PERSICA L. Peach. 2n=16. Primary centre in China (p. 42). Secondary centre in Italy and Spain.

CRATAEGUS AZAROLUS L. (syn. C. aronica Bosc.). Azerolier. 2n=   . S. Europe, N. Africa and the Orient (p. 85). This shrub or small tree is often cultivated for its edible fruits. Var. aronica L. is found wild on Crete.

   Rutaceae

CITRUS AURANTIUM L. spp. bergamia (Risso & Poit.) Wight & Arn. Bergamot. 2n=18. Calabria (Italy. Primary centre probably in SE. Asia (p. 63). Cultivated for bergamot oil in Calabria.

CITRUS LIMON (L.) Burm. Lemon. 2n=18, (36). Primary centre probably in SE. Asia (p. 63). Secondary centre in the Mediterranean Region, especially in Sicily.

CITRUS SINENSIS (L.) Osbeck (syn. C. aurantium L. var. sinensis L.). Sweet orange. 2n=18, (27, 36). Primary centre probably in S. China or Cochinchina (p. 63). Secondary centres in Israel (e.g. the varieties Shamuti, Beladi, Khalili) and in Spain (e.g. the variety Valen-

cia, blood orange).

RUTA CHALEPENSIS L. Fringed rue. 2n=36. Mediterranean area. Cultivated there and elsewhere as a medicinal plant.

RUTA GRAVEOLENS L. Common rue, Rue. 2n=72, 81. Wild in the Mediterranean area. Introduced into many tropical countries. The leaves are used as a condiment and medicinally.

   Scrophulariaceae

DIGITALIS PURPUREA*

   Solanaceae

ATROPA BELLADONNA L. Belladonna. 2n=72. From Spain, the Balkans, Asia Minor to India (p. 79). Cultivated in Europe, India and USA as a medicinal plant. A. martiana F.Q. is cons d- ered a hybrid of A. belladonna and A. baetica Willk. (2n=72), which is found in Spain.

HYOSCYAMUS NIGER L. Black henbane. 2n=34. Mediterranean area. A medicinal plant cultiva- ted in some countries for its alkaloids.

   Ulmaceae

CELTIS AUSTRALIS L. (syn. C. excelsa Salisb.). Hackberry. 2n=40. Mediterranean area. Tree cul- tivated there as an ornamental and in Asia Minor for its edible fruits (Mansfeld, 1959).

ULMUS spp. Semi-cultivated by the Romans as a support for grapevines and so distributed. The leaves are used as fodder in dry summers.

   Umbelliferae

AMMADAUCUS LEUCOTRICHUS (Coss. & Bur.). 2n=14. N. Africa. Cultivated there.

AMMI MAJUS L. (syn. Apium ammi Crantz). Bish- op's weed. 2n=22. Mediterranean area to Iran and to Switzerland and Belgium. Cultivated since the Middle Ages for its aromatic seeds and for medicinal purposes.

ANETHUM GRAVEOLENS L. (syn. A. sowa Kurz.). Satapashpi, Sowa, Suwa. 2n=22. Eurasia. Culti- vated in India. It has longer fruits than the Indian type (p. 79).

APIUM GRAVEOLENS L. Celery. 2n=22. Cultivation started in the Mediterranean area. The wild parent A. graveolens var. silvestre Presl. (syn. var. graveolens) is cosmopolitan. Not much is known about the development of the three botanical varieties of A. graveolens: var. sil- vestre f. secalinum Alef. (syn. var. secalinum Alef.), Leafy celery, Smallage or Soup celery var. rapaceum (Mill.) DC., Celeriac, Turnip- rooted celery or German celery; var. dulce (Mill.) Pers., Blanching celery, Pascal celery or Stalk celery.

CORIANDRUM SATIVUM L. Coriander. 2n=22. Mediterranean area and W. Asia. Cultivated for its aromatic fruits.

CRITHMUM MARITIMUM L. Samphire, Sea samphire, Sea fennel, Piercestone. 2n=20, (22). Canary Islands, Madeire, coasts of Portugal to S. England and those of the Mediterranean area and Crimea. Cultivated in the USA as a kitchen herb.

CUMINUM CYMINUM L. Cumin. 2n=14. Mediterranean area to Turkistan. Cultivated in SE. Europe, N. Africa, India and China.

DAUCUS CAROTA L. Yellow carrot. 2n=18. Wild species from Afghanistan (p. 86) to the Mediterranean area. Although yellow carrots may have arisen in other areas where purple carrots were cultivated, it is thought that the true yellow carrots developed in the Mediterranean Region from crosses with the wild D. carota ssp. agg. carota (syn. ssp. maximus (Desf.) Ball).

FOENICULUM VULGARE Mill. (syn. F. officinale Gaertn.). Fennel. 2n=22. Mediterranean area. Cultivated there for a long time and introduced into many other temperate countries.
    Var. piperitum (Ucr.) Cout. (syn. F. piperitum Acr., 2n=22) is Bitter fennel. Var. dulce (Mill.) Thell. (syn. F. dulce Mill., 2n=22) is the Florence fennel, Sweet fennel or Roman fennel. Cultivated for its blanched petioles in S. France and the Mediterranean area. Var. azoricum (Mill.)Thell. (syn. F.azoricum Mill.), Carosella or Italian fennel, originated in Italy. It has very broad leaf-stalk bases.

MEUM ANTHAMANTICUM Jacq. Signel. 2n=22. A herb of C. and S. Europe, once cultivated in N. England for its roots.

PETROSELINUM CRISPUM (Mill.) Nym. ex A.W. Hill (syn. Carum petroselinum Benth.). Parsley. 2n=22. S. Europe. Widely cultivated there and elsewhere. Mansfeld (1959) has classified the wild and cultivated types.

SIUM SISARUM L. Skirret, Chervin. 2n=20, 22. E. Asia and Mediterranean area. Occasionally cultivated for its edible tuberous roots (var. sisarum).

SMYRNIUM OLUSATRUM L. Alisander, Alexanders, Maceron. 2n=22. Mediterranean area, S. and W. Europe and Caucasia. Formerly much cultivated but now replaced by celery.

    Urticaceae

SOLEIROLIA SOLEIROLII (Req.) Dandy. 2n=   . Islands of W. Mediterranean area. Cultivated.

    Valerianaceae

FEDIA CORNUCOPIAE Gaertn. African valerian, Valeriane d'Alger. 2n=32. Mediterranean area. Cultivated as a pot-herb and during famine.

VALERIANA ERIOCARPA Desv. Italian corn salad. 2n=   . Mediterranean area. Cultivated for salad.

    Verbenaceae

VITEX AGNUS-CASTUS L. Chaste tree. 2n=24, 32. Mediterranean area. Cultivated in the Old and New Worlds for various purposes.

    Violaceae

VIOLA ODORATA L. (syn. V. officinalis Cr.). Sweet violet, Sweet scented violet, Common violet. 2n=20. Europe and SW. Asia. Var. parma is cultivated in N. Italy and S. France as a source of an essential oil for perfumery.

    Vitadaceae

VITIS VINIFERA L. Common grape, European grape.

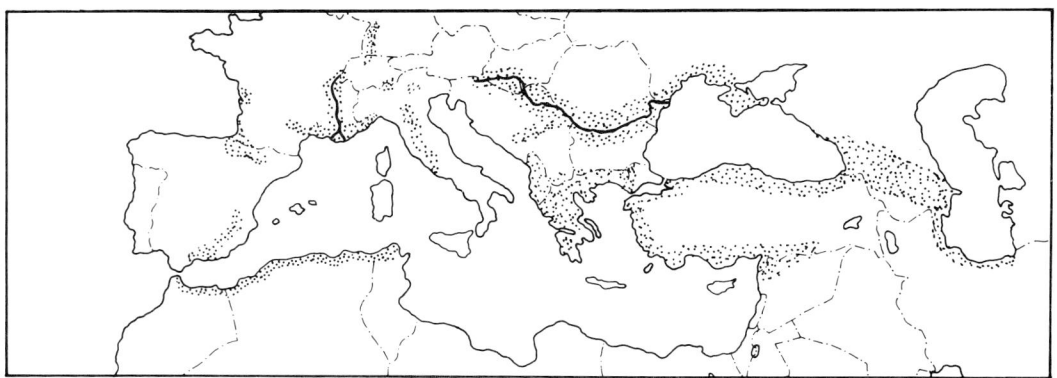

Wild grape (Vitis vinifera. var. silvestris) (Zohary & Spiegel-Roy, 1975).

2n=38, (40, 57, 76). The Mediterranean Region
is one of the three primary centres of diversity. On p. 102 the domestication of the grape
is discussed and other data are presented.
The grape reached Greece and Italy c. 1000 BC.
and spread northwards to enter France c. 55 AD.
There by introgression, it absorbed genes for
adaptation to cooler and more humid climates
(Rives, 1975). There are several secondary centres, e.g. the varieties for currants in Greece,
and the varieties for wine in Italy, Spain and
Algeria.

8 African Region

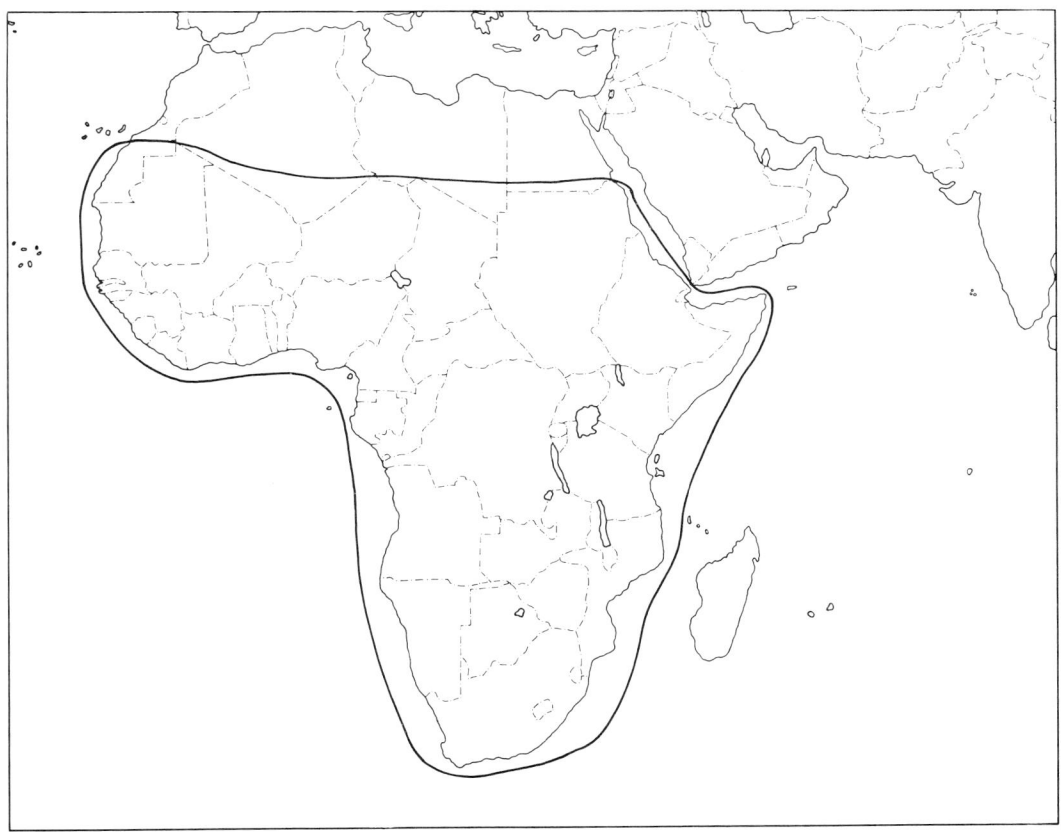

The African Region includes all of Africa south of the Sahara. Portères (1950) recognized four major centres of plant domestication in Africa: a Mediterranean cradle, which forms part of the Mediterannean Region (Chap. 7); an Ethiopian cradle, which corresponds with the Abyssinian Centre of Vavilov (1928) and the Ethiopian Centre of Darlington (1956); an East African cradle; and a West African cradle. Portères divided his West African cradle into Senegambian, Central Niger, Benin and Adamawa subcradles. An independent origin of agriculture in the West African savanna was also proposed by Anderson (1960) and Murdock (1960), but several research workers have presented evidence against this hypothesis (Wrigley, 1960; Clark, 1962; Harris, 1967). Agriculture in Africa north of the Sahara is typically Near Eastern in origin. South of the Sahara, agriculture is based primarily on native African crops. A notable exception is the Highlands of Ethiopia, where wheat and barley have been grown since at least the beginning of the Christian Era.

The antiquity of native agriculture in Africa is not known. Archaeological remains of finger millet (Eleusine coracana) from Ethiopia suggests that this cereal has been cultivated in Africa for at least five millennia. This archaeological race of finger millet has lost the ability to disperse seec naturally, so cereal cultivation in Africa must be substantially older than 5000 years (Hilu et al., 1979). Remains of pearl millet (Pennisetum americanum) dating back to the fifth millennium BC. were uncovered from lake edge settlements in Mauritania (Munson, 1976). A sequence from gathering wild grasses to growing cereals such as pearl millet and possibly sorghum (Sorghum bicolor) is obvious in these settlements. However, these crops probably reached Mauritania fully domesticated. Wild races of pearl millet occurs in C. Sahel and Highlands of C. Sahara, and wild sorghum is native to the savanna regions, where these two cereals were probably domesticated (Brunken et al., 1977; de Wet, 1978).

The pollen record shows that the Sahara was substantially wetter some 8000 years ago than now. People with cattle, goats and sheep camped along the edges of numerous shallow lakes in C. Sahara, and harvested wild cereals and other plant foods in areas that are now desert (Clark, 1976). The Sahara became progressively drier over several subsequent millennia, and it was probably these nomadic herdsmen who domesticated the native cereals of West Africa as they migrated south into what is now savanna (Harlan et al., 1976)

Acanthaceae

ADHATODA SCHIMPERIANA (Hochst.) Nees. 2n= E. Africa. In Ethiopia cultivated as a hedge-plant (Jansen, 1981).

JUSTICIA INSULARIS T. And. 2n=   . Africa. Cultivated in W. Africa for its edible leaves.

Agavaceae

AGAVE FOURCROYDES Lem. Henequen agave. 2n= c. 140. Yucatan (p. 185). Secondary centre possibly in Africa. Cultivated for fibre.

DRACAENA ARBOREA Link. (syn. D. mannii Baker). Asparagus tree, Soap tree; D. fragrans (L.) Carol; and D. smithii ex Hook.f., Cocked hat, Cockade bush. 2n=   . These four species are native to Africa. Cultivated as living fences and live sticks.

SANSEVERINIA GUINEENSIS (L.) Willd. Bowstring hemp. 2n=   . Africa. A fibre crop cultivated on a small scale in Mexico.

SANSEVERINIA LONGIFLORA Sims. Florida bowstring hemp. 2n=   . Africa. Cultivated in Trinidad, S. Florida and S. Carolina.

SANSEVERINIA THYRSIFLORA Thunb. 2n=   . S. Africa. Cultivated for its fibres in the tropics.

SANSEVERINIA TRIFASCIATA Prain. African bowstring hemp. 2n=   . Trop. W. Africa. Cultivated (often as S. guineensis*) in the tropics. Var. laurentii (De Wildem.) N.E. Brown is cultivated as an ornamental in Zaïre.

Aizoaceae

MESEMBRYANTHEMUM ANGULATUM Thunb. Marigold.

2n=18. S. Africa. An annual cultivated in Zaïre and the Mediterranean area as a spinach.

MESEMBRYANTHEMUM CRYSTALINUM L. (syn. Cryophytum crystallinum (L.) N.E. Brown). Ice plant, Crystalline. 2n=18. S. Africa. Cultivated as salad vegetable or as a soil stabilizer.

MESEMBRYANTHEMUM EDULE L. (syn. Carpobrotus edulis (L.) L. Bolus). Hottentot fig. 2n=18 S. Africa. A dune stabilizer, leaves used as forage and as a source of water.

Amaranthaceae

CELOSIA TRIGYNA L. 2n=18. Trop. Africa, Madagascar and Arabia. Cultivated as a vegetable in Africa.

Annonaceae

XYLOPIA AETHIOPICA (Dun.) A. Rich. African pepper, Guinea pepper, Ethiopian pepper, Spice tree. 2n=   . Trop. Africa. (Semi-)cultivated in W. Africa.

Apocynaceae

CARISSA GRANDIFLORA A.DC. Natal plum. 2n=22. S. Africa. Cultivated for its fruits and as an ornamental.

FUNTUMIA ELASTICA (Preuss) Stapf. Lagos silk rubber. 2n=22. W. Africa. Large plantations of this tree were established in W. Africa, after the discovery that it was a source of rubber. However, these plantations cannot compete with Hevea rubber.

TABERNANTHE IBOGA Baillon. Iboga. 2n=22. Gabon, Congo and the NW. Zaïre. Cultivated in Gabon. The roots contain several indole alkaloids. The most important is ibogaine which is a

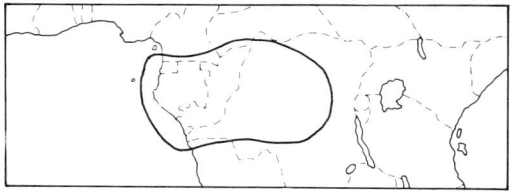

Tabernanthe iboga (Pope, 1969).

stimulant and in large doses a hallucinogen.
Roots of wild plants are collected which has
resulted in the almost extinction of this plant
in several districts in Gabon.

VINCA ROSEA L. Madagascar periwinkle, Cape
periwinkle. 2n=16, (32). Probably Madagascar.
A herb cultivated as a medicinal plant.

Bignoniaceae

KIGELIA AFRICANA (Lam.) Benth. 2n=40. Sausage
tree. Trop. W. Africa. Cultivated for medicine
and witchcraft.

Bombacaceae

CEIBA PENTANDRA Gaertn. Kapok tree, Silk cotton
tree. 2n=72, 80, 88. Some authors believe in
an American/African origin of the kapok tree
(p. 187). If America is the sole centre of
origin, then the African centre is secondary.
The African kapok tree is divided in the Caribbean forest type and the Caribbean savanna
type. The latter type, which has a broadly
spreading crown, is planted in market places.
It is possible that this type arose from cuttings of plagiotropic branches (Zeven, 1969).

Burseraceae

CANARIUM EDULE Hook.f. (syn. Pachylobus edulis
G. Don, Dacryodes edulis (G. Don.) Lam). Bush
butter tree, Native pear. 2n=   . Trop. Africa.
Occasionally cultivated for its edible fruits.

COMMIPHORA OPOBALSAMUM Engl. Mecca myrrh tree,
Harobol myrrh. 2n=   . Arabia and Somalia. Formerly (11th-17th Century) cultivated in Egypt
and Palestine (Mansfeld, 1959).

Cannaceae

CANNA SPECIOSA Rosc. 2n=   . W. Africa. Cul-
tivated in Sierra Leone. It is the source of
African Turmeric. The tubers resemble those of
Curcuma longa*.

Celastraceae

CATHA EDULIS Forsk. Khat, Miraa. 2n=   . Ethiopia and Somalia, south to Natal and Transvaal
in South Africa, and in Yemen and Saudi Arabia
where it probably was introduced. Cultivated in

Ethiopia and Arabia for its leaves that contain
a mild narcotic. The fresh leaves and twigs are
used as a stimulant particularly in Arabia, Somalia, Ethiopia and Tanzania. Leaves are either
chewed, or a refreshing tea is brewed from them.
In Ethiopia, the leaf has been used as a protection against pestilence, and especially in
Arabia against bubonic plague. In Yemen, khat
is an important item at birth, circumcision,
and at marriages and funerals. In Harrar, twigs
of khat are placed on graves for seven days.

Cleomaceae

GYNANDROPSIS GYNANDRA (L.) Briq. (syn. G. pentaphylla DC.). Cat's whiskers. 2n=30, 32, 34.
(Sub)trop. Africa and India. Cultivated in
Africa, in the West Indies and in Malaya. Used
as vegetable and as ornamental.

Compositae

CRASSOCEPHALUM BIAFRAE S. Moore. 2n=   . W.
Africa. Cultivated as a vegetable. Several
types are known (Terra, 1967).

CRASSOCEPHALUM CREPIDIOIDES (Benth.) S. Moore.
2n=40. Vegetable of Nigeria.

GUIZOTIA ABYSSINICA (L.f.) Cass. Niger seed.
2n=30. Centre of diversity Ethiopia (Baagoe,
1974) and spread southwards to Malawi and to
India, where it has run wild. Used for oil-
seed.

GYNURA CERNUA Benth. 2n=20. W. Africa. A herb
cultivated for its leaves.

LACTUCA TARAXACIFOLIA (Willd.) Schum. (syn.
Sonchus taraxacifolius Willd.). Wild lettuce,
Langue de vaches. 2n=   . Trop. Africa especially in Sierra Leone, Ghana, S. Nigeria
and Nile region. Cultivated in W. Africa as
a vegetable and as fodder.

LAUNAEA TARAXACIFOLIA (Willd.) Amin ex C. Jeffrey. Wild lettuce. 2n=   . Vegetable of Nigeria.

SENECIO BIAFRAE Oliv. 2n=   . Africa. Occasionally cultivated in W. Africa.

SENECIO GABONICUS Oliv. 2n=   . Trop. W. Africa. Occasionally cultivated.

STRUCHIUM SPARGANOPHORA (L.) O. Ktze. Water
bitterleaf. 2n=   . Vegetable of Nigeria.

Crassulaceae

BRYOPHYLLUM PINNATUM (Lam.) Oken. Never-die,
Resurrection plant. 2n=   . Africa. Cultivated
there as a medicinal crop and elsewhere as an
ornamental.

Cruciferae

BRASSICA CARINATA A.Br. Abyssinian mustard. 2n=34, genome formula BBCC. Unknown wild. Cultivated in Ethiopia as a vegetable and as an oil crop. A natural amphidiploid of ♀ B. nigra* and ♂ B. oleracea* (Uchimiya & Wildman, 1978).

BRASSICA JUNCEA (L.) Czern. & Coss. (syn. Sinapsis juncea L.). Sarepta mustard, Brown mustard, Leaf mustard, Indian mustard. 2n=36, genome formula AABB. Africa. However, Hemingway (1976) suggested a centre of domestication in C. Asia-Himalayas with secondary centres of diversity in India, China and Caucasia. Spread to E. Europe and China. Now distributed from Europe to E. Asia. Often as a weed. It is cultivated for its oily seeds and as a condiment.
    This species originated from the natural amphidiploid of ♀ B. campestris* and ♂ B. nigra* (Uchimiya & Wildman, 1978). Through artificial amphiploidization of hybrids of the parental species it has been possible to introduce characteristics of both parents into Sarepta mustard.

ERUCA PINNATIFIDA (Desf.) Pomel. 2n=   . Sahara. Occasionally cultivated in oases as fodder.

LEPIDIUM SATIVUM L. Garden cress, Common cress. 2n=16, 32. Wild type var. silvestre Thell. From Sudan area to the Himalayas. Cultivated in ancient times in Europe as a vegetable. It may have reached Europe from the Levant as a flax weed. In Africa, there are red, white and black varieties and seeds are used for medicinal purposes, oil production and as a vegetable.

    Cucurbitaceae

CITRULLUS LANATUS (Thunb.) Mansf. (syn. C. vulgaris Schrad.). Water-melon. 2n=22. Tropical and subtropical Africa. The wild race is commonly eaten by animals. An edible wild race, the tsama occurs in the Kalahari Desert, where it is often the principal source of water for animals and the bushmen. Food is often cooked directly in the tsama. Cultivated since ancient times in Mediterranean area and India. Now cultivated in many countries of the Old and New Worlds so that secondary centres of diversity have arisen. Var. citroides (Bailey) Mansf. is found in Sudan. Cultivated in USA (Citron, Preserving melon) and USSR.
    The citron - a fodder melon - is adapted to very dry areas. It has both weedy and cultivated races.
    The wild form, var. colocynthoides (syn. C. colocynthoides Pang.) is characterized by its white or yellow flesh with bitter flavour or not and the cultivated form var. edulis (syn. C. edulis Pang.) has red or yellow flesh with sweet flavour (Shimotsuma, 1965).

COCCINIA ABYSSINICA (W. & A.) Cogn. Anchoté. 2n=   . Ethiopia. Sporadic cultivation in SW. of Ethiopia for its tubers but its fruits are not eaten. The tubers and fruits of the wild plants are inedible.

CUCUMEROPSIS EDULIS (Hook.f.). Cogn. 2n=   . W. Africa. Cultivated in gardens and on roofs.

CUCUMEROPSIS MANNII Naud. 2n=   . W. and C. Africa. Cultivated there.

CUCUMIS ACULEALUS Cogn. 2n=40. Wild perennial from Ethiopia.

CUCUMIS AFRICANUS L.f. 2n=24. Wild in S. Africa. Resistant to cucumis green mottle mosaic virus and powdery mildew (Visser & de Nijs, 1980).

CUCUMIS ANGURIA L. 2n=24. Gherkin. The will type is var. longipes A. Meeuse (syn. C. longipes Hook.) occurring in Ethiopia and E. Africa. Introduced to the Caribbean, where the cultigen West Indian gherkin (var. auguria developed (Meeuse, 1958). Esquinas-Alcazar (1978) found similar electrophoretic patterns for enzymes of both varieties, but Puchalsi et al. (1979) did not. Some accessions of both varieties resistant to cucumis squash mottle mosaic virus and powdery mildew (Visser & de Nijs, 1980).

CUCUMIS DIPSACEUS Spach. Teasel gourd. 2n=24. Africa. An ornamental.

CUCUMIS FICIFOLIUS A.Rich. 2n=24, (48). A perennial from Ethiopia southwards.

CUCUMIS FIGAREI Naudin. 2n=72. Wild in Nigeria.

CUCUMIS HEPTADACTYLUS Naudin. 2n=48. Africa. Perennial (Dane et al., 1980).

CUCUMIS MELO L. Musk-melon, Melon, Cantelou e. 2n=24. As most Cucumis species come from Africa, the species probably originates from trop. Africa, whence it spread to other regions, producing secondary gene centres in Iran (p. 89), China (p. 36), Iran and S. USSR (p. 82) (Leppik, 1966).

CUCUMIS METULIFERUS Naudin. African horned cucumber. 2n=24. Cultivated as an ornamental and in some parts of Africa for its fruits. This self-compatible species is a source of resistance to southern root-knot nematode, aphids and squash mosaic virus for C. sativa.

CUCUMIS MYRIOCARPUS Naudin. 2n=24. S. Africa. Wild. Closely related to C. africanus* and C. leptodermis Schweik., 2n=24 (A.P.M. de Nijs, pers. comm. 1980). Resistance to powdery mildew (Visser & de Nijs, 1980).

CUCUMIS ZEYHERI Sond. 2n=(24), 48. A perennial from S. Africa (Dane et al., 1980).

LAGENARIA SICERARIA (Molina) Standl. (syn. L. vulgaris Ser.). Bottle gourd, White-flowered

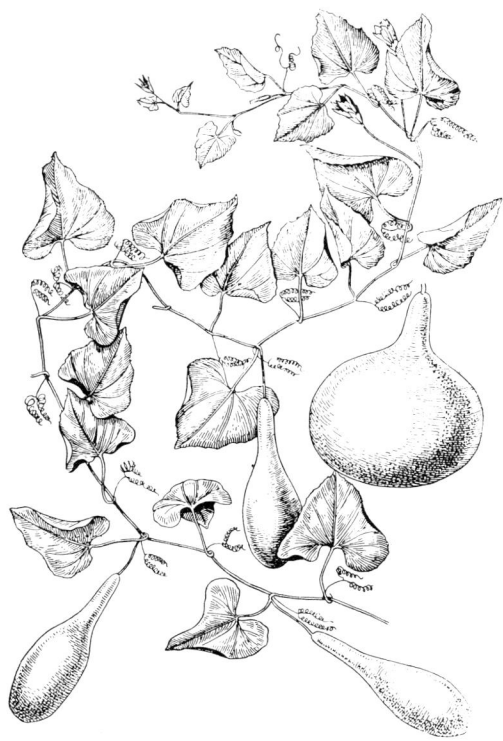

Lagenaria siceraria

gourd, Calabash gourd. 2n=22. Widespread in
Africa, now pantropic. Although an extensive
variation occurs in Africa both subspecies
asiatica Kob.(found in Asia) and afrikana
Kob. (found in Africa) also occur in Papua New
Guinea, where the penis gourd developed
(Heiser, 1973a, 1973b).

It now occurs subspontaneously and is cultivated in trop. Africa, Asia and America. It
has been shown that gourds float for a long
time and seeds remain viable. This may explain
very early spread to other continents by sea
currents. Remains of plant material tentati-
vely identified as belonging to Lagenaria have
been found in the Spirit Cave, Thailand and have
been dated 10000-6000 BC. (Gorman, 1970). Remains of the bottle gourd were found in Mexico
dated 7000-5500 BC. (Whitaker & Cutler, 1971)
in Peru 4000-3000 BC., in the Egyptian tombs
dated 3500-3000 BC. (Purseglove, 1968) and in
China 500 AD. (Li, 1969). Material found in
Mexico and dated 700-1300 AD. appears to be
more closely related to the modern races punctatum and latifolium than it is to other races
(Whitaker & Cutler, 1971).

It must be the oldest crop cultivated in the
tropics (Purseglove, 1968). Related species
are: L. abyssinica (Hook.f.) C. Jeffrey (syn.
Adenopus abyssinicus Hook.f., A. reticulatus

Gilg) (2n=   ), L. guineënsis (G. Don.) C.
Jeffrey (syn. Bryonia guineënsis G. Don., Adenopus longiflorus Benth., A. guineënsis (G.
Don.) Exell, A. pynaerti De Wild.) (2n=   )
and L. rufa (Gilg) C. Jeffrey (syn. Adenopus
rufus (Gilg) (2n=   ) (Jeffrey, 1962).

TELFAIRIA OCCIDENTALIS Hook.f. Fluted pumpkin.
2n=   . Trop. Africa. Cultivated there for its
seeds.

Cupressaceae

JUNIPERUS PROCERA Hochst. 2n=   . E. Africa.
Mainly a timber tree; also used for soil conservation and for medicinal purposes.

Dioscoreaceae

DIOSCOREA ABYSSINICA Hochst. 2n=40. Ethiopia,
savanna of Africa. Cultivated to a limited extent as a food crop, especially in Uganda
(Burkill, 1939; Coursey, 1967).

DIOSCOREA BULBIFERA L. (syn. D. latifolia
Benth.). Potato yam, Aerial yam, Bulbil-bearing yam. 2n=36, 40, 54, 60, 80, 100. Wild and
cultivated in trop. Asia (p. 52) and Africa.
It could have been domesticated in both regions.

DIOSCOREA CAYENENSIS Lam. Yellow yam, Yellow
Guinea yam, Twelve-month yam, Cut-and come
yam. 2n=36, 54, 60, 80, 140 and aneuploids.
W. Africa. Also cultivated in W. Indies.

DIOSCOREA COLOCASIIFOLIA Pax. False water yam.
2n=   . W. Africa. Cultivated in E. Ghana,
Cameroons and Mayumbe area of Zaïre.

DIOSCOREA DUMETORUM (Kunth) Pax. Bitter yam,
Cluster yam. 2n=36, 40, 45, 54. Cultivated
throughout Africa between 15°N and 15°S.
Closely related to the Asian D. hispida*.

DIOSCOREA ELEPHANTIDES (L'Hér.) Engl. Elephant's foot. 2n=   . S. Africa, in the rocky,
semi-deserts. Collected and eaten by Hotten-
tots. In Europe and N. America, it is cultivated as a curiosity (Coursey, 1967). The tuber
can grow to 350 kg.

DIOSCOREA HIRTIFLORA Benth. 2n=40. Savanna of
Africa. Cultivated in N. Nigeria.

DIOSCOREA LIEBRECHTSIANA De Wild. 2n=   .
Africa. Cultivated.

DIOSCOREA OVINALA Baker. Ovinala. 2n=   . Madagascar. Cultivated there. Almost replaced
by D. alata* and Manihot utilissima* (Coursey,
1967).

DIOSCOREA PRAEHENSILIS Benth. Bush yam, Forest yam. 2n=40, 80. W. Africa. Cultivated
there. Probably ancestor of D. rotundata*.

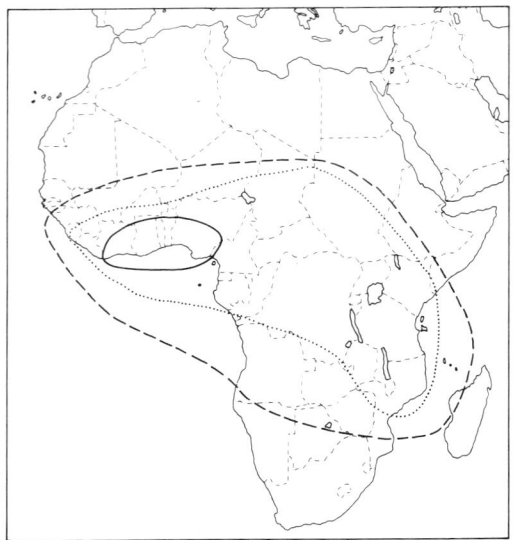

Dioscorea cayenensis and D. rotundata (——), D. dumetorum (···) and D. bulbifera (---)(Harris, 1972).

DIOSCOREA ROTUNDATA Poir. White yam, White Guinea yam, Guinea yam, Ibo yam. 2n=40, 60. W. Africa. The most important yam cultivated there. Probably derived from D. praehensilis*. Widely variable. Closey related to D. cayenensis* and often included it.

DIOSCOREA SANSIBARIENSIS Pax. (syn. D. macroura Harms, D. welwitschii Renole). Africa. Cultivated there.

DIOSCOREA SEMPERFLORENS Illine. 2n=   . Cultivated in Congo.

DIOSCOREA SOSO Jun. & Perr. 2n=   . Formerly cultivated in Madagascar, but now replaced by Manihot utilissima*.

DIOSCOREA ZARA Baudon. 2n=   . Cultivated to some extent in C. Africa. This name is applied to what is possibly a form of either D. sagittifolia Pax. or D. lecardii De Wild.

Ehretiaceae

CORDIA AFRICANA Lam. Sudan teak. 2n=   . Trop. Africa, trop. Arabia. Occasionally cultivated in Ethiopia, the leaves being used for medicinal purposes and the wood for building and furniture (Jansen, 1981).

Euphorbiaceae

BRIDELIA MICRANTHA (Hochst.) Baillon. 2n=   . Trop. Africa. Cultivated as food plant of the African silk caterpillar.

EUPHORBIA DREGEANA E. Mey. 2n=   . Namaqualand, S. Africa. Somethimes cultivated for rubber (Uphof, 1968).

EUPHORBIA KAMERUNICA Pax. Solo. 2n=   . W. Africa. A tall xerophytic tree. Cultivated for the latex used for tattooing and to poison arrows (Uphof, 1968).

MANIHOT ESCULENTA Crantz. Cassava. 2n=36. S. and C. America (p. 170). Secondary centre in Africa.

PLUKENETIA CONOPHORA Muell. Arg. (syn. Tetracarpidum conophorum Hutch. & Dalz.). 2n=   . A woody vine of trop. Africa. Cultivated as a source of oil.

RICINODENDRON HEUDELOTII (Baill.) Pierre ex Pax. 2n=22. W. Africa up to Angola and Usambara Highlands (Tanzania). Fruits and seeds are used as a source of oil. Also cultivated in Cameroons.

RICINUS COMMUNIS L. Castor bean, Castor-oil plant. 2n=20, (21). Trop. E. Africa and India. Now cultivated in most tropical countries where it runs wild in clearings, roadsides and dumpheaps. It probably originated as camp-follower, evolving into an oil plant, a drug and an ornamental (Anderson, 1952). The only species of this genus.

Flacourtiaceae

ONCOBA ECHINATA Oliver (syn. Caloncoba echinata (Oliver) Gilg.). 2n=   . Trop. W. Africa. Cultivated in C. and S. America for medicinal seed oil.

Geraniaceae

PELARGONIUM X ASPERUM Ehrh. ex Willd. (syn. P. radula L'Hér. var. roseum Willd., Pelargonium roseum Willd.). Rose geranium. 2n=77, 81. S. Africa. Cultivated for its geranium oil. The plant is male-sterile. Autetraploids (2n=4x= 154) are fertile. Crossed with autotetraploid P. denticulatum and backcrossed with 4x P. x asperum resulted in plants with 40-55% more oil than P. roseum (Tamai & Tokumasu, 1968). P. x asperum is probably a hybrid of P. radens x P. denticulatum* (Clifford, 1958) or P. graveolens* x P. radens (Moore, 1955). P. radens Moore. (2n=   ) is a plant of S. Africa.
   If the first parentage is correct, the new oil-rich hybrids are a cross of a 4x hybrid (p. radens x P. denticulatum) with 4x P. denticulatum and of backcrossing with the 4x original hybrid.
   This species, P. quercifolium Ait. (2n=auto 4x=44; Oak-leaved geranium) and P. crispum* have identical zymograms for esterase, peroxidase and acid phosphatase (Tokumasu et al., 1977), which points to a close relationship.

PELARGONIUM CRISPUM (L.) L'Hér. ex Ait. (syn

P. rigidum Willd.). 2n=2x=22. S. Africa. Cultivated for its lemon-scented oil. It varies considerably in the wild and there are several forms.

PELARGONIUM DENTICULATUM Jacq. 2n=90. S. Africa. Was cultivated as a fragrant pelargonium in Japan where it was replaced in 1954 by P. roseum*. It has a pine scent.

PELARGONIUM GRAVEOLENS L'Hér. (syn. P. terebinthinaceum (Cav.) Small). Rose geranium. 2n= 90. S. Africa. A pelargonium with rose-scented leaves. Cultivated for it oil. There are many cultivars. P. capitatum Willd., is a derivative of P. graveolens (Moore, 1955). Cultivated in Algeria and Isle of Réunion.

PELARGONIUM KAROOENSE Kunth. 2n=   . S. Africa. Cultivated for its geranol.

PELARGONIUM ODORATISSIMUM (L.) Ait. 2n=16. Trop. Africa. Extensively cultivated for its apple-scented geranium oil.

PELARGONIUM TOMENTOSUM Jacq. 2n=   . S. Africa. Cultivated for its peppermint-scented oil. It crosses readily with P. graveolens*.

Gramineae

ACROCERAS AMPLECTANS Stapf. (syn. Panicum zizanoides Hbk. var. angustatum Stapf). 2n= . W. Africa. Cultivated in Gambia as a vegetable (Terra, 1967).

ACROCERAS MACRUM Stapf. Nilegrass. 2n=36. S. and E. Africa. Cultivated as a pasture grass.

ANDROPOGON GAYANUS Kunth. Gamba. 2n=20, 40. N. Nigeria. It has been divided into var. gayanus (syn. var. genuinus Hack.), var. squamulatus (Hochst.) Stapf., var. bisquamulatus (Hochst.) Hack., and var. tridentatus (Hochst.) Hack. The second and third varieties have been used for selection. The tetraploid plants found in var. tridentatus are perhaps hybrids of A. gayanus (2n=20) in the far north of Nigeria and A.tectorum (2n=20)in the S. part of N. Nigeria.

ARUNDINARIA ALPINA K. Schum. Alpine bamboo. 2n=   . Kenya, Tanzania, Uganda, Sudan, Ethiopia, Rwanda and Burundi in mountain forests at an altitude of about 2400-3000 m. Its stems are used in paper industry and as building material.

AVENA ABYSSINICA Hochst. Ethiopian oats, Abyssinian oats. 2n=28, genome formula AABB. Obligate weed in wheat and barley fields above 2000 m on the Ethiopian Plateau. It resembles domesticated cereals in that it has lost the ability of natural seed dispersal. Ethiopian oats are unintentionally harvested and sown with the crop it accompanies, as a mimictic weed. A spontaneous race (A. vaviloviana (Malz.) Mordv.) also occurs in Ethiopia. Natural seed

dispersal mechanisms in A. abyssinica are controlled by two independent loci that are homozygous recessive in the non-brittle, obligately weedy race. Ethiopian oats is derived from the Mediterranean tetraploid (AABB) A. barbata Pott. ex Link. (Ladizinsky, 1975b; Ladizinsky & Zohary, 1971).

AVENA STRIGOSA Schreb. abyssinica type. Abyssinian oat. 2n=28, genome formula AsAsBB. This type has also been described as A. abyssinica Hochst. This is the non-brittle form while the semi-brittle form (vaviloviana type, A. vaviloviana Malz.) is also found in Ethiopia. The abyssinian type is harvested and threshed together with barley. Both types probably derive from introduced barbata type of A. strigosa* (Ladizinsky & Zohary, 1971).

BRACHIARIA BRIZANTHA (Hochst.) Stapf. Palisade grass. 2n=(x=9), 36, 54. Trop. and S. Africa, cultivated esp. in Sri Lanka and Brazil.

BRACHIARIA DECUMBENS Stapf. Signal grass. 2n= 4x=36. Trop. Africa. Cultivated throughout the tropics for fodder. An obligate aposporous apomict.

BRACHIARIA DEFLEXA (Schumach.) C.E. Hubbard. Animal fonio. 2n=20. Guinea coast to Yemen, and south to S. Africa and Botswana. Var. sativa Portères is cultivated as a cereal on the Fouta Djalon Highlands of Guinea in W. Africa. Often invades cultivated fields as a weed, and is frequently harvested as a wild cereal. In Angola, an aggressive colonizer race is a tolerated wild cereal in maize fields (de Wet, 1977). This species grades morphologically into B. ramosa (L.) Stapf, a species that is cultivated as a cereal in S. India.

BRACHIARIA MUTICA (Forsk.) Stapf (syn. B. purpurascens (Raddi) Henri). Para grass, Mauritius grass, Watergrass. 2n=36. Throughout tropics and subtropics. Grown as a fodder.

BRACHIARIA RUZIZIENSIS Germain & C. Evrard. Congo signal grass, Ruzi grass. 2n=18. E. Africa. In Australia Kennedy ruzi grass is cultivated. It is self-incompatible.

CENCHRUS BIFLORUS Roxb. (syn. C. barbatus Schum., C. catharticus Del.) Cramcram. 2n= 30, 34, 36. Aggressive colonizer of disturbed habitats in African savanna, extending to India. Widely harvested in W. Africa as a cereal, and important fodder in the arid savanna.

CENCHRUS CILIARIS L. Buffel grass, African foxtail, Rhodesian foxtail. 2n=mainly 36. Cultivated in Australia. Obligate and facultative apomixis and sexual propagation (Bray, 1972). Related to C. setigerus Vehl, Birdwood grass, 2n=34, 36, 37.

CHLORIS GAYANA Kunth. Rhodes grass. 2n=20, 30,

40. E. Africa from Ethiopia to South Africa. Excellent natural forage. Cultivated widely as a fodder in the tropics and subtropics.

CHLORIS ROXBURGHIANA Schult. 2n=20. Kenya.

CYNODON DACTYLON (L.) Persoon. Kweek grass, Bermuda grass. 2n=18, 36. Africa and Eurasia; introduced to the New World. Several varieties are recognized (Harlan et al., 1970). Selections from var. dactylon are widely planted as lawn-grasses. Coastal Bermuda grass (Burton, 1947), a widely planted fodder in SE. USA reproduced vegetatively from a hybrid between var. dactylon (2n=36) and var. elegans (2n=36). Var. coursii (2n=36) is an important natural fodder in Madagascar, as is var. elegans in S. Africa. Var. aridus (2n=18) is drought-tolerant, and extends from the S. Karroo (S. Africa), across the Near East to India. See p. 73.

CYNODON INCOMPLETUS Nees. var. hirsutus (Stent) De Wet & Harlan (syn. C. bradleyi Stent). 2n= 18. S. Africa. Widely cultivated lawn-grass.

CYNODON X MAGENISII Hurcombe. Magenis, Sunturf. This triploid represents a natural hybrid between C. dactylon var. dactylon (2n= 36) and C. transvaalensis (2n=18). Widely planted lawn-grass from a single hybrid clone near Johannesburg in South Africa.

CYNODON NLEMFUENSIS Vanderyst. Giant star grass. 2n=18, 36. Ethiopia, Uganda and south to Angola and Zimbabwe. An excellent natural fodder. Cultivated in trop. Africa. A cultivar grown in SW. Nigeria was derived from a cross between this species (2n=36) and C. dactylon* var. coursii (2n=36).

CYNODON PLECTOSTACHYUS (Schumach.) Pilger. Star grass. 2n=18. Ethiopia to Zaïre and Zambia. An excellent natural fodder, but cultivated in Kenya. Often confused with C. nlemfuensis*, but readily distinguished by its minute glumes.

CYNODON TRANSVAALENSIS Burtt-Davy. Transvaal Bermuda, African Bermuda grass (US). 2n=18. South Africa. An excellent fine hardy lawn-grass.

DIGITARIA ABYSSINICA (Hochst.) Stapf. Abyssinian finger grass. 2n=   . Trop. Africa. Used in S. Africa to control erosion; useful fodder.

DIGITARIA DECUMBENS Stent. Digit grass, Pangola (finger) grass. 2n=27. S. Africa. An excellent natural fodder. An introduction from S. Africa is grown as a fodder in the Americas as Pangola grass.

DIGITARIA EXILIS (Kippist) Stapf. Fonio, Acha, Fundi. 2n=18, 36. W. Africa. Cultivated as a cereal in the W. African savanna (Portères, 1955). Its closest wild relative is D. longiflora (Retz.) Persoon, which is widely distributed in the tropics. Portères (1976) recognizes five races of fonio. However, these races have no geographic unity and grade morphologically into one another. The most primitive is var. gracilis with two racemes and spikelets that are mostly grouped into threes along the rachis. In these traits, var. gracilis resembles D. longiflora except that the spikelets are glabrous. The lower part of each raceme is devoid of spikelets in var. stricta. The other three varieties have usually more than two racemes per inflorescence. Var. densa is characterized by crowded spikelets. Var. rustica and var. mixta include robust plants that are late to mature.

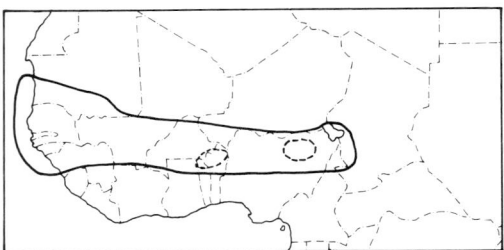

Digitaria exilis (—) and D. iburua (---)(Portères, 1950).

DIGITARIA IBURUA Stapf. Iburu, Black fonio, Hungry rice. 2n=36. W. Africa. Cultivated as a cereal by the Hausa of Nigeria between Jos and Zaria, and sporadically around Zinder in Niger, Azagive in the Ivory Coast, Kande and Atalote in Togo, and between Birni and Natitingou in Benin. It is often grown in between rows of sorghum or pearl millet, and frequently as a mixture with D. exilis*. The closest wild relative of black fonio is D. barbinodis Henr., an aggressive natural colonizer in W African savanna.

DIGITARIA PENTZII Stent. Taiwan pangola grass. 2n=(18, 27), 36, (45), 54. S. Africa. Related and perhaps identical with D. decumbens*. Source of resistance to virus diseases.

DIGITARIA TRICOSTULATA (Hack.) Henr. 2n= Africa. Related to D. iburua*.

DIGITARIA VALIDA Stent. Giant pangola grass. 2n=24, 30, 36. S. Africa. A source of disease resistant for D. decumbens*. Introduced in Florida and Surinam.

ECHINOCHLOA COLONA (L.) Link. 2n=54. Widely distributed in the tropics and subtropics. Formerly cultivated in Egypt and Tanzania. Now cultivated as inferior cereal in India. An important wild cereal and good fodder across the dry African savanna and as fodder in N. America.

EHRHARTA CALYCINA Smith. Perennial veldtgrass.
2n=24, 30, 48. S. Africa. Used as a soil stabilizer in W. of USA. Cv. California veldtgrass has an open panicle and sheds its caryopses. The new cv. Mission veldtgrass has a compact panicle and is non-shedding.

ELEUSINE CORACANA (L.) Gaertn. ssp. africana
(Kenn.-O'Bryan) Hilu & de Wet (syn. E. africana Kennedy-O'Bryan). Wild finger millet. 2n=
36. Guinea coast of W. Africa to Ethiopia and
south to the Cape Province (S. Africa). Differs from E. indica* in being tetraploid, not
diploid, and in having more obviously sculp-
tured grains (Phillips, 1972).

ELEUSINE CORACANA (L.) ssp. coracana. (syn.
E. coracana (L.) Gaertn). Finger millet. 2n=
36. Widely cultivated as a cereal along the
highlands of E. Africa from Uganda and Ethiopia to South Africa. Mehra (1963) recognizes
an African highland race with open inflorescence. Hilu & de Wet (1976) show that the
African highland race is widely cultivated on
the E. African highlands and was derived under cultivation from ssp. africana. This race
gave rise to an African lowland race that was
introduced to India, where it evolved into a
morphologically distinct cereal complex. The
oldest known domesticated finger millet occurs in the archaeological record of Ethiopia

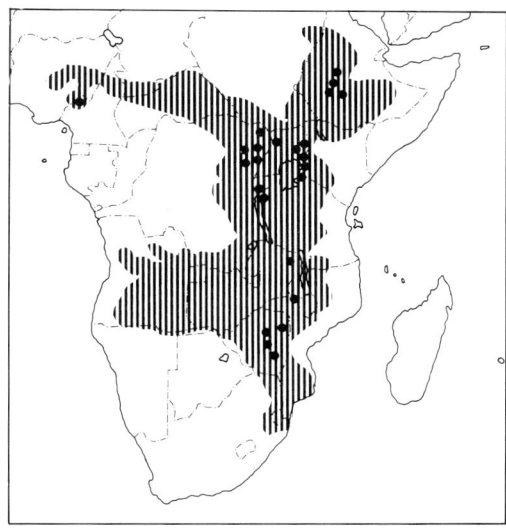

Eleusine coracana in Africa (grey) African highland race, (●) African lowland race.

south as the Transvaal of South Africa by the
beginning of the Bantu Iron Age.

ELEUSINE INDICA (L.) Gaertn. Goosegrass. 2n=
18. Eurasia and Africa. Introduced to the New
World, where it is an aggressive weed. Jameson (1970) proposed that the Indian races of
finger millet were derived from E. indica while
E. coracana* ssp. africana is the progenitor
of domesticated African finger millets. Cytogenetic evidence refutes this hypothesis. Ssp.

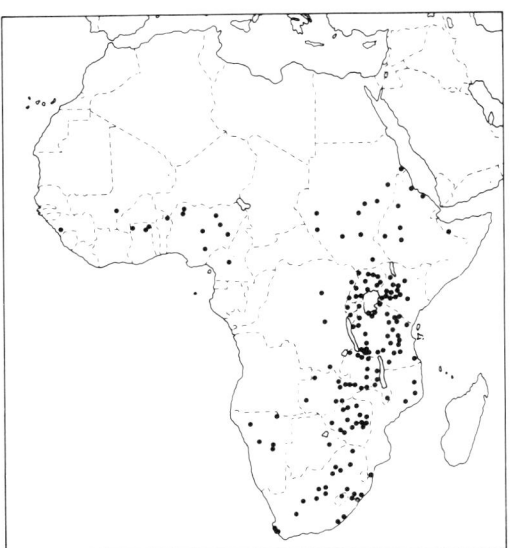

Eleusine africana (Phillips, 1972).

dating back some 5000 years (Hilu et al., 1979).
It never spread into the W. African savanna,
probably because of competition with other
millets such as the fonios (Digitaria sp.).
However it became widely cultivated as far

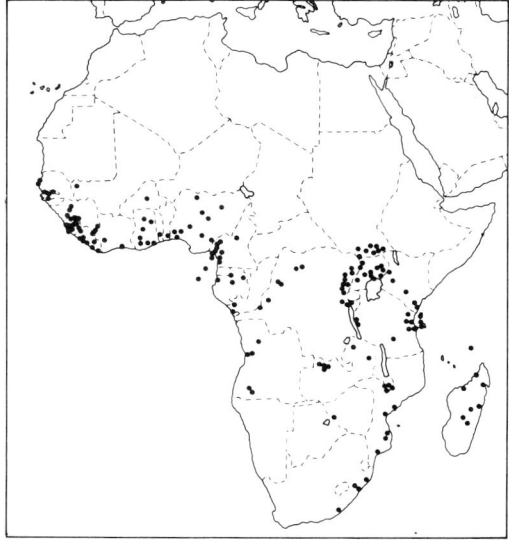

Eleusine indica (Phillips, 1972).

africana (2n=36) crosses readily with both African and Indian finger millets to produce fertile hybrids (Chennaveeraiah & Hiremath, 1974).

ENTEROPOGON MACROSTACHYUS Schum. Bush rye. 2n= 20. E. Africa.

ERAGROSTIS CURVULA (Schrad.) Nees. Weeping lovegrass, Boer lovegrass. 2n=20, 30, 40, 50, 60, 70, 80, 30-70, x=10. S. Africa. There is no relation between region of provenance and 2n. Most plants belong to type robusta. The reproduction is sexual, obligate and facultative apomixis. Used as sand stabilizer.

ERAGROSTIS SUPERBA Peyr. Tickgrass. 2n=40. E. Africa. Cultivated there.

ERAGROSTIS TEF (Zucc.) Trotter. (syn. E. abyssinica (Jacq.) Link.). Teff, Teffgrass. 2n= 40. The large and widely distributed genus Eragrostis includes this one domesticated cereal species. Teff is an endemic cereal crop of the Ethiopian highlands (Tadessa, 1975). Widely grown in S. Africa as a fodder for livestock; introduced in USA. The wild progenitor of teff is not certain. Its closest wild relative E. pilosa (L.) Beauv. is widely distributed across warm temperate parts of the world, and is harvested as a wild cereal in E. Africa (Rozhevicz, 1928).

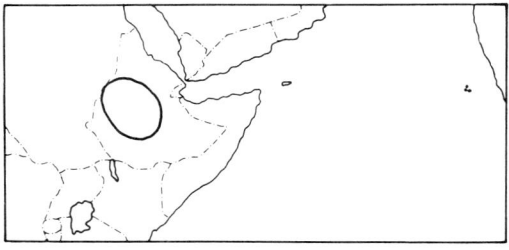

Eragrostis tef (Portères, 1950).

HEMARTHRIA ALTISSIMA (Poir.) Stapf & C.E. Hubb. Limpograss. 2n=18, 36, (54). SE. Africa. Domesticated in Florida, USA as a perennial, vegetatively propagated forage grass.

HYPARRHENIA RUFA (Nees) Stapf. (syn. Andropogon rufus Kunth). Jaragua grass. 2n=20, 30, 36, 40. Trop. Africa. Cultivated in N. and S. America.

MELINIS MINUTIFLORA Beauv. Molasses grass, (Brazilian) stink grass, Honey grass. 2n=4x =36. Africa. Cultivated as a fodder plant. Naturalized in Brazil.

OREOBAMBOS BUCHWALDII K. Schum. 2n=   . The mountains of trop. Africa.

ORYZA BARTHII A. Chev. (syn. O. breviligulata A. Chev., O. stapfii Roshev., O. perennis Moench. ssp. barthii (A. Chev.) A. Chev.). 2n= 24. From the Guinea coast of W. Africa across the savanna to Zambia. Growing in water, often as a weed in rice fields (Clayton, 1972). It probably represents derivatives of hybrids between O. longistaminata* and O. glaberrima*.

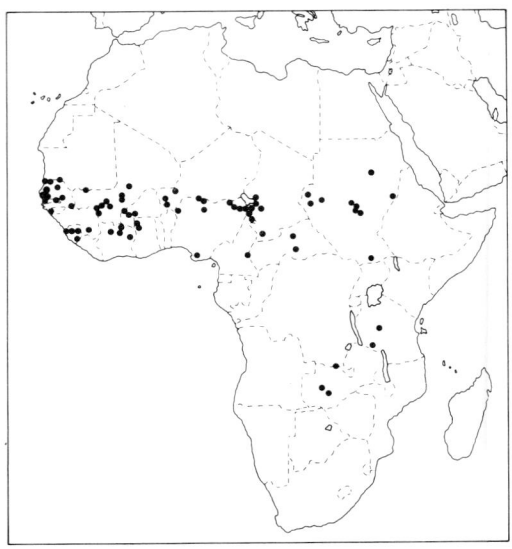

Oryza barthii (Harlan, 1973).

ORYZA BRACHYANTHA A. Chev. & Roehr. (syn. O. guineensis A. Chev.). 2n=24. From the Guinea coast of W. Africa across N. Zaire to the S. Sudan. This species usually occurs in shallow pools that dry out after the rainy season. In permanent pools it behaves as a perennial.

ORYZA EICHINGERI A. Peter (syn. O. latifolia Hook.f. var. collina (Trimen) Hook.f.) 2n=48. This slender species grows in damp places as a forest undergrowth and is distributed from the Ivory Coast to Uganda and Tanzania, and also occurs in Sri Lanka. The name O. eichingeri was also used for types now included in O. punctata*, and O. schweinfurthiana non Prod. (Gopalakrishnan & Sampath, 1966).

ORYZA GLABERRIMA Steud. African rice. 2n=24, genome formula A^gA^g. An indigenous cultivated rice grown in flood plains of savanna. From Senegal to Lake Chad. It is generally accepted that this species evolved under cultivation from O. longistaminata*, which is widely collected as a wild cereal in the African savanna. Nayar (1973) postulated that African rice originated as a derivative of introduced Asiatic rice, O. sativa which according to him reached

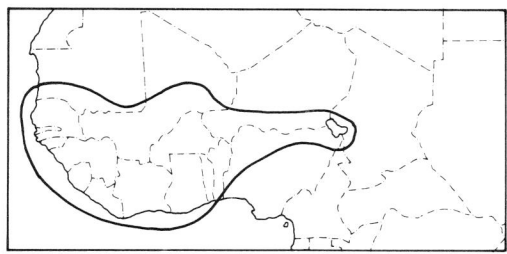

Oryza glaberrima (Portères, 1950).

Egypt during the fourth century BC. There is, however, no botanical or genetic evidence to support this hypothesis. Variation is discussed by Portères (1956).

ORYZA LONGISTAMINATA A. Chev. & Roehr. African wild rice. 2n=24. Throughout trop. Africa including N. Transvaal of South Africa. This perennial occurs in shallow pools and along the banks of rivers. It resembles O. sativa* (Asiatic rice) in having long ligules on the lower leaves.

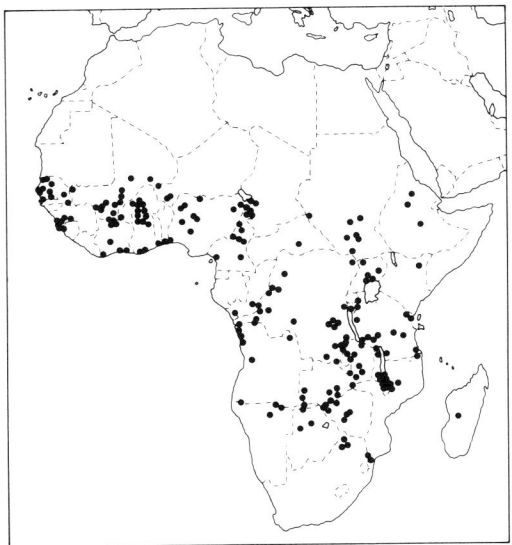

Oryza longistaminata (Harlan, 1973).

ORYZA PUNCTATA Kotschy & Steud. (syn. O. schweinfurthiana Prod.). 2n=24. Swampy streamsides from the Guinea coast to the Sudan, south to Angola. Also in Madagascar and S. Asia.

OXYTENANTHERA ABYSSINICA Munro (syn. Bambusa abyssinica Rich.). Woody bamboograss. 2n=c.60. Senegal to Ethiopia. Cultivated for its stems

which are used for boats and rafts, as well as for paper-making.

PANICUM BULBOSUM HBK (syn. P. maximum var. gongylodes Doell). Texas grass. 2n=6x=54, 70, 8x=72. Distributed in Texas, Mexico, C. and S. America. Forage grass.

PANICUM COLORATUM L. Small buffalo grass. 2n= 18, 36, 44, (54). S. Africa. A good fodder. Closely allied to P. maximum*. Var. makarikariense Goossens, makarakeri grass, 2n=44 is a native of Zimbabwe. It is more drought tolerant than var. coloratum and cultivated in S. Africa as a forage grass.

PANICUM LAETUM Kunth (syn. albidulum Steud.). Haze. 2n=   . An important wild cereal and good fodder forming large stands in the Sahel from Senegal to Eritrea. A potential cereal for arid regions.

PANICUM MAXIMUM Jacq. Guinea grass, Panic. 2n =18, (32)- 36, (48). Trop. and S. Africa, Madagascar, Mascarene Islands and Yemen. Cultivated as a pasture grass in many warm countries.

PENNISETUM AMERICANUM (L.) Leeke ssp. americanum. (syn. P. typhoides (Brum.) Stapf & Hubb., P. spicatum (L.) Koern.). Pearl millet. 2n=14. African savanna, also India and the Near East. This subspecies is recognized to include all cultivated taxa of pearl millet grown primarily as cereals (Brunken, 1977). The cultivated types commonly recognized (Stapf & Hubbard, 1934) are divided among four races. Race typhoides is characterized by obovate grains and includes the primitive pearl millets from which other races were derived. Grown across the African savanna and in India. Race nigritarum has grains with angular cross-section and is an important cereal from Sudan to Senegal. Race globosum has spherical grains and is grown from Upper Volta to Sudan. Race leonis is characterized by acute oblanceolate grains. It is primarily a pearl millet of Sierra Leone, but is sporadically grown also in S. Mauritania. Its wild ancestor is ssp. monodii*; a weedy type is ssp. stenostachyum*.

PENNISETUM AMERICANUM (L.) Leeke ssp. monodii (Maire) Brunken (syn. P. violaceum Lam.). 2n= 14. Wild pearl millet. W. Africa, Sahel from Dakar to C. Sudan, and the mountains of the C. Sahara. It is an aggressive colonizer of man disturbed habitats, and is the wild progenitor of pearl millet (P. americanum ssp. americanum*). Distribution suggests that pearl millet was domesticated along the C. Saharan highlands at the onset of the present dry phase in N. Africa, probably between 4000 and 5000 years ago.

PENNISETUM AMERICANUM (L.) Leeke ssp. stenostachyum (Klotzsch ex A.Br. & Bouche) Brunken (syn. P. stenostachyum Klotzsch). Shibra, Weed pearl millet. 2n=14. The pearl millet gene pool includes wild (ssp. monodii*) and cultivated

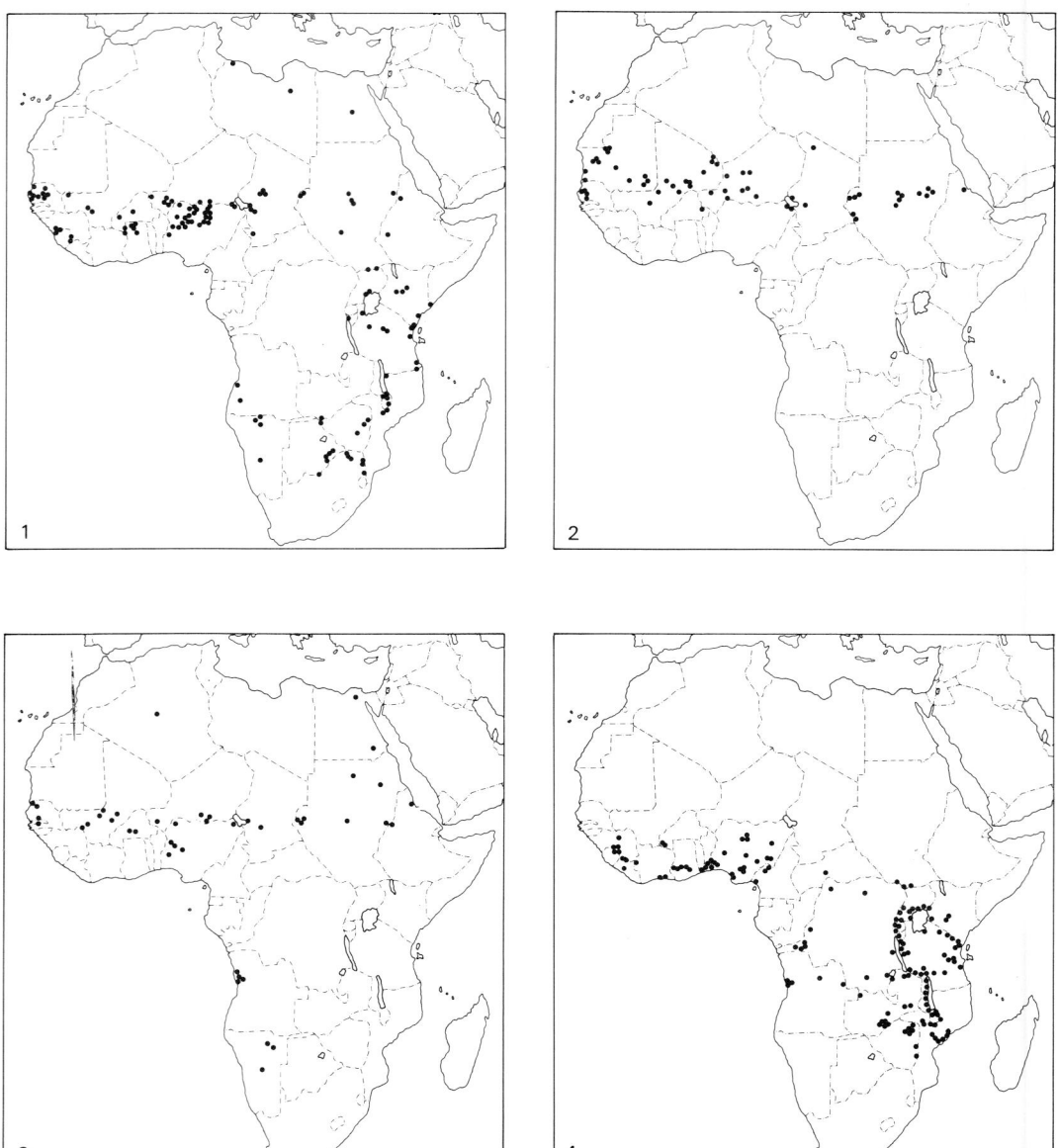

Pennisetum **sect.** Pennisetum americanum in Africa. 1 subspecies americanum, 2 subspecies monodii, 3 **subspecies** stenostachyum, 4 P. purpureum (Brunken, 1977).

(ssp. americanum*) kinds, as well as numerous spontaneous, weedy plants that mimic the crop in vegetative and floral morphology. Until maturation, these weeds are often difficult to distinguish from the race of pearl millet they accompany as a weed. However, their inflorescences disarticulates at maturity, and ssp. stenostachyum is spontaneous in man-disturbed habitats. Shibras originate from hybrids between cultivated races of pearl millet and subspecies monodii.

PENNISETUM CLANDESTINUM Hochst. ex Chiov. Kikuyu grass. 2n=36. Trop. E. Africa. An excellent natural fodder, and widely cultivated in the tropics and subtropics, as a soil stabilizer, lawn grass and fodder. Hermaphroditic and male-sterile.

PENNISETUM PURPUREUM Schumach. Napier grass. 2n=14. Trop. Africa. This species does particularly well in areas with an annual rainfall exceeding 1000 mm per year. It is an aggressive natural colonizer of wet disturbed sites. Napier grass was introduced during the 20th Century to many parts of the world as a fodder, and has become naturalized in most of the world's wet tropics. Bana grass in Kenya is a hybrid with P. americanum*.

PENNISETUM SETACEUM (Forsk.) Chiov. Fountain grass. 2n=27. African savanna. Cultivated as a fodder and in S. Africa also as an ornamental.

PENNISETUM UNISETUM (Nees) Benth. Natal grass, Drakenberg silky grass. 2n= . African Highlands. Cultivated in S. Africa as a forage grass.

PENNISETUM VULPINUM Stapf & Hubbard. 2n= . Africa. Cultivated in Sudan.

SACCHARUM SPONTANEUM L. Wild cane. 2n=104-128. From India (p. 75) plants with 2n=54 spread to Africa. In Uganda and adjacent Tanzania it is actually cultivated. In Africa originally used as a source of salt by burning, later it became used as hedges, for erosion control and for household. Grassl (1964) suggested that the high number of chromosomes may derive from hybridization of the original S. spontaneum and an African related species e.g. Sorghum bicolor*.

SECALE AFRICANUM Stapf. 2n=14. E. Karoo Plateau, S. Africa. Whether this species is a Pleistocene immigrant to S. Africa or a derivative of a relatively recent introduction of seeds of S. montanum from Spain or Italy as a contaminant of wheat and barley is not known (Khush, 1960). It has the same chromosome arrangement as S.montanum* and must have derived from this species (Stutz, 1972). Owing to its separation from the Secale-area, it adopted self-fertilization as a means of perpetuation. It has a fragile rachis and a perennial habit.

SETARIA PORPHYRANTHA Stapf. 2n= . Purple pigeon grass. Zimbabwe. Perennial grass culti-

vated in Australia.

SETARIA SPHACELATA (Schum.) Stapf & Hubbard. Setaria, Golden timothy grass. 2n=18, 36, 54. Africa. Cultivated there, Australia and elsewhere. Some cultivars have a high oxalic acid content which may result in the death of cattle. In Australia, it is often called S. anceps Stapf ex Massey, which species is closely related. Self-incompatible.

SORGHUM BICOLOR (L.) Moench ssp. bicolor (syn. vulgare Pers.). Sorghum. 2n=20. This subspecies is recognized to include the 28 cultivated taxa of Snowden (1936). It is widely cultivated in Africa, was introduced to India at least 3000 years ago, and has become an important crop in the New World during the last century. It is not known when sorghum was first brought into cultivation. Murdock (1959) proposes that it is a W. African crop. Doggett (1965) proposes that domestication took place somewhere in the NE. quadrant of Africa. Distribution indicated that sorghum must have been domesticated in the savanna zone south of the Sahara, and that the crop must have been cultivated for at least 3000 years (Harlan & Stemler, 1976). However, known identifiable archaeological remains of cultivated sorghum in Africa date back only to the early centuries of the Christian Era (de Wet, 1978). Cultivated kinds of grain sorghums are divided among races bicolor, kafir, durra, guinea, caudatum and several intermediated races (Harlan & de Wet, 1972).

Race bicolor (subser. Bicoloria Snowden) is characterized by open inflorescences and long clasping glumes that usually enclose the elliptic grain at maturity. Bicolor sorghums resemble spontaneous weedy sorghums, but they lack the ability of natural seed dispersal. Members of race bicolor, particularly those far removed from their African centre of origin, probably represent relics of ancient cultivated kinds. Others may have originated as selections from derivatives of hybrids between modern cultivated races and wild members of S. bicolor. Bicolor sorghums are low yielding as cereals. They are rarely an important crop, but are grown across the range of sorghum cultivation in Africa and Asia. Some selections are grown strictly for their sweet stems, while in Africa other kinds are grown for their bitter grains that are used to flavor sorghum beer. The race is morphologically heterogeneous. It includes S. dochna and S. bicolor of the Bicoloria, S. exsertum of Guineensia, and S. splendidum and S. nervosum of the subseries Nervosum Snowden.

Race kafir (subseries Caffra Snowden, excl. S. caudatum). It is characterized by more or less compact inflorescences that are often cylindrical in outline. Sessile spikelets are typically elliptic with the ripe glumes tightly clasping the usually much longer grain. The name is derived from 'kafir' the Arabic for unbeliever, referring to the Bantu who grow this race. Kafir sorghums are important staples

Sorghum bicolor

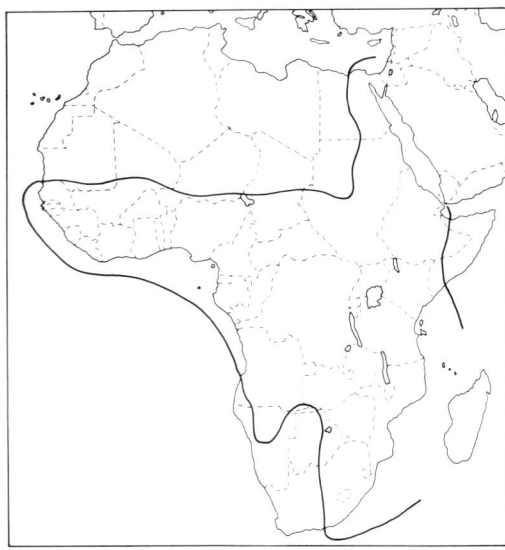

Sorghum bicolor (de Wet et al., 1972).

across E. and S. savanna from Tanzania to S. Africa. The race includes the usually recognized S. caffrorum and S. coriaceum.

Race caudatum is based on S. caudatum and S. nigricans of subseries Caffra. Caudatum sorg-

hums have turtle-backed grains flat on one side and distinctly curved on the other. The grains are usually exposed between the shorter glumes at maturity. Inflorescences range in shape from compact to open. This race is closely associated with speakers of Chari-Nilotic languages in Africa (Stemler et al., 1975). It is widely grown in Chad, Sudan, NE. Nigeria and Uganda. It is an old race of grain sorghum. Carbonized grains from Daima, dated to the ninth century (Connah, 1967) belong typically with race caudatum.

Race durra includes S. durra and S. cerruum of subseries Durra. The name is derived from the Arabic name for sorghum, and the distribution of race durra is closely associated with Islamic people in India and Africa. Inflorescences are usually compact. Sessile spikelets are flattened and ovate and the lower glume is either creased near the middle or has the tip of a distinctly different texture from the lower two-thirds. Durra sorghums are widely grown along S. fringes of Sahara, across arid W. Africa, the Near East and parts of India. A sheath of sorghum discovered in a building at Qasr Ibrim and dated to Meroitic time (Plumley, 1970) is composed of durra-like sorghums.

Race guinea is based on subseries Guineensia. It is characterized by long and gaping glumes that reveal the obliquely twisted grain at maturity. Inflorescences are usually large and open, with the branches often pendulous at maturity. The race is primarily a sorghum of W. Africa, but is also grown along the E. African Rift Valley from Malawi south to Swaziland. Some cultivars are adapted for cultivation in high rainfall areas, and others are used in decrue agriculture (Harlan & Pasquereau, 1969). Guinea sorghums are grown extensively in N. Nigeria where hybridization with drought-tolerant kinds of race durra is evident. Race guinea includes three well defined cultivated groups (de Wet et al., 1972). The one complex includes S. margaritiferum with its varieties, and is characterized by small (3.0-5.0 mm long) grains that are shorter than the glumes. This complex is grown in the high rainfall areas of W. Africa and the fog belt of E.S. Africa. In W. Africa, the flinty grains are cooked and eaten as rice. The Snowdenian S. guineense, S. conspicum and S. gambicum have larger (5.0-9.0 mm long) grains that are about equal in length to the gaping glumes. This complex is widely grown in the broad-leaf savanna of W. Africa, and the savanna of Malawi. In Malawi the inflorescences are often picked unripe and the sweet grains are eaten raw after drying. S. roxburghii is intermediate in spikelet morphology between races guinea and kafir. This complex extends across the range of sorghum cultivation in Africa and S. Asia.

Besides S. roxburghii, several Snowdenian species do not typically belong with any one of the five basic races. S. ankolib, S. rigidum and S. subglabrescens are intermediate in spikelet morphology between races bicolor and durra. Derivatives of hybridization between races guinea and caudatum are represented by S. dulcicaule and some varieties of S. elegans and S. notabile. S. melaleucum and S. mellitum are guinea-bicolor in spikelet morphology, and the intermediate kafir-bicolor complex includes S. basutorum, S. miliiforme, S. simulans and some cultivars of S. elegans and S. nervosum. Some cultivars of S. nigricans as recognized by Snowden are derivatives of kafir-caudatum hybridization. Hybrid races occur primarily where two or more basic races overlap. However, the hybrid morphology of some intermediate races has become fixed and several of these kinds are grown beyond probable centres of origin.

SORGHUM BICOLOR (L.) Moench. ssp. arundinaceum (Desv.) de Wet & Harlan (syn. S. arundinaceum (Desv.) Stapf, S. aethiopicum (Hack.) Rupr., S. verticilliflorum (Steud.) Stapf, S. virgatum (Hack.) Stapf). Wild sorghum. 2n=20. African savanna, into trop. forest and semidesert. Widely grazed. There are several more or less well defined ecotypes (de Wet, 1978). The savanna ecotype was domesticated to produce grain sorghums.

SORGHUM BICOLOR (L.) Moench ssp. drummondii (Steud.) de Wet & Harlan (syn. S. drummondii (Steud.) Millsp., S. sudanense (Piper) Stapf.). Chicken corn, Weed sorghum. 2n=20. Africa wherever grain sorghums are grown. These weeds represent derivatives of hybrids between grain sorghums and members of ssp. arundinaceum. Grain sorghums also introgress with S. halepense* in S. Asia and other parts of the world where this rhizomatous perennial became established, to form annual diploid and perennial tetraploid weeds. The widely distributed chicken corn of SE. USA probably originated from an abandoned cultivated grain sorghum. It is characterized by fragile racemes, but disarticulation takes place by breaking of the rachis rather than through callus formation as is typical for other spontaneous sorghums.

SORGHUM HALEPENSE (L.) Pers. (syn. S. miliaceum (Roxb.) Snowden, S. controversum (Steud.) Snowden). Johnson grass. 2n=40. Mediterranean area to Pakistan and S. India. This rhizomatous perennial was introduced as a fodder to all warmer parts of the world. The leaves and stems contain HCN, but the species makes an excellent hay. Sometimes a bad weed. In the Americas, S. halepense has introgressed with grain sorghums to produce the widely distributed and productive columbus grass (Celarier, 1958), which is drought-resistant. Derivatives of such introgression are known as S. almum* Parodi in Argentina (Saez, 1949).

TRICHOLAENA ROSEA Nees (syn. Rhynchelytrum repens (Willd.) Hubbard). Natal grass, Wire grass, Ruby grass. 2n=   . Trop. and SE. Africa. Cultivated as a forage grass and as an ornamental.

TRITICUM AESTIVUM (L.) Thell. ssp. vulgare (Vill.) MK. (syn. T. vulgare Vill.). Bread wheat, Common wheat. 2n=42, genome formula AABBDD. The bread wheats in Africa are also cultivated in the Sahara oases and Sudan zone. In the oases, special types exist, sometimes called T. vulgare ssp. oasicolum Duc. Other speltoid types have been referred to as T. spelta var. saharense; inflatum and sphaerococcoid forms (T. sphaerococcum) have also been found. Perhaps the Sahara oases could be a secondary centre of ssp. vulgare. Bread wheats of the Sahel zone came from Saudi Arabia - Sudan and N. Africa - Sahara (Zeven, 1980b).

Spelt wheats may have been introduced by the Romans. African spelt carries an Rf tim. gene like some European spelts (Zeven, 1971).

TRITICUM TURGIDUM (L.) Thell. Cultivated tetraploid wheats. 2n=28, genome formula AABB. Tetraploid cultivated wheats were introduced into Ethiopia. A secondary centre of T. turgidum* ssp. dicoccum; ssp. turgidum conv. turgidum, conv. durum and conv. polonicum arose there. Typical Ethiopian types have been classified as abyssinicum.

Leppik (1968) showed that Ethiopia is also the primary centre of wheat stem rust (Puccinia graminis Pers.).

ZEA MAYS L. Maize. 2n=20. Domesticated in C. America (p. 190). An example of the diversity of maize is given by Plarre (1972) for the Karamoja District of Uganda. Secondary centres in W. Africa, S. Africa, E. Africa (Somalia, Kenya and Ethiopia) (Brandolini, 1970).

Labiatae

ACOLANTHUS PUBESCENS Benth. 2n=36. Trop. Africa. Cultivated as a salad.

COLEUS EDULIS Vatke (syn. C. tuberosus Richard.). 2n=   . E. Africa. Cultivated in Ethiopia (Cufodontis, 1957).

COLEUS FORSSKAHLII (Poir.) Briquet (syn. C. barbatus Benth., Ocimum asperum Roth.). Kaffir potato. 2n=18. E. Africa and India. Cultivated in some parts of India (Uphof, 1968).

COLEUS ROTUNDIFOLIUS Chev. & Perrot (syn. Plectranthus rotundifolius Spreng.). Hausa potato. 2n=   . From W. and C. Africa to Transvaal, and Madagascar. Introduced into India, Malaysia, Indonesia and Philippines. Cultivated for its tubers.

HYPTIS SPICIGERA Lam. 2n=32. Trop. Africa. Cultivated there for its oily seeds.

OCIMUM KILIMANDSCHARICUM Guerke. 2n=76. Africa. Cultivated during World War II for the preparation of camphor.

ORTHOSIPHON RUBICUNDUS Benth. (syn. Plectranthus tuberosus Roxb.). 2n=28. Trop. Africa.

Cultivated for its tubers.

PLECTRANTHUS ESCULENTUS N.E.Br. (syn. Coleus dazo A. Chev., C. esculentus (N.E.Br.) Tayl., C. langouasiensis A. Chev.). Dazo, Kaffir potato. 2n=24. Africa. Cultivated there for edible tuber.

SOLENOSTEMON OCYMOIDES Schum. & Thonn. 2n= . Trop. Africa. Cultivated as a vegetable.

Leguminosae

ACACIA KARROO Hayne. (syn. A. horrida Willd.). Mimosa thorn, Allthorn acacia, Sweet thorn. 2n=52, 104. S. Africa. This tree is planted as an ornamental, in hedges and as sandbinder.

ACACIA NILOTICA (L.) Willd. ex Del. (syn. A. arabica (Lam.) Willd.). Babul acacia. 2n=52, 104. Trop. Africa extending to India. Cultivated there for its bark tannin. It also yields babul gum (Purseglove, 1968).

ACACIA SENEGAL (L.) Willd. (Sudan) gum arabic. 2n=26. Dry trop. Africa extending to the Red Sea and NW. India. The gum is mainly obtained from wild and semi-cultivated trees in the Sudan (Purseglove, 1968).

ALYSICARPUS GLUMACEUS (Vahl.) DC. 2n=20. Uganda, Kenya, Tanzania and Mozambique. Cultivated there as fodder.

ALYSICARPUS RUGOSUS (Willd.) DC. (syn. A. violaceus (Forsk.) Schindler). 2n=16. Dry trop. Africa. Used as a cover crop and fodder. Sometimes incl. in A. vaginalis*.

ALYSICARPUS VAGINALIS DC. Alyce clover, One-leaved clover. 2n=16, 20. Trop. Africa. Cultivated now in all tropics for soil improvement, as a cover crop and as a fodder crop. Var. nummarifolius (A. nummarifolius DC.) developed in the West Indies. It has a low spreading habit with buds located in the root crown. This makes it an ideal pasture plant (Whyte et al., 1953).

ARACHIS HYPOGAEA L. Groundnut, Peanut. 2n= 40. S. America (p. 172). Introduced into Africa where it is cultivated widely. Bunting (1955, 1958) has described numerous varieties for trop. Africa, which points to a secondary centre in this region.

ASPALATHUS CONTAMINATUS (Thunb.) Druce. Rooibos tea-bush. 2n= . S. Africa. There are two forms: the prostrate one is found on the Cape Peninsula and the erect cultivated form (A. cedarbergensis Bolus) is observed in the Cedarbergs in the Clanwilliam and Citrusdal regions. The latter is the cultivated type (Cheney & Scholts, 1963).

ASTRAGALUS VENOSUS (A. Rich.) Hochst. 2n=16. E. Africa. Cultivated as horse fodder.

BAPHIA NITIDA Lodd. Camwood. 2n=44. W. Africa. Formerly cultivated as a source of red dye, now only as an ornamental.

BAUHINIA ESCULENTA Burch. Gemsbuck bean, Tamany berry. 2n= . Arid savanna of S. Africa, often abundant. Seeds are excellent to eat after roasting or boiling as porridge. Young tubers make a good vegetable, and may be boiled or baked. Although not cultivated, seeds and tubers are often for sale in native markets of Botswana. A potential cultivated plant.

CAJANUS CAJAN (L.) Millsp. Pigeon pea. 2n=22, 44, 66. Native to India (De, 1974; van der Maesen, 1980), where wild plants and related species occur. Its early introduction into Africa, its wide variation and run wild plants there confused earlier authors who indicated this area as its native region. A secondary centre of diversity developed in this region.

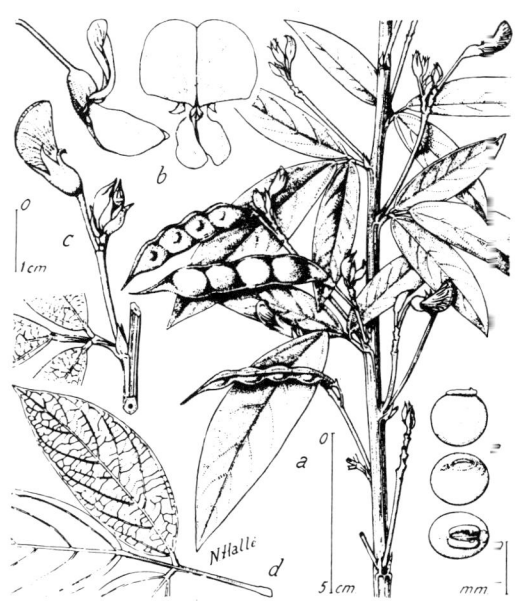

Cajanus cajan

CALPURNIA AUREA (Ait.) Bentham. 2n= . Angola, S. Africa, highlands of trop. E. Africa, Etiopia and S. India. Hedgeplant in Ethiopia. Shade-tree in coffee plantations. Ornamental in S Europe and elsewhere (Jansen, 1981).

CANAVALIA REGALIS Dunn. 2n=22. Probably an old African domesticate known only in cultivation. It is probably derived from C. virosa (Roxb) Wight & Arn. (2n=22), which occurs in Afric. south of the Sahara and also in India (Sauer, 1964).

CASSIA ANGUSTIFOLIA Vahl. Indian senna, Tinne-velly senna. 2n=(26), 28. Somali and Arabia. Cultivated in India for senna (laxative) (Pur-seglove, 1968).

CASSIA SENNA L. (syn. C. acutifolia Del). Alex-andrian senna. 2n=   . Egypt, Sudan region and Sahara. Leaves and pods are taken from wild and cultivated plants (Purseglove, 1968).

CLITORIA TERNATA L. Butterfly pea, Kordofan pea. 2n=16. Probably from Madagascar (Lowry & Chew, 1974). It is widespread in the tropics and cultivated as a fodder and soil cover crop. In Malaysia, actinomorphic flowers with bluer anthocyanins than normal are used to colour rice cakes. That type is not cultivated, but is conserved if noticed (Lowry & Chew, 1974).

CROTALARIA CANNABINA Schweinf. 2n=   . Sudan. A fibre crop.

CROTALARIA GOREENSIS Guill. & Pur. Gambia pea. 2n=16, (32). Trop. Africa. Cultivated in Queensland as green manure.

CROTALARIA INTERMEDIA Kotschy. Slenderleaf crotalaria. 2n=16. Trop. Africa. Cultivated in N. America and elsewhere especially for soil improvement, and also for grazing, hay and silage.

CROTALARIA SPECTABILIS Roth. (syn. C. seri-cea Retz., C. retzii A. Hitchc.). 2n=16. Trop. Africa. A green manure cultivated in (sub)-tropical countries. Wild in India and else-where.

CROTALARIA USARAMOENSIS E.G. Baker f. (syn. C. zanzibarica Benth.). 2n=(14), 16, (20). E. trop. Africa. A cover crop and green manure.

CYAMOPSIS SENEGALENSIS Guill. & Perr. 2n=14. Semi-arid savanna zone south of the Sahara from Senegal to Saudi Arabia. An annual herb. Probably the parental species of C. tetrago-noloba* (Hymowitz, 1973). Valuable fodder in Senegal.

CYAMOPSIS TETRAGONOLOBA (1.) Taub. (syn. C. psoralioides DC.). Cluster bean, Guar. 2n=14. Purseglove (1968) suggested that its origin lies in India, but Anderson (1960) stated an African domestication of this crop (see fur-ther p. 76). Cultivated in S. India.

DESMODIUM SALICIFOLIUM (Poir. ex Lam.) DC. 2n =20, 22. Trop. Africa. Used as green manure.

DIPOGON LIGNOSUS (L.) Verdc. (syn. Dolichos lignosus L., D. benthamii Meisn., D. gibbosum Thunb., Verdcourtia lignosus (L.) Wilczek). 2n=22. C. Africa. Cultivated in Africa, S. America and Australia where it has run wild (Verdcourt, 1970).

DOLICHOS AXILLARIS E. Mey. (syn. Macrostyloma

axillare (E. Mey.) Verdc.). Cultivated in E. Africa.

ERYTHRINA SENEGALENSIS DC. Coral flower. 2n= 42. W. Africa. Used as a hedge plant, as an ornamental and for medicinal purposes.

INDIGOFERA ARRECTA Hochst. Natal indigo. 2n= 16. E. Africa. Formerly cultivated for dye, and now as a green manure.

INDIGOFERA ENDECAPHYLLA Jacq. Wineleaf indigo, Creeping indigo. 2n=32, 36. Africa and Asia. Cultivated as fodder crop, usually in pastures, but poisons calves and horses.

INDIGOFERA TINCTORIA L. (syn. I. indica Lam., I. sumatrana Gaertn.). True indigo plant. 2n= 16. Probably W. Africa (Mansfeld, 1959). Cul-tivated as a dye plant. Also used as a green manure.

LABLAB PURPUREUS (L.) Sweet (syn. Dolichos lab-lab L., D. purpureus L., Lablab niger Medik.). Hyacinth bean, Bonavit bean, Lablab bean, Seins bean, Indian bean, Lubia bean, Egyptian bean. 2n=22, 24. Wild type (ssp. uncinatus Verdc., syn. Lablab uncinatus A. Rich.) in trop. Af-rica from W. Africa to Sudan and Ethiopia and to S. Africa. The commonly cultivated forms belong in general to ssp. purpureus unless they have linear kidney bean-like pods. Var. purpureus of this subspecies is a distinct due to all parts of the plant being purple. From Kenya, the cultivated ssp. bengalensis (Jacq.) Verdc. (syn. Dolichos bengalensis Jacq.) is reported (Verdcourt, 1970).

LOTONONIS BAINESII Baker. Miles lotononis. 2n=36. N. Transvaal and Zimbabwe. A perennial cultivated in Queensland.

MACROSTYLOMA GEOCARPUM (Harms) Maréchal & Baudet (syn. Kerstingiella geocarpa Harms, Voandzeia poissonii Chev.). Geocarpa bean, Geocarpa groundnut, Ground bean, Harms seeds, Kersting's groundnut. 2n=20, 22. W. Africa. Wild plants are classified as var. tisserantii (Pellegrin) Hepper (syn. Kerstingiella tis-serantii Pellegrin), 2n=20, and domesticated types as var. geocarpa, 2n=22.

NEONOTONIA WIGHTII (Arnott) Lackey (syn. Gly-cine wightii (Arnott) Verdc.). 2n=22, 44. Af-rica. A perennial relative of soya (Glycine max*). Cultivars in Australia originate from Malawi, 2n=44.

PHYSOSTIGMA VENENOSUM Balf. Calabar bean, Or-deal bean. 2n=   . W. Africa. Cultivated for its beans which are used as poison for ordeals.

PISUM SATIVUM ssp. abyssinicum (A. Braun) Alef (syn. P. abyssinicum Braun). 2n=14. Ethiopia and Yemen. Rarely found wild. Closely related to ssp. jomardi (p. 115).

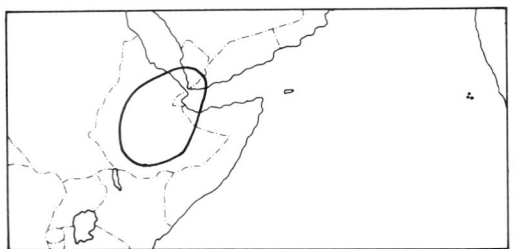

♦ Pisum savitum spp. abyssinicum (Govorov, 1937).

PSOPHOCARPUS GRANDIFLORUS Wilczek. 2n= .
Ethiopia to Uganda and Zaïre in uplands at
alt. c. 1750 m. Cultivated in Ethiopia (Westphal, 1974; Verdcourt & Halliday, 1978). Closely related to P. tetragonolobus*.

PSOPHOCARPUS PALUSTRIS Desv. 2n=16, 18, 20.
From Senegal to Sudan. The Ethiopian cultivar
Wondo Surprise (Westphal, 1974) belongs to P.
grandiflorus* (Verdcourt & Halliday, 1978).
Closely related to P. tetragonolobus*.

PSOPHOCARPUS SCANDENS (Endl.) Verd. 2n=18. E.
Africa. Cultivated in Indonesia, Sri Lanka,
India, Burma, Brazil and Jamaica for its fruits.
Closely related to P. tetragonolobus*; it is
not its direct parent (Pickersgill, 1980).

PSOPHOCARPUS TETRAGONOLOBUS (L.) DC. Goa bean,
Asparagus bean, Winged bean, Manilla bean. 2n=
18, (20). The origin of this species is much
discussed and Hymowitz & Boyd (1977) concluded
on 'meagre evidence' (as they call it) Papua
New Guinea. However like Burkill (1935), Smartt
(1980) advocated E. Africa. Smartt based his
conclusion on the absence of related species
in Asia and their presence in Africa. Among
the last, there is the closest related wild P.
grandiflora* found in E. Africa from Ethiopia
through Uganda to Zaïre in upland areas at c.
1750 m above sea level. Wild material could
have been taken to Asia and domesticated there
(Smartt, 1980). All parts of this protein-rich
vegetable are edible. It can also be used as
a restorative intercrop and as a cover crop
and the stalks can be used as fodder. It is
drought-sensitive (Hymowitz & Boyd, 1977).

SPHENOSTYLIS SCHWEINFURTHII Harms. Yam bean.
2n= . Trop. Africa. A woody plant. Cultivated for seeds and tubers.

SPHENOSTYLIS STENOCARPA (Hochst. ex A. Rich.)
Harms. African yam bean, Yam bean. 2n=18. W.
and E. Africa. Cultivated in Central African
Republic,Zaïre, Ethiopia and along the Rift
Valley of E. Africa for its edible tubers and
seeds. Probably domesticated independently at
several places across its native range (Okigbo,
1973).

STYLOSANTHES FRUTICOSA (Retz.) Alston (syn. S.

mucronata Willd.). Wild lucerne. 2n= . Trop.
Africa and SE. Asia. Cultivated as a fodder
crop in Brazil and Australia. Also naturalized
there.

STYLOSANTHES HUMILIS H.B. & K. Townsville
lucerne, Townsville stylo. 2n=20. S. Africa.
Cultivated in N. Australia in pastures.

TAMARINDUS INDICA L. Tamarind. 2n=24. The
savannas of trop. Africa. Introduced to India
long ago and recently to other parts of the
tropics. The tree and its parts have many uses
(Purseglove, 1968).

TEPHROSIA DENSIFLORA Hook.f. 2n= . W. Africa.
Cultivated and used to stupefy fish. Closely
related to T. vogelii*.

TEPHROSIA VOGELII Hook.f. Vogel tephrosia. 2n=
22. Trop. Africa. Cultivated for its rotencids
which are used as insecticides and piscicides.
Also cultivated as a green manure and a cover
crop.

TERAMNUS LABIALIS (Linn.f.) Spreng. 2n=20.
Asia and Africa. Cultivated in E. Africa and
Australia.

TERAMNUS REPENS (Taub.) Bak.f. 2n= . E. and
S. Africa, and India. Cultivated in E. Africa
and Australia.

TRIFOLIUM SEMIPILOSUM Fres. Kenya white clover,
E. African white clover. 2n=16. Kenya. Domesticated in Australia as a forage crop.

VIGNA UNGUICULATA (L.) Walp. (syn. V. sinensis (L.) Savi). Cowpea, Black eye, Southern
pea. 2n=22, 24. Primary centre W. and C. Africa. Probably domesticated in W. Africa. Introduced into the Indian subcontinent where ssp.
sesquipedalis (L.) Verdc. (syn. V. sesquipedalis (L.) Fruw., Dolichos sesquipedalis L.),
Asparagus pea, Yardlong pea (2n=22, 24), and
ssp. cylindrica (L.) Van Eseltine (syn. V.
cylindrica Skeels., V. catjang (Burm.f.) Walp.),
catjang (2n=22), developed. Ssp. sesquipedalis
has a long flabby pod, and is cultivated as
a snap bean while ssp. cylindrica is developed
as a forage crop. It has small seeds (Faris,
1965) (p. 76).

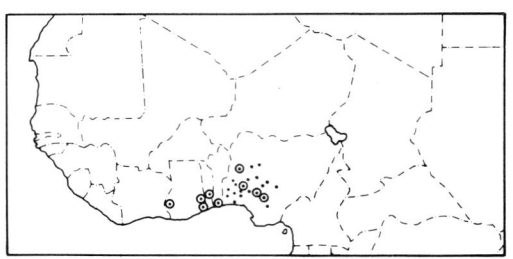

Vigna unguiculata (Harlan, 1973)

VIGNA VEXILLATA (L.) A. Rich. (syn. V. capensis auctt. non (L.) Walp., V. senegalensis A. Chev.). Wild mung. 2n=22. Grows wild in trop. Asia, Africa and Australia. Its tubers are collected in the wild. Cultivated in E. Africa.

VIGNA SUBTERRANEA (L.) Verdc. (syn. Voandzeia subterranea (L.) DC.). Bambara groundnut, Congo coober. 2n=22. Wild in W. Africa. Distributed throughout Africa and later to the Americas and Asia. Hepper (1963) described the wild type as var. spontanea (Harms) Hepper and the cultivated ones as var. subterranea Hepper.

Liliaceae

TUBAGHIA VIOLACEA Harv. Wild garlic, Wild knoflook. 2n=12. S. Africa. The Zulu of Natal often plant this species around their huts to keep snakes away, supposing that the odour repels all vermin. The leaves are cooked as a spinach and the bulb is used as a emetic love medicine (Watt & Breyer-Brandwijk, 1962).

Linaceae

LINUM USITATISSIMUM L. Flax 2n=30, (32). For possible origin see p. 99. Ssp. indo-abyssinicum Vav. & Ell. is cultivated in Ethiopia and Eritrea. Identical types are cultivated in India and may formerly have been introduced there from Africa.

Lythraceae

LAWSONIA ALBA Lam. (syn. L. inermis L.). Henna, Camphire. 2n=24. A shrub from trop. Asia and Africa with several uses.

Malvaceae

ABELMOSCHUS ESCULENTUS (L.) Moench. (syn. Hibiscus esculentus L.). Okra, Lady's finger, Gombo. 2n=72-132. See for origin p. 77. Siemonsma (1980) classified the gombo cultivars in W. Africa into the true type which is cultivated throughout the world, and the Guinean gombo. The first has 2n=c. 130 and the second 2n=c. 194. He suggested that the Guinean type, also called West African gombo, is an amphiploid of A. esculentus (true type) and A. manihot*, 2n=c. 66.

GOSSYPIUM ANOMALUM Wawr. & Peyr. 2n=26, genome formula B_1B_1. Along S. fringe of the Sahara, in SW. Africa and Angola. It can be crossed with G. herbaceum* and G. arboreum*.

GOSSYPIUM ARBOREUM L. Tree cotton. 2n=26, genome formula A_2A_2. Race soudanense. NE. and W. Africa. Hutchinson (1962) suggested that it was introduced from India, but Chowdhury and Buth (1970, 1971) thought that it is native to Africa. They found material dated about 3000 BC. at an early Neolithic site. It was probably used as stock feed, because cotton

hairs intermediate between lint hairs and the hairs of wild species were found in goat dung. The form was probably cultivated by the people of Meroë, an ancient Nubian kingdom, dated about 500 BC.

GOSSYPIUM BARBADENSE L. Egyptian cotton. 2n= 52 genome formula $(AADD)_2$. Peru (p.176). Spread to Africa. A perennial type from S. Nigeria made a 'Green Revolution' of cotton growing in the Nile Delta possible after 1820. This lead to introduction of other cottons. Only Sea Islands was successful. Vigourous and fertile hybrids of these two types occurred from which Egyptian was developed. It combines the annual habit and some of the quality of Sea Islands and some of the vigour and cropping characteristic of the perennial. It can be grown twice a year.

GOSSYPIUM HERBACEUM L. Short-staple cotton. 2n= 26, genome formula A_1A_1. Wild G. herbaceum var. africanum (Watt) Hutch. & Chose is a perennial shrub found in the bushveldt across a belt from Mozambique to Angola and SW. Africa.

Hutchinson (1971) suggested a likely centre of domestication in S. Arabia and Baluchistan. As wild G. herbaceum plants were found on the coast of Sind near Karachi, domestication may have taken place within the area of the Harappan culture at Mohenjo-Daro (Pakistan) about 2400 BC. However fragments of textile and a string found at that site and dated 2500-1700 BC. have been identified as G. arboreum*. Hutchinson (1962) suggested that cotton must have been brought from the area of present Zimbabwe by early traders to the north. The earliest domesticants were probably selected between there and Ethiopia or Arabia. From that variety, the primitive cultivated race acerifolium was selected, which was formerly found in Ethiopia, S. Arabia and Baluchistan.

Chowdhury & Buth (1970, 1971) found cotton seed and hairs in Egyptian Nubia with an age of about 2500 BC. They suggested that the cotton was used as sheep fodder, since no textile was found. The ancient Nubian cotton resembles G. herbaceum var. africanum and G. arboreum race soudanensis*.

Race persicum*, race kuljianum* and G. arboreum race indicum* derived from race acerifolium.

Either G. herbaceum reached S. America from America or G. arboreum reached Peru from Asia by way of the Pacific islands to form the amphiploid G. hirsutum* and G. barbadense*.

Many varieties belonging to G. hirsutum and G. barbadense are grown in Africa. G. hirsutum varieties (Upland and Cambodia) are cultivated in W. and C. Africa (race punctanum) in Congo and E. Africa, while G. barbadense (Egyptian) is found in the Nile Valley and Delta.

Var. africanum has a very simple proteinbanding pattern (Cherry et al., 1970).

GOSSYPIUM LONGIOCALYX Hutch. & Lee. 2n=26, ge-

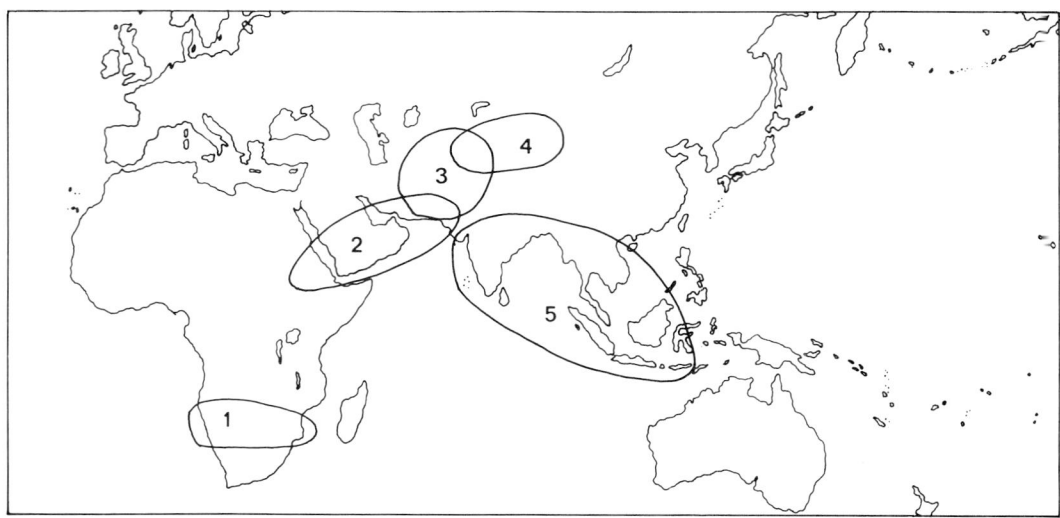

Distribution of the Old World cottons in the 13th Century: Gossypium herbaceum var. africanum (1), G. herbaceum var. acerifolium (2), G. herbaceum var. persicum (3), G. herbaceum var. kuljianum (4) and G. arboreum var. indicum (5)(Hutchinson, 1962)

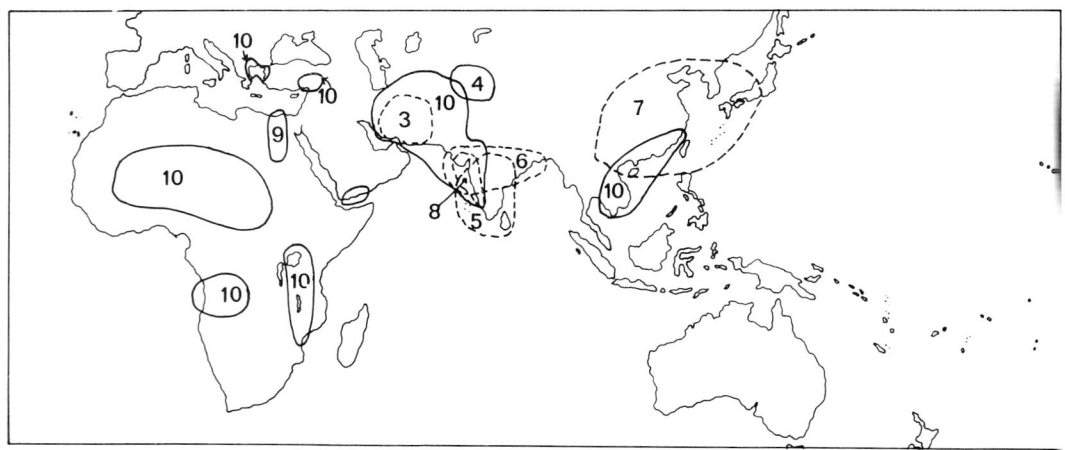

Distribution of annual cottons in the Old World in 1960: Gossypium herbaceum var. persicum (3), G. herbaceum var. kuljianum (4), G. arboreum var. indicum (5), G. arboreum var. bengalense (6), G. arboreum var. sinense (7), G. herbareum var. wightianum (8), G. barbarense Egyptians (9), G. hirsutum uplands and Cambodias (10)(Hutchinson, 1962)

nome formula E_5E_5. Uganda and Tanzania. It has an entire leaf like the American G. klotzschianum*.

GOSSYPIUM SOMALENSE (Guerke) Hutch. 2n=26, genome formula E_2E_2. Sudan, Somali and Kenya. A variable species.

GOSSYPIUM TRIPHYLLUM (Harv. ex Harv. & Sond.) Hochr. 2n=26, genome forumula B_2B_2. Desert of SW. Africa and S. Angola. It can be crossed with G. herbaceum* and G. arboreum*.

HIBISCUS ACETOSELLA Welw. ex Hiern. Azedas,

Red-leaved hibiscus, Bronze hibiscus. 2n=72. Genome formula AABB. Tanzania, Zaïre, Zimbabwe and Angola. Cultivated in SW. Africa as a vegetable. Introduced as H. eetveldeanus De Wild. & Dur. into Indonesia. Cultivated in the (sub)tropics as an ornamental.

The A genome is almost homologous to the A genome of H. asper*. The B genome is from H. surattensis* (Wilson & Menzel, 1964; Menzel & Martin, 1970), which grows in W. trop. Africa. The closely related H. radiatus* comes from Asia.

H. noldeae Baker f. is a spiny, inedible (primitive?) wild or weedy form of H. acetosella (Wilson & Menzel, 1964).

HIBISCUS ASPER Hook.f. 2n=36, genome formula AA, 72. Wild in W. and C. trop. Africa. Wild plants are collected for bast fibre. Occasionally cultivated for this purpose. Its A genome is close to the A genome of H. cannabinus*. It is one of the parents of H. sabdariffa* and H. acetosella* (Menzel & Martin, 1970). The A genome is also found in the African H. meeusei Exell (2n=72), genome formula AAXX (Menzel & Martin, 1971).

HIBISCUS CANNABINUS L. Kenaf. 2n=36, genome formula AA. Probably (sub)trop. Africa. Also wild in Asia but these plants might derive from naturalized plants. Its A genome is related to that of H. asper*. Kenaf is the A-genome donor of H. radiatus*.

HIBISCUS SABDARIFFA L. Rosella, Jamaica sorrel, Guinea sorrel, Florida cranberry, rozelle, sorrel, red sorrel, Indian sorrel, sour-sour, Queensland jelly plant, jelly okra, lemon bush. 2n=(36), 72, genome formula AAYY. Africa. Angola is apparently its primary centre of dispersal. Probably first domesticated as a dooryard or weedy plant for its seeds. Later it became a vegetable and finally a fibre crop (var. altissima Webster). It is a ruderal species of Angola, SW. Africa, Zaïre and Tanzania. Its A genome is derived from H. asper* (Menzel & Martin, 1970). Its Y genome donor is not yet known. Wilson and Menzel (1964) noted the relationship of roselle and H. mechowii Garcke. Var. sabdariffa is used on Jamaica to produce a sorrel drink.

HIBISCUS SCHIZOPETALUS Hook.f. 2n=45. E. Africa. Used there and elsewhere for hedges and as an ornamental. Its uneven chromosome number suggests a hybrid origin, H. rosa-sinensis L., 2n=36, 46, 72, 92, c.144, 168 being one parent. Van Borssum Waalkes (1966) concluded that, as H. schizopetalus was first collected in E. Africa, H. rosa-sinensis might have an African origin. However, Negroid people in general do not cultivate ornamentals and therefore a domestication of H. rosa-sinensis in Africa is unlikely. More probable is that H. schizopetalus arose in E. Africa after introduction of H. rosa-sinensis, probably from Asia. Judging from the variable number of this last species it might have a hybrid origin too.
    H. x archeri W. Watson is an artificial hybrid of H. rosa-sinensis and H. schizopetalus.

HIBISCUS SURATTENSIS L. 2n=36, genome formula BB, (72). Africa. It also occurs in India, SE. Asia, Indonesia and Philippines. The B donor of H. acetosella* and H. radiatus*.

Marantaceae

THAUMATOCOCCUS DANIELLII Benth. 2n=   . W. African rainforest from Sierra Leone to Zaïre. It produces proteins which are a non-sugar

sweetener.

Melastomataceae

SAKERSIA LAURENTIA Cogn. 2n=   . Zaïre. Cultivated there for its leaves (Terra, 1967).

Menispermaceae

CISSAMPELOS OWARIENSIS Beauv. Velvet leaf. 2n=   . W. Africa. Cultivated near coast as a medicinal (Dalziel, 1937).

JATEORHIZA PALMATA (Lam.) Miers (syn. J. columba (Roxb.) Miers, J. miersii Oliv.). 2n=   . Trop. Africa. Cultivated as a medicinal.

Moraceae

CHLOROPHORA EXCELSA (Welw.) Benth. Iroko. 2n=   . Africa. Cultivated there for its timber.

FICUS OVATA Vahl. 2n=26. Africa. Planted in S. Ethiopia as a sacred tree.

FICUS PALMATA Forsk. 2n=26. Ethiopia, Sudan, Egypt, Arabia, Yemen. According to Aweke (1979), this species could be the ancestor of F. carica (p. 99).

FICUS TILIAEFOLIA Bak. Voara. 2n=   . Madagascar. Cultivated there for its fibre.

Moringaceae

MORINGA PEREGRINA (Forsk.) Fiori. 2n=   . Egypt and Somalia. Cultivated in the (sub)tropics for the seeds which are the source of bennu oil. This species is closely related to M. oleifera*.

Musaceae

ENSETE VENTRICOSUM (Welw.) Cheesm. (syn. E. edule (Horan) Cheesm.). Ensete, Inset, Abyssinian banana. 2n=18. Ethiopia, the mountains of Kordofan (Sudan) and the lower part of the montane forest belt of Mount Ruwenzori (border of Uganda and Zaïre). Cultivated for the flour obtained from the pseudostem and also for its fibres. It is propagated by offshoots and by seeds from cultivated types or occasionally from wild plants. The cultivated plants are grown at higher altitudes than the wild plant. Several cultivated types are recognized. It is suggested that there are about forty types of ensete. The back of the leaf of the Koba type is red to purple. This variety has been described as var. montbeliardi D. Bois (Smeds, 1955).
    It is suggested that ensete is one of the oldest cultivated plants of Ethiopia.

MUSA cultivars of the AAA group. Banana. 2n= 33. Primary centre in the Malayan region (p. 59). Secondary centre in the uplands of E. Africa. There it has long been cultivated. The

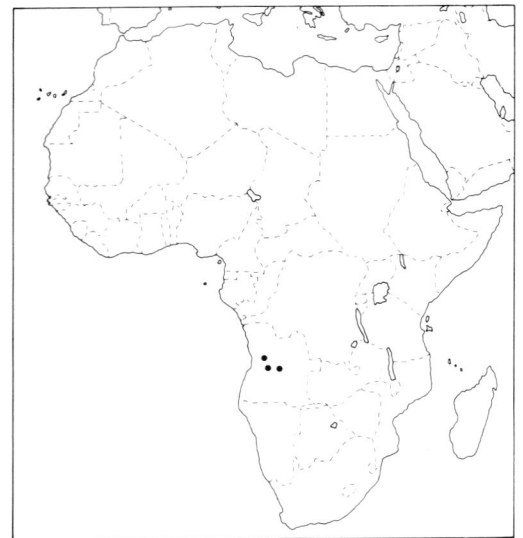

Hibiscus acetosella (Menzel & Wilson, 1969).

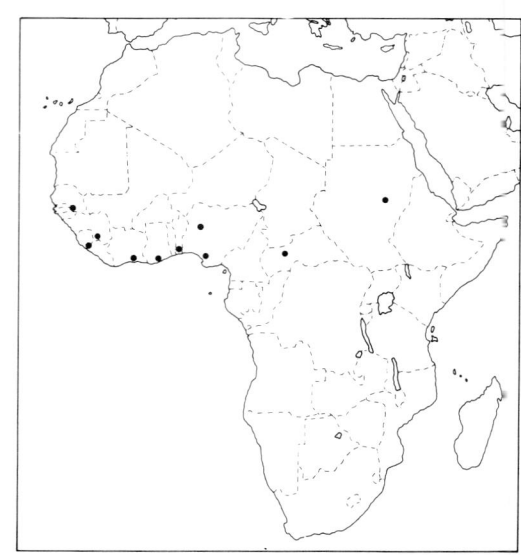

Hibiscus asper (Menzel & Wilson, 1969).

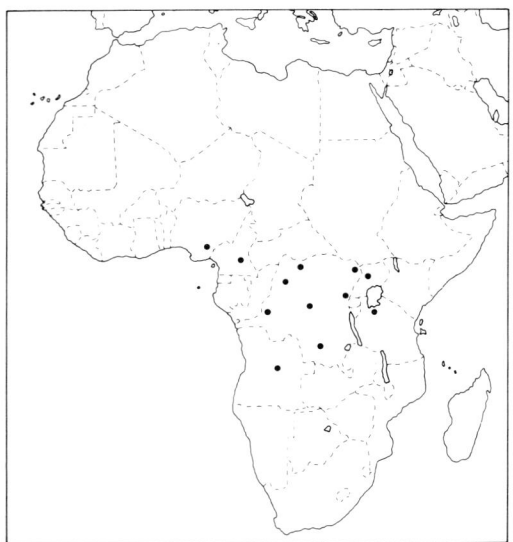

Hibiscus noldeae (Menzel & Wilson, 1969).

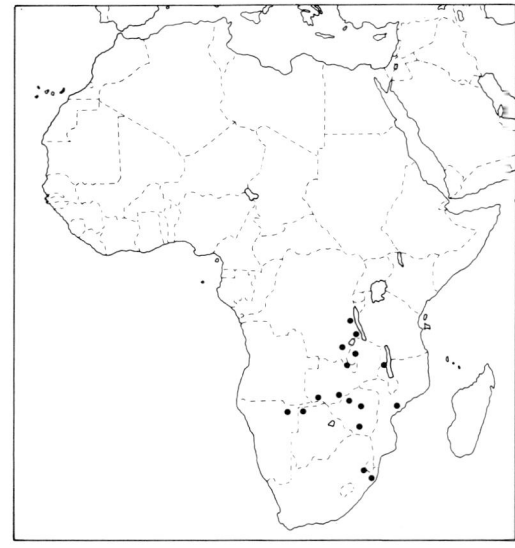

Hibiscus meeusei (Menzel & Wilson, 1969).

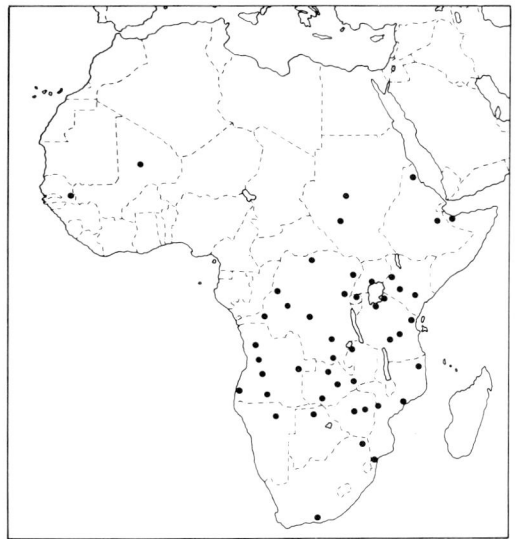

Hibiscus cannabinus (Menzel & Wilson, 1969).

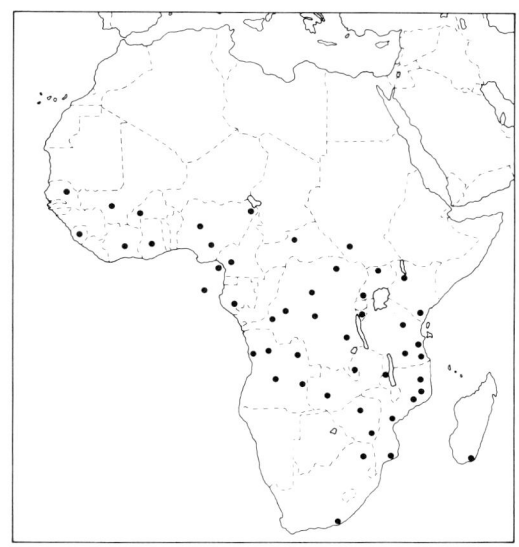

Hibiscus surattensis (Menzel & Wilson, 1969).

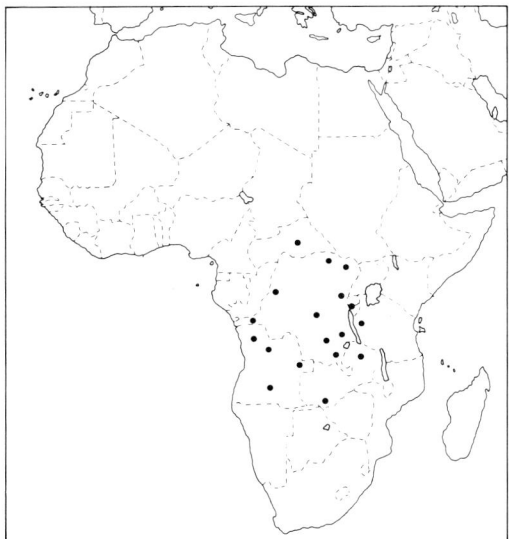

Hibiscus mechowii (Menzel & Wilson, 1969).

AAB plantain also occurs in Ghana and probably elsewhere in W. Africa.

Palmae

BORASSUS FLABELLIFER L. Lontar, Palmyra palm. 2n=36. India and Malay Archipelago. Cultivated there. Unknown wild. Probably a cultigen of the African B. aethiopum Mart. (2n=   ).

ELAEIS GUINEENSIS Jacq. Oil palm. 2n=32. The coastal belt from Sierra Leone to Angola. Primary centre in Africa. Large areas are covered by semi-wild palms. The oil palm was domesticated only in a few areas before the establishment of 'European' plantations and 'development' farmer's plots (Zeven, 1967, 1972). Large plantations are found in Africa, SE. Asia and in C. America.

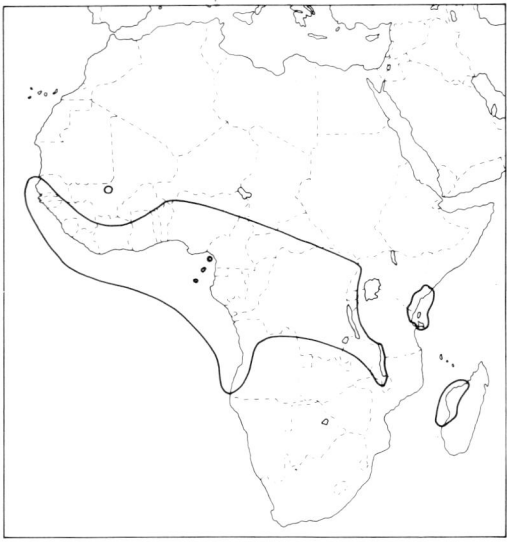

Elaeis guineensis (Zeven, 1967).

PHOENIX ATLANTICA Chev. False date palm. 2n= 36. Africa. It closely resembles Ph. dactylifera*. Near Marrakesh in Morocco var. marocana Chev. is cultivated. It has fairly tasty fleshy fruits while those of this species are, in general, of poor quality (Meunier, 1962).

PHOENIX CANARIENSIS hort. (syn. Ph. jubae Christ.) 2n=36. The Canary Islands. Spread as an ornamental to N.Africa and S.France. Closely related to Ph. dactylifera* and easily hybridizes with this and other Phoenix species.

PHOENIX DACTYLIFERA L. Date palm. 2n=28. Primary gene centre: probably N. Africa. One of the oldest cultivated plants and cultivated for a long time from the Atlantic to NW. India.

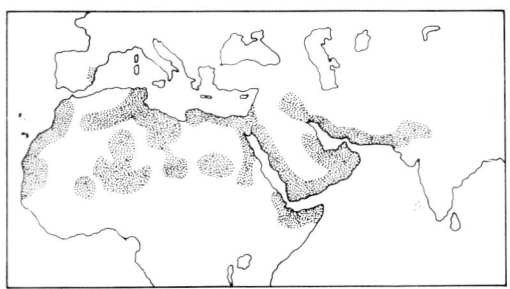

Phoenix dactylifera (Oudejans, 1969).

Phoenix species easily hybridize. This may have resulted in an increased variation. Perhaps all mentioned Phoenix* species should be included in one species.

PHOENIX HUMILIS Chev. 2n=   . Cameroons. There palms are wild and semi-wild. In the latter case, they are protected, but not planted. They are in a pre-domestication stage.

PHOENIX RECLINATA Jacq. False date palm. 2n= 36. W. Africa. Some reports refer to this palm as being cultivated as a wine palm. However these may refer to Ph. humilis* (Portères, 1955b).

PHOENIX SYLVESTRIS Roxb. Wild date palm. 2n= 36. Pakistan, India and S. Iran. Cultivated there as a source of sugar and wine. Closely related to Ph. dactylifera* and may have been derived from it, or they may have a common progenitor.

RAPHIA HOOKERI Mann & Wendl. Wine palm. 2n= . The 100-250 km wide coastal belt of W. Africa (Russell, 1965). Highly valued for its wine and fibre, and therefore cultivated and cared for. In SE. Nigeria, pedlars sold germinated fruits from the Imo River banks to farmers up to 100 km away.

Pandanaceae

PANDANUS UTILIS Bory. 2n=   . Africa. Introduced elsewhere as an ornamental, while leaves are used for various purposes. Cultivated in Mauritius for making sugar bags.

Pedaliaceae

CERATOTHECA SESAMOIDES Endl. Bungu. 2n=32. W. Africa. Cultivated in some northern areas. It yields leaves for soups and seeds for oil.

SESAMUM ALATUM Thonn. Tacoutta. 2n=26. Trop. Africa or India. Occasionally cultivated for its seeds in W. Sudan zone.

SESAMUM INDICUM L. (syn. S. orientalis L.). Oriental sesame, Beni seed. 2n=26, (52, 58).

Unknown wild. Secondary centre in India (p. 78) and in China/Japan (p. 42). An ancient crop, much cultivated, at present, in India, China, Japan, Burma, NW. Africa, Americas and Europe. As all wild Sesamum species but one (S. prostratum Retz. (2n=32), wild in E. India) occur in Africa it is thought that its progenitor(s) are African. Spontaneous tetraploids have been observed.

Nayar & Mehra (1970) considered S. indicum var. malabaricum (2n=26) as a possible 'companion weed' of sesame. It may have originated from hybrids between sesame and some sympatric wild Sesamum species.

SESAMUM RADIATUM Schum. & Thonn. 2n=64. Trop. Africa. Cultivated in C. and W. Africa for its oil seeds.

Perioplocaceae

CRYPTOSTEGIA GRANDIFLORA Br. 2n=24. Trop. Africa or India (p. 78). Occasionally cultivated for its Palay rubber and often as an ornamental.

Piperaceae

PIPER CLUSII DC. 2n=   . W. Africa. Cultivated as a spice.

PIPER GUINEENSE Schum. & Thonn. Guinea pepper, Ashanti pepper. 2n=   . W. Africa. Cultivated there as a spice.

Polygalaceae

POLYGALA BUTYRACEA Heck. Cheyi, Numbuni. 2n=   . W. Africa. This plant probably does not exist in the wild. It is probably a relic of an ancient tropical W. African culture. However, more evidence is needed. Cultivated in W. Africa for its fibre and edible seed.

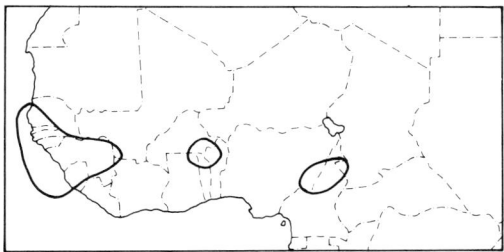

Polygala butyracea (Portères, 1950).

Polygonaceae

RUMEX ABYSSINICUS Jacq. Spanish rhubarb dock. 2n=   . Ethiopia. Cultivated in the Congo basin for its brick-red pigment.

Portulacaceae

TALINUM CUNEIFOLIUM (Vahl) Willd. 2n=   . Africa and Arabia. Cultivated in E. Africa as a vegetable.

TALINUM PANICULATUM (Jacq.) Gaertn. 2n=24. Vegetable of Nigeria.

TALINUM PORTULACIFOLIUM (Forsk.) Aschers. 2n=   . Trop. Africa and Asia. Cultivated in Africa as a vegetable.

TALINUM TRIANGULARE Willd. 2n=48, 72. Probably C. or S. America or trop. Africa. Cultivated in Brazil (p. 178), West Indies and W. Africa as a vegetable. The cultivation in forest regions may indicate an African origin, but as species of this genus are native to Africa and to the New World further investigation is necessary.

Rosaceae

HAGENIA ABYSSINICA J.F. Gmel. (syn. Brayera anthelmintica Kunth). 2n=   . Ethiopia. Cultivated there for its flowers used as medicine against tapeworm.

Rubiaceae

COFFEA ARABICA L. Arabica coffee. 2n=22, 44, (66, 88). Primary centre: SW. Ethiopia (Meyer, 1969). Secondary centre: Yemen (p. 101). Traditionally the arabica coffee has only been known in cultivation. Cultivated now over large areas.

Arabica coffee is the only known Coffea species being allopolyploid and self-compatible. Its parental species are not known, but closest relatives occur in C. and W. Africa (Meyer, 1969). Kammacher & Capot (1972) suggested that one of the genomes has a similar structure to the genome of C. canephora*.

Various botanical and agricultural varieties are known and so are many mutants. An example is the mutant discovered on Réunion, formerly Bourbon, which became the highly productive Bourbon coffee (Meyer, 1965). Icatu is a hybrid of C. arabica and C. canephora*.

COFFEA CANEPHORA Pierre ex Froehner (syn. C. robusta Linden). Robusta coffee. 2n=22, 44. W. to C. (sub)trop. Africa, from Guinea and Liberia to Sudan and Uganda. It has the highest cafein content of the Coffea species (Charnier & Berthaud, 1975). Self-incompatible. Icatu is a hybrid of C. arabica* and C. canephora. The greatest diversity has been described for Zaïre.

Before the arrival of the Europeans in Africa, it was already cultivated there. Cultivated now especially in Indonesia and, because it is used to prepare 'instant' coffee, its cultivation increased in other tropical Asian and African countries.

It is a cross-fertilizer and hence very polymorphic. This has resulted in several synonyms.

'Congusta' coffee is probably a hybrid of C. canephora and C. congensis* although the latter is considered to be a form of C. canephora. Some botanical and agricultural varieties are described.

COFFEA CONGENSIS Froehner. 2n=22, (44). Congo Basin. It resembles C. arabica*. Possibly a form of C. canephora*. 'Congusta' coffee is a hybrid product of C. congensis and C. canephora. Form 'de la Nana' is a heterogeneous population most closely resembling this species (Berthaud & Guillaumet, 1978).

COFFEA EUGENIOIDES S. Moore. 2n=22. Wild in the Lake Kivu area of Zaïre, W. Uganda and W. Tanzania. Cultivated there. It resembles a slender form of C. arabica*.

COFFEA LIBERICA Hiern. Liberica coffee. 2n= 22, 44. Guinea to Angola. Cultivated to some extent in Liberia, Surinam and a few other countries. It is a cross-fertilizer and hence very polymorphic. It has been crossed with C. arabica to produce hybrids which are cultivated.

This species includes the Excelsa coffee (C. excelsa Chev., syn. C. liberica var. dewevrei De Wild. & Dew., C. arnoldiana De Wild.).

There is a possibility that in the ancestry of this species some introgression with C. canephora* has occurred (Chinnappa, 1970).

VANGUERIA MADAGASCARIENSIS J.F. Gmel. (syn. V. edulis Vahl.). 2n=   . Trop. Africa and Madagascar. Cultivated for its edible fruits.

Rutaceae

ADENANDRA FRAGRANS (Sims.) Roem. & Schult. 2n=   . S. Africa. Cultivated there for its leaves which are used to decoct tea.

BAROSMA BETULINA (Berg) Bartl. & Wendl.f. Buchu. 2n=   . SW. and S. Africa. Cultivated on a small scale in the Clanwilliam district. Leaves of wild and cultivated crops are used for their medicinal properties (Gentry, 1961).

CITROPSIS GILLETIANA Swing. & Kell. and other Citropsis species. Trop. Africa. Closely related to Citrus. They can be used as citrus rootstocks.

Sapindaceae

BLIGHIA SAPIDA Koenig. Akee. 2n=32. Forests of W. Africa. Cultivated in Jamaica and W. Africa. In Jamaica, it is naturalized.

Sapotaceae

ARGANIA SPINOSA (L.) Skeels (syn. A. sideroxylon Rom. & Schult.). Argan, Arganier. 2n=20. SW. Morocco. A wild tree, communally owned and harvested for their fruits which are a source of argan oil, used like olive oil (G . Barbeau, pers. comm., 1979). This tree is suitable for domestication.

BUTYROSPERMUM PARKII (Don.) Kotschy (syn. B. paradoxum (Gaertn.f.) Hepper ssp. parkii (Don.) Hepper, Vitellaria paradoxa Gaertn.f.). Karité, Shea butter tree. 2n=24. Semiwild in the savannas of W. Africa.

CHRYSOPHYLLUM AFRICANUM A. DC. African star apple. 2n=26. Trop. Africa. Cultivated for its fruits.

Solanaceae

SOLANUM ACULEASTRUM Dunal. 2n=24. Trop. Africa. This non-tuberous plant is used for hedges.

SOLANUM AETHIOPICUM L. 2n=24. Trop. Africa. This non-tuberous plant is cultivated for its edible leaves and fruits.

SOLANUM ANOMALUM Thonn. Children's tomato. 2n =   . Trop. Africa. This non-tuberous plant is sometimes cultivated for its red berries used as condiment.

SOLANUM BURBANKII Bitter. Wonderberry, Msoba. 2n=6x=72. Probably derived from S. African msoba (Heiser, 1969). It is apparently not a hybrid of S. sarrachoides (syn. S. villosum) (2n=   ) and S. melanocerasum Allioni (syn S. guineense Lam. non L.), Garden Shuckleberry (2n=72), but a contaminant.

SOLANUM DUPLOSINUATUM Klotsch. 2n=   . Trop. and S. Africa. Cultivated for its edible fruits and leaves.

SOLANUM GILO Raddi. 2n=24. Vegetable of Nigeria.

SOLANUM INCANUM L. 2n=24. Africa. Occasionally cultivated. Hybridisation with S. melongena* succeeded only when S. incanum was taken as mother. The two species are closely related (Baksh, 1979).

SOLANUM MACROCARPON L. African eggplant. 2n=36. Mascarene Islands. Cultivated for its leaves and fruits (Ghana, Togo, Benin and Nigeria). The cultivar type is described as var. caljum Bitter. Its triploid number of chromosomes may point to a hybrid origin.

SOLANUM NIGRUM L. Black nightshade. 2n=(x=12), 24, (36, 40, 48), 72 genome formula AAAASS, (96, 144). Native region not known. The 6x is amphidiploid of S. americanum Mill., 2n=2x=24 and S. villosum Mill., 2n=4x=48, genome formula SSXX. The S genome derives from S. sarrachoides Sandtn., 2n=24 (Edmonds & Glidewel, 1977). The hybrid S. nigrum (2n=6x) x S. sarrachoides is named S. x procurrens Leslie (2n=4x=48). It is sterile.

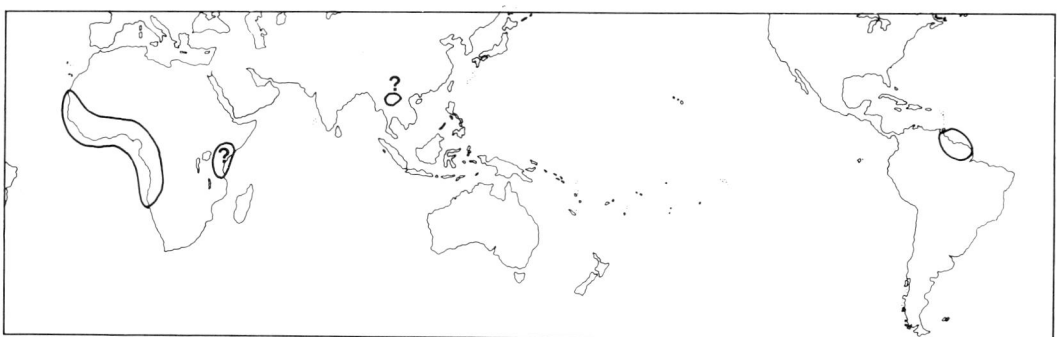

Aframomum melegueta (van Harten, 1970).

SOLANUM NODIFLORUM Jacq. 2n=24, 72. The Sahara and Nigeria. Cultivated for its leaves. May have run wild elsewhere.

SOLANUM OLIVARE Paill. 2n=   . Cultivated in Ivory Coast, Benin and Congo.

SOLANUM ROTUNDIFOLIUM Moric. ex Dun. (syn. S. nelsoni Dun.). Hausa potato. 2n=   . Believed to come from Ethiopia. Spread to W. Africa and other parts of Africa.

Sterculiaceae

COLA ACUMINATA (P. Brenan) Schott. & Endl. Abata kola. 2n=40. Nigeria to W. Gabon. Spread to Zaïre and Angola, to the West Indies and elsewhere. Cultivated esp. in W. Nigeria, but is second in importance to C. nitida*.

COLA ANOMELA K. Schum. Bamenda kola. 2n=   . Cameroon, esp. in Bamenda. Cultivated there.

COLA NITIDA (Vent.) Schott & Endl. Gbanja kola. 2n=40. Sierra Leone to Benin, with its highest frequency in the forest area of Ivory Coast and Ghana. The genus Cola has its primary centre in W. Africa (van Eijnatten, 1969, 1970). Fruits were taken to the Caribbean, where this kola already grew in 1630. Introduced to other tropical countries. This is the main kola of commerce. Subspecies refer to fruit colour, but this may be caused by some genes conditioning these colours.

COLA VERTICILLATA (Thonn.) Stapf ex Chev. Owe kola. 2n=   . From Ivory Coast to lower Congo. Often found as stray individuals in plantings, of C. nitida*. On the Mambilla Plateau in N. Nigeria, it is the only kola found (van Eijnatten, 1970).

Tamaricaceae

TAMARIX ARTICULATA Vahl. 2n=   . The Sahara, Arabia and Iran. Great numbers are found in S. Morocco and Mauritania. Cultivated as a windbreak for orange cultivation, as a sandbinder, for fuel and as ornamental.

Tiliaceae

CORCHORUS TRILOCULARIS L. Al Moulinouquia. 2n=14. Senegal to India. Sometimes cultivated as a vegetable, e.g. near Timbuktu (Mali) (Uphof, 1968).

Verbenaceae

LIPPIA ADOENSIS Hochst. Gambian teabush. 2n=   . Zaïre. A pot-herb cultivated there. In W. Africa it is used as a tea substitute.

VITEX CIENKOWSKII Kotschy & Peye. 2n=32. Trop. Africa. A tree planted on compounds or semi-cultivated for its edible fruits.

Zingiberaceae

AFRAMOMUM CORRORIMA (Braun) Jansen. Korarima. 2n=   . Ethiopia. Also cultivated there and elsewhere as a condiment and for medicine (Jansen, 1981).

AFRAMOMUM MELEGUETA (Rosc.) K. Schum. Melegueta pepper. 2n=   . W. African coastal belt from Guinea to Angola, including Fernando Po and San Thomé (van Harten, 1970). Probably not cultivated in W. Africa. After its introduction into S. America, cultivated in Surinam and Guyana. It is the historically known 'grains of paradise', giving its name to the West African Pepper Coast, Grain Coast or Malagueta Coast.

9 European-Siberian Region

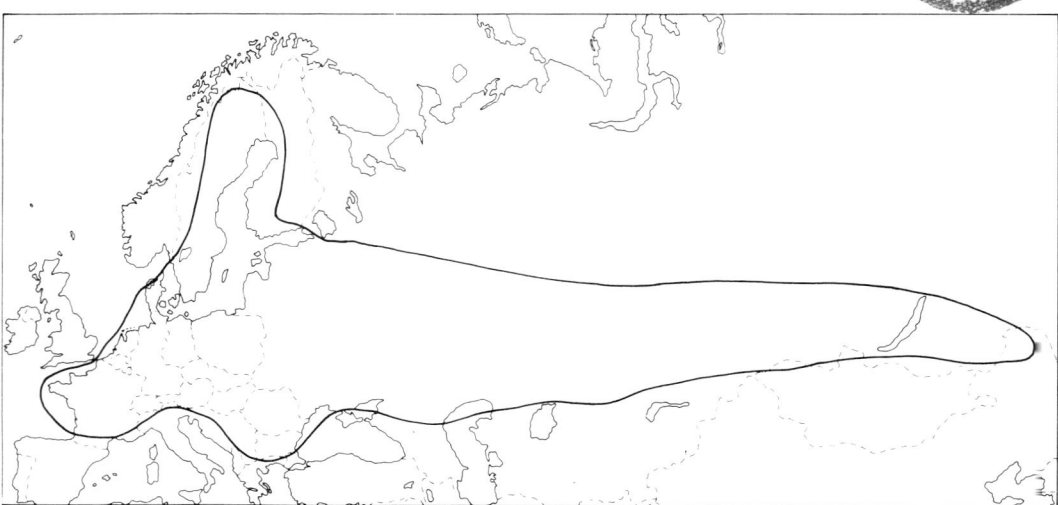

The European-Siberian Region was not indicated by Vavilov. Darlington (1953) was the first to refer to Europe as a region of origin of crop plants. Zhukovskij (1968) recognized it as a megacentre of diversity of a relatively small importance.

Agriculture reached the region from the Near Eastern Region and arrived in NW. Europe about 4000 BC.

Important crops have been developed in this region including fruit-trees, grasses, Brassica sp., Cannabis sativa, Cichorium sp., Digitaria sanguinalis, Fragaria sp., Lactuca sativa, Humulus lupulus, Medicago sp., Ribes sp., Rubus sp. and Trifolium sp.

Alliaceae

ALLIUM AMPELOPRASUM L. Levant garlic. Perennial sweet leek. 2n=16, 24, 32, genome formula AAA'A'', 40, (48, genome formula AAA'A'A''A'', AABBBB), (56). Europe, Asia Minor, Caucasia to Iran and N. Africa. Cultivated in S. France and around Nuremberg, Germany for its bulbs (Kuckuck, 1962). Some cultivation also in Kashmir (p. 70) and Iran (p. 87).

ALLIUM SCORODOPRASUM L. Giant garlic. 2n=16 + 0-2B, 24, 32, 38 + 1B, 40 + 0-4B, 48 + 0-1B. C. and S. Europe and Asia Minor. Tutin et al. (1976) describe 4 subspecies: ssp. rotundum (L.) Stearn (syn. A. rotundum L.), 2n=16 + 0-2B, 32, 38 + 1B, 40 + 1-4B, 48 + 1B, ssp. waldsteinii (G. Don) Stearn (syn. A. waldsteinii G. Don), 2n=16, 32, 40, 48, ssp. jajlae (Vved.) Stearn (syn. A. jajlae Vved.), 2n=   and ssp. scorodoprasum, 2n=16, 24. The last is probably derived from ssp. rotundum and its wide and scattered distribution are probably partly due to former cultivation as a culinary plant. According to Kuckuck (1962), it is still cultivated in USSR.

Araceae

ACORUS CALAMUS L. Sweet flag, Sweet root, Calamus. 2n=18, 24, 36, (44, 45, 48, 54). N. Europe, temperate Asia and E. North America. Used as a medicinal plant, as an ornamental and for the root that is used for various purposes such as preparation of oil. Widely cultivated now, but roots of wild plants are still collected and used.

Aristolochiaceae

ARISTOLOCHIA CLEMATIS L. 2n=14. Probably E. and S. Europe. Formerly cultivated as a medicinal herb in most of Europe and now naturalized.

Asclepiadaceae

CYNANCHUM VINCETOXICUM (L.) Pers. Swallows-
wort. 2n=22. Europe to Himalayas and Altai,
and in N. Africa. A perennial herb cultivated
formerly in gardens as a medicinal plant.

Berberidaceae

BERBERIS VULGARIS L. European berberry. 2n=28.
Most of Europe and Caucasia. Difficult to as-
sess its territory because it was formerly
planted for its edible berries and now as an
ornamental. Wood and bark were used to produce
a yellow dye. It is an intermediate host of
stem rust (Puccinia graminis Pers.) and has
therefore been eradicated in many parts.

Boraginaceae

LITHOSPERMUM OFFICINALE L. Gromwell. 2n=28.
Spp. officinale throughout Europe, W. Asia,
Caucasia and Iran. Formerly cultivated in Bo-
hemia for preparing Bohemian or Croatian tea.
Spp. erythrorhizon is cultivated in China and
Japan (p. 34).

Campanulaceae

CAMPANULA RAPUNCULUS L. Rampion, Ramps. 2n=20,
102. Europe, N. Africa, SW. Asia and Siberia.
Cultivated in the Middle Ages for its fleshy
roots.

Cannabidaceae

CANNABIS SATIVA L. Hemp. 2n=20. The wild form
is found in C. Asia. It is marked by a horse-
shoe-shaped scar at the base of the achene. C.
sativa is one of the earliest cultivated crops.
It had reached China by 2500 BC. Cultivated for
its fibre and for its seeds, for food or as
a source of hemp seed oil. 'C. ruderalis Ja-
nisch' is a weedy non-toxic type. The Indian
type, 'C. indica' (p. 71) is cultivated as a
source of narcotics. Special cultivar groups
have been developed for different purposes.
Exceptionally tall types are found in NE.
China (p. 33).

HUMULUS LUPULUS L. Hop. 2n=2x=20 with X-Y sex
chromosome system. Var. lupulus is cultivated
in Europe, Asia and N. America. It has been domesticated in Europe and its present distribution probably reflects dispersion by man. Hop
is grown for its cones (female inflorescences)
which are used to flavour beer. A perennial
mainly propagated by rhizomes.
   Var. neomexicanus, var. pubescens and var.
lupuloides occur in N. America (p. 199), while
var. cordifolius is found in Japan and China
(p. 34) (Small, 1978a).

Caryophyllaceae

SAPONARIA OFFICINALIS L. Soapwort, Soaproot.
2n=28. Europe and Asia. Occasionally cultivated in Germany (Mansfeld, 1959).

SPERGULA ARVENSIS L. (syn. Spergularia arvensis Cambess.). Corn spurrey. 2n=18. Europe. Var.
sativa (Boenningh.) Mert. & Koch (syn. S. sativa Boenningh.). Cultivated as a fodder crop
or as a green manure. Var. arvensis is a widespread weed, while var. maxima (Weihe) Mert.
& Koch. is a weed in flax fields.

Chenopodiaceae

ATRIPLEX HORTENSIS L. Mountain spinach, Garden
orach. 2n=18. Wild in temperate Europe and
Asia. Formerly cultivated in Europe as a vegetable.

BETA VULGARIS L. var. rapa. Fodder beet. 2n=
18. Distribution of the wild type is given on
p. 104. Probably developed in the Netherlands,
perhaps from types introduced from Spain. Secondary centre in Region 5 (p. 81). Spread to
Germany and elsewhere. It may have played a
role in the development of sugar-beet, var.
saccharifera (syn. var. altissima). Sugar-beet
probably developed in Silesia by hybridization
of an old garden form and fodder beet. The
land variety "Weisser schlesischer Zückerrübe"
is the parent of all sugar-beet varieties.
Fuel beets are sugar-beets suitable for alco-
hol production but not for sugar extraction.

CHENOPODIUM ALBUM L. Goosefoot, Fat hen, Lambs-
quarters. 2n=18, 36, 54. Probably cultivated
in Europe in Neolithic times. Now it is a weed.

CHENOPODIUM BONUS-HENRICUS L. (syn. Ch. esculentus Salisb.). Allgood, Good King Henry. 2n=
36. Native to the temperate Old World. Formerly cultivated as a pot-herb.

CHENOPODIUM FOLIOSUM Aschers. 2n=18. Europe and
the Orient. Formerly cultivated as a vegetable
(Uphof, 1968).

Compositae

ANTHEMIS TINCTORIA L. (syn. Cota tinctoria (L.)
Gay). Dyer's chamomile, Golden chamomile. 2n=
18. Europe and W. Asia. Cultivated as a dye
plant.

ARCTIUM LAPPA L. (syn. Lappa arctium Gaertn.).
Great burdoc, Cocklebur. 2n=32, 36. Europe and
Asia. Cultivated in Europe as a medicinal
plant, and also in China and Japan (p. 34).

ARTEMISIA ABROTANUM L. Southern wood. 2n=18.
S. Europe and temp. Asia. Cultivated as a medicinal crop for flowers and as an ornamental.

ARTEMISIA ABSINTHIUM L. Absinthe. 2n=18. Europe, S. Siberia, Kashmir and Mediterranean
area. Cultivated in S. Europe, N. Africa and
USA for the production of absinthe.

ARTEMISIA LAXA Fritsch. 2n=18. C. and S. Europe. Cultivated.

ARTEMISIA MARITIMA L. 2n=18, 36, 54. Europe to Mongolia. Cultivated as a medicinal crop.

ARTEMISIA VULGARIS L. Mugwort. 2n=16, 18. Temp. N. Hemisphere. Cultivated in Indonesia and elsewhere for several uses.

CHAMAEMELUM NOBILE (L.) All. (syn. Anthemis nobilis L.). Noble chamomile. 2n=18. S. and W. Europe. Cultivated as a medicinal and as an ornamental.

CHAMOMILLA RECRUTICA (L.) Rauschert (syn. Matricaria chamomilla L.). Chamomile, German chamomile. 2n=18. Europe, Iran and Afghanistan. Cultivated in Europe as a medicinal and as a source of an essential oil used for flavouring and perfumery. A substitute of Chamaemelum nobile*.

CICHORIUM INTYBUS L. Chicory, Succory, Brussels witloof, Sugar-loaf chicory. 2n=18. Europe, Siberia, N. Africa and the Near East to Iran, Baluchistan and Lake Baikal. Wild type (var. intybus) was used as a salad and for medicinal purposes. Var. sativum Lam. & DC. is cultivated in Europe and elsewhere to produce a coffee substitute while var. foliosum Hegi, the Brussels witloof, was first developed around Brussels since c. 1830 from var. sativum, whose young leaves had already been traded as lettuce since c. 1800 and were known as barba de capucin (Moens, 1974).

HELIANTHUS ANNUUS L. Sunflower. 2n=34. Wild in N. America (p. 200). Secondary centre in USSR. Domesticated and cultivated in N. America. Largeheaded forms introduced in Europe.

LACTUCA QUERCINA L. 2n=18. Europe, esp. in Germany, France to USSR and the Balkans. A biennal. Sometimes cultivated near Clermont-Ferrand (France) for its narcotic properties (Uphof, 1968).

LACTUCA SATIVA L. Lettuce. 2n=18. Primary centre: the Middle East. Lettuce derives from L. serriola L., prickly lettuce. This species occurs in S. and C. Europe to Denmark, Caucasia, Transcaucasia, Iran, Iraq, Syria, Saudi Arabia, Siberia to Altai, and N. Africa to the Canary Islands. However, Lindqvist (1960) believed that lettuce probably derives by hybridization of other Lactuca species including L. saligna L. and that L. serriola arose from the same or subsequent hybridization. L. serriola is now a weed. L. saligna like L. serriola has its main distribution centre round the Mediterranean Sea (Lindqvist, 1960).

The first record of lettuce dates from 2500 BC.; a long-leaved form was depicted in the Egyptian tombs.

The present marked variation of lettuce is probably a product of hybridization with L. serriola, but may also have been induced by some natural mutation (Whitaker, 1969).

Var. asparagina Bailey (syn. L. angustana

Vilm., L. sativa var. angustana Irish), Asparagus lettuce of Celtuce, forms a single thickened straight stem 90 cm or more long, which is eaten as salad when young.

L. saligna from Israel is a source of resistance to downy mildew, Bremia lactucae Reg.

TANACETUM VULGARE L. (syn. Chrysanthemum vulgare (L.) Bernh. non (Lam.) Gaterau, C. tanacetum Karsch. non Vis. incl. T. audibertii (Req.) DC). Common tansy. 2n=18. Almost throughout Europe. Cultivated as a pot-herb, medicinal and ornamental.

TARAXACUM HYBERNUM Steven. Krim sagiz. 2n=32, 40. Italy, Balkans, Asia Minor, Syria and Crimea. Cultivated in USSR as a rubber crop.

TARAXACUM OFFICINALE Weber. Dandelion, Lionstooth, Milk-gowan, Puffball. 2n=8, 24 (and others). Europe and W. Asia. In France and elsewhere, improved varieties are cultivated. These varieties "Pissenlit à coeur plein amélioré" and "Pissenlit vert de Montmagny" differ from wild plants (pissenlit ordinaire) as they have less bitter leaves. Young etiolated leaves of wild plants covered by molehills are collected as dandelion salad.

Crassulaceae

SEDUM REFLEXUM L. Jenny stonecrop. 2n=34, c. 56, 68, c. 112. S. Europe. Cultivated in W. and C. Europe and used to flavour soup and salad.

SEMPERVIVUM TECTORUM L. Hen-and-Chickens, Roof houseleek. 2n=(36), 72. Europe. Cultivated as a medicinal plant.

Cruciferae

ARMORACIA RUSTICANA (Lam.) Gaertner. Mey & Schreb., (syn. Cochlearia armoracia L.). Horseradish. 2n=28, 32. Finland, to Poland, the Caspian Sea and the deserts of Cuman and in Turkey. Primary centre in temperate E. Europe (Counter & Rhodes, 1969). Cultivated as condiment and hence naturalized.

BARBAREA PRAECOX R.Br. (syn. B. verna Asch.). Scurvy grass, Winter-cress, Upland cress. 2n=16. Europe. Cultivated as a vegetable.

BARBAREA VULGARIS R.Br. Yellow rocket, Common winter-cress, Upland cress. 2n=16. Temp. Europe, Asia and N. Africa. Spread throughout the world. Cultivated as a pot-herb.

BRASSICA CAMPESTRIS L. Turnip group. 2n=20, genome formula AA. The wild form ssp. sylvestris (L.) Jancken grows as a weed and ruderal in most of Europe, Asia and N. Africa. The various oily (ssp. oleifera (Metzg.) Sinsk., oil-seed turnip) and fodder (ssp. rapifera (Metzg.) Sinsk., "stubble turnip", Dutch turnip) cultivars have developed independently.

There are three main groups: the Asian (p.

35), the Mediterranean and the West European.
The turnip-rape, var. oleifera (Metzg.) Sinsk.,
possibly developed in Belgium. Leafy types of
turnip are cultivated especially in Finland.

The A genome is also found in the diploid B.
chinensis* and the diploid B. japonica*. This
genome is related to the Ad genome of B. adpressa Boiss., the F genome of B. fruticulosa
Cyril. and the D or T genome of B. tournefortii Gouan (Mizushima, 1969).

B. campestris is one of the parents of B.
juncea* and B. napus*, and also of the artificially made B. napocampestris (2n=58, genome
formula $A_1A_1AAC_1C_1$).

BRASSICA NAPOBRASSICA (L.) Mill. (syn. B. napus
L. var. napobrassica (L.) Rchb.). Rutabaga,
Swedish turnip. 2n=38. Unknown wild. Primary
gene centre in the Mediterranean area (p. 106).
Secondary gene centre in Europe. Probably a derivative of B. oleracea* x B. napus*. The roots
are more elongated and oval and larger than
those of turnip. They are eaten as a vegetable.

BRASSICA NIGRA (L.) Koch. Black mustard. 2n=
16, genome formula BB. Europe, especially in
C. and S. parts. However, Hemingway (1976) suggested a centre of domestication in Asia Minor
or Iran. Cultivated since ancient times. Seeds
are pressed for black mustard seedoil. The B
genome is related to the F genome of B. fruticulosa (Mizushima, 1969). Black mustard is one
of the parents of B. juncea* and B. carinata*.
An artificial amphiploid of B. tournefortii*
and this species is called B. amarifolia (2n=
36), genome formula TTBB or DDBB).

BRASSICA OLERACEA L. Wild kale. 2n=18, genome
formula CC. Atlantic coast of Europe. Occurrence
on Heligoland is probably spontaneous. It may
have already been present there in medieval
times. The wild kales of Atlantic Europe are
closely related to the wild kales of the Mediterranean (see B. oleracea, p. 106).

BRASSICA OLERACEA L. var. gemmifera DC. Brussels sprouts. 2n=18, genome formula CC. Developed in Belgium probably from var. ramosa.

COCHLEARIA OFFICINALIS L. Spoonwort, Scorbute
grass, Scurvy grass. 2n=(14), 24, genome formula $A_6A_6A_6A_6$, (28, 36). N. and W. Europe. Cultivated formerly as a medicinal plant.

CRAMBE MARITIMA L. Sea kale. 2n=60. Sea coast
of Europe. Cultivated in England as a vegetable.

HESPERIS MATRONALIS L. Damask. 2n=24. C. and
S. Europe. Cultivated for its seeds which are
a source of oil and as an ornamental. Escapes
are common.

NASTURTIUM OFFICINALIS R. Br. (syn. Rorippa
nasturtium-aquaticum (L.) Hayek). Watercress.
2n=2x=32, (28, 64). W. Asia and S. Europe and
Great Britain, where it is cultivated. The

leafy stems are eaten as salad.
It is also cooked as a vegetable. In New Zealand, it is a serious weed of rivers. The almost sterile hybrid (N. x sterile (Shaw) Oe-
fel, 2n=3x=48) of watercress and N. microphyllum (Boenn.) Rchb., 2n=4x=64 is also cultivated for salad (Purseglove, 1968). It is vegetatively propagated. Watercress and N. x sterile have both run wild in Florida, USA.

Cucurbitaceae

BRYONIA ALBA L. White bryony. 2n=20. C. Europe,
USSR, the Balkans and N. Iran. Cultivated formerly as a medicinal plant.

BRYONIA CRETICA L. Red berry bryony. 2n=20. S.,
SC. and W. Europe to Great Britain and N. Af-
rica. Cultivated formerly as a medicinal crop.
Spp. cretica is found in the Aegean region,
spp. dioica (Jacq.) Tutin (syn. B. dioica Jacq.)
has a wide distribution, while spp. acuta Desf.)
Tutin (B. acuta Desf.) is found in Tunesia and
Libya.

Cyperaceae

CAREX ARENARIA L. (syn. C. spadicea Gilib.).
2n=58, 60-64. Europe, especially the littoral
areas. Cultivated as a soil stabilizer.

SCIRPUS LACUSTRIS L. (syn. S. validus Vahl.).
Great bulbrush. 2n=(38, 40), 42. A world wide
distribution. Cultivated in the Netherlands
and Germany, to promote land reclamation and
improve impoldered land. In Germany cultivated
to clean polluted water and so it is expected
that the planting will increase and better varieties of this plant will be bred. Its culms
contain 80% air taken from the atmosphere. They
absorb air pollutant gases, sodium, phosphorus,
zinc and copper.

Gramineae

AGROPYRON CANINUM P.B. (syn. Roegneria canina
(L.) Nevski). 2n=28, genome formula S'S'H'H'.
Cultivated in the USSR.

AGROPYRON CRISTATUM L. Gaertn. Crested wheatgrass. 2n=14 mainly, 28, (42). Europe and Asia.
Introduced into N. America. Cultivated there
as a hay crop. This species includes a number
of other species like A. desertorum (Fisch.)
Schult., A. pectiniforme Roem. & Schult., A.
michnoi Roshev. and A. sibiricum (Willd.) P.B.

AGROPYRON INTERMEDIUM (Host) Beauv. (syn. A.
glaucum, Elytrigea intermedia (Host) Nevski).
2n=(28), 42, genome formula $B_2B_2E_1E_1E_2E_2$. Intermediate wheatgrass. S. and C. Europe to
Iran, Pakistan and Caucasia. Self-compatible.

AGROPYRON REPENS (L.) Beauv. (syn. Elytrigia
repens (L.) Desv.). Couchgrass, Twitch, Quack-
grass. 2n=18, 6x=42, genome formula $S_1S_1S_2S_2XX$,
(56). Temperate Eurasia. Aggressive weed with

wide adaptation. Spread to all continents.
Sometimes used as palatable high-quality
forage grass. It easily crosses with A. spicatum*, which introgresses as the F_1 is fertile
(Dewey, 1976).

AGROSTIS CANINA L. 2n=14, 28, (35, 42, 56).
Europe. Cultivated in the Netherlands.

AGROSTIS GIGANTEA Roth. (syn. A. alba auct.
non L.). Fiorin, Red top. 2n=42, genome formula
$A_1A_1A_2A_2A_3A_3$. Europe, Asia and N. America. Cultivated as a pasture grass and as a hay crop.

AGROSTIS TENUIS Sibth. (syn. A. vulgaris
With.). Rhode Island bent, Colonial bent. 2n=
28, genome formula $A_1A_1A_2A_2$. Most of Europe,
N. Asia Minor, Armenia, Caucasia, Siberia, N.
Africa and N. America. Hybrids with A. gigantea* have been found in Germany and called A.
intermedia C.A. Weber.

ALOPECURUS PRATENSIS L. Meadow foxtail. 2n=
28, (42). Most of Europe, N. Asia and Caucasia.
Cultivated as a meadow grass.

AMMOPHILA ARENARIA Link (syn. A. arundinacea
Host.). Beachgrass. 2n=28. The coastal areas
of Europe. A perennial cultivated as a sand
binder.

ANTHOXANTHUM ODORATUM L. Sweet scented vernal
grass, Spring grass. 2n=10, 20. Europe, Asia,
W. part of N. Africa. Cultivated as a forage
grass. It has a low food value. The diploid
is also described as A. alpinum Löve & Löve.
Autoploidy has played an important role in the
genesis of the tetraploid (Hedberg, 1970).
Teppner (1970) suggested the following genome
formula for A. alpinum and A. odoratum:

species	ploidy	genome formula	region
A. alpinum	2x	AA	general
A. alpinum	4x	AAAA	Cantal, France
A. odoratum	2x	CC	Italy
A. odorarum	2x	DD	Italy, Yugo-slavia, Greece
A. odoratum	2x	DE	Serbia
A. odoratum	4x	BBDD	Southern C. and W. Europe
A. odoratum	4x	BBFF	W. Europe

A comparison of Austrian, Swiss, Swedish and
Polish populations showed that diploids from
Austria and Switzerland are morphological
closer to those from Poland than to those in
Scandinavia (Hedberg, 1969).

ARRHENATHERUM AVENACEUM Beauv. (syn. A. elia-
tor Beauv.). Tall meadow oatgrass. 2n=40. Europe. A valuable pasture grass.

ARRHENATHERUM TUBEROSUM Druce (syn. Avena tuberosa Gilib., Arrhenatherum avenaceum Beauv.).
Onion couchgrass. 2n=18. In neolithic times

possibly cultivated for its tubers.

AVENA SEPTENTRIOLANIS Malz. (syn. A. fatua
spp. septentrionalis (Malz.) Malz.). 2n=42. N.
and NE. European USSR to W. Siberia. There it
usually grows in undisturbed habitats. Baum
(1972) stated that is is probably the most
closely related taxon to A. sativa* and that
it resembles the hypothetical ancestor of the
predomesticated oats.

BROMUS ERECTUS Huds. (syn. B. arvensis Poll.).
2n=(28, genome formula AeAeAeAe), 42, 56, (70,
84, 112). C. and S. Europe, N. Africa, Ante-
Asia up to Caucasia. Cultivated especially in
S. France, Switzerland, S. Germany and USSR.
Some people regard this species and its synonyms as two species.

BROMUS INERMIS Leyss. Awnless brome, Smooth
brome, Hungarian brome. 2n=(28, genome formula
AiAiBiBi, 42, 49), 56, genome formula AiAiAi
AiBiBiBiBi, (54-58). N., C., and SE. Europe,
Caucasia, temperate Asia and China. Cultivation started at various places in Europe. Introduced to N. America.

BROMUS SECALINUM L. Chess, Rye brome. 2n=28.
A cultivated hulled cereal of prehistory grown
together with emmer (Triticum dicoccum*) and
einkorn T. monococcum*). It has a very high
multiplication factor (2500 caryopses per
plant). It is now a weed mainly of winter cereals, but types with a spring habit are also
found (Knörzer, 1965).

CYNOSURUS CRISTATUS L. Crested dogtail, Dogs-
tail grass. 2n=14. Primary centre in C. and W.
Europe, Caucasia and Asia Minor.

DACTYLIS GLOMERATA L. Cocksfoot, Orchard grass.
2n=28. Stebbins (1956) suggested that D. glomerata is a tetraploid derived from two related diploids. One of them could be D. aschers-
oniana Aschers. & Graebn. (2n=14). This species is distributed over C. Europe, Himalaya
and W. China. Another diploid is D. smithii
Link which exists in the Canary Islands. It
is likely that all diploids derive from one
common diploid. Hybridization of diploids and
doubling of the number of chromosomes and a-
gain hybridization within the tetraploid group
and with the diploids has led to the very variable D. glomerata. Cultivated as a pasture
and hay grass.

DIGITARIA SANGUINALIS Scop. 2n=18, 28, 36 (-48,
54, 76). Bluthirse, Millet sanguin. S. Europe,
Asia Minor, Central Asia, N. and S. America,
in temperate zones. There is a great variation
of the species. The cultivated type is var. esculenta (Gaudin) Caldesi. Among this variety
var. frumentacea Henr. and spp. aegyptiaca
(Retz) Henr. are found. Primary centre is not
known. Probably first cultivated in Illyria
preceeded by a long time of collection of wild
plants. Cultivated formerly in a large area

in Europe. Another area of cultivation is in
India (p. 73). Whether the origin of cultivation independently arose here, or whether this
cereal spread to India·from Europe or the reverse is not known (Portères, 1955a). Spp.
pectiniformis Henr. of E. Europe, the Near East
and NE. Africa. Not cultivated. Spp. aegyptiaca has an 'eastern' origin but it is probably
not in Egypt. From this subspecies the cultivated var. frumentacea is derived. Spp. vulgaris (Schrander) Henr. is very variable and
widely distributed.

FESTUCA ARUNDINACEA Schreb. 2n=(28), 42, (70).
Europe, N. Africa and Asia (Syria, Siberia,
Japan) Not much cultivated, due to its coarse-
ness although seeds have been commercially
available for a long time.
    According to Borrill (1972) the tetraploid
and hexaploid cytotypes have affinities with
F. pratensis*, while the octoploid and decaploid possess a genome pair of F. scariosa
Aschs. & Graebn. (2n=14). This species is endemic in the Spanish Sierra Nevada.
    F. arundinacea has been rather widely intro-
duced as a meadow and pasture grass in northern
USA.

FESTUCA OVINA L. Sheep's fescue. 2n=14, (21),
28, 42, (49), 56, 70. Europe, the Caucasus,
the Himalaya and N. America. Cultivated in Europe. An important grass of Australia and S.
Africa. Many 4x and 6x types have been described as Festuca species.

FESTUCA PRATENSIS Huds. (syn. F. elatior L.).
Fescue grass, Meadow fescue, English bluegrass.
2n=14, FpFp, (28, 42, 70). Europe, Caucasia,
Iran, the Urals and Siberia. Cultivated in Europe and N. America. Natural hybrids with Lolium perenne* are described as Festulolium
loliaceum (Huds.) P. Fourn. (syn. Festuca lo-
liacea Huds.), 2n=2x=14, LpFp, loloid 3x=FpLp
Lp, festucoid 3x=FpFpLp.
    According to Jauhar (1975), F. pratensis and
Lolium perenne are closely related and probably
evolved from a common progenitor, as there is
no effective intergeneric barrier to gene flow.

FESTUCA RUBRA L. Red fescue. 2n=14, (28), 42,
56, (70 and aneuploids). Europe, temperate A-
sia, Africa and N. America. Much cultivated as
a pasture grass. In New Zealand chewings fescue is cultivated. It is a red fescue of the
non-creeping type (spp. fallax). Var. genuina
is creeping red fescue.

GLYCERIA FLUITANS R. Br. Manna grass. 2n=(20),
28, 40. Was collected in a large part of E.
Europe.

HOLCUS LANATUS L. Soft meadow grass, Woolly
soft grass, Yorkshire fog, Velvet grass. 2n=
14. Europe and temperate Asia. Cultivated for
pasture and hay. A secondary centre of diversity is developing in New Zealand (p. 65).

LOLIUM MULTIFLORUM Lam. var. westerwoldicum
Wittm. (syn. spp. multiflorum (Husnot) Becher-
er). Westerwolds ryegrass. 2n=14. Annual types
derived from populations of spp. italicum were
selected at Westerwolde, NE. Netherlands.

LOLIUM PERENNE L. Perennial ryegrass. 2n=14.
Not know where and when it was domesticated,
but probably in Europe. However, the parent
plants may have come from the Mediterranean
area of SW. Asia. The first true grass sown in
a pure, or relatively pure state. Cultivated
now in the Old and New Worlds. Tetraploids and
amphiploids with Festuca pratensis* are cultivated. Natural hybrids between these two species are described as Festulolium loliaceum
(Huds.) P. Fourn. Hybrids of L. perenne and
L. multiflorum* have been called L. x hybridum
Hausskn. These last two species are closely related.

PHALARIS ARUNDINACEA L. Red canary grass. 2n=
14, 28. Most of Europe, W., N. and E. Asia.
Cultivated in the Old and New Worlds.

PHLEUM PRATENSE L. Timothy, Herdsgrass. 2n=
mostly 42, genome formula $NNA_1A_1A_2A_2$. Europe,
N. Asia and N. Africa. An amphiploid of P.
alpinum L. (Alpine timothy, 2n=28) and P. nodosum L. (syn. P. pratense var. nodosum (L.)
Richter) (2n=14, genome formula NN(?)). A tetraploid type similar to this species was developed
from the diploid Ph. nodosum after doubling the
number of chromosomes. Ph. pratense is cultivated in Europe and N. America as a forage and
hay crop.

PHRAGMITES COMMUNIS Trinius. Reedgrass. 2n=
(36), 48, (54, 84, 96). A cosmopolite grass
used for land reclamation and bank protection.
Young sprouts are eaten, while the culms have
many uses.

POA BULBOSA*

POA PALUSTRIS L. Fowl bluegrass. 2n=18, (42).
Arctic zone of Europe, Asia and N. America.
Various varieties have been developed in Eu-
rope.

POA PRATENSIS L. Bluegrass, Kentucky bluegrass,
Birdgrass. 2n=38-147. Europe, Asia, N. Africa
and northern N. America. The great variation in
chromosome number owing to autoploidization has
resulted in many species descriptions, but they
can be considered as synonyms. Furthermore as
apomixy of this species is not constant, types
with different chromosome number may be selected. So it was possible to select plants similar
to P. pratensis from P. trivialis*. If this pro-
ves that P. pratensis derives from P. trivialis
then P. pratensis must have originated in the
Old World. Various varieties have been bred in
Europe and Canada (p. 202) and elsewhere.

POA TRIVIALIS L. Roughish meadow grass. 2n=14,
(28). Europe and S. Siberia. Not much cultiva-

ted. It might be the parent species of P. pratensis*.

SPARTINA ANGLICA C.E. Hubbard, Cordgrass. 2n= 122. Originated in W. Europe after introduction of the American S. alternifolia Lois. (2n= 62) and hybridization with the European S. maritima (Curt.) Fern. (2n=60). The hybrid is named S. x townsendii H. & J. Groves (2n=62). From this hybrid the amphiploid S. anglica evolved, which has ousted out its parent S. maritima (Adema & Mennema, 1979). Cultivated for soil reclamation and stabilization.

TRISETUM FLAVESCENS (L.) Beauv. (syn. T. pratense Bers.). Yellow catgrass, Golden oatgrass. 2n=24, 28. It probably derives from T. sibiricum Rupr. (2n=14, 24). This species occurs in Kamtschatka, Siberia. From here it spread westwards.

TRITICUM AESTIVUM (L.) Thell. spp. compactus Host.). Clubwheat. 2n=42, genome formula AAB-BDD. The clubwheats of the Austrian alpines, except for the research of E. Mayr. are much neglected. They are probably derivatives of the wheat (T. antiquorum Heer) cultivated by the Swiss Lake Dwellers in the Neolithicum. They are nearly extinct.

TRITICUM AESTIVUM (L.) Thell. spp. spelta (L.) Thell. Spelt. 2n=42, genome formula AABBDD. Cultivated from the Belgian Ardennes to Switzerland and to Schwaben, Germany and in Spain. Formerly the spelt area in Europe must have been much larger running from Sweden to Spain and may be up to Africa (p.135). In Spain (Asturia) spelt is harvested in the same way as in Transcaucasia. It is remarkable that many German/Belgian spelts, the relic Swedish spelt (from Gotland) and one from Africa carry an Rf_{tim}-gene (Zeven, 1971).

ZEA MAYS L. Maize. 2n=20. Secondary centres in S. Europe and the Mediterranean Region (p. 112) in the European corn belt and the Atlantic and Continental maize growing regions (Brandolini, 1970). Domesticated in C. America (p. 190). Flint maize - indurata Sturt. - is common in all these areas.
    Siberian ecotypes are recognized by germination at 5-6°C, cold resistance of seedlings to 4-5°C, rapid growth, earliness, high assimilation rate and protogyny (Gerasenkov, 1968).

    Grossulariaceae

RIBES ACICULARIS Smith. 2n=   . The mountains of Siberia especially in the Altai. The most precocious Ribes-species with a high winter-hardiness and mildew resistance. These characteristics are useful in Ribes-breeding.

RIBES GROSSULARIA L. (syn. R. uva-crispa L.). (European) Gooseberry. 2n=16. Eurasia and in the mountains of W. Asia and the Mediterranean countries. Cultivated in temperate zones. Re-

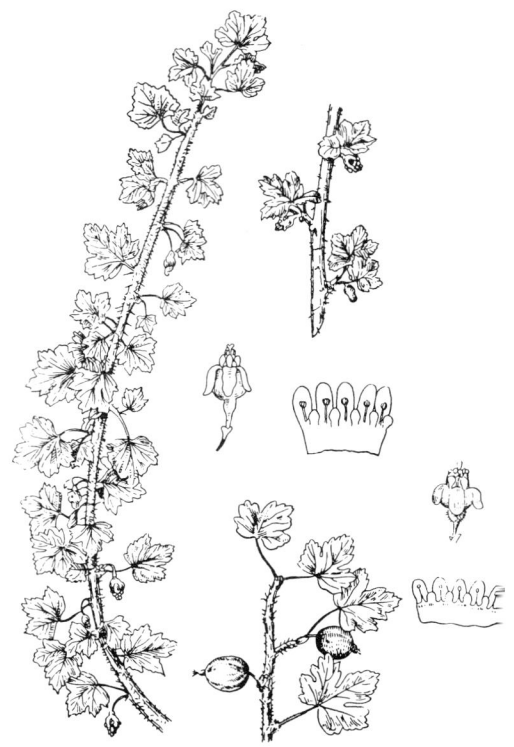

Ribes acicularis

lated N. American Ribes-species R. oxyacanthoides Mill. (2n=16), R. hirtellum Mix. (2n=16), R. divaricatum Dougl. (2n=16), R. cynosbati L.* (2n=16), R. pinetorum Greene (2n=   ) and R. niveum Lindl. (2n=16) carry resistance to mildew, while R. niveum and R. divaricatum may be used as source of mildew resistance and to improve fruit characteristics. Resistance to Nasononia ribisnigri Mosley is found in R. roezlii Regel (2n=16) and R. sanguineum Pursh (2n=16), while the latter species and R. cereum Dougl. (2n=16) are sources of resistance to Hyperomyzus lactucae L. (Keep & Briggs, 1971).
    Hybrids between R. grossularia and R. sanguineum are named R. fontenayense Jancz. (2n=   ). Spineless types are also found of R. oxyacanthoides.

RIBES NIGRUM L. (European) Black currant. 2n= 16. Eurasia and sporadically in N. America. The cultivated type was derived from the wild one. In N. Scandinavia very precocious, winterhardy types are found. The American R. americanum Mill. (2n=   ) and the Asiatic R. dikuscha Fish. are related to the black currant. They have breeding value.
    Cultivars of var. sibiricum F. Wolf. of this species and R. ussuriense* are sources of resistance to the blackcurrant gall mite. Phy-

toptus ribis Nal.
  Spontaneous hybrids with R. procumbens (2n=
) occur in the USSR.

RIBES PETRAEUM Wulfen. Rock red currant. 2n=
16. The Pyrena to the Carpates and N. Africa.
Cultivated in the Alps. One of the parents of
the present-day red currant (R. sativum*).

RIBES SATIVUM Syme (R. rubrum L., R. multiflorum Kitt. and R. petraeum Wulf.). 2n=16.
The wild R. sativum grows in W. Europe. In N.
America it has run wild. R. rubrum is found
wild in W. and C. Europe and N. Asia. R. petraeum* grows in the mountains of Europe and
Asia. R. sativum is probably the originally
cultivated species. Later it hybridized with
the other two, so these three species are the
parents of the present-day red currant.

RIBES SPICATUM Robson. 2n=16. NE. Europe.
Sometimes cultivated.

Guttiferae

HYPERICUM PERFORATUM L. Saint Johns wort. 2n=
32, (36). Cultivated on a small scale in the
Netherlands as a medicinal crop.

Juglandaceae

JUGLANS REGIA L. Walnut, Persian walnut, English walnut. 2n=32, 36. Primary centre of diversity in Region 5. Secondary centre in SW.
Europe and Moldavia.
  Almost all varieties in Germany are apomictic.

Labiatae

MENTHA CARDIACA Gerard ex Baker. Scotch mint,
Scotch spearmint. 2n=   . Temp. Europe. Culti-
vated for its volatile oil. Closely related to
M. x gentilis L. (2n=54, 60, 84, 96, 108, 120).
It is believed that these two species are hy-
brids of M. arvensis* and M. spicata*.

MENTHA x GENTILIS L. (syn. M. sativa var. gentilis (L.) Reichenb.). 2n=54, 60, 84, 96, 108,
120. A hybrid of M. arvensis* and M. spicata*.
Usually sterile. Cultivated frequently.

MENTHA x PIPERITA L. Peppermint. 2n=(36, 48,
64-69), 72, (84, 108, 122, 144). Probably a
natural hybrid of M. aquatica* and M. spicata*.
This hybridization probably took place in England. f. piperita (blackmint, black mitcham)
is cultivated in C. Europe and Great Britain.
while f. pallescens Camus (white mint, white
mitcham) is cultivated especially in France.
In USA existing clones were replaced by the
cultivar Mitcham in 1890. This is still the
main clone cultivated.

MENTHA ROTUNDIFOLIA (L.) Huds. (syn. M. spicata var. rotundifolia L.). Apple mint, Woolly
mint. 2n=24, genome formula RR. Europe and

Canary Islands. Cultivated. Probably the parental form of M. spicata* and one of the parents
of M. japonica Mak., M. arvensis* and M. a-
quatica* (Ikeda & Ono, 1969). This species is
related to M. longifolia* and M. spicata*.

MENTHA x SMITHIANA R.A. Graham (syn. M. rubra
Sm., non Miller). 2n=54, 120. Rarely cultivated (Tutin et al., 1972). It is a hybrid of M.
aquatica* x M. arvensis* x M. spicata*. Usually sterile, spreading vegetatively.

MENTHA SPICATA (L.) Hudson (syn. M. viridis
L.). Spearmint, Green mint, Lamb mint. 2n=36,
48, genome formula RRSS (48+2B, 64). Temp. Europe. It might derive from an autotetraploid
plant of M. rotundifolia* after which one genome pair RR changed into SS. Tutin et al.
(1972) suggested that this species arose in
cultivation as a segmental allopolyploid of
M. suaveolens (see M. x rotundifolia*) and M.
longifolia*. Var. crispata Schrader (syn. M.
crispa L.) has genome formula RRS^{C}S^C. This
species is one of the parents of M. x piperita*.
It might be one of the parents of M. x villosa*.
  Murray et al. (1972) artificially crossed M.
aquatica (2n=96) and M. spicata (2n=48). This
resulted in very variable F1 due to the hetero-
zygosity of the pollen parent. Some hybrids resembled the natural strains of M. x piperita,
others did not.

MENTHA SUAVEOLENS Ehrh. (syn. M. rotundifolia
auct., non (L.) Hudson). 2n=24. Cultivated as
a potherb.

MENTHA x VILLOSA Hudson (syn. M. cordifolia
auct., M. gratissima Weber). 2n=36. This
species is a hybrid of M. spicata* and M. suaveolens*.

NEPETA CATARIA L. (syn. Cataria vulgaris
Moench.). Catnip, Catmint. 2n=(32), 34, (36).
Europe. A perennial herb cultivated for medi-
cinal purposes.

ORIGANUM VULGARE L. Wild majoram. 2n=30. An
extremely variable species from the Azores,
Madeira, the Canary Islands, Europe throughout
the Mediterranean Region, W., C. and E. China
to Taiwan. Its great variation has resulted in
numerous synonyms (Ietswaart, 1980). Cultivated as a medicinal plant.

Leguminosae

ANTHYLLIS VULNERARIA L. Kidney vetch, Spring
vetch, Lady's fingers, Wound-wort, Amer, Tare.
2n=12. Temp. Europe, Caucasia, Ante-Asia, N.
Africa and Ethiopia. Cultivated since 1858
(Mansfeld, 1959) and is now usually mixed with
pasture grasses.

ASTRAGALUS CICER L. Milk vetch. 2n=64. Europe.
A perennial pasture plant well-adapted for grass

mixtures (Whyte et al., 1953).

ASTRAGALUS FALCATUS Lam. Sicklepod milk vetch. 2n=16. W. Asia. A forage plant cultivated in USSR and France.

ASTRAGALUS GLYCYPHYLLUS L. Milk vetch. 2n=16. Europe and Siberia to Altai. A perennial herb cultivated as a fodder.

CORONILLA VARIA L. Crown vetch. 2n=24. C. and S. Europe extending to C. Russia. Cultivated as an ornamental, a fodder crop and a cover crop.

GALEGA OFFICINALIS L. Galega, European goat's rue. 2n=16. E., C. and S. Europe, Caucasia, Asia Minor and Iran. Cultivated as a forage crop and as an ornamental.

GLYCYRRHIZA ECHINATA L. 2n=16. SE. Europe to Hungary and Italy. Cultivated to produce liquorice.

GLYCYRRHIZA GLABRA (syn. G. glandulifera Waldst. & Kit.). Common licorice, Liquorice. 2n=16. Europe and the Mediterranean region. A perennial herb. Var. typica Regel & Herder is cultivated to produce Spanish or Italian licorice and var. glandulifera Waldst. Russian licorice.

HEDYSARUM HEDYSAROIDES (L.) Schinz. & Thell. (syn. H. alpinum Jacq.). 2n=14. S. Europe, Asia Minor, America and Caucasia. Cultivated as a fodder crop especially in the Alps.

LATHYRUS SYLVESTRIS L. Flat pea, Wood pea. 2n=14. Europe. Cultivated for forage and as an ornamental plant.

LATHYRUS TUBEROSUS L. Groundnut peavine, Earth chestnut. 2n=14. Europe and W. Asia. Cultivated for its tubers. In the 16th Century its flowers were distilled for perfumes (Uphof, 1968).

LOTUS CORNICULATUS L. Birds-foot trefoil. 2n= 12, 24. Europe, moderate Asia and N. Africa to Ethiopia. Formerly and at present in USA in use in seed mixtures for a ley crop and for pastures. Landolt (1970) and Somarov & Grant (1971) suggested that the diploid is a hybrid and the tetraploid an allotetraploid of L. alpinus Schleicher (2n=12) of the Alp and the submediterranean L. pilosus Jord. (2n=12).

The erect, broad-leaved type probably from C. European origin is spread now as a contaminant of grass seed for road sides throughout W. Europe (Jones, 1973).

LOTUS ULIGINOSUS Schkuhr. Greater birds-foot trefoil. 2n=12, (24). Europe, N. Africa, Ante-Asia to Tibet. Cultivated in C. Europe and Great Britain as a fodder crop (Mansfeld, 1959).

MEDICAGO FALCATA L. Yellow lucerne. 2n=16, 32.

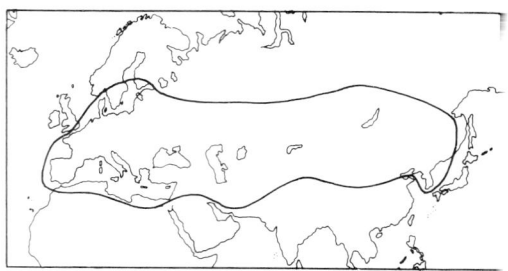

Medicago falcata (Fischer, 1938).

In Europe and Asia from longitude 10° to 85° E. and latitude 42° to 60° N., and mountains near the S. limits. The 4x is common while 2x is rare but occurs in the whole area. The 2x ssp. romanica (Prod.) Hayek possesses some rare characteristics and may derive from an older 2x stock (Lesins & Lesins, 1979).

MEDICAGO GLOMERATA Balbis. 2n=16, (32?). Maritime Alps. Useful as gene source of M. sativa*.

MEDICAGO LUPULINA L. Hop clover, Black medic. 2n=16, genome formula SS, 32, (64). Europe, most of Asia and N. Africa. It is naturalized in N. America. The 4x type has been found in C. Siberia. Occasionally included in seed mixtures for pastures. Cultivated since 1659 in England and 1785 in France, and now in the Old and New Worlds as a green fodder, hay crop and green manure (Lesins & Lesins, 1979).

MEDICAGO SATIVA L. Lucerne, Blue alfalfa. 2n= (16, genome formula SS), 32, (48, genome formula SSSSSS, 64). Transcaucasia (p. 97). Two populations - one from the Balkans and one from France - "met" in Thuringia, Germany. This resulted in a hybrid swarm from which winterhardy types were introduced in Minnesota, USA in 1857.

MELILOTUS ALBUS Medik. White sweet clover, Bokhara clover, Honey clover, White melilot. 2n= 16. Europe and W. Asia. Cultivated in the Old World and particularly in the USA as a fodder crop and green manure.

It can be divided into two groups 1) the annual wild type and 2) the bushy type. The latter might be a mutant of group 1, or derive from a natural cross of M. albus. From both groups cultivars have been selected.

The very low variation of this species may point to only a few introductions.

MELILOTUS ALTISSIMUS Thuill. 2n=16. Europe and temp. Asia. Sometimes cultivated for horse fodder.

MELILOTUS DENTATUS (Waldst. & Kit.) Pers. 2n= 16. E. and C. Europe to N. Sweden. Coumarin deficient and salt tolerant. Used to breed coumarin free cultivars of M. albus*.

MELILOTUS MACRORHIZUS Pers. 2n=16. Asia and
Europe. Cultivated in China for its roots which
are eaten as a vegetable. Closely related to M.
altissimus*.

MELILOTUS OFFICINALIS Lam. Biennal yellow sweet
clover, Field melilot, Yellow melilot. 2n=16.
W. Europe to W. China. Cultivated in Europe
and also in the USA. It is a biennal with sporadically some annuals.

ONOBRYCHIS VICIIFOLIA Scop. (syn. O. sativa
s.1.Lam.). Esparcette, Sainfoin. 2n=18. Temp.
Europe, SW. Asia to Altai and Transbaikal. Cultivation was probably started in S. France resulting in spp. sativa. There are three subspecies: arenaria (Kit & Koch.) Thellung, sand
esparcette, montana (Lam. & D.C.), the mountain
esparcette and sativa (Lam.) Thellung, the cultivated esparcette. The last name is confusing,
because spp. arenaria (also described as var.
transcaucasia, syn. O. transcaucasia Grossh.)*
is cultivated too.

SAROTHAMNUS SCOPARIUS (L.) Wimm. ex Koch. Broom.
2n=(14), 46, 48. W. and C. Europe. Cultivated
as a soil stabilizer.

TRIFOLIUM HYBRIDUM L. (syn. T. fistulosum
Gilib.). Alslike clover. 2n=16. Temp. Europe,
SW. Asia and N. Africa. Possibly first cultivated in Sweden. Introduced to other European
countries and N. America. Often found in fields
of red clover. Very likely not the ancestral
form of T. repens*. The cultivated type spp.
hybridum is probably derived from the wild
type spp. elegans (Savi) Asch. & Graebn. In
Anatolia spp. anatolicum (Boiss.) Hossain is
found.

TRIFOLIUM PANNONICUM Jacq. Hungarian clover.
2n=c. 96, 98, c. 126, c. 130, c. 180. E., C
and S. Europe. Cultivated.

TRIFOLIUM PRATENSE L. Red clover. 2n=14, genome formula AA, (28). Europe, W. and C. Asia
and N. Africa. Primary centre in Region 9. It
was probably first cultivated in the Netherlands, in the beginning of the 16th Century.
The Classics already mentioned 2000 years ago
that local ecotypes were developed in SE. Europe and Asia Minor. Spread to Germany and
through Flanders to England. In the beginning
of the 17th Century seed of red clover was exported from the Netherlands to the Scandina-
vian countries and France. From England red
clover was spread to USSR and N. America. The
wild type has more leaves and new shoots emerge
from internodes at the butt end, while the cultivated type has less leaves and new shoots
emerge from the leaf rosett. The variable wild
type is described as var. pratense Bobr. and
the cultivated as var. sativum (Crome) Bobr.
(syn. T. sativum (Sturm) Crome.
     Late red clover (var. serotinum) may have de-
veloped from contaminants or spontaneous mutants in USSR from introduced early types (var.

praecox).
     Autotetraploid types are widely cultivated
now. Var. americanum C.O. Hartz was cultivated
between 1883 and c. 1910 in C. Europe. It originated from a N. American introduction. It is
often erroneously described as T. expansum
Waldst. & Kit. Var. maritimum Zabel (var. villosum Wahlberg) is found wild on the S. coast
of the Balkan Peninsula and var. frigidum
Gaudin occurs wild in the Alps.
     Red clover is closely related to the annual
T. diffusum Ehrh., 2n=16, to the annual T.
pallidum Waldst. & Kit., 2n=16 and the perennial T. noricum Wulf., 2n=16.

TRIFOLIUM REPENS L. White clover. 2n=32, (48,
64). Wild type (var. sylvestre). In meadows
throughout Eurasia and N. Africa. Cultivation
started probably in N. Italy (p. 115) and in
the Netherlands. Very variable.
     Brewbaker & Keim (1953) suggest that T. ni-
grescens Viv., Ball clover (2n=16) is one of
the parents. Chen & Gibson (1970) believe that
it is an autotetraploid while T. nigrescens
and T. occidentale D. Coombe (2n=16) are related to it. T. uniflorum L. (2n=32) might also be a parent. This species is found in E.
Mediterranean area to Sicily. It includes T.
savianum Guss. of Sicily and Calabria, Italy.
It is probably an autotetraploid. Navalikhina
(1977) suggested that white clover is an allopolyploid of T. nigrescens, T. occidentale
and T. uniflorum.

TRIFOLIUM RESUPINATUM L. (syn. T. suaveolens
Willd.). Persian clover. 2n=(14), 16. The Mediterranean area to Iran, Afghanistan and India. Cultivated as a fodder crop. Var. majus
Boiss. is syn. to T. suaveolens Willd.

TRIGONELLA COERULEA (L.) Ser. Sweet trefoil.
2n=16. Cultivated and also found as a weed or
ruderal. It may be derived from T. procumbens
(Besser) Reichenb. (syn. T. besserana Ser.,
T. coerulea spp. procumbens (Besser) Thell.).
This species is a native to EC. and SE. Europe.

ULEX EUROPAEUS L. Common corse. 2n=96. W. Europe to Italy. Cultivated formerly for fodder,
bedding and as hedges.

VICIA CRACCA L. Gerard vetch. 2n=12, 14, (21,
24), 28. W. Europe to Kamtchaska, E. China and
Japan. Cultivated.

VICIA HIRSUTA (L.) S.F. Gray. Common tare,
Hairy tare. 2n=14. Europe, N. Africa and W.
Asia. Cultivated in W. of USSR together with
barley.

VICIA PANNONICA Crantz. Hungarian vetch. 2n=
12. Primary centre in SW. Asia (p. 98). Secondary centre in Hungary.

     Liliaceae

ASPARAGUS OFFICINALIS L. Garden asparagus. 2n

=20. Primary centre probably in the saltsteppes of E. Europe. A. officinalis var. prostratus Richter is a tetraploid (Braak & Zeilinga, 1957).

CONVALLARIA MAJALIS L. Lily-of-the-valley. 2n =32, 36, 38. Europe, temp. Asia and Japan. A perennial herb cultivated as a medicinal crop and as an ornamental.

Linaceae

LINUM USITATISSIMUM L. Flax, Linseed. 2n=30, (32). For origin see p. 99. Helbaek (1971) supposed two ways of introduction of flax. One through Greece and the Donau valley into C. and W. Europe and the other west of the Black Sea in a northern direction into Russia. The first was probably a winter-annual which is the parent of "Winterlein" cultivated in Germany. The other was probably a summer-annual. In the first millenium B.C. the latter was introduced to C. and W. Europe. It is at present described as spp. eurasiaticum Vav. & Ell. In NW. USSR there is a centre of flax containing some of the finest fibre flax varieties.
  In W. Europe and Ukraine the weed rattle flax, L. crepitans Dumort. (2n=30), now included in L. usitatissimum is probably the weedy type of flax.

Malvaceae

ALTHAEA OFFICINALIS*

Paeoniaceae

PAEONIA OFFICINALIS L. Peony, Piney. 2n=20. S. Europe, Asia Minor and Armenia. A perennial herb cultivated for its medicinal merits.

Plantaginaceae

PLANTAGO LACEOLATA L. Rib grass. 2n=12, (13, 12 + 2B). Cultivated on a small scale in the Netherlands and elsewhere as a medicinal crop.

Polygonaceae

RUMEX ACETOSA L. Garden sorrel. 2n=14 ♀ , 15 ♂ and other numbers. Temp. Europe and Asia. A perennial herb. Var. hortensis Dierb. (syn. R. ambiguus Gren.) is cultivated in the Old and New Worlds.

RUMEX ALPINUS L. Alpine dock, Monk's rhubarb. 2n=20. C. Europe, the Balkans and Caucasia. Cultivated formerly in C. Europe as a vegetable.

RUMEX OBTUSIFOLIUS L. Broad-leaved dock, Bitter dock. 2n=40,(60). Europe and temp. Asia. Cultivated.

RUMEX PATIENTIA L. Patience dock, Spinach dock, Herb patience. 2n=(40), 60. Probably C. Europe to W. Asia. Cultivated as a vegetable.

RUMEX SCUTATUS L. (R. alpestris Jacq.). French sorrel. 2n=20, (40). C. and S. Europe, Alpine regions, Caucasia, India. Cultivated as a vegetable (var. hortensis Lam. & DC.).

Portulacaceae

PORTULACA OLERACEA L. Purslane. 2n=2x=18, 4x= 36, 6x=54. Purslane is a cosmopolitan weed whose origin is doubtful (Danin et al., 1978). The cultivated type (ssp. sativa (Haw.) Celak., 2n=54) is a vegetable, which probably developed in Europe from the Eurasian weedy type ssp. oleracea, 2n=54. The distribution of the 2x, 4x and 6x wild and weedy subspecies indicates that one of the centres of diversity is Mexico (p.   ) (Danin et al., 1978).

Ranunculaceae

ACONITUM NAPELLUS L. Monkshood. 2n=24, 32. C. Europe. Cultivated as a medicinal crop and also as an ornamental.

AQUILEGIA VULGARIS*

NIGELLA SATIVA*

Resedaceae

RESEDA LUTEOLA*

Rhamnaceae

RHAMNUS CATHARTICUS L. Buckthorn. 2n=24. Europe up to Transcaucasia and W. Siberia, and in Algeria. Formerly the fruits of this tree were used as a source of yellow dye.

RHAMNUS FRANGULA L. Alder buckthorn. 2n=20, 22, 26. Europe, Asia and N. Africa. A tree formerly cultivated.

Rosaceae

AGRIMONIA ODORATA (Gouan) Mill. 2n=56. It is included in A. eupatoria L., Agrimony. Cultivated as a medicinal crop.

AMYGDALUS BESSERIANA Schott. (syn. A. nana L., Prunus nana (L.) Stokes, P. tenella Batsch.). Dwarf almond, Dwarf Russian almond, Steppe almond. 2n=16. Primary centre in E. Europe and Siberia. Also wild in the Balkan, Asia Minor, Causasus and China (p. 42). It is the commonest wild almond species and it is very frost resistant which makes it extremely valuable as a rootstock of A. communis.

AMYGDALUS LEDEBOURIANA Schlecht. (syn. Prunus ledebouriana Schlecht.) 2n=   . A shrub from Tarbagatai and Altai.

AMYGDALUS PERSICA L. Peach. 2n=16. Primary centre in China (p. 42). Secondary centre in Moldavia, USSR.

ARMENIACA BRIGANTINA (Vizl.) Pers. (syn. Prunus brigantina Vill.). Briançon apricot. 2n=
. Originated in SE. France. The seeds are the source of the perfumed oil "Huile de Marmotte" (Uphof, 1968). It might be a gene source of late flowering.

ARMENIACA SIBIRICA Pers. (syn. Prunus sibirica L., P. armeniaca var. sibirica K. Koch.). Siberian apricot. 2n=16. Intern Mongolia to the Sowjet Far East and Lake Baikal. This species has the largest distribution of all apricot species (Zylka, 1970). It is very cold resistant.

Armeniaca sibirica

FRAGARIA X ANANASSA Duch. (syn. F. grandiflora Ehrh.). Pineapple strawberry. 2n=56. Arose spontaneously in W. Europe (in a garden near Haarlem, the Netherlands) after hybridization of F. virginiana* from N. America and F. chiloensis* from S. America. F. ovalis (Rydb.) Lemm. from NW. USA is used as a source of winterhardiness.

FRAGARIA MOSCHATA Duch. Hautbois strawberry. 2n=42. Europe and European USSR. Cultivated formerly, and run wild in other countries.

FRAGARIA VESCA L. Wild strawberry, Alpine

Fragaria moschata

strawberry. 2n=14, genome formula AA. Europe, Asia and N. America (p. 204). Darrow (1955) stated that var. semperflorens Duch. is the parent of the cultivated strawberry. It was domesticated N. of the Italian Alps. Cultivated from seed and vegetatively.

FRAGARIA VIRIDIS Duch. Polunitsa. 2n=14. European part of Region 9. Cultivated formerly.

MALUS BACCATA (L.) Borkh. var. baccata. Siberian crab apple. 2n=34. Wild in Transbaikal and Ante-Baikal territories. Primary gene centre in Siberia. Resistant to frost.

MALUS PRUNIFOLIA (Willd.) Borkh. (syn. Pyrus prunifolia (Willd.). Chinese crab apple. 2n=34, (51, 68). Wild and cultivated in the extreme eastern sector of Region 9. Primary centre China.

MALUS PUMILA Mill. (syn. Pyrus malus L.) Apple. 2n=34, 51, 68. The Balkans and SW. USSR (p. 85), eastwards through Transcaucasia, Iran, Turkestan, and northwards to the Altai mountains. It occurs along the ancient and mediaeval routes of commerce and migration between Europe and E. Asia. Man has greatly promoted its distribution (Wilcox, 1962). It is considered as the principal ancestor of the

Malus baccata

cultivated apple. M. sylvestris* hybridizes
with this species and hence may also have
played a small part as an ancestor.
    European USSR is the primary centre for many
old cultivars as Antonovka, Aport, Borovinka.
In early 19th Century, Bolotov, described 600
Russian cultivars; about 10 000 cultivars exist
in the world today. This shows the very polymorphic nature of this species which has also
arisen due to introgression with other species.

PRUNUS CERASUS L. Sour cherry. 2n=32, genome
formula CC. C. Asian centre (p. 101). The population Vladimirskaya vishnia with large dark-
scarlet fruits that are very palatable and aromatic, originated in Region 9, extending westward and southward to the Rhine and Balkans.

PRUNUS DOMESTICA L. Garden plum, Domestic
plum. 2n=48, genome formula CCSSSS or CdCdSS
S_1S_1 or $CdCdD_1D_1D_2D_2$. For origin see p. 101.
Werneck (1958) considered Upper Austria as a
place where the garden plum has arisen. Bush
seedling would have been transplanted to compounds where further domestication may have
occurred. The Lake Bank Dwellers of neolithic
Switzerland knew the garden plum.

PRUNUS FRUTICOSA Pall. (syn. Cerasus fruticosa Pall.). Dwarf Cherry, Bush Cherry, Ground
Cherry, Mongolian Cherry, Steppe Cherry. 2n=
16, 32. Extended over Europe. It occurs in
great diversity beyond the Volga, in S. Ural,
SW. Siberia and Bashkirskaya. One of the parents of P. cerasus*. It withstands -52°C.

PRUNUS INSITITIA L. (syn. P. domestica var.
insititia (L.) C.K. Schneider, P. domestica

spp. italica (Borkh.) Hegi). Bullace plum,
Damson plum. 2n=48. S. and SE. Europe and adjacent parts of Asia. Occurs now throughout
temp. Europe and W. Asia. Probably only known
as a cultigen and naturalized. If so, it is
obviously an allohexaploid. It is frost resistant.

PRUNUS MAHALEB L. Mahaleb cherry, St. Lucie
cherry. 2n=16. C. and S. Europe and W. Asia.
Fruits are not edible. Used as rootstock for
cultivated cherries. Mainly self-incompatible.

PYRACANTHA COCCINEA M.J. Roemer. 2n=34. S.
Europe and westwards to NE. Spain. Cultivated
as an ornamental and for its fruits.

PYRUS COMMUNIS L. (syn. P. domestica Med.).
Common pear. 2n=34, (51). Europe and W. Asia
It has been divided into spp. pyraster L. (syn.
P. pyraster Burgsd., P. communis var. achras
Wallr.), spp. nivalis Jacq. (syn. P. nivalis
Jacq.) and spp. salvifolia (syn. P. salvifolia
DC.). Spp. pyraster is the most important one,
it grows in C. Europe and W. Asia. Spp. nivalis,
the snow pear grows in W. Switzerland and
France. It is used as a rootstock. Spp. salvifolia is found in the same areas. The cultivars
are derived from these subspecies by selection
and by crossing with P. serotina*, P. ussuriensis*, P. longipes, P. caucasica*, P. amygdaliformis* and P. salicifolia*. Pavlov (1969a,
1969b) reported that types of W. and S. Europe
derive from crosses with P. nivalis* and P.
amygdaliformis*, because they have hairiness
and a high number of stomata per area like these
two species.
    Some cultivars in Caucasus show characteris-
tics obviously derived from P. caucasica*. The
E. European cultivars show a direct derivation
from the wild P. communis.

PYRUS CORDATA Desv. 2n=   . W. Europe. Cultivated in hedges and for its wood.

ROSA x ALBA L. French rose. 2n=28, 42. Cultivated in Bulgaria and S. France for the perfumery industry. Probably a hybrid of R. arvensis* x R. gallica*, and a white flowered mem-
ber of the Sect. Canina.

ROSA ARVENSIS Hudson. 2n=14. S., W. and C. Europe. It is one of the parents of R. x alba*.

ROSA x BIFERA (Poiret) Pers. (syn. R. damascena auct., non Miller). Damask rose. 2n=28.
Probably a hybrid of R. moschata* and R. gallica*. Cultivated in Bulgaria, S. France and
Turkey. The petals are used to produce oil of
roses which is used in perfumery.

ROSA CANINA L. Brier, Dog rose, Doghip. 2n=35.
Europe, temperate Asia and N. Africa. It is a
common rootstock of garden roses. The named
selections are often less prickly than the wild
ones.

ROSA GALLICA L. French rose. 2n=28. S. and C. Europe up to Belgium and C. France and W. Asia. Probably a parent of R. x bifera* and R. x alba*. The petals are used in perfumery.

ROSA RUBIGINOSA L. (syn. R. eglanteria auct.). Sweet briar. 2n=35. W. and C. Europe. Cultivated for its flowers and as rootstock.

ROSA VILLOSA L. Apple rose. 2n=28. Var. pomifera (Herrm.) Crép. Europe and SW. Asia.

RUBUS ARCTICUS L. Arctic bramble, Nectarberry. 2n=14. Europe and N. Asia. Used in breeding work with R. idaeus*. Fruits have a distinct aroma and rich in Vit. C. A hardy, high yielding, disease resistant plant.

RUBUS CHAMAEMORUS L. Cloudberry, Yellowberry, Salmonberry, Bake apple. 2n=56. Europe and N. Asia used in breeding with R. idaeus*. Easily domesticated (Larson, 1969). Seed and esp. subterranean runners are used to propagate this dioecious species.

RUBUS IDAEUS L. European red raspberry. 2n=14. Spp. vulgatus wild in Europe. It is domesticated. The present cultivars often are hybrids of this subspecies and its NE. American counterpart spp. strigosus.
    The tetraploid subspecies: melanolasis Focke from NW. America and Siberia, sachalinensis Léveillé from Sakhalin and sibiricus from Kamchatka, have been grouped as R. sachalinensis Levl. Some cultivars derive from R. idaeus x R. chamaemorus*, cloudberry (2n=56). Crosses have also been made between this species and R. R. xanthocarpus Bur. & Franch from W. China, R. arcticus* L., Arctic bramble (2n=14) and P. parviflorus L., Japanese raspberry (2n=14). Other Rubus species have also been used in breeding work. Ever bearing types have been developed.

RUBUS LACINIATUS Willd. Evergreen blackberry. 2n=28. C. Europe. A cultivar was brought to N. America where hybridization took place with another European immigrant, R. procerus P.J. Muell. (2n=14, 28, 49), Himalaya berry. In 1925, a mutant was found in Oregon and named 'Thornless Evergreen'. This cultivar and its minor mutants are commonly grown in the USA.

RUBUS SAXATILIS L. Stoneberry. 2n=18. Europe and N. Asia. In Sweden a species has been found to be resistant to rust and other diseases. The fruit has only a few drupelets and lacks flavour (Larsson, 1969).

SANGUISORBA MINOR Scop. 2n=18, (54, 56). Europe and temp. Asia. Sometimes cultivated to flavour soup or for salads (Mansfeld, 1959).

SANGUISORBA OFFICINALIS L. Great burnet, Garden burnet. 2n=18, (42, 56, c. 70). Europe, Asia and N. America. Sometimes cultivated as a vegetable (Mansfeld, 1959).

SORBUS AUCUPARIA L. (syn. Mespilus aucuparia All.). Rowan tree, European mountain ash. 2n=34. The "Mährische Eberesche" (var. moravica) was found in 1810 in Czechoslovakia. It has been improved and distributed. Before its domestication var. rossica and var. rossica-major were already cultivated in USSR. It is an important source of Vitamin C (Mueller-Stoll & Michael, 1949).

SORBUS DOMESTICA L. Service tree, Mountain ash. 2n=34. S. Europe, N. Africa and W. Asia. Cultivated in Europe for its fruits which are eaten or made into wine and as an ornamental. Largefruited forms are found in forests in Crimea (p. 101).

Rubiaceae

RUBIA TINCTORUM L. Madder. 2n=44. S. Europe and Asia Minor. Cultivated in Europe as a dye plant.

Salicaceae

SALIX ACUTIFOLIA L. Caspic willow. 2n=38. A tree of USSR and Manchuria. Cultivated for twig production.

SALIX ALBA L. (syn. S. aurea Salisb.). White willow. 2n=76. In large area of Europe and Asia (p. 86) and N. Africa. Introduced into N. America. Cultivated in Europe for twig production for dike building.

SALIX CAPREA L. Goat willow, Common willow. 2n=38, (57, 76). Europe and N. Asia. Cultivated for its twigs.

SALIX FRAGILIS L. Brittle willow, Crack willow. 2n=(38), 76, (114). Europe, Asia Minor, Syria, Iran and W. and C. Siberia. Often planted for twig production. It is one of the parents of S. x rubens Schrank.

SALIX PURPUREA L. Purple willow, Purple osier willow. 2n=38. A large part of Europe, and in Asia to Japan, and in N. Africa. Cultivated for twig production for dike works and basketry.

SALIX TRIANDRA L. (syn. S. amygdalina L.). French willow, Almond-leaved willow. 2n=38, 44, (57, 88). Spread from W. Europe to E. Asia. Planted for twig production. One of the parental species of the cultivated S. x mollissima Ehrh. (2n=38).

SALIX VIMINALIS L. (syn. S. longifolia Lam.). Twiggy willow, Common osier, Basket willow, Osier willow. 2n=38. C. Europe and a large part of Asia. Much cultivated in N. and S. Europe and elsewhere for twig production. Many of the willows planted in the Netherlands for dike work belong to this species and to S. triandra*. They are often cultivated in mixed stands which leads to cross fertilization and development of hybrids.

S. dasyclados Wimmer (2n=38, 57, 76, 114) is probably a complex hybrid of S. caprea x S. cinera x S. viminalis. S. helix L. is a hybrid of S. purpurea* x S. viminalis. In Great Britain, this willow is planted as a windbreak and to shelter cattle.

Sambucaceae

SAMBUCUS EBULUS L. Dwarf elder. 2n=36. From Netherlands and Ukraine southwards. Formerly cultivated as a medicinal plant. Naturalized elsewhere.

SAMBUCUS NIGRA L. European elder. 2n=36. Europe. Cultivated. Recently there has been a new interest in this tree because of the processing of alcohol-free beverage (Strauss & Novak, 1971).

Saxiphragaceae

BERGENIA CRASSIFOLIA (L.) Fritsch. 2n=34. Siberia, Altai and N. Mongolia. A perennial herb cultivated since 1927 in USSR as a tea plant (Mansfeld, 1959).

Scrophulariaceae

DIGITALIS LANATA Ehrh. 2n=56. SE. Europe . Elsewhere in Europe it may have run wild. Cultivated as a medicinal crop.

DIGITALIS PURPUREA L. Purple fox-glove. 2n= 56. S. (p. 118) and C. Europe. Cultivated as a medicinal plant and as an ornamental.

VERBASCUM THAPSIFORME Schrad. 2n=32. Spread throughout Europe. Cultivated for its medicinal properties and as an ornamental.

Solanaceae

CAPSICUM ANNUUM L. Bell pepper, Paprika, Cayenne pepper. 2n=24. Mexico (p. 196). Secondary centre in Europe.

PHYSALIS ALKEKENGI L. Strawberry tomato, Winter cherry. 2n=24. C. and S. Europe. A perennial herb cultivated for its fruits.

SCOPOLIA CARNIOLICA Jacq. Scopalia. 2n=46-48, 48. Europe. Cultivated as a medicinal crop.

SOLANUM TUBEROSUM L. Potato. 2n=48. Domesticated in S. America. In Europe spp. tuberosum developed. Its genetic basis is very small. This is probably caused by only a few introdutions, and afterwards by the selection for short-day forms and by mass killing during blight epidemics in the 1840's.

Umbelliferae

ANGELICA ARCHANGELICA L. Angelica. 2n=22. Temperate Europe, Himalaya, Siberia and Kamtschatka. Cultivated for its aromatic petioles. Spp.

archangelica includes the cultivated type.

ANTHRISCUS CEREFOLIUM (Waldst. & Kit.) Sprengel. Garden chervil. 2n=18. Probably EC. and SE. Europe. Var. cerefolium has glabrous fruits It includes the cultivated type.

BUNIUM BULBOCASTANUM L. (syn. Ligusticum bulbocastanum Crantz). 2n= . W. Europe. Formerly cultivated for its edible tubers.

CARUM CARVI L. (syn. Apium carvi Crantz). Caraway. 2n= 20, 22, (23, 25). Europe and W. Asia. Cultivated in temperate regions, N. India and Sudan (see C. roxburghianum*, C. copticum*)

CHAEROPHYLLUM BULBOSUM L. Turnip-rooted chervil. 2n=22. Europe and W. Asia. Its cultivation as a vegetable is on the decline.

DAUCUS CAROTA L. White carrot, Orange carrot. 2n=18. Afghanistan (p. 86). The origin of the white type is not clear. It probably arose as a mutant from a yellow type, most likely in France. The orange carrot probably originated in the Netherlands. This type of carrot is now cultivated widely by peoples of European stock. It has suppressed the growth of the purple carrot, which colours soups and food preparations purple (Banga, 1957, 1963). The poor storage quality of the purple types (Small, 1978b) may also have encouraged their replacement by other types. Even before the introduction of domesticated carrots, wild plants were grown in gardens as medicinal crops (W. Brandenburg, pers. comm., 1980).

LEVISTICUM OFFICINALE Koch. (syn. Angelica levisticum Ball.). Garden lovage, Bladder seed. 2n=22. Cultivated mainly for flavouring.

MYRRHIS ODORATA (L.) Scop. Garden myrrh, Sweet scented myrrh. 2n=22. Europe and Caucasia. Cultivated for flavouring and for fodder.

PASTINACA SATIVA L. Parsnip. 2n=22. Europe. Var. sativa is cultivated there and elsewhere for its sweet, fresh tap-root. The wild type has a sour root.

PEUCEDANUM CERVARIA (L.) Lapeyr. Hart's wort. Much-good, Broad-leaved spignel. 2n=22. S. and C. Europe. Cultivated formerly as a medicinal.

PEUCEDANUM OSTRUTHIUM (L.) Koch. Master wort Pellitory of Spain, Hogfennel. 2n=22. Europe Cultivated for its scenting root since the 16th Century, as a medicinal and as herb. Its cultivation has almost disappeared now.

Valerianaceae

VALERIANA LOCUSTA (L.) Betcke. (syn. V. olitoria Pollich). Corn salad, Lamb's lettuce. 2n= . Europe, N. Africa, Caucasia. Cultivated to be used for salads.

VALERIANA OFFICINALIS L. Valerian. 2n=2x=14,
4x=28, 8x=56. Most of Europe and temp. Asia.
Subsp. officinalis (syn. V. exaltata Mikan f.
ex Pohl), 2n=14, ssp. collins (Wallr.) Nyman
(syn. V. collina Wallr.), 2n=28, and ssp. sam-
bucifolius (Mikan f.) Cecak (syn. V. sambuci-
folius Mikan f., V. exelsa Poiret), 2n=56,
are recognized, but other chromosomal numbers
occur within a subspecies. These ploidy levels
and occasional hybrids have led to many synonyms (Schrantz, 1961). Cultivated for its
rhizome which yields the drug valerian.

VALERIANA PROCUMBENS Wallr. 2n=56. Spain,
Great Britain, France and Germany. Cultivated
in Germany. This species might be included in
V. officinalis*.

VALERIANA SAMBUCIFOLIA Mikan f. ex Pohl. 2n=
56. Wild in N., C. and E. Europe. Cultivated
in Thuringia, Germany for its seeds. This species might be included in V. officinalis*.

   Violaceae

VIOLA TRICOLOR L. 2n=26. Europe, Siberia up
to Altai and India. Spp. arvensis Gaud. (V.
arvensis Murr., 2n=34) is a cosmopolitan weed.
This subspecies and spp. tricolor (2n=26) are
cultivated for their medicinal and ornamental
purposes.

   Vitidaceae

VITIS VINIFERA L. Common grape, European grape.
2n=38, (57, 76). For primary centres see p.
102). In Europe, the wild grape played a role
in the development of old and modern cultivars.
The wild type is declining (Schumann, 1977).

10 South American Region

The South American Region was restricted to the Andes by Vavilov (1949/50) and recognized as the Andean Centre which he divided into two areas: (1) Peru, Ecuador and Bolivia; (2) the island of Chiloe in Chile. The area between the coast of Venezuela, Guyana, Surinam and Cayenne, and S. Brazil and Paraguay was added by Darlington & Janaka Ammal (1945) as a third centre. Zhukovskij recognized a megacentre for the whole of S. America, and Harlan (1971) demonstrated the lack of well defined centres of origin for cultivated plants in this region.

The oldest known remains of cultivated plants in S. America are Phaseolus vulgaris from Guitarrero Cave in Peru, dating back some 8000 years (Kaplan et al., 1973). This, however, is not necessarily the centre of origin of agriculture in the New World. Plants were domesticated on the Andean Highlands as well as the tropical Lowlands (Reed, 1977), and a knowledge of food production may have evolved independently in these regions. Tuberous crops such as Xanthosoma were domesticated in the humid tropics while others such as Oxalis, Solanum and Ullucus are more typically crops of the High Andes. S. America provided the world with numerous fruits and vegetables, but a single cereal, Bromus mango endemic to Chiloe of Chile (Cruz, 1972). Maize (Zea mays) was introduced from C. America early in its evolution into S. America, and there evolved a major secondary centre of diversity.

Acanthaceae

JUSTICIA PECTORALIS Jacq. 2n=   . West Indies
and trop. America. Var. stenophylla Leonard
semi-cultivated in E. Colombia to adjacent Amazonian Brazil. It is a smaller plant, has
smaller and longer leaves, and has shorter inflorescences than the common type.

Agavaceae

FURCRAEA FOETIDA (L.) Haw. (syn. F. gigantea
Venth.). Piteira, Piteira gigante. 2n=(18, 19,
34), 60. S. and C. America. The Mauritius hemp
comes from var. willemettiana Roem. which is
cultivated on Mauritius and elsewhere.

FURCRAEA MACROPHYLLA (Hook.) Baker. Fique. 2n
=   . Colombia. Cultivated there on a small
scale. Some varieties have developed. Fique
fibre also comes from other Furcraea species
such as F. andina Trel. (2n=60), a wild growing
species from Equador and Peru, and T. humboldt-
iana Trel., a wild growing species from Venezuela.

Aizoaceae

MESEMBRYANTHEMUM CHILENSE Mol. (syn. Carpobrotus chilensis (Mol.) N.E. Brown). Sea fig.
2n=   . Chile. A shrub used in N. America to
stabilize dunes.

Amaranthaceae

AMARANTHUS CAUDATUS L. Inca wheat, Quihuicha.
2n=32, 34. S. America, Asia and possibly in
Africa. Cultivated as a grain crop. In Andean
region of Peru, Bolivia and NE. Argentina and
in China, India, Nepal and Afghanistan. Its
leaves are also eaten. A form with red flower-
spikes used as a garden ornamental ('love-lies
-bleeding') should not be confused with quinoa
(Chenopodium quinoa*. Quinoa is of S. American
origin (Sauer, 1950)). It resembles A. edulis*
and the wild S. American A. quitensis H.B.K.,
2n=32.

AMARANTHUS DUBIUS Mart. ex Thell. 2n=64. Trop.
America. Cultivated there as a potherb and
for its grains. It also is a common weed. It
resembles A. cruentus*. Perhaps it is a tetraploid from this latter species. See for hybridization with A. spinosus (p. 165).

AMARANTHUS HYBRIDUS*

AMARANTHUS MANTEGAZZIANUS Passer (syn. A. edulis Spegazzini). 2n=32. Cultivated in Argentina. The wild S. American A.quitensis H.B.K.(2n=
32) closely resembles it.It is also included in
A.caudata* as ssp. mantegazzianus (Passer)Hanelt.

AMARANTHUS QUITENSIS H.B.K. Sangorache. 2n=   .
Cultivated in Ecuador for its brilliant red
inflorescences, which are a source of dye. Selection for bigger flowers (Heiser, 1964).

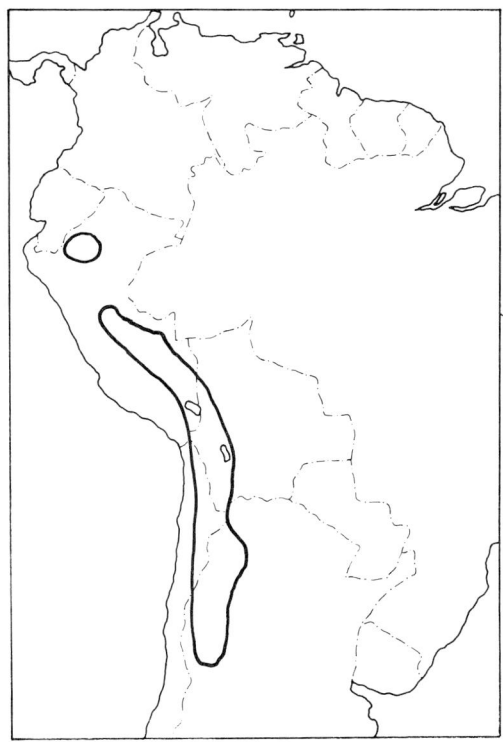

Amaranthus caudatus (Sauer, 1976).

AMARANTHUS SPINOSUS L. Thorny pigweed. 2n=34.
S. and C. America. Widespread tropical noxious
weed. Cultivated as a vegetable (Mansfeld, 1959)
in Singapore. Because of the spines it is un-
like any of the grain amaranths (Sauer, 1950).
Where it grows together with A. dubius* sterile
hybrids easily arise: A. braunii Thell. and A.
caracasamus H.B.K. In general A. spinosus is
the female parent. Grant (1959) supposed that
A. spinosus is one of the parents of A. dubius,
but Pal (1972) does not support this.

Anacardiaceae

ANACARDIUM OCCIDENTALE L. Cashew. 2n=42. Trop.
America from Mexico to Peru and Brazil and also
the West Indies. Cultivated now in many tropical
countries which may form secondary centres of
diversity. Thus Northwood (1966) showed the
great variation in yield and nut size in the
cashew populations in Tanzania.

SCHINUS MOLLE L. Californian pepper tree, Brazil pepper tree. 2n=28, 30. Mexico to Chile and
Uruguay. Cultivated in the tropics as a medicinal plant, as a shade tree and as an ornamental.

SPONDIAS MOMBIM L. (syn. S. lutea L.). Yellow
mombim, Jobo, Hog plum. 2n=32. Trop. America.

A fruit tree now cultivated in the tropics.

SPONDIAS PURPUREA L. (syn. S. mombim L.). Red mombim, Spanish plum. 2n=   . Trop. America, C. America and Mexico. A small fruit tree.

SPONDIAS RADLKOFERI J. Donn. Sm. 2n=   . Lower C. America and Panama. Derived from S. mombin* under selection for late fruiting.

Annonaceae

ANNONA CHERIMOLA Mill. Cherimoya. 2n=14, 16. Wild in the Andean valleys of Ecuador and Peru. There is its primary centre. A small tree. Cultivated now in the tropics. Its karyotype is similar to that of A. reticulata* and A. squamosa*. Several cultivars are known. Atemoya is a hybrid with A. squamosa*.

ROLLINIA DELICIOSA Safford. 2n=   . Brazil. A tree cultivated for its fruits.

ROLLINIA LONGIFOLIA St. Hil. (syn. R. dolabripetala (Reddi) St.-Hil.) 2n=   . Brazil. A tree cultivated for its fruits.

ROLLINIOPSIS DISCRETA Safford. 2n=   . Brazil. A shrub cultivated for its fruits.

Apocynaceae

PLUMERIA ACUTIFOLIA Poir. (syn. P. acuminata Roxb., P. obtusa Lour.). 2n=36. Mexico and S. America. Cultivated in the tropics as a medicinal tree.

THEVETIA NEREIFOLIA Juss. (syn. T. peruviana Schum.). Exile tree, Yellow oleander. 2n=20, 22. Trop. America and West Indies. A shrub cultivated in the tropics as a medicinal plant.

Aquifoliaceae

ILEX PARAGUENSIS D. Don. (syn. I. paraguariensis St.-Hil.). Paraguay tea, Yerba maté. 2n= 40. S. America. Cultivated for its leaves which are used to prepare tea.

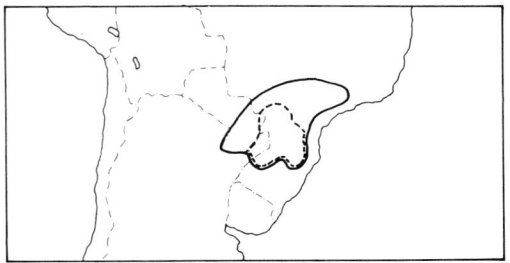

Dispersion (——) and cultivation of Ilex paraguensis (---)(Patiño, 1968).

Araceae

XANTHOSOMA ATROVIRENS C. Koch et Bouche (syn. X. peregrinum Griseb.). Yautia Amarilla, Nut Edo., 2n=   . Wild in the llanos of Venezuela. Widely cultivated for its tubers in the Antilles and N. South America. It is characterized by intensely dark green upper leaf-blades, and tubers with yellow flesh. A race grown in Cuba has small tubers, and the race temba taia of Brazil is characterized by soft tubers. A race grown in Puerto Rico with somewhat hairy leaves is known as jengibrilla.

XANTHOSOMA BELOPHYLLUM (Willd.) Kunth. (syn. Caladium belophyllum Willd., X. versicolor Hort. ex Schott). Ocumo, Carouany. 2n=   . Cultivated in the coastal mountains of Colombia and Venezuela, and east to Guyana. The tubers of this species is short and stocky, with white flesh. A race, d'espinagas (spinach) is grown in the mountains of Venezuela and adjacent Colombia for its edible leaves.

XANTHOSOMA BRASILIENSE Engler. Belember, Herbe a Calalou. 2n=   . Wild in S. Brazil. Cultivated for its leaves that are cooked as a vegetable in Puerto Rico and other Caribbean islands.

XANTHOSOMA CARACU C. Koch et Bouche. Rolliza, Yautia blanca (Puerto Rico), Lampaza, Rejolgar (Mexico), Manola (Jamaica), Malanga (Cuba), Ocumo (Venezuela). 2n=   . Widely grown, also in Africa. Tubers are almost cylindrical with white or rarely orange flesh.

XANTHOSOMA MAFAFFA Schott. (syn. X. blandum Schott, X. poeppigii Schott). Mafaffa. 2n= . Tropical forests of Colombia, Brazil, Peru and Bolivia. This species is typically a crop of the wet tropics. It is grown for its tubers in the Amazon Basin of Colombia.

XANTHOSOMA SAGITTIFOLIUM (Linn.) Schott. (syn. X. edule (Mey.) Schott., X. xanthorrhizon (Jacq.) C. Koch, Arum sagittaefolium Linn.). Yautia palma. 2n=24, 26. Mountains of Venezuela. Widely cultivated in the Antilles and S. America. Stem up to 1 m tall bearing tubers with white flesh. In Jamaica, it is sometimes known as Yautia panama, although probably introduced to the Caribbean from S. rather than C. America.

XANTHOSOMA UNDIPES (C. Koch et Bouche) C. Koch (X. jacquinii Schott.). Yautia palma, Malanga, Chau milon, Grande tayove. 2n=   . This species resembles X. sagittifolium in developing and aerial stem. But, the leaves are purplish rather than green, and the tubers are white or orange inside. Yautia palma is cultivated, and occurs as a weed from C. Mexico throughout the Antilles to Equador.

XANTHOSOMA VIOLACEUM Schott. (syn. X. nigrum Vell.). Jamaica tanier (Trinidad), Oto (Panama), Pica uncucha (Peru), Ocumo (Venezuela), Yautia morada, Prieta (Puerto Rico), and Malanga (Cuba). 2n=24, 26. Widely grown in the Antilles, C. and S. America. The species is characterized by its usually violet pink to purple leaves, and tubers with white flesh but usually purplish outside.

Basellaceae

BOUSSINGAULTIA CORDIFOLIA Ten. (syn. B. baselloides H.B.K.). Madeira vine, Mignonette vine. 2n=c. 20, 36. S. and C. America. Cultivated as a leafy vegetable or for its tubers.

ULLUCUS TUBEROSUS (Lindl.) Lozano. Ulloco (Peru, Bolivia), Chiqua (Colombia), Melloco (Equador), Timbo (Venezuela), Papa lisa (Spanish). 2n=24. Cultivated for its tubers from Venezuela to Argentina. Its wild ancestor, U. aborigineus Brücher 2n=   is a high Andean species of Argentina and Chile. Tubers are eaten fresh or dehydrated, and in some Andean villages ulloco ranks second as a staple only to potatoes. It is beautifully depicted on pottery of the Tiawanako culture (Leon, 1964, illustrations). Tubers are of various colours and sizes, and numerous local races are recognized.

Bixaceae

BIXA ORELLANA L. Annato. 2n=14, 16. Trop. America and the West Indies. Introduced into many other tropical countries where it may have run wild. It is a dye crop.

Bombacaceae

QUARARIBEA CORDATA (H. & B.) Garcia-Barriga & Hernandez (syn. Matisia cordata H. & B.) South American sapote. 2n=   . NW. South America. Within this region this fruit is cultivated. No superior strains have been developed yet.

Bromeliaceae

ANANAS COMOSUS (L.) Merr. (syn. A. sativus Schult.f., Bromelia comosa L.). Pineapple. 2n=50, (75, 100). It is suggested that the Tupi-Guarani domesticated pineapple in the Paraná-Paraguay river drainage area and that from this region pineapple was spread to all (sub)-tropics. However, Brücher (1971) suggested that the domestication of pineapple might have taken place in the highlands of Guyana and alongside the rivers there. In the first area, wild related species A. bracteatus (Lindl.) Schultes (2n=   ), A. ananassoides (Bak.) L.B. Smith (2n=   ) and Pseudananas sagenarius (Arudda) Camarcq. (2n=   ) occur. A. bracteatus var. typicus is occasionally cultivated for its fruits, while A. ananassoides var. nanus is an ornamental.

ANANAS PARGUAZENSIS Card.-Cam. & Smith. 2n=   . This species occurs where the Rio Par-

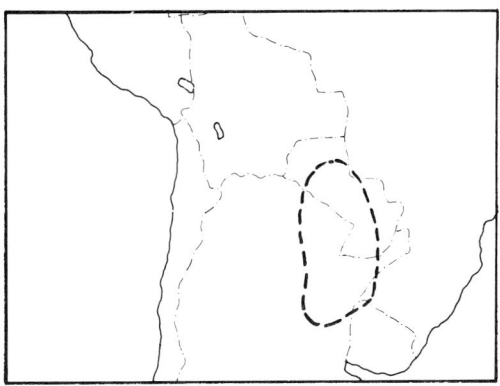

Putative area of domestication of Ananas comosus (Pickersgill, 1976).

guazo discharges into the Rio Orinoco, Venezuela. Brücher (1971) suggested that primitive fibre and fruit cultivars have been selected. This selection work could have been carried out - independently of each other - in the region Guyana-Orinoco, and between Maranhao and Pernambuco.

PSEUDANANAS MACRODONTES (Harms) Morr. 2n=c. 100. Argentina and Brazil. There its primary centre is found. Cultivated on a large scale on Polynesian and Melanesian islands.

Cactaceae

CEREUS HEXAGONUS (L.) Mill. 2n=   . Venezuela, West Indies, N. South America. Cultivated there for its fruits and as a hedge plant.

CEREUS PERUVIANUS (L.) Mill. 2n=24. Probably S. America (Hammer, 1976). Cultivated in the tropics as a hedge plant and ornamental.

ERIOCEREUS MARTINII (Lab.) Riccob. 2n=   . Cultivated in Argentina as source of an alkaloid.

HYLOCEREUS POLYRHIZUS (Weber) Britt. & Rose. 2n=   . Equador, a hedge plant.

OPUNTIA BOLDINGHII Britt. & Rose. 2n=   . NW. coast of Venezuela, Trinidad and Curaçao. Cultivated in Venezuela and on Curaçao as a hedge plant and for its fruits.

OPUNTIA ELATIOR Mill. 2n=   . Panama, Colombia, Venezuela. Cultivated there and in Mexico, India, Indonesia and Australia for its fruits. The wild types bear many long spines, whereas in the domesticated types fruits are naked or bear a few short thorns (Hammer, 1976).

OPUNTIA EXALTATA Berger. 2n=   . Peru. Cultivated as a hedge plant, and there and elsewhere as an ornamental.

OPUNTIA VULGARIS Mill. 2n= 22, 33, 66. Brazil,

Uruguay, Argentina and probably Paraguay, where it may have run wild (Hammer, 1976). Cultivated as a hedge plant in India, S. Africa and Australia. In Australia it has run wild. Formerly cultivated in India, Sri Lanka, Indonesia and E. Africa for cochenille.

PERESKIA ACULEATA Mill. Barbados cherry, Sweet Mary, West Indian gooseberry, Lemon vine. 2n= 22. Trop. America. Cultivated for its fruits and as a hedge plant. Naturalized in Florida, USA.

PERESKIA BAHIENSIS Gürke. 2n=   . Brazil. Cultivated in hedges.

PERESKIA BLEO (H.B.K.) DC. 2n=   . Colombia, Panama, Venezuela and Brazil. Cultivated there and elsewhere.

PERESKIA GUAMACHO Weber. 2n=   . Venezuela, Marguerita Island. Cultivated there and on Curaçao for hedges (Hammer, 1976).

PERESKIA SACHAROSA Griseb. 2n=22. Paraguay and Argentina. Cultivated there for hedges.

RITTEROCEREUS DEFICIENS (Otto & Dietr.) Backeb. 2n=   . Venezuela and Curaçao. Hedges on Curaçao.

RITTEROCEREUS GRISEUS (Haw.) Backeb. 2n=   . Venezuela. Cultivated in trop. America and Mexico for hedges and fruits.

TRICHOCEREUS BRIDGESII (Salm-Dyck) Britt. & Rose. 2n=   . Bolivia. Cultivated there as hedge plant.

TRICHOCEREUS CUZCOENSIS Britt. & Rose. Peru. Cultivated there as a hedge plant.

TRICHOCEREUS PACHANOI Britton & Rose. 2n=   . Andean parts of Ecuador and Peru. Apparently widely cultivated throughout the C. Andes (Schultes & Hofmann, 1973).

Cannaceae

CANNA EDULIS Ker. Achira, Queensland arrowroot. 2n=18, (27). Probably NW. South America. Spread to Mexico, C. America, West Indies and N. South America. Achira is cultivated in the West Indies, Australia, S. America, parts of Asia and Pacific Islands. Remains of achira have been found at Huaca Prieta, N. Peru (Bird, 1948). They have been dated c. 2400 BC. It could not be established whether they had been collected or cultivated.
  Mukherjee & Khoshoo (1971) suggested that the triploid (2n=3x=27) is probably an inter-varietal hybrid involving genetically related varieties. It is vigorous and robust and has large rhizomes.
  In S. America rhizomes of other Canna species (C. coccinea Mill., C. paniculata R. & C. and C. indica L.) have been collected and eaten

(Gade, 1966).

Caricaceae

CARICA CANDAMARCENSIS Hook.f. (syn. C. pubescens Lenne & Koch). Mountain papaya. 2n=   . The Andes of Colombia and Ecuador. A tree cultivated there and also in E. Africa for its fruits (Mansfeld, 1959).

CARICA CHRYSOPETALA Heilb. 2n=   . Ecuador. A tree cultivated for its fruits (Mansfeld, 1959). Badilla (1967) suggested that this species is a natural hybrid product of C. candamarcensis* and C. stipulata Badilla from Ecuador. He further suggested that this species, C. pentagona* and C. frutifragans Garcia & Hernandez another hybrid of the same parents (from Colombia) should be grouped in C. x heilbornii Badilla.

CARICA PENTAGONA Heilb. 2n=   . Ecuador. A tree cultivated for its fruits (Mansfeld, 1959). Badilla (1967) suggested that this species is a natural hybrid product of C. candamarcencis* and C. stipulata Badilla from Ecuador.

Caryocaraceae

CARYOCAR NUCIFERUM L. 2n=   . Brazil and Guyana. A tall tree cultivated in the West Indies for its edible Suari nuts.

Chenopodiaceae

CHENOPODIUM PALLIDICAULE Aellen. Cañihua. 2n= 36. Andes. Cultivated on the Alti Plano of Peru and Bolivia as a marginal grain crop (Dale, 1970).

CHENOPODIUM QUINOA Willd. Quinoa, Andean grain chenopod. 2n=allo 4x=36. Andes. Cultivated in the Andes as a grain crop. This cultivation is on its decline. The weedy C. hircinum Schrad. (sensu Aellen), 2n=36 forms with quinoa a weed-cultigen complex (Wilson, 1976). Quinoa is closely related to C. nuttalliae*, which may derive from imported quinoa.

Chrysobalanaceae

CHRYSOBALANUS ICACO L. Icaco plum, Coco plum. 2n=   . (Sub)trop. America. Cultivated for its fruits.

Compositae

EUPATORIUM TRIPLINERVE Vahl. (syn. E. ayapana Vent.). 2n=51. Trop. America. A perennial herb introduced in Java where it is cultivated as a medicinal plant.

MADIA SATIVA Molina. Madia, Tarweed. 2n=32. Cultivated formerly in Chile as an oil-seed crop. Attempts have been made to grow it elsewhere, but without success. The culture is almost extinct now.

POLYMNIA SONCHIFOLIA Poepp. & Endl. (syn. P. edulis Weddell.). Yacon strawberry. 2n=60. Andes. Cultivated there and elsewhere for its tubers.

SPILANTHES OLERACEA L. (syn. S. acmella Murr.). Para cress, Brazilian cress. 2n=14, 24, 52. Brazil, West Indies and also India. Cultivated as a vegetable or salad.

STEVIA REBAUDIANA Bertoni. 2n=22. N. Paraguay. Annual and biennial. The leaves contain stevioside, which is 300 times sweeter than canesugar. However it acts female sterilizing.

TAGETES MINUTA L. Marigold. 2n=   . Trop. America. Spread to many other countries. Cultivated for its medicinal properties (Neher, 1968). It may reach a height of 3 m or more when cared for. Has run wild in France, Yugoslavia and Greece.

Convolvulaceae

MERREMIA MACROCARPA (L.) Roberty. 2n=   . Brazil and West Indies. Cultivated for its medicinal tubers.

MERREMIA TUBEROSA (L.) Rendle (syn. Ipomoea tuberosa L.). 2n=30. Brazil, West Indies, trop. Africa and India. Origin is unknown. Cultivated as a medicinal and also as an ornamental. It may have spread from West Indies and Brazil because in these areas M. macrocarpa* grows wild and is cultivated.

Cruciferae

LEPIDIUM MEYENII Walp. Maca. 2n=   . Peru and Bolivia. Cultivated in Peru for its root. A relic crop.

Cucurbitaceae

CUCURBITA MAXIMA Duch. ex Lam. Pumpkin, Winter squash. 2n=40. Cultivated all over the world. Secondary gene centre in India and adjacent areas (p. 72). Whitaker & Davis (1962) suggested a common origin for C. maxima, C. ficifolia*, C. moschata* and possibly C. pepo* and C. mixta* from C. lundelliana Bailey (2n=40).

C. lundelliana grows in S. Mexico, Guatemala and Honduras. From this parent, C. maxima developed in N. Argentina, Bolivia and S. Peru. In this area the related species C. andreana Naud. grows wild. It is probably a weedy derivative of the cultigen.

The wild C. ecuadorensis Cutler & Whitaker (2n=40) is closely related to this species and C. andreana (Cutler & Whitaker, 1969).

SICANA ODORIFERA (Vell.) Naud. Casa banana, Curaba. 2n=   . Peru, Brazil to Mexico and West Indies. This vine is cultivated in trop. America.

Cyperaceae

SCIRPUS CALIFORNICUS (C.A. Meyer) Steudel. (syn. S. tatara Kunth). Totora. 2n=64, 68, 70. Widely distributed in the Americas, on Easter Island and Hawaii. Material of wild plants are used for many purposes like making rafts, houses and roofs, and as food for man and animals. Sometimes cultivated in Peru (Heiser, 1978).

Dioscoreaceae

DIOSCOREA PIPERIFOLIA Humb. & Bonpl. 2n=   . Brazil. Cultivated there.

DIOSCOREA TRIFIDA L.f. Cush-cush yam, Yampi. 2n=54, 72, 81. S. America and Antilles, cultivated throughout Caribbean. A race with purple tubers is grown on Puerto Rico.

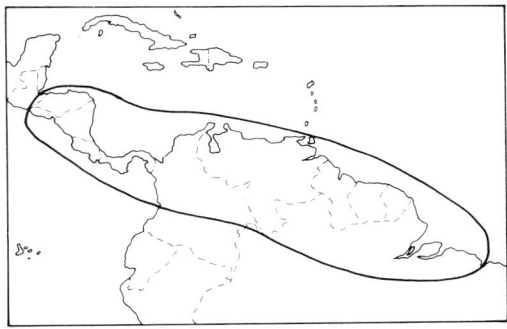

Dioscorea trifida (Coursey, 1967).

Erythroxylaceae

ERYTHROXYLUM COCA Lam. Coca, Guarigos. 2n=24. Unknown wild. Probably from high Andes of Peru and Bolivia. Cultivated at high altitudes in Peru, Bolivia, Argentina, Colombia and Brazil.

Some taxonomists include E. novogratense*, E. truxillense Rusby and E. bolivianum Burck in this species.

ERYTHROXYLUM NOVOGRANATENSE (Morris) Hieron. Truxillo coca. 2n=   . Andes. Cultivated at a lower altitude than E. coca*. It was distributed to the tropics.

Euphorbiaceae

HEVEA BENTHAMIANA Muell.-Arg. 2n=36. The Amazone basin, Brazil, Peru and Bolivia. A tree cultivated for its rubber.

HEVEA BRASILIENSIS (Willd.) Muell.-Arg. Brazilian hevea, Para rubber tree. 2n=36. The Amazon basin. This is the primary gene centre. Secondary gene centre in Malaya (p. 52). Cultivated now in Malaya, Indonesia, Sri Lanka and in some other countries. In Africa rubber has been cultivated as a farmer's crop and as

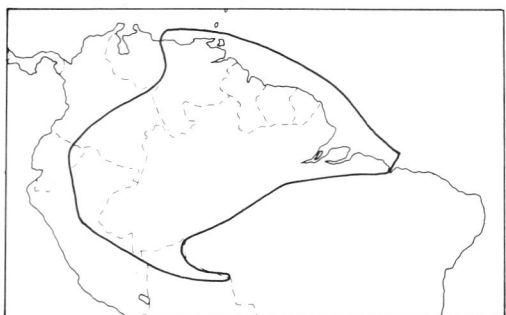

Hevea brasiliensis (Dijkman, 1951).

a plantation crop. A farmer's plot often consists of a few trees. Bouharmont (1960) suggested that H. brasiliensis originated by amphiploidization of two yet unknown diploid
species.

JATROPHA CURCAS L. French purging nut, Physic
nut. 2n=22. Mexico and Bermudas up to Chile
and Paraguay. Cultivated in these and other
tropical countries for its curcas oil. In Brazil it is planted as a living fence.

JATROPHA MULTIFIDA L. Chicaquil, Tortora, Yuca
cimarrona. 2n=22. Trop. America up to Mexico
and West Indies. A shrub cultivated there as
a medicinal crop and elsewhere as an ornamental.

JATROPHA URENS L. Pendo tree. 2n=   . Trop.
America. This tree is cultivated in the Philippines for its leaves which are used as a vegetable (Terra, 1967).

MANIHOT ESCULENTA Crantz. Cassava, Manihot,
Manioc, Yucca. 2n=36. According to Nassar
(1978), there are c. 40 wild Manihot species
in Brazil especially in S. Goias and W. Minas
Gerais. Some cross readily with domesticated
cassava. It should be established which species
are really wild and which are weedy introgres-
sants of wild/weedy x domesticated. Cassava is
a staple throughout the tropics. Secondary gene
centres almost certainly exist in Africa (p.
126 and Indonesia (p. 53). Cassava can be divided into sweet cassava and bitter cassava
(M. esculenta Crantz, 2n=36, M. utilissima
Pohl., 2n=36).
The sweet cassava was probably first domesticated in Meso-America (p. 190), from where it
spread to S. America. Bitter cassava was domesticated in northern S. America (Renvoize,
1972). In Brazil the diversity increased
through intraspecies crosses and by hybridization with wild Manihot species. The weedy M.
saxicola Lanj. (2n=   ), M. melanobasis Muell.
-Arg. and other weedy species may derive from
the cultigen (Roger, 1963). The first species
is found in NE. of S. America, M. glaziovii*
is a source of resistance to cassava mosaic

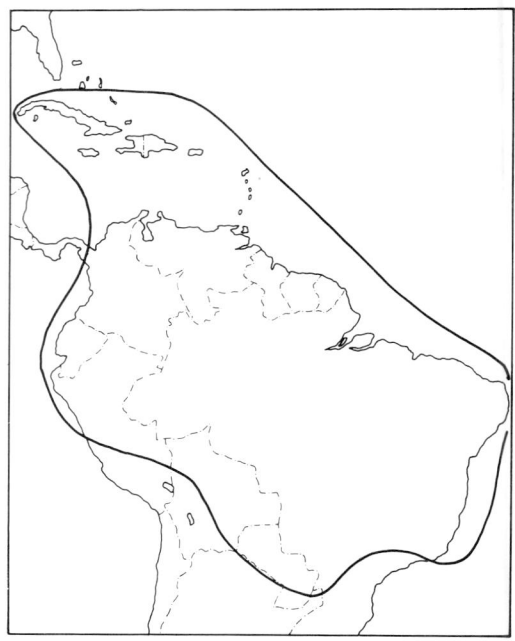

Manihot esculenta (Harris, 1972).

disease and drought.

MANIHOT GLAZIOVII Muell.-Arg. Ceara rubber.
2n=36. Brazil. Attempts were made to establish
plantings for rubber production in Asia and
Africa, but the cultivation was abandoned in
favour of para rubber (Purseglove, 1968).

OMPHALEA MEGACARPA Hemsl. 2n=   . S. America,
especially Brazil and also West Indies. A shrub
cultivated for its seeds.

PLUKENETIA VOLUBILIS L. (syn. P. peruviana
Muell.-Arg.) 2n=   . N. South America and West
Indies. A vegetable and a fodder crop.

SAPIUM JENMANI Hemsl. 2n=   . Guyana. Cultivated there.

Gramineae

BRASILOCALAMUS PUBESCENS (Doell) Nakai. 2n=
. Brazil. Related to the Asiatic Bambusa.

BROMUS MANGO Desv. Mango. 2n=   . NW. Argentina and adjacent Chile. Mango was grown as a
biennial cereal by the Araucano Indians of
Chiloe in the municipality of Castro in Chile
until at least the middle of the 19th Century.
In the first year, livestock were allowed to
graze the fields. During the second year, the
plants were allowed to mature, inflorescences
were harvested, threshed and the grains were
toasted and ground into flour. Mango was used

to make unleavened bread called covgue or a Chicha drink (Gay, 1865; Parodi & Hernandez, 1964). Cultivation of this cereal was eventually abandoned to make room for the far superior wheat introduced from Europe. Today mango occurs as a wild and weedy species in NW. Argentina and adjacent Chile.

BROMUS UNIOLOIDES H.B.K. (syn. B. catharticus Vahl., B. schraderi Kunth). Rescue grass, Schrader's brome. 2n=28, 42, 56. S. of USA, S. America, Australia and Europe. It probably developed in S. America particularly Argentina. In the Andean region it (syn. B. haenkeanus (Presl) Kunth) (2n=42) grows wild.

BROMUS WILLDENOWII Kunth (syn. B. unioloides (Willd.) Respail, Festuca unioloides Willd.). Common rescue grass. 2n=28, 42. A plant from S. America cultivated as a fodder grass.

CHUSQUEA ANDINA Phil. 2n=   . Chile, where it reaches the snow boundaries. The genus Chusquea Kunth includes over 70 species native to S. America, Mexico and E. India. It is typical for the Andes, where the species form dense thickets. Many of them are very ornamental and may be very valuable for introduction to the humid subtropical areas of USSR and elsewhere because they are very hardy.

CHUSQUEA CULEON E. Desv. ex C. Gray. 2n= Chile.

CHUSQUEA DEPAUPERATA Pilg. 2n=   . Peru, up to 3400 m.

CHUSQUEA ULIGINOSA Phil. 2n=   . Chile.

CORTADERIA ARGENTEA Stapf (syn. Gynerium argenteum Nees). Pampas grass. 2n=70. S. America. A grass cultivated as a source of pulp.

ERIOCHLOA POLYSTACHYA H.B.K. Carib grass. 2n= . West Indies, Brazil to Ecuador. A grass cultivated as a forage grass in SE. USA.

GUADUA ANGUSTIFOLIA H.B.K. 2n=   . Colombia and Ecuador up to 1500 m and in humid areas it forms thickets. Cultivated in Puerto Rico, Guatemala, Ecuador, Haiti, Honduras, Peru, USA, and elsewhere. The stems may grow 18-30 m long. It is the most valuable species in the Western Hemisphere. The wood is strong and easy to work with. Its stems are used for buildings. The genus Guadua contains 35 species. They are native to Mexico and S. America. Several species are cultivated in and beyond the natural area. This genus is near to the Asiatic genus Bambusa.

GYNERIUM SAGITTATUM (Aubl.). P. Beauv. Indian arrowleaf. 2n=   . Cultivated in Venezuela for its shafts which are used for making long arrows.

ORYZA ALTA Swallen. 2n=48, genome formula CC-

DD. C. and S. America.

ORYZA GRANDIGLUMIS Desv. 2n=48, genome formula CCDD. C. and S. America. Closely related to O. alta*. Gopalakrishman & Sampath (1966) suggested that O. grandiglumis derives from O. alta.

ORYZA LATIFOLIA Desv. 2n=48, genome formula CCDD. C. and S. America.

PASPALUM DILATATUM Poir. Dallis grass. 2n= (x=10) (30), 40, 50, (60). Probably Chaco Savanna. The common type has 2n=50, genome formula $A_1A_1B_1B_1C$. Type pauciciliatum has 2n=40, $A_1A_1B_1C$. Type uruguaiana has 2n=60, $A_1A_1B_1B_1$ C E, and the asynaptic type torres also has 2n=60. These types are apomictic. The only sexual type is 'yellow anther' with 2n=40, A_1 $A_1B_2B_2$. It has one genome in common with P. conspersum Schrad. ex Schult, 2n=40 (Burson & Bennett, 1976). In Japan, sexual and apomictic types occur with 2n=30.

PASPALUM NOTATUM Fluegge. Pensacola Bahia grass. 2n=(x=10) 20, (30), 40, genome formula $X_1X_1X_2$ X_2 or $X_1X_1Y_1Y_1$. It is not clear whether Pensacola Bahia grass originated in Florida or that it came from interior of S. America (Burton, 1967), where a wide variation of types on the Berduc Island of Rio Paraná, Uruguay was found. Widespread in S. USA. There it was first found in Pensacola, Florida.

PASPALUM PLICATULUM Michaux. 2n=(x=10), 20, genome formula H_1H_1, 40, $H_1H_1H_1H_1$, (60). S. America. Cultivated in Australia.

SORGHUM HALEPENSE (L.) Pers. (syn. S. almum Parodi). Black Sorgo, Columbus grass. 2n=40. Grown as a forage in Argentina, where this weed evolved as a derivative of a cross between the Mediterranean S. hapense and cultivated grain sorghum (S. bicolor*).

TRIPSACUM ANDERSONNI Gray. Guatemala grass. 2n=64. This sexually sterile species is widely grown as a fodder in the tropics. It probably originated in the mountains of Venezuela or Colombia as a natural hybrid between a species of Tripsacum and cultivated maize (Zea mays*). In pre-Columbian and early Columbian times, it was grown as a fodder for guinea-pigs.

TRIPSACUM AUSTRALE Cutler & Anderson. Gramalote. 2n=36. Widely distributed in S. America, cultivated as a fodder in Colombia.

ZEA MAYS L. Maize, Corn. 2n=20. Maize derives from teosinte, Z. mexicana*, which grows wild in C. America (p. 190). From here it spread south and north. After its introduction into S. America, its development there became agriculturally more advanced than in its area of domestication. This might be a result of the absence of its wild and weedy relatives. A secondary centre in S. America. These S. Ameri-

Tripsacum australe (Hernandez, 1973).

can primitive maize varieties were taken to C. America. In Mexico they were described as Pre-Columbian exotic races (p. 190). In the 19th Century a secondary centre of diversity arose here when cultivars from the Amazonian and Para-guayan lowlands mixed with 'coastal tropical' flint from the West Indies and with flint cultivars from the southern slopes of Bolivia (Brandolini, 1970).

Primitive Races - all belonging to the pop-corn type - have been found in Colombia, Ecuador, Bolivia, Peru and Chile. In Colombia the Primitive Races are called Pollo and Pira. Pollo might be related to the Peruvian Confite Morocho. Collections of Pollo made at Medellin, at an altitude considerably lower than their normal habitat, segregate plants which in their general aspects are almost identical to maizoid teosinte in Mexico. Such plants at the silking stage can easily be mistaken for teosinte (Roberts et al., 1957). It is thought that the cause might be a virus inducing profuse branching. Pira might have also occurred in Venezuela and Bolivia. It is related to the Peruvian Confite Morocho and Confite Puntiagudo.

At a later stage less primitive and developed races originated in S. America. In the coastal eastern S. America the race 'Coastal Tropical Flint' was cultivated. This race was also found in the West Indies, it was probably introduced from the continent. However, it is possible that in both areas a similar race developed from identical parents (Hatheway, 1957).

Owing to the high variation of maize in S. America this region is considered as a secondary centre of diversity. For instance, Grobman et al. (1956) concluded that Peru appears to be the home of pericarps colour genes. In the dept. Ancash all three alleles of the A locus and all 7 of the P locus are found.

Guttiferae

MAMMEA AMERICANA L. Mammey apple, Mamey. 2n= . Trop. America and West Indies. Cultivated there for its edible fruits and for its scented flowers which are used to prepare the liquor Eau de Créole.

RHEEDIA ACUMINATA (Ruiz & Pav.) Planch. & Triana. 2n= . Colombia up to Peru. Cultivated as a compound tree in NW. of S. America.

Juglandaceae

JUGLANS HONOREI Dode. Ecuador walnut. 2n= . Rootstock of J. regia*.

Lauraceae

NECTANDRA CINNAMOMOIDES Nees. 2n= . Equatorial Andes. A tree cultivated in Ecuador as a spice plant.

PERSEA LEIOGYNA Blake. 2n= . Probably trop. America. A fruit tree.

Lecythidaceae

BERTHOLLETIA EXSELSA Humb. & Bonpl. Brazil nut, Para nut. 2n=34. The Amazon forests. The kernels and oil are eaten. The oil/kernel ratio is quite high: 60-70%.

LECYTHIS ZABUCAJO Aubl. Sapucaia nut, Paradise nut, Monkey pot. 2n= . The forests of the Guyanas and Brazil. Not much cultivated.

Leguminosae

ACACIA CAVENIA Bert. Cavenia acacia, Espino cavan. 2n=26, 52. S. America. A small tree cultivated as a source of perfume. Related to A. farnesiana*.

ACACIA FARNESIANA (L.) Willd. Sweet acacia. 2n =52, (104). Probably trop. America (Purseglove, 1968). This shrub is cultivated esp. as an ornamental and for its perfumery, where it has run wild in the tropics. In S. France the very fragrant Cassie Flowers are the source of Cassie Ancienne.

AESCHYNOMENE AMERICANA L. (syn. A. glandulosa Poir.). 2n= . Trop. America. Used in Indonesia and elsewhere as a green manure, soil cover and as a forage crop.

ALBIZIA CARBONARIA. 2n= . Colombia and C. America. Cultivated in Puerto Rico (Whyte et al., 1953).

ARACHIS GLABRATA Benth. Arb peanut. 2n=40. Brazil, Argentina and Bolivia. Perennial used for pastures and hay (Prine, 1964).

ARACHIS HYPOGAEA L. Groundnut, Peanut. 2n=40, genome formula $A^hA^hB^hB^h$. Primary gene centre

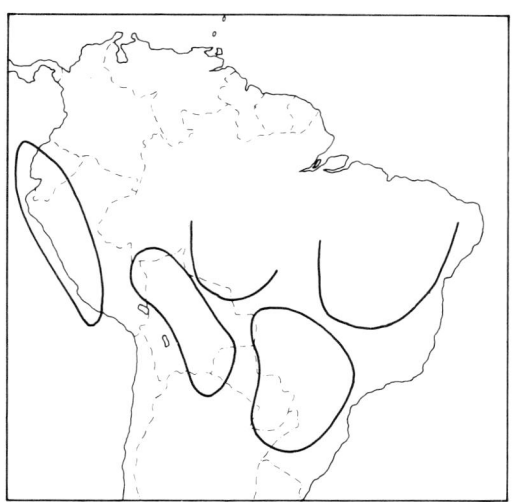

Gene centres of Arachis hypogaea (Krapovickas, 1972).

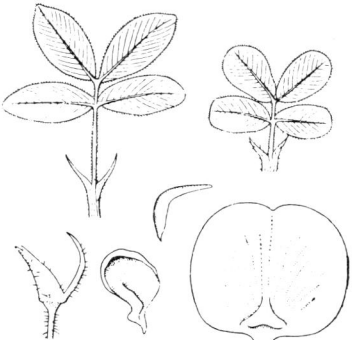

Arachis monticola

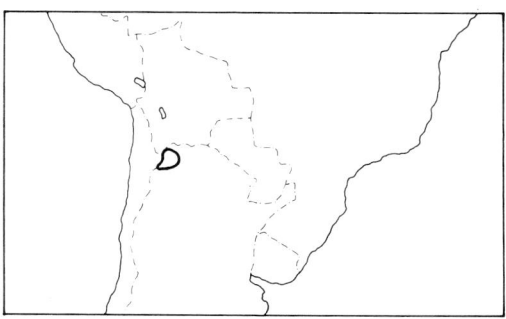

Arachis monticola (Zhukovsky, 1971).

in Argentina and Bolivia. Secondary centres in W. Africa and Congo. The species was probably domesticated in the Gran Chaco area. It is cytogenetically conspecific with A. monticola Krapov. & Rig, 2n=40, which is probably the wild ancestor of domesticated peanut. This species grows wild in the mountains of the Jujuy Province, NW. Argentina. It crosses easily with the groundnut. It can be used to improve disease resistance etc. of the groundnut. A. villosa Benth. (2n=20) has the genome formula $A^v A^v$ (Raman, 1973).

Krapovickas (1969) pointed to five S. American centres of diversity: 1. the Guarami region, the basins of the Paraguay and Parana rivers, which is the centre of variation for the ssp. fastigiata Waldron var. vulgaris Harz., the Spanish type, 2. The region of Goias and Minas Gerais where ssp. fastigiata var. fastigiata, 3. The region of Rondonia and NW. Mato Grosso. This region is not yet fully studied. It includes ssp. hypogaea var. hypogaea (syn. A. africana Lour., A. nambyquarae Hoehne), the Brazilian or Virginia type, and the distantly related cultivated A. villosulicarpa , 4. The region of the eastern foothills of the Andes in in Bolivia, which contains a great variation of var. hypogaea. Some introgression may occur with var. fastigiata resulting in the forms Overo, Pintado and Cruceno, and 5. Peru, which is the centre of variation of ssp. hypogaea var. hirsuta Kohler (syn. A. asiatica Lour.). Ashri (1976) discovered three types of cytoplasm, which together with three nuclear loci conditioned the growth habit of the plant.

ARACHIS VILLOSULICARPA Hoehne. 2n=20. Cultivated by the indians of Juruena and Diamantino of the Mato Grosso in Brazil. Perennial and not closely related to A. hypogaea* (Krapovickas, 1969).

CANAVALIA ENSIFORMIS (L.) DC. Jack bean, Horse bean. 2n=22. S. America. Secondary centre in India. Sauer & Kaplan (1969) mentioned C. boliviana Piper (2n=   ), C. brasiliensis Mart. ex Benth. (2n=   ), C. dictyota Piper (2n=   ), C. maritima (Aubl.) Thou. (2n=   ) and C. piperi Killip & MacBride (2n=22), as possible ancestors. An ancient legume, now cultivated in the tropics as a green manure or fodder crop.

CANAVALIA PLAGIOSPERMA Piper. 2n=22. Probably trop. S. America. Possible ancestor of the Andean C. piperi Killip & MacBride (2n=22) (Sauer, 1964). One of the earliest cultivated crops in S. America, but not cultivated at present. It resembles C. ensiformis*.

CENTROSEMA PLUMIERI (Turp.) Benth. 2n=20. Trop. America. This cover crop and green manure has been distributed throughout the tropics.

CENTROSEMA PUBESCENS Benth. 2n=20. Trop. America. This cover crop and green manure is distributed throughout the tropics.

CROTALARIA ANAGYROIDES H.B.K. 2n=16. Trop. America. Cultivated for green manure and as a vegetable (Terra, 1967).

DESMODIUM DISCOLOR Vog. 2n=22. Brazil. A forage plant.

DESMODIUM INTORTUM (Mill.) Urb. Greenleaf. 2n= 22. C. America and Brazil. Cultivated in Australia (Hutton, 1970).

DESMODIUM UNCINATUM (Jacq.) DC. Silverleaf. 2n =22. S. America. Cultivated in Australia (Hutton, 1970).

DIPTERYX ODORATA Willd. Tonka bean, Dutch tonka. 2n=32. Forests of trop. America, Venezuela, the Guyanas and lower Amazon basin. The tree is cultivated now in Venezuela, Malaya, West Indies and some other tropical countries (Cobley, 1963).

ERYTHRINA GLAUCA Willd. 2n=42. S. America. A shade tree in cacao plantations.

ERYTHRINA MICROPHERYX Poepp. Anauca. 2n= . Peru. A shade tree in cacao plantations.

GLIRICIDIA SEPIUM (Jacq.) Steud. (syn. G. maculata Benth.). 2n=20, 22. Mexico, C. America and N. South America. A shade tree, green manure and fodder crop.

INDIGOFERA ANIL L. (syn. I. suffruticosa Mill.). Indigo plant. 2n=12. S. America. Once much cultivated in the tropics for its dye (indigo) (Heiser, 1965).

INGA FEUILLEI DC. (syn. I. reticulata Spr.). 2n= . Peru. This tree is cultivated there for sweet fruit pulp (Uphof, 1968).

INGA PREUSSII Harms. 2n= . El Salvador. Used as a shade tree.

INGA PUNCTATA Willd. 2n= . S. and C. America. Used as a shade tree.

LEUCAENA LEUCOCEPHALA*

LONCHOCARPUS UTILIS Smith. 2n=44. Peru. Cultivated as a source of rotenone.

LUPINUS BOGOTENSIS Benth. 2n= . Bolivia. Cultivated there.

LUPINUS MONTANUS H.B.K. 2n= . Peru, Bolivia, Guatemala and Mexico. Cultivated in Bolivia.

LUPINUS MUTABILIS-TAURIS-CUNNINGHAMII-CRUCKSHANKSII species group. 2n=48. Andes region between Bolivia and Venezuela. This group of species, also named L. mutabilis Sweet/L. tauris Hook. is not yet well described. Formerly widely cultivated in its native centre. Still cultivated in Bolivia. Apparently farmers have not tried to select for sweet types. At present this species is used as 'bitter protection rows' around fields of Vicia faba and Pisum sativum to stop animals entering fields. Types have been developed that grow well un-

der tropical short-day conditions, that have pods which do not open and soft-coated seeds rich in protein and of low alkaloid content (Brücher, 1970; Hackbarth & Pakendorf, 1970). The big seeds are used to prepare tarwi or ullu. Other wild, but possible valuable Lupinus -species of the American continents should be domesticated. They are often shrubby and have small seeds (Brücher, 1970).

MIMOSA INVISA*

MYROXYLON BALSAMUM (L.) Harms. Balsam of Peru. 2n=28. Var. pereira (Royle) Harms is spread in Guatemala and El Salvador. It is a source of balsam. It was cultivated in the imperial gardens of the Aztecs in Mexico (Mansfeld, 1959).

PACHYRHIZUS APIHA (Wedd.) Parodi. 2n=22. Probably a cultigen developed by the indians in Bolivia and N. Argentina.

PACHYRHIZUS TUBEROSUS (Lam.) Spreng. Yam bean, Potato bean, Jicama. 2n=22. The headwaters of the Amazon. From there it was distributed to other parts of S. America and parts of the West Indies. The young pods and tubers are eaten.

PHASEOLUS ABORIGINEUS Burk. 2n=22. Forests of NW. Argentina Andes. Probably extended through Bolivia, Peru, Ecuador up to Honduras (Burkart & Bücher, 1953). It might be the progenitor of P. vulgaris* in Peru (Heiser, 1965).

PHASEOLUS LUNATUS L. Lima bean, Sieva bean, Butter bean, Madagascar bean, Burma bean. 2n= 22. C. America, and in the Andes from Peru to Argentina. Kaplan (1965) showed that the big lima bean of Peru was first domesticated in the Andean highlands and that the small lima bean of Mexico may have arisen in the Pacific coastal foothills of Mexico (p. 193). A small-seeded subspecies (ssp. microsperma, Sieva or Small Lima) originated by natural selection. It spread to the Antilles.

PHASEOLUS VULGARIS L. Common bean. 2n=22. For origin see p. 194. The earliest remains of cultivated common beans have been found in the Guitarrero Cave in Peru. It dates from about 6000 BC. The 'domesticated' characters are especially dark red brown and dark red beans (Kaplan et al., 1973).

PITHECELLOBIUM SAMAN Benth. Rain tree, Saman, Cow tamarind. 2n=26. Trop. America. It is used as a shade tree in cacao and coffee plantation.

PROSOPIS CHILENSIS (Molina) Stuntz emend. Burkart. 2n= . From Peru and Bolivia to C. Chile and NW. Argentina. An unarmed tree suitable for domestication as a shade, timber and fuel tree, and for its sweet pulpy fruits eaten by man and cattle (Burkart, 1976).

PROSOPIS JULIFLORA DC. Mesquite. 2n=28, 52, 56. Cultivated in Brazil, India and elsewhere as a

shade and timber tree, and for forage. The
shrubby type is an aggressive invader in Hispaniola and Pakistan (Burkart, 1976).

PROSOPIS STROMBULIFERA (Lam.) Bentham. 2n=28.
W. Argentina and N. Chile. At one time cultivated in Chile for its fruits, which ease
toothache. Wild fruits are gathered for this
purpose. Var. ruiziana Burkart, perhaps a
tetraploid (2n=4x=56) (Burkart, 1976), has
fruits twice the size of var. strombulifera.

PROPOSIS TAMARUGO T. Philippi. Tamarugo tree.
2n= . Tree for desert forestation and for
raising Merino sheep and Angora goat, which
feed on falling leaves and legumes. The leaves
absorb atmospheric moisture (Burkart, 1976).

RHYNCHOSIA MINIMA (L.) DC. 2n=22. S. America.
Cultivated in Australia and elsewhere as a
fodder and pasture crop.

STYLOSANTHUS GUIANENSIS SW. (syn. S. surinam-
ensis Miq.). 2n=20. Guyana. Used as a food
plant for livestock and as a soil conservator.

VICIA GRAMINEA Smith. 2n=14. Argentina and
Chile. Occasionally cultivated for its seeds
as a source of anti-N-lecitin (Nijenhuis et
al., 1969). This is used as a test serum for
the human N-blood group.

   Malpighiaceae

BANISTERIOPSIS CAAPI (Spruce ex Griseb.) Morton. 2n=20. S. America. A woody vine cultivated in the Amazon region as a drug and narcotic.

BUNCHOSIA ARMENIACA (Cav.) DC. 2n=   . The
Andean region. A shrub cultivated in Ecuador
for its fruits.

MALPIGHIA GLABRA L. (syn. M. punicifolia L.).
Barbado cherry, West Indian cherry. 2n=   .
West Indies and N. South America. Cultivated
there and elsewhere for its fruits. It also
makes a good hedge, like M. coccigera L.
(Purseglove, 1968).

   Malvaceae

ABUTILON OXYCARPUM F. Von Muell. 2n=14. South
America and Australia. Cultivated for its
fibres.

GOSSYPIUM BARBADENSE L. (syn. G. vitifolium
Lam., G. peruvianum Cav.). Sea island cotton.
2n=52, genome formula $(AADD)_2$. It has been pro-
posed that G. barbadense arose from a cross
and amphidiploidization of G. arboreum* and
G. raimondii*. G. arboreum could have been in-
troduced into Peru by way of Asia and the Pa-
cific islands. Another hypothesis is that an
African diploid reached S. America by way of
Atlantic. This diploid would probably have been
G. herbaceum*.
   As Bird (1948) found G. barbadense material

Distribution of the New World cottons in the
13th century: Gossypium barbadense (11), G.
hirsutum var. marie-galante (12) and G. hirsutum punctatum (13)(Hutchinson,1962).

at Huaca Prieta, Peru which was dated 2400 BC.
the introduction of the African Gossypium species and its amphidiploidization with G. raimondii must have taken place long before that
time. The main point is how this African species reached Peru.
   However, the centre of origin N. Peru is in
the arid mountainous interior of the prov.
Tumbes. The ssp. darwinii is closely related
and is endemic in the Galapagos Islands. At
present it is 'contaminated' by hybridization
with exotic introductions. Secondary centre
in Peru.
   In S. America G. barbadense spread south and
eastwards to NW. Argentina. Some other forms
are found in S. America. The Tanguis variety
is a selection from Tumbes. In Chile and Peru the Pacific assemblage is found, characterized by broad leaves and intense hairiness
of the underside of the leaf. This character
induces resistance to jassids, Empoasca ssp.
The lint of G. barbadense is usually coarse
with a length up to 34.5 mm. The lint of an
Ecuador type, of Sea Islands and Egyptian is
fine and silky with a length up to 37.5 mm. It
is possible that the Ecuador type is the parent
of the Sea Islands/Egyptian complex (p. 84,
139) (Harlan, 1970). The Atlantic assemblages
include the kidney cottons (seeds fused in a
kidney-shaped cross). They have a wide distribution in N. South America and the islands of
C. America. They have been taken to Africa,
India, Sri Lanka, Indonesia and elsewhere.
   Secondary centres in Egypt (p. 139) and in
Turkmenistan – Tadjikistan – S. Uzbekistan,
USSR (p. 84).
   On the Sea Islands of S. Carolina, USA the
Sea Island cottons developed after cottons
from Bahamas or Jamaica (p. 194) were intro-
duced (Hutchinson, 1962).

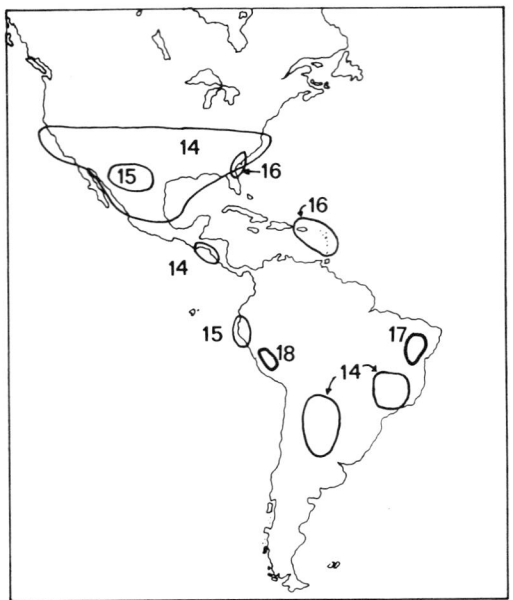

Distribution of annual cottons in the New World at 1960: Gossypium hirsutum var. uplands (14), G. barbadense var. Egyptians (15) and G. barbadense var. Sea Islands (16)(Hutchinson, 1962). G. mustelinum (17) and G. raimondii (18)(Pickersgill et al., 1975).

GOSSYPIUM HIRSUTUM L. Upland cotton. 2n=52, genome formula (AADD)$_1$. The common theory is that G. hirsutum arose from an amphiploidization of the Old World G. arboreum* or G. herbaceum* and G. raimondii. G. raimondii is the parent of the D genome and one of the first two the donor of the D genome. It is not known when this amphiploidization took place, but material collected from Tehuacan Valley in Mexico and dated 3500-2300 BC. appears to be fully domesticated (Smith & Stephens, 1971). It is also not known whether G. barbadense reached Peru by way of Asia or whether G. herbaceum reached eastern S. America from W. Africa. Harland (1970) observed wild plants of an exceedingly primitive perennial race marie galante in the state Rio Grande do Norte, N. Brazil. He suggested that this area is almost certainly the centre of origin of the whole Upland group. From here this cotton dispersed first northward to the Amazon, then along the Amazon and across the Andes into Ecuador, W. Colombia and possibly still further north. In another direction this cotton dispersed northward through the Guyanas passing the West Indies to E. Colombia and further northward into C. America via Yucatan. C. America must be considered as a secondary centre of diversity (p. 194). Wild and semi-wild marie galante cotton were observed in Florida until some years ago. Upland cotton also dispersed southward to E. Brazil. At present this race is also grown in Ghana.

It is a source of resistance to Verticillium.

A second important perennial is race punctatum, which is found around the coast of the Gulf of Mexico from Yucatan to Florida and the Bahamas and some other islands (p. 199). At present G. hirsutum Cambodia (a latifolium type) is cultivated in S. India. Their way of spread was probably S. America-Philippines-Cambodia-S. India.

GOSSYPIUM KLOTZSCHIANUM Andersson. 2n=26, genome formula $D_{3-K}D_{3-K}$. Galapagos Islands. Var. davidsonii is found on the shores of Gulf of California and the Revilla Gigedo islands (p. 139).

GOSSYPIUM MUSTELINUM Miers ex Watt. (syn. G. caicoense Aranha, Leitao & Gridi-Papp). 2n= 52, genome formula AADD. NE. Brazil. A wild species distinct from G. hirsutum* and G. barbadense*, and not derived from either of them (Pickersgill et al., 1975).

GOSSYPIUM RAIMONDII Ulbr. 2n=26, genome formula D_5D_5. Formerly N. Peru. Now extinct in its original habitat and only found in collections (Harland, 1970). This species is a source of hairiness gene H_6 conditioning resistance to jassid, Empoasca ssp. Probably one of the parental species of G. barbadense* and G. hirsutum.

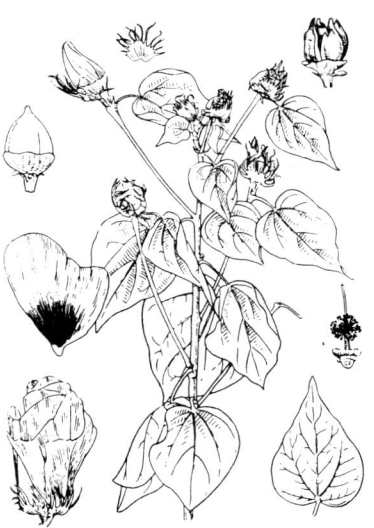

Gossypium raimondii

GOSSYPIUM TOMENTOSUM Nutt. ex Seem (syn. G. sandvicense Parl.). 2n=52, genome formula (AADD)$_1$. Hawaii. A fuzzy-seeded but not limited species. At one time it was believed that if the origin and relationship of this species were elucidated the problem of the origin of G. barbadense* and G. hirsutum* could be solved. However it appears that its origin is independent of those of the New World species (Hutchinson, 1962).

WISSADULA CONTRACTA (Link.) R.E. Fries. 2n= 14. Trop. America. Cultivated in W. Java for fibre (van Borssum Waalkes, 1966).

WISSADULA PERIPLOCIFOLIA (L.) Presl ex Thw. 2n=14. Probably introduced in Sri Lanka as a source of fibre for which purpose it is still used (van Borssum Waalkes, 1966). The degree of variability of this species is very small in Malaysia. Some varieties and forms have been described for American representatives. This may point to an American origin. A pan-tropical weed.

Marantaceae

CALATHEA ALLOUIA (Aubl.) Lindb. Sweet corn root, Leren. 2n=   . Native to Hispaniola, Puerto Rico, Lesser Antilles, the Guyanas, Brazil, Venezuela, Colombia, Ecuador and Peru. Introduced into Asia. A minor tuber crop.

MARANTA ARUNDINACEA L. Arrowroot, Bermuda arrowroot. 2n=18, 48. N. South America and the Lesser Antilles. Cultivated in the tropics for its rhizomes containing starch and as a medicinal crop.

Musaceae

MUSA cultivars. 2n=22, 33. Not much is known yet about the distribution of the clones of the various genome groups. In Venezuela, the relative frequency of these groups is AA 1, AAA 8, AAB c. 10 and ABB c. 3 (Borges, 1972). Trop. America is a secondary centre for the Plantain subgroup French Plantain or Horn Plantain, 2n=33, AAB.

Myrtaceae

ABBEVILLEA FENZLIANA Berg. 2n=   . Brazil. A small tree cultivated for its edible fruits.

BRITOA ACIDA Berg. Para guava. 2n=   . Brazil. A shrub cultivated for its fruits.

CAMPOMANESIA GUAVIROBA Benth. & Hook. 2n= S. Brazil. Cultivated for its edible fruits.

CAMPOMANESIA LINEATIFOLIA Ruiz. & Pav. (syn. C. cornifolia H.B.K.). 2n=   . E. Andes. Cultivated as a fruit tree in Peru (Mansfeld, 1959).

EUCALYPTUS CAMALDULENSIS Dehn. Longbeak eucalyptus. 2n=22. Primary centre: Australia (p. 66). Secondary centres: Brazil, Argentina and the Mediterranean area (p. 117).

EUGENIA DOMBEYANA DC. Grumichama. 2n=   . Peru and S. Brazil. A tree cultivated for its fruits.

EUGENIA UNIFLORA L. Pitange, Surinam cherry.

2n=22. Brazil. Cultivated in the tropics and subtropics.

EUGENIA UVALHA Camb. Uvalha. 2n=   . S. Brazil. Cultivated for its fruits.

FEIJOA SELLOWIANA Berg. Feijoa. 2n=22. S. Brazil, Uruguay, Paraguay and N. Argentina. Also its primary centre of diversity. Sometimes cultivated for its fruit in hot countries e.g. the Caucasian coast of the Black Sea where it grows well.

MYRCIARIA CAULIFLORA Berg. (syn. Eugenia cauliflora (Berg.) DC.). Jabotica. 2n=   . Brazil. Cultivated for its fruits (Purseglove, 1968).

MYRCIARIA JABOTICABA Berg. 2n=   . Brazil. Cultivated in the tropics for its fruits.

PSIDIUM GUINEENSE SW. 2n=   . The West Indies and trop. America. Occasionally cultivated.

PSIDIUM LITTORALE Raddi (syn. P. cattleianum Sabine). Strawberry guava. 2n=88. Brazil. A small tree introduced in the tropics and subtropics. Var. lucidum Degener, Chinese strawberry guave yields fruits of improved quality (Uphof, 1968).

Nyctaginaceae

MIRABILIS JALAPA L. Marvel of Peru, Four o'clock, False jalap. 2n=(54), 58. S. America. Spread over the whole world and in W. Africa as a fetish plant. Cultivated as an ornamental. Tuberous roots were used as jalap. Elsewhere a subtropical weed.

Onagraceae

FUCHSIA MAGELLANICA Lam. Fuchsia. 2n=22, 44. S. America. Planted as hedges in Azores, Ireland and W. Britain.

Oxalidaceae

OXALIS TUBEROSA Mol. Oca. 2n=(14), 60, 63-64, 68-70. Cultivated in the Andes from Colombia to Bolivia for an extremely long time. Introduced also in Europe where it was cultivated like the Mexican O. deppei Lodd. (2n=14, 56) as a vegetable by amateurs (Uphof, 1968). Several colours of the tubers have been observed. It should not be confused with Tropaeolum tuberosum*.

Palmae

COPERNICIA PRUNIFERA Moore. Carnauba wax palm. 2n=36. Brazil. Mostly semi-wild; some plantations for wax production.

COROZO OLEIFERA (H.B.K.) Bailey. (syn. Elaeis melanococca Gaertn.). Nolipalm. 2n=32. C. America to Colombia and Amazon area. Cultivated for its oily fruits. It can be crossed with the African oil palm, Elaeis guineensis* producing fertile hybrids.

GUILIELMA GASIPAES (H.B.K.) L.H. Bailey. Peach palm, Peribaye. 2n= . S. and C. America. Cultivated in S. America.

OENOCARPUS BACABA Martius. 2n= . Amazon area to Surinam and Guyana. A palm cultivated on compounds for its oily fruits.

Passifloraceae

PASSIFLORA ALATA Dryand. Winged passion flower, Maracuja. 2n= . Peru and Brazil. A woody vine cultivated in Brazil for its fruits.

PASSIFLORA ANTIOQUIENSIS Karst. (syn. P. vanvolxemii (Lem.) Triana & Planch.). 2n= . Banana passion fruit. Colombia. A woody vine cultivated e.g. in New Zealand for its fruits. P. x militaris hort. derives from P. antioquiensis x P. manicata (Juss.) Pers., 2n=18, and P. x exoniensis Bailey derives from P. antioquiensis x P. mollissima* (Ohle, 1975).

PASSIFLORA CAERULEA L. 2n=18. Blue passion flower. Brazil, Argentina, Paraguay. Cultivated for its fruits and as an ornamental.

PASSIFLORA COCCINEA Aubl. 2n= . Brazil, Bolivia, Amazon district of Peru.

PASSIFLORA EDULIS Sims. Passion fruit, Purple granadilla. 2n=18. S. Brazil. Widely distributed throughout the tropics and subtropics. The fruits are especially used for juice preparation. The mountain form. f. edulis occurs from Brazil to N. Argentina and in the tropics. It has run wild in Assam. The lowland form flavicarpa Degener is a mutant of it (Ohle, 1975).

PASSIFLORA FOETIDA L. Stinking passion flower, Love-in-a-mist. 2n=18, 20, 22. West Indies and S. America. Weedy. Distributed to many tropical countries in Africa and Asia, where it has naturalized. Its fruits are sometimes eaten. In Malaya and E. Africa it has been used as a cover crop.

PASSIFLORA LAURIFOLIA L. Water-lemon, Golden apple, Yellow grandilla, Jamaica honeysuckle, Belle apple, Pomme de liane. 2n=18. Thickets and forest fringes in the West Indies and NE. South America. Cultivated for its fruits in the 17th Century. Spread throughout the tropics (Purseglove, 1968). Cultivated on Java and in India as an ornamental and as a medicinal plant.

PASSIFLORA LIGULARIS Juss. Sweet granadilla. 2n=18. Trop. America. Spread to C. America. Its sweet fruits are much used in the mountainous regions of Mexico and C. America (Purseglove, 1968).

PASSIFLORA MALIFORMIS L. Curuba. 2n=18. Trop.

America. A vine cultivated for its fruits.

PASSIFLORA MIXTA L.f. 2n=18. Venezuela, Colombia, Ecuador, S. Peru, P. x rosea (Karst.) Killip, 2n= . Derives from P. mollissima* x P. mixta.

PASSIFLORA MOLLISSIMA (H.B.K.) Bailey. Banana passion fruit, Tasco, Caruba de Castilla. 2n= 18. The Andes. Especially cultivated in Ecuador and Bolivia. Introduced in other countries.

PASSIFLORA PINNATISTIPULA Cav. 2n= . Andes. Cultivated Colombia, Chile and Peru. It hybridizes with P. mollissima*.

PASSIFLORA POPENOVII Killip. 2n= . Andes (Ecuador). Resembles P. laurifolia* (Ohle, 1975).

PASSIFLORA PSILANTHA (Sodiro) Killip. Gullan. 2n= . Ecuador. A hybrid of P. mollissima* x P. partita* (Ohle, 1975). A vine cultivated for its fruits.

PASSIFLORA QUADRANGULARIS L. Giant granadilla, Barbadine. 2n=18. Trop. S. America. Cultivated since 18th Century for its fruits. Now widely distributed in the tropics. Possibly a hybrid (Ohle, 1975).

PASSIFLORA SERRATO-DIGITATA L. (syn. P. cearensis Barb.). 2n= . Trop. S. America, Amazon Basin.

PASSIFLORA TRIPARTITA (Juss.) Poir. Tasco. 2n= 18. Ecuador. Cultivated there.

Peperomiaceae

PEPEROMIA PELLUCIDA H.B.K. 2n= . S. America. In Africa this pantropical weed is cultivated as a vegetable and medicinal crop.

Phytolaccaceae

PHYTOLACCA CHILENSIS Miers. 2n= . Chile. A perennial herb cultivated for its berries which are a source of red dye.

PHYTOLACCA DIOICA L. 2n=36. Temp. and subtrop. S. America. Cultivated as an ornamental and shade plant.

RIVINA HUMILIS L. Rouge plant. 2n=108. The tropics of the Old and New Worlds. Cultivated in Colombia for its berries which are a source of red dye.

Piperaceae

PIPER ADUNCUM L. 2n= . Trop. America. Used as a soil conservant.

Portulacaceae

TALINUM TRIANGULARE*

Rhamnaceae

COLUBRINA RUFA Reiss. 2n=   . Brazil. Cultivated for its medicinal bark and other purposes.

Rosaceae

FRAGARIA CHILOENSIS L. Chiloe strawberry, Beach strawberry, Ambato strawberry. 2n=56, genome formula AAA'A'BBBB. The Pacific coastal region of N. and S. America and Hawaii. Dioecious; polygamodioecious or hermaphroditic types are occasionally found. Formerly cultivated there. It is one of the parents of F. x ananassa*.

RUBUS BRASILIENSIS Mart. 2n=   . Brazil. A shrub cultivated for its fruits.

RUBUS GLAUCUS Benth. 2n=   . Costa Rica to Ecuador. Cultivated in the Andes.

RUBUS MACROCARPUS Benth. Colombian berry. 2n=   . Colombia and Ecuador. Cultivated for its very large fruits (5 cm long).

Rubiaceae

CEPHAËLIS IPECACUANHA (Stokes) Baill. Ipecac, Ipecacuanha. 2n=22. Brazil. Introduced into India and Malaya. There small plantings were established. Roots of wild and cultivated plants are the source of ipecac or ipecacuanha used to treat amoebic dysentery.

CINCHONA LEDGERIANA Moens ex Tremen (syn. C. calisaya var. ledgeriana How., C. officinalis L., C. calisaya Wedd. and C. succirubra Pav. ex Klotzsch.). Quinine. 2n=34 (all species). These species are taken together. They all come from the same centre of diversity: Andes mountains of S. Peru, Bolivia and S. Ecuador. Here many Cinchona species are found and the great diversity of botanical varieties is caused by natural hybridization between the species and varieties. Plantations in Indonesia and Sri Lanka and recently in E. Africa. The original introductions in the Asian countries were very probably a mixture of true species and their hybrids. From this material C. ledgeriana was derived but it is thought to be a variety of C. calisaya, and is also considered a hybrid of C. calisaya, C. succirubra and C. lancifolia Mutis. C. succirubra which is used as rootstock is probably a variety of C. pubescens Vahl. (van Harten, 1969).

Sapindaceae

MELIOCOCCUS BIJUGATUS Jacq. Kanappy tree, Kinnup tree, Bullace plum, Honey berry, Spanish lime, Geneps. 2n=32. Trop. America. Cultivated there for its edible fruits (Mansfeld, 1959).

PAULLINIA CUPANA (H.B.K.) Guarana. 2n=   . S. America. Cultivated in Brazil for its seeds, used as a coffee.

SAPINDUS SAPONARIA L. Soap wood tree, Soap tree, Soap berry tree. 2n=   . Trop. America. Cultivated there and elsewhere for its fruits.

Sapotaceae

LUCUMA NERVOSA A. DC. (syn. L. rivicoa Gaertn. f., Pouteria campechiana (H.B.K.) Baenhi). Egg fruit, Canistel. 2n=   . NE. South America. Cultivated in trop. America for its fruits.

LUCUMA OBOVATA H.B.K. (syn. Pouteria lucuma (Ruiz & Pav.) O. Kuntze). Lucumo. 2n=   . Chile and Peru. This tree is cultivated for its fruits.

LUCUMA PROCERA Mart. (syn. Urbanella procera Pierre). Macarandiba. 2n=   . This fruit tree is cultivated in Brazil.

MANILKARA BIDENTATA (A. DC.) Chev. (syn. Mimusops balata Pierre). Balata, Bully, Bullet, Purgio, Quinilla. 2n=   . S. America and Trinidad. The wild trees are tapped for latex (balata).

POUTERIA CAIMITA (Ruiz & Pav.) Radlk. 2n=   . Peru to E. Ecuador and Guyanas. A tree cultivated for its fruits.

Simaroubaceae

QUASSIA AMARA L. Surinam quassis, Bitter wood. 2n=   . N. South America. Cultivated for its wood which is used medicinally, and also as an ornamental tree.

Solanaceae

CAPSICUM BACCATUM H.B.K. (syn. C. angulosum Miller). Pepper. 2n=24. The wild type is var.

Capsicum bacatum var. baccatun (o) and var. pendulum (●)(Eshbough, 1975).

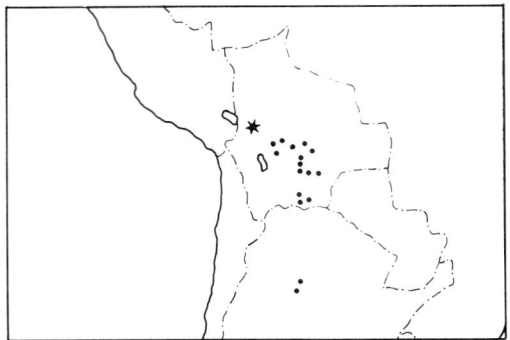

Capsicum eximium (●) and C. cardenasii (*)
(Eshbough, 1980)

baccatum (syn. C. microcarpum Cav.). It occurs
in Peru, Bolivia, Paraguay, N. Argentina and
S. Brazil. It is the parental type of the cultivated type var. pendulum (Willd.) Eshbaugh
(syn. C. pendulum Willd.). This cultigen was
originally found in the same area as var. baccatum and in S. Colombia, Ecuador and in Chile.
Now it is also cultivated elsewhere (Eshbaugh,
1970).

CAPSICUM CHINENSE Jacq. (syn. C. sinense Jacq.).
2n=24. This pepper was originally cultivated in
the West Indies and lowland S. America, from
S. Bolivia to S. Brazil. Closely related to C.
frutescens*. It may have originated from it
(Pickersgill, 1969).

Capsicum frutescens (o) and C. chinense (●)
(Eshbough, 1975)

CAPSICUM PUBESCENS Ruiz & Pavon. 2n=24. Cultivated in the highlands of S. and C. America.
It is related to the wild self-incompatible C.
cardenasii Heiser & Smith, 2n=24, and the wild
pseudo-self-compatible C. eximium Hunziker, 2n
=24; these species together with C. tovari, 2n
=24, form the purple-flowered group of Capsicum (Jensen et al., 1979). C. cardenasii is an
endemic of the La Paz district of Bolivia; C.
eximium is widely distributed from N. Argentina to C. Bolivia (Eshbaugh, 1977, 1980).
Both species hybridize naturally and the hybrids are fully fertile. They also cross to
a lesser extent with C. pubescens and may form
one species complex deriving from a common wild
ancestor (McLeod et al., 1979).

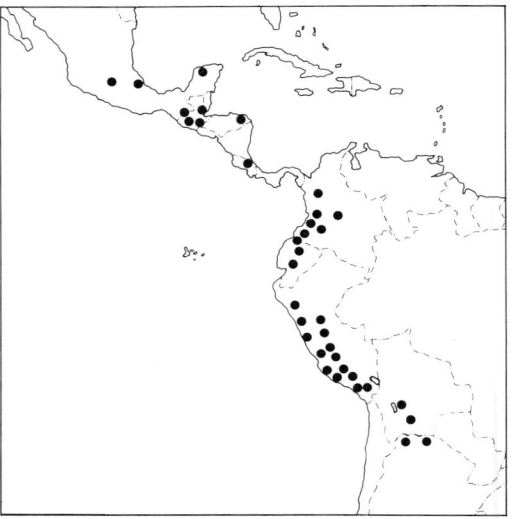

Capsicum pubescens (Eshbough, 1975).

CYPHOMANDRA BETACEA (Cav.) Sendt. (syn. C.
crassifolia). Tree tomato. 2n=24. Peru. Unknown wild. Cultivated in the Andean region
especially in Ecuador. Other species of this
genus are found in S. America and partly in
C. America. One of them, is C. hartwegi Sendt.;
its fruits are harvested in Colombia, Chile and
Argentina.

LYCOPERSICON CHEESMANII Riley (syn. L. esculentum Mill. ssp. minor Rick, L. minutum Rick).
Galapagos tomato. 2n=24. Coasts of Galapagos
Islands. Characterized by a very dense pubescence, compound yellow-green leaves, yellow
or orange fruit (rich in beta-carotens), a
calyx that expands after fertilization and
seeds with a deep dormancy. The plants are
drought and salt tolerant. They are eaten by
the Galapagos tortoises and seeds can germinate after passing through their digestive
tracts (Rick & Bowman, 1961).

LYCOPERSICON CHILENSE Dun. 2n= . The coastal strip of Peru and N. Chile. A wild tomato often found growing together with L. peruvianum. They do not cross. This species is characterized as a source for resistance to all tomato diseases except Phytophthora.

LYCOPERSICON CHMIELEWSKII Rick, Kesicki, Fobes & Holle. 2n= . C. and N. Peruvian Andes. Sympatric with its derivative L. parviflorum*. Formerly belonging with this species to 'L. minutum'. Cross-fertilizer (Rick et al., 1976).

LYCOPERSICON ESCULENTUM Mill. Tomato. 2n=24. The centre of the genus Lycopersicon is a narrow belt of the S. American west coast limited by the equator and 30°S and the Andes and the Galapagos Islands. The greatest variation of the tomato is however outside this area, in the Veracruz-Puebla area in Mexico (Jenkins, 1948). This area was very likely the source of the cultivated tomatoes of the Old World. The putative ancestor of the tomato is probably var. cerasiforme (Dun.) Alef. This variety was originally confined to the Peru and Ecuador area from where it spread in pre-Columbian times as a weed of fields and compound yards throughout much of trop. America, either with or without man's active co-operation. In Mexico it became cultivated because of its similarity to another food plant, Physalis ixocarpa*.

Outside its primary gene centre the tomato plant is self-compatible. In Peru and Ecuador it spontaneously crosses with L. pimpinellifolium*. Tomato flowers pollinated by pollen of L. peruvianum* result in the induction of parthenocarpic fruits. Some F_1 seeds may be set resulting in hybrid plants with varying degree of fertility.

Rick (1971) studied the geographical distribution of the alleles Ge^c, Ge^p, and Ge^n. He found that most European and US cultivars have the genotype Ge^nGe^n, only a few have Ge^cGe^c or Ge^pGe^p. The C. American varieties have Ge^nGe^n and occasionally Ge^cGe^c. In Ecuador Ge^n is also common among the cultivars. The C. American sources of var. cerasiforme have Ge^nGe^n, and an Ecuador source has Ge^c. So in Ecuador the cultivars differ from the wild type, but more sources should be investigated. Sources of L. pimpinellifolium* ex Ecuador carried Ge^n. This would suggest gene exchange between L. pimpinellifolium and the cultivars. The Peruvian cultivars carry Ge^p; the same allele is found in Peruvian sources of L. pimpinellifolium. This suggests gene exchange too. Rick concluded that the European and US tomato cultivars are qualitatively closer related to the cultivars of Peru, and quantitatively to those from C. America and Mexico.

LYCOPERSICON HIRSUTUM Humb. & Bonpl. 2n=24. The western slopes of the Andes in Peru. A green-fruited species. The glabratum is self-compatible. It is characterized by disease resistance, e.g. tomato mosaic virus (Marmon

tabaci Holmes).

LYCOPERSICON PARVIFLORUM Rick, Kesicki, Fobes & Holle. 2n= . C. and N. Peruvian Andes. Compatric with its ancestor L. chmielewskii*. Formerly classed with this species to 'L. minutum'. Strict self-fertilizer (Rick et al., 1976).

LYCOPERSICON PERUVIANUM (L.) Mill. 2n=24. Chile and Peru. A green, small-fruited wild species. Most plants are gametophytic self-incompatible, although some plants have been found to be self-compatible (Hogenboom, 1968). It is a source of tomato mosaic virus tolerance.

LYCOPERSICON PIMPINELLIFOLIUM Mill. (syn. L. esculentum ssp. pimpinellifolium (Mill.) Brezhn.). Currant tomato. 2n=24. Primary centre: coastal Ecuador and Peru. This red-fruited species crosses with L. esculentum* and its genes introgress into tomato (Rick & Fobes, 1975). Because of the high frequency of outcrossing, it is highly heterogenous (Rick et al., 1977). It is cultivated and occurs as a weed. A source of tolerance for tomato.

METHYSTICODENDRON AMESIANUM R.E. Schultes. 2n = . S. America. Cultivated as a medicinal and witchcraft plant.

NICOTIANA RUSTICA L. Aztec Tobacco, Makhorka, Nicotine Tobacco. 2n=48. Unknown wild, with a possible exception of var. pavonii (Dunal) Goodspeed. This variety occurs as a ruderal in the Andes. Aztec Tobacco is a tetraploid having probably originated in Peru by amphiploidization of apparently N. paniculata L. (2n=24) and N. undulata Ruiz & Pavon (2n=24). Both species occur wild in Peru. Its cultivation is limited to some areas such as the USSR and India. In most other areas it is replaced by N. tabacum* which has a low nicotine content.

NICOTIANA TABACUM L. Tobacco. 2n=48, genome formula SSTT. Clausen (1932) showed that tobacco is a natural amphitetraploid of N. sylvestri Speg. & Comes, 2n=24, genome formula S'S' and N. tomentosiformis Goodsp., 2n=24, genome formula T'T'. Isozymic (Sheen, 1972) and cytoplasmic (Gray et al., 1974; Kawashima et al., 1976) evidence supports his view. The occasional wild plants are escapes of cultivation.

Interspecific crosses have been made to introduce male-sterilizing cytoplasma and genes conditioning resistance to diseases.

PHYSALIS PERUVIANA L. Cape gooseberry. 2n=24, 48. Andes. Cultivated in some S. American countries for its berries. Often observed as a weed or semi-wild.

SOLANUM ABANCAYENSE Ochoa. 2n= . Peru. Tubers are very small and white.

SOLANUM ACAULE Bitt. 2n=48, genome formula

$A_2A_2A_3A_3$. Wild tetraploid from C. Peru, Bolivia and NW. Argentina. A parent of S. x juzepczukii*. Frost resistant and resistant to X-virus disease, nematodes and the Colorado beetle. Very susceptible to Phytophthora.

SOLANUM AJANHUIRI Juz. & Buk. 2n=2x=24. Cultivated in N. Bolivia (dept. La Paz) and S. Peru. It derives from S. tuberosum* group stenotomum x S. megistacrolobum Bitt., 2n=24 (Huaman et al., 1976). It is frost resistant, the tubers are long and irregularly shaped. Also resistant to virus diseases.

SOLANUM CHACOENSE Bitt. 2n=24, (36). N. and C. Argentina, Paraguay, Uruguay and S. Brazil. A very polymorphic wild species. Only once an autotriploid was observed. This triploid has been described as 'S. calvescens Bitter'. 'S. muelleri Bitter' also belongs to S. chacoense (Brücher, 1975). Rich in tomatine alkaloid which is poisonous to the Colorado beetle.

Introgression between this species and S. microdontum exists in Argentina and possibly elsewhere. This resulted in an extension of this originally low altitude species of open places of the Argentinean plain to mountainous region (Hawkes, 1962a). Used as a source of resistance to common scab, virus diseases and Colorado beetle.

SOLANUM x CHAUCHA Juz. & Buk. (syn. S. tuberosum group chaucha). 2n=3x=36. This species is a hybrid of S. tuberosum* group Andigena x group Stenotomum or group Phureja, but Bukasov (1970) suggested that it is a triploid derivative of group Phureja. The hybridization may have occurred several times and because of the variation of the parents this species is very polymorphic. Cultivated from C. Peru to N. Bolivia. It has a rather low yield (Jackson et al., 1976).

This species has run wild in Simla hills, India. Initially it was established by vegetative propagation. The older the population the more plants flower and the more self-incompatibility breaks down (Nayar & Gohal, 1970).

SOLANUM COMMERSONII Dun. 2n=24, 36. E. Central Argentina, Paraguay, Uruguay and S. Brazil. 'S. acroleucon Bitter' belongs to this species (Brücher, 1975). A source of resistance to potato cancer and Colorado beetle. It withstands frost of -6°C.

SOLANUM CONTUMAZAENSE Ochoa. 2n= . N. Peru. With white-yellow tubers of 15-25 mm length.

SOLANUM x CURTILOBUM Juz. & Buk. 2n=60. The high Andes of Bolivia and Peru, where it has been cultivated. Probably a hybrid of S. x juzepczukii* and x S. tuberosum group Andigena. It reproduces itself vegetatively, although it is moderately fertile. It crosses readily with S. tuberosum group Tuberosum. Less frost resistant than its parent S. x juz-

epczukii (Hawkes, 1962b).

SOLANUM x FLAVOVIRIDENS Ochoa. 2n= . Humid trop. Bolivia. Its glandular hairs provide resistance to virus-spreading aphids. Its parents are not yet fully known.

SOLANUM GONIOCALYX Juz. & Buk. 2n=24. This potato is cultivated in C. Peru (dept. Junin). It is a northern derivative of S. tuberosum* group Stenotomum. It may be included in this species as an extreme variant (Hawkes, 1958). Bukasov (1970) suggested that it was a derivative of S. multi-interruptum. The tubers have a pale-yellow flesh owing to their richness in carotinoids. They have an excellent flavour.

SOLANUM HUMECTOPHILUM Ochoa. 2n= . Peru. With white-hyaline tubers of 8-12 mm length.

SOLANUM IMPROVIDUM Brücher. 2n=24. La Rioja and Catamarca, W. Argentina. Wild potato of deserts (Brücher, 1979).

SOLANUM x JUZEPCZUKII Buk. 2n=36. High Andes of Bolivia to Mendoza Prov. of W. Argentina. Wild potato of deserts. Self-incompatible. Source of resistance to nematode and tolerance to frost (Brücher, 1979).

SOLANUM KURTZIANUM Bitter & Wittmack. 2n= . S. Bolivia to Mendoza Prov. of W. Argentina. Wild potato of deserts. Self-incompatible. Source of resistance to nematode. and tolerance to frost (Brücher, 1979).

SOLANUM MACOLAE Bukasov. 2n=24. Mendoza Prov. of W. Argentina. Wild potato of deserts, with high content of solanin in tubers (Brücher, 1979).

SOLANUM MAGLIA Molina 2n=24, 36. The 2x 'andinum' occurs wild in the Cordillera Foothills of Mendoza, W. Argentina, and the 3x 'pacificum' grows wild on the Pacific coast between Valpraiso and Loquimbo. Both are partially male-sterile (Brücher, 1979).

SOLANUM MURICATUM Ait. Pepino morado. 2n=24. Unknown wild. Probably domesticated in the Andes. Cultivated in C. and S. America. Extremely variable and many types of fruits are recognized. There are two closely related species, either of which could be the parental species. These are S. caripense Humb. & Bonpl. (2n=24) and S. tabanoense Correll (2n=24). Both occur in Ecuador and Colombia. Pepino is cultivated for its fruits (Heiser, 1964).

SOLANUM NUBICOLA Ochoa. 2n=48. The Huánuco region, Peru. A tetraploid species of the Tuberosum group.

SOLANUM OCEANICUM Brücher. 2n=36. A weedy potato of the Pacific coast of Chiloe Island, Chile.

SOLANUM PELOQUINIANUM Ochoa. 2n=24. Wild potato species from the Peruvian Andes.

SOLANUM PENNELLII Corr. 2n=   . Closely related to S. lycopersicoides Dunal. (2n=   ). Both species are representatives of a transition between Solanum and Lycopersicon. It can be crossed with L. esculentum* and it is a source of resistance to Tomato Mosaic Virus.

SOLANUM PHUREJA see S. tuberosum.

SOLANUM QUITOENSE Lam. Naranjillo, Lulo. 2n= 24. Unknown wild. Cultivated for its fruits in Colombia and Ecuador. Var. septentrionale R.E. Schultes & Cautrecasan is spineless (Heiser, 1971). Closely related to S. pectinatum Dun. (syn. S. hirsutissimum Standl.), 2n=24.

SOLANUM RAPHANIFOLIUM Card. & Hawkes. 2n=24. The dept. of Cuzco, Peru. There it occurs as a weed. A stabilized hybrid of S. megistacrolobum Bitt. (2n=24), and S. canasense Hawkes (2n=24) (Ugent, 1970a).

SOLANUM RUIZ-LEALII Brücher. 2n=24. Mendoza Prov. of W. Argentina. Wild and self-incompatible. Source of resistance to nematode and tolerance to drought. Brücher (1979) concluded that it is not a hybrid of S. chacoense* and S. kurtzianum*.

SOLANUM SPARSIPILUM Bitt. 2n=24. Peru and Bolivia. A weedy species. Probably a clonal mixture of diploid hybrids of S. tuberosum groups Stenotomum and Phureja* and diploid related species like S. canasense Hawkes, S. raphanifolium Card. & Hawkes, and others which Ugent (1970a) grouped in one complex species S. brevicaule* Bitt. This weedy species may form a bridge for a gene flow from S. brevicaule s.l. to S. tuberosum* and vice versa (Ugent, 1970a)

SOLANUM STENOTOMUM see S. tuberosum.

SOLANUM SUCRENSE Hawkes. 2n=48. Bolivia. A weedy potato in potato crops. It is a hybrid of S. tuberosum ssp. andigena and S. oplocense, 2n=48. Source of resistance to several pathotypes of Globodera nematodes (Astley & Hawkes, 1979).

SOLANUM TOPIRO Humbolt & Bonpland ex Dunal. Jibara, Uvilla, Cocona. 2n=24. S. America. Var. topiro is commonly cultivated for its fruits in the Upper Amazon valley. There are two fruit forms: ovoid named jibara and globose called uvilla. The latter has been described as S. alibile R.E. Schultes. A common weed in Ecuador is var. georgicum (R.E. Schultes) Heiser (syn. S. georgicum R.E. Schultes). Var. topiro has no spines and big fruits, while var. georgicum has spines and small fruits. It is believed that these differences are a result of domestication. The greatest variation in size, shape and content of anthocyanins of the fruits is found in the W. Amazon Basin (W.

Brazil) (von der Pahlen, 1977). Self and cross compatible.
    Artificial intervarietal hybrids have been made. It has been suggested that in nature such hybrids also occur (Heiser, 1971).

SOLANUM TUBEROSUM L. Potato. 2n=24, 48. There are two geographical regions where the largest number of the wild and cultivated potatoes grow; 1. C. Mexico (p. 197, 198) and 2. Andes of C. Peru, Bolivia and NW. Argentina. The greatest number of tuberous Solanum species is found in Peru where the potato was probably first domesticated.
This species is divided into 4 groups:
1. group Stenotomum (syn. S. stenotomum Juz. & Buk.), 2n=24, a cultivated type of very high altitudes from Peru to N. Bolivia. It is the parent of groups Andigena and Phureja, S. x chauca* and S. x juzepczukii*. Some provenances

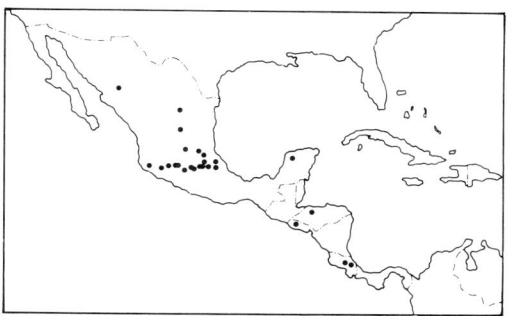

Solanum tuberosum group Andigena (Ugent, 1968)

are frost-resistant, have a high yield of good quality. If introduced into Europe, its self-incompatibility may have hindered its small-scale propagation at that time (Zeven, 1980a).
2. group Phureja (syn. S. phureja Juz. & Buk.), criollo potato, 2n=24, genome formula A_1A_1, cultivated in most lowlands of Venezuela, Colombia, Ecuador, Peru and N. Bolivia. The tubers are the largest of the diploid species. Dormancy is very short (1-13 days) and may have prevented its introduction into Europe in the 16th Century and later (Zeven, 1980). It matures early. It is a selection of group Stenotomum with a short dormancy.
3. group Andigena (S. tuberosum ssp. andigena, S. andigena Juz. & Buk.), 2n=48, found in the Andes of Venezuela, Colombia, Ecuador, Peru, Bolivia and NW. Argentina. It evolved from group Stenotomum in C. Andes. Parental type of group Tuberosum.
4. group Tuberosum (syn. S. tuberosum ssp. tuberosum, S. tuberosum sensu stricto), derived from group Andigena introduced into the coastal region of S. Central Chile (Island of Chiloe and adjacent coastal mainland) (Brücher, 1971; Glendinning, 1975) and into Europe and N. America (Hawkes, 1958). Naturalized and culti-

vated Tuberosum from Chile and elsewhere have
identical cytoplasmic factors (Grun, 1979). The
evolution of Andigena into Tuberosum was simu-
lated by Simmonds (1968). The distinction between Andigena and Tuberosum is that Tuberosum
has less dissected leaves with wider leaflets,
generally arched and set at a wider angle to
the stem. The tubers form with long days, or
in the tropics with short days only at lower
altitudes.

In the Canary Islands, cultivar Negra has
been cultivated. It is a triploid (2n=36) (Zubeldia et al., 1955). Sanudo (1970) suggested
that it is a hybrid of group Stenotomum and
group Andigena. Zubeldia L. et al. (1955) believed that it was introduced from Peru in the
early part of the 17th Century together with
tetraploid material.

Naturalized potatoes grow in the Kilimandjaro
Mountains of Tanzania, in Lesotho and Botswana.
They probably derive from cultivars introduced
from Europe (Brücher, 1966). He described 30
types.

Andigena is a source of resistance to potato
virus Y. Some plants have tubers with a very
black flesh, which can be used as a source of
pigments.

SOLANUM VIARUM Dunal. (syn. S. khasianum C.B.
Clarke var. chatterjeeanum Sen Gupta). 2n=24.
S. America. Fruits are source of solanidin.
Related species are S. myriacanthum Dunal (syn.
S. khasianum C.B. Clarke), 2n=24, naturalized
in the Khasia Mountains of Assam; S. retro-
flexum Schrank, 2n=48; and S. platanifolium
Hook., 2n=24, which is rare. S. viarum is na-
turalized in several places in trop. Asia (Babu
& Hepper, 1977). A shrub.

Sterculiaceae

GUAZUMA GRANDIFLORA G. Don. (syn. Theobroma
grandiflora Schum.). 2n=   . Brazilian Amazon
basin. A tree cultivated for its fruits.

THEOBROMA BICOLOR*

THEOBROMA CACAO L. Cacao. 2n=16, 20, 26. Primary gene centre: the area of the 'Upper waters of the Amazon'. Spread by man. Only in
Mexico was the domestication of the cacao com-
pleted by the Maya. Elsewhere cacao was wild
or semidomesticated. Cuatrecasas (1964) described 22 Theobroma species, which all are
found in trop. S. and C. America. Relative
isolation of cacao populations and their original parentage resulted in the development of
two more or less uniform groups distinguished
as Criollo (T. cacao ssp. cacao) and Forastero
(ssp. sphaerocarpum).

The Criollo is located in C. America (Central American Criollo) and in N. Colombia
(South American Criollo). The Forastero can
be divided into the Upper Amazonian Forastero,
indigenous to the Upper Amazon basin and the
lower Amazonian Forastero, also named and
found in the Guyanas (Cheesman, 1944; Toxo-

peus, 1969) and in Africa where it is known as
the West African amelonado.

The Trinitario is a recently originated hybrid swarm of Criollo from C. America and A-
melonado.

THEOBROMA MICROCARPA Mart. 2n=   . Brazil.
Cultivated in Bahia.

Thymelaeaceae

FUNIFERA BRASILIENSIS (Raddi) Mansf. 2n=   .
Brazil. Cultivated in the West Indies for its
fibres.

Tropaeolaceae

TROPAEOLUM LEPTOPHYLLUM G. Don. 2n=   . Ecuador and Peru. Cultivated for its tubers.

TROPAEOLUM MAJUS L. Nasturtium. 2n=28. S. A-
merica. A herbaceous vine cultivated as an
ornamental plant. The flower buds and young
fruits are used for flavouring vinegar. They
are also used as capers.

TROPAEOLUM TUBEROSUM Ruiz & Pav. Tuber nasturtium. 2n=42. A very old cultivated food plant
unknown wild in Peru, Chile and Bolivia. In
Bolivia it is still cultivated in the mountains above Lake Titicaca.

Umbelliferae

ARRACACIA XANTHORRHIZA Bancr. (syn. A. esculenta DC). Arracacha, Apio arracacia. 2n=   .
Unknown wild. Cultivated mainly in Venezuela
and Colombia, also in Bolivia and Peru, and
introduced into Brazil, C. America, E. Africa
and India.

Verbenaceae

LIPPIA CITRIODORA H.B.K. (syn. L. triphylla
(L. 'Hér.) Kuntze). Lemon verbena. 2n=36. S.
America. Formerly much cultivated for its ver-
bena oil, now as an ornamental.

11 Central American and Mexican Region

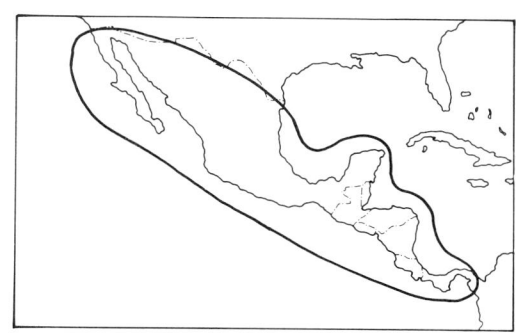

The Central American and Mexican Region has been described by Vavilov as the Central American and South Mexican Centre of Origin. Darlington & Janaki Ammal (1945) named Mexico as a centre of origin, while Darlington (1956) added C. America to Mexico. In this region agriculture developed since the 7th Millenium BC. Harlan (1971) called it centre C1 Mesoamerican centre.

Old farming sites have been discovered at Tamaulipas and in the Tehuacán Valley of Mexico. To the earliest plant remains belong Amaranthus sp., Avocado persica, Capsicum annuum, Cucurbita pepo, C. mixta, Gossypium hirsutum and Lagenaria siceraria.

Relatively a few but important crops have been domesticated in this region e.g. fruit trees, Agave sp., Capsicum sp., Cucurbita sp., Gossypium sp., Ipomoea batatas, Phaseolus sp., Zea mays etc.

Agavaceae

AGAVE AMERICANA L. Century plant, Magvey. 2n= 60, 120, (180, 240 and aneuploids). Mexico. Cultivated in Mexico, Europe, Africa and N. America as an ornamental, foliage plant, a hedge plant and for pulp.

AGAVE ATROVIRENS Salm-Dyck (syn. A. latissima Jacobi). Pulque. 2n=150, 180. Mexico. Extensively cultivated in Mexico. The inflorescence is cut off and the sweet juices that collect in the cavity produced are allowed to ferment to produce the alcoholic drink pulque or mexcal de pulque.

AGAVE CANTALA (Haw.). Roxb. (syn. A. candelabrum Tod.). Cantala. 2n=90. Probably Mexico. There a wild form occurs on the western coast. Smaller than the cultivated types. It was taken to the Philippines and later to Indonesia where it is cultivated for its fibre. In India cultivated as a hedge and anti-erosion plant (Purseglove, 1972).

AGAVE COMPULVIATA Trel. Pulque. 2n= . Mexico. Cultivated around Comitán in Mexico. Comiteca, a fine liquor, is distilled from a mixture of fermented sugar-cane juice and a mash made from the stems and leaves of this species.

AGAVE CRASSISPINA Trel. Maguey manso. 2n= Mexico. Cultivated there.

AGAVE DEWEANA Trel. Zapupe verde, Zapupe de Tantoyuca. 2n= . Cultivated for a long time by the Tantoyuca Indians in Mexico.

AGAVE FOURCROYDES Lem. Henequen agave. 2n=c. 140. Yucatan, Mexico. Primary centre also there. Secondary centre probably in E. Africa (p. 122). Cultivated in many countries for its excellent fibre.

AGAVE HETERACANTHA Zucc. (syn. A. funkiana Koch & Bouche). Ixtle de Juamava. 2n= . Arid NE. Mexico. Cultivated for its fine fibre, used to make cordage and brushes.

AGAVE LECHEGUILLA Torr. Lechuguilla, Tula Istle. 2n= . Texas and N. Mexico. Cultivated for fibre, used to make rugs, mats and brushes.

AGAVE LETONAE F.W. Taylor. Letona, Salvador henequen. El Salvador. Cultivated there for centuries.

AGAVE LOPHANTA Schiede. Lechuguilla. 2n= . Mexico. Cultivated by natives for its fibre.

AGAVE SCHOTTII Engllm. Amole. 2n= . Sonora of Mexico and arid Arizona. Cultivated by Amerindians. Dried pulp of leaves used as soap.

AGAVE SISALANA Perr. (syn. A. rigida Mill.): Sisal agave. 2n=(c. 138, 147, 149), 150. Mexico and C. America. Primary centre in Yucatan,

Mexico. Introduced to Florida and from here to most sisal-growing countries.

FURCRAEA FOETIDA*

HESPEROYUCCA FUNIFERA (Koch.) Trel. (syn. Yucca funifera Koch.). 2n=   . Mexico. Cultivated for its leaves which are a source of fibre.

POLIANTHES TUBEROSA L. 2n=(50), 60. Tuberose. Very likely from Mexico (Dressler, 1953). Unknown wild. It has probably a long history of domesticated ornamental because of its great variation. Spread to other countries where it is used for perfumery and other purposes. It may derive from P. gracilis Link. (Mansfeld, 1959).

YUCCA ELEPHANTIPES Regel. 2n=   . Probably Veracruz, Mexico (Dressler, 1953). Cultivated for hedges especially in C. America, where it was apparantly introduced. The flowers are used as a vegetable.

Alstroemeriaceae

BOMAREA EDULIS (Tuss.) Herb. 2n=   . Mexico to S. America. Apparently very variable. Probably the species of Bomarea cultivated by the Mexicans for the edible, tuberous roots, and as an ornamental (Dressler, 1953).

Amaranthaceae

AMARANTHUS CRUENTUS L. 2n=32, 34. Cultivated in Guatemala and other parts of C. America as a grain crop. It evidently derived from A. hybridus* (Sauer, 1969).

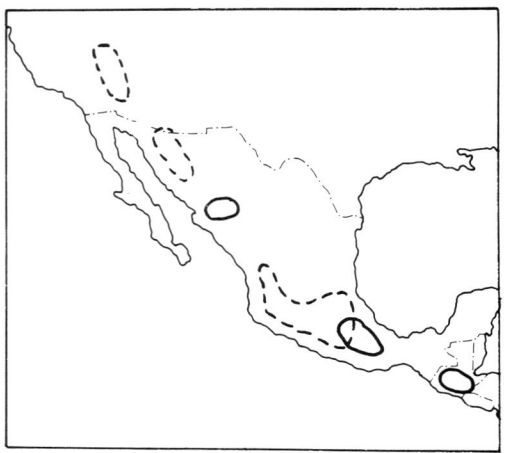

Amaranthus cruentus (—) and A. hypochondriacus (---)(Sauer, 1976).

AMARANTHUS HYBRIDUS L. Slim amaranth. 2n=32. C. America. Cultivated in India and neighbouring regions as a grain crop and as an ornamental. Derived from A. cruentus* (Sauer, 1969). Hybridization with other Amaranthus species and with species of the genus Acnida has been observed (Sauer, 1950).

AMARANTHUS HYPOCHONDRIACUS L. (syn. A. leucocarpus S. Wats.). Huauhtli. 2n=32. A main crop in the Columbian times. Still cultivated in Mexico and Guatemala, and also in Asia (India, Iran?). An ornamental in Europe and N. America. Most of the Mexican populations are pale-seeded, as are those of Asia although there are more black-seeded forms than found in Mexico. The plants cultivated as ornamentals in Europe and N. America are invariably black-seeded (Sauer, 1950). It is evidently derived from A. powellii S. Wats. (2n=34) (Sauer, 1969). It is also morphologically close to A. hybridus*.

Anacardiaceae

ANACARDIUM OCCIDENTALE*

CYRTOCARPA PROCERA H.B.K. Chupandilla. 2n=   . Tehuacán Valley of Mexico. A small fruit tree. Archeological seed-remains date from about 6500 BC. (Smith, 1968).

SCHINUS MOLLE*

SPONDIAS PURPUREA*

Annonaceae

ANNONA DIVERSIFOLIA Safford. Itama. 2n=   . S. Mexico, Guatemala, El Salvador and other countries of C. America. Cultivated there and in Florida.

ANNONA MONTANA Macf. Mountain soursop. 2n=16. The West Indies. Cultivated.

ANNONA MURICATA L. Soursop, Guanabana, Corossol. 2n=14, (16). Gene centre in the Antilles. A small tree cultivated from C. America to the coastal valleys in Peru and elsewhere in the tropics. It develops the biggest fruits of all Annona species. Some fruits may weigh 2 kg.

ANNONA PURPUREA Moc. & Sessé. Soncoya. 2n=   . S. Mexico and C. America. Cultivated there.

ANNONA RETICULATA L. Bullock's heart, Common custard apple, Corazon. 2n=14, (16). Gene centre lies in the Antilles. Spread to trop. America and later to other tropical countries.

ANNONA SCLERODERMA Safford. Posh té. 2n=   . C. America especially from S. Mexico to Guatemala. Cultivated.

ANNONA SQUAMOSA L. Sweetsop, Sugar apple, Custard apple. 2n=14, (16). Gene centre in the Antilles. Spread to trop. America. Later is was brought to other tropical countries. Atemoya is a hybrid product with A. cherimola*.

CYMBOPETALUM PENDULIFLORUM Baill. 2n= . Mexico and Guatemala. A shrub cultivated for its vanilla-scented petals.

Araceae

MONSTERA DELICIOSA Liebm. (syn. Philodendron pertusum Kunth). Ceriman. 2n=24, 56, 60. Mexico and Guatemala. A liane cultivated for its fruits.

XANTHOSOMA ROBUSTUM Schott. Pixi, Capota, Quequesque, Marac, Quiscamote. 2n=26. S. Mexico and C. America. There often cultivated as an ornamental. The huge leaves are used as umbrellas. Roots and leaves are also used medicinally and as a stimulant.

Basellaceae

BOUSSINGAULTIA CORDIFOLIA*

Bignoniaceae

CRESCENTIA CUJETE L. Calabash tree, Calabazo, Cujete. 2n=40. Trop. America. Cultivated in the tropics. The thin shell of the fruits is used for containers. In Guatemala three varieties are recognized. It should not be confused with Lagenaria siceraria*.

PARMENTIERA CERIFERA Seem. Candle tree. 2n=40. C. America. Cultivated in the West Indies and other tropical regions for its fruits.

PARMENTIERA EDULIS DC. Cuachilota, Food candle tree. 2n=40. C. America. Cultivated there and in Mexico for its fruits.

Bombacaceae

CEIBA PENTANDRA Gaertn. Kapok tree, Silk cotton tree. 2n=72, 80, 88. Toxopeus (1950) believed that the kapok tree originated in an area which was later divided by the Atlantic Ocean. So this species is native both to America and Africa (p. 123). He based his conclusion mainly on the great variation of this plant and on the high frequency of dominant inherited characteristics in these two continents. However, Bakhuizen van den Brink (1933) and Chevalier (1949) thought that seeds may have come from America in prehistoric times and that later introduction increased the variation.
    Its chromosome number suggest a polyploid origin and if this supposition is correct the kapok tree can only have arisen in that area where its parents occur. As all other Ceiba species are restricted to America this would also indicate an American origin.
    The variety found in America and Africa is C. pentandra var. caribaea (DC) Bakh.

Bromeliaceae

BROMELIA PINGUIN L. Pegwe. 2n=96. West Indies, C. America and Venezuela. A perennial herb cultivated as a living hedge. The fruits are edible.

Cactaceae

ESCONTRIA CHIOTILLO (Weber) Ross. Mexico. 2n= . Cultivated in Mexico for its fruits and flowers ('immortals').

HYLOCEREUS NAPOLEONIS (Grah.) Britt. & Rose. West Indies and Mexico. Cultivated as a hedge plant and for its fruits.

HYLOCEREUS OCAMPONIS (Salm-Dyck) Britt. & Rose. 2n= . Mexico. Cultivated there as a hedge plant and ornamental, and for its fruits.

HYLOCEREUS UNDATUS (Haw.) Britt. & Rose. 2n= 22. Mexico. Cultivated there and in (sub)trop. America and elsewhere for its edible fruits and as a hedge plant.

LOPHOCEREUS SCHOTTII (Eng.) Bitt. & Rose. 2n= 22. N. Mexico and S. USA. Cultivated in N. Mexico as a hedge plant and for its edible fruits.

MARGINATOCEREUS MARGINATUS (DC.) Backeb. 2n= . Mexico. Cultivated there as a hedge plant.

MARSHALLOCEREUS ARAGONII (Weber) Backeb. 2n= . Costa Rica. Cultivated there as a hedge plant.

MARSHALLOCEREUS THURBERI (Eng.) Backeb. 2n= . S. Arizona (USA) and Mexico. Cultivated in Mexico as a hedge plant and for its edible fruits.

NOPALEA COCHENILLIFERA (L.) Salm-Dyck. Nopal. 2n=22. Mexico, trop. America, Jamaica. Cultivated in the (sub)tropics, formerly used to obtain its red pigment, cochenilla, now grown as an ornamental, for its edible fruits and for forage.

NOPALEA DEJECTA Salm-Dyck. Nopal. 2n=22. Probably Panama. Occasionally cultivated in trop. America for its edible fruits.

NOPALEA KARWINSKIANA (Salm-Dyck) Schumann. 2n= . Mexico. Cultivated there as a hedge plant.

NYCTOCEREUS SERPENTINUS (Lag. & Rodz.) Britt. & Rose. 2n=22. Known only as a cultigen. Cultivated in Mexico, California and Chile. Hammer (1976) believes that it originated on the E. Coast of Mexico.

OPUNTIA AMYCLAEA Tenore. 2n= . Mexico. Cultivated there and in Italy for its edible fruits.

OPUNTIA CRASSA Haw. 2n= . Probably Mexico, wild form not known. Occasionally cultivated in Mexico and trop. America.

OPUNTIA CRYSTALENIA Griff. 2n=   . Mexico. Cultivated there for its edible fruits.

OPUNTIA DILLENIA (Ker-Gawler) Haw. Pest pear. 2n=22, 66. S. USA, Bermuda, West Indies, N. South America. Cultivated there and on Tenerife (Canaries), Italy, W. Africa, India, E. Asia and Australia for its edible fruits. It has often run wild.

OPUNTIA FICUS-INDICA (L.) Miller. Indian fig, Nopal, 2n=22, 88. Probably Mexico (Hammer, 1976). Cultivated in (sub)tropics for its edible fruits, and as a forage and hedge plant.

OPUNTIA FUSICAULIS Griff. 2n=   . Not known wild. Thornless species cultivated in Mexico and S. USA as forage.

OPUNTIA HYPTIACANTHA Weber. 2n=   . Mexico. Cultivated for its fruits.

OPUNTIA LANCEOLATA (Haw.) Haw. 2n=88. Mexico. Occasionally cultivated in the (sub)trop. Americas for its fruits.

OPUNTIA LEUCOTRICHA DC. 2n=44. Mexico. Cultivated there and around the Mediterranean area for its fruits, and as an ornamental and hedge plant.

OPUNTIA LINDHEIMERI Eng. 2n=   . SW. Louisiana, SE. Texas (USA), and NE. Mexico. Cultivated for its fruits and as a forage.

OPUNTIA MAXIMA Mill. 2n=   . Probably Mexico. Occasionally cultivated in the (sub)trop. Americas and Asia. Not known wild.

OPUNTIA MEGACANTHA Salm-Dyck (syn. O. castillae Griffith). Tuna, Nopal. 2n=   . Mexico. Cultivated there and in Jamaica, S. California and Hawaii. Thornless strains cultivated as forage. Naturalized on Hawaii (Hammer, 1976).

OPUNTIA ROBUSTA Wendl. 2n=   . Mexico. Cultivated there for its fruits.

OPUNTIA STREPTACANTHA Lem. 2n=   . Mexico. Cultivated there. Var. streptacantha is thorny and is used as an animal deterrant, whereas var. pachona (Griff.) Hammer (syn. O. pachona Griff.) is thornless and is cultivated for its fruits.

OPUNTIA TOMENTOSA Salm-Dyck. 2n=44. Mexico. Cultivated there. Formerly used as feed for cochenilla.

OPUNTIA UNDULATA Griff. 2n=   . Mexico. Cultivated there for its edible fruits.

PACHYCEREUS PECTEN-ABORIGINUM (Eng.) Britt. & Rose. 2n=   . Mexico. Hedge plant.

PACHYCEREUS PRINGLEI (S. Wats.) Britt. & Rose. 2n=   . Mexico. Cultivated as a hedge plant.

PERESKIOPSIS CHAPISTLE (Weber) Britt. & Rose. 2n=   . Mexico. Cultivated as a hedge plant.

PERESKIOPSIS SPATHULATA (Otto) Britt. & Rose. 2n=   . S. Mexico. Hedge plant.

RITTEROCEREUS PRUINOSUS (Otto) Backeb. 2n= C. and S. Mexico. Cultivated as a hedge plant and for its edible fruits.

SELENICEREUS GRANDIFLORUS (L.) Britt. & Rose (syn. Cereus grandiflorus Mill.). 2n=22. Jamaica, Cuba, Mexico. Cultivated as a source of drug, and widespread as an ornamental.

STENOCEREUS STELLATUS (Pfeiff.) Riccob. 2n= . Mexico. Cultivated for its edible fruit and as a hedge plant.

Caricaceae

CARICA PAPAYA L. Papaya, Pawpaw. 2n=18. Lowlands of C. America somewhere in the region between S. Mexico and Nicaragua. Unknown wild. The history of its domestication is not known. Papaya has now spread to all tropical countries and may have run wild as was observed in the forest fringes in N. trop. Argentina. Closely related to C. pelta Hook. & Arn., which also occurs in this area. This species may have contributed by hybridization (Purseglove, 1968).

Chenopodiaceae

CHENOPODIUM NUTTALLIAE Safford. 2n=allo 4x=36. This self-compatible species is grown as a vegetable (inflorescence) and a grain crop in C. Mexico. It is closely related to C. quinoa* and may derive from it. The weedy C. berlandieri Moq., 2n=36, forms a weed-cultigen complex with C. nuttalliae. C. berlandieri occurs from C. Mexico to W. USA where it is very polymorphic (Wilson, 1976). See for additional information Wilson & Heiser (1979) and Wilson (1981).

Compositae

DAHLIA VARIABILIS Desf. (syn. D. rosea Cav). Dahlia. 2n=64. Mexico. A tuberous amphiploid of D. pinnata, 2n=32 and D. coccinea Cav., 2n =32, 64. Probably domesticated as a food crop but now grown as an ornamental.

PARTHENIUM ARGENTATUM A. Gray. Guayule. 2n= 36, 54, 72, 108 and many aneuploids. Mexico and Texas, USA. Cultivated as a rubber producer.

TAGETES ERECTA L. Big marigold. 2n=24, genome formula AeAe. Mexico. Cultivated as an ornamental and for its medicinal properties. Also used in religious rituals and celebrations (Neher, 1968). Probably a parent of T. patula*. The genus Tagetes extends from SW. USA into Argentina and the area of the greatest diversity is in S. Central Mexico (Neher, 1968).

TAGETES PATULA L. Marigold, Flor del muerto. 2n=48, genome formula ApApBpBp. Mexico. Probably originated by hybridization of T. erecta* and T. tenuifolia Cav. (2n=24, genome formula BtBt) or closely related species. Cultivated as an ornamental and for its medicinal properties. Spread throughout the world. At one time it was thought to have an Old World origin because of the sacred role in the Hindu religion (Anderson, 1952). However, its role might have been promoted by the sacredness of the yellow colour in India.

Convolvulaceae

IPOMOEA BATATAS (L.) Poir. in Lam. Sweet potato. 2n=6x=90, genome formula BBBBBB. Unknown wild. With long cultivation, mutation and hybridization, sweet potato is very variable and many types have been classed as separate species, like I. tiliacea (Willd.) Choisy and I. triloba L. So descriptions of Ipomoea species before Austin (1977, 1978) should be treated with care. Nishiyama's I. trifida is a feral I. batatas; Nishiyama's K233, Jones' 67.50 both from Mexico and Jones' 71.3 from Colombia and Jones' 73.1 from Ecuador are 4x derivatives of I. batatas x I. trifida* (Austin, 1977).

Sweet potato was already cultivated in Polynesia in pre-Columbian times. Whether it was brought there as tubers by man or reached it as capsules or on drifting material by sea-currents (Purseglove, 1968) is not yet known. Sweet potato is cultivated in many tropical countries.

IPOMOEA PURGA (Wender.) Hayne (syn. Exogonium purga (Wender.) Benth.). Jalap. 2n=24-28. E. Mexico, S. Mexico and C. Panama. Cultivated in Mexico, the West Indies and later India for its medicinal tubers.

IPOMOEA TRIFIDA (H.B.K.). G. Don. 2n=2x=30. Mexico and Caribbean to N. Colombia and Venezuela. Common weed. Many chromosome counts attributed to this species refer to I. batatas*. According to Austin (1977), Nishiyama's I. trifida is a feral I. batatas.

Cucurbitaceae

CUCURBITA FICIFOLIA Bouché. Malabar gourd, Fig-leaf gourd. 2n=40, (42). Highlands of Mexico and America. This species might be a derivative of C. lundelliana* (Whitaker & Davis, 1962).

CUCURBITA MIXTA Pang. Pumpkin, Winter squash, Walnut squash. 2n=40. It probably derives from C. lundelliana Baily in C. America and S. Mexico. It appears that it was widely distributed in N. Mexico and SW. USA in pre-Colombian times (Purseglove, 1968). It is a primitive horticultural crop with little fruit flesh. It crosses with C. moschata* and has been described as belonging to this species. It developed later than C. maxima* and C. pepo*.

CUCURBITA MOSCHATA Duch. Cushaw, China squash, Pumpkin, Winter squash. 2n=(24), 40. From Mexico to Peru. Domesticated in 1800-1400 BC. (Willey, 1962). Cultivated throughout the world. Whitaker & Davis (1962) suggested it to be a derivative of C. lundelliana*.

CUCURBITA PEPO L. Marrow, Zucchini, Pumpkin. 2n=(24, 28), 40, (40-42, 44-46). Whitaker & Davis (1962) suggested that his species is a possible derivative of C. lundelliana Bailey, wild gourd, 2n=40, spreading into N. Mexico and SW. USA. In Texas the related wild C. texana Gray is found. This species is either a weedy offspring of C. pepo or may have been involved in the latter's formation. Whitaker & Cutler (1969) observed one seed in a layer dated c. 8750-7840 BC. in a cave in Mexico.

Var. ovifera (L.) Alef. is cultivated for its ornamental fruits.

CYCLANTHERA PEDATA Schrad. 2n=32. Cultivated in Mexico for its young fruits and shoots.

POLAKOWSKIA TACACCO Pitt. Tacaco. 2n= . Costa Rica. Semi-cultivated for its fruits.

SECHIUM EDULE Schwartz (syn. Chayote edulis Jacq.). Chayote, Guisquil, Christophine. 2n=24. Mountanous America and Mexico. Centre of variation is from Guatemala to Panama. It was a common crop among the Aztecs before Spanish conquest. A perennial vine now grown in subtrop. N. America, Africa and Europe. Insect pollination, resulting in selfing, crossing and vivipary.

Dioscoreaceae

DIOSCOREA FLORIBUNDA Mart. & Gal. 2n=36, 54. S. Mexico and adjacent areas of C. America. Cultivated in America to yield sapogenin (Coursey, 1967).

Ebenaceae

DIOSPYROS EBENASTER Retz. Black sapote, Zapote negro. 2n= . Probably Mexico. Cultivated for its fruits.

Ehretiaceae

CORDIA DODECANDRA DC. Copte, Siricote. 2n= . Mexico. A tall tree cultivated for its fruits.

Elaeocarpaceae

MUNTINGIA CALCABURA L. Panama berry, Capulin. 2n= . Widely cultivated for its sweet edible fruits.

Euphorbiaceae

JATROPHA ACONITIFOLIA Mill. (syn. Cnidoscolus chayamansa McVaugh.). 2n= . A shrub. Cultivated in the Yucatan area, Mexico. Young shoots and leaves are eaten as a pot herb. During do-

mestication, forms with fewer stinging hairs
were selected for (Dressler, 1953).

MANIHOT ESCULENTA Crantz. Cassava, Manioc,
Manihot, Yucca. 2n=36. Schmidt (1951, cited
by Nassar, 1978) stated that cassava was taken
by Amer-indians from the N. Amazon to Mexico
some 1000 years ago. But Roger (1963) mentioned
that cassava could have been domesticated in
Mexico too, because there is no reason to ex-
clude domestication of roots in the Mexican
seed-type agriculture. If so, one would expect
wild ancestral species there.

Cassava is cultivated in W. and S. Mexico,
C. America including parts of Guatemala. There
are only sweet cultivars in Mexico, where they
have been developed and whence they have spread.
However sweet types in Brazil could have developed locally. More research is needed.

Gramineae

AXONOPUS COMPRESSUS (Swartz) Beauv. Carpet
grass. 2n=40, 50, 60. C. America and the West
Indies. A perennial tropical grass suitable
for lawns and permanent pasture.

ORYZA ALTA*

ORYZA LATIFOLIA*

ORYZA PERENNIS Moench. 2n=24, genome formula
AA. For distribution see p. 74. In America var.
cubensis (O. cubensis Ekman), the American race
(2n=24, genome formula AA) of this species developed. Gopalakrishnan & Sampat (1966) suggested that O. perennis entered America as a
weed of O. sativa in post-Columbian times.

PANICUM SONORUM Beal. Sauwi. 2n=   . Sonora of
of Mexico and adjacent Arizona. Cultivated by
Guarijio Indians as a cereal (Dressler, 1953;
Gentry, 1942).

PANICUM VIRGATUM L. Switch grass. 2n=36, 72
and aneuploids. N. and C. America. Cultivated
as cattle food.

SETARIA GENICULATA (Lam.) Beauv. 2n=36, 72. An
early crop in Tehuacan Valley, Mexico; now replaced by maize and European food crops.

SETARIA MACROSTACHYA HBK. 2n=54, 72. An early
crop in Tehuacan Valley, Mexico; now replaced
by maize and European food crops.

TRIPSACUM ANDERSONII Gray. Guatemala grass.
2n=64. C. and S. America. This species combines 54 Tripsacum and 10 Zea chromosomes in
its genome. It is widely cultivated in trop.
America as a fodder, and to indicate property
boundaries (de Wet et al., 1976).

TRIPSACUM DACTYLOIDES (L.) L. Gamma grass. 2n=
36, 72. C. USA to Paraguay. Excellent cultivated fodder grass, often irrigated. Gene exchange with Zea mays is possible (Randolph,

1970; de Wet & Harlan, 1974).

TRIPSACUM LANCEOLATUM Rupr. ex Fourn. (syn. T.
lemmoni Vasey). 2n=72. Mountains of arid S.
Arizona and adjacent Sonora. Excellent fodder.

TRIPSACUM LATIFOLIUM Hitchc. 2n=36, 72. C.
America. Excellent trop. fodder.

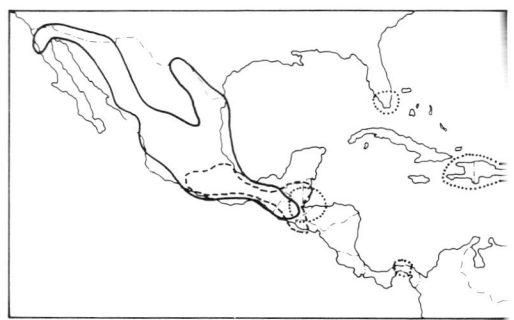

Tripsacum latifolium (···), T. lanceolatum
(—) and T. laxum (---)(Randolph, 1970).

TRIPSACUM LAXUM Nash. 2n=36, 72. Veracruz Oaxaca,
Mexico. Excellent fodder, for the wet tropics.

TRIPSACUM MAIZAR Hern. & Randolph. 2n=36, 72
C. Mexico. Robust species, widely grazed when
young.

TRIPSACUM PILOSUM Scribn. & Merr. 2n=36, 72.
C. America. Excellent fodder.

TRIPSACUM ZOPILOTENSE Hern. & Randolph. 2n=72,
76. Arid W. Central Mexico. The only Tripsacum
species without rhizomes. Extensively grazed

ZEA DIPLOPERENNIS Iltis, Doebley & Guzman. Diploid perennial teosinte. 2n=20. Jalisco, Mexico. Crosses with maize to produce fertile hybrids (Iltis et al., 1979).

ZEA LUSURIANS (Durieu & Ascherson) Bird. Guatemala teosinte. 2n=20. Guatemala and Honduras.
Crosses readily with maize to produce fertile
hybrids.

ZEA MAYS L. ssp. mays. Maize, Corn. 2n=20. The
'origin' of maize has been subject to much discussion and research. The present conclusion
is that teosinte (Z. mexicana) is the wild
parent of maize (de Wet et al., 1971; de Wet
& Harlan, 1972; Galinat, 1971; J.G. Waines,
see Galinat, 1971). Other theories were that
maize derived from hybridization of primitive
maize, teosinte and Tripsacum ssp. when the
first reached C. America from S. America. If
so wild maize - a podcorn - tunicata Sturt. -
should have been extinct by now. This complete
disappearance of wild maize would have been
caused by a number of factors such as intro-

gression of genes of domesticated maize, the use of the habitats of wild maize for maize cultivation and the grazing of Old World animals.

The earliest finds of maize were tiny cobs (2-3 cm) in the Bat Cave of Tehuacan, Mexico. They have been dated about 3600 BC. Two types have been observed: 1. a podcorn and 2. a popcorn - everata Sturt. (syn. praecox) (Mac-Neish, 1964; Mangelsdorf et al., 1964). In another cave, early Bat Cave-like maize and teosints have been identified. The material dates from about 2200 BC. Early tripsacoid maize dates from 2300-1500 BC. MacNeish (1964a, b) supposed that about 5000 BC. wild maize i.e. teosinte was cultivated.

From C. America maize reached S. America where its development became more advanced (p. 171). Advanced varieties were returned to C. America. For Mexico they have been described as Pre-Columbian Exotic Races comprising of 4 varieties: Cacahuacinthe, Harinoso de Ocho, Olotón and Maize Dulce (Wellhausen et al., 1952). Where they hybridized with primitive Mexican Ancient Indigenous Races: Palomero Toluqueno, Arrocillo Amarillo, Chapalote and Nal-Tel. This resulted in a new group of varieties called: Prehistoric Mestizos. Introgression with teosinte most likely has taken place too. Wellhausen et al. (1952) described 13 races.

Modern incipient Races have developed since the Conquest. Wellhausen et al. (1952) described four of them. Some being very recently developed. The same development took place in Guatemala (Wellhausen et al., 1957).

From C. America maize also spread to N. America (p. 203).

De Wet et al. (1972) suggested that the 'tripsacoid' races of maize in S. America were originally introduced from Mexico or C. America where they inherited their 'tripsacoid' characteristics through introgression with teosinte. It is also possible that these races represent relics which retain some original teosinte-like characteristics inherited from the maize progenitor.

The oldest domesticated maize varieties had a string (slender) cob. This primitive characteristic is still found in some relic cultivars like Confite Morocho, which is the most primitive living cultivar (Galinat, 1969). It comes from Peru. The domesticated recessive character thick cob is conditioned in the Corn Belt dent by 3 major loci. One allele derives from northern flint which obtained it from Maize de Ocho. It is possible that this allele introgressed from Tripsacum sp. probably T. dactyloides*. Perhaps this introgression could be traced to S. America by way of the cultivars Cabuya and Sabanero (Galinat, 1969). However, de Wet et al. (1972) believed that no introgression exists between maize and Tripsacum species. So cv. Chococena is not a hybrid of cv. Confite (ex Peru) and a Columbian Tripsacum as has been suggested.

The source(s) of other two recessive alleles is not fully understood. One of these alleles produces high condensation of staminate spike-lets in the tassel branches and the other increases tassel branching. If the first allele is absent the expression of the second is complete resulting in profuse branching like the mutant ramosa. Some cultivars of the southern dent and 'bear paw' popcorn appear to have this high condensation-ramosa type of thick cob. The degree of fasciation with which this type of thick cob may be asociated seems to have been modified by teosinte introgression, teosinte gene(s) suppressing fasciation. It is suspected that the Corn Belt dents obtained these two pairs of recessive alleles from the southern dents (Galinat, 1969).

Other morphological changes due to domestication are a development of a complete husk coverage of the mature ear, the development of female inflorescense, a reduction of the glumes of the female inflorescense, an arrangement of spikelets in a higher row number, a development of the cupules and an increase of the length of the styles (silk). Some cultivars have an ear length up to 45 cm. Hybrid maize varieties may produce more than 1000 kernels per cob while the Tehuacan maize has about 40 kernels per cob.

The terminal inflorescense becomes entirely staminate being a lax plume with waving branches (Galinat, 1969).

A flow of teosinte genes to maize still exists where maize cultivation is primitive and teosinte is present. Maize x teosinte hybrids are actually cultivated. Maize may show pronounced signs of 'tripsacoid' i.e. teosinte germ plasm such as induration of the lower glume and a straight rigid ear.

Less genes flow from maize to teosinte since the genetic incorporation of a maize-like rachis results in the inability to disperse seed and so to the extinction of teosinte introgressed with maize (Wilkes, 1970). Extensive gene exchange in both directions is evident around Chalco, S. of Mexico City, where the weedy teosinte race mimics the local race of maize in size, colour and pubescence. These weeds remain teosintoid with respect to female inflorescense structure. In many other areas of Mexico, particular the Rio Balsas Valley on the W. escarpment, W. of Mexico City, teosinte behaves essentially as a wild grass, but modern development leads to an increased infiltration of maize genes into teosinte.

Several types of maize are cultivated. An improved popcorn is being cultivated in USA, Mexico and elsewhere. Softcorn - amylacea Sturt. - predominates in the Andean region. Flint maize, flint corn - indurata Sturt. - predominates in N. Colombia and E. S. America. Sweet corn - saccharata Sturt. (syn. rugosa Bonof.) - was cultivated for the preparation of South American and Mexican beer. At present it is mainly cultivated in USA. Waxy maize - ceritina Kulesh. - cultivated in the Americas and in E. Asia. Dent maize - indenta Sturt. is the main type of the Corn Belt of USA and N. Mexico. A hybrid of a late-maturing dent Gourd Slide cultivated in the south, and an early ma-

turing flint maize, mainly cultivated in the
north. The latter derives from Maiz Ocho.

From C. and S. America maize was taken to
Europe (p. 135), Asia (p. 33) and Africa (p.
117), where secondary centres of diversity
developed.

At present flint maize, flint corn - indurata Sturt. - is quite common in C. America.

Derivatives of Z. mays /2* Z. mexicana are
used for fodder. These are called maisinte
(Prasad & Chaudhuri, 1968).

ZEA MAYS ssp. mexicana (Schrader) Iltis (syn.
Z. mexicana (Schrader) Kunze, Euchlaena mexicana Schrader). Mexican teosinte. 2n=20. C.
Plateau and Valley of Mexico. MacNeish (1964a,
b) suggested that about 5000 BC. wild maize i.e.
teosinte was cultivated. It is the ancestor
of maize, Zea mays*. Owing to natural hybridization between maize and teosinte there is a
gene flow from teosinte to maize, while that

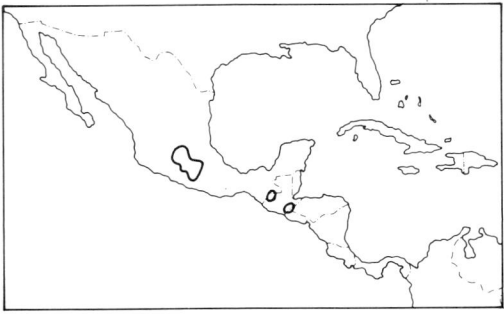

Zea mexicana (Wilkes, 1967).

gene flow from teosinte to maize, while that
of maize to teosinte is very small (see p.
190). This may happen between the earliest
flowering teosinte plants and the latest of
maize. Teosinte plants may grow unnoticed in
a maize field and may be harvested together
with its leader crop. Seeds may be spread either during the transport or storage of the
crop or in manure (Wilkes, 1967). Attempts
have been made to cultivate teosinte as a fodder, but it yields less than sorghum. This
subspecies is often found as a weed in fields
of maize, and introgresses naturally with domesticated maize. See also Z. mays ssp. par-
viglumis*.

Iridaceae

TRIGIDIA PAVONIA (L.f.) DC. Cacomite, Tiger
flower. 2n=26, 28. Mexico. Naturalized in most
of C. America, Colombia, Bolivia, Peru and Brazil. Easily cultivated. Soon escapes into maize
fields etc. as a weed. The Aztecs cultivated
this species for almost a 1000 years. Cultivated now as an ornamental which resulted in
spontaneous variations in colour and size (Mol-

seed, 1970).

Juglandaceae

CARYA PECAN (Marsch.) Engl. & Graebn. Pecan.
2n=32. N. Mexico. Cultivated there. It resembles the walnut, Juglans regia* but the seed
has a better taste.

JUGLANS MOLLIS Engelm. Guatemala walnut. 2n=
. Mexico and Guatemala. Similar to the walnut
(J. regia*).

Labiatae

HYPTIS SUAVEOLENS Poit. 2n=28, 32. Cultivated
mainly in Mexico. A variable and weedy plant
now occurring in many parts of the tropics.

SALVIA CHIA Fern. Chia. 2n=   . Mexico. Seeds
are used to prepare a beverage and for pain-
ting or medicine.

SALVIA DIVINORUM Epling & Jativa-M. 2n=   .
Wild unknown. Cultivated in NE. Oaxaca, Mexico.
Vegetatively propagated (Schultes & Hofmann,
1973). Perhaps one clone. Closely related to
S. cyanca Lindl. (2n=   ) of C. Mexico.

Lauraceae

PERSEA AMERICANA Miller. Avocado. 2n=24, (36,
48). Mexico and C. America. There are three
geographical races: (1) Mexican (also named
P. americana var. drymifolia Mez. syn. P.
drymifolia Cham. & Schlecht.) from the Mexican
highlands where wild progenitors have been
found. Its anisescented leaves, hardiness and
small fruits are characteristics. (2) Guatemalan, from the Guatemalan highlands. Wild
progenitors have been found in this area. (3)
West Indian, from the Guatemalan lowlands which
has only spread to the West Indies in post-
Columbian times (Purseglove, 1968). Where these
races grow together - either in their native
region or elsewhere - hybrids originate (Bergh,
1969). Electrophoretic studies showed that the
Guatemalan race is the most ancient form (Gar-
cía & Tsunewaki, 1977). The Mexican and West
Indian races have been described as var. americanum.

PERSEA FLOCCOSA. 2n=24. Semi-cultivated in
Puebla-Veracruz area of Mexico.

PERSEA SCHIEDEANA Ness. Coyo avocado. 2n=24.
From Guatemala to Mexico. Semi-cultivated
chiefly in Orizaba, Mexico for its edible
fruits (Bergh, 1969).

Leguminosae

CALOPOGONIUM MUCUNOIDES Desv. 2n=   . Trop. A-
merica. A cover crop and green manure. Cultivated in the tropics where it has naturalized.

CANAVALIA CAMYLOCARPA Piper. Babricon bean.

2n=   . The West Indies. Cultivated as a green manure.

CROTALARIA LONGIROSTRATA Hook. & Arn. Much of Mexico and C. America (Dressler, 1953). A large herb cultivated in Guatemala as a potherb.

DESMODIUM TORTUOSUM (Sw.) DC. (syn. Meibomia purpurea (Mill.) Vail.). Florida clover, Giant beggarsweed. 2n=22. C. America, Florida, West Indies and N. South America. A perennial herb used as a green manure and forage crop.

DESMODIUM UNCINATUM*

ENTEROLOBIUM CYCLOCARPUM (Jacq.) Griseb. 2n= 26. Mexico, C. America, N. South America and West Indies. Cultivated as a shade tree.

INGA DULCIS. 2n=   . Mexico. Used as a shade tree and hedge plant.

INGA EDULIS Mart. Food inga. 2n=26. Mexico and C. America. Used as a shade tree.

INGA GOLDMANII Pittier. 2n=   . C. America. Used as a shade tree.

INGA LAURINA (Sw.) Willd. Sackysac. 2n=   . C. America and the West Indies. It has edible fruits. Used as a shade tree in coffee plantations in the New World (Purseglove, 1968).

INGA LEPTOLOBA Schlecht. 2n=   . Mexico, C. and S. America. Used as a shade tree.

INGA PITTIERI Micheli. 2n=   . C. America. Used as a shade tree.

LEUCAENA LEUCOCEPHALA (Lam.) de Wit (syn. L. glauca (Willd.) Benth., L. latisiliqua (L.) Gillis. Leucaena. 2n=104. C. America, spread to the Caribbean islands, the Philippines, SE. Asia and elsewhere. Var. glabrata is L. glabrata Rose.

Three types are recognized: (1) Hawaiian type, a short bush with year round flowering causing a high seed production and easily becoming a pest weed. (2) Salvador type, a tall tree of the inland forests of C. America. Mexican material coming through the Philippines to Hawaii was the source of the Hawaiian Giants cultivar group bred for timber. (3) Peru type, an extensively branching tree extremely rich in foliage. Forage cultivars derive from this type; forage cultivar Cunningham is a hybrid of Salvador type and Peru type. Cultivars poor in mimosin are bred for.

Leucaena is autogamous. Since 1900 hybrids (2n=80) of L. leucocephala and L. pulverulenta (Schlecht.) Benth., 2n=56, have developed in Indonesia and shade trees and forage cultivars low in mimosin. They are partially sterile and cannot become a pest weed (Vietmeyer & Cottons. (1977).

MACROPTILUM ATROPURPUREUM (DC) Urb. (syn. Pha-

seolus atropurpureus DC). Siratro. 2n=22. S. Texas, New Mexico (USA), Mexico, C. America, Colombia, Ecuador, Peru and Argentina. Material from Mexico has recently been domesticated in Australia for tropical pasture.

MIMOSA INVISA Mart. 2n=24, 26. C. and S. America. In Java and elsewhere it is used as a cover and green manure. The spiny stem is a disadvantage. Var. inermis Adelb. is a useful selection.

PACHYRHIZUS EROSUS (L.) Urban. (syn. P. angulatus Rich. ex DC., P. bulbosus (L.) Kurz.). Yam bean, Jicama. 2n=22. Mexico and N. Central America. Cultivated there in pre-Columbian times. Taken to Asia and cultivated there. In S. China and Thailand it has run wild (Clausen, 1944). Var. palmatilobus (DC.) Clausen is probably P. palmatilobus Benth. & Hook.

PHASEOLUS ACUTIFOLIUS Gray. Tepary bean. 2n= 2x=22. From N. Central Arizona (USA) to Guatemala. Found in Mexico in layers dating from 3000 BC. A very polymorphic species with drought resistance, high protein content and high productivity. Wild specimens are annuals with indeterminate climbing habit and cleistogamous flowers. They belong to var. tenuifolius Gray; cultivated types belong to var. latifolius Freeman (Baudet, 1977b). However Nabham & Felger (1978) stated that some wild types belong to the latter variety.

PHASEOLUS COCCINEUS L. Scarlet Runner, Runner bean. 2n=22. Mexico and Guatemala. Domesticated there before 300 BC., perhaps for its thick roots. The cultivated form is var. coccineus, the wild form has not yet been described. Cultivated in the Americas and Eurasia for food, for fodder and as an ornamental. For Ph. vulgaris* it is a source of halo blight resistance, absence of parchment and string. Smartt (1973) suggested that the cultigen ssp. darwinianus Hdz. X. & Miranda C. may have an independent domestication of a yet unknown ancestral form. He stated that a special taxonomic treatment may be necessary. Baudet (1977b) suggested that this subspecies is also described as Ph. polyanthus Greenm. but Smartt (1973) stated that this latter species is related to Ph. vulgaris*. It sometimes crosses with Ph. vulgaris*.

PHASEOLUS LUNATUS L. Sieva bean, Lima bean. 2n=22. C. America and in the Andes from Peru to Argentine. Kaplan (1965) showed that the small lima bean of Mexico may have arisen in the Pacific coastal foothills of Mexico and that the big lima bean of Peru was first domesticated in the Andean highlands (p. 174).

Baudet (1977a) divided the species into a wild form var. silvester Baudet and the cultivated form var. lunatus, which is subdivided into three cultivar groups: (1) Lima (Big Lima/True Lima) with large flat seeds corresponding to Ph. inamoenus L.; (2) Sieva (Small Lima) with medium-sized seeds corresponding to Ph. lunatus

L. sensu stricto; and (3) Potato with small globular seeds corresponding to Ph. bipunctatus
Jacq.

PHASEOLUS RETUSUS Benth. Metcalf bean. 2n=   .
Texas, Arizona and New Mexico, USA. Occasionally
cultivated.

PHASEOLUS VULGARIS L. Common bean. 2n=22. Kaplan (1981) suggested a multiple domestication
within C. America from a widespread and poly-
morphus species. It has been suggested that
this domestication may have taken place between
5000 and 3000 BC. From C. America it would have
spread to other parts of America (Kaplan, 1965).
However, Heiser (1965) believed in an independent domestication from the closely related Ph.
aborigineus Burk. (syn. Ph. vulgaris L. var.
aborigineus (Burk.) Baudet), 2n=22, which occurs
wild in N. Argentina, Bolivia, Peru, Ecuador,
Colombia and Venezuela. In Argentina and Venezuela, the wild plant is harvested (Berglund-
Brücher & Brücher, 1976). When Ph. vulgaris
reached the area of Ph. aborigineus, aborigineus
genes may have introgressed into vulgaris. However, Gentry (1969) and Baudet (1977b) suggested
that Ph. aborigineus could be a naturalized type.
    Gentry (1969) pointed out that a wild type of
Ph. vulgaris grows in C. America and is the parent of the cultivated forms. From this wild
type the cultivated forms derive.
    Ph. arborigineus was reduced by Burkart &
Bücher (1953) to a subspecies level of Ph. vulgaris. They suggested that this subspecies was
not taken to S. America. A study of the wild
and cultivated beans of this area should cla-
rify whether this is so or whether ssp. arbori-
gineus is an escape of early cultivated forms
(Gentry, 1969). Its primary centre of diversity
is in Mexico. Here introgression between cultivated and wild Ph. vulgaris and P. coccineus*
occurs (Wall, 1970). The purple-marbled culti-

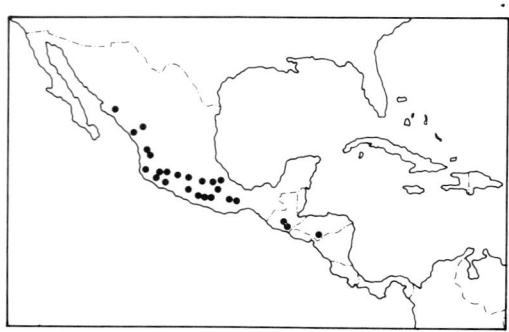

Phaseolus vulgaris (Gentry, 1969).

vars like Kievitsboon in the Netherlands may
derive from such introgression. Secondary centres in Eurasia (p. 40).

PITHECELLOBIUM DULCE Benth. Manila tamarind.
2n=26. Mexico to N. South America. The arillus
is edible. A tree planted in hedges.

SOPHORA SECUNDIFLORA (Ort.) Lagasca ex De Candolle. Mescal bean, Red bean, Coral bean. 2n=
18. N. Mexico to Texas and New Mexico. Used
as hallucinogen. Often planted as an ornamental.

TEPHROSIA SINGAPOU (Buc'hoz) A. Cheval. (syn.
T. toxicaria (Sw.) Pers.) 2n=22. Mexico and C
America to Peru and N. Brazil. Cultivated as
a fish poison.

    Malpighiaceae

BUNCHOSIA COSTARICENSIS Rose. 2n=   . Costa
Rica. Cultivated for its fruits.

MALPIGHIA URENS L. Barbados cherry. 2n=   .
The West Indies. Cultivated for its fruits.

    Malvaceae

GOSSYPIUM ARIDUM (Rose & Standley) Skovsted.
2n=26, genome formula D_4D_4. Mexico.

GOSSYPIUM ARMOURIANUM Kearney. 2n=26, genome
formula $D_{2-1}D_{2-1}$. San Marcos Islands, Gulf of
California.

GOSSYPIUM GOSSYPIOIDES (Ulb.) Standley. 2n=26,
genome formula D_6D_6. Mexico. It crosses poorly
with most of the species of the D genome. Its
seed-protein pattern is different from the D
genome species. However, it is similar to the
pattern of G. klotzschianum* (Cherry et al.,
1970).

GOSSYPIUM HARKNESSII Brandg. 2n=26, genome formula $D_{2-2}D_{2-2}$. The islands and coasts of the
Gulf of California. Var. davidsonii is, ac-
cording to Bahavandoss & Jayaraman (1973), the
progenitor of the D genome found in 4x species.

GOSSYPIUM HIRSUTUM L. Upland cotton. 2n=52, genome formula (AADD). The current theory is that
this species originated in C. America. Harland
(1970) suggested that its centre of origin is
in S. America (p. 176), while C. America is an
important secondary centre of diversity. Upland
cotton is cultivated in USA, in Africa except
for the Nile Delta (p. 176), in C. Asia, India
(Cambodia type, p. 59), S. America, SE. China,
Indochina and elsewhere. In C. America and the
West Indian islands race marie galante is found
while race punctatum is found around the coasts
of the Gulf of Mexico from Florida to Yucatan
in the Bahamas and on some West Indian islands.
It was taken to W. Africa where it spread in the
zone south of the Sahara, to Réunion, the Malabar Coast of India, Polynesia, the Marquesas,
Fiji and N. Australia. A great diversity was
found in N. Australia.
    Race yucatense is probably a cotton that has
run wild and is now naturalized into natural
vegetation of the coastal sand dunes of the

Progeso area, Mexico.

Race morilli is found in Oaxaca, Peubla and Morelos, C. Mexico. A perennial cotton with a bushy form and broad, intensely hairy leaves.

Race palmeri in the state Guerrero, Mexico. It has deeply dissected leaves and strong anthocyanin pigmentation.

Race latifolium is found in Chiapas, Mexico and neighbouring regions of Guatemala. An annual cotton. Throughout its territory a small-fruited form is found. A large-fruited form grows in the vicinity of Acala, Chiapas. This race appears to be the foundation stock of all the annual G. hirsutum cottons (Hutchinson, 1962).

GOSSYPIUM KLOTZSCHIANUM Andersson var. davidsonii (Kellogs) Saunders. 2n=26, genome formula $D_{3-D}D_{3-D}$. Shores of the Gulf of California and the Revilla Gigedo islands. Related to the plants of this species found on the Galapagos Islands (p. 176).

GOSSYPIUM LOBATUM Gentry. 2n=26, genome formula D_7D_7. Mexico.

GOSSYPIUM THURBERI Todaro. 2n=26, genome formula D_1D_1. Arizona, USA and Sonora and SW. Chihuahua, Mexico. At one time it was thought to be the American parent of G. herbaceum* and G. barbadense*.

GOSSYPIUM TRILOBUM (Sess. & Moc. ex DC.) Skovsted. (syn. Ingenhouzia triloba Moc. & Sess. ex DC.). 2n=26. C. Mexico (Fryxell & Parks, 1967).

Moraceae

BROSIMUM ALICASTRUM Swartz. Ramon, Ramon breadnut tree. 2n=26. Trop. America. Seeds are edible when roasted. Probably planted by the Maya (Lundell, 1937).

CASTILLA ELASTICA Cerv. Arbol del Hule. 2n=28. S. Mexico and C. America. Cultivated in C. America, Trinidad and Tobago, and Java at the end of the 19th Century. Now replaced by hevea rubber.

Myrtaceae

PIMENTA DIOICA (L.) Merr. (syn. P. officinalis Lindl.). Allspice, Pimento. 2n=22. The West Indies and C. America. Spread to other countries.

PSIDIUM FRIEDRICHSTHALIANUM (Berg.) Nied. Costa Rican guava. 2n= . C. America. A small tree cultivated for its acid fruits.

PSIDIUM GUAJAVA L. Guava. 2n=22, 4x=44. Trop. America. Cultivated there. In 1526 Oviedo reported that improved forms were cultivated in the West Indies. Spread through the tropics, where guava may be found naturalized.

PSIDIUM MOLLE Bertol. Guisare. 2n=5x=55. S.

Mexico and C. America. Cultivated for its fruits.

PSIDIUM SARTORIANUM (Berg.) Nied. Pichiché, Arrayan, Guayabillo. 2n= . Mexico. Cultivated there.

Onagraceae

OENOTHERA BIENNIS L. (syn. Onagra biennis Scop.). Evening primrose. 2n=14. N. America to Mexico. Run wild over a large part of the world. Cultivated as a fodder crop.

Orchidaceae

VANILLA FRAGRANS (Salisb.) Ames. (syn. V. planifolia Andrews). Vanilla. 2n=(28-32), 32. C. America, SE. Mexico and the Antilles. A perennial vine cultivated in the tropics and S. Mexico for its aromatic fruits.

VANILLA POMPONA Schiede (syn. V. grandiflora Lindl.). West Indian vanilla. 2n=32. SE. Mexico, C. America and N. South America. A perennial vine on Tahiti, Martinique and Guadeloupe for its aromatic fruits.

Palmae

CHAMAEDOREA TEPEJILOTE Liebm. 2n=32. Ch. wendlandiana (Oerst.) Hemsl. 2n= . At least one, and probably several, species of this genus are cultivated in S. Mexico and C. America. The young staminate flower clusters are used as a vegetable (Dressler, 1953).

GUILIELMA GASIPAES*

Papaveraceae

ARGEMONE MEXICANA L. Mexican prickly poppy. 2n=28. SW. USA and Mexico. Cultivated in Mali. Seeds are used to prepare oil. Also an ornamental.

Passifloraceae

PASSIFLORA SEEMANNII Griseb. 2n=18. Panama and Andes of Colombia.

Polygonaceae

COCCOLOBA UNIFERA L. Seaside grape. 2n= . Trop. America. A shrub or tree cultivated for its edible fruits.

RUMES HYMENOSEPALUS Torr. Canaigre, Wild rhubarb, Pie dock, Sour dock, Tanner's dock. 2n=100. SW. USA and adjacent Mexico. A perennial herb occasionally cultivated.

Portulacaceae

CLAYTONIA PERFOLIATA Donn. ex Willd. (syn. Montia perfoliata How.). Winter purslane, Miner's lettuce. 2n=36. N. America and Mexico. Cultivated as a vegetable.

PORTULACA OLERACEA L. Purslane. 2n=2x=18, 4x=
36, 6x=54. Widespread. The distribution of the
2x, 4x and 6x wild and weedy subspecies shows
that Mexico is one of the centres of diversity
(Danin et al., 1978). The cultivated type probably developed in Europe (p. 158).

Rosaceae

CRATAEGUS PUBESCENS (H.B.K.) Steud. (syn. C.
stipulosa (H.B.K.) Steud.). 2n=34. A tree widely cultivated in Mexico and Guatemala for its
fruits.

Rutaceae

CASIMIROA EDULIS La Llave & Lex. White sapote,
Zapote Blanco. 2n=36. Highlands of Mexico and
C. America. A fruit tree introduced to other
subtropical countries.

CITRUS PARADISI Macf. Grapefruit. 2n=18. Unknown wild. Closely related to C. grandis and
it probably is a bud mutation or a hybrid product of C. grandis and sweet orange (C. sinensis*). This must have occurred in the West Indies some time before 1750 (Purseglove, 1968).
It is widely cultivated in the (sub)tropics.
    Hybrids with other Citrus-species have been
obtained, Sopomaldin is a hybrid with C. mitis
(Calamondin), Siamelo with C. reticulata* (King
Orange), Tangelo with the same species var. deliciosa (Tangerine), Satsumelo with the same
species (Satsuma) and Chironja with C. sinensis* (Sweet Orange). Tangelolo is a hybrid
of grapefruit with Tangelo.

Sapotaceae

CALOCARPUM SAPOTA (Jacq.) Merr. (syn. C. mammosum Pierre, Achras mammosa L.). Mamey sapote,
Sapote, Marmelade plum, Mamey colorado. 2n=   .
C. America. A tree cultivated in the tropics
for its fruits.

CALOCARPUM VIRIDE Pitt. Green sapote. 2n=   .
Guatemala to Costa Rica. A tree cultivated for
its fruits.

CHRYSOPHYLLIUM CAINITO L. Star apple. 2n=52.
West Indies and C. America. The pulp is edible.
Also an ornamental.

LUCUMA BIFERA Mol. Egg fruit. 2n=   . Chile and
Peru. Cultivated there for its fruits.

LUCUMA SALICIFOLIA H.B.K. (syn. Pouteria campechiana (H.B.K.) Baenhi). Yellow sapote, Zapote amarillo. 2n=   . Mexico and C. America.
Cultivated for its fruits.

MANILKARA ACHRAS (Mill.) Fosberg (syn. Achras
zapota L., M. zapotilla (Jacq.) Gilly). Sapo-
dilla, Chiku. 2n=26. Mexico and C. America.
Cultivated now in the tropics for its fruits
and gum (chickle) for chewing-gum production.

Simaroubaceae

SIMAROUBA GLAUCA DC. Aceituno. 2n=   . S. Florida to Costa Rica. In El Salvador and elsewhere attempts are made to cultivate it as an
oil crop.

Simmondsiaceae

SIMMONDSIA CHINENSIS (Link) Nutt. (syn. S.
californica Nutt). Jojoba, Pignut, Goatnut.
2n=56, c. 100. California and adjacent Mexico.
Dioecious. It is now being domesticated in
California. It yields a stable liquid wax, jojoba oil.

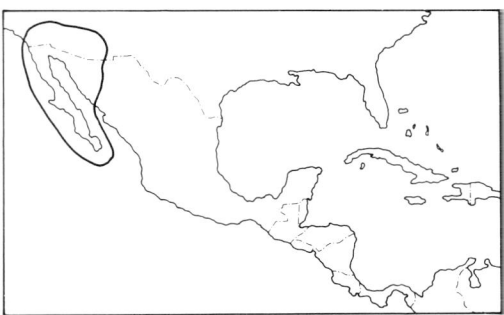

Simmondsia chinensis (Gentry, 1958).

Solanaceae

CAPSICUM ANNUUM L. Bell pepper, Cayenne pepper,
Mexican chili. 2n=24. Wild variety in S. USA
West Indies, Mexico, C. America and Colombia
Primary centre in Mexico. Secondary centres
in Europe (p. 162) and Asia (p. 79). Originally
the cultivars were limited to C. America. The
wild type is the bird pepper, var. aviculare
(Dierbach) D'Arcy & Eshb. (syn. glabriusculum
(Dunal) Heiser & Pickersgill). The domesticated
type is var. annuum.

CAPSICUM FRUTESCENS L. Tobasco pepper. 2n=24
This species consists of wild types and derived cultivars, like the Tobasco peppers. Widespread as a weed and as cultivars in Mexico,
C. America and lowland S. America. It might be
the parental species of C. chinense*.

PHYSALIS IXOCARPA Brot. Tomatl, Miltomate, Husk
tomato, Tomatillo. 2n=24. Mexico. There and
in Guatemala this vegetable is cultivated.

SOLANUM AGRIMONIFOLIUM Rydb. 2n=48. From C.
Mexico to Bolivia.

SOLANUM BRACHISTOTRICHUM (Bitt.) Rydb. 2n=24
NW. Mexico, in open pine and juniper forests
and amongst bushes and rocks. Resistant to the
green peach aphid, Myrus persicae Sulzer.

SOLANUM BREVICAULE Bitt. 2n=24. Ugent (1970a) grouped in this species wild diploid species as S. canasense Hawkes, S. brevicaule Bitt. s.s., S. raphanifolium Card. & Hawkes, S. leptophyes Bitt., S. soukupii Hawkes, S. multiinterruptum Bitt., S. abbottianum Juz., S. liriunianum Card. & Hawkes, S. spegazzinii Bitt. and S. vidaurrei Cárdenas. It is likely that from this complex species the diploid S. stenotomum* arose.

SOLANUM BULBOCASTANUM Dun. 2n=24, genome formula BB, (36, BBB). At medium altitudes from C. Mexico to Guatemala in grassland, waste places and forest glades and clearings. There are three subspecies (Hawkes, 1966):
   Ssp. Bulbocastanum (2n=24, 36) is found in S. Mexico, ssp. dolichophyllum (2n=24) in the Mexican states Morelos and Guerrero and ssp. partitum (2n=24) in S. Mexico and Guatemala.
   This B genome also constitutes two of the genomes of S. polytrichon* A_4A_4BB. The B genome is related to the A_4 genome and to the A_1 genome of S. phureja*. S. bulbocastanum crosses with S. tuberosum* and is used as a source of resistance to Phytophthora, X-virus, Y-virus, Colorado beetle and several aphids (vectors of virus diseases).

SOLANUM CARDIOPHYLLUM Lindl. 2n=24, 36. S. Mexico. In dry stony grassy and waste places, often as a weed in maize and bean fields. Ssp. ehrenbergii is found in N. Central to W. Mexico, ssp. cardiophyllum occurs in C. Mexico and ssp. lanceolatum in SE. to S. Mexico. Triploid forms are frequent in ssp. cardiophyllum. Ssp. ehrenbergii is one parent of S. sambucinum*.

SOLANUM CLARUM Corr. 2n=24. Guatemala, in the high mountains. Probably a link between Bulbocastana and Morelliformia series.

SOLANUM DEMISSUM Lindl. 2n=(36, 48), 72, genome formula $A_1A_1A_4A_4BB$. Nw. Mexico to Guatemala. An important source of disease resistance (Phytophthora, X-virus, Y-virus). The A_1-genome may have come from S. verrucosum*. One of the parental species of S. x edinense* and S. X semidemissum.

SOLANUM X EDINENSE Berthault. Mexican weed potato, Papa morado. 2n=60. Clones occur in and along the edges of cultivated field, irrigation ditches, roadsides thickets and forest fringes in the Central Volcani Cordillera of Mexico between 2000 and 3500 m. A source of Phytophthora and frost resistance. This 5x hybrid is a cross between S. tuberosum (group Andigena, 2n=4x=48) and S. demissum Lindl. (2n=6x=72) (Hawkes, 1966). S. demissum genes may introgress in the cultivated potato by backcrossing. Harvest of potato may contain tubers of S. X edinense and by trading the potato this weedy potato is also spread (Ugent, 1967).

SOLANUM GUERREROENSE Correll. 2n=72, genome formula $A_1A_1A_4A_4BB$. SW. Mexico. The A_1 genome may have come from S. verrucosum*.

SOLANUM HJERTINGII Hawk. 2n= . NE. Mexico, in pinon scrub and cultivated fields. Very similar to S. fendleri*. A source of resistance to the potato aphid, Macrosiphum euphorbiae Thomas.

SOLANUM HOUGASII Corr. 2n=72, genome formula $A_1A_1A_4A_4BB$. W. Central Mexico. The A_1 genome may have come from S. verrucosum*. Source of resistance to potato Y-virus.

SOLANUM IOPETALUM (Bitt.) Hawk. 2n=72, genome formula $A_1A_1A_4A_4BB$. W. and S. Mexico. It includes S. brachycarpum Corr. The A_1 genome may have come from S. verrucosum*.

SOLANUM JUGLANDIFOLIUM Dunn. 2n=24. Costa Rica. Little value to potato breeders because it does not bear stolons or tubers.

SOLANUM LEPTOSEPALUM Correll. 2n= . NE. Mexico and possibly in USA.

SOLANUM LESTERI Hawkes & Hjerting. 2n=24. Oaxaca, Mexico.

SOLANUM MICHOACANUM (Bitt.) Rydb. (syn. S. trifida Corr.). 2n=24. Michoacan and Jalisco, Mexico. In the pine forests and fields. Resistant to the green peach aphid, Myrus persicae Sulzer.

SOLANUM MORELLIFORME Bitt. & Muench. 2n=24. C. Mexico, southwards to Guatemala.

SOLANUM OXYCARPUM Schiede. 2n=48. E. Central Mexico, Honduras, Costa Rica and adjacent Panama.

SOLANUM PAPITA Rydb. 2n= . Similar to S. fendleri*.

SOLANUM PINNATISECTUM Dun. 2n=24. N. Central Mexico. A maize field weed. A source of resistance to Phytophthora, Y-virus and Colorado beetle. A parent of S. sambucinum*.

SOLANUM POLYADENIUM Greenm. 2n=24. C. Mexico. A source of Phytophthora resistance and, owing to its glandular hairs, of resistance to tarsonemid mite (Polyphago tarsonemus latus Banks).

SOLANUM POLYTRICHON Rydb. 2n=48, genome formula A_4A_4BB. NW. to N. Central Mexico. In waste places, shrubland and cultivated fields. Its genomes are related and also to the A_1 genome of S. phureja*. S. bulbocastanum* has the genome formula BB. S. polytrichon is used as a source or resistance to Phytophthora and potato aphid.

SOLANUM X SAMBUCINUM Rydb. 2n=24. In maize fields in N. Central Mexico. A natural hybrid of S. pinnatisectum* x S. cardiophyllum* ssp. ehrenbergii* (2n=24) and S. pinnatisectum* (2n=24) (Hawkes, 1966).

SOLANUM X SEMIDEMISSUM Juz. 2n=60. Clones of
this 5x plant in roadside thickets in Mexico.
A source of Phytophthora and frost resistance.
It is thought that it is a hybrid of S. demissum
x S. tuberosum, the reciprocal of the cross
yielding S. x edinense. It is sterile (Ugent,
1967). This may block introgression of S. demissum into the potato.

SOLANUM STOLONIFERUM Schlechtd. & Bouché. 2n=48,
genome formula A_4A_4BB. N. Mexico. A source of
resistance to Y-virus, A-virus, Phytophthora,
Pseudomonas and the potato aphid, Macrosiphum
euphorbiae Thomas. One of the parents of S. x
vallis-mexici*. One genome is the same as that
of S. acaule*.

SOLANUM X VALLIS-MEXICI Juz. 2n=36, genome formula A_1A_4B, 60 $A_1A_4A_4B$, 72, $A_1A_1A_4A_4BB$. The
Valley of Mexico. A natural hybrid of S. stoloniferum* and diploid S. verrucosum*. Amphiploids have also been found. Seed collected
from 5x plants produced aneuploid plants resembling either S. stoloniferum* or S. demissum*. Plants of the first group had 2n=47-55,
while those of the second group had 2n=61-69.
Intercrossing between the hybrid, the aneuploids and the species could account in part,
for the extensive polymorphism found in S. stoloniferum and S. demissum populations (Marks
& Montelongo-Escobedo, 1970).

SOLANUM VERRUCOSUM Schlechtd. 2n=24, genome formula A_1A_1, (36, 48, 72). NE., C. and S. Mexico.
Also cultivated there. The tubers have a good
flavour (Abdalla & Hermsen, 1973). A source of
resistance to Phytophthora infestans, X-virus,
Y-virus, and several insects. The diploid
forms a link between the Demissa and the Tuberosa series of S. America. It is similar to
the Colombian S. andreanum*.

SOLANUM WOODSONII Corr. 2n=   . Dry specimens
came from Costa Rica, Panama and Venezuela.
No living material has been collected yet.

   Sterculiaceae

THEOBROMA BICOLOR H. & B. Nicaraguan cacao.
2n=20. From Mexico to Brazil. Cultivated outside its natural range for the edible pulp
round the seeds. The seeds themselves are used
like those of Th. cacao* (Purseglove, 1968).

THEOBROMA PANTAGONA Bern. Cacao lagarto. 2n=
    . Costa Rica to Panama. Cultivated there.

12 North American Region

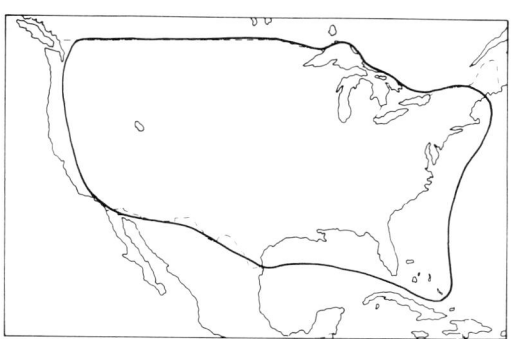

Darlington & Janaki Ammal (1945) established the USA Centre of Origin. Zhukovsky (1968) enlarged this area to the southern half of N. America. Agriculture must have been introduced from Region 1 in the third millenium BC., although there are indications that chenopods and amaranths were deliberately cultivated. However, they may have belonged to the ruderal flora the seeds being collected as food. One of the earliest introduced crops is Zea mays.

A few but important crops have been domesticated in this Region: Fragaria virginiana, Helianthus sp., Prunus sp., Rubus sp., Vaccinium sp., Vitis sp. etc.

Aceraceae

ACER SACCHARUM Marsh. Sugar maple, Rock maple. 2n=26. E. North America. The sap is a source of maple sugar and maple syrup. Also cultivated. Mansfeld (1959) suggested that A. saccharinum L. is a synonym, but his species has 2n =52.

Amaranthaceae

AMARANTHUS HYBRIDUS*

AMARANTHUS POWELLII see A. hypochondriacus

AMARANTHUS SPINOSUS*

Anacardiaceae

MANGIFERA INDICA L. Mango. 2n=40. Assam and Chittagong Hills. See further p. 71. In Florida, a secondary centre of diversity developed.

Araceae

ACORUS CALAMUS*

Araliaceae

PANAX QUINQUEFOLIA L. American ginseng. 2n= . E. North America. Cultivated for its roots, which are used as a stimulant.

Asclepiadaceae

ASCLEPIAS SYRIACA L. (syn. A. cornuti Decne).

2n=(20), 22, (24). E. North America. Run wild in cultivated ground and dry grassland (Tutin et al., 1972). Cultivated formerly in Europe for fibre and as a food-plant for bees.

Berberidaceae

PODOPHYLLUM PELTATUM L. 2n=12. May apple. E. North America. Herb of interest as possible medicinal crop.

Campanulaceae

LOBELIA INFLATA L. Indian tobacco. 2n=14, (16). N. America. Cultivated there as a medicinal plant. It has attracted attention again recently because it has been discovered to be a source of the lobeline used in anti-smoking preparations.

Cannabidaceae

HUMULUS LUPULUS L. Hop. 2n=2x=20 with X-Y sex chromosome system. Var. neomexicanus Nelson & Cockerell (syn. H. neomexicanus (Nelson & Cockerell) Rydberg) occurs mainly in the W. Cordillera. In the prairies of Canada, its variation overlaps with that of var. lupuloides E. Small (syn. H. americanus Nuttall). In N. America, var. pubescens E. Small is also found. Var. lupulus occurs especially in E.N. America where it derives from hop cultivated for its cones used to taste beer and as an ornamental (Small, 1978a).

Chenopodiaceae

ATRIPLEX CANESCENS (Pursh.) Nutt. American shad scale, Hoary saltbush, Wing scale, Four-wing saltbush. 2n= . W. North America up to Mexico. Cultivated as a fodder plant on saline soils and as a hedge plant (Mansfeld, 1959). A. gardnesi (Moq.) Standl. (2n=) is from the same area and A. truncata (Torr.) A. Gray (2n=) is from Utah, USA.

CHENOPODIUM NUTTALLIAE Safford. 2n=4x=36. This species is named now Ch. berlandieri Moq. ssp. nuttalliae (Safford) Wilson & Heiser. It is cultivated in the highlands of C. Mexico and Arkansas and Missouri (USA). The weedy Ch. bushianum Aellen of E. North America is closely related (Wilson & Heiser, 1979; Wilson, 1981).

Compositae

HELIANTHUS ANNUUS L. Sunflower. 2n=14, genome formula Ba_1Ba_1. N. America. It is difficult to be more specific because of its spread as a food plant and weed. The wild type may have resembled ssp. jaegeri, a small-headed type found in SW. Utah and NE. Arizona to S. California in USA. In new areas the sunflower has introgressed with related species so that the morphological variation has increased. An important species is H. bolanderi A. Gray (2n= 34) of C. and N. California. It may derive from crosses of H. annuus with H. exilus Gray, 2n= . Other species H. agrophyllus Torr. & A. Gray (2n=34) of Texas, H. debilis Nutt. ssp. cucumerifolius (2n=34) of Texas and H. petiolaris Nutt. (2n=34) of W. of N. America have also hybridized with the sunflower.

Various subspecies and varieties are recognized: ssp. lenticularis (Dougl.) Ckll, which is near to the original wild type and is found from W. Canada to N. Mexico. Ssp. texanus grows mainly in Texas. It may have arisen by hybridization of ssp. lenticularis and H. debilis.

Ssp. annuus L. is a ruderal weed, a weed sunflower, found in the settlements in the Midwest. It possibly derives from ssp. lenticularis. Var. macrocarpus (DC.) Ckll is probably the parental form of the cultivated types. It grows in NE. USA and Canada. It probably originated from ssp. annuus or this subspecies and var. macrocarpus developed together from ssp. lenticularis.

A weedy sunflower may have reached the Middle West where no other annual Helianthus species are found. Here the giant, large-headed sunflower may have developed (Heiser, 1955, 1965).

From N. America the sunflower was introduced into Europe where in USSR a secondary centre of diversity arose (p. 130).

HELIANTHUS EXILIS A. Gray. Serpentine sunflower. 2n= . Moist serpentine soils of Inner Coastal Range in California, USA. Almost extinct. H. bolanderi A. Gray, 2n=34, resulted from introgression of H. exilis genes into H. annuus* (Jain et al., 1977). Cold-tolerant.

HELIANTHUS TUBEROSUS L. Jerusalem artichoke. 2n=102, genome formula $At_1At_1At_2At_2Bt_1Bt_1$. N. America. Run wild in S. Ukraine and N. Caucasus. A perennial species introduced to Mexico and Eurasia.

The Bt_1 genome is related to the Ba_1 genome of H. annuus*. H. tuberosus is probably an amphiploid of a species with genome formula $At_1At_1At_2At_2$ and a B genome donor. This might be H. annuus or else a closely related species.

H. x laetiflorus Pers. (2n=102), a wild perennial species of USA is probably a hybrid of H. subrhomboidus Rydb. (2n=102) and H. tuberosus. The first parent is also native to USA (Clevenger & Heiser, 1963).

IVA ANNUA L. (syn. I. ciliata Willd.). Sump weed, Marsh elder. 3n=34. A large-'seeded' type (var. macrocarpa) is an extinct oil-crop cultivated from the early 1st Millenium BC. to the first half of the 2nd Millenium AD. (Yarnell, 1972).

STOKESIA LAEVIS (Hill) Green. Stokes aster. 2n= . A perennial native to Georgia, Florida, Alabama, Mississippi and Louisiana (USA), grown as an ornamental. A possible oil-crop?

Cucurbitaceae

CUCURBITA FOETIDISSIMA HBK. Feral buffala gourd, Fetid gourd, Missouri gourd, Calabazilla. 2n= . Will probably be domesticated (Bemis et al., 1978).

Cupressaceae

JUNIPERUS VIRGINIANA L. Eastern red cedar. 2n = . E. North America. Much variation is due to introgressive hybridization with other Juniperus species (Hemmerly, 1970).

Ebenaceae

DIOSPYROS VIRGINIANA L. Common persimmon. 2n= . E. North America. Cultivated for its fruits. Also used as a rootstock of D. kaki*.

Ericaceae

VACCINIUM ASHEI Reade. Rabbiteye. 2n=72. N. America. Cultivated there. Wild plants are also harvested. According to Camp (1945) the wild types derive from hybridization of the tetraploid species V. arkansanum, V. australe Small, Southeastern highbush blueberry, V. darrowi-4x and V. myrsinites Lam., Ground blueberry.

VACCINIUM CORYMBOSUM L. Highbush berry. 2n= 72. N. America. Cultivars have developed from the wild type which arose from hybridization of the tetraploid species V. lamarckii Camp (syn. V. angustifolium Ait.), V. alto-montanum Asche, V. simulatum and V. australe Small, Southeastern highbush blueberry.

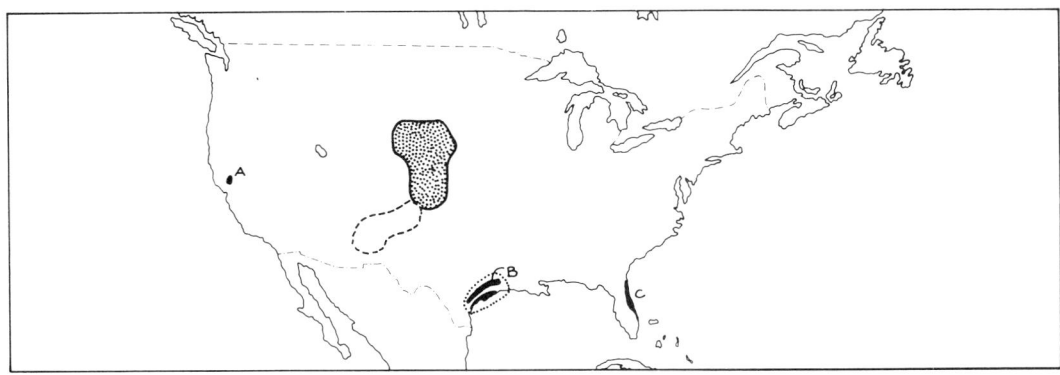

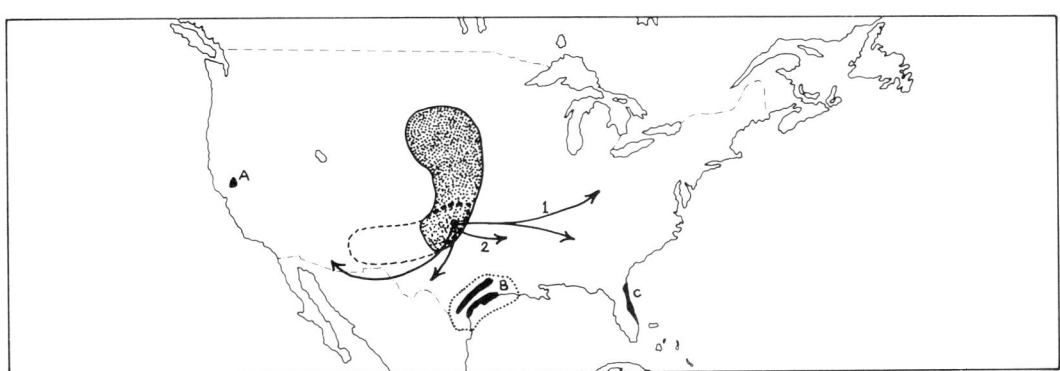

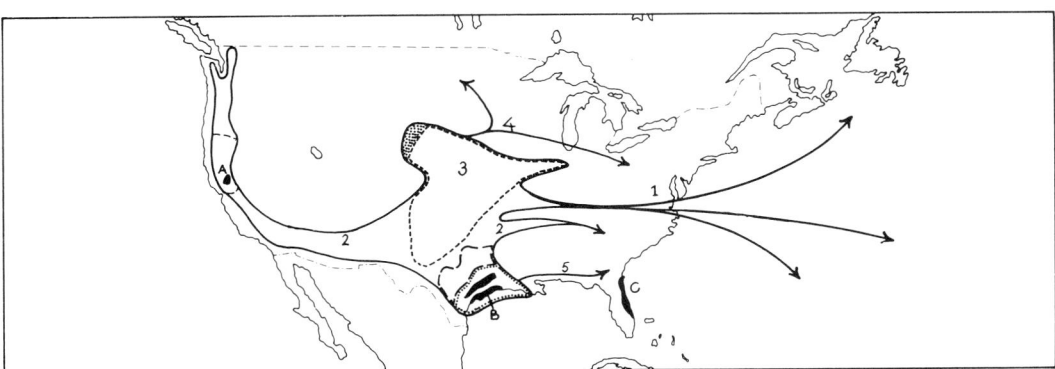

Distribution of Helianthus spp. in pre-human (above), pre-columbian (middle) and modern(below) times. (H. annuus (---), H. petiolaris (speckled), H. exilis (A), H. argophyllus (B), H. debilis var. cucumerifolius (···), H. debilis var. debilis (C), H. bolanderi (——), cultivated sunflower (1), campflower (2), Great plains annuus (3), weed petiolaris (4) and weed cucumerifolius(5) (Anderson, 1956; based on Heiser's research).

Fruits of wild plants are still picked, as are those of other wild species like V. myrtillus L., (European) blueberry, Whortleberry, Billberry (2n=24).

VACCINIUM MACROCARPON Ait. Cranberry. 2n=24, genome formula MaMa. NE. North America. Cultivars selected and cultivated in N. America and on Terschelling, the Netherlands. Related to the N. American wild V. oxycoccos L. (2n=48) genome formula $Mi^OMi^OMa^OMa^O$. The Mi^O genome is related to Mi of V. microcarpum (Turez.) Hook. (2n=24) (Ahokas, 1971).

Euphorbiaceae

ALEURITES FORDII Hemsl. Tung oil tree. 2n=22. S. Central China (p. 37). Secondary gene centre probably in the large planting.

Fagaceae

CASTANEA DENTATA (Marsh.) Borkh. American chestnut. 2n=24. E. North America. A tree cultivated for its edible sweet nuts.

CASTANEA PUMILA (L.) Mill. Common chinquapin. 2n=   . N. America (from Pennsylvania to Florida and Texas). A tree cultivated for its nuts.

Gramineae

AGROPYRON DASYSTACHUM (Hook.) Scribn. (syn. tetraploid 'A. smithii'). Western wheatgrass. 2n=28, genome formula SSHH (Dewey, 1975). Used to control erosion and as a forage crop. Hexaploid plants (2n=42, genome formula SSSHHH) occur in many populations (Sadasivaih & Weijer, 1981). A. smithii Ryd. has 2n=56, genome formula SSHHJJXX.

AGROPYRON PAUCIFLORUM (Schweinitz) Hitchc. (syn. A. trachycaulum (Link.) Malte). Slender wheatgrass, Bald wheatgrass, Western ryegrass. 2n=28. N. America. A forage crop. A. subsecundus (Link.) Hitch., 2n=28 is the awned version.

AGROPYRON SMITHII Rydb. Western wheatgrass. 2n =28. N. America. Used to control erosion and as a forage crop.

AGROPYRON SPICATUM (Pursh) Scribn. & Smith. Bluebunch wheatgrass. 2n=14, genome formula SS, 28, SSSS. N. America. Cultivated as a forage crop. Var. inerme is Beardless bluebunch wheatgrass. A latiglume (Scribn. & Smith) Rydb., (2n=28), A. scribneri Vasey (2n=28), A. trachycaulum (Link.) Malte ex H.F. Lewis (2n=28, SS HH) and Sitanion hystrix (Nutt.) J.C. Smith (2n=28) also possess a pair of S genomes. It easily crosses with A. repens*, producing fertile hybrids and a new forage crop (Dewey, 1976).

AGROSTIS GIGANTEA*

AGROSTIS TENUIS*

BOUTELOUA CURTIPENDULA (Michx.) Torr. Side-oats grama. 2n=20-103. N. America. An important pasture grass.

BOUTELOUA ERIOPODA Torr. Black grama, Grama grass. 2n=20, 21, 28. SW. USA and N. Mexico. Used as a pasture grass.

BOUTELOUA FILIFORMIS (Fourn.) Griff. Grama grass. 2n=14, 20, 21, 22, 46. W. USA and N. Mexico. A pasture grass.

BOUTELOUA GRACILIS (H.B.K.) Lag ex Steud. Blue grama. 2n=20-84. N. America, ranging from Canada to Mexico.

BROMUS MARGINATUS Nees. Mountain brome. 2n= 28, 42, 56, 70. N. America. Cultivated in Australia, E. Africa and N. America.

DESCHAMPSIA INSIGNIS Pierre (syn. D. caespitosa (L.) Beauv.). Tufted hairgrass, Tussock grass. 2n=(24, 25), 26, (27), 28, (49). W. North America. Cultivated for hay and pasture.
   Putnam & Klein (1971) suggested that from this species D. elongata (Hook.) Munro (2n= 26) and D. holciformis Presl. (2n=26) have been derived. From D. elongata comes the annual D. danthonioides (Trin.) Munro. These four species are found in N. America and Europe.

DIGITARIA ADSCENDENS (H.B.K.) Henrard. 2n=54. N. America. A weedy grass sometimes included in D. sanguinalis*, but Gould (1963) classified 2n=6x=54 plants as D. adscendens and 2n= 4x=36 plants as D. sanguinalis. These species are closely related.

ELYMUS CANADENSIS L. Canada wild rye. 2n=28, (42), genome formula $S^+S^+H^+H^+$. N. America. A grass used as pasture and hay crops.

PANICUM VIRGATUM*

PASPALUM DISTICHUM L. 2n=40, genome formula X_5X_5WW, (48), 60. Lowlands of the world. Used in the USA as a soil stabilizer.

POA COMPRESSA L. Canada bluegrass, Wire grass. 2n=(14), 42, 56 and aneuploids. Europe to the Ural and Caucasia, and in N. America. Selection work was done particularly in N. America.

POA NEMORALIS L. Wood meadow grass. 2n=28, 42, 56, c. 70 and aneuploids. Europe, N. Africa, temperate Asia, N. America. Cultivated in N. America.

POA PRATENSIS L. Field meadow grass, Bluegrass, Kentucky bluegrass, Birdgrass. 2n=38-147. For origin see p. 153. Europe, Asia, N. Africa and N. North America. Various varieties have been developed in Europe, Canada and elsewhere. Natural hybrids with P. ampla Merr. have been found in W. North America.

PUCCINELLIA NUTTALLIANA (Schult.) Hitchc. Nut-tal alkali grass, Meadow grass. 2n=42, 56. N. America. Cultivated as a forage grass especially on alkaline soils.

STIPA VIRIDULA Trin. Green needle-grass. 2n= 82. N. America. This perennial bunch grass has been adapted to the N. Great Plains for rangeland.

TRIPSACUM DACTYLOIDES (L.) L. 2n=36, 72. See p. 190. Tetraploid types of Florida, USA have a thick rachis which apparently developed as an adaptation to dispersal by floating (Galinat, 1969).

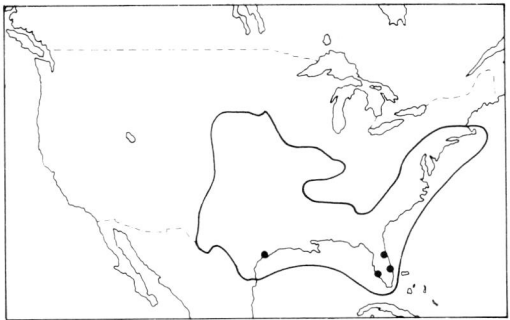

Tripsacum dactyloides (——) and T. floridanum (●●)(Randolph, 1970).

UNIOLA PANICULATA L. Sea cats. 2n=40. S. North America. A dune stabilizer.

ZEA MAYS L. Maize, Corn. 2n=20. Secondary centres in N. America. Domesticated in C. America (p. 190). There local races and those introduced from the Mexican lowlands and the West Indies, hybridized (Brandolini, 1970). Dent maize, dent corn - indentata Sturt. - is common here.

ZIZANIA AQUATICA L. Indian rice, Wild rice, Tuscarora rice. 2n=30. S. Canada and USA in the area of the Great Lakes. Seeds are collected.

Grossulariaceae

RIBES CYNOSBATI L. American wild gooseberry, Frickle gooseberry. 2n=16. E. North America. Cultivated there. Its characteristic mildew resistance is useful in breeding European gooseberry cultivars (p. 154).

RIBES ODORATUM Wendland. Buffalo currant. 2n= 16. N. America. Types with large fruits are cultivated.

Hydrastidaceae

HYDRASTIS CANADENSIS L. Golden seal, Orange root. 2n=26. E. North America. Cultivated there

as a medicinal crop and as an ornamental.

Hydrophyllaceae

PHACELIA TANACETIFOLIA Benth. Valley vervenia. 2n=(18), 22. California, USA. Cultivated as a crop for honey bees.

Juglandaceae

CARYA ILLINOINENSIS (Wangenh.) K. Koch. (syn. Carya pecan Engler & Graebn.). Pecan. 2n=32. N. America. A tree cultivated for its nuts. One of the parents of C. x lecontei Little, bitter pecan (2n=   ). The other parent is probably C. aquatica (Michx.f.) Nutt., water hickory (2n=32).

CARYA OVATA (Mill.) K. Koch (syn. C. alba Nutt.). Shagbark hickory, Shellbark hickory. 2n=   . N. America. Cultivated also as an ornamental.

JUGLANS HINDSII Jepson. C. Californian black walnut. 2n=   . C. California, USA. Cultivated as rootstock of J. regia*.

JUGLANS NIGRA L. Black walnut. 2n=32. Most of the eastern half of the USA and S. Ontario between Lake Huron and Lake Ontario. Pure, natural stands are rare and usually small, it generally occurs as individual trees scattered through the forest. This walnut is mainly selected for its fruits, but also some selections have been made for distinctive foliage and for wood (Funk, 1969).

Labiatae

MENTHA CANADENSIS L. (syn. M. arvensis L.). American wild mint. 2n=54, 96, N. America. Occasionally cultivated.

Leguminosae

AMPHICARPAEA MONOICA (L.) Ell. (syn. Falcata comosa (L.) Kuntze). Hog pea, Ground peanut. 2n=20. E. and S. USA. Formerly cultivated for its seeds.

APIOS TUBEROSA Moench. (syn. A. americana Medik., Glycine apios L.). Potato bean, Ground nut. 2n=2x=22, 3x=33. E. North America, Florida and Texas. Cultivated for its edible tubers and as an ornamental or as a curiosity.

GLEDITSIA TRIACANTHOS L. Honey locust, Sweet bean. 2n=28. C. and E. North America. This tree is cultivated in hedges and as an ornamental.

LUPINUS PERENNIS L. 2n=48, 96. E. North America. Cultivated as an ornamental, fodder crop and green manure.

LUPINUS POLYPHYLLUS Lindl. 2n=48. Pacific N. America. Cultivated as an ornamental, fodder crop and green manure.

ROBINIA HISPIDA L. 2n=30. SE. North America.
Cultivated as an ornamental and in hedges.

ROBINIA PSEUDACACIA L. Locust, Black locust.
2n=20, c. 20, 22. C. and E. North America. This
tree is planted as an ornamental and as a soil
stabilizer.

SESBANIA EXALTATA (Raf.) Rydb. 2n=12. USA.
Cultivated there as a green manure.

SESBANIA MACROCARPA Muhl. 2n=12. USA. Cultivated there. Closely related to S. exaltata* or
is a synonym of this species.

VICIA LEAVENWORTHII Torr. & Gray. Leavenworth
vetch. 2n=14. Missouri and Arkansas to Texas
in USA. Occasionally cultivated.

Liliaceae

CAMASSIA LEICHTLINII (Baker) S. Wats. Camas.
2n=30. E. North America. Uncultivated bulb
beds are divided into family plots, which have
been passed down from generation to generation.
These plots are not farmed, but stones, weeds
and shrubs are removed every year. In most
cases the plants are marked in bloom so that
the bulb can be harvested when it is fully
grown (Chapman Turner & Bell, 1971).
    The camas is semi-domesticated i.e. the wild
plant is protected and the growing circum-
stances are improved. The latter may result in
more sites for the plant to grow.

CAMASSIA QUAMASH (Pursh) Greene. Blue camas.
2n=   . E. North America. See further C.
leichtlinii*.

Limnanthaceae

LIMNANTHES ALBA Benth. Meadow foam. 2n=10.
NW. Pacific states of USA. Potential oil-crop.
Erect types have been developed for cultivation.
Self- and cross-compatible.

Malvaceae

GOSSYPIUM BARBADENSE L. Sea Islands cotton.
2n=52, genome formula (AADD)$_2$. Peru (p. 176).
Sea Islands cotton developed on the Sea Islands of S. Carolina, USA after introduction
from Bahamas or Jamaica. Cultivated in E. USA
and some Caribbean islands. Maybe similar types
in Ecuador are its parental material (Harlan,
1970).

Martyniaceae

PROBOSCIDEA LOUISIANICA (Mill.) Thell. (syn.
Martynia proboscidea Glox.). Unicorn plant,
Ram's horn, Double claw, Proboscis flower. 2n
=   . N. America. A herb cultivated for its
fruits and as an ornamental.

Moraceae

MACLURA POMIFERA (Rafin.) C.K. Schneider (syn.
M. aurantiaca Nuttall). Osage orange. Texas,
Oklahoma and Arkansas, USA. Widely planted as
living fence in USA from 1850-1875. Naturalized.
Also used as a source of bows, yellow dye and
building material. Dioecious, wind-pollinated.
Macludrania hybrida André is a natural hybrid
of Cudrania trisuspidata x Maclura pomifera
var. inermis (Smith & Perino, 1981).

Passifloraceae

PASSIFLORA INCARNATA L. May-Pop, Yellow-fruited
Virginian passion flower, Apricot-Vine. 2n=18,
36. E. North America, Florida and Texas. It
was cultivated by indians in Virginia. Resembles P. edulis*.

Phytolaccaceae

PHYTOLACCA AMERICANA L. 2n=36. USA. It has run
wild in S. Europe. Cultivated as a dye plant
(berries) and ornamental. The berries are also
used to colour wine.

Rosaceae

AMYGDALUS PERSICA L. Peach. 2n=16. Primary centre: China (p. 42). Secondary centre: California, USA.

FRAGARIA CHILOENSIS*

FRAGARIA OVALIS Lehm. 2n=8x=56. W. North America. Used in breeding F. x ananassa*.

FRAGARIA VESCA L. Wild strawberry. 2n=14, genome formula AA. Europe (p. 159), Asia and N
America. In California, it is found in a broad
range of environments from the coastal fog
belt to the Sierra Nevada and Cascade Mountains
and from San Jacinto Mountains near the Mexican
border to Oregon. Hermaphroditic, self-compatible, reproducing sexually and asexually by
runners. There are many ecotypes, which aid
survival under this wide range of environments
(Hancock & Bringhurst, 1978). Some clones are
used to test for viruses in F. x ananassa*.

FRAGARIA VIRGINIANA Duch. Virginian strawberry.
2n=56. N. America, especially in the eastern
part. Cultivated. One of the parents of F. x
ananassa* Duch. (syn. F. grandiflora Ehrh.),
the pineapple strawberry (2n=56).

PRUNUS. The American Prunus species are valuable
because of their longevity and winterhardiness.

PRUNUS AMERICANA Marsh. American Plum. 2n=16
A large territory of N. America between Mani-
toba and Texas. This small tree usually grows
slowly. Cultivated. Valuable because of its
longevity and winterhardiness. Cultivars have
been developed from interspecific crosses.

PRUNUS ANGUSTIFOLIA Marsh. (syn. P. chicasa Mich.). Chickasaw plum, Florida sand plum, Mountain cherry. 2n=16. S. Delaware to Florida and westward to the Texas and S. Oklahoma. A small tree with a dense crown. The cultivated species lack hardiness. It hybridizes easily with P. munsoniana*.

PRUNUS BESSYI Bailey. Western sand cherry. 2n =16. N. America on sandy and saline soils. This perennial shrub is characterized by a good longevity, frost resistance and sweet, edible fruits. A source of a bush-type habit for ease of mechanical harvesting.It hybridizes with Armeniaca vulgaris* and Prunus ssp.

PRUNUS HORTULANA Bailey. Hortulan plum. 2n=16. C. USA. This tree is very cold resistant and has good fruits. It flowers late (Zylka, 1970). It hybridizes easily with other American Prunus species. According to Bailey (1898) it is a hybrid of P. angustifolia* and P. americana*.

PRUNUS MARITIMA Marsh. (syn. P. maritima Wangh., P. acuminata Michx.). Beach plum, Sand plum. 2n=16. E. USA and adjacent Canada. Some cultivars have been selected (Zylka, 1970) in the USA. Also used as a source of late flowering, cold resistance and very high fertility in the breeding of other cultivars. It is an ornamental.

PRUNUS MUNSONIANA Wight & Hedrick. Wild Goose Plum. 2n=16. N. Texas, E. Oklahoma and Missouri. It flowers late and the fruits are of good quality. It has a good longevity and winterhardiness. It hybridizes easily with P. angustifolia* and other species. Cultivars were bred from such interspecific crosses.

PRUNUS NIGRA Ait. Canada plum. 2n=16. The territory between S. New Foundland to the Strait of Mackinac and southward to Lansing, Michigan. Cultivated there to some extent. This species is valuable because of its longevity and winterhardiness. Cultivars have been developed from interspecific crosses.

PRUNUS PENSYLVANICA L. (syn. P. persicifolia Desf.). Bird cherry, Pigeon cherry, Pin cherry, Wild red cherry. 2n=16. N. America, from New Foundland to British Columbia and Colorado. A source of late flowering and cold resistance.

PRUNUS SEROTINA Ehrh. Black cherry, Run cherry. 2n=32. N. America from Ontario and North Dakota to Texas and Florida. The fruits are unpalatable. It could be a source of late flowering and frost resistance.

PRUNUS VIRGINIANA L. Common choke cherry, Eastern choke cherry, Choke cherry. 2n=30, 32. W. North America. Micurin selected Vinogradnaja from this species (Zylka, 1971b).

RUBUS ACAULIS Michx. 2n=14. The Canadian counter part of R. articus (Larsson, 1969). It

could be one parent of R. stellatus*. Also named ssp. acaulis of R. arcticus.

RUBUS FLAGELLARIS Willd. (syn. R. villosus Ait.). Northern dewberry. 2n=63. E. North America. Cultivated for its fruits. Var. roribaccus Bailey is the Lucretia dewberry (Uphof, 1968).

RUBUS IDAEUS L. (syn. R. strigosus Michx.). American red raspberry. 2n=14. The NE. American counterpart of this species. Present cultivars are often hybrids between this subspecies and ssp. vulgatus*, the European red raspberry. Natural hybrids between ssp. strigosus and R. occidentalis* have been described as R. neglectus Peck., Purple cane raspberry (2n=14). They have been occasionally cultivated. In N. America such hybridization has led to introgression between the two parental species. See for other hybrids p. 141. Cultivars are often unarmed or have simple leaves. The loganberry (2n=42), genome formula $V_1V_1V_2V_2II$, is derived from the cross of a tetraploid form R. ursinus Cham. & Echt. (2n=28), genome formula $V_1V_1V_2V_2$ and R. idaeus (2n=14). Mayberry is a hybrid product of R. palmatus Thunb. x ssp. strigosus and Youngberry (2n=42, 49) of loganberry x Mayes dewberry (R. baileyanus x R. argutus). Other Rubus species like R. arcticus* have also been used in breeding work.

RUBUS OCCIDENTALIS L. Black raspberry. 2n=14. NE. North America, Colorado and British Columbia. It is cultivated. Present cultivars often derive from hybrids with R. idaeus*. Natural hybrids with the N. American ssp. strigosus of R. idaeus have been named R. neglectus Peck., purple cane raspberry (2n=14). This hybridization has led to introgression between these two parental species. It is for R. idaeus* a source of resistance to the rubus aphid, Amphorophora rubi Kalt.

RUBUS STELLATUS Sm. 2n=14. Wild from Alaska, Aleutian Islands and Kamchatka. Closely related to R. arcticus* and has been described as ssp. stellatus of this latter species. It could be a hybrid of R. arcticus and R. acaulis* (Larsson, 1969).

Salicaceae

SALIX RIGIDA Mühlenberg (syn. S. cordata Mühl.) American willow. 2n=44. N. America. Introduced in Europe for twig production.

Solanaceae

DATURA STRAMONIUM L. Thorn-apple, Jimson weed. 2n=24. N. America. Pantropical now. A poisonous plant cultivated as a medicinal plant yielding stramonium.

NICOTIANA QUADRIVALVIS Pursh. 2n=48. SW. USA along rivers and in rocky soils. The Indians cultivated it for smoking leaves and flowers.

An annual, frost-resistant, early maturing
species. It hybridizes easily with N. tabacum*.

PHYSALIS PUBESCENS L. Strawberry tomato, Dwarf
Cape gooseberry. 2n=24. N. America. Cultivated
in Ukraine and elsewhere.

SOLANUM FENDLERI A. Gray. Navajo potato. 2n=
48, genome formula A_4A_4BB. Arizona, New Mexico and W. Texas, USA and NW. Mexico. Very similar to S. hjertingii* and similar to S. papita*. It is resistant to Y virus.

SOLANUM JAMESII Torr. 2n=24, 36. Arizona, New
Mexico and Colorado (USA) and in Mexico near
the Arizona boundary.

Valerianaceae

VALERINA EDULIS Nutt. 2n=   . N. America. This
perennial herb is cultivated for its roots.

Vitadaceae

VITIS BERLANDIERI Planch. 2n=38. SE. USA to
Texas. Used as a rootstock. Rootstocks of V.
riparia* x V. berlandieri are also used. It
can be crossed with V. vinifera*.

VITIS CINEREA Engelm. Downy grape, Sweet winter grape. 2n=38. SE. USA. Resistant to fungal
diseases and to phylloxera. Viteus vitifolii
Shimer, but it cannot be crossed with V. vinifera*.

VITIS CORDIFOLIA Michx. 2n=30, 38. SE. USA. It
can be crossed with V. vinifera* to introduce
resistance to fungal diseases.

VITIS LABRUSCA L. Fox grape. 2n=38. E. North
America. It appears to have run wild in Georgia, USSR (p. 102). Introduced into the Old
World. It is cultivated. It has been crossed
with V. vinifera* to improve it and for this
species it is used as a rootstock.

VITIS RIPARIA Michx. (syn. V. vulpina L.).
2n=38. E. and C. USA and in Ontario, Canada.
Used as a rootstock. It can be crossed with V.
vinifera* to introduce resistance to phylloxera,
Viteus vitifolii Shimer. Such hybrids occur
wild in USA and have been described as V. bour-
quina. Rootstocks of V. riparia x V. berlandieri* are also used.

VITIS ROTUNDIFOLIA Michx. Muscadine grape,
Southern fox grape. 2n=40. Florida, the southern coast of USA and the east coast of Mexico.
Dioecious, but hermaphrodite cultivars have
been developed. Cv. Scuppernong was developed
in 1584 from wild material in NE. North Carolina.

VITIS RUPESTRIS Scheele. 2n=   . SW. USA. Used
as a rootstock. It can be crossed with V. vinifera* to introduce resistance to phylloxera,
Viteus vitifolii Shimer.

Species without an identified region

Some species could not be listed in one of the Regions. They have a very wide geographical distribution. Either their locality of cultivation has not been reported or they are cultivated at several places. Thus it is not known whether their wide distribution occurred before their domestication or not, i.e. it is not mentioned whether the wild species grew in a large area where it has been domesticated at several places, or whether wild plants were domesticated on one site after they had been spread by man.

Agavaceae

YUCCA GLORIOSA L. 2n=50. Cultivated in Georgia, (USSR).

Amaranthaceae

GOMPHRENA GLOBOSA L. Batchelor's button. 2n= 32, 40-44, 44-48. The tropics. Cultivated in some villages of mainly coastal districts in W. Africa as a curiosity and as a fetish plant. In Europe and elsewhere it is an ornamental.

Anacardiaceae

SPONDIAS CYTHEREA Sonner (syn. S. dulcis Forst.f.). Otaheita apple, Ambarella, Hog plum. 2n= . Cultivated for its fruits. Mansfeld (1959) reported the presence of var. cytherea on the Society Islands, Tahiti, Fidji, Samoa and Madagascar, var. mucroniserrata (Engl.) Mansf. in Mexico, var. macrocarpa (Engl.) Mansf. in Brazil, var. acida (BL.) Mansf. in Malaysia and var. integra (Engl.) Mansf. in Amboina.

Apocynaceae

APOCYNUM VENETUM L. (syn. A. sibiricum Pall. ex Roem. & Schult.). Kendyr. 2n=16, 22. Italy to E. Asia. A perennial fibre crop brought into cultivation in USSR.

Chenopodiaceae

CHENOPODIUM BOTRYS L. Jerusalem oak. 2n=18. S. Europe, Orient and C. Asia. Occasionally cultivated (Mansfeld, 1959).

Corynocarpaceae

CORYNOCARPUS LAEVIGATUS J.F. Forst. & G. Forst. Kopi, karaka. 2n=44. This species occurs wild on the New Hebrides and New Caledonia as C. similis and C. dissimilis respectively. The large kernels can be eaten after removing the poisonous karakin by heating. Therefore they were taken to New Zealand (Stevenson, 1978) where the species ran wild and became semi-domesticated.

Cruciferae

CRAMBE ABYSSINICA Hochst. ex. R.E. Vries. 2n= 90. Its wild distribution is obscure, but it may have developed in Turkey. Cultivars have been released in USA. See p. 89.

Cucurbitaceae

MOMORDICA BALSAMINA L. Bitter gourd, Bitter cucumber, Balsam pear, Balsam apple. 2n=22. Tropics of the Old World, especially India and SE. India. Leaves and stem are used for fodder.

MOMORDICA CHARANTIA L. Bitter gourd, Bitter cucumber, Balsam pear. 2n=22. Tropics of the Old World. Naturalized in nearly all tropics and subtropics. An edible, medicinal and toxic plant (Morton, 1967).

Cyperaceae

CYPERUS ARTICULATUS L. 2n= . Cultivated for its sweet scented roots.

MARISCUS UMBELLATUS Vahl. 2n= . The tropics of the Old World. Cultivated for its rhizomes.

Euphorbiaceae

EUPHORBIA TIRUCALLI L. 2n=20. Trials at Arizona (USA) to grow this plant for its sap as a raw material for petrol.

Gramineae

EREMOCHLOA OPHIUROIDES (Munro) Hack. 2n=28. Some cultivation on Puerto Rico.

HETEROPOGON HIRTUS Pers. (syn. H. contortus Beauv. ex Roem. & Schult., Andropogon contortus L.). Spearhead, Tangle grass. 2n=20, 40, (42-44, 50), 60, (80, c. 70-80). The Old and New World, subtropics and tropics. Cultivated as a fodder for live stock. Plants with 2n=20 come from India, with 2n=40 from Java, India, Madagascar, Tanzania, Kenya, Uganda, Zimbabwe and Zaïre, and with 2n=60 from S. Africa, Mexico and N. America.

Leguminoseae

CROTALARIA MUCRONATA Desv. (syn. C. striata DC.). 2n=16. Distributed in tropics and subtropics as a cover crop and green manure.

CROTALARIA RETUSA L. 2n=16. This fibre crop is widespread throughout the tropics. In E. Africa it is used for its pigments and in Florida as an ornamental.

DESMODIUM ADSCENDENS DC. 2n=22. Tropics. Cultivated in many regions as a cover crop and green manure.

DESMODIUM GANGATICUM DC. 2n=   . Trop. Asia and Australia. Cultivated as a fodder plant and green manure.

INDIGOFERA HIRSUTA L. (syn. I. schimperi Jaub. & Spach.). Hairy indigo. 2n=16. Many tropical countries. It is cultivated.

TEPHROSIA PURPUREA Pers. Purple tephrosia. 2n =22, (24, 44). The tropics. Cultivated as a green manure and cover crop. Grows wild in N. India on waste places and road sites.

Malvaceae

ABUTILON GRAVEOLENS Sweet. 2n=14, 36. The tropics of the Old World. Cultivated especially in USSR for its oily seeds.

MALACHRA CAPITATA L. 2n=56. The tropics. A herb cultivated for its fibre.

URENA LOBATA L. Aramina fibre, Congo jute. 2n=28, 56. Wild or naturalized in the tropics and subtropics. Centre of origin very likely in the Old World (Purseglove, 1968).

Rutaceae

EVODIA HORTENSIS J.R. & G. Forst. (syn. Fagara euoda L.f., F. evoda L.f., Zanthoxylum varians Benth.). 2n=   . A widespread shrub. Cultivated in many parts of the Pacific. Leaves are used for medicinal purposes.

Solanaceae

SOLANUM MAMMOSUM L. 2n=   . It spread as a campfollower over C. and S. America. Its native habitat is not clear but it appears to be wild in the Caribbean. Primitive types are found in the savanna of Venezuela and Colombia, and it is widely used as fish poison and ornamental, and in fetish. In Panama, it is cultivated as a fish poison (Nee, 1979).

Umbelliferae

CONIUM MACULATUM L. Hemlock, Poison hemlock. 2n=16, 22. Europe, Asia, N. Africa and Ethiopia. Occasionally cultivated. Often occurring as a ruderal. Used as a poison and medicinal plant.

Urticaceae

BOEHMERIA STIPULARIS Wedd. Hawaian false nettle, Akola. 2n=   . Probably from the Mascarene islands. According to Uphof (1968) this fibre crop grows wild on Hawaii, where it was formerly cultivated. This has resulted in many varieties.

TOUCHARDIA LATIFOLIA Gaudich. Olona. 2n=   . The Hawaian Islands. At one time cultivated for its fibre (Hutchinson, 1962).

References

Abdalla, M.M.F. & G. Günzel, 1979. Protein content and electrophoresis seed proteins of certain Vicia faba L. stocks and their assumed ancestors. PflZücht. 83:148-154.

Abdalla, M.M.F. & J.G.Th. Hermsen, 1973. An evaluation of Solanum verrucosum Schlecht. for its possible use in potato breeding. Euphytica 22:19-27.

Abdallah, M.S. & H.C.D. de Wit, 1978. The Resedaceae. A taxonomical revision of the family (final instalment). Meded. Landbouwhogeschool Wageningen 78-14, p. 95-416.

Adema, F. & J. Mennema, 1979. De Nederlandse slijkgrassen. Gorteria 9: 330-334.

Ahokas, H., 1971. Cytology of hexaploid cranberry with special reference to chromosomal fibres. Hereditas 68:123-136.

Allchin, F.R., 1969. Early cultivated plants in India and Pakistan. In: P.J. Ucko & G.W. Dimbleby (Eds): The domestication and exploitation of plants and animals. Duckworth and Company, London.

Anand, I.J., J.N. Singh & P.P. Khanna, 1975. Interrelationships and diversity in Indian colza. Indian J. agric. Sci. 45:253-258.

Anderson, E., 1949. Introgressive hybridization. New York/London. 109 p.

Anderson, E., 1952. Plants, man and life. University of California Press. 251 p.

Anderson, E., 1956. Man as a maker of new plants and new plant communities. In: W.L. Thomas (Ed.). Man's role in changing the face of the earth. Chicago. p. 763.

Anderson, E., 1960. The evolution of domestication. In: Tax, 1960, p. 67-84.

Angulo, M.D. & Sanchez de Rivera, A.M., 1977. Comparative chromosomal study of Spanish ecotypes and Australian cultivars of Trifolium subterraneum L. Cytologia 42:473-482.

Anon., 1975. The winged bean, a high-protein crop for the tropics. Nat. Acad. Science Washington 1975, p. 1-39.

Arora, R.K., 1977. Jobs tears (Coix lacryma-jobi) a minor food and fodder crop of northeastern India. Econ. Bot. 31:358-366.

Ashri, A., 1976. Plasmon divergence in peanuts (Arachis hypogaea): a third plasmon and locus affecting growth habit. Theor. Appl. Genet. 48:17-21.

Ashri, A. & P.F. Knowles, 1960. Cytogenetics of safflower (Carthamus L.) species and their hybrids. Agron. J. 52:11-17.

Astley, D. & J.G. Hawkes, 1979. The nature of the Bolivian weed potato species Solanum sucrense Hawkes. Euphytica 28:685-696.

Austin, D.F., 1977. Hybrid polyploids in Ipomoea section batatas. J. Hered. 68:259-260.

Austin, D.F., 1978. The Ipomoea batatas complex. I. Taxonomy. Bull. Torrey Bot. Club 105:114-129.

Aweke, G., 1979. Revision of the genus Ficus L. (Moraceae) in Ethiopia. Meded. Landbouwhogeschool Wageningen 79-3. 115 p.

Ayensu, E.S. & D.G. Coursey, 1972. Guinea yams. Econ. Bot. 26:301-308.

Baagøe, J., 1974. The genus Guizotia (Compositae). A taxonomic revision. Bot. Tiddskr. 69:1-39.

Babu, C.R. & F.N. Hepper, 1977. Taxonomy and nomenclature of Solanum khasianum and some of its relatives. Kew Bull. 34:1-39.

Badilla, V.M., 1967. A cerca de la naturaleza hybrida de Carica pentagona, C. chrysophylla y C. fructifragrans, frutales des Ecuador y Colombia. Rev. Fac. Agron. Maracay 4(2):92-103. Pl. Breed. Abstr. 38 (3334).

Bahavandoss, M. & N. Jayarama, 1973. Leaf shape expression and spontaneous amphidiploidy in species hybrids of Gossypium and their evolutionary significance. Madras agric. J. 60:1540-1544.

Bai, K., K. Vijaya, M.L. Magoon & R. Krishnan, 1971. Meiosis and pollen mitosis in diploid and triploid Colocasia antiquorum Schott. Genetica 42:187-198.

Bailey, E.T. & C.M. Francis, 1971. Isoflavone concentrations in the leaves of the species of the genus Trifolium, section Caly-comorphum. Austral. J. agric. Res. 22:731-736.

Baker, H.G., 1962. Comments on the thesis that there was a major centre of plant domestication near the headwaters of the River Niger. J. Afric. Hist. 3:211-233.

Baker, H.G. & G.L. Stebbins (Eds.), 1965. The genetics of colonizing species. Acad. Press New York/London. 588 p.

Bakhuizen van den Brink, H.C., 1933. De Indische flora en haar eerste Amerikaanse indringster. Natuurk. Tijdschr. Ned.-Indië 93:20-55.

Baksh, A., 1979. Cytogenetic studies on the F_1 hybrid Solanum incanum L. x Solanum melongena L. variety 'Giant of Banaras'. Euphytica 28:793-800.

Banga, O., 1957. Origin of the European cultivated carrot. Euphytica 6:54-63.

Banga, O., 1963. Main types of the Western carotene and their origin. Tjeenk Willink, Zwolle. 153 p.

Baranov, A., 1966. Recent advances in our knowledge of the morphology, cultivation and uses of ginseng (Panax ginseng C.A. Meyer). Econ. Bot. 20:403-406.

Barrau, J., 1959. The sagopalms and other food plants of marsh dwellers in the South Pacific islands. Econ. Bot. 13:151-163.

Barrau, J., 1961. Subsistance agriculture in Polynesia and Micronesia. Bernice P. Bishop Museum Bull. 223. 94 p.

Barrau, J. (Ed.), 1963. Plants and the migrations of Pacific peoples. Bishop Museum Press. 136 p.

Barrett, H.C. & A.M. Rhodes, 1976. A numerical taxonomic study of affinity relationships in cultivated Citrus and its close relatives. Syst. Bot. 1:105-136.

Basu, R.K. & K.K. Mukherjee, 1975. Investiga-on a new Beta (Chenopodiaceae). Canad. J. Bot. 53:1166-1175.

Bates, D.M., 1968. Notes on the cultivated Malvaceae. Abelmoschus. Baileya 16:99-112.

Baudet, J.C., 1977a. The taxonomic status of the cultivated types of lima bean (Phaseolus lunatus L.). Trop. Grain Legume Bull. No. 7:29-30.

Baudet, J.C., 1977b. Origine et classification des espèces cultivées du genre Phaseolus. Bull. Soc. r. Bot. Belg. 110:65-76.

Baum, B.R., 1972. Avena septentrionalis and the semispecies concept. Can. J. Bot. 50:2063-2066.

Baum, B.R., 1977. Oats: Wild and cultivated. Canad. Dept. Agric. Biosyst. Res. Inst. Monogr. 14. Thorn Press, Ottawa.

Beadle, G.W., 1980. The ancestry of corn (maize). Scient. Amer. 247(1):86-103.

Beaumont, P.B. & A.K. Boshier, 1972. Some comments on recent findings at Border cave, Northern Natal. S. Afr. J. Sci. 68:22-24.

Becker, G., 1962. Knollensellerie, Apium graveolens L., var. rapaceum (Miller) DC. In: Kappert & Rudorf, 1962, p. 104-130.

Beddows, A.R., 1953. The ryegrasses in British agriculture. Welsh Plant Breed. Stn. Bull. Ser. H. (17):1-81.

Bell, G.D.H., 1965. The comparative phylogeny of the temperate cereals. In: Sir Joseph Hutchinson (Ed.): Crop plant evolution. Cambridge Univ. Press, Cambridge.

Bemis, W.P., L.D. Curtis, C.W. Weber & J. Berry, 1978. The feral buffalo gourd, Cucurbita foetidissima. Econ. Bot. 32:87-95.

Ben-Ze'ev, N. & D. Zohary, 1973. Species relationships in the genus Pisum L. Israel J. Bot. 22:73-91.

Berg, R.G. van den, 1978. Pollen morphology of the genera Pometia, Cubilia, Otonephelium and Litchi (Sapindaceae-Nephelieae). Blumea 24:369-294.

Bergh, B.O., 1969. Avocado, Persea americana Miller. In: Ferwerda & Wit, 1969, p. 23-51.

Berglund-Brücher, O. & H. Brücher. The South-American wild bean (Phaseolus aborigineus Burk.) as ancestor of the common bean. Econ. Bot. 30:257-272.

Berthaud, J. & J.-L. Guillaumet, 1978. Les caféiers sauvages en Centrafrique. Café Cacao Thé 22:171-186.

Bezbaruah, H.P. & S.C. Gogoi, 1971. An interspecific hybrid between tea (Camellia sinensis L.) and C. japonica L. Proc. Indian Acad. Sci. 76, sec. B(5):219-220.

Bird, J.B., 1948. America's oldest farmers. Nat. Hist. 57:296-303.

Biswas, M.R. & S. Dana, 1975. Phaseolus aureus x P. lathyroides cross. The Nucleus 18:81-85.

Bolkhovskikh, Z., V. Grif, T. Matvejeva & O. Zakharyeva, 1969. Chromosome numbers of flowering plants. Leningrad. 926 p.

Bor, N.L., 1970. Graminaceae, In: Reichinger (Ed.): Flora Iranica. Graz. 573 p.

Bor, N.L., 1955. The genus Digitaria Heist. in India and Burma. Webbia 11:301-367.

Borges, O.L., 1972. Taxonomia y descripcion de clones del genero Musa (Platanos y Cambures) cultivados en Venezuela. Rev. Fac. Agron. 6(3):17-63.

Borrill, M., 1972. Studies in Festuca. III. The contribution of F. scariosa to the evolution of polyploids in sections Bovinae and Scariosae. New Phytol. 71:523-532.

Borssum Waalkes, J. van, 1966. Malesian Malvaceae revised. Blumea 14:1-251.

Bouharmont, J., 1960. Recherches taxonomiques et caryologiques chez quelques espèces du genre Hevea. Serie Scient. INEAC, 64 p.

Braak, J.P. & A.E. Zeilinga, 1957. Production of colchicine-induced tetraploid asparagus. Euphytica 16:201-212.

Braidwood, R.J., H. Çambel & P.J. Watson, 1969. Prehistoric investigations in southeastern Turkey. Science, N.Y. 164:1275-1276.

Braidwood, R.J. & B. Howe, 1962. Southwestern Asia beyond the lands of the Mediterranean Littoral. In: R.J. Braidwood & G.R. Willey (Eds.): Courses towards urban life. Aldine Publ. Comp., Chicago. p. 132-146.

Brandolini, A., 1970. Maize In: Ueko & Dimbleby, 1970, p. 273-309

Bray, R.A., 1978. Evidence for facultative apomixis in Cenchrus ciliaris. Euphytica 27: 801-804.

Bremer, G., 1966. The origin of the North Indian sugar canes. Genetica 37:345-363.

Brewbaker, J.L., 1979. Diseases of maize in the Wet Lowland tropics and the collapse of the Classic Maya civilization. Econ. Bot. 33:101-118.

Brewbaker, J.L. & W.F. Keim, 1953. A fertile interspecific hybrid in Trifolium (4n T. repens L. x 4n T. nigrescens VIV.). Am. Nat. 87:323-326.

Brieger, F.C., 1963. Collection and evaluation of indigenous races of maize. Genet. Agr. 17:259-264.

Brücher, H., 1966. Wildkartoffeln in Afrika. Z. PflZucht, 56:147-163.

Brücher, H., 1970. Beitrag zur Domestication proteinreicher und alkaloidarmer Lupinen in Südamerika. Angew. Bot. 44:7-27.

Brücher, H., 1971. Zur Widerlegung von Vavilovs geographisch-botanischer Differentialmethode. Erdkunde 25:20-36.

Brücher, H., 1975. Brasiliens Wildkartoffeln, die Sektion Tuberarium des Genus Solanum in Südbrasilien. Ber. dt. bot. Ges. 88: 399-410.

Brücher, H., 1979. Uber seltene und wenig bekannte Wildkartoffeln aus dem ariden Westen Argentiniens. Angew. Botanik 53:1-14.

Brunken, J.N., 1977. A systematic study of Pennisetum sect. Pennisetum (Gramineae). Amer. J. Bot. 64:161-176.

Brunken, J.N., J.M.J. de Wet & J.R. Harlan, 1977. The morphology and domestication of pearl millet. Econ. Bot. 31:163-174.

Bukasov, S.M., 1970. Cytogenetic problems of evolutions of the potato species of the section Tuberosum (Dun.) Buk., Genus Solanum. Genetika Moscow. 6(4):84-95.

Bunting, A.H., 1955. A classification of cultivated groundnuts. Emp.J.exp. Agric. 23: 158-170.

Bunting, A.H., 1958. A further note on the classification of cultivated groundnuts. Emp.J.exp. Agric. 26:254-258.

Burkart, A. & H. Brücher, 1953. Phaseolus aborigineus Burkart, die mutmassliche andine Stammform der Kulturbohne. Züchter 23:65-72.

Burkart, A., 1976. A monograph of the genus Prosopis (Leguminosae subfam. Mimosoideae) J. Arnold Arboretum 57:450-525.

Burkill, I.H., 1935. Dictionary of the economic products of the Malay Peninsula. Oxford. Vol. I, II.

Burkill, I.H., 1939. Notes on the genus Dioscorea in the Belgian Congo. Bull. Jardin bot. Etat Bruxelles 15:345-392.

Burkill, I.H., 1951-52. Habits of man and the origins of the cultivated plants of the Old World. Proc. Linn. Soc. Lond. 164:12-42.

Burrows, V.D., 1970. Yield and disease-escape potential of fall-sown oats possessing seed dormancy. Can. J. Pl. Sci. 50:371-377.

Burson, B.L. & H.W. Bennett, 1976. Cytogenetics of Paspalum conspersum and its genomic relationship with yellow-anthered P. dilatatum and P. malacophyllum. Can. J. Genet. Cytol. 18:701-708.

Burton, G.W., 1967. A search for origin of Pensacola Bahia grass. Econ. Bot. 21:379-382.

Cahana, H. & G. Ladizinsky, 1978. The cytogenetic position of Avena damasoena among the diploid oats. Can. J. Genet. Cytol. 20: 399-404.

Cambel, H. & R.J. Braidwood, 1970. An early farming village in Turkey. Scient. American (March) 223:50-56.

Cameron, J.W. & R.K. Soost, 1969. Citrus, Citrus ssp. In: Ferwerda & Wit, 1969, p. 129-162.

Camp, W.H., 1945. The North American blueberries with notes on other groups of Vacciniaceae. Brittonia 5:203-275.

Celarier, R.P., 1958. Cytotaxonomic notes on the subsection Halepensia of the genus Sorghum. Bull. Torrey bot. Club 85:49-62.

Chang, K.-C., 1970. The beginnings of agriculture in the Far East. Antiquity 44:175-185.

Chang, T.T., 1970. Rice. In: Frankel & Bennet, 1970, p. 267-272.

Chang, T.T., 1964. Present knowledge of rice genetics and cytogenetics. Intern. Rice Res. Inst., Techn. Bull. 1:1-96.

Chang, T.T., 1976a. The rice culture. Phil. Trans. R. Soc. London B275:143-157.

Chang, T.T., 1976b. The origin, cultivation, dissemination and diversification of Asian and African rices. Euphytica 25:425-441.

Chang, T.T., 1976c. Rice, In: Simmonds, 1976. p. 98-104.

Chapman Turner, N. & M.A.M. Bell, 1971. The ethnobotany of the Coast Salish Indians of Vancouver Islands. Econ. Bot. 25:63-104.

Charrier, A. & J. Berthaud, 1976. Variation de la teneur en caféine dans le genre Coffea. Café Cacao Thé 19:251-264.

Chatterjee, D., 1951. Note on the origin and distribution of wild and cultivated rices. Indian J. Genet. 11:18-22.

Cheesman, E.E., 1944. Notes on the nomenclature, classification and possible relationship of cacao populations. Trop. Agric., Trin. 21:144-159.

Chen, Chi-Chang & P.C. Gibson, 1970. Chromosome pairing in two interspecific hybrids of Trifolium. Can. J. Genet. Cytol. 12: 790-794.

Cheney, R.H. & E. Scholz, 1963. Rooibos tea, a South African contribution to world beverages. Econ. Bot. 17:186-194.

Chennaveeraiah, M.S. & S.C. Hiremath, 1974. Genome analysis of Eleusine coracana (L.) Gaertn. Euphytica 23:489-495.

Cherry, J.P., F.R.H. Katterman & J.E. Endrizzi, 1970. Comparative studies of seed proteins of species of Gossypium by gel electrophoresis. Evolution 24:431-447.

Chevalier, A., 1949. Nouvelles observations sur les arbres à kapock de l'Ouest africain. Rev. int. Bot. appl. Agric. trop.

29:377-385.

Chinnappa, C.C., 1970. Interspecific hybrids of Coffea canephora and C. liberica. Genetica 41:141-145.

Chowdhury, K.A., & G.M. Buth, 1970. 4,500 year old seeds suggest that true cotton is indigenous to Nubia. Nature Lond. 227:85-86.

Chowdhury, K.A. & G.M. Buth, 1971. Cotton seeds from the Neolithic in Egyptian Nubia and the origin of the Old World cotton. Biol. J. Linn. Soc. 3:303-313.

Churcher, C.S. & R.E.L. Smith, 1972. Kom Ombo: preliminary report on the fauna of late Paleolithic sites in Upper Egypt. Science 177:259-261.

Ciferri, R., 1939. Frumenti e granicoltura indigena in Etiopia. Agric. Col. 33(6): 15 p.

Clark, J.D., 1962. Africa south of the Sahara. In: R.J. Braidwood & G.R. Willey (Eds.): Courses toward urban life. Aldine Publ. Comp., Chicago. p. 1-33.

Clark, J.D., 1963. The evolution of culture in Africa. Am. Nat. 97:15-28.

Clark, J.D., 1976. Prehistoric populations and pressures favoring plant domestication in Africa. In: J.R. Harlan, J.M.J. de Wet & A.B.L. Stemler (Eds.): Origins of African plant domestication. Mouton, The Hague/ Paris. p. 67-105.

Clausen, R.E., 1932. Interspecific hybridization in Nicotiana. XII. Further data as to the origin of N. tabacum. Svensk. bot. Tidskr. 26:123-136.

Clausen, R.F., 1944. A botanical story of yam beans (Pachyrrhizus). Cornell Univ. Agric. Exp. Sta. Mem. 264. 35 p.

Clayton, W.D., 1972. Gramineae, p. 459-463 in F.N. Hepper (Ed.). Flora of West Tropical Africa III, 2. London.

Clevenger, S. & C.B. Heiser Jr., 1963. Helianthus laetiflorus and Helianthus rigidus - hybrids or species. Rhodora 65(762):121-133.

Clifford, D., 1958. Pelargoniums including the popular 'Geranium'. Blandford Press. 299 p.

Cobley, L.A., 1963. An introduction to the botany of tropical crops. Longman, Green & Co., London. 15 + 357 p.

Coenen, J. & J. Barrau, 1961. The breadfruit tree in Micronesia. S. Pac. Bull., Oct., p. 37-39, 65-67.

Coffman, F.A., 1946. Origin of cultivated oats. J. Am. Soc. Agron. 38:983-1002.

Connah, G., 1967. Progress report on archaeological work in Bornu. North. Hist. Res. Scheme, 2nd Inter. Report, Zaria.

Coursey, D.G., 1967. Yams. Longmans. 230 p.

Courter, J.W. & A.M. Rhodes, 1969. Historical notes on horseradish. Econ. Bot. 23:156-164.

Craig, I.L., B.L. Murray & T. Rajhathy, 1974. Avena canariensis: morphological and electrophoretic polymorphism and relationships with the A. magna - A. murphyi complex and A. sterilis. Can. J. Genet. Cytol. 16:

677-689.

Crane, M.B., 1950. The origin and improvement of cultivated plants. J.R. hort. Sco., 75: 427-435, 466-474.

Cruz, A.W., 1972. El Bromus mango, planta desaparecida. Idesia 2:127-131.

Cuatrecasas, J., 1964. Cacao and its allies, a taxonomic revision of the genus Theobroma. Contr. U.S. natn. Herb. 35:379-614.

Cufodontis, G., 1957. Bemerkenswerte Nutz- und Kulturpflanzen Aethiopiens. Botanische Ergebnisse der Expedition des Frobenius-Instituts der Universität Frankfurt am Main nach Süd-Aethiopien, 1954-1956. I. Senckerberg biol. 38:405-415.

Cutler, H.C. & Th.W. Whitaker, 1969. A new species of Cucurbita from Ecuador. Ann. Mo. bot. Gdn. 55:392-396.

Dalziel, J.M., 1937. The useful plants of West Tropical Africa. Crown Agents, London. 612 p.

Dane, F., D.W. Denna & T. Tsuchiya, 1980. Evolutionary studies of wild species in the genus Cucumis. Z. PflZücht. 85:8-109.

Dane, F. & T. Tsuchiya, 1976. Chromosome studies in the genus Cucumis. Euphytica 25: 367-374.

Danin, A., I. Baker & H.G. Baker, 1978. Cytogeography and taxonomy of the Portulaca oleracea L. polyploid complex. Israel J. Bot. 27:177-211.

Darlington, C.D., 1952. The coming of heredity. Discovery 13:139-143.

Darlington, C.D., 1956. Chromosome botany and the origins of cultivated plants. Revised 2nd ed. G. Allen & Unwin Ltd. 231 p.

Darlington, C.D., 1969. The evolution of man and society. G. Allen & Unwin Ltd., London. 753p.

Darlington, C.D. & E.K. Janaki Ammal, 1945. Chromosome atlas of cultivated plants. G. Allen & Unwin Ltd., London. 397 p.

Darrow, G.M. 1955. Effect of temperature and daylength on varietal adaptation of strawberry. Fruit Var. hort. Dig. 10:37-40, 51-54.

Dart, R.A. & P.B. Beaumont, 1971. On a further radiocarbon data for ancient mining in Southern Africa. S. Afr. J. Sci., p. 10-11.

De, D.N., 1974. Pigeon pea. In: J.B. Hutchinson (Ed.): Evolutionary studies in world crops. Cambridge. University Press, p. 79-87.

De, D.N., 1976. Origin, evolution and distribution of Cajanus and Phaseolus: Western Ghats as a microcentre (Abstract). Indian J. Genet. Plant Breed. 36:141-142.

De Wet, J.M.J., 1975. Evolutionary dynamics of cereal domestication. Bull. Torrey bot. Club 102:307-312.

De Wet, J.M.J., 1977. Domestication of African cereals. Afr. Econ. Hist. 3 (Spring): 15-32.

De Wet, J.M.J., 1978. Systematics and evolution of Sorghum sect. Sorghum (Gramineae). Am. J. Bot. 65:477-484.

De Wet, J.M.J., 1979. Principles of evolution and cereal domestication. In: Zeven & Van

Harten, 1979, p. 269-282.

De Wet, J.M.J., L.M. Engle, C.A. Grant & S.T. Tanaka, 1972. Cytology of maize - Tripsacum introgression. Am. J. Bot. 59:1026-1026.

De Wet, J.M.J., J.R. Gray & J.R. Harlan, 1976. Systematics of Tripsacum (Gramineae). Philologia 33:203-227.

De Wet, J.M.J., J.R. Harlan & C.A. Grant, 1971. Origin and evolution of teosinte (Zea mexicana (Schrad.) Kuntze). Euphytica 20:255-265.

De Wet, J.M.J. & J.R. Harlan, 1972. Origin of maize: the tripartite hypothesis. Euphytica 21:271-279.

De Wet, J.M.J. & J.R. Harlan, 1974. Tripsacum - maize interaction: a novel cytogenetic system. Genetics 78:493-502.

De Wet, J.M.J. & J.R. Harlan, 1975. Weeds and domesticates: Evolution in the man-made habitat. Econ. Bot. 29:99-107.

De Wet, J.M.J., J.R. Harlan & B. Kurmarohita, 1972a. Origin and evolution of guinea sorghums. E. Afr. agric. For. J. 38:114-119.

De Wet, J.M.J., J.R. Harlan, R.J. Lambert & L.M. Engle, 1972b. Introgression from Tripsacum into Zea and the origin of maize. Caryologia 25:25-31.

De Wet, J.M.J. & J.P. Huckabay, 1967. The origin of Sorghum bicolor II. Distribution and domestication. Evolution 21:787-802.

Dewey, D.R., 1975. The origin of Agropyron smithii. Am. J. Bot. 62:524-530.

Dewey, D.R., 1976. Derivation of a new forage grass from Agropyron repens x Agropyron spicatum hybrids. Crop Science 16:175-180.

Doebley, J.F. & H.H. Iltis, 1980. Taxonomy of Zea (Gramineae). I. A subgeneric classification with key to the taxa. Am. J. Bot. 67:982-993.

Doggett, H., 1965. The development of cultivated sorghums. In: Hutchinson, 1965, p. 50-69.

Doggett, H., 1970. Sorghum. Harlow, London. 16 + 403 p.

Dorofeev, V.F., 1971. Die Weizen Transkaukasiens und ihre Bedeutung in der Evolution der Gattung Triticum L. 3. Die Spelzweizen Transkaukasiens (T. macha Dek. et Men., T. spelta L. ssp. spelta Dorof., ssp. Kuckuckianum Gökg. und ssp. vavilovii Sears). Z. Pfl.Zücht. 66:335-360.

Dressler, R.L., 1953. The pre-Columbian cultivated plants of Mexico. Bot. Mus. Leafl., Harv. Univ. 16:115-172.

Duke, J.A., B.N. Okigbo & C.F. Read, 1977. Macrotyloma geocarpum (Harms, Marechal and Baudet). Trop. Grain Legume Bull. No 10:12-13.

Dutt, B. & R.P. Roy, 1971. Cytogenetic investigations in Cucurbitaceae. I. Interspecific hybridization in Luffa. Genetica 42:139-156.

Dutta, P.K., I.C. Chopra & L.D. Kapoor, 1963. Cultivation of Rauvolfia serpentina in India. Econ. Bot. 17:243-251.

Edmonds, J.M. & S.M. Glidewel, 1977. Acrylamide gel electrophoresis of seed proteins from some Solanum (Section Solanum) species. Plant Syst. Evol. 127:277-291.

Engelbrecht, Th., 1916. Ueber die Entstehung einiger feldmässig angebauter Kulturpflanzen. Geogr. Z. 22:328-334.

Eshbaugh, W.H., 1970. A biosystematic and evolutionary study of Capsicum baccatum (Solanaceae). Brittonia 22:31-43.

Eshbaugh, W.H., 1977. The taxonomy of the genus Capsicum (Solanaceae). In: E. Pochard Ed.): Capsicum-77. I. Taxonomy and cytogenetics. Montfavet. p. 13-26.

Eshbaugh, W.H., 1980. Variation and evolution in Capsicum eximium Hunz. In: I.W. Boukema (ed.): Synopses of the Eucarpia Working Group IVth meeting, October 1980, Wageningen. Also Capsicum - 1980, Wageningen: 10-11. p. 10-14.

Esquinas-Alcazar, J.T., 1978. Alloenzyme variation and relationships in the genus Cucumis (Abstract). Diss. Abstracts Intern. B 38:4634B. Cited from Pl. Breed. Abstr. 50 (1980), No 682.

Evreinoff, V.-A., 1944. Le prunier japonais (Prunus salicina Lindl.), son origin, ses variétés, sa culture. Rev. Hort., Paris 115:307-310, 323-325.

Evreinoff, V.-A., 1954. Les ancêtres de nos abricots. J. Agric. trop. Bot. appl. 1:431-440.

Eijnatten, C.L.M. van, 1969. Kolanut, Cola nitida (Vent.) Schott & Endl. and C. acuminata (P. Brenan) Schott & Endl. In: Ferwerda & Wit, 1969, p. 289-307.

Eijnatten, C.L.M. van, 1970. Kola; its botany and cultivation. Comm. Dep. agric. Res. R. trop. Inst. Amsterdam. 59 p.

Ezumah, H., 1970. Miscellaneous tuberous crops. Tropical root and tuber crops tomorrow 1:166-171.

Faris, D.G., 1965. The origin and evolution of the cultivated forms of Vigna sinensis. Can. J. Genet. Cytol. 7:433-442.

Feldman, M., 1979. New evidence on the origin of the B genome of wheat. Proc. 5th Int. Wheat Genetics Symp. New Felhi 1978, p. 120-132.

Feldman, M., I. Strauss & A. Vardi, 1979. Chromosome pairing and fertility of F_1 hybrids of Aegilops longissima and Ae. searsii. Can. J. Genet. Cytol. 21:261-272.

Ferwerda, F.P. & F. Wit (Ed.), 1969. Outlines of perennial crop breeding in the tropics. Misc. Pap. 4, Agricultural University Wageningen. 511 p.

Fiskenjö, G., 1975. Chromosomal relationships between the species of Allium as revealed by C-banding. Hereditas 81:23-31.

Flach, M. & A.M. Cruickshank, 1969. Nutmeg, Myristica fragrans Houtt. and Myristica argentea Warb. In: Ferwerda & Wit, 1969, p. 329-338.

Flannery, K.V., 1965. The ecology of early food production in Mesopotamia. Science, N.Y. 147:1247-1256.

Fosberg, F.R., 1960. Introgression in Arto-
    carpus (Moraceae) in Micronesia. Brittonia
    12:101-113.
Fouzdar, A. & S.L. Tandon, 1976. Cytogenetical
    evolution in the genus Pisum. Cytologia 41:
    91-104.
Frankel, O.H. & E. Bennett (Ed.), 1970. Genetic
    resources in plants, their exploration and
    conservation. Oxford/Edinburgh. 21 + 554 p.
Frey, K.J. (Ed.), 1967. Plant breeding. State
    Univ. Press. Ames, Iowa. 430 p.
Fryxell, P.A. & C.R. Parks, 1967. Gossypium
    trilobum: an addendum. Madrono 19:117-123.
Funk, D.T., 1969. Genetics of black walnut
    (Juglans nigra). USDA Forest Serv. Res. Pap.
    WO-10. 13 p.
Gade, D.W., 1966. Achira, the edible canna, its
    cultivation and use in the Peruvian Andes.
    Econ. Bot. 20:407-415.
Gade, D.W., 1970. Ethnobotany of canihua (Cheno-
    podium pallidicaule), rustic seed crop of
    the Altiplano. Econ. Bot. 24:55-61.
Galil, J., M. Stein & A. Horovitz, 1976. On the
    origin of the sycomore fig (Ficus sycomorus
    L.) in the Middle East. Gdn's Bull., Singa-
    pore 29:191-205.
Galinat, W.C., 1969. The evolution under domes-
    tication of the maize ear: string cob maize.
    Bull. Mass. agric. Exp. Stn. 577. 10 p.
Galinat, W.C., 1971. The origin of maize. Ann.
    rev. Genetics 5:447-478.
Garćia, A. & K. Tsunewaki, 1977. Cytogenetical
    studies in the genus Persea (Lauraceae).
    III. Electrophoretical studies on peroxi-
    dase isozymes. Japan J. Genet. 52:379-386.
Gay, C., 1865. Historia fisica y politica de
    Chile. 2 vol. Paris.
Gentry, H.S., 1955. Introducing black-pepper
    into America. Econ. Bot. 9:256-268.
Gentry, H.S., 1961. Bucku - a new cultivated
    crop in South Africa. Econ. Bot. 15:326-331.
Gentry, H.S., 1969. Origin of the Common bean,
    Phaseolus vulgaris. Econ. Bot. 23:55-69.
Gentry, H.S., 1971. Pisum resources, a preli-
    minary survey. Pl. Genetics Resourc. Newsl.
    (25):3-13.
Gentry, M.S., 1942. Rio Mayo Indians. Carnegie
    Inst. Washington. Publ. 527.
Gerašenkov, B.L., 1968. (Siberian forms - a dis-
    tinct ecotype of maize). Sb. nauch. Rab.
    Sib. (14):137-141. Pl. Breed. Abstr. 42
    (2369).
Gladstones, J.S., 1970. Lupins as crop plants.
    Field Crops Abstr. 23:123-148.
Glendinning, D.R., 1975. Chilean potatoes: an
    appraisal. Potato Res. 18:306-30.
Gökgöl, M., 1941. Uber die Genzentrentheorie
    und den Ursprung der Weizen. Z.PflZücht.
    23:562-578.
Gopalakrishnan, R. & S. Sampath, 1966. The
    American species of Oryza. Oryza 3 (1):35-
    40.
Gorman, C.F., 1969. Hoabinhian: a pebble-tool
    complex with early plant associations in
    Southeast Asia. Science, N.Y. 163:671-673.
Gould, F.W., 1963. Cytotaxonomy of Digitaria
    sanguinalis and D. adscendens. Brittonia
    15:241-244.
Grant, M.D., 1959. Cytogenetic studies in Ama-
    ranthus. II. Natural interspecific hybri-
    dization between Amaranthus dubius and A.
    spinosus. Can. J. Bot. 37:1063-1070.
Grassl, C.O., 1964. Problems relating to the
    origin and evolution of wild and cultiva-
    ted Saccharum. Indian J. Sug.cane Res. Dev.
    8:106-116.
Grassl, C.O., 1967. Introgression between
    Saccharum and Miscanthus in New Guinea anc
    the Pacific area. I.S.S.C.T. Proc. 12th
    Congr., Puerto Rico, 1965.
Grassl. C.O., 1968. Saccharum names and their
    interpretation. I.S.S.C.T. Proc. 13th Congr.,
    Taiwan, p. 868-875.
Grassl, C.O., 1977. The origin of the sugar
    producing cultivars of Saccharum. Sugarcane
    Breeder's Newsletter 39:8-33.
Gray, J.C., 1978. Serological reactions of
    Fraction I proteins from interspecific hy-
    brids in the genus Nicotiana. Pl. Syst.
    Evol. 129:177-183.
Grobman, A., W. Salhuana & P.C. Mangelsdorf,
    1956. Races of maize in Peru. Maize Genet.
    Coop. New Lett. 30:27-30.
Grubben, G.J.H., 1977. Tropical vegetables and
    their genetic resources. FAO, Rome. 197 p.
Grun, P., 1979. Evolution of the cultivated
    potato: a cytoplasmic analysis. In: J.G.
    Hawkes, R.N. Lester & A.D. Skelding: The
    biology and taxonomy of the Solanaceae.
    Academic Press. p. 655-665.
H(...), T.R. & T.T. C(hang), 1978. History of
    rice offers clues for rewarding germ plasm
    preservation. The IRRI reporter (1/78):
    1-3.
Hackbart, J. & K.W. Pakendorf, 1970. Lupinus
    mutabilis Sweet., eine Kulturpflanze der
    Zukunft. Z. PflZücht. 63:237-245.
Hammer, K., 1976. Die kultivierten Kakteenarten.
    Kulturpflanze 24:249-282.
Hammer, K. & R. Fritsch, 1977. Zur Frage nach
    der Ursprungsart des Kulturmohns (Papaver
    somniferum L.). Kulturpflanze 25:113-124.
Hammer, K. & H. Knüpffer, 1979. Eine Methode
    zur Abgrenzung infraspezifischer Sippen
    anhand quantitativer blütenökologischer
    Merkmale bei Aegilops tauschii Coss. Fed-
    des Rep. 90:179-188.
Hancock, J.F. & R.S. Bringhurst, 1978. Inter-
    populational differentiation and adaptation
    in the perennial, diploid species Fragaria
    vesca L.. Amer. J. Bot. 65:795-803.
Hanelt, P., 1961. Zur Kenntnis von Carthamus
    tinctorius L. Kulturpflanze 9:114-145.
Hanelt, P., 1972. Die intraspezifische Varia-
    bilität von Vicia faba L. und ihre Glie-
    derung. Kulturpflanze 20:75-128.
Harlan, J.R;, 1951. Anatomy of gene centres.
    Am. Nat. 85:97-103.
Harlan, J.R., 1961. Geographic origin of plants
    useful to agriculture. In: R.E. Hodgson
    (ed.): Germ plasm resources. Washington.
    p. 3-19.
Harlan, J.R., 1967. Plant introduction and bio-
    systematics, p. 55-83 In: K.J. Frey, 1967.

Harlan, S.C., 1970. Gene pools in the new world tetraploid cottons. In: Frankel & Bennett, 1970. p. 335-340.

Harlan, J.R., 1971. Agricultural origins: centres and noncentres. Science, N.Y. 174: 468-474.

Harlan, J.R., 1973. Genetic resoruces of some major field crops in Africa. Survey of Crop Genetic resources in their centres of diviersity. First Report, FAO. 45.

Harlan, J.R. & Pasquereau, 1969. Decrue agriculture in Mali. Econ. Bot. 23:70-74.

Harlan, J.R. & A.B.L. Stemler, 1976. Races of sorghum in Africa. In: J.R. Harlan, J.M.J. de Wet & A.B.L. Stemler (Eds.): Origin of African plant domestication. Mouton Press, The Hague.

Harlan, J.R. & J.M.J. de Wet, 1965. Some thoughts about weeds. Econ. Bot. 19:16-24.

Harlan, J.R. & J.M.J. de Wet, 1969. Sources of variation in Cynodon dactylon (L.) Pers. Crop Sci. 9:774-778.

Harlan, J.R. & J.M.J. de Wet, 1972. A simplified classification of cultivated sorghum. Crop Sci. 12:172-176.

Harlan, J.R., J.M.J. de Wet, W.W. Huffine & J.D. Deakin, 1970. A guide to the species of Cynodon (Gramineae). Oklahoma State Univ. Exp. Stn. Bull. B-673:1-37.

Harlan, J.R., J.M.J. de Wet & A.B.L. Stemler, 1976. Origins of African plant domestication. Mouton Press, The Hague.

Harlan, J.R. & D. Zohary, 1966. Distribution of wild wheats and barleys. Science, N.Y. 153: 1074-1080.

Harland, S.C., 1970. Gene pools in the New World tetraploid cottons. In: O.H. Frankel & E. Bennett (Eds.): Genetic resources in plants - their exploitation and conservation. Blackwell Scient. Publ., Oxford/Edinbourgh. p. 335-340.

Harries, H.C., 1978. The evolution, dissemination and classification of Cocos nucifera L. Bot. Rev. 44:265-319.

Harris, D.R., 1967. New light on plant domestication and the origins of agriculture: a review. Geogr. Rev. 57:90-107.

Harris, D.R., 1972. The origins of agriculture in the tropics. Am. Scient. 60:180-193.

Harten, A.M. van, 1969. Cinchona, Cinchona spp. In: Ferwerda & Wit, 1969, p. 111-128

Harten, A.M. van, 1970. Melegueta pepper. Econ. Bot. 24:208-216

Hashimoto, M. & T. Shimura, 1978. (Morphological studies on the origin of tea V. A proposal of one place of origin theory based on cluster analysis). Jap. J. trop. Agric. 53:93-101. Cited from Pl. Breed. Abstr. 48 (1978) No 8815.

Hatheway, W.H., 1957. Races of maize in Cuba. NAS-NRC Publ., Washington Publ. 453, 75 p.

Hawkes, J., 1958. Kartoffel. I. Taxonomy, cytology and crossability. In: Kappert & Rudorf, 1958, p. 1-43.

Hawkes, J., 1962a. Introgression in certain wild potato species. Euphytica 11:26-35.

Hawkes, J., 1962b. The origin of Solanum juzep-

czukii Buk. and S. vertilobum Juz. & Buk. Z. PflZücht. 47: 1-14.

Hawkes, J., 1963. A revision of the tuber-bearing Solanums (second edition). Report Scottish Plant Breeding Station.

Hawkes, J., 1966. Modern taxonomic work on the Solanum species of Mexico and adjacent countries. Am. Potato J. 43:81-103.

Hawkes, J.G., 1969. The ecological background of plant domestication. In: Ucko & Dimbleby, 1969, p. 17-29.

Hawkes, J.G., 1970. Problems and results of evolutionary and taxonomic studies on cultivated plants, with special reference to New World taxa. Kulturpf. Beih. 6:141-156.

Hawkes, J.G. & W. Lange (Eds.), 1973. European and regional gene banks. Eucarpia, Wageningen. 107 p.

Hawkes, J.G., R.N. Lester & A.D. Skelding, 1979. The biology and taxonomy of the Solanaceae. Academic Press, London. 738 p.

Hedberg, I., 1969. Cytotaxonomic studies on Anthoxanthum odoratum L., s. lat. III. Investigations of Swiss and Austrian population samples. Svensk bot. Tidskr. 63:233-250.

Hedberg, I., 1970. Cytotaxonomic studies on Anthoxanthum odoratum L. s. lat. IV. Karyotypes, meiosis and the origin of tetraploid A. odoratum. Hereditas 64:153-176.

Heiser, C.B., 1955. The origin and development of the cultivated sunflower. Am. Biol. Teach. 17:162-167.

Heiser, C.B., 1964a. Origin and variability of the pepino (Solanum muricatum): a preliminary report. Baileya 12:151-158.

Heiser Jr, C.B., 1964b. Sangorache, an amaranth used ceremonially in Ecuador. Am. Anthrop. 66:136-140.

Heiser, C.B., 1965. Sunflowers, weeds and cultivated plants. In: Baker & Stebbins, 1965, p. 391-398.

Heiser, C.B., 1969. Nightshades the paradoxial plants. W.H. Freeman & Co. Ltd., Kent. 200 p.

Heiser, C.B., 1971. Notes on some species of Solanum (Sect. Leptostemomum) in Latin America. Baileya 28:50-65.

Heiser, Ch.B. Jr, 1973a. Variation in the bottle gourd. In: Maggers et al., p. 121-128.

Heiser, Ch.B. Jr, 1973b. The penis gourd of New Guinea. Ann. Ass. Am. Geogr. 63:312-318.

Heiser, Ch.B., 1978. The totora (Scirpus californicus) in Ecuador and Peru. Econ. Bot. 32:222-236.

Helbaek, H., 1960. Ecological effects of irrigation in Ancient Mesopotamia. Iraq 22:186-196.

Helbaek, H., 1966. Commentary on the phylogenesis of Triticum and Hordeum. Econ. Bot. 20:350-360.

Helbaek, H., 1971. Notes on the evolution and history of Linum. Kuml. Aarhus. p. 103-129.

Helm, J., 1963a. Morphologisch-taxonomische Gliederung der Kultursippen von Brassica oleracea. Kulturpflanze 11:92-210.

Helm, J., 1963b. Die Chinakohle im Sortiment

Gatersleben. III. 3. Brassica narinosa L.H. Bailey. Kulturpflanze 11:416–421.

Hemingway, J.S., 1976. Mustards, Brassica spp. and Sinapis alba (Cruciferae). In: N.W. Simmonds (Ed.): Evolution of crop plants. Longman. p. 56–59.

Hemmerly, Th.E., 1970. Economic uses of eastern red cedar. Econ. Bot. 24:39–41.

Hepper, F.N., 1963. Plants of the 1957–58 West African Expedition. II. The bambara groundnut (Voandzeia subterranea) and Kersting's groundnut (Kerstingiella geocarpa) wild in West Africa. Kew Bull. 16:395–407.

Hermann, F.J., 1962. A revision of the genus Glycine and its immediate allies. Tech. Bull. 1268, Washington.

Hernandez X., E., 1973. Genetic resources of primitive varieties of Mesoamerica. Zea spp. Phaseolus spp., Capsicum spp. and Cucurbita ssp.. In: Survey of crop genetic resources in their centres of diversity. FAO. p. 76–115.

Heybroek, H.M., 1963. Diseases and lopping for fodder as possible causes of a prehistoric decline of Ulmus. Acta bot. neerl. 12:1–11.

Higgs, E.S. & M.R. Jarman, 1969. The origins of agriculture: A reconsideration. Antiquity 43:31–41.

Higgs, E.S. & M.R. Jarman, 1972. The origins of animal and plant husbandry. In: Higgs, E.S. (Ed.): Papers in economic prehistory. Cambridge Univ. Press, Cambridge. p. 3–13.

Hilu, K.W. & J.M.J. de Wet, 1976. Domestication of Eleusine coracana. Econ. Bot. 30:194–208.

Hilu, K.W., J.M.J. de Wet & J.R. Harlan, 1979. Archaeobotanical studies of Eleusine coracana ssp. coracana (finger millet). Am. J. Bot. 66:330–333.

Hjelmqvist, H., 1972. A find of Nelumbo nucifera from Old Cyprus. With some note on the history of the species. Bot. Notiser 125:383–388.

Ho, P., 1969. The loess and the origin of Chinese agriculture. Am. Hist. Rev. 75:1–36.

Ho, P., 1976. The cradles of the East. Hongkong/Chicago. 12 + 440 pp.

Ho, P., 1977. The indigenous origins of Chinese agriculture. In: C.A. Reed (Ed.): Origins of agriculture. Mouton Press, The Hague. 1013 p.

Ho, T.-T., 1969. Huang-t'u yü Chung-kuo Nung-yeh ti Ch'i-yüan. Hongkong. Cited by Chang 1970.

Hogeboom, N.G., 1968. Self-compatibility in Lycopersicon peruvianum (L.) Mill. Euphytica 17:220–223.

Holub, J., 1969. (The origin of peach trees and their variability with respect to our natural conditions). Sb. csl. Akad. zemed. Ved., Rostlinná Vyroba 15:531–538. Pl. Breed. Abstr. 40(3707).

Hu, S.Y., 1976. The genus Panax (Ginseng) in Chinese medicine. Econ. Bot. 30:11–28.

Huaman, Z., J.G. Hawkes & P.R. Rowe, 1976. Studies on the origin of Solanum ajanhuiri Juz. et Buk., a South America cultivated diploid potato. Am. Potato J. 53:372.

Hutchinson, J., 1969. Evolution and phylogeny of flowering plants. Academic Press. London/New York. 717 p.

Hutchinson, J. (Ed.), 1965. Crop plant evolution. Cambridge University Press, London. 7 + 244 p.

Hutchinson, J.B., 1962. The history and relationships of the world's cotton. Endeavour 21:5–15.

Hutchinson, J.B., 1971. Changing concepts in crop plant evolution. Expl. agric. Rev. 7 273–280.

Hutton, E.M., 1970. Tropical pastures. Adv. Agron. 22:1–73.

Hymowitz, T., 1970. On the domestication of the soybean. Econ. Bot. 24:408–421.

Hymowitz, T., 1973. The trans-domestication concept as applied to guar. Econ. Bot. 26 49–60.

Hymowitz, T. & J. Boyd, 1977. Origin, ethnobotany and agricultural potential of the winged bean - Psophocarpus tetragonolobus Econ. Bull. 31:180–188.

Hymowitz, T. & C.A. Newell. 1980. Taxanomy, speciation, domestication, dissemination, germplasm resources and variation in the genus Glycine. In: R.J. Summerfield & A.H Bunting (Eds.): Advances in legume science. Royal Botanical Garden Kew, Publication, London.

Ietswaart, J.H., 1980. A taxonomic revision of the genus Origanum (Labiatae). Leiden Univ. Press (Leiden Botanical Series 4). 153 p.

Ikeda, N. & S. Ono, 1969. Studies on Mentha aquatica L. and its genome analysis. II. Genome analysis in the genus Mentha. Part 7. Jap. J. Breed. 19: 357–365.

Ikeda, N., S. Shimizu, O. Karasawa, T. Origasa, & S. Ono, 1970. Mentha arvensis L. var. piperascens Mal. which grows wild in the north-eastern part in Japan II. General characters and cytogenetical analysis. Scient. Rep. Fac. Agric. Okayama Univ. 36:1–11.

Iltis, H.H. & J.F. Doebley, 1980. Taxonomy of Zea (Gramineae). II. Subspecific categories in the Zea mays complex and a generic synopsis. Am. J. Bot. 67:994–1004.

Iltis, H.H., J.F. Doebley, R. Guzman-M. & B. Pazy, 1979. Zea diploperennis (Gramineae) A new teosinte from Mexico. Science N.Y. 203:186–188.

Imrie, B.C. & P.F. Knowles, 1970. Inheritance studies in interspecific hybrids between Carthamus flavescens and C. tinctorius. Crop Sci. 10:349–352.

Jackson, M.T., P.R. Rowe & J.G. Hawkes, 1976. The enigma of triploid potatoes: a reappraisal (Abstract). Am. Potato J. 53:393.

Jacques, W.A., 1974. Yorkshire fog (Holcus lanatus). Its potential as a pasture species. Proc. N. Z. Grassld Ass. 35:249–257.

Jagadishchandra, K.S., 1975. Recent studies on Cymbopogon Spreng. (Aromatic grasses). J. Pl. Crops 3:1–5.

Jain, S.K., 1977. Genetic diversity of weedy rye populations in California. Crop Sci.

17:480-482.

Jain, S.K. & D.K. Banerjee, 1974. Preliminary observations on the ethnobotany of the genus Coix. Econ. Bot. 28:38-42.

Jain, S.K., A.M. Olivieri & J. Fernandez-Martinez, 1977. Serpentine sunflower, Helianthus exilis, as a genetic source. Crop Sci. 17:477-478.

Jain, S.K., C.O. Qualset, G.M. Bhatt & K.K. Wu, 1976. Geographical patterns of phenotypic diversity in a world collection of durum wheat. Crop Sci. 16:700-705.

Jameson, J.D., 1970. Agriculture in Uganda. Oxford University Press, Oxford.

Jansen, P.C.M., 1981. Species, condiments and medicinal plants in Ethiopia, their taxonomy and agricultural significance. Agric. Res. Rep. 906. Pudoc, Wageningen. 327 p.

Jauhar, P.P., 1975. Chromosome relationships between Lolium and Festuca (Gramineae). Chromosome 52:103-121.

Jeffrey, C., 1962. Notes on Cucurbitaceae, including a proposed new classification of the family. Kew Bull. 15:337-371.

Jenkins, J.A., 1948. The origin of the cultivated tomato. Econ. Bot. 2:379-392.

Jensen, R.J., M.J. McLeod, W.H. Eshbaugh & S.I. Guttman, 1979. Numerical taxonomic analyses of allozymic variation in Capsicum (Solanaceae). Taxon 28:315-327.

Jensma, J.R., 1957. Teelt en veredeling van bloemkool. Meded. Inst. Vered. Tuinb. Gewass. 96. 61 p.

Johnson, B.L., 1972. Protein electrophoretic profiles and the origin of the B genome of wheat. Proc. Nat. Acad. Sci., USA 69:1398-1402.

Jones, D.A., 1973. On the polymorphism of cyanogenesis in Lotus corniculatus 5. Denmark. Heredity 30:381-386.

Jones, H.A. & L.K. Mann, 1963. Onions and their allies. Botany, cultivation and utilization. Leonard Hill Books Ltd., London. 286 p.

Jones, J.K. & B.U. Majisu, 1968. The homoeology of Aegilops mutica chromosomes. Canad. J. Genet. Cytol. 10:620-626.

Kabulov, Z.L., 1969. (The pistachio in Turkmenia). Sborn. Trud. Asp. molod. nauc. Sotrud. vses. nauc. issled. Inst. Rasten 10: 567-568. Pl. Breed Abstr. 40(1567).

Kammacher, P. & J. Capot, 1972. Sur les relations caryologiques entre Coffea arabica et Coffea canephora. Café-Cacao-Thé 16 (4): 289-293.

Kaplan, L., 1965. Archaeology and domestication in American Phaseolus beans. Econ. Bot. 19 :356-368.

Kaplan, L., 1981. What is the origin of the common bean. Econ. Bot. 35:240-254.

Kaplan, L., T.F. Lynch & C.E. Smith Jr., 1973. Early cultivated beans (Phaseolus vulgaris) in intermontane Peruvian valley. Science, N.Y., 179:76-77.

Kappert, H. & W. Rudorf, 1962. Handbuch der Pflanzenzüchtung. 6. Züchtung von Gemüse, Obst, Reben und Forstpflanzen. 2nd ed. Ber-

lin/Hamburg. 913 p.

Kato, M. & T. Simura, 1978. Cytogenetical studies on Camellia species. III An interspecific hybrid between Camellia japonica L. and C. sinensis (L.) O. Kuntze. Jap. J. Breed. 28:147-150.

Katznelson, J. & F.H.W. Morley, 1965a. Speciation processes in Trifolium subterraneum. Israel J. Bot. 14:15-35.

Katznelson, J. & F.H.W. Morley, 1965b. A taxonomic revision of sect. Calycomorphum of the genus Trifolium. I. The geocarpic species. Israel J. Bot. 14:112-134.

Kaul, R.K., 1974. Job's tears. In: J.B. Hutchinson (Ed.): Evolutionary studies in world crops. Cambridge University Press, Cambridge.

Kaur, M., H.C. Das & G.S. Randhawa, 1973. Systematic status of round melon (Citrullus vulgaris var. fistulosus) as studied by leaf phenolics. Curr. Sci. 42:730-731.

Kawashima, N., Y. Tanake & S. Iwai, 1976. Origin of Nicotiana tabacum detected by primary structure of Fraction I Protein. Biochim. Biophys. Acta 427:70-77.

Kazakova, A.A., 1971. (The most widely distributed species of onion, their origin and intraspecific classification). Trudy prikl. Bot. Genet. Selek. 45:19-41. Pl. Breed. Abstr. 42(9176).

Kazimierski, T., 1960. An interspecific hybrid in the genus Lupinus. Genet. pol. 1: 3-60.

Keep, E. & J.B. Briggs, 1971. A survey of Ribes species for aphid resistance. Ann. appl. Biol. 68:23-30.

Kempanna, C., 1969. Phytogeographical studies of Eleusine corocana. Mysore agric. J. 3 (1):22-31. Pl. Breed. Abstr. 40(892).

Khidir, M.O. & P.F. Knowles, 1970. Cytogenetic studies of Carthamus species (Compositae) with 32 pairs of chromosomes. II. Intersectional hybridization. Can. J. Genet. Cytol. 12:90-99.

Khush, G.S., 1960. Cytogenetic and evolutionary studies in the genus Secale. Thesis Univ. of California, Davis. 145 p.

Khush, G.S., 1963. Cytogenetic and evolutionary studies in Secale III. Cytogenetics of weedy ryes and origin of cultivated rye. Econ. Bot. 17:60-71.

Kihara, H., 1969. History of biology and other sciences in Japan in retrospect. Proc. Int. Congr. Genetics 3:49-70.

Kihara, H., K. Yamashita & M. Tanaka, 1956. A new strain of Triticum polonicum. Wheat Inf. Serv. 4:3.

Kimber, G. & R.S. Athwal, 1972. A reassessment of the course of evolution of wheat. Proc. Natn. Acad. Sci. USA. 69:912-915.

Knörzer, K.-H., 1965. Die Roggentrespe (Bromus secalinum L.) als prähistorische Nutzpflanze. Archaeo-Physika 2:30-38.

Knowles, P.F., 1969. Centres of plant diversity and conservation of crop germ plasm in safflower. Econ. Bot. 23:324-329.

Kollmann, F., 1972. Allium ampeloprasum - a polyploid complex. II. Meiosis and interre-

lationships between the ploidy types. Caryologia 25:295-312.

Koul, A.K. & R.N. Gohil, 1970. Cytology of the
tetraploid Allium ampeloprasum with chiasma
localization. Chromosome 29:12-19.

Krapovickas, A., 1969. The origin, variability
and spread of the groundnut (Arachis hypogaea). In: Ucko & Dimbleby, 1969, p. 427-
441.

Krapovickas, A., 1973. Evolution of the genus
Arachis. In: R. Moav (Ed.): Agricultural
genetics. John Wiley & Sons, New York & To-
ronto. p. 135-151.

Kraus, B.H. & R.A. Hamilton, 1970. Bibliography
of the Macadamia. Part I. Author Index. Res.
Rep. 176, Hawaii Agricultural Experimental
Station. College of tropical Agriculture
University of Hawaii. 12 p.

Kuckuck, H., 1962. Vavilov's Genzentrentheorie
im heutigen Sicht. 3rd Congr. Eur. Ass.
Res. Pl. Breed. Eucarpia, Paris. p. 177-
196. Abridged: Present views on Vavilov's
gene-centre theory. Pl. Introd. Newsl. (12)
(1963):8-10.

Kuckuck, H., 1973. Present situation of genetic
resources of small grains in Syria, Iraq,
Iran, Afghanistan and West-Pakistan. In:
Hawkes & Lange, 1973, p. 74-77.

Kuckuck, H. & G. Kobabe, 1962. Küchenzweibel,
Allium cepa L., In: Kappert & Rudorf, 1962.
p. 270-312.

Kupzow, A.J., 1932. The geographical variability
of the species Carthamus tinctorius L. Bull.
Appl. Bot. Genet. Pl. Breed. 9th Ser. p. 99-
181.

Kupzov, A.J., 1955. (Geographical distribution
of cultivated flora and its historical development). Bull. All Union Geogr. Soc. 87
:220-231. Cited by Darlington (1963).

Kuruvilla, K.M. & A. Singh, 1981. Karyotypic
and electrophoretic studies on taro and its
origin. Euphytica 30:405-413.

Ladizinsky, G., 1973. Genetic control of bi-
valent pairing in the Avena strigosa polyploid complex. Chromosoma 42:105-110.

Ladizinsky, G., 1975a. A new Cicer from Turkey.
Notes R. bot. Gdn Edinb. 34:201-202.

Ladizinsky, G., 1975b. Oats in Ethiopia. Econ.
Bot. 29:238-241.

Ladizinsky, G., 1975c. On the origin of the
broad bean, Vicia faba L. Israel J. Bot.
24:80-88.

Ladizinsky, G., 1978. Chromosomal polymorphism
in the wild populations of Vicia sativa.
Caryologia 31:233-241.

Ladizinsky, G., 1979. Species relationships in
the genus Lens as indicated by seed protein electrophoresis. Bot. Gaz. 140:449-
451.

Ladizinsky, G. & R. Temkin, 1978. The cytogenetic structure of Vicia sativa aggregate.
Theor. Appl. Genet. 53:33-42.

Ladizinsky, G. & D. Zohary, 1971. Notes on species delimitation, species relationships
and polyploidy in Avena L. Euphytica 20:
380-395.

Landolt, E., 1970. Mitteleuropäische Wiesen-

pflanzen als hybridogene Abkömmlinge von
mittel- und südeuropäischen Gebirgsippen
und submediterranen Sippen. Feddes Rep.
81:61-66.

Langhe, E., De, 1969. Bananas, Musa ssp. In:
Ferwerda & Wit (Eds.), 1969, p. 53-78

Larsen, E. & D.A.N. Cromer, 1970. Exploration,
utilization and conservation of Eucalypt
gene resources. In: Frankel & Bennet
(Eds.), 1970, p. 381-388.

Larsson, E.G.K., 1969. Experimental taxonomy
as a base for breeding in northern Ruki.
Hereditas 63:283-351.

Leenhouts, P.W., 1978. Systematic notes on the
Sapindaceae-Nepheliaeae. Blumea 24:395-
403.

Leggett, J.M., 1980. Chromosome relationships
and morphological comparison between the
diploid oats Avena prostrata, A. canariensis
and the tetraploid A. maroccana. Can. J. Genet. Cytol. 22:287-294.

Leon, J., 1964. Plantas alimenticias Andinas.
Inst. Interam. Cienc. Agric. Andina Bol.
Tec. 6:1-112.

Leppik, E.E., 1968. Introduced seed-borne
pathogens endanger crop breeding and plant
introduction. FAO Plant Protection Bull.
16 (4): 57-63.

Leppik, E.E., 1965. A pathologist's view on
plant exploration and introduction. Pl.
Introd. Newsl. (15):1-6.

Lesins, K. & I. Lesins, 1966. Little-known
Medicagos and their chromosomes. Can. J.
Genet. Cytol. 8:8-13.

Lesins, K.A. & I. Lesins, 1979. Genus Medicago
(Leguminosae); a taxogenetic study. Dr W.
Junk Publishers, the Hague-Boston-London.
228 p.

Li, H.-L., 1969. The vegetables of Ancient
China. Econ. Bot. 23:253-260.

Li, H.-L., 1970. The origin of cultivated
plants in Southeast Asia. Econ. Bot. 24:
3-19.

Lindqvist, K., 1960. On the origin of cultivated lettuce. Hereditas 46:319-349.

Lowry, J.B. & L. Chew, 1974. On the use of extracted anthocyanin as food dye. Econ. Bot.
28:61-62.

Lumholtz, C., 1902. Unknown Mexico. Scribner's
Sons, New York.

Lumpkin, T.A. & D.L. Plucknett, 1980. Azolla:
botany, physiology, and use as a green manure. Econ. Bot. 34:111-153.

Lundell, C.L., 1937. The vegetation of Petén.
Carnegie Institute, Washington O.C. Cited
by J.L. Brewbaker, 1979.

Maan, S.S., 1973. Cytoplasmic and cytogenetic
relationships among tetraploid Triticum
species. Euphytica 22:287-300.

Maan, S.S., 1976. Cytoplasmic homology between
Aegilops squarrosa L. and Ae. cylindrica
Host. Crop Sci. 16:757-761.

Maan, S.S., 1980. Cytoplasmic homology between
Aegilops triuncialis and Ae. umbellulata.
Can. J. Genet. Cytol. 22:197-212.

McCollum, G., 1974. Chromosome behavior and
sterility of hybrids between the common

onion, Allium cepa, and the related wild
A. oschaninii. Euphytica 23:699-709.

McFarlane, J.S., 1975. Naturally occurring
hybrids between sugarbeet and Beta macrocarpa in the Imperial Valley of California.
J. Am. Soc. Sugarbeet Techn. 18:245-251.

Mac Key, J., 1966. Species relationship in Triticum. Hereditas Suppl. (2):237-276.

McLeod, M.J., W.H. Eshbaugh & S.I. Guttman,
1979. An electrophoretic study of Capsicum
(Solanaceae): the purple flowered taxa.
Bull. Torrey Bot. Club 106:326-333.

MacNeish, R.S., 1964a. The food-gathering and
incipient agricultural stage of prehistoric
Middle America. In: West, 1964, p. 413-426.

MacNeish, R.S., 1964b. Ancient American civilization. Science, N.Y. 173:531-537.

Maesen, L.J.G., van der, 1972. Cicer L., a monograph of the genus, with special reference to the chickpea (Cicer arietinum L),
its ecology and cultivation. Thesis, Wageningen. Also published as Meded. Landbouw-
Hogesch. Wageningen 72-10. 342 p.

Maesen, L.J.G., van der, 1980. India is the
native home of pigeonpea. In: J.C. Arends,
G. Boelema, C.T. de Groot & A.J.M. Leeuwen-
berg (Eds.): Liber gratulatorius in honorem
H.C.D. de Wit. Miscell. Papers Landbouwhogeschool, Wageningen 19:257-262.

Maggers, B.J., E.S. Ayensu & W.D. Duckworth
(Eds.), 1973. Tropical forest ecosystems
in Africa and South America: A comparative
review. Smithsonian Institution, Mass.
Washington.

Malik, C.P. & R.C. Tripathi, 1968. Cytogenetical evolution within the Cynodon dactylon
complex. Biol. Zbl. 87:625-627.

Mangelsdorf, P.C., R.S. MacNeish & W.C. Galinat, 1964. Domestication of corn. Science,
N.Y. 143:538-548.

Mansfeld, R., 1959. Vorläufige Verzeichnis land-
wirtschaftlich oder gärtnerisch kultivierter
Pflanzenarten. Kulturpflanze Suppl. 2.,
Berlin. 659 p.

Marks, G.E., & H. Montelongo-Escobeda, 1971. A
new pentaploid Mexican wild potato and its
progeny. Evolution 24:745-749.

Martin, F.W. & A.M. Rhodes, 1979. Subspecific
grouping of eggplant cultivars. Euphytica
28:367-383.

Masefield, G.B., M. Wallis, S.G. Harrison & B.
E. Nicholson, 1969. The Oxford book of food
plants. Oxford University Press. 206 p.

Massal, E. & J. Barrau, 1956. Food plants of
the South Sea Islands. Noumea: S. Pac. Comm.
Tech. Pap. 94.

Meeuse, A.D.J., 1958. The possible origin of
Cucumis anguria L. Blumea Suppl. 4:196-204.

Mehra, K.L., 1963. Considerations on the African
origin of Eleusine corocana (L.) Gaertn.
Curr. Sci. 32:300-301.

Mehra, P.N. & O.P. Sood, 1974. Floating chromosomal populations in Saccharum spontaneum.
Cytologia 39:681-698.

Menzel, M.Y. & D.W. Martin, 1970. Genome affinities of four African diploid species of Hibiscus sect. Furcaria. J. Heredity 61:178-
184.

Menzel, M.Y. & D.W. Martin, 1971. Chromosome
homology in some intercontinental hybrids
in Hibiscus sect. Furcaria. Am. J. Bot. 58:
191-202.

Menzel, M.Y. & F.D. Wilson, 1969. Genetic relationships in Hibiscus sect. Furcaria. Brittonia 21:91-125.

Meunier, P., 1962. Sur la présence du faux
dattier, Phoenix atlantica Chev., en Adrar
maurétanien. Fruits d'outre mer 17:208-210.

Meyer, F.G., 1965. Notes on wild Coffea arabica
from Southwestern Ethiopia, with some historical considerations. Econ. Bot. 19:136-151.

Meyer, F.G., 1969. The origin of Arabica coffee
(Coffea arabica L.). Abstr. Pap. XI. Int.
Bot. Congr. 146. Pl. Breed. Abstr. 41(8522).

Minessy, F.A., F.M. Kitat & M.M. Ebrahim, 1970.
Cytological studies on some citrus hybrids.
Alex. J. agric. Res. 18:197-205.

Mizushima, U., 1969. Phylogenetic studies on
some wild Brassica species. Kromosomo (75):
2427-2429.

Moens, J., 1974. Bijdrage tot de geschiedenis
van de witloofteelt. Wetenschapp. Tijdingen
33:k315-k324.

Molseed, E., 1970. The genus Tigridia (Iridaceae) of Mexico and Central America. Univ.
Calif. Publ. Bot. 54:1-113.

Moore Jr., H.E., 1966. Pelargoniums in cultivation. Baileya 3:5-25, 41-46, 70-97.

Moreno, M.-T. & J.I. Cubero, 1978. Variation
in Cicer arietinum L. Euphytica 27:465-485.

Morinaga, T., 1968. Origin and geographical
distribution of Japanese rice. JARQ 3:1-5.

Morton, J.F., 1967. The balsam pear - an edible,
medicinal and toxic plant. Econ. Bot. 21:
57-68.

Mueller-Stoll, W.R. & K. Michael, 1949. Unter-
suchungen über die Eigenschaften der Beeren
und Blätter von süszen und bitteren Eberes-
chen (Sorbus aucuparia L.). Züchter 19:233-
247.

Mukherjee, I. & T.N. Khoshoo, 1971. Genetic-
evolutionary studies on cultivated cannas,
V. Intraspecific polyploidy in starch
yielding Canna edulis. Genet. Iber. 23:37-
42.

Mukherjee, S.K., 1951. The origin of mango. Indian J. Genet. Pl. Breed. 11:49-56.

Munson, P.J., 1976. Archaeological data on the
origins of cultivation in the southwestern
Sahara and its implications for West Africa.
In: J.R. Harlan, J.M.J. de Wet & A.B.L.
Stemler (Eds): Origins of African plant do-
mestication. Mouton Press, The Hague.

Murdock, G.P., 1959. Staple subsistence crops
of Africa. Geogrl Rev. 50:521-540.

Murdock, G.P., 1960. Africa, its people and
their culture history. McGraw-Hill Book
Company, Inc. 456 p.

Murray, M.J., D.E. Lincoln & P.M. Marble, 1972.
Oil composition of Mentha aquatica x M.
spicata F_1 hybrids in relation to the origin of M. x piperita. Can. J. Genet. Cytol.
14:13-29.

M'yakushko, T.Ya. & V.K. M'yakushko, 1970. Diversity of forms of wild sweet cherry (Cerasus avium Moench.) in the Ukrain. Ukr. Bot. J. 28:219-326. Pl. Breed. Abstr. 42 (3411).

Nabham, G.P. & R.S. Felger, 1978. Teparies in Southwestern North America. Econ. Bot. 32: 2-19.

Nagato, K., 1979. (Interspecific and intraspecific relationships in the genus Camellia in our country based on isozyme variation). Jap. J. Breed. 29:49-58.

Nakagahara, M., 1977. The differentiation, classification and center of genetic diversity of cultivated rice (Oryza sativa L.) by isozyme analysis. p. 77-82 In: A.A. Muhammed & R.C. von Borstel (Eds): Genetic diversity in plants. Pt II. Plenum Press. 159 p.

Nakai, Y., 1977. (The origin of Aegilops triuncialis revealed by esterases isozymes); Abstract. Jap. J. Genet. 52:463. Cited from Pl. Breed. Abstracts 49(1979) No 960.

Nakai, Y., 1979. Isozyme variations in Aegilops and Triticum, IV. The origin of the common wheats revealed from the study on esterase isozymes in synthesized hexaploid wheats. Japan. J. Genetics 54:175-189.

Nassar, N.M., 1978. Wild Manihot species of Central Brazil for cassava breeding. Can. J. Pl. Sci. 59:257-261.

Navalikhina, N.K., 1977. (Role of polyploidy in the origin of white clover). Uspekhi poliploidii: 155-165. Pl. Breed. Abstr. 49(1979) No 2809.

Nayar, N.M., 1973. Origin and cytogenetics of rice. Genet. 17:153-292.

Nayar, N.M. & M.S. Gokal, 1970. Establishment and colonization by a wild potato species in the Old World - in the Simla hills, India. Curr. Sci. 39:362-363.

Nayar, N.M. & K.L. Mehra, 1970. Sesame: its uses, botany, cytogenetics and origin. Econ. Bot. 24:20-31.

Nee, M., 1979. Patterns in biography in Solanum, section Acanthophora. In: Hawkes et al., 1979, p. 569-580.

Neher, R.F., 1968. The ethnobotany of Tagetes. Econ. Bot. 22:317-325.

Nieuwhof, M., 1969. Cole crops; botany, cultivation and utilization. World Crops Books, London. 353 p.

Nishiyama, I., 1971. Evolution and domestication of the sweet potato. Bot. Mag., Tokyo. 84: 377-387.

Northwood, P.J., 1966. Some observations on flowering and fruitsetting in cashew, Anacardium occidentale L. Trop. Agric., Trin. 43:35-42.

Nijenhuis, L.E., H.J. Venema & H.C.D. de Wit, 1961. Vicia graminea Sm. Belmontia IV. Incid. Ser. fasc. 5:22-27.

Ohle, H., 1975. Beiträge zur Kenntnis der als Obstpflanzen kultivierten Passiflora-Arten. Kulturpflanze 23:107-129.

Oka, H.I. & T.T. Chang, 1961. Hybrid swarms between wild and cultivated rice species, Oryza perennis and O. sativa. Evolution 15 418-430.

Oka, H.I., 1974. Experimental studies on the origin of cultivated rice. Genetics 78: 475-486.

Okigbo, B.N., 1973. Introducing the yam bean, Spenostylis stenocarpa (Hochst. ex A. Rich) Harms. Proc. first IITA Grain Legume Improvement Workshop. Intern. Inst. Trop. Agric., Ibadan, Nigeria, p. 224-238.

Oudejans, J.H.M., 1969. Date palm (Phoenix dactylifera L.). In: Ferwerda & Wit. p. 243-257.

Pahlen, A. von der, 1977. (Solanum topiro [Humb. & Bonpl.), una fruteira da Amazônia). Acta Amazonia 7:301-307. Cited from Pl. Breed. Abstracts 48(1978) No 9007.

Pal, M., 1972. Evolution and improvement of cultivated amaranths. III. Amaranthus spinosus-dubius complex. Genetica 43:106-118.

Parodi, L.R. & J.C. Hernandez, 1964. El Mango, cereal extinguido en cultivo, sobrevive en estado salvage. Cience. Invest. 20:543-549.

Parthasarathy, N., 1946. The probable origin of North Indian sugarcanes. J. Indian Bot. Soc. 133-150.

Parthasarathy, N., 1948. Origin of noble sugarcane (Saccharum officinarum L.). Nature, Lond. 161:608.

Patino, V.M., 1968. Guayusa, a neglected stimulant from the eastern Andean foothills. Econ. Bot. 22:310-316.

Pavlov, A.V., 1969a. (Morphological characteristics of the flowers in the cultivated pear and the problem of the origin of cultivars). Sborn. Trud. Asp. molod. nauc. Sotrud. vses. nauc. issled. Inst. Rasten 10:567-568. Pl. Breed. Abstr. 40 (1482).

Pavlov, A.V., 1969b. (Characteristic features of the leaf epidermis in cultivated pears, as related to the origin of varieties). Bot. Zh. Moscov 54:750-755. Pl. Breed. Abstr. 40 (1483).

Perdue, Jr., R.E. & C.J. Kraebel, 1961. The rice-paper plant - Tetrapanax papyriferum (Hook.) Koch. Econ. Bot. 15:165-171.

Phelan, J.R. & J.G. Vaughan, 1976. A chemotaxonomic study of Brassica oleracea with particular reference to its relationship to Brassica alboglabra. Biochem. Syst. Ecol. 4 173-178.

Phillips, S.M., 1972. A survey of the genus Eleusine Gaertn. (Gramineae) in Africa. Kew Bull. 27:251-270.

Pickersgill, B., 1969. The domestication of chili peppers. In: Ucko & Dimbleby, 1969, p. 443-450.

Pickersgill, B., 1976. Pineapple, Ananas comosus (Bromeliaceae). In: Simmonds, 1976, p. 14-18.

Pickersgill, B., 1980. Cytology of two species of winged bean, Psophocarpus tetragonolobus (L.) DC. and P. scandens (Endl.) (Leguminosae). Bot. J. Linn. Soc. 80:279-291.

Pickersgill, B., S.C.H. Barrett & D. de Andrade-Lima, 1975. Wild cotton in Northeast Brazil. Biotropica 7:42-54.

Plarre, W., 1972. Die Entstehung eines Genzentrums in Ostafrika. Ein Beitrag zur Genzen-tren-Theorie. Z. PflZücht. 68:124-128.

Plumley, J.M., 1970. Qasr Ibrim. J. Egypt. Archaeal. 56:12-18.

Polunin, O., 1960. Introduction to plant geography and some related sciences. Longmans, 640 p.

Polunin, O. & A. Huxley, 1972. Flowers of the Mediterranean. Chatto & Windus, London. 260 p.

Pope Jr., H.G., 1969. Tabernanthe iboga: an African narcotic plant of social importance. Econ. Bot. 33:174-184.

Portères, R., 1950. Vieilles agricultures de l'Afrique intertropical. Agron. trop. 5: 489-507.

Portères, R., 1955a. Les céréales mineures de genre Digitaria en Afrique et en Europe. J. Agric. trop. Bot. appl. 2:350-386, 477-510, 620-675.

Portères, R., 1955b. Cultures de Phoenix reclinata Jacq. dans le golfe du Bénin pour l'obtention de vin de palme. J. Agric. trop. Bot. appl. 2:340-341.

Portères, R., 1956. Taxonomie agrobotanique des riz cultivés, Oryza sativa et O. glaberrima. J. Agric. trop. Bot. appl. 3:343-384, 541-580, 627-700, 821-856.

Portères, R., 1962. Berceaux agricoles primaires sur le continent africain. J. afric. Hist. 3:195-210.

Portères, R., 1976. The African cereals: Eleusine, Fonio, Black Fonio, Teff, Brachiaria, Paspalum, Pennisetum, and African rice. In: J.R. Harlan, J.M.J. de Wet & A.B.L. Stemler (Eds): Origins of African plant domestication. Mouton Press, The Hague.

Prakash, S. & A. Narain, 1971. Genomic status of Brassica tournefortii Gouan. Theor. appl. Genet. 41:203-204.

Prasad, B. & A.P. Chaudhary, 1968. Maisinte, a promising hybrid for fodder. Indian Dairym. 20(2):223-224. Pl. Breed. Abstr. 41 (964).

Price, S. & J. Daniels, 1968. Cytology of South Pacific sugarcane and related grasses with special reference to Fiji. J. Hered. 59: 141-145.

Prine, G.M., 1964. Forage possibilities in the genus Arachis. Proc. Soil Crop Sci. Soc. Fla. 24:187-196.

Puchalski, J.T., R.W. Robinson & J.W. Shail, 1979. Comparative electrophoresis of isozymes of Cucumis species. Cucurbit Genetics Coop. No 1, p. 39.

Purseglove, J.W., 1968. Tropical crops. Dicotyledons I. Longmans. 322 p.

Purseglove, J.W., 1972. Tropical crops. Monocotyledons, I. 1-334, II:335-607.

Putman, D.L. & W.M. Klein, 1971. Biosystematic studies of Deschampia Beauv. Am. J. Bot. 58:466.

Rachie, K.O. & L.V. Peter, 1977. The Eleusines. ICRISAT, Hyderabad. 179 p.

Rajhathy, T., 1971. Chromosome polymorphism in Avena ventricosa. Chromosoma 35:206-216.

Rajhathy, T. & B.R. Baum, 1972. Avena damascena: a new diploid oat species. Can. J. Genet.

Cytol. 14:645-654.

Rajhathy, T., D.A. Shearer & E.M. Warner, 1971. A thin-layer chromatographic study of some amphiploids in Avena. Can. J. Genet. Cytol. 13:749-759.

Raman, V.S., 1973. Genome relationships in Arachis. Oléagineux 28:137-140.

Randolph, L.F., 1970. Variation among tripsacum populations of Mexico and Guatemala. Brittonia 22:305-337.

Rappard, F.W., 1961. De wijze van voorkomen, het gebruik en de cultuur van matao, Pometia pinnata Forst. door papoea's. Nieuw Guinea Studiën 5:1-8. Summ. In: Belmontia III. Hort. fasc. 5 (29).

Rappaport, R.A., 1971. The flow of energy in an agricultural society. Scient. Am. 225 (3): 116-122, 127-132.

Reed, C.A. (Ed.), 1977. Origins of agriculture. Mouton Press, The Hague. 1013 p.

Reed, C.F. & R.O. Hughes, 1970. Selected weeds of the United States. Agric. Handbook 366. U.S. Government Printing Office, Washington, D.C.

Rehder, A., 1947. A manual of cultivated trees and shrubs, hardy in North America, exclusive of the subtropical and warmer temperature regions. 2nd ed., New York. 996 p.

Renvoize, Barbara S., 1972. The area of origin of Manihot esculenta as a crop plant - a review of the evidence. Econ. Bot. 26:352-360.

Rhodes, A.M., C. Campbell, S.E. Malo & S.G. Carmer, 1970. A numerical taxonomic study of the mango, Mangifera indica L. J. Am. Soc. Hort. Sci. 95:252-256.

Rick, C.M., 1971. The tomato Ge locus: linkage relations and geographic distribution of alleles. Genetics. 57:75-89.

Rick, C.M. & R.I. Bowman, 1961. Galápagos tomatoes and tortoises. Evolution 15:407-417.

Rick, C.M. & J.F. Fobes, 1975. Allozyme variation in the cultivated tomato and closely related species. Bull. Torrey Bot. Club 102:376-384.

Rick, C.M., J.F. Fobes & M. Holle, 1977. Genetic variation in Lycopersicon pimpinellifolium: evidence of evolutionary change in mating systems. Plant Syst. Evol. 127:139-170.

Rick, C.M., E. Kesicke, J.F. Fobes & M. Holle, 1976. Genetic and biosystematic studies on two new sibling species of Lycopersicon from Interandean Peru. Theor. Appl. Genetics 47:55-68.

Rimpau, J. & R.B. Flavell, 1974. The repeated sequence DNA in B-chromosomes in rye. In: P.L. Pierson (K.R. Lewis (Eds): Chromosome today 5, p. 147-157.

Rithidech, K. & D.A. Ramirez, 1974. Cytological survey of Saccharum spontaneum L. in the Philippines. Philipp. Agric. 58:205-224.

Rives, M., 1975. Les origins de la vigne. Recherche 6:120-129.

Rjadnova, I.M., 1967. (Origin of cultivated forms of Prunus avium L.). Nauc. Trud. Krasnodar. pedag. Inst. no. 82:19-29. Pl.

Breed. Abstr. 41 (3689).

Roach, B.T., 1972. Chromosome numbers in Saccharum edule. Cytologia 37:155-161.

Roberts, L.M., U.J. Grant, E.R. Ramirez, W.H. Hatheway & D.L. Smith, 1957. Races of maize in Colombia. Nat. Acad. Sci. - Nat. Res. Centre Washington Publ. 510. 153 p.

Rogers, D.J., 1963. Studies of Manihot esculenta Crantz and related species. Bull. Torrey Bot. Club 90:43-54.

Rousi, A., 1969. Cytogenetic comparison between two kinds of cultivated tarragon (Artemisia dracunculus). Hereditas 62:192-193.

Russell, T.A., 1965. The raphia palms of West-Africa. Kew Bull. 19:173-196.

Rybin, W.A., 1936. Spontane und experimentell erzeugte Bastarde zwischen Schwarzdorn und Kirschpflaume und das Abstammungsproblem der Kulturpflaume. Planta 25:22-58.

Rozhevicz, R.J., 1928. Bread plant from Ethiopia. Eragrostis teff (Zucc.) Trotter. Bull. appl. Bot. Pl. Breed. (Trudy prikl. Bot. Genet. Selek.) 18:389-403.

Sadasivaiah, R.S. & J. Weijer, 1981. The origin and meiotic behaviour of hexaploid Northern wheatgrass (Agropyron dasystachyum). Chromosoma 82:121-132.

Saez, F.A., 1949. En torno a la meiosis de Sorghum almum Parodi. Lilloa 19:111-118.

St. John, H., 1965. Revision of the genus Pandanus Stickman, 19. Additional Malayan species of Pandanus. Pacif. Sci. 19:224-237.

St. John, H. & A.C. Smith, 1971. The vascular plants of the Horne and Wallis Islands. Pac. Sci. 25:313-348.

Sanudo, A., 1970. Estudios citogenéticos en el gen. Solanum. IV. Un triploide cultivado desde antiguo en las islas Canarias. An. int. nat. Investnes Agron. 19:225-235.

Sauer, C.O., 1952. Agricultural origins and dispersals. The M.I.T. Press, New York, 175 p.

Sauer, J. & L. Kaplan, 1969. Canavalia beans in American prehistory. Am. Antiq. 34:417-423.

Sauer, J.D., 1950. The grain amaranths: a survey of their history and classification. Ann. Mo. bot. Gard. 37:561-632.

Sauer, J.D., 1964. Revision of Canavalia. Brittonia 16:106-181.

Sauer, J.D., 1969. Identity of archaeologic grain amaranths from the valley of Tehuacán, Puebla, Mexico. Am. Antiq. 34:80-81.

Sauer, J.D., 1976. Grain amaranths, in: Simmonds, 1976, p. 4-7.

Scholz, H., 1979. The phenomenon of mimetic weeds in the African Pennisetum americanum- - a critique. In: G. Kunkel (Ed.): Taxonomic aspects of African Economic Botany. A.E.T.F.A.T. publ., Las Palmas. p. 230-233.

Schratz, E., 1961. VI. Baldrian, Valeriana officinalis L. In: Kappert & Rudorf, 1961, p. 470-474.

Schroeder, C.A. & W.A. Fletscher, 1967. The Chinese gooseberry (Actinidia chinensis) in New Zealand. Econ. Bot. 21:81-92.

Schultes, R.E. & A. Hofmann, 1973. The botany and chemistry of hallucinogens. C.C. Thomas. 267 p.

Schultze-Motel, J., 1972. Die archäologischen Reste der Ackerbohne, Vicia faba L. und die Genese der Art. Kulturpflanze 19:321-358.

Schultze-Motel, J., 1979. Die urgeschichtlicher Reste des Schlafmohns (Papaver somniferum L.) und die Entstehung der Art. Kulturpflanze 27:207-215.

Schumann, F., 1977. Zur Erhaltung der Wildrebe Vitis vinifera L. var. silvestris Gmelin in den rheinischen Auwäldern. Pfalzer Heimat 28:150-154.

Scora, R.W., 1975. On the history and origin of Citrus. Bull. Torrey Bot. Club 102:369-375.

Scora, R.W. & M.N. Malik. 1970. Chemical characterization of Citrus as a tool in phylogeny. Taxon 19:215-228.

Sealy, J., 1958. A revision of the genus Camellia. London. 239 p.

Seetharam, A., 1972. Interspecific hybridization in the genus Linum. Euphytica 21:489-495.

Seetharaman, R. & D.P. Ghorai, 1976. Occurrence of types with characters of Oryza glaberrima in Assam rice collection. Current Science 45:67.

Sharma, B.D., K. Vivekananthan & N.C. Rathkrishnan, 1974. Cassia intermedia (Caesalpiniaceae) - a new species from South India. Proc. Indian Acad. Sci. 80:301-306.

Sharma, S.D. & V.S. Shastry, 1965a. Taxonomic studies in genus Oryza L. III. O. rufipogon Griff. sensu stricto and O. nivara Sharma et Shastry nom. nov., Indian J. Genet. 25:157-167.

Sharma, S.D. & V.S. Shastry, 1965b. Taxonomic studies in genus Oryza L. VI. A modified classification. Indian J. Genet. 25:173-178.

Sheen, S.J., 1972. Isozymic evidence bearing on the origin of Nicotiana tabacum L. Evolution 26:143-154.

Shimotsuma, M., 1965. Watermelons collected in Afghanistan and Iran. In: Yamashita, 1965, p. 201-206.

Siemonsma, J.S., 1980. Bilan des études corduites sur le gombo. Rapport Annuel 1979-1980 de Centre Néerlandais à Adiopodoumé. Agricultural University, Wageningen. p. 35-43.

Simmonds, N.W., 1962. The evolution of the bananas. Longmans, Green & Co. Ltd., London, 12 + 170 p.

Simmonds, N.W., 1964. Bananas. Longmans. 466 p.

Simmonds, N.W., 1968. Change of leaf size in the evolution of the Tuberosum potatoes. Euphytica 17:504-506.

Simmonds, N.W., 1976. Evolution of crop plants. Longmans. 339 p.

Simura, T., M. Hasimoto & S. Matusika, 1967. The tea plant grown in Burma. Sci. Rep. Fac. Agric., Meijo Univ. 4:10-16.

Singh, B.V. & M.R. Ahuja, 1977. Phaseolus sublobatus Roxb.: a source of resistance to yellow mosaic virus for cultivated mung

Indian J. Genet. Pl. Breed. 37:130-132.

Singh, D. & M.M. Bhandari, 1963. The identity of an imperfectly known hermaphrodite luffa, with a note on related species. Baileya 11:132-141.

Singh, H.B. & R.K. Arora, 1972. Raishan (Digitaria sp.). A minor millet of the Khasi Hills, India. Econ. Bot. 26:376-380.

Singh, L.B., 1976. Mango, Mangifera indica (Anacardiaceae). In: Simmonds, 1976, p. 7-9.

Singh, R.J. & G. Röbbelen, 1975. Comparison of somatic Giemsa banding pattern in several species of rye. Z. PflZücht 75:270-285.

Sinskaja, E.N., 1931. The wild radish. Bull. appl. Bot. Genet. Pl. Breed. (Trudy prikl. Bot. Genet. Selek.) 26:3-50.

Sinskaja, E.N. & A.A. Beztuzheva, 1931. The forms of Caenelina sativa in connection with climate, flax, and man. Bull. appl. Bot. Genet. Pl. (Trudy prikl. Bot. Genet. Selek.) Breed. 25:98-200.

Siskesjö, G., 1975. Chromosomal relationships between three species of Allium as revealed by C-banding. Hereditas 81:23-32.

Small, E., 1978a. A numerical and nomenclatural analysis of morph-geographic taxa of Humulus. Syst. Bot. 3:37-76.

Small, E., 1978b. A numerical taxonomic analysis of the Daucus carota complex. Can. J. Bot. 56:248-276.

Small, E., H.D. Beckstead & A. Chan, 1975. The evolution of cannabinoid phenotypes in Cannabis. Economic Bot. 29:219-232.

Smartt, J., 1973. The possible status of Phaseolus coccineus L. ssp. darwinianus Hdz X & Miranda C. as a distinct species and cultigen of the genus Phaseolus. Euphytica 22:424-426.

Smartt, J., 1980. Some observations on the origin and evolution of the winged bean (Psophocarpus tetragonolobus). Euphytica 29: 121-123.

Smeds, H., 1955. The ensete planting culture of Eastern Sidamo, Ethiopia. Acta Geogr. 13(4):1-39.

Smith, A.C., 1971. Studies of Pacific Islands plants 23. The genus Diospyros (Ebenaceae) in Fiji, Samoa and Tonga. J. Arnold Arbor. 52:369-403.

Smith Jr., C.E., 1968. Archaeological evidence for selection of chupandilla and cosahuico under cultivation in Mexico. Econ. Bot. 22: 140-148.

Smith Jr., C.E. & S.G. Stephens, 1971. Critical identification of Mexican archaeological cotton remains. Econ. Bot. 25:160-168.

Smith, J.L. & J.V. Perino, 1981. Osage orange (Maclura pomifera): history and economic uses. Econ. Bot. 35:24-41.

Snogerup, S., 1979. Experimental and cytological studies of the 'Brassica oleracea' group. Webbia 34:357-363.

Snogerup, S., 1980. The wild forms of the Brassica oleracea group (2n=18) and their possible relations to the cultivated ones., p. 121-132 in S. Tsunoda, K. Hinata & C.

Gómez-Campo. Brassica crops and wild allies, biology and breeding. Japan Scientific Societies Press, Tokyo. 354 p.

Snowden, J.D., 1936. The cultivated races of Sorghum. Allard and Son, London.

Solheim, W.G., 1972. An earlier agricultural evolution. Sci. Am. 226(4):34-41.

Somarov, B.H. & W.F. Grant, 1971. Phylogenetic relationships between certain diploid Lotus species and L. corniculatus (Abstr.). Can. J. Genet. Cytol. 13:646.

Spencer, J.E., 1963. The migration of rice from the mainland southeast Asia into Indonesia. In: J. Barrau (Ed.): Plants and the migrations of pacific people. Bishop Museum Press, Honolulu. p. 83-89.

Spinden, H.J., 1917. The origin and distribution of agriculture in America. Proc. 19th Intern. Congr. Amer. 1915. p. 269-276.

Stapf, O. & C.E. Hubbard, 1934. Pennisetum. F. Tr. Afr. 9.

Stebbins, G.L., 1956. Cytogenetic and evolution of grasses. Am. J. Bot. 43:890-905.

Steer, M.W. & H. Thomas, 1976. Evolution of A. sativa: origin of the cytoplasmic genome. Can. J. Genet. Cytol. 18:769-771.

Stemler, A.B.L., J.R. Harlan & J.M.J. de Wet, 1975. Caudatum sorghums and the speakers of Chari-Nile languages in Africa. J. Afr. Hist. 16:161-183.

Stevenson, G., 1978. Botanical evidence linking the New Zealand Maoris with New Caledonia and the New Hebrides. Nature 276:704-705.

Storey, W.B. & I.J. Condit, 1969. Fig, Ficus carica L. In: Ferwerda & Wit, 1969, p. 259-267.

Strauss, E. & R. Novak, 1971. Anbauversuche mit Holunder (Sambucus nigra). Mitt. Klosterneuburg 21:416-426.

Stutz, H.C., 1971. Genotypically controlled chromosome breakage as an isolation barrier in the origin of Secale ancestrale Zhuk. Am. J. Bot. 58 (5 pt. 2):466.

Stutz, H.C., 1972. On the origin of cultivated rye. Am. J. Bot. 59:59-70.

Stutz, H.C., 1976. Genetically controlled chromosome breakage as an isolation barrier in the origin and maintenance of Secale ancestrale. Can. J. Genet. Cytol. 18:105-109.

Swamy Rao, T., 1971. Varietal differentiation in brown sarson. Can. J. Genet. Cytol. 13: 720-722.

Tadessa, E., 1975. T'ef (Eragrostis tef). The cultivation, usage, and some of the known diseases and insect pests. Haile Sallasie I Univ., Call. Agric. Exp. St Bull. 60: 1-56.

Tahbaz, F., 1971. L'Allium 'Tarée irani' du groupe ampeloprasum L. cultivé en Iran, région de Téhéran. Bull. Soc. Bot. France 118:753-761.

Tahbaz, F., 1976. Étude comparée des caryotypes de 2 Allium du group Ampeloprasum cultivés en Iran. C.R. Acad. Sci. Paris 283 série D:1185-1188.

Takahashi, R., 1964. Further studies on the

phylogenetic differentiation of cultivated barley. Barley Genetics I:19-26.

Tamai,T. & S. Tokumasu, 1968. Breeding a new type of Pelargonium by means of chromosome doubling and interspecific hybridization. Proc. 12th Int. Congr. Gen. I:263.

Tateoka, T., 1964. Taxonomic studies of the genus Oryza. In: Rice genetics and cytogenetics. Elsevier Publ. Co, Amsterdam. p. 15-23.

Tax, S. (Ed.), 1960. The evolution after Darwin. II. The evolution of man. University of Chicago Press. 473 p.

Teppner, H., 1970. Karyotypen europäischer, perennierender Sippen der Gramineen-Gattun Anthoxanthum. Oesterr.Z. 118:280-292.

Terra, G.J.A., 1967. Tropical vegetables. Commun. 54, Dept. Agric. Res., Trop. Inst., Amsterdam. 107 p.

Thoday, J.M., 1972. Disruptive selection. Proc. R. Soc. London Ser. B 182:109-143.

Todd, W.A. & M.J. Murray, 1968. New essential oils from hybridization of Mentha citrata Ehrh. Perfum. essent. Oil Rec., London. February:1-6.

Tokumasu, S., F. Yano & M. Kato, 1977. Estimation of genetic relationships among Pelargonium species by the electrophoretic patterns of isozymes. Jap. J. Genet. 52: 197-205.

Torres, A.M., R.K. Soost & K. Diedenhofer, 1978. Leaf isozymes as genetic markers in Citrus. Am. J. Bot. 65:869-881.

Toxopeus, H., 1969. Cacao, Theobroma cacao L. In: Ferwerda & Wit, 1969, p. 79-109.

Toxopeus, H.J., 1950. Kapok. In: van Hall & van de Koppel, 1950, p. 53-102.

Toxopeus, H.J., 1952. Studies in the breeding of Derris elliptica and Derris malaccensis. I. Variation and the origin of the cultivated material. Euphytica 1:34-42.

Tozu, T., 1965. Luffa acutangula Roxb. collected by KUSE, 1955. In: Yamashita, 1965. p. 257-258.

Tsuji, S. & K. Tsunewaki, 1976. Genetic diversity of the cytoplasm in Triticum and Aegilops. IV. On the origin of the cytoplasm of two hexaploid Aegilops species. Japan. J. Genet. 51:149-151.

Tutin, T.G., V.H. Heywood, N.A. Burges, D.M. Moore, D.H. Valentine, S.M. Walters & D.A. Webb, 1972. Flora Europaea. 3. Diapensiaceae to Myoporaceae. Cambridge Univ. Press. 370 p.

Tutin, T.G. c.s., 1976. Flora Europaea. Vol. 4. Cambridge Univ. Press. 505 p.

Uchimiya, H. & S.G. Wildman, 1978. Evolution of fraction I protein in relation to origin of amphidiploid Brassica species and other members of the Cruciferae. J. Hered. 69:299-303.

Ucko, P.J. & G.W. Dimbleby, 1969. The domestication and exploitation of plants and animals. London. 26 + 581 p.

Ugent, D., 1967. Morphological variation in Solanum x edinense, a hybrid of the common potato. Evolution 21:696-712.

Ugent, D., 1968. The potato in Mexico: geography and primitive culture. Econ. Bot. 22:109-123.

Ugent, D., 1970a. Solanum raphanifolium, a Peruvian wild potato species of hybrid origin. Bot. Gaz. 131:225-233.

Ugent, D., 1970b. The potato. What is the botanical origin of this important crop, and how did it first become domesticated. Science, N.Y. 170:1161-1166.

Ulbrich, E., 1934. Chenopodiaceae. In: Engler & Prangl: Die naturlichen Pflanzenfamilien. 16c:379-584.

Uphof, J.C.T., 1968. Dictionary of economic plants. 2nd ed. 591 p.

Valiček, P., 1977. Some notes on the taxonomy of the new cotton species Gossypium calcoense Aran., Leit. & Gridi. Agric. Trop et Subtrop. 10:119-128.

Valiček, P., 1979. Gossypium nelsonii Fryx and its relation to other species of the subsection Hibiscoidea. Coton & Fibres Trop. 34:315-319.

Vardi, A. & D. Zohary, 1967. Introgression in wheat via triploid hybrids. Heredity 22: 541-560.

Vavilov, N.I., 1917. On the origin of cultivated rye. Bull. appl. Bot. (Trudy Byuro prikl. Bot) 10:561-590.

Vavilov, N.I., 1926. Studies on the origin of cultivated plants. Bull. appl. Bot. (Trudy Byuro prikl. Bot.) 26 (2). 248 p.

Vavilov, N.I., 1928. Geographische Genzentren unserer Kulturpflanzen. Int. Kongr. G. Vererb. Wiss. (1927). Z. indukt. Abstramm.-u. Vererblehre Suppl. 1:342-369.

Vavilov, N.I., 1930a. Wild progenitors of the fruit trees of Turkestan and the Caucasus and the problem of the origin of fruit trees. Rep. Proc. 9th int. Hort. Congr. 1930. Group B: 271-286.

Vavilov, N.I., 1930b. The problems of the origin of cultivated plants and domestic animals, as conceived at the present time. Proc. Congr. Genet., Leningrad. II, 5-18.

Vavilov, N.I., 1931. The problem of the origin of the world agriculture in the light of the latest investigations. Science at the Cross Roads, London. p. 1-10.

Vavilov, N.I., 1935. (Theoretical bases of plant breeding, Part I). Moscow-Leningrad. 1043 p.

Vavilov, N.I., 1940. The new systematics of cultivated plants. In: Huxley, J. (Ed.): The new systematics. Oxford University Press p. 519-566. Also issued in 1941 and 1945.

Vavilov, N.I., 1957. World resources of cereals, grains leguminous crops and flax and their utilization in plant breeding. General part: agroecological survey of the principal field crops. Moskva/Leningrad. 462 p. (also transl. by M. Paenson & Z.S. Cole, Jerusalem. 442 p.).

Vavilov, N.I., 1949/1950. The origin, variation, immunity and breeding of cultivated crops. Chron. Bot. 13, 364 p.

Verdcourt, B., 1970. Studies on the Legumino-

sae-Papilionoideae for the 'Flora of Tropical East Africa'. III. Kew Bull. 2:379-447.

Verdcourt, B. & P. Halliday, 1978. A revision
of Psophocarpus (Leguminosae-Papilionoideae
-Phaseoleae). Kew Bull. 33:101-227.

Vietmeyer, N.D. & B. Cottons, 1977. Leucaena:
promising forage and tree crop for the
tropics. Nat. Acad. of Sciences, Washington. 115 p.

Vishnu-Mittre, 1974. Paleobotanical evidence
in India. In: J.B. Hutchinson (Ed.): Evolutionary studies in world crops. Cambridge
Univ. Press, Cambridge.

Visser, D.L. & A.P.M. de Nijs, 1980. The Cucumis species collection at the IVT (Wageningen). Cucurbit Genetics Cooperative
Rept. No 3. p. 68-74.

Visser, T., 1969. Tea, Camellia (L.) O. Kuntze.
In: Ferwerda & Wit, 1969. p. 459-493.

Vosa, C.G., 1976. Heterochromatic patterns in
Allium. Heredity 36:383-392.

Waard, P.W. de & A.C. Zeven, 1969. Pepper,
Piper nigrum L.. In: Ferwerda & Wit, 1969.
p. 409-426.

Wall, J.R., 1970. Experimental introgression
in the genus Phaseolus. I. Effect of mating systems on interspecific gene flow.
Evolution 24:356-366.

Watson, J.B., 1968. Pueraria: names and tra-
ditions of a lesser crop of the Central
Highlands, New Guinea. Ethnology 7:268-
279.

Watt, J.M. & M.G. Breyer-Brandwijk, 1962. Medicinal and poisonous plants of southern
and eastern Africa. Livingstone Lts.,
Edinburgh.

Wein, K., 1964. Die Geschichte des Rettichs
und des Radieschens. Kulturpflanze 12:33-
74.

Wellhausen, E.J., O.A. Fuentes & A.H. Corzo,
1957. Races of maize in Central America.
Nat. Acad. Sci-Nat. Res. Council, Washington. Publ. 511. 128 p.

Wellhausen, E.J., L.M. Roberts & E. Hernandez
X., 1952. Races of maize in Mexico, their
origin, characteristics and distribution.
The Bussey Institution of Harvard Univ.
223 p.

Wendello, P., 1971. Alliaceae. In: Rechinger
(Ed.): Flora Iranica (76):1-100. Akad.
Druck. Graz.

Wendorf, F. and 7 coworkers, 1979. Use of barley in the Egyptian Late Paleolithic.
Science, N.Y. 205:1341-1347.

Werneck, H.L., 1951. Ur und fruhgeschichtliche
Roggenfunde in den Ostalpen und am Ost-
rande des Bohmerwaldes. Der Züchter 21:
107-108.

Werneck, H.L., 1958. Die Formenkreise der bo-
denständigen Pflaumen in Oberösterreich,
ihre Bedeutung für die Systematik und die
Wirtschaft der Gegenschaft. Mitt. Klosterneuburg (Ser. B) 8:59-82.

West, R.C. (Ed.). Handbook of Middle American
Indians. I. University Texas Press. 570 p.

Westphal, W., 1974. Pulses in Ethiopia, their
taxonomy and agricultural significance.

Agric. Res. Rep. 815, Pudoc, Wageningen.
261 p.

Whitaker, Th.W., 1969. Salades for everyone -
a look at the lettuce plant. Econ. Bot. 23:
261-264.

Whitaker, T.W. & H.C. Cutler, 1969. Pre-histo-
ric cucurbits from the valley of Oaxaca,
Mexico. Abst. Pap. 11, Int. bot. Congr.:
236. Pl. Breed. Abstr. 41 (9094).

Whitaker, T.W. & H.C. Cutler, 1971. Prehistoric cucurbits from the valley of Oaxaca,
Mexico. Abst. Paper 11. Intern. Bot. Congress 1969. 236.

Whitaker, T.W. & G.N. Davis, 1962. Cucurbits.
London/New York. 12 + 250 p.

Whitehead, R.A., 1976. Coconut, Cocos nucifera
(Palmae). In: Simmonds, 1976, p. 221-225.

Whyte, R.O., G. Nilsson-Leissner & H.C. Trum-
ble, 1953. Legumes in agriculture. FAO,
Rome. 367 p.

Widler, B.E. & G. Bocquet, 1979. Brassica insularis Moris.: Beispiel eines messinischen
Verbreitungsmusters. Candollea 34:133-151.

Wijesekera, R.O.B., A.L. Jayewardena & B.D.
Fonseka, 1973. Varietal differences in the
constituents of citronela oil. Phyto-
chemistry 12: 2697-2704.

Wilcox, A.N., 1962. I. Systematics (of the
apple). In: Kappert & Rudorf, 1962, p.
637-645.

Wilde-Duyfjes, B.E.E. de, 1976. A revision of
the genus Allium L. (Liliaceae) in Africa.
Meded. LandbwHogesch. Wageningen 76-11.
237 p.

Wilke, Ph.J., R. Bettiner, Th.F. King & J.F.
O'Connell, 1972. Harvest selection and
domestication in seed plants. Antiquity
46:203-209.

Wilkes, H.G., 1967. Teosinte, the closest relative of maize. Cambridge, 159 p.

Wilkes, H.G., 1970. Teosinte introgression in
the maize of the Nobogame valley. Bot. Mus.
Leafl. Harvard Univ. 22:297-311.

Williams, J.F., A.M.C. Sanchez & M.T. Jackson,
1974. Studies on lentils and their variation. I. The taxonomy of the species.
Sabrao J. 6:133-145.

Willis, J.C., 1922. Age and Area. A study in
geographical distribution and origin of
species. Cambridge, 10 + 259 p.

Willis, J.C., 1966. A dictionary of the flowering plants and ferns. University Press.
Cambridge. 22 + 1214 + 53 p.

Wilson, F.D. & M.Y. Menzel, 1964. Kenaf (Hibiscus cannabinus), roselle (Hibiscus sabdariffa). Econ. Bot. 18:80-91.

Wilson, H.D., 1976. Genetic control and distribution of leucine aminopeptidase in the
cultivated chenopods (Chenopodium) and related weed taxa. Biochem. Genet. 14:913-
919.

Wilson, H.D., 1981. Domesticated Chenopodium
of the Ozark Bluff Dwellers. Econ. Bot.
35:233-239.

Wilson, H.D. & Ch.B. Heiser Jr., 1979. The
origin and evolutionary relationships of
'Huazontle' (Chenopodium nuttalliae Saf-

ford), domesticated chenopod of Mexico. Am. J. Bot. 66:198-206.

Winter, H.F., 1963. Ceylon spinach (Basella rubra). Econ. Bot. 17:195-199.

Wit, F., 1969a. The clove tree, Eugenia caryophyllus (Sprengel) Bullock & Harrison. In: Ferwerda & Wit, 1969, p. 163-174.

Wit, F., 1969b. Tungtrees, Aleurites fordii Hensl. and A. montana (Lour.). In: Ferwerda & Wit, 1969, p. 495-507.

Wrigley, C., 1960. Speculations on the economic prehistory of Africa. J. Afric. Hist. 1 (2):189-203.

Wu, C.T., Y.H. Chia, C.H. Feng & C.M. Tsai, 1970. Morphological observations on wild tea on Mount Meiyuan in Taiwan. I. Taiwan agric. Q. 6(1):15-27. Pl. Breed. Abstr. 41 (8515).

Yabuno, T., 1968. Biosystematic studies of the genus Echinochloa. Proc. 12th Int. Congr. Genetics I, p. 184.

Yamashita, K. (Ed.), 1965. Cultivated plants and their relatives. Results of the Kyoto University Scientific Experiments (KUSE) to the Karakoram and Hindukush, 1955. I. Kyoto. 361 p.

Yarnell, R.A., 1972. Iva annua var. macrocarpa: extinct American cultigen. Am. Anthropologist 74:335-341.

Yen, D.E. & J.M. Wheeler, 1968. Introduction of taro into the Pacific: the indication of the chromosome number. Ethnology J. 7:259-267.

Zeist, W. van & J.A.H. Bakker-Heeres, 1975. Evidence for linseed cultivation before 6000 BC. J. Archaeol. Sci. 2:215-219.

Zeist, W. van & S. Bottema, 1971. Plant husbandry in early neolithic Nea Nikomedeia, Greece. Acta Bot. neerl. 20:524-538.

Zeven, A.C., 1967. The semi-wild oil palm and its industry in Africa. Rep. Agric. Res. Rep. 689. Pudoc, Wageningen. 378 p.

Zeven, A.C., 1969. Kapok tree, Ceiba pentandra Gaertn. in: Ferwerda & Wit, 1969, p. 269-287.

Zeven, A.C., 1971. Fifth supplementary list of wheat varieties classified according to their genotype for hybrid necrosis and geographical distribution of Ne-genes. Euphytica 20:239-254.

Zeven, A.C., 1972. The semi- and complete domestication of the oil palm (Elaeis guineensis Jacq.) and its centres of diversity. Econ. Bot. 26:274-279.

Zeven, A.C., 1973. The introduction of the nypa palm (Nypa fruticans Wurmb.) to West Africa. J. Nig. Inst. Oil Palm Res. 5(18):35-36.

Zeven, A.C., 1974. Indigenous bread wheat varieties from Northern Nigeria. Acta bot. neerl. 23:137-144.

Zeven, A.C., 1975. A possible contribution of environmentally induced changes to the domestication of plants. Euphytica 24:369-370.

Zeven, A.C., 1979. The prehistoric spread of bread wheat into Asia. Proc. 5th Intern. Wheat Genetics Symp., New Delhi-1978.

p. 103-107.

Zeven, A.C., 1980a. Polyploidy and domestication: the origin and survival of polyploids in cytotype mixtures. In: W.H. Lewis (Ed.): Polyploidy: biological relevance. Plenum Press, New York. p. 385-407.

Zeven, A.C., 1980b. The spread of bread wheat over the Old World since the Neolithicum as indicated by its genotype for hybrid necrosis. J. Agric. Trad. Bot. appl. 27: 19-53.

Zeven, A.C. & A.M. van Harten (Eds), 1979. Proceedings of the conference, Broadening the genetic basis of crops, Wageningen, Netherlands 3-7 July 1978. Pudoc, Wageningen. 347 p.

Zhukovsky, P.M., 1962. Cultivated plants and their wild relatives. Moscow. 107 p. Abridged translated by P.S. Hudson. Commonwealth Agriculturel Bureaux.

Zhukovsky, P.M., 1964. Cultivated plants and their wild relatives. 2nd ed. Kolos, Leningrad. 791 p.

Zhukovsky, P.M., 1965. Main gene centres of cultivated plants and their wild relatives within the territory of the U.S.S.R. Euphytica 14:177-188.

Zhukovsky, P.M., 1968. (New centres of origin and new gene centres of cultivated plants including specifically endemic microcentres of species closely allied to cultivated species). Bot. Zh. 53:430-460. Pl. Breed. Abstr. 38(38).

Zhukovsky, P.M., 1970. (World genofund of plants for breeding. Mega-gene centres and endemic microcentres). Leningrad, 87 p. Translated by E.E. Leppik.

Zhukovsky, P.M., 1971. Cultivated plants and their wild relatives. Systematics, geography, cytogenetics, resistance, ecology, origin and use. Kolos, Leningrad. 751 p.

Zohary, D., 1970. Centres of diversity and centres of origin. In: Frankel & Bennett, 1970, p. 33-42.

Zohary, D., 1969. The progenitors of wheat and barley in relation to domestication and agricultural dispersal in the Old World. In: Ucko & Dimbleby, 1969, p. 47-66.

Zohary, D., 1971. The fate of natural 'hybrid swarms' between Hordeum spontaneum and H. vulgare. In: Nilan, 1971, p. 63-64.

Zohary, D., 1972. The wild progenitor and the place of the origin of the cultivated lentil: Lens culinaris. Econ. Bot. 26:326-332.

Zohary, D., 1973. The origin of cultivated cereals and pulses in the Near East. Chromosomes Today 4:307-320.

Zohary, D., 1976. Lentil, Lens culinaris (Leguminosae-Papilionatae). In: Simmonds, 1976, p. 163-164.

Zohary, D., 1977. Comments on the origin of cultivated broad bean, Vicia faba L. Israel J. Bot. 26:39-40.

Zohary, D. & J. Basnizky, 1975. The cultivated artichoke - Cynara scolymus; its probable wild ancestors. Econ. Bot. 29:233-235.

Zohary, D. & U. Plitmann, 1979. Chromosome polymorphism, hybrixation and colonization in the Vicia sativa group (Fabaceae). Pl Syst. Evol. 131:143-156.

Zohary, D. & P. Spiegel-Roy, 1975. Beginnings of fruit growing in the Old World. Science, N.Y. 187:319-327.

Zubeldia Lizarduy, A., G. López Campos & A. Sanudo Palazuelos, 1955. Estudio, descripción y clasificación de un grupo de variedades primitivas de patata cultivadas en los isles Canarias. Bot. Inst. Invest. agron., Madrid 15:287-325. Pl. Breed. Abstr. 26 (2587).

Zylka, D., 1970. Die Verwendung von Wildarten der Gattung Prunus in der Sortenzüchtung und als Unterlage. Giessen. 223 p.

Zylka, D., 1971a. Die Verwendung von wilden Kirscharten in der Sortenzüchtung und als Unterlagen. I. Prunusarten der Sektion Eucerasus. Gartenbauwissenschaft 2:261-291.

Zylka, D., 1971b. Die Verwendung von wilden Kirschenarten in der Sortenzüchtung und als Unterlage. III. Prunusarten der Sektion Mahaleb und des Subgenus Padus. Gartenbauwissenschaft 3:557-572.

Index of botanical names

The following pages give four blank distribution maps.
1. The Americas
2. Europe, the Middle East and Africa
3. Asia and Australia
4. World map

Maps 1-3 can be joined. -.-, national fron-
tiers; --- borders of states and provinces.
They can be photocopied by plant geographers
to make their own distribution maps.